"Politics is neighboring, negotiating a con[...] strangers, enemies, and the friendless, and pointical theology requires a kaleidoscopic approach, brilliantly instantiated in this book, that disrupts canon, shifts geography, and eschews sovereign placement in favor of active listening. A transformative contribution!"

— JENNIFER A. HERDT
Yale Divinity School

"Bretherton's brilliant scholarship, on display in this book, his deliberate choice of interlocutors, and his astute selection of spheres of social life for analysis are a demonstration of what the common life in Christ looks like in theologizing. Bretherton opens things up to multiple voices not as a politically correct ploy, but as a genuine and rigorous engagement with others."

— NIMI WARIBOKO
Boston University

"Luke Bretherton has written a solid textbook on political theology. He refreshingly explicates a range of historical and contemporary political theologies (humanitarianism, Black Power, Catholic social teaching, Pentecostalism, Anglicanism) as he makes a case for democratic politics as a work of love. Amid twenty-first-century political strife, Bretherton offers Christians a map for traversing the terrain."

— MARCIA Y. RIGGS
Columbia Theological Seminary

"*Christ and the Common Life* offers one of the most comprehensive and insightful examinations of the intersecting terrains of North Atlantic political theology while building a careful, rich, and compelling theological defense of democracy. Whether or not one fully agrees with Bretherton's assessments and proposals, *Christ and the Common Life* compels nuanced engagement and sets a new standard for political theology."

— C. MELISSA SNARR
Vanderbilt University Divinity School

"Deeply learned and humane, Bretherton's book surveys the landscape of political theology while making its own argument for 'why Christians should be committed to democracy as a vital means for pursuing a flourishing life.' Bretherton's five case studies—on humanitarianism, Black

Power, Pentecostalism, Catholic social teaching, and Anglicanism—are nothing short of a master class in different Christian conceptions of political flourishing."

— Cathleen Kaveny
Boston College

"Bretherton's work is always rich, brimming with ideas and thought-provoking arguments. But this is a new kind of gift—an introduction to the whole field of political theology, taking seriously both the political and the theological aspects of the field. Ambitious and lucid, the book makes surprising and fruitful connections as it takes readers on a journey through a bewildering maze of topics—and you never feel lost. I don't know of another book that can compete with it. Highly recommended, to those seasoned in the field and to those just starting out."

— Charles Mathewes
University of Virginia

"Luke Bretherton's highly original and challenging book cuts across the dominant polarities characterizing political theology—religious/secular, church/state, and private/public—in order to challenge Christianity to embrace the political dimensions of its very public faith without reducing theology to pragmatic political considerations. His conception of political theology brings together the prophetic and corporate dimensions of the Christian faith for the sake of a shared common good in our increasingly pluralist context."

— Rubén Rosario Rodríguez
Saint Louis University

Christ and the Common Life

Political Theology and the Case for Democracy

Luke Bretherton

[handwritten inscription and signature]

WILLIAM B. EERDMANS PUBLISHING COMPANY
GRAND RAPIDS, MICHIGAN

Wm. B. Eerdmans Publishing Co.
4035 Park East Court SE, Grand Rapids, Michigan 49546
www.eerdmans.com

Hardcover edition 2019
Paperback edition 2022

Printed in the United States of America

28 27 26 25 24 23 22   1 2 3 4 5 6 7

ISBN 978-0-8028-8179-3

2022-04

Library of Congress Cataloging-in-Publication Data

Names: Bretherton, Luke, author.
Title: Christ and the common life : political theology and the case for democracy /
    Luke Bretherton.
Description: Grand Rapids : Eerdmans Publishing Co., 2019. | Includes
    bibliographical references and index.
Identifiers: LCCN 2018048359 | ISBN 9780802881793 (pbk. : alk. paper)
Subjects: LCSH: Political theology. | Christianity and politics. | Christian democracy. |
    Democracy—Religious aspects—Christianity.
Classification: LCC BT83.59 .B73 2019 | DDC 261.7—dc23 LC record available at
    https://lccn.loc.gov/2018048359

In memoriam
Michael Stocking
(1967–2016)

Contents

CONTENTS

Introduction

This book provides an introduction to historical and contemporary theological reflection on the meaning and purpose of politics, while at the same time making a case for why Christians should be committed to democracy as a vital means for pursuing a flourishing life. It is born out of involvement in or teaching about the interaction of Christianity and politics throughout my working life. Whether in the European or North American context, I consistently encounter the same question being asked by those I work alongside or teach as they try to make sense of the social, economic, and political problems and conflicts they face. The question goes something like this: "It's all very well being told to love our neighbors, but when it comes to politics, of what does neighbor love consist?" Like a triangle, this question has three sides to it. The first is, what is the appropriate response to the poverty, suffering, and injustice one encounters in trying to love one's neighbors? Much theological thinking about politics is inspired by and taken up with debates about how best to answer this question.

The second side is this: In loving my neighbor, how can I keep faith with my distinctive commitments while also forming a common life with neighbors who have a different vision of life than I do? Another way to put this question is, how should our own roots, our sense of what counts as home, identity, or belonging—that is, what makes us distinctive and particular—be coordinated with and ordered in relationship to those we find strange or who don't share our beliefs and practices? Again, much of political theology tries to answer this second question, as the creation and sustaining of a common life between "Christians" and "non-Christians"—or church and world—is a central concern.

The third, often unacknowledged side to the issue of neighbor love in politics is the question of what kind of power shapes the relationship be-

1

tween oneself and another and how this power is distributed. This third question is fundamental to any account of human flourishing and identifies a central problem that politics addresses. Politics is about forming, norming, and sustaining a common life between those who are the same and those who are different (however conceived), as configurations of power shape the conditions of life together at various scales from the local to the global. A common life with and for others (including nonhuman life) is a prerequisite for human flourishing: the good or flourishing life cannot be reduced to individual happiness as we are not atomized monads but mutually vulnerable, interdependent creatures whose flourishing depends on being embedded in just and loving forms of common life. Therefore, a central concern of political theology is how power is constructed, circulated, and distributed within patterns of shared life, at whatever scale that life takes. Keeping these three concerns in play throughout, this book examines different theological ways of answering questions about how to respond to poverty and injustice, how to form a common life with strangers and enemies, and how to handle and distribute power constructively.

Amid the perils and paradoxes that the interaction of Christianity and politics brings, it is easy to get confused or lost. Like a map, this book aids the navigation of political life and its positive and negative roles in fostering faithful, hopeful, and loving ways of being alive with and for others. Its chapters add up to a kind of field guide, providing orientations and markers to help readers traverse the contemporary political landscape, name its features, and identify some of the characteristic ways Christians make sense of politics and go about trying to love their neighbors. At the same time, like a seasoned guide marking a trail through swampy and mountainous terrain, the book charts its own pathway, one that leads beyond the boundaries of what is familiar or perhaps even comfortable.

A basic premise of the book is that talk of God and talk of politics are coemergent and mutually constitutive. Underlying this descriptive statement is a more substantive claim that politics is a crucial arena of human activity through which we come to grasp the truth of many theological concepts, learn how to love our neighbors, and discover what it means to flourish as creatures. It was not merely for convenience' sake that those who wrote the New Testament foraged Greco-Roman ideas about political life. Politics was a crucible through which the New Testament writers articulated what it meant to be the church; for example, *ekklēsia* (church) and *leitourgia* (liturgy) are political terms turned to ecclesial ends. Early theologians continued this process of converting political categories into ecclesial ones and thereby reorienting and recalibrating them. A paradigmatic example is Augustine's reconceptualization of Cicero's definition of a people.[1] The nature and form of political life were crucial to understanding something about the nature and form of divine-human relations. Conversely, participation in ecclesial practices enabled new kinds of moral and political judgment to be made, generating new understandings of what it means for humans to flourish as inherently social animals.

Over time, the relationship between theological and political concepts became a thicket of entangled ideas. As Christianity became more widespread and influential, theological categories and concepts were used to theorize political life. To complicate matters further, theological uses of political terms were then borrowed back to understand political life, but still with the imprint of their theological meaning embedded within them. The historical development of human rights is a case in point. It draws on prior theological notions of natural rights and natural law, but today many churches adopt nontheological discourses of human rights as a way of framing their political claims. Contrary to stories of a one-way drive toward secularization, the traffic continues to flow in both directions. This process of interweaving should not be surprising, as it reflects how knowledge is produced. Social life is rarely composed of a single, monolithic, and transparent set of beliefs and practices. Neither is it lived as a stark clash of two or more such worldviews, language games, or civilizations. Rather, in both the ancient and modern world, our forms of life are constituted by the interaction of often contradictory beliefs and practices and involve multiple loyalties that pull us in different, sometimes conflicting, directions (to family, work, state, congregation, etc.). Moreover, the advent of Christianity, whether in the Roman Empire, among the Kievan Rus' in the tenth century, or in the Kingdom of Kongo in the fifteenth century, leaves neither Christianity nor the cultural and political milieu unchanged. This book tries to display how to read the ways in which talk of God and talk of politics are mutually constitutive and refract each other, and show how, for better or worse, this interrelationship shapes *both* ecclesial and political life.

By attending to the analogies and disanalogies between talk of God and talk of politics, I show how understanding politics demands paying attention to theology and how understanding theology necessitates attention

---

1. See Augustine, *City of God* 19.24. All references refer to Augustine, *The City of God*, trans. William Babcock (New York: New City Press, 2013).

to politics. Engagement with political philosophy and social theory may, at times, help with such an endeavor. A guiding assumption of this book is that the richer our engagement with ways of understanding the relationship between ecclesial and political life, the deeper will be our understanding of what it means to be the church and of the nature of faithful witness. Or to put this another way, ecclesiology, missiology, and political theology address interwoven concerns. A further assumption is that given the dynamic and provisional nature of the relationship between ecclesial and political life, no one-size-fits-all blueprint can or should be given for the relationship between Christianity and politics. Rather, reflection on how best to order one in relation to the other should begin with forms of context-sensitive practical reasoning. Echoing this assumption, each chapter oscillates between the descriptive and the prescriptive, both of which are shaped and colored by theological considerations. This oscillation reflects the nature of moral and political judgment, which simultaneously entails discernment and decision. Just or right judgment has a retrospective element (as an act of discernment, it pronounces upon an existent state of affairs), and as a decision it has a prospective and prescriptive aspect (it establishes or opens up a way toward a common field of action in which moral and political relations are possible).[2] Thus each chapter attends to both retrospective and prescriptive dimensions of judgment, giving an account of the conditions for coming to judgment (so aiding discernment) while at times offering specific, normative prescriptions that reflect my own position on a matter. My adjudications are contestable and contingent, but as prescriptions they display something of how political theology enables specific judgments. For example, the chapter on secularity reviews debates about the nature of the secular, and in doing so describes how secularity shapes the conditions of political decision making in the contemporary context; *and* it offers my take on how to construct secularity to optimize the conditions for faithful and wise political deliberation.

An intentional limitation of scope is the book's primary focus on Europe and North America. This is the context the book grows out of and addresses. However, precisely because of this context, the book pays attention to how modern conceptualizations of terms such as "democracy," "sovereignty," and "citizenship" *do not* emerge pristine from Europe to be exported elsewhere. There is no single point of origin. Drawing on Édouard Glissant's work, modern political theology is "creole," wrought in the com-

---

2. Oliver O'Donovan, *The Ways of Judgment* (Grand Rapids: Eerdmans, 2005), 7–12.

mercial and violent entanglements of Europe, the Middle East, Africa, and the Americas.[3] As Glissant, C. L. R. James, Cedric Robinson, Paul Gilroy, and others have argued, a crucible of modern political concepts is the "Black Atlantic" and the configurations and disruptions of the relationship between metropole and colony that circulated within it.[4] For example, as Barnor Hesse notes: "The modern framing of freedom, particularly in association with the democratic imaginary, was deeply embedded in colonial antagonisms of Atlantic slavery, shaped both by European and American governmental indifference to racial equality and passions aroused by the challenge or threat posed by black politics."[5] Moreover, the formation of liberal democratic nation-states in Europe was made possible by colonial political economies spread across the globe. While this formation is not the primary focus of this book, the chapters do draw lines of connection to it, and in some it is an explicit focus (see the chapters on humanitarianism, Black Power, Anglicanism, and humanity). And given this history, and because Eurocentric political theologies have mostly ignored or concealed the creolized nature of modern political terms and their colonial and racialized formation, it is necessary to shift the geography of political theology.[6] The main focus of this volume is the Atlantic world, even as other geographic registers and circuits of exchange are tacit within and occasionally show up in the book.[7]

---

3. Édouard Glissant, *Caribbean Discourse: Selected Essays*, trans. J. Michael Dash (Charlottesville: University Press of Virginia, 1989). The English and French meaning of "creole"/*créole* is *not* equivalent to the Spanish meaning of *criollo*. The parallel terms in Spanish are *mestizaje, mulatez*, and *mezcolanza*.

4. Paul Gilroy, *Black Atlantic: Modernity and Double Consciousness* (Cambridge, MA: Harvard University Press, 1993).

5. Barnor Hesse, "Symptomatically Black: A Creolization of the Political," in *The Creolization of Theory*, ed. Françoise Lionnet and Shu-mei Shih (Durham, NC: Duke University Press, 2011), 53.

6. This is to parse the Caribbean Philosophical Association's strapline "shifting the geography of reason."

7. Other circuits include that between Europe, the Levant, and the Middle East; that between Europe, India, and China; and later, that between North America and the countries of the Pacific Rim. An example of the way exchanges with India and across religious boundaries shaped political theology in the West is that between foundational figures in the American civil rights movement and the nonviolent movement led by Mahatma Gandhi. On this see Sarah Azaransky, *This Worldwide Struggle: Religion and the International Roots of the Civil Rights Movement* (Oxford: Oxford University Press, 2017). Azaransky's book is a good example of the shift in the geography of political theology I am calling for.

Political theology, as I see it, is an interpretive art for discovering faithful, hopeful, and loving judgments about how to act together in response to shared problems. And it is an art best practiced in the company of others, and through active listening to outsiders, whether inside or outside of our primary community. Without such shared deliberation and the modes of association it entails, we are liable to, on the one hand, error, bias, and false assumptions, and on the other, failing to serve that which is a raison d'être of political theology, namely, a faithful practice of politics.[8] I should also make clear that political theology is only ever an aid to judgment. Having either a "theologically sound" or "ideologically correct" political theology in no way guarantees making a wise political judgment. The possibility of that depends on a host of other factors, including character, imagination, what is desired, the quality of practical reasoning, and the comprehension of the good being sought and the context of its realization. And for a judgment to be faithful, hopeful, and loving, it depends on such factors as attunement to the work of the Holy Spirit through prayer and worship. Ultimately, the worth of any judgment rests with Christ, not conformity to this or that political theology.

Given my caution about using blueprints, I do not use a single framework of analysis such as natural law, or follow a theme such as liberation, or resort to a single method such as narrative theology, or apply a fixed set of axioms. Rather, I begin with a set of questions and problems we invariably confront when trying to address poverty and injustice, generate a common life with others, and negotiate or transform asymmetries of power. The interpretations and judgments developed in response to these questions and problems are woven from a mixture of threads that include biblical exegesis, intellectual and social history, moral and political philosophy, critical and social theories, ethnographic description, and theological analysis. And given my location, what is presented is primarily addressed

---

8. For a more extensive account of the methodology that informs my approach, and how it contrasts with, on the one hand, accounts that begin with a theological trope, axiom, or ideal that is then applied to reality and, on the other hand, accounts that begin with experience or context that is then correlated to theology, see Luke Bretherton, "Coming to Judgment: Methodological Reflections on the Relationship between Ecclesiology, Ethnography and Political Theory," *Modern Theology* 28, no. 2 (2012): 167-96. The key distinction is that I take theological and political conceptualizations to be always already in circulation with each other. There can be an ad hoc and contingent commensurability between them, but this can only be discerned and discovered rather than predetermined, systematized, or rejected.

to a Western context.[9] But my claim here goes beyond a call for attention to context, the need for self-reflexivity about structural location, and the importance of beginning with practical rather than theoretical reason when undertaking political theology. It is also a theological claim that the stitched-together character of the book reflects something of what kind of creatures we are, namely, the sort who must find ways of coming to and making shared judgments if common action is to be possible, but whose judgments about how to live together are frail and contingent, subject to dissolution and revision through time. Furthermore, contrary to much political theology and political philosophy, this book gives a positive assessment of the demotic energies that often shape politics. Instead of pathologizing them as irrational or seeking to control and order them through law, government, or prescribed forms of rationality (e.g., "public reason"), the book attempts a discernment of spirits to see where the Holy Spirit may be at work within and beyond the church in the life of the people. If the church is to witness to the work of Spirit, who is poured out on all flesh, part of faithful political judgment is discerning where the Spirit is at work in the world healing wounds, exorcising oppression, and bringing new life. Given this emphasis, my focus is on the political rather than the juridical dimensions of public life.

Part 1 lays out some frameworks through which Christians make sense of politics today. It is not an exhaustive set of political theologies, neither is it representative. Rather, given the central problems under consideration—namely, how to address suffering and injustice, and how to create and sustain a common life orientated to mutual flourishing amid difference and asymmetries of power—the political theologies reviewed are influential and paradigmatic approaches to these problems that are good to think with, thereby serving as invitations to reflect on one's own ways of thinking about politics. As case studies, they rehearse how to (a) understand the mutually

9. The canon, primary interlocutors, and points of reference would change depending on the regional orientation of a book of this nature. For example, in China, Confucius rather than Aristotle would be a primary interlocutor, and figures such as Hong Xiuquan, Wu Yaozong, or Lin Zhao would be modern points of reference. In Africa, what Henry Odera Oruka calls "African sage philosophy" would form a backdrop to deliberations, while contemporary figures ranging from John Mbiti to Mercy Amba Oduyoye would be contemporary interlocutors. That being said, given the meshwork of influences from around the world that informs Christian political thought throughout its history, there is no clear dividing line between one region and another. Yet a global introduction to political theology is beyond the scope of this volume.

constitutive relationship between talk of God and talk of politics; (b) see how political theologies emerge and take shape in response to different historical and political conditions that are the context needed to make sense of their judgments and theological emphases; (c) construct a coherent vision of political life shaped and grounded in theological commitments; and (d) foster more faithful, hopeful, and loving forms of political judgment and practice in response to different contexts and challenges. Two of the positions examined are explicit political theologies (Catholic social teaching, Anglican political theology). Two are movements with tacit political theologies that often go unrecognized as having one (humanitarianism, Pentecostalism). The chapter on Black Power assesses a position that is influenced by earlier political theologies, but that was complexly religious and nonreligious, carrying within it explicit political theologies (notably, black Christian nationalism), and was a catalyst for many broader developments in political theology—most directly, black liberation theology.

Part 1 begins with chapters on humanitarianism and Black Power, as these represent different beginning points for coming to address issues of suffering, injustice, and understanding the nature and purpose of a common life. Both seek to address poverty, but the former begins from what we share, the latter, from how we are different. These chapters also represent two different structural locations from which to do political theology: humanitarianism wrestles with the perplexities of privilege, while Black Power is derived from and confronts the ravages of oppression and the question of how to act politically in the face of systemic exclusion.[10] And while humanitarianism emphasizes how humans are the same, it often ignores questions of power. By contrast, Black Power makes questions of power central, challenging a key way in which power is distributed unjustly: namely, via white supremacy. Both are influential discourses informing how Christians imagine political life. For many churches, love of neighbor is understood within humanitarian terms as a kind of pastoral care. The legacy of Black Power and the political theology that emerged in its wake—black liberation theology—shape theological debates about race and identity central to contemporary cultural and political concerns about issues such as policing, mass incarceration, gentrification, and educational and health disparities.

10. Pentecostalism, Catholic social teaching, and Anglicanism are neither one nor the other of these beginning points and structural locations, combining elements—to a greater or lesser degree—of both.

Like the chapters on humanitarianism and Black Power, the chapters on Pentecostalism, Catholic social teaching, and Anglicanism also address different ways in which privilege and power construct sameness and difference. But their focus is more explicitly on how these dynamics play out in the relationship between church and world. All the chapters in part 1 review political theologies that emerge out of or are deeply shaped by the Atlantic world, but for Pentecostalism and Catholic social teaching the focus is on political theologies informing the most vibrant and numerically sizable streams of Christianity worldwide. Pentecostalism is arguably the largest social movement of the past hundred years and represents a seismic shift in the center of gravity of Christianity away from the West, even as non-Western Pentecostal churches shape Christianity in the West through patterns of migration and "reverse mission." The chapter on Pentecostalism thereby reckons with a "glocalized" form of political theology.[11] If Pentecostalism represents an emerging, populist strand of political theology, Catholic social teaching represents an established, top-down, and formal political theology that nevertheless takes as foundational the life of the people as basic to faithful political witness. A further contrast is that Pentecostalism tends to emphasize the distinctiveness of Christianity over and against the world—establishing an at-times antagonistic relationship between the two—whereas a characteristic feature of Roman Catholic political theology is emphasizing the continuity between church and world through the use of natural law and a notion that a Christian moral and political vision can be shared by all people of "good will."

Anglicanism is another stream of Christianity that exists worldwide, but one that combines Protestant and Catholic elements. Alongside the Pentecostal/charismatic movement, it is the tradition that I am situated within, and so including it is a way of locating myself on the map. Anglican political theology is the fruit of an established church, but it is a church that was always internally and externally contested, and so the relationship between power, plurality, and a common life is central to its formation. It also represents a different kind of political imaginary to that of Catholic social teaching and Pentecostalism, one which informs much of the insti-

---

11. Ogbu Kalu identifies Pentecostalism as "glocal" in form as a way of naming how it sits at the intersection of global processes and local identities. See Ogbu Kalu, *African Pentecostalism: An Introduction* (Oxford: Oxford University Press, 2008), 188–92. The neologism "glocal" is a disruptive term meant to deconstruct false dichotomies that oppose the local and global. It points to how each refracts and produces the other. See Roland Robertson, *Globalization: Social Theory and Global Culture* (London: Sage, 1992), 130.

tutional architecture and political discourses of the modern world as part of the afterlife of the British Empire. What it shares with Pentecostalism and Roman Catholicism is an acceptance of democracy as the normative form of political order. Yet each of these traditions gives a different kind of rationale for this commitment.

While distinct, each chapter in part 1 helps illuminate and intersects with all the other chapters. For example, the Anglican Church invests heavily in humanitarian work, and humanitarianism shapes the political imagination of many Anglicans. Large parts of the Anglican Communion have been "Pentecostalized." At the same time, racism and colonialism have been formative of the Anglican Church, while, from the black Episcopal abolitionist Peter Williams Jr. through Anna Julia Cooper, Pauli Murray, and Desmond Tutu, a concern for black liberation and black self-determination has also been a current in Anglican political thought. So Black Power critiques of white supremacy, and liberation theologies more generally, should be an important interlocutor for the further development of Anglican political theology. And Anglican political theology cannot be understood apart from its ongoing dialogue with Catholic social teaching. Nest-like, parallel points of connection interlace the other chapters in part 1. Subsequent sections excavate and develop further the key concepts, terms, and issues at work in these initial chapters.

Part 2 focuses on the challenges that corrode a common life over time amid asymmetries of power and identifies practices that sustain it. Each chapter in this section addresses issues that, if not responded to constructively, lead to the fracture and dissolution of a common life as a realm of mutual flourishing. Additionally, the question of how to coordinate commonality, plurality, and power, and how failure to coordinate them justly and lovingly generates much suffering and oppression, permeates my thinking throughout. The part begins with a chapter on class analyzed through the prism of how social hierarchies of one form or another shape the common life of a congregation, and then turns to a chapter on the difference between secularism and secularity. Its focus is the need for Christians to coordinate pursuit of the kingdom of God (and a distinctive form of life) with pursuit of penultimate goods held in common with non-Christian others through constructing a common life that is secular yet open to theological claims. The third chapter is on toleration and hospitality understood as constructive responses to the challenge of generating a common life with those we object to, find scandalous, or strange. Each chapter in this section follows on from and builds on the one before it.

Part 3 sets out key concepts and terms for thinking about democracy as a means for generating patterns of common life characterized by mutual flourishing. However, instead of starting with the formal institutions of the modern liberal democratic state, I offer an approach to thinking about politics from the vantage point of the everyday and the quotidian that, at the same time, tries to keep in view the ironic and ambivalent nature of political life in this age before Christ's return. Picking up on themes explored in the first two parts, part 3 opens with a chapter on humanity, setting out a theological anthropology for understanding how difference and sameness are constitutive of any form of life together with others, including nonhuman ways of being alive. It also argues that understanding what it means to be human necessitates attending to questions of politics and power if our very conceptions of humanity are to avoid legitimizing forms of oppression. A chapter on the meaning and purpose of economics follows, as economics is a central part of creating and sustaining a common life. It argues that economic relations must be understood as embedded within prior moral and political relations if they are to help generate forms of human and ecological flourishing. This chapter, along with that on humanity, thereby sets up the importance of subsequent chapters that explore the twin poles of democracy: sovereignty and the people. The chapter on sovereignty addresses primarily European debates about the nature of political authority, as these debates form key conceptual terrain over which contemporary political theology travels. Next there is a chapter on the people and populism understood as simultaneously theological and political categories. Politically, the people are the justificatory basis of modern sovereignty, and the formation and demarcation of "the people" is the primary site of democratic politics. Populism—whether democratic or antidemocratic—is taken to be an inherent feature of this process of formation and demarcation. Part 3 concludes with a summary, somewhat polemical chapter on the term "democratic politics," outlining how it is as relevant to what goes on in church or on a school board as to what is done in Congress.

If a central theme underlying part 2 is how Christians should orient themselves within existing democratic polities, the primary focus of part 3 is setting out a constructive political theology of democratic politics as a means through which to pursue the flourishing of creation. Understanding the relationship between Christianity and democracy is vital for three reasons. The first is historical. Democracy was a primary means through which Western churches responded to processes of modernization such as industrialization, the rise of nation-states and capitalism, and the new forms of social and ecological relationships that emerge through them. Understanding how Christianity situates itself in relation to the contemporary context means, at least in part, understanding its relationship to democracy. The second reason is normative. Christians do not need democracy to practice their faith, but democracy enshrines some central Christian commitments, and so, as a judgment of practical reason, democracy should be an aspirational feature of political order for Christians. But the theo-logic of this judgment and aspiration needs spelling out, as it is neither immediately obvious nor well known. The third is apologetic. Atrophy or outright rejection increasingly threatens democracy as a way of ordering political life, solving shared problems, and pursuing human and ecological flourishing. The book enumerates the ways it is threatened and undermined. The likes of William Temple, Jacques Maritain, and Reinhold Niebuhr stated the theological case for democracy when faced with adherence to totalitarian and authoritarian regimes in the 1930s and 1940s, and there is a similar need to do so today. But the context and threats are somewhat different, and so a different kind of case needs to be made.

All the chapters in the book stand on their own and so can be read as individual essays. However, like a Cubist portrait that connects multiple dimensions and angles of vision, seen together, these essays paint a composite theological picture of social, political, and economic relations in the contemporary Western context. Rather than following a single linear genealogical road, I plot multiple intersecting pathways through the same landscape.[12] An overly neat approach that posits a uniform line of development from a single point of origin makes determinative one history, geography, and set of experiences. Arguably, such an approach is "unbiblical," as the Bible itself is a multigenre, polyglot text that traverses multiple histories and geographies. As already noted, I situate my account of political theology within the Atlantic world and its cross-cutting interchanges. Doing so recognizes multiple points of origin and enables a broader range of voices to inform what is taken to be political theology. The organization of the book also means that, as a portrait of the relationship between Christianity and contemporary politics, it steps beyond a single genre to combine elements of a collection of essays, a companion, and an introduction.

12. An example of the linear approach is Oliver O'Donovan and Joan Lockwood O'Donovan, eds., *From Irenaeus to Grotius: A Sourcebook in Christian Political Thought, 100-1625* (Grand Rapids: Eerdmans, 1999).

Priority is given to topics and terms that are both constitutive of and definitional for politics and political theology (as defined in the first chapter). Some chapters examine background dynamics that shape politics today—dynamics with which the church must contend—namely, capitalism, class, secularism, and white supremacy.[13] Themes—notably ecology, gender, power, justice, and love—not addressed by an individual chapter are touched on in many of the chapters. Other chapters contain a focused analysis of key terms—notably "poverty" and "privilege" in chapter 2, and "citizenship" in chapter 3. However, the book does not aim to be either comprehensive or encyclopedic. Neither is it a dictionary. Inevitably, therefore, there are shortcomings and elisions. There are some highly pertinent topics I do not address; for example, the way either war or sexuality impacts politics.[14] There are terrains I do not map; for example, the multifarious strands of political theology that feed into evangelicalism. There are trails I do not explore; for example, the interconnection between Christian and Jewish political theology and political thinkers—but which are nevertheless present in the text, as evidenced in references to figures such as Martin

---

13. I treat elsewhere some of these background terms and conditions, notably, what is meant by the term "civil society." See Luke Bretherton, *Resurrecting Democracy: Faith, Citizenship, and the Politics of a Common Life* (Cambridge: Cambridge University Press, 2015), 179–218. I steer away from using the term "civil society" in this volume because when it comes to the political role of churches and other religious associations, "civil society" confuses more than it clarifies. On this see Jacob Levy, *Rationalism, Pluralism, and Freedom* (Oxford: Oxford University Press, 2015), 17–22.

14. The central focus of this book is the nature and form of politics. But I recognize the contingency of this starting point. There is a strand of political thought that sees war as the basis of politics—politics is war by other means. My approach explicitly rejects such a framework (see chap. 1). More recently, an alternative starting point for thinking about political order is represented by queer theory. It contends that unless one begins with the instabilities of how sexuality and gender are constructed, and the way norms about sexual identity organize social, economic, and political relations, one is masking *a*, if not *the*, fundamental way in which human life together is ordered and power distributed. In political theology, the work of Marcella Althaus Reid exemplifies this kind of analysis. This is a compelling account but not one I have taken to frame this book, as I think it makes overdeterminative one aspect of a common life. However, the account I develop has points of connection to the work of some queer theorists (e.g., José Esteban Muñoz and Judith Butler), while for others it would be seen as wholly antithetical (e.g., Lee Edelman). Moreover, some will question the absence of a chapter devoted to sexuality. While that is debatable, I focus on race (chapter 3) and class (chapter 7), and their interstitial operations, as paradigmatic of all other structures of oppression.

Buber, Hannah Arendt, and Walter Benjamin. And there are strands of thought in which I have emphasized some voices over others; for example, within feminist theology broadly construed, I focus on womanist, black feminist, and *mujerista* theology.

The book can be used as the basis for an introductory course in Christian political theology, or individual chapters can be incorporated into broader ethics or theology courses. The book can also be used for discussion groups in a variety of settings. To aid these uses, each chapter is accompanied by a set of suggested scriptural texts as well as readings, mostly in primary sources, that can be used as the basis for further discussion. For the readings, I have selected one or two classic texts from an earlier period to put into dialogue with a range of modern texts, each of which illuminates and shares a set of concerns with the chapter in question.[15] The readings are of such a length that, depending on the time available, either one or a cluster could be selected for use in a single class.[16] As structured, the book moves from the ground up, beginning with some significant ways Christians are already making sense of political life and then unfolding key terms and debates through which to understand the interaction of Christianity and politics. However, it can also be read or taught in the reverse order. Those who like to understand key concepts first, and then see how they are at work in a series of interlinked positions, can begin with the last essay and work backward.

In summary, the book consists of a series of intersecting essays that together constitute an inquiry into some of the primary vocabulary, ideas, themes, and schools of thought that shape Christian reflection on politics in the West. I include material from my prior publications, but in a revised and often more explicitly theological way. The chapters combine systematic overviews and historical descriptions with normative judgments. Together, these provide a deep field of vision for understanding the contemporary relevance of the terms and arguments discussed.

Overall, this book explores what it means for Christians to speak and act faithfully, hopefully, and lovingly in the contemporary Western political context. This is a context in which, on a daily basis, I find myself boxed into choosing between, on the one hand, a politics that reduces human flourish-

---

15. The readings are listed in the order of original publication date. When a suggested reading is not explicitly discussed in the chapter, a short line explaining why it is included is given.

16. To that end, many of the primary sources suggested are from abridged versions, and so of a manageable length.

ing to securing material prosperity and consuming better and, on the other hand, a set of polarizing social scripts that reduce politics to conforming to a brittle ideological checklist, whether of the left or the right. If the former provides a comforting familiarity, the latter compensates with a sense of drama and moral urgency. In my settled moments, I know that neither option abides with the spiritual, physical, psychological, and interpersonal complexities of living a life with and for my friends, colleagues, neighbors, and family members, let alone those I find strange or threatening. Yet such a life is the reality of what I, and I think most of us, seek to nourish, while at the same time having a care for those around us who suffer, whether at home or abroad. Like others, I find myself bewildered in the face of what it means to live a flourishing life with and for others and need help trying to meaningfully and purposefully reach toward inhabiting one. In these pages, I have tried to address this need by articulating a political theology that speaks beyond either bourgeois or ideological pieties, and which is capacious enough to address the profound desire many have for faith, hope, and love amidst the struggles and indignities of everyday life, and the personal and political catastrophes and injustices that afflict those around us. While I can provide neither comfort nor drama, I hope that what follows helps generate wisdom and passion for how to live well as political animals who confess Jesus Christ as Lord amidst the perplexities and tragedies of a human life.

I begin by examining how to understand two terms central to the book: "political theology" and "politics." The next chapter is programmatic for the book as a whole. It combines the genealogy of political theology as a field and definitions of some core terms used throughout the book with a constructive vision for how to understand the relationship between Christianity and politics.

CHAPTER 1

What Is Political Theology? What Is Politics?

We are immersed in talk of politics. It dominates the news cycle and conversations with friends and family. It shapes critical aspects of our lives and can even determine our sense of identity. Political talk arouses strong emotions, divides society, and can lead to war. It should therefore matter a great deal what kinds of speech count as political speech, how we talk together about politics, and whether we understand what people mean when they use a term like "democracy," "state," or "government."

How anyone speaks about politics matters, but a specific challenge exists for Christians: many political terms are also terms Christians use to talk about who God is and who we are in relation to God. Words like "ruler" and "kingdom" have obvious political overtones. But even seemingly churchy words like "liturgy," "ecclesial," and "bishop" are explicitly political in origin. The symbiosis between talk of God and talk of politics sets up all sorts of potential connections, conflations, and confusions. Political concepts can illuminate but also be overidentified with theological ones, and vice versa. For example, when we talk of God's sovereignty, is that the same as talking about the sovereignty of a state? Or should we understand these uses of "sovereignty" very differently? The potential for confusion becomes even more pronounced when we talk about the interaction between church and state or between the Christian life and political life. The attempt to talk rightly about the interaction between Christianity and politics generates different schools of thought, which articulate divergent understandings. For example, how Calvinists frame church-state relations (as involving a connected but mutually disciplining relationship) differs markedly from how Anabaptists understand it (as necessitating separation). If Christians are to understand each other, let alone their non-Christian neighbors, then greater clarity is needed about the ways in which different Christians approach political life. Added to this is the need for more generative and theologically robust ways of articulating how Christians should talk and act with others as moral and political animals. This book aims to address both needs.

Theological reflection on politics has come to be called, perhaps unsurprisingly, "political theology." But what, precisely, is meant by this term? To answer this question, I first examine how confessing Jesus Christ as Lord and Savior inherently makes a claim about the nature and purpose of politics, but also, how all theological claims emerge from a political process. Second, I set out a theological rationale for politics. Third, I reflect on how political theology is not just a confessional endeavor. It can also constitute a form of "political philosophy"; that is, it can be a way of thinking about the nature and purpose of politics independent of whether or not someone confesses Jesus Christ as Lord. The division between confessional and nonconfessional approaches to political theology raises the question of how to classify different political theologies. This question is taken up in the fourth section. These initial parts focus on the theological dimensions of political theology. The fifth section analyzes its political aspects, exploring how politics is two-faced. On the one hand, politics denotes statecraft—top-down, unilateral, and coercive ways of ordering life together. On the other hand, it denotes a relational, bottom-up, and nonviolent craft for forging and sustaining a common life. Building on this distinction, I delineate in the sixth part how political theology both works with and reconfigures Greco-Roman ways of understanding the nature and purpose of politics, arguing that the ways it does so is paradigmatic for subsequent interactions between confessional political theology and other political philosophies. The final part extends this analysis to show how political theology also generates ways of reimagining economic and familial relations.

Political Theology as Theology

Politics is a foundational part of forging a good or flourishing life. The good life is not reducible to individual happiness: we are social creatures whose flourishing emerges out of and depends on being embedded in some form of common life. Moreover, a truly good, happy, and meaningful life cannot be built on the domination of others. Therefore, to ask what the good or moral life is necessitates asking about how such a life is symbiotic with the flourishing of others. It requires asking what the interpersonal, structural, ecological, and cosmic conditions of human flourishing are, and conversely, how their absence constitutes a form of suffering.

As the central way humans create and order their common life, politics determines whether this common life is just or unjust, generous or heartless, peaceable or violent. Politics is therefore central to the nature and form of the good or moral life, and thus any analysis of the nature and form of morality must include reflection on the nature of political life.[1] Unsurprisingly then, from the Bible onward, political life has figured largely in theological reflection on the meaning, purpose, and ordering of human life in response to the revelation of God given in Jesus Christ. But such reflection is also always already contextual, as theological and political questions arise through having to negotiate a common life in a specific time and place.

Theology is not reducible to politics. That is to say, politics does not exhaust the meaning and purpose of theology. However, theology always has a political valence, and its formulation and articulation involve political, economic, and social processes. An example of this is the Nicene Creed, which, after Scripture, is a primary document of Christian confession. It is a vital formulation of Christian belief and means of *paradosis* (the handing on of faith between generations). It contains reflection on the nature and form of politics. And it was written as the result of a political process involving Roman imperial authorities. But no single one of these three elements should wholly determine how to interpret the creed. Rather, each of these elements is important for understanding this creed as a form of Christian confession.

To pick up on just one of these elements, the creed testifies to the centrality of politics to questions about who God is and who we are in relation to God. Alongside Mary and Jesus, the figure of Pontius Pilate is the only other human person named in both the Apostles' Creed and the Nicene Creed. His inclusion signifies something vital about the nature of politics and the nature of the relationship between Christianity and all forms of political order.[2] Politics is always time and site specific, involving particu-

---

1. I take political theology to be a constitutive part of and subset within Christian ethics/moral theology. Moral theology is not reducible to or wholly conflated with political theology, but political theology needs to be a dimension of any full-orbed response to moral questions.

2. For a parallel reflection on the encounter between Jesus and Pilate as definitional for political theology, see Karl Barth, "Church and State," in *Community, State, and*

lar persons making judgments in specific places. When talk about politics becomes too abstract, it loses touch with how granular histories are the forge in which political life is cast. Political theology must account for how sweeping historical forces such as capitalism, or systemic injustices such as racism and sexism, determine conditions for action. But a Christian account of political life must avoid any fervor to see the world wholly in structural terms. Rather, it should always keep in view how it is nameable persons who must take responsibility and be held accountable for the right and wrong judgments they make or omit to make.[3] Here the contrast between Pilate and Mary is instructive. Mary, someone without status and oppressed in multiple ways, acts in faith and love toward God, and in so doing changes the cosmos. Pilate, someone with high status and authority over life and death, acts out of fear and pride, rejects God, but his actions achieve nothing but their own negation.

Pilate points to how God judges and condemns the Roman Empire and the form of political order it represents and embodies. Jesus was judged to be an enemy of the dominant religious-political order, and so was condemned to be shamed and humiliated through crucifixion. The form this humiliation took was a parodic exaltation designed to make a grotesque spectacle of and thereby mock the pretensions of Jesus to be a king. But God the Father glorified Jesus, inverting the parody, thereby mocking and shaming the established authorities of the day. As a way of humbling the self-proclaimed rulers of the age, Christ's crucifixion, resurrection, and ascension are a twofold response. First, there is a reversal that upends sovereignty understood in imperial, tyrannous, and exploitative terms so that such forms of lordship are dethroned and shown to be anti-Christic.[4] The drama and radical newness of this reversal—whereby ancient forms of dignity and glory are revealed to be preposterous and pretentious, and

---

Church: Three Essays (Eugene, OR: Wipf & Stock, 2004 [1960]), 108–14. Barth condemns Pilate for allowing injustice to run its course, but he does not reckon with how Pilate's actions are a form of judgment and how Pilate's failure to defend Jesus speaks to the often arbitrary and unaccountable actions of political authorities.

3. An extreme example that clearly illustrates this interaction is how a nuclear strike is ordered in the USA. The president must decide to activate the codes, but his or her agency is not possible without large-scale material, economic, and military infrastructures and meshworks of social relations that are the condition for the existence and upkeep of the weapons and make possible their launch. Use of the weapons requires both individual agency and structure.

4. The creeds thereby witness against their own context of composition.

a seditious, possibly lunatic slave embodies and becomes the criterion for identifying what is true, good, and beautiful—are often lost on contemporary readers.[5] Pilate is in the creeds because this reversal is vital for understanding why the gospel is good news. Pilate, far from being the center of the story (and in the archive of recorded history, it is the Pilates of this world who are always the center of the story), is a marginal figure. Jesus is the main character, and in the creeds, Jesus's story is the turning point of all history.

Second, Christ's crucifixion, resurrection, and ascension reveal the impotence of fallen principalities and powers, who, when challenged, can only constrain, punish, and kill, and in doing so expose the limits of their power and their fear of their own limits. In contrast to Pilate, and in him all worldly authorities of which he is a type, the resurrection and ascension unveil the deepest and only life-giving source of power: the power of the Spirit. The Spirit brings calm out of storms, health out of disease, and resurrection out of death. And at Pentecost, this power is poured out on all flesh so that all may have abundant life. By implication, at the most basic level of confession, Christians are to realize that the institutions and structures of this world, and those who rule them, while fearsome, are not in control, and do not have the last word. Jesus is the Alpha and Omega and, as Lord of the cosmos, relativizes and points beyond all human structures and

---

5. Even if the person crucified was not legally a chattel slave, crucifixion was associated with the execution of slaves and identified those crucified with the status of a slave. Through crucifixion, Jesus was therefore configured as someone who had no status or agency whatsoever within the existing order of things and on whom any manner of brutality and degradation could be unleashed. This brutality served to inscribe on and through the body of the crucified, via the imaginations of the onlookers, the sovereign status of the existing political order. In reference to the crucifixion as the event through which to interpret Christ, Phil. 2 explicitly identifies Christ as a slave, thereby turning upside down accepted status hierarchies (the divine as slave). Moreover, Philippians and the passion narratives point back to Exodus and the books of the law that remind us that salvation cannot be understood, let alone lived into, unless the status of the slave seeking liberation is the perspective from which it is remembered and the future contemplated (e.g., Lev. 26:13; Deut. 5:15). The significance of the crucifixion for challenging all patterns of earthly sovereignty is enormous yet rarely reckoned with, particularly in Western societies still living in the afterlife of modern forms of chattel slavery. Naming Jesus as a slave refuses to sanitize the horror of what is happening but at the same time makes clear the critique of all forms of earthly sovereignty it enacts. I am grateful to Matt Elia, on whose unpublished work I draw for this insight. The mocking of Jesus as mad or foolish is something the Western tradition has drawn on more explicitly in art, literature, ecclesial life, and theology. Traditions of the holy fool are but one example.

authorities that shape our common life. His Lordship admits no other—there is only one, and this one is like no other—meaning that it defines and relativizes all other claims to rule (Deut. 6:4-5). Conversely, politics and economics neither exhaust nor explain what it means to be human; while bread is necessary to live, we cannot live by bread alone.

Echoing how the creeds position Pilate, political theology is bifocal. It articulates the nature, form, and purpose of political life in the light of the revelation of God given in Jesus Christ while at the same time attending to the historical realities in which that life is lived. Political theology discerns the consonance and dissonance between the form of rule incarnated and inaugurated by Jesus Christ and the orders and authorities shaping this age between Christ's ascension and return. At times, it identifies how penultimate authorities obey Christ, while at other times it detects how they are anti-Christic. Political theology aids our discernment of how to act appropriately in *this* time, in both its historical and its eschatological register. To be Christian, any process of discernment must itself be subject to the gospel, which is no easy matter, as the gospel is anarchic, fissile material, at once disruptive and creative in its political effects.

So What Is *Theological* about Political Theology?

As already indicated, "theology" in the term "political theology" refers to reflection on the nature and form of political life in response to Jesus Christ as the revelation of God. Thus, it is woven into and out of theological anthropology, that is, the articulation of what humans are as creatures and sinners who are redeemed and fulfilled in and through Jesus Christ and in the power of the Holy Spirit. Theological anthropology constitutes the normative basis of political theology. And it is the Bible, along with its reception in myriad subsequent confessions of belief and practice (e.g., the creeds), that is the primary point of reference for envisioning and describing what it means to be human and how to situate political life within a wider drama of divine-human relations. This book tracks various understandings of what it means to be human—some more theological than others—and has a whole chapter devoted to just this question. Put schematically, driving the constructive elements of my arguments is the attempt to think through political theology from the standpoint of what it means to be a *creature*, to be in *covenantal relation* with God and neighbor (whether through the institutions of the church or not), and to be open to *conversion* (to be a sinner in need of and receptive to the work of the Spirit in healing and delivering creation, thereby reopening creation to its eschatological fulfillment).

As creatures, situated in various covenantal relations, and in need of conversion, we are always already in relationship with others. Our personhood is the fruit of a social and wider ecological womb as much as a single physical one; that is, we come to be in and through others not like us, including nonhuman others. This means we cannot exist without some kind of *common life* with a plurality of human and nonhuman ways of being alive. The theological claim is that we cannot enjoy a fullness of existence without communion with God. Given what it means to be a fallen, finite, and frail creature whose survival and flourishing depend on the care of others, the formation of a common life is necessary to live. And the formation of any form of common life entails politics. We act politically, for better or worse, when we do the work of forging and sustaining patterns of common life. The character and form of a distinctively Christian vision of political relations—and thence the basis of a common life—are based on neighbor love. I spell out below what I mean by neighbor love and how it incorporates love of the stranger, the enemy, and the friendless.

If one foundational warrant for political theology is our relationship to God and others, another is our relationship to time and space. If humans are to participate more lovingly and justly in forms of common life with each other, with nonhuman life, and with God, then the current social, political, and economic structures need to change. That the current spatial and temporal order of things is not inevitable or necessary, and that it can and should change, is a central scriptural theme. Abram and Sarai must leave Haran to become Abraham and Sarah. God delivers Israel from Egypt. The institutions of kingship in Israel are ambiguous in origin and wayward in practice, so that prophets must remind the king of a higher law than their own writ. Babylon is a place of exile, not the way things should be. And while Jesus Christ has come, creation still groans as we await Christ's return. In these stories and tropes, the Bible deconstructs and offers an alternative to any attempt to write a particular social, economic, and political order into the cosmic order in such a way that a contingent and fallen way of ordering time and space is inscribed with an immutable character and posited as inevitable, natural, or "just the way things should be." However, the tension between the world as it is and the world as it will be in the kingdom of God gives rise to a dilemma at the heart of political theology. We must strive to see present political arrangements from the standpoint of eternity so that we can understand them as spatially and temporally contingent. However, to make political judgments as if one is already a full-fledged inhabitant of God's eternal realm is to render what is contingent sacrosanct and unchangeable. Instead, we must accept the contingency and frailty of our judgments (however righteous the cause) as the price of admitting we are temporal, not eternal. To be faithful, political judgments must be held lightly (thereby resisting making this age a final home), even as they are made with the intention to live now in the light of eternity.

However strong the temptation, the political, social, and economic order of the day should not be equated with God's *oikonomia*, that is, God's cultivation of the cosmos. The church often forgets this injunction, with terrible consequences, but prophetic figures and movements are raised up by the Spirit to help the church remember it. From the martyrs' refusal to bow the knee to the Roman emperor as Lord, through to modern confessions such as Mary Wollstonecraft's *Vindication of the Rights of Woman* (1792), David Walker's *Appeal to the Colored Citizens of the World* (1829), the Barmen Declaration (1934) against the Nazis, and Martin Luther King Jr.'s "Letter from Birmingham Jail" (1963), it is a foundational (if often ignored) political insight of Christianity that there is a need to deconstruct and offer an alternative to any attempt to sanctify a political order or to say it is immutable. At the same time, pursuit of the kingdom of God is inseparable from pursuit of penultimate goods in common. Down the centuries, political theologies have at times coordinated pursuit of the kingdom of God and pursuit of penultimate goods and at other times conflated them.

Political Theology as Political Philosophy

What I have outlined so far is a Christian conception of political theology. But the term has a history both before and outside of Christian usage. As a term, it can refer to how pre-Christian Stoic philosophy envisaged the beliefs and practices associated with state cults that divinized and personified the political order through divine figures such as Athena or Jupiter. The "political theology" of a polity was contrasted with "natural theology," said to transcend any given political order and be universal. More recently, the term has been associated with a stream of thinkers who raid the Christian archive to furnish themselves with categories and concepts for reflection on modern politics. They utilize the Christian archive out of recognition that, at least in the West, much of the language and conceptual grammar of political life has roots in theological beliefs and practices. Nevertheless, this is nonconfessional, "postsecular" political theology. At the same time, it is entwined with and contributes to explicitly confessional forms of political theology.

A synonym for political theology could be Christian political philosophy. However, as already noted, this does not quite capture the ways non-Christians have taken up the theological archive for reflection on politics. And feeding into contemporary political theology is the complex intellectual history of the relationship between political philosophy and theology in the West, so that figures such as Augustine, Thomas Aquinas, John Calvin, Thomas Hobbes, G. W. F. Hegel, Jane Addams, and Martin Luther King Jr. are part of both the canon of political theology and the canon of "secular" political thought. Conversely, avowed non-Christian thinkers such as Karl Marx, Friedrich Nietzsche, and Hannah Arendt deploy theological terms and can be vital interlocutors in explicitly Christian political theology. Political theology can thereby be confessional or nonconfessional. Dante and Leo Tolstoy are confessing Christians whose work addresses the church but who are also read to illuminate explicitly nonconfessional political projects. In contrast, contemporary figures such as the Italian philosopher Giorgio Agamben and the Slovenian philosopher Slavoj Žižek write explicitly nonconfessional political theology that can, nevertheless, be read and appropriated confessionally. Such contemporary figures stand in continuity with one of the seminal figures of early modern political theology, Baruch Spinoza (1632–1677). Then there are those who write non-Christian political theology by engaging with the Christian archive but within a different religious or philosophical tradition. A prominent example is Mahatma Gandhi; others include the German-Jewish philosopher Jacob Taubes and the Chinese democratic activist and dissident Liu Xiaobo.

Political Theology or Political Theologies? The Problem of Classification

Alongside a division between confessional and nonconfessional are a range of other fissures that shape and order what is understood to be the purpose, content, and form of politecal theology. These fractures are then used to create a taxonomy. One such is a broad division between sapiential (wisdom-focused, prudential) and apocalyptic forms of political theology. However, alongside sapiential and apocalyptic forms, most theologians and schools of thought deploy a variety of genres, including tragic, comedic, and, on occasion, epic styles (for example, Augustine's *City of God* is a monumental prose epic).[6] This diversity is right. Political theology needs multiple genres to articulate the realities of which it speaks.

A widely taught but problematic approach to narrating the field is to divide political theology, in all its forms, between two broad currents of reflection: the Augustinian-Reformed and Aristotelian-Thomistic traditions of moral and political thought. The key divide is theological, turning on whether political life is understood as a post-Fall development or whether it is an original part of creation. If the former, politics is a symptom of the introduction of sin into creation; if the latter, politics is a good in itself rather than at best a providential good that inhibits things getting worse. A lot follows from this division. If the former, political authority and political life are primarily about restraining evil. If the latter, politics is part of human flourishing, even though, after the Fall, it is caught up in and manifests idolatrous and sinful patterns. In this book, I split the difference. Politics is a creational good, the goal of which is a just and loving common life, embodying as it does the good of association. Statecraft, which entails the use of coercive, unilateral power, is a postlapsarian endeavor that at its best inhibits evil.

To state things as they are often taught, following the Aristotelian-Thomistic line will supposedly lead to a more positive view of human efforts and political authority in forming moral persons and communities. By contrast, the Augustinian-Reformed approach is said to lead to greater skepticism about what humans are capable of and tends to emphasize the priority of divine rather than human action in the formation of just and loving persons and communities. The primary problem with this portrayal is that Augustine and Aquinas are closer than this account presumes, and there is much overlap in the strands of thought they are said to spawn. While there are divisions in the tradition over whether political life is either good but fallen or intrinsically sinful, the nomenclature is misplaced: Augustine and Aquinas fall on neither one side nor the other of this division.

---

6. Arguably, all tragedy is a form of political theology. However, while the tragedies of Sophocles, Euripides, and Shakespeare focus on the fate of the powerful and prosperous, in the modern, democratic age, the tragic figure is ordinary, quotidian, and lowly. Although, as Peter Burian argues, even though its settings were not democratic, ancient Athenian tragedy was itself a form of democratic discourse. See "Athenian Tragedy as Democratic Discourse," in *Why Athens? A Reappraisal of Tragic Politics*, ed. D. M. Carter (Oxford: Oxford University Press, 2011), 95-117.

Rather, they share a sense of humans as political animals whose temporal and eschatological fulfillment requires the formation of a common life; of political rule as a potentially virtuous activity orientated to promoting human flourishing; and of the importance of well-ordered institutions (e.g., household and commonwealth) to structuring the pursuit of a good life.[7]

A parallel but no less problematic binary is sometimes drawn between Augustine and Eusebius, that is, between political theologies that understand established political authorities to be contingent (Augustine) and those that sacralize the existing political order (Eusebius). The modern reception of Eusebius portrays him as a propagandist of empire. However, even as he validates imperial rule as having a place in God's providential ordering of the cosmos, he renders it contingent, while at the same time seeking to school the emperor by emphasizing the pastoral dimensions of rule. Variations of the divide between Augustine and Eusebius are between "non-Constantinian" and "Constantinian" as well as dissenting and establishment streams of political theology. Closer inspection reveals blurred lines and many points of overlap between the seeming polarities of these positions.

There is a further, very significant weakness of the taxonomy that focuses solely on supposed divisions between Augustinian-Reformed and Aristotelian-Thomistic strands of political theology. It is one that ignores and marginalizes less formal and more radical traditions. One example is black political theologies articulated by figures such as Nat Turner, Olaudah Equiano, Martin Delany, Ida B. Wells, Frederick Douglass, and Albert Cleage Jr. As I will argue throughout the book, it is vital that political theology not simply canvass a broad range of voices when formulating a position but give priority to those who speak from the "underside of history." But to do so requires problematizing three things: the geography, historiography, and canon of political theology. I problematized the geography of political theology in the introduction by drawing attention to how it is a creolized set of discourses born out of the commercial and colonial entanglements of the Atlantic and other worlds. Our notion of history also needs troubling, as modern conceptions of history are mostly an attempt to give an account of life together through time without reference to God or the status of humans as creatures. Such an approach

---

7. Eric Gregory and Joseph Clair, "Augustinianisms and Thomisms," in *The Cambridge Companion to Christian Political Theology*, ed. Craig Hovey and Elizabeth Phillips (Cambridge: Cambridge University Press, 2015), 176–96.

generates genealogies of political theology as if God does not exist. And the canon of texts—and what and who counts as doing political theology—needs revising. Modern intellectual history, political philosophy, and political theology presume an archive and therefore focus on those who had status of some kind or produced records. In modern Western political theology, this was primarily white men imbricated in one kind of colonizing project or another. Up to now political theology has primarily focused on textual analysis and commentary, so the challenge is how to listen to those who are without an archive and increase the range of figures who count as doing political theology. Going forward, a range of other disciplines and methods needs to be incorporated such as oral history, folklore, archeology, and ethnography.[8] This is not a call to abandon the notion of a canon. A canon of texts, cases, and concepts is necessary for thinking through political questions in a robust and responsible way with others, over generations. It is rather a call to reconfigure how the canon of political theology is imagined and narrated.

The work of people like Turner, Wells, and Douglass—and the way their work problematizes the geography, historiography, and canon of political theology—poses a further question, that of how to situate white, Eurocentric streams of political theology in relation to nonwhite, non-Eurocentric approaches. This very formulation illustrates the problem. Is one side defined by a negative or mimetic relation to the other? Or is one a form of dissent or subversion of a "mainstream" set of positions? Or are these incommensurable traditions locked in a permanent struggle, with the affirmation of one constituting the negation of the other? Or is the relationship dialectical? All these formulations of the relationship are problematic because they all rest on one kind of binary or another. Echoing my critique of prior divisions, I contend it is crucial to resist setting up binaries between traditional and radical, conservative and progressive, mainstream and subversive, premodern and modern, Western and non-Western, or colonial and decolonial frames of reference. Such binaries can make for compelling rhetoric, but too often they are reductive attempts to stabilize and simplify what are inherently dynamic and often paradoxical relations, thereby concealing more than they reveal. Chapter 4 on Pentecostalism exemplifies what I am getting at, as Pentecostalism does not fit straightforwardly on to either one side or the other of the categories just outlined.

8. This is something I have undertaken in my previous work through the use of ethnography.

All political theologies do, however, exist on an axis between death and hope. To even begin to make sense of the world, they must contemplate the tears, blood, and shit that ground and suffuse our political orders. But to find meaning and purpose in this world, they must discover a way to speak—however tentatively—of brutality and tragedy in the voice of hope. In the context of political theology, to speak of death in the locution of hope demands wrestling with how processes of cross-cultural transmission exist within systemic oppression, points of dialogue within domination, fragments of loving intimacy amid trauma. Such wrestling reflects the conditions of theology as faith seeking wisdom when caught between crucifixion and ascension. When so situated, the quest for wisdom begins either at the site of a wound or in a place of wonder. And both are places of loss and disorientation.

In attempting to navigate a bleak landscape illumined by shards of light, this book in no way sponsors a narrative of progress. Nor does it wrap a blanket of consolation around the wounds and sores of history, thereby hiding them from view. I take it that if we are to tell the truth, then alongside the agony of oppression, the agency of the oppressed—and their aspirations for and experiences of a better world—also needs remembering.[9] Conversely, when contemplating the contribution of Western theology to the formation of Christian belief and practice, we can neither simply vilify nor laud it. Rather, as part of how God heals and exorcises the spirit of the Western world, the need is to provincialize Western theology as one contribution among many, identify and repent its idolatries and pathologies, and deconstruct its pretensions to be the highest form that everyone else should conform to. Then, as part of the ongoing journey of conversion, the need is to reimagine and revise Eurocentric ways of knowing, sensing, desiring, and acting in the world so that such ways more faithfully, hopefully, and lovingly participate in the Holy Spirit's gathering of witnesses to and making present Jesus Christ. After all, a mark of faith, hope, and love is the decentering of "our" world so that "we" might be opened out to life with and for others, particularly the suffering and despised.

---

9. As Vincent Lloyd notes, "The idea of pure oppression is illusory, as is the idea of pure domination" (*Religion of the Field Negro: On Black Secularism and Black Theology* [New York: Fordham University Press, 2018], 37). For a critique of conceptions of slavery as a condition without any form of political agency, see Neil Roberts, *Freedom as Marronage* (Chicago: University of Chicago Press, 2015). On how all discourse is polyvalent and provides both stumbling blocks and stepping-stones toward reconfiguring oppressive relations, see Michel Foucault, *The History of Sexuality*, vol. 1, *An Introduction*, trans. Robert Hurley (New York: Random House, 1980), 100-101.

I use the term "conversion" to describe the process of transformational change that a Christian conception of politics should seek, as conversion captures the paradoxical, nonprogressive view of change that informs this book. As exemplified in baptism, a theological vision of change is simultaneously retrospective and prospective. It involves the recovery of an originally good but currently fallen way of being alive and the movement into a new, eschatologically given form of life that transfigures what currently exists. Conversion also entails events of definitive change and, at the same time, a chronological process framed as a journey or pilgrimage. But conversion is not linear or unidirectional (forward or backward, up or down). Depending on the circumstances, it entails a turn back, a turn away from, or a turn toward something.[10] If we shift the semantic framework from a spatio-temporal register to a relational one, conversion generates degrees of identification with and participation in how the Spirit is making Christ present in the world. Such personal and communal attunement and reorientation create more-or-less intense patterns of identification and disidentification with the world.[11] At times who or what is to be identified with lies outside the church, and at other times one is to identify with the church over and against the world.

To avoid misleading binaries, the approach I take here is simply to posit political theology as a shared terrain across which there are mul-

10. The New Testament builds on the Hebrew Bible/Old Testament usages of *shûb*, which denotes a turn back or return to something but also a change of heart or consciousness; for example, the prophets calling the people to recover covenant faithfulness. The verb *epistrephō* (Greek) or *convertere* (Latin) means to turn around, which, as noted here, can mean a turn back, a turn away from, a turn toward something new, or a change of course. In the Gospels (particularly Luke) and in Acts, cognates of *epistrephō* (*epistrephein* and *epistrophē*) can be synonymous with *metanoeō* (to undergo a change of mind/consciousness/way of being in the world/repent) and *metanoia* (repentance). Paul's letters emphasize being called by God as the framework for conversion. Calling is understood as a creative summons to and enablement of faithful participation in the body of Christ. New Testament motifs for conversion include a change from fruitlessness to fruitfulness, blindness to sight, lost to found, darkness to light, sick to healed, and also include being born again and becoming a new creation. These combine a sense of either recovery or rectification with a transformational sense of both newness and fullness.

11. A parallel can be drawn here with José Esteban Muñoz's notion of "disidentification" as neither assimilating nor wholly rejecting, but of working on, with, and against a dominant culture or ideology so as to reorganize and "transfigure" it. José Esteban Muñoz, *Disidentifications: Queers of Color and the Performance of Politics* (Minneapolis: University of Minnesota Press, 1999), 11-12, 39-56.

tiple pathways. "Political theology" as a term can be given an adjective, as in "Anglican political theology" or "Lutheran political theology," or it can name a specific formulation within one tradition—notably, Catholic social teaching. Each term denotes a pathway emerging from or situated within a particular tradition of Christian belief and practice. Staying with the cartographic metaphor, different ecclesial traditions (e.g., Reformed, Anabaptist, Roman Catholic) and movements (e.g., evangelicalism, Social Gospel, Pentecostalism) generate distinct pathways that nevertheless intersect with each other. These pathways ramble from, to, and across the terrain of premodern and modern schools of theology (e.g., Augustinian, Thomistic, liberation theology), philosophy (e.g., Platonic, deontological, utilitarian), and critical social theories (e.g., Marxist, queer, decolonial) that make up the topography of political theology as a landscape. These pathways can converge at various intersections to generate specific political theories: for example, Christian socialism, Christian democracy, and Christian anarchism. Through points of shared genealogy and interchange, the landscape of Christian political theology overlaps with political thinking in other faiths—most immediately, Judaism and then Islam, but also Hinduism, Buddhism, Taoism, and a range of other identifiably non-Christian traditions of belief and practice.

"Political theology" is not just a generic term or common noun for numerous pathways that marry political and theological reflection; it also refers to one particular pathway. As a distinct path, its development illustrates how different political theologies cut across and connect with other ways of walking the same landscape. As a singular pathway, this particular political theology emerges out of debates in Germany between the two world wars about whether or not there is a necessary identification between theological and political concepts and the implications of this for understanding the nature of political order.[12] While the controversial German Catholic legal theorist and onetime Nazi Carl Schmitt was a catalytic and formative presence in this strand of political theology, other key figures include the Catholic historian Erik Peterson, the historian Ernst Kantorowicz, the jurist Hans Kelsen, and the Marxist-influenced philosophers Walter Benjamin and Ernst Bloch (all of Jewish origin, three of whom had to flee the Nazis). After the Second World War, this debate was developed in constructive,

---

12. One of the earliest modern uses of the term "political theology" in this formal sense is by the anarchist thinker Mikhail Bakunin in his 1871 treatise "The Political Theology of Mazzini and the International."

theological directions by two Protestant theologians—Dorothee Sölle and Jürgen Moltmann—and one Catholic theologian—Johannes Baptist Metz. Sölle, Moltmann, and Metz envisaged their species of political theology as a corrective to the privatization of Christianity and the way in which modern theology overly spiritualized Christian beliefs and practices and legitimized oppressive regimes. They called on the church to become a "social-critical institution," envisaging salvation as having as much to do with matters of political, economic, and social transformation in the here and now as with the eternal destiny of the soul. Sölle, Moltmann, and Metz's work was in dialogue with and contributed to the emergence of Latin American liberation theology—a political theology that includes both Protestants and Catholics.

The broader question their work raised was whether it was the role of political theology, in any form, to provide rationales for or critiques of "secular" political programs and social movements. The alternative role for political theology is to articulate how the church has its own politics that may or may not conform to either progressive or conservative political programs. Contemporary figures such as Stanley Hauerwas, John Milbank, and Oliver and Joan Lockwood O'Donovan represent this alternative view. At the heart of this debate are a set of questions that haunt contemporary political theology, and which black liberation theology, womanist, feminist, queer, and decolonial theologies have posed with great perspicuity. Can Christians imagine and narrate Christianity against itself when faced with the complicity of Christians, acting in the name of Christ, in generating forms of life that warrant such things as ecological devastation, patriarchy, white supremacy, and genocide? Or has the Holy Spirit moved beyond the historic churches? And is the Spirit better identified with non-confessional social movements such as feminism or the environmental movement? I take the view that reformation and renewal are possible. This book should be read as a contribution to this task, a task that is perennially before the church.

At base, political theology emerges in the tension-filled and ambiguous time between the world as it is and the world as it will be in Christ—that is, between mortality and natality, death and hope, fasting and feasting, lament and praise. This in-between time is the time of politics. But saying this raises the question of how to understand politics as a concept and activity.

What Does the Word "Political" Signify
in the Term "Political Theology"?

"Politics" as a term has an affective, descriptive, and evaluative register. Affectively, to call something political is to invoke feelings of attraction or aversion. For example, to say "they're playing politics with the issue" is to communicate that even if what they are doing is not illegal or immoral, they are acting in a way that feels wrong or inappropriate. Descriptively, politics denotes a bounded activity. For example, voting is political, shopping is economic. But, like the terms "murder" or "hospitality," the term "politics" not only describes an action but also signifies a moral evaluation of an action or arena of human endeavor. Some see politics as, at best, a necessary evil or inherently corrupting and so morally bad or suspect. It is therefore to be avoided or superseded. For examples, utopias often envisage pre- or postpolitical forms of life that do away with the need for politics altogether. By contrast, politics is defined here as a moral good. While politics is often corrupt, bad, or evil, normatively I see it as necessary for human survival and flourishing.

Politics as a moral good has three dimensions. The first dimension of politics as a good refers to the nature and form of the *polis*, the thing that is shared. Other terms for this common life include the "commonwealth," "commonweal," "public life," or *res publica*. The good that inheres in the form and structure of the polity is the good of association or common life and the structures, practices, and processes that enable this good to be tilled and tended. As a good, association is both an intrinsic good and a means through which to fulfill other kinds of substantive common goods (e.g., health and education).[13] As a good, politics is directed to the flour-

13. I focus on common goods or goods in common rather than either public goods or *the* common good. The notion of a public good is nonmoral and economistic. Public goods are used by individuals qua individuals and are goods and services that everyone needs such as sewers, the use of which neither inherently excludes others nor entails competition. Public goods are provided or protected by state-centric means. In contrast, common goods are irreducibly social since they can only be achieved and used by participating in some form of association (e.g., health, education, citizenship). They have a moral end, as participation in and fulfillment of these goods are constitutive of human flourishing. Moreover, their realization is not inherently dependent on the state. Under conditions of a fallen and finite political life, the idea that there can be an all-encompassing common good is highly problematic. Determining the common good of a family, workplace, or small-scale community is possible and, arguably, necessary, for politics of the kind I outline here to be achievable. But beyond that scale, a claim to

ishing of the whole rather than the part, the common rather than either a factional or private interest.

Secondly, the political is that which shapes and structures this common life so that, as a good, it can be sustained over time. The political thereby includes such things as laws, constitutions, the means of governance (bureaucracy, etc.), electoral systems, and the like. Politics in this second sense is a synonym for statecraft: the exercise of sovereignty and governance through the management of and competition for control of state apparatus. Modern political theology as reflection on statecraft focuses on a number of interrelated themes, most notably: the nature and purpose of the public sphere; the role of theological speech and the institutions of the church within the public sphere (often referred to as church-state relations); the construction of what is public and what is private; conceptualizing the interrelationships between state, market, civil society, and kinship structures; regimes of law, constitutional order, and structures of governance; processes for the legitimization and representation of rule, such as voting systems; and the basis and formation of a demos, people, or nation, and thereby the character and ground of sovereignty.[14] Politics as statecraft is an instrumental and functional good that serves the ordering and maintenance of a common life as a realm of human flourishing. Failure to be subordinated to this good means statecraft is disordered and potentially

---

know *the* common good of a conurbation, region, nation, or the globe is antipolitical. It denies the plurality and contestability of moral visions in complex societies and the conflicts that arise in pursuit of divergent moral goods, all of which must be negotiated through politics. Although, arguably, a notion of the common good understood as an ever-deferred horizon of possibility can still operate as a helpful regulative ideal or guiding point of reference for large-scale social formations.

14. An implication of my account is that something called "public theology" is a category mistake. It assumes that it is necessary to translate theological concepts into the idioms and frameworks of liberalism on the assumption that liberalism is the determinative discourse shaping the public realm. But liberalism is already a translation of Christian terms and concepts, even if much got lost in translation. The impetus for public theology is a felt need to banish talk of demons, angels, Jesus, and the Bible to the naughty step of political discourse, when these are the very charisma that political theology contributes. To use Charles Mathewes's terms, a "theology of public life," taken to mean theological reflection on what is common or relating to the *res publica*, needs distinguishing from "public theology," understood as the attempt to shoehorn political theology into rationalistic and secularizing frames of reference (Charles Mathewes, *A Theology of Public Life* [Cambridge: Cambridge University Press, 2007], 1). I take a theology of public life to be a synonym for political theology.

anti-Christic. However, the term "political" does not just refer to formal means and structures for ordering an instantiation of common life.

Thirdly, "politics" refers to the relational practices through which a common world of meaning and action is created and cultivated. This sense refers to the craft of politics understood as the formation and negotiation of a common life between friends and strangers, including their estranged or competing interests and visions of the good. Or, to put it another way, politics in its third dimension is the craft of maintaining commonality by recognizing and conciliating conflict with others in pursuit of goods held in common. It involves discovering a shared vision of human flourishing in the face of the inevitable and intractable disagreements and differences that emerge in any form of life with others.

This third sense is different from the second; while statecraft includes formal, institutional practices for sustaining commonality amid difference, statecraft does not exhaust the ways and means of undertaking this work. Politics as an informal, relational craft takes place in multiple settings and is not coextensive with control of the state or even dependent on there being a state. Nomads in the desert outside of any formal state structures still generate a rich form of political life through customary practices of hospitality, greeting, etc., through which they sustain a common life based on shared goods (e.g., access to water). Elders and pastors negotiating changing service times in a church are practicing the craft of politics. Neighbors sorting out complaints about noise between themselves are likewise doing politics in this third dimension.

Politics as a craft for building relationships and making judgments about what is common entails acting in a way appropriate to the time/*kairos*. Hence it entails the need for judgments about what is best for these people, in this place, at this time: How, when, and where should we act and what should we do? As action in time, politics involves questions of power: How to act, and who does what to whom, and how to achieve our goals? This, in turn, raises questions about legitimacy: Why should we act this way rather than that way, who gets to act, and what is the meaning and purpose of our actions? And finally, politics involves what I call wily wisdom: the local knowledge, strategic analysis, and practical skills necessary to respond appropriately to a constantly changing and ambiguous environment.

Politics as a set of practices demands attention to virtue and the interaction of personal and structural transformation. Sustaining relationship amid conflict, disagreement, and asymmetries of power requires cultivating certain dispositions. Justice and prudence are obvious examples of

34

virtues needed to sustain a political life. As I will argue in chapter 9, so are tolerance and hospitality. However, what character traits are needed will vary according to the nature and goods of the political life in question, and this will change, depending on the historical and cultural context. The virtues required to sustain political life are also relative to structural location. The privileged must address internalized attitudes of domination that distort and damage them and prevent their flourishing, or mask how what they take to be flourishing is really a form of domination. Those who oppress develop callousness, cruelty, and various other attitudes that make them unable to relate in ways that sustain a just and compassionate common life. Conversely, as the feminist virtue ethicist Lisa Tessman argues, internalized oppression and its distortions of character must also be addressed. The oppressed can develop an inferior sense of self that may lead to self-destructive forms of behavior, or they might become resentful, vengeful, and bitter in ways that distort their character and inhibit the ability to pursue their flourishing in relation to others.[15] If we are to transform the subjective and objective dimensions of a common life, the cultivation of virtue must go hand in hand with addressing systemic barriers to human flourishing.

The three-dimensional nature of politics outlined here indicates that politics is categorically not war by other means. To be at war or engage in armed revolt (whether just or not) is to move into a qualitatively different kind of human interaction, one that signals the end of politics and the start of something else. The bullet and the ballot box are mutually exclusive routes to solving shared problems.[16] At a basic level, politics as a good is the alternative to unrestrained violence and cycles of revenge. Consequently, it is inappropriate to use "politics" as a synonym for talk of power understood as a wholly negative and violent phenomenon. The primary focus of politics—particularly in its first and third dimensions—is relational power (power with). As statecraft, politics deploys command and control or unilateral forms of power (power over).[17] To build relational power demands

15. Lisa Tessman, *Burdened Virtues: Virtue Ethics for Liberatory Struggles* (New York: Oxford University Press, 2005).

16. This is not a comment on the use of force in self-defense of one's home or immediate community when legal authorities don't act or refuse to act or are the source of intimidation or domination. That is a separate moral debate. My concern here is with the proactive use of violence by nonstate actors to achieve political ends in the public sphere.

17. Hannah Arendt sketched an initial conception of relational power ("On Violence," 105-98, in *On Revolution* [London: Penguin Books, 2006 (1963)], 166-67). The

listening to and negotiating with others rather than forcing them to do what you want using coercion or an oppressive system. A commitment to politics grounded on relational power requires a tacit commitment to nonviolence as a better form of human interaction, a commitment explicitly developed in philosophical, spiritual, and tactical ways in a wide range of political movements. These include the anti-imperial Indian movement struggling for independence from Great Britain; the American civil rights movement; the United Farm Workers movement in California; the "Velvet Revolution," which overthrew communism in Czechoslovakia; "People's Power," ending the Marcos dictatorship in the Philippines; and "Mass Action for Peace" by Christian and Muslim women in Liberia, which helped end the recent civil war there.

For politics to be possible, those engaged in it must assume that while not everyone is or should be the same, a common world of meaning and action is possible despite manifold differences. Politics, as a tacitly nonviolent form of interaction, entails a commitment to conditions in which worlds of shared meaning and action can be created or sustained. By contrast, the proactive use of physical violence—beatings, kidnapping, torture, bombing, and the like—by state and nonstate actors to achieve political ends represents the destruction of the institutions, customs, practices, and habits through which mutual communication and relationship are made possible. The commitment to discovering some form of a shared world of meaning and action displays the basic moral requirement that politics entails: a commitment to the dignity of friends *and* strangers (which includes those we find scandalous or objectionable). Politics thereby involves a vision of a common life that can be sustained and renewed through time and as something more than the aggregation of individual choices. Yet moral conviction without humility, often arising out of a belief in our innocence and the absolute rightness of our cause, inhibits the kinds of negotiations and neighborly relations necessary to forge a common life between friends and strangers. Moreover, the use of political authority not simply to restrain evil but to enforce virtue can be as much of a problem as is its use for cor-

---

distinction between "power with" and "power over" originates with Mary Parker Follett, *Creative Experience* (New York: Longmans, Green, 1930 [1924]). Examples of the theological deployment of this kind of distinction include Bernard Loomer, "Two Conceptions of Power," *Process Studies* 6, no. 1 (1976): 5-32, and Emilie M. Townes, "Living in the New Jerusalem: The Rhetoric and Movement of Liberation in the House of Evil," in *A Troubling in My Soul: Womanist Perspectives on Evil and Suffering*, ed. Emilie M. Townes (Maryknoll, NY: Orbis, 1993), 86-87.

rupt and oppressive ends. Terror and totalitarianism are as often born of zeal for righteousness as from a malevolent desire to dominate.

Antipolitical Forms of Domination:
Tyranny, Technocracy, and Majoritarianism

Even at its best, politics in a fallen world is caught up in sustaining idolatrous structures of domination and generating forms of "slow violence."[18] However, there are modern, distinctly antipolitical forms of domination from which politics should be distinguished. The first and most obvious kind of antipolitics consolidates the rule of the one over and against the many. This may take the form of one party, despot, dictator, movement, or ideology, with any alternative centers of power or forms of life viewed as a threat to the sovereign rule of the one. As exemplified in the Soviet Union, Nazi Germany, and Western colonial forms of rule, totalitarianism, authoritarianism, and other kinds of tyrannous, unjust, unaccountable, and arbitrary rule are the manifestations of modern forms of this kind of antipolitics.

The second kind of unilateral antipolitics is technocracy, which is constituted by the rule of the few over and against the many. It grows out of attempts to overcome the need for learning and practicing the craft of politics—and the contingency, uncertainty, and lack of control it entails—through different forms of legal, bureaucratic, and market-based procedures. Technocracy often poses as the alternative to and remedy for tyranny. It is not. Rather, technocratic regimes attempt to close or corrode various "informal"—that is, non-state-centric— forms of political life and thereby undermine the ability of ordinary persons to learn the craft of politics. As a paradoxically antipolitical form of "politics," technocracy is about following a bureaucratic procedure, conforming to regulations, or applying an economic "law" regardless of whether these actions contribute to building up a just and merciful common life. Massive amounts of human suffering can result from demanding conformity to a procedure, policy, or law, but that suffering is either ignored or seen as collateral damage needed to make the system (whether administrative, legal, or economic) work efficiently and effectively. For the political theorist Hannah Arendt, a

---

18. On the concept of slow violence, see Rob Nixon, *Slow Violence and the Environmentalism of the Poor* (Cambridge, MA: Harvard University Press, 2011).

pointed example of exactly this dynamic was Adolf Eichmann, who refused to exercise judgment in the name of conforming to legal and bureaucratic regulations. He thereby aided and abetted the Holocaust. As the example of Eichmann illustrates, technocracy can be aligned with modern kinds of tyranny, particularly its totalitarian forms. Another example is how capitalism immiserates the working conditions of millions of people; such practices are justified by referencing the "laws" of economics. Ignoring the human and ecological cost of following procedures is not accidental. What the sociologist Max Weber called the "iron cage" of bureaucratic, legal, and economic calculation and control is a deliberate attempt to separate moral questions from political and economic ones in the name of creating a more rational and well-ordered social and political life. Within this technocratic framework, morality and religious beliefs and practices are understood as private and personal, while political and economic life are identified as public, "neutral," disenchanted, reasonable, and amoral. The iron cage is one of the dominant frameworks within which politics is imagined today—both on the left and the right. Political theology refuses this separation, seeing political and economic judgments as always already moral judgments and political life as inherently sacred and secular. Imagining politics through the lens of the iron cage is the primary framework used in the fields of economics and political science, and it generates a top-down, antipolitical vision of politics—a vision much given to careless experiments in social engineering.

Alongside tyranny and technocracy, we must also attend to how politics, even at its best, can generate forms of domination. Here the problem can be framed as the rule of the many over and against either the few or the one perceived as "other." This is the third kind of antipolitics, known as either majoritarianism or democratic despotism. To understand this dynamic in the contemporary context, it is helpful to see how it operated in the Greco-Roman world, from which many key Western political concepts and words come. In that ancient context, authentic politics could only take place within a city/*polis*. The *polis* was the basis of a "civilized" common life. But not everyone involved in the cultivation of this civilized common life was considered equal. One grouping—women, slaves, and children—was confined to the *oikos* (household), understood as a private sphere that served, but was segregated from, the arena of politics. Another group was composed of foreigners, who were not considered part of the common life of the city. Both those confined to the *oikos* and those perceived as external to the *polis* were judged as being incapable and unworthy of enjoying the good/moral life, and so were excluded from practicing the craft of politics. Only property-owning men were capable of a truly flourishing life, so only they were qualified to participate in political life, which was the primary and most significant arena of human flourishing. Before we discuss more fully those confined to the *oikos*, we take up the status of the foreigner/barbarian in this classical framework, as this has analogies with how we still view noncitizens as uncivilized and subject to suspicion.

The *Polis*: Citizen and Noncitizen, Friends and Enemies

Those judged to be outsiders/noncitizens, whether resident within the boundaries of the city or living elsewhere, were potential, if not actual, enemies. Their way of life threatened the very existence of the city, which was the condition for the possibility of its citizens flourishing. The physical, moral, and spiritual flourishing of the individual citizen was coterminous with the flourishing of the city, and vice versa. Other, alien forms of life, not identified as sharing in and contributing to the flourishing of the city, were necessarily either potentially seditious (if they were resident aliens) or a threat (if they were foreign). It was necessary to guard against alien forms of life, and if they disturbed the peace they were either repressed (if inside the walls) or repelled (if outside). Internal and external "others" were also a means by which the common life of "our" city came to be defined and understood. "We, the people" were not like "them," and all that the other was imagined to be (effeminate, uncivilized, treacherous, cruel, etc.) was all that "we" were not (virile, loyal, brave, honest, rational, etc.). See, for example, numerous ancient Greek depictions of the Persians.

Notoriously, Carl Schmitt made a virtue of friend-enemy relations, seeing them as the basis of political life.[19] We need not make a virtue of them, but we cannot ignore his insight that they are a central feature of politics. Different civilizations have imagined themselves over against different internal and external others, and friend-enemy relations are deeply constitutive of the nature and form of fallen political life. This is no less true of Christendom than of city-states like Athens, or the Roman, Ottoman, or Ming empires, or atheistic states like the former Soviet Union. Euro-

---

19. Carl Schmitt, *The Concept of the Political*, trans. George Schwab (Chicago: University of Chicago Press, 2007).

pean, confessionally Christian civilization historically imagined itself over against the internal other of Jews and the external other of Muslims. This self-understanding thereby justified the repression or subjugation of Jews and Muslims, and then of various nonwhite peoples.

This repression and subjugation echo the tendency of all worldly political orders to absolutize friend-enemy distinctions and see in them points of moral and spiritual difference. For example, when those identified as white are seen as purer and of greater worth than those identified as black, this justifies the oppression of black people and their exclusion from citizenship. Theologically, friend-enemy relations ought to be relativized but cannot be wholly superseded, at least not until Jesus returns. The universal scope of God's love and presence calls into question any attempt to absolutize them. The heretic Samaritan and the pagan Syrophoenician woman, no less than the faithful Jewish man, can teach us something about God, how to live well, and that God can be present in "their" form of life, despite it being very different from "ours."[20] This is not to deny that Christians have a distinctive vision of the good life that others can threaten and undermine, but it should prohibit any attempt to stabilize and institutionalize distinctions between Christians and non-Christians politically. Friend-enemy relations are fallen rather than created; thus, they can be redeemed. Non-Christian others participate with Christians in a common, penultimate world in which God is nevertheless active and present. If politics is simply a contingent, penultimate, "secular" endeavor that is nevertheless located within a cosmos that has meaning and purpose, then I can relinquish control, trusting that the other and I exist in a common world of meaning and action. I can thereby compromise without compromising the end of history. As a fallen and finite human who participates with others in a penultimate yet common world of meaning and action, I can trust that the other may well have something to teach me about how to live well and that even if I profoundly disagree with them, a common life is still possible.

20. The New Testament echoes the logic of the Hebrew Scriptures. It is Tamar (Gen. 38) and Ruth who are the forebears of David. Two marginal, and acutely vulnerable, figures (childless widows) from peoples despised by the Israelites—the Canaanites and the Moabites—are nevertheless paradigms of faithfulness. And before Ruth, it is Rahab, a marginal and vulnerable woman of questionable status (a prostitute) from an avowed enemy, who is the first person to recognize what God is doing in the promised land and respond faithfully, not the male Israelite spies (Josh. 1–2). Enemies and those we find scandalous can know better who God is and teach those self-identified as the people of God what it means to be faithful, loving, and just.

This theme is central to chapter 9 on toleration and hospitality and is also touched on in chapter 4 on Pentecostalism.

The divine call to listen to and learn from others should prohibit Christians from turning conflicts over material needs (oil, water, land, etc.) and penultimate goods (education, health, etc.) into ultimate, Manichaean conflicts of good against evil and thereby rejecting the possibility of a common life in the face of disagreement. When Christians do this, it is because they are overinvested in worldly projects of salvation, having lost sight of the ultimate by making a god of the penultimate. The theological term for this kind of overinvestment is idolatry, and it is unequivocally condemned as evil. Moreover, the crucified Jesus shatters all attempts to stabilize any one way of life as the unique basis of true humanity to which all others should conform. Everyone needs conversion, and the church is always in need of reformation. Conversely, building a common life with strangers and enemies is a profound act of faith that in Christ all things are created and will be reconciled.

The constructive way in which political theology should frame relations with others is in terms of loving one's neighbor. That said, I want to suggest that politics is not merely an arena for practicing neighbor love; it can of itself be a form of neighbor love. This is only possible when a Christian conception of neighbor love reconfigures how core political relations, notably, friend-enemy relations, are understood. Love of neighbor should disrupt how we imagine and construct friend-enemy relations, extending our sense of whom to include in political life. One way of conceptualizing this, which mostly draws inspiration from the work of Aristotle, is by understanding politics as a means of generating public friendship. But unlike being a friend, being a neighbor is a vocation that does not depend on liking, having a rapport with, or being equal to others. Neither is it a condition, state of being, or preassigned role. Unlike such things as family, class, ethnicity, or gender, who my neighbor is cannot be predetermined. Neighbors have neither assigned social identities (e.g., father, sister, etc.) nor institutionally constructed roles (e.g., doctor, police officer, etc.). We only discover our neighbor within contingent and contextual relationships, and we can encounter a neighbor in any one of our roles and beyond those with whom we identify. Indeed, the encounter with a neighbor confronts us with a need to interrogate our own settled identities, roles, and habits and the ways these inhibit our ability to love our neighbor. Neighbor love therefore disrupts hierarchal, institutional, and identity-based ways of structuring status. It also cuts across vocational and ideological lines.

On occasion, the call of the neighbor supersedes prior commitments and loyalties, whether professional, religious, social, political, or ideological. The dynamics of neighbor love are therefore *unlike* ripples in a pond, which begin at a fixed point such as the family or nation and become weaker and weaker the further they move away from an animating center. Rather, the call to respond to another as one's neighbor disrupts linear or sequential ways of ordering human relations. It can, at times, demand greater intensity of devotion to distant neighbors than to family members, whether that distance be cultural, ideological, economic, or geographic.

Folded into the love of neighbor is the call to love our enemies. But Christian enemy-love tends to fall into one of three traps. Either we make everyone an enemy (the sectarian temptation to denounce anyone who is not like "us"). Or we make no one an enemy, denying any substantive conflicts and pretending that if we just read our Bible and pray, things like racism and economic injustice will get better by means of some invisible process (the temptation of sentimentalism that denies we are the hands and feet of the body of Christ). Or we fail to see how enemies claim in problematic ways to be our friend (the temptation of naïveté that ignores questions of power). In relation to this last trap, we must recognize that the powerful mostly refuse to recognize they are enemies to the oppressed and claim they are friends with everyone. A loving act in relation to those in power who refuse to acknowledge their oppressive action is to force those who claim to be friends to everyone (and are thereby friends to no one) to recognize that their actions perpetuate injustice and domination and need renouncing. This involves struggle culminating in an ongoing dance of conflict and conciliation. With too much conflict, we cannot hear each other. Political debate thereby dissolves into sloganeering, denunciation, and eventually violent strife. With too much conciliation, we paper over real points of disagreement, foreshortening the debate, and thereby concealing the truth of the matter and the truth about ourselves. Thus, like any good dance, politics as a form of neighbor love requires cultivating a sense of motion in balance through learning certain moves, cultivating particular dispositions and habits (e.g., patience, courage, etc.), and developing the ability to live with tension. But this dance of conflict and conciliation means we must learn to see enemies as neighbors capable of change and recognize that we ourselves must move and change. Agitational democratic politics can be a means for actively building relationship with enemies in order to "seek the welfare of the city" (Jer. 29:7) so that it displays something of what a just and compassionate common life might look like.

Building any form of just and loving common life through a dance of conflict and conciliation entails reckoning with a hard truth: everyone must change, and in the process, we must all lose something to someone at some point. Change is part of what it means to live as frail, finite, and fallen creatures. Loss, and therefore compromise and negotiation, are inevitable, if the flourishing of all is to take place. The temptation and sin of the privileged and powerful are to fix the system so that they lose nothing and others always lose, no matter how hard they work. The fight is to ensure that the loss is not borne disproportionately by the poor and marginalized. Such a fight is a critical part of what it means to love our neighbor in a way that is faithful to the life, death, and resurrection of Jesus Christ.

It follows that politics as a form of neighbor love does not end at the border of the state, nor is it restricted to citizens of the same state. Anyone anywhere is a potential neighbor to be loved, and a person's status as a creature of God and neighbor for whom Christ died is prior to and transcends the status ascribed to him or her by a nation-state. Refugees and the provision of sanctuary to them are a case in point. Sanctuary of refugees, as a practice, witnesses to the claim that the authority and rule of Christ transcend any political boundary. If Christ is King, then no fallen sovereign or community has the right to utterly exclude or make an exception of anyone from the status of a human being. The church is a witness to this, and sanctuary of refugees is one such means of faithful witness, one that exemplifies how an ecclesial form of witness can simultaneously combine a gesture of pastoral care with a form of political action. As love of neighbor, this love is embodied in form and thereby contrasts with abstract, cosmopolitan visions of an undifferentiated humanity that shape modern conceptions of humanitarianism. It also contrasts with a liberal understanding of humans as individual, rights-bearing, autonomous subjects with which humanitarianism is often aligned. I explore the contrast between neighbor love and an abstract concern for other humans in chapter 2 on humanitarianism and chapter 10 on humanity.

Sanctuary for refugees exemplifies how politics as a form of neighbor love includes love of the civically and economically friendless. Alongside the enemy, the friendless is another antonym of the friend. The irreducibly relational nature of human being—we come to be through not merely a physical but also a social womb—means that to be without friends is to lack power. Whatever the reason, to be cut off or alienated from family or friends (i.e., friendless) is to lack the necessary conditions for surviving, let alone thriving. By extension, to lack social, economic and political friends, or at the very least those who might be friendly towards you, is to lack agency. In political terms, the friendless are those with either a severely constrained capacity to act for themselves or who lack the ability to appear on their own terms. Another term for the friendless is "the poor." I explore powerlessness as the primary form of poverty in chapters 2 and 3. To be friendless is also to be without standing or recognition in a community: you just don't matter to those with privilege and power. Banishment and exile are therefore harsher than execution in some ancient contexts; even though sentenced to death, the executed still have standing within a divine and human community.[21] Scripturally, the paradigmatic examples of the friendless are the orphan, the widow, and the resident alien: they lack status; are economically, politically, and socially vulnerable; and are situated in relations of dependency. In the contemporary context, the friendless include socially, economically, and politically marginalized or excluded groups. Like slaves, colonial subjects, or Jews under the Nazi regime, the friendless are those whose distinct human face is locked inside an iron mask of stereotype and stigma and who are without rights or recognition. While neighbor love for the friendless should include works of mercy, as a political relation it goes beyond pastoral care. It demands "binding and loosing" (Matt. 18:18) existing social, political, and economic relations so that fitting patterns of differentiation and interdependence are either created or maintained. Politics as neighbor love helps reconstitute the conditions of human flourishing by enabling judgments about what is alienated or broken apart and so needs binding, and what is in bondage or falsely tied together and so needs loosing. Politics as a process of neighboring thereby counters the dynamics of exclusion, erasure, and alienation. Amid these fallen conditions, politics-as-neighboring reweaves the fragile fabric of reciprocal relations that holds society together.

In summary, politics, as a craft through which relations with strangers, enemies, and the friendless can be created and sustained, is a mode of neighboring. And neighbor love should be the primary frame of reference for responding to the three forms of antipolitics outlined earlier. First,

21. Giorgio Agamben draws on this aspect of being friendless in his use of the ancient legal category of *homo sacer*. The *homo sacer* was "bare life" who, though human, could be killed with impunity or without the charge of homicide, but could not be sacrificed to the gods nor submitted to sanctioned forms of execution. The *homo sacer* exists in a zone of indistinction, excluded or banned from participation in both the divine and human community. Giorgio Agamben, *Homo Sacer: Sovereign Power and Bare Life*, trans. Daniel Heller-Roazen (Stanford, CA: Stanford University Press, 1998).

against tyrannous forms of rule that serve the one, neighbor love embodies the need to treat everyone with dignity and worth and to help build forms of life that are just and merciful to all. Second, against the technocratic rule of the few, neighbor love upholds the need to put people before program or procedure. Third, against the rule of the many over the few or the one judged to be other or an enemy or friendless, neighbor love recognizes that faithfulness to Christ means we are called to love enemies, those we find strange, and those without friends. On a theological account, the remedy for democratic despotism (the unilateral and tyrannous rule of the many over the one or the few) is not, as liberalism supposes, a one-size-fits-all program of humanitarian concern coupled with rights-based procedural-ism. Rather, it is in multiple relational practices of neighboring (and the dance of conflict and conciliation/binding and loosing this entails). The remedy also necessitates prudential judgments about how to embody jus-tice and love with *this* person or *these* people in *this* place, at *this* time.

The *Oikos*: Familial and Economic Relations

I have examined how confessional political theology reconfigures core po-litical relations, notably friend-enemy relations. Such a process of transfor-mation also applies to how economic and kinship relations are conceived. The body called into being by Christ breaks open and reimagines the status and role of those confined to the *oikos*. Through Christ, familial and eco-nomic life ceases to be an immutable realm of necessity and becomes open to change. Rather than a strict separation of public and private, the *ekklēsia* (the public assembly of the people of God) forms a hybrid *oikos-polis*. Those who were previously excluded from the public realm—women, slaves, chil-dren, and the disabled and diseased—are now addressed as citizens. Men, the only ones who had political agency, and who were the *patresfamilias* with absolute sovereignty over their households, are now asked to identify themselves as brothers—that is, equals—to slaves, women, and children. As Galatians 3 suggests, ethnic, gender, political, and economic differences do not count when it comes to being included as a citizen in the city of God, and as the Gospel of Matthew puts it, "whoever does the will of my Father in heaven is my brother and sister and mother" (Matt. 12:50).

What it means to be a part of the *oikos-polis* of Christ is in dynamic inter-play with—and so contests and reconfigures—how we understand earthly kinship, economic, and political relations. As will be examined in chapters

7 and 11, on class and economy, respectively, this interplay has profound implications for how to understand our relations as producers and consumers. Chapter 5 on Catholic social teaching lays out a political theology that makes central the dynamic relation between the *oikos* and the *polis*. And tacit throughout, but made explicit in chapter 10, is the view that, as Joan Tronto and other feminists have emphasized time and again, freedom is not premised on the transcendence of relations of dependency and care: that is, the movement is not from the *oikos* understood as the realm of necessity to the *polis* understood as the realm of liberty, autonomy, and equality.[22] Rather, freedom pertains to both *oikos* and *polis*, premised as it is on the structural and interpersonal capacity to inhabit relations of dependency, intimacy, and care more justly and lovingly. Interdependency and mutual care are a condition for the possibility of autonomy understood as purposeful agency; equality defined as parity, not sameness; and freedom conceived of as the liberty to act with and for others as participants in a political economy within which kinship relations are situated.[23] In short, the realization of human dignity comes through, not despite, relations of dependency and care, relations that suffuse both *oikos* and *polis*.

If, on the one hand, a Christian political theology must guard against falsely separating *oikos* and *polis* (often marked by divisions between public and private), on the other hand, it must also guard against inverting the relationship between *oikos* and *polis*, either by making the *oikos* determine the nature and form of the *polis* or by ignoring the need for a common life. As already noted, in classical and some modern forms of political thought, the political or public life was considered the domain of true freedom. To focus on what was economic and private was to turn away from the realm of freedom and corrupt politics because it was to prioritize the realm of necessity over the realm of liberty. However, some prevalent streams of modern thought make economics—rather than politics—the domain of human freedom. They correspondingly elevate the pursuit of private interests above public interests. Within such streams, humans are not primarily political and social animals but *homo economicus*. This inversion of the relationship between politics and economics is at the root of the final form of antipolitics that I consider: the view that politics at best serves economics or at worst

22. Joan Tronto, *Caring Democracy: Markets, Equality, and Justice* (New York: New York University Press, 2013).

23. Parity requires both commutative and distributive justice, denoting as it does a differentiated and proportional equivalence.

is a hindrance to commerce and that, in an ideal world, economics would replace politics. There are left-wing and right-wing versions of this view, but its most virulent contemporary version is a libertarian ideology whose patriarchs are Ludwig von Mises and Friedrich von Hayek. For Mises and Hayek, the market system was neutral, spontaneous, and self-regulating, and any attempt to limit it by subjecting it to moral or political judgment was to limit not merely economic efficiency but human freedom. Within a libertarian view, social harmony and human flourishing no longer issue from and are embedded within a prior set of institutional, historical, and morally and politically determined arrangements, but flow from the spontaneous equilibrium of economic forces. Within such a vision the status of the citizen becomes absorbed into that of the producer, consumer, and debtor. Political theologies do not always reject such a position—but they should. Liberty and the formation of a just and compassionate common life are not a by-product of economics but the fruit of combined social, economic, and political labors. If money, markets, and property are to serve morally fruitful purposes, economic life must be embedded in and serve the formation of just and loving social and political relations. Chapters 11, 12, and 14 explore this dynamic in more detail.

Conclusion

I have sketched a vision of politics that cuts across many of the typical ways it is understood. One type I reject is that politics is only about law, the exercise of unilateral power, and elections; another is that politics is primarily about the rational administration of scarce resources and how to maximize economic efficiency (which prioritizes technocracy rather than democracy). In contrast to these anemic visions, politics should, first and foremost, be understood as the negotiation of a common life between friends, strangers, enemies, and the friendless.

In theological terms, a human can only know the truth about God and what it means to be a sane and humane creature through *finitude*—that is, by risking negotiated historical relations with others, including nonhuman others. Through participation in the world around us, we humans may discover and then make sense of who we are in relation to God and neighbor. However, this requires attentiveness to and reception of a world we did not make and others we do not control, and yet, for myriad reasons, with whom we must order our social, economic, and political relationships.

Attentiveness and reception—characterized by a posture of listening or contemplation—are the precursor of shared speech and action, and thence the coming into being of a common life. The promise of politics is that, within and through our differences, some form of common life can be discovered. But if the process of discovery is to be faithful, hopeful, and loving, we must render ourselves vulnerable to others we don't understand, don't like, and may even find scandalous or threatening. Politics understood as action in time through which forms of peaceable, just, and merciful common life are cultivated, is a necessary part of any such process of discovery. However, before Christ's return, the tragic dimensions of social and political life cannot be avoided, and failure is often the result of our shared political action. Yet faith, hope, and love demand the risk still be taken.

Threshold

Part 1 opens with an essay on humanitarianism, as this is a primary framework through which Christians in the West express their commitment to a common life with those who are different from them. Humanitarianism also frames how they understand the nature and basis of a common life: rooted as it is in how we imagine humans as the same as each other.

PART ONE

Case Studies in Political Theology

CHAPTER 2

Humanitarianism

The most significant political revolution of the modern era was not that of America, France, Haiti, or Russia but the longer-lasting, deeper-rooted, and more pervasive revolution that constitutes "humanitarianism." Rather than a change in one form of political order, it was a revolution of moral sentiment that affects all political orders. While humanitarianism emerged in the Atlantic world from a combination of Christian mission, cosmopolitan philosophical ideas, and various social movements, most notably the antislavery movement of the nineteenth century, it is now a distinct, global phenomenon.[1] It has its own apparatus, which includes treaties and legal codes such as the Geneva Conventions and 1951 Refugee Convention, and its own institutions, which range from the international, such as the United Nations refugee agency UNHCR (United Nations High Commissioner for Refugees), to the transnational, such as the International Committee of the Red Cross, to the national, such as USAID (United States Aid for International Development). Underneath this institutional and legal canopy are myriad initiatives channeling millions of dollars to help those in distress.

At the heart of the revolution in moral sentiment that these institutional and legal developments reflect are two premises. The first is that "we" (tacitly assumed to be privileged Westerners) should care for distant strangers irrespective of whether they agree with us or share our way of life. That is to say, whatever the differences between oneself and another, the duty to be

1. On the historical roots of humanitarianism, see Michael N. Barnett, *Empire of Humanity: A History of Humanitarianism* (Ithaca, NY: Cornell University Press, 2011), and Peter Stamatov, *The Origins of Global Humanitarianism: Religion, Empires, and Advocacy* (Cambridge: Cambridge University Press, 2013). On its philosophical roots, see Charles Taylor, *Sources of the Self: The Making of the Modern Identity* (Cambridge: Cambridge University Press, 1992).

humane should never be overridden by any other kind of claim. An underlying assumption of this first premise is that humans are the same. The second premise is that "we" can effectively alleviate the poverty and suffering of others.[2] Humanitarianism thereby transcends any one political community and acts as a criterion of evaluation by which all polities are judged and found wanting. The fruit of this revolution is that the acme of moral action is no longer love for a proximate "brother" but love for a remote "other."

This chapter asks whether humanitarianism is a Christian ethic for addressing poverty and unjust distributions of power, and a way of imagining the nature and basis of a common life with strangers, enemies, and the friendless. One way of approaching this task would be to pose a binary between Christianity and humanitarianism that frames humanitarianism as the secularized rival and antitheological alternative to Christian notions of neighbor love. But the reality is more ambiguous, and this ambiguity complicates the task of this inquiry. A theological critique of humanitarianism must reckon with how Christianity is both an insider and an outsider, committed to and, at the same time, detached from humanitarianism.[3] On the one hand, Christianity is a vital part of the genealogy of modern humanitarianism and is still heavily invested in humanitarian work.[4] On the other hand, humanitarianism emerged partly as an alternative to explicitly Christian approaches for framing moral concerns. Part of its conceptual backdrop is the transmutation of theological categories such as sin and charity into more immanent and moralized ones such as vice and altruism. For the likes of August Comte, who coined the term "altruism," this process of transmutation was a self-conscious effort to supplant theological categories with humanist ones.[5] For Nietzsche, this shift represented the death

2. For a prominent defense of this premise, see Peter Singer, *The Life You Can Save: How to Do Your Part to End World Poverty* (New York: Random House, 2010).

3. Didier Fassin, *Humanitarian Reason: A Moral History of the Present Times* (Berkeley: University of California Press, 2012), 244-47.

4. Peter Redfield and Erica Bornstein, "An Introduction to the Anthropology of Humanitarianism," in *Forces of Compassion: Humanitarianism between Ethics and Politics*, ed. Erica Bornstein and Peter Redfield (Santa Fe, NM: School for Advanced Research Press, 2011), 3-34; Barnett, *Empire of Humanity*; Peter Stamatov, "Activist Religion, Empire, and the Emergence of Modern Long-Distance Advocacy Networks," *American Sociological Review* 75, no. 4 (2010): 607-28; Michael Barnett and Janice Gross Stein, "Introduction: The Secularization and Sanctification of Humanitarianism," in *Sacred Aid: Faith and Humanitarianism* (Oxford: Oxford University Press, 2012), 1-36; and Fassin, *Humanitarian Reason*, 248-49.

5. "Altruism" was developed by Comte in explicit rejection of Christian notions of

of Christianity by its own hand. Yet it is wrong to see this transmutation as a sign of secularization understood in sociological terms as the decline in the public significance of religion. Rather, it represents the sacralization of Christian commitments in a different discursive register, that of humanitarianism. Agapic love for strangers may now operate within an "immanent frame," but that does not necessarily make it less "religious."[6] Rather than a neutral, nonreligious, and tradition-free way of framing concern for suffering others, humanitarianism is a form of faith, one that is simultaneously Christ-forgetting and Christ-haunted, playing off a christological pattern of atonement and redemption while pursuing a wholly immanent eschaton.[7] To put this contentiously, humanitarianism is a continuation of Christianity by other means.

The anthropologist Didier Fassin contends that humanitarianism is the primary form political theology takes in the modern world.[8] He argues that how modern democratic political orders valorize life as sacred and suffering as inherently negative is a vestigial form of theological com-

---

love (see Thomas Dixon, "The Invention of Altruism: Auguste Comte's *Positive Polity* and Respectable Unbelief in Victorian Britain," in *Science and Beliefs: From Natural Philosophy to Natural Science, 1700-1900*, ed. David M. Knight and Matthew D. Eddy [Aldershot, UK: Ashgate, 2005], 195-211). Alongside and in parallel to critiques of humanitarianism are critiques of "altruism." Rather than a "neutral" and tradition-free way of framing concern for others, it is understood as coterminous with and a buttress to conceptions of egoistic and individualistic self-interest that undergird capitalism (see Jonathan Parry, "The Gift, the Indian Gift and the 'Indian Gift,'" *Man* 21, no. 3 [1986]: 453-73). Altruism is seen also as a conceptual foundation stone in the construction of what Charles Taylor calls an "exclusive humanism" that marginalized and rendered "private" religious beliefs and practices in the formation of modern European and colonial regimes of secularity (Charles Taylor, *A Secular Age* [Cambridge, MA: Harvard University Press, 2007], 246-80).

6. Taylor, *A Secular Age*. On the relationship between humanitarianism and processes of secularization and sacralization, see Barnett, *Empire of Humanity*; Gilbert Rist, *The History of Development: From Western Origins to Global Faith*, new ed. (London: Zed, 2002); and Redfield and Bornstein, "An Introduction to the Anthropology of Humanitarianism."

7. Barnett contends that humanitarianism has become a form of "faith" (*Empire of Humanity*, 237-39). He, along with other critics of humanitarianism, sees humanitarianism as a means of atonement for the suffering the West has caused "the rest" that goes along, paradoxically, with a commitment to save the "underdeveloped" by incorporating them into a new "civilized" world order (Barnett, 17-18 and 26-29; Fassin, *Humanitarian Reason*, 249 and 251; Redfield and Bornstein, "An Introduction," 3-34).

8. Fassin, *Humanitarian Reason*, 249-52. Hereafter, page references from this work will be given in parentheses in the text.

mitments (251). What he calls "humanitarian reason" is the form these theological commitments take: "Humanitarian reason, by instituting the equivalence of lives and the equivalence of suffering, allows us to continue believing—contrary to the daily evidence of the realities that we encounter—in this concept of humanity which presupposes that all human beings are of equal value because they belong to one moral community. Thus humanitarian government has a salutary power for us because by saving lives, it saves something of our idea of ourselves, and because by relieving suffering, it also relieves the burden of this unequal world order" (252). On Fassin's account, for all its good intentions, humanitarian reason enacts a division between "the West" and "the rest" premised on inequality and a hierarchy of human life. "This tension between inequality and solidarity, between a relation of domination and a relation of assistance, is constitutive of all humanitarian government" (3). For example, Western aid agencies value their own workers more than those the agencies seek to help on the ground (223-42). Fassin does not thereby dismiss humanitarianism as hypocritical. Rather, he sees it as tragic and—despite the inequalities it reinscribes—as a way to discursively legitimize and sustain a more humane politics.

As part of asking whether humanitarianism is a Christian ethic, I examine whether humanitarianism, as Fassin contends, is a form of political theology, and if so, how to evaluate it theologically. The chapter unfolds in six parts. First, I enumerate several critiques of humanitarianism to identify where its ethical problems lie. Second, to establish a framework of evaluation, I set out a theological definition of poverty. "Poverty" is shown to be a multivalent term signifying some combination of destitution, powerlessness, affliction, and humility. Third, building on the second section, I explore further the meaning of poverty understood as humility, examining how it both justifies forms of privilege and is the basis for a moral response to being privileged. Fourth, echoing Fassin, I argue that the need to benefit the poor and suffering has become a key diagnostic of what constitutes "good" rule. Going beyond Fassin, I then suggest that this rule can embody two divergent forms of political theology: an "order of beneficence" and an "order of blessing." The former reinforces structures of privilege, while the latter seeks the flourishing of goods in common rather than the benefit of the one, the few, or even the many. Fifth, I establish a christological framework for understanding poverty as primarily a moral and political problem. Lastly, I propose that democratic politics is a more theologically congruent and ethical paradigm than humanitarianism for responding to poverty. My aim overall is not to condemn or reject humanitarianism but rather to suggest how a theological analysis sheds light on, and is perhaps even a therapy for, some of the ambiguities and internal contradictions of humanitarianism as a form of political theology.

Central to humanitarianism is a particular conception of poverty, one that foregrounds material lack and biological need, which in turn emphasizes apolitical means of addressing this need. While recognizing the importance of meeting material needs, a central argument of this chapter is that poverty is never simply a condition of material scarcity; it is always a moral and political problem as well. A more expansive, moral and political conception of poverty also challenges reductive, economistic accounts of poverty that inform and reinforce apolitical ways of addressing human need. Ever since Charles Booth's *Inquiry into the Life and Labour of the People in London* (1886-1903), there have been attempts to map, quantify, and provide an objective definition of poverty.[9] Booth's approach, along with all other wholly quantitative analyses of poverty, norms certain ways of imagining and acting in relation to "the poor." Within quantitatively driven frameworks of analysis, poverty becomes envisaged as an aberration or exception rather than as something produced by the economic system as such. Moreover, a singular focus on poverty as an economic problem reduces the poor to biological artifacts, disembedded from any form of social and political life. Wholly quantitative and economistic approaches thereby mask how poverty is first and foremost a moral and political problem. Poverty is not just material lack; it is also a lack of agency. A lack of agency undermines the ability of the poor to act with parity within and take responsibility for the body politic. Efforts to address poverty should therefore address the need the poor have not just for food, shelter, or warmth but also for power. Some recent critiques of humanitarianism pick up this point, noting how humanitarianism can reinforce inequality and reproduce structures of domination. It is to these critiques that I now turn.

9. For an overview of sociological and economic ways of defining poverty, see Caterina Ruggeri Laderchi, Ruhi Saith, and Frances Stewart, "Does It Matter That We Do Not Agree on the Definition of Poverty? A Comparison of Four Approaches," *Oxford Development Studies* 31, no. 3 (2003): 243-74.

Humanitarianism as a Moral Problem

It is no longer clear, if it ever was, what humanitarianism is for and whether the ideals that inspired it are valid. The historian of humanitarianism, Michael Barnett, contends that the issue is now "whether and how humanitarianism can preserve its ethics."[10] Increasingly questioned are the purpose, efficacy, and morality of humanitarianism along pragmatic, radical, and revisionist lines. Pragmatic critiques are generated by those running and funding the institutions and agencies of international aid and development. They express worries about failures in management and efficiency. Such failures are unjust, as they lead to the unfair distribution of scarce resources. One response is to introduce greater accountability and transparency.[11] Another is to recast aid and development work as "investments" to encourage fairer and more strategic interventions. Aligned with this perspective, a new breed of donors envisages themselves as "venture philanthropists" bringing new methods and entrepreneurial savvy to the field that can generate greater efficiency and effectiveness and thereby be more just in the allocation of scarce resources.[12]

The radical critique focuses on questions of governance and the role of humanitarian work in aiding or undermining democratization. These critics worry that for all the high-flown ideals, humanitarian aid and development work is more often than not a technocratic and utilitarian exercise driven by self-appointed "experts" that undermines indigenous attempts to address collective problems. A postcolonial strain of criticism along these lines, championing a "postdevelopment" perspective, questions the validity of the enterprise as such and asks whether development and aid work are anything more than the assertion of capitalism and the normativity of a Western and white way of life.[13] There is much validity to this

10. Michael Barnett and Thomas Weiss, "Humanitarianism: A Brief History of the Present," in *Humanitarianism in Question: Politics, Power, Ethics*, ed. Michael Barnett and Thomas Weiss (Ithaca, NY: Cornell University Press, 2008), 7.

11. Key criteria and standards are provided by the Paris Declaration on Aid Effectiveness (2005) and the Accra Agenda for Action (2008) and are now measured by Quality of Official Development Assistance (QuODA) and the Commitment to Development Index compiled each year since 2003 by the Center for Global Development. The work of William Easterly has been central to this development.

12. The Bill and Melinda Gates Foundation is the most well known of these.

13. See, for example, Rist, *The History of Development*, and Ilan Kapoor, *The Postcolonial Politics of Development* (London: Routledge, 2008).

postdevelopment critique. Many of the rationales for humanitarian work bear a striking resemblance to those given to justify European colonialism in the nineteenth century.[14] Some critical theorists, mirroring the postdevelopment critique, see humanitarianism as part of how the "poor"— whether distant or near—are managed and governed.[15] Such critiques call into question the viability of what have become core principles of humanitarianism, notably neutrality, impartiality, independence, and universality. They suggest that humanitarianism is a social imaginary that negatively shapes the West's responses to poverty and suffering.[16] A further critique is that beyond issues of hegemony and inequality, humanitarianism is inherently anthropocentric as a framework. This anthropocentrism gives rise to the question of whether humanitarianism inhibits the need to address the ecological challenges at the root of much poverty in the contemporary context.

Finally, there are revisionist critics like Fassin who see a need for something like development work and emergency aid in a world of poverty and suffering but, as a kind of therapeutic intervention within this work, seek to articulate the ambiguities, contradictions, and failures of humanitarianism.[17] One such critic is Jennifer Rubenstein. She identifies a cluster of ethical predicaments that humanitarian agencies regularly face. She notes that, far from being neutral, these agencies are constitutively involved in forms of governance and are inherently political actors. As she argues, they provide basic services to large populations for extended periods that are analogous to what governments "conventionally" understood provide. These services include access to food, shelter, clean water, medical care, education, sanitation facilities, and information. They influence the coercive policies and practices of conventional governments and in some cases set those policies. And they make large-scale decisions about resource use

14. Barnett, *Empire of Humanity*, and Carol Lancaster, *Foreign Aid: Diplomacy, Development, Domestic Politics* (Chicago: University of Chicago Press, 2007), 9.

15. Alyosha Goldstein, *Poverty in Common: The Politics of Community Action during the American Century* (Durham, NC: Duke University Press, 2012); Uma Kothari, "Power, Knowledge and Social Control in Participatory Development," in *Participation: The New Tyranny?*, ed. Bill Cooke and Uma Kothari (London: Zed, 2004); Gilles Deleuze, "Postscript on the Societies of Control," *October* 59 (1992): 3–7.

16. See, for example, Giorgio Agamben, *Homo Sacer: Sovereign Power and Bare Life*, trans. Daniel Heller-Roazen (Stanford, CA: Stanford University Press, 1998).

17. Alongside Fassin, Peter Redfield, Erica Bornstein, and Craig Calhoun fit this category of critic.

that have public effects.[18] Yet, they not only govern less than conventional governments, but they also often govern less well.[19] Rubenstein names this the dilemma of being "second-best actors." In certain situations, these second-best actors are the only form of government available and so act as an agency of last resort. Being an agency of last resort, however, leads to a further predicament. Their actions can often perpetuate violence or corruption and prolong the situations that cause suffering. But if agencies do not act or stop acting in order to avoid complicity in causing harm, then the impoverished may suffer more or die. A paradigmatic instance of this was how aid organizations in refugee camps in Zaire contributed to catalyzing and perpetuating the 1994–1999 Rwandan civil war by providing shelter for the perpetrators of the genocide, enabling them to regroup and then attack the Rwandan government. Rubenstein calls this "the problem of spattered hands."

Another ongoing dilemma humanitarian agencies face is always existing in a triage situation and having to make decisions about where to invest scarce resources and what to prioritize. Rubenstein identifies this as the "cost-effectiveness conundrum." It entails ethical judgments about what to prioritize and why. Yet on what basis are these judgments to be made? How is one kind of suffering to be prioritized over another kind? A final dilemma revolves around the need to raise money, which generates what Rubenstein calls "the moral motivation tradeoff."[20] This dilemma relates particularly to portrayals of poverty and how humanitarian agencies frame the call for donations and motivate donors to give. Representations of "third world" poverty that accompany appeals for funding often play off racialized, demeaning, and infantilizing stereotypes. Images of poverty, war, and disaster—what Susan Sontag calls the "iconography of suffering"—invoke sympathy, indignation, and alarm (often accompanied by an unacknowledged yet ever-present voyeuristic curiosity about the gruesome, the excruciating, and the calamitous).[21] As Sontag notes, the modern representation of the suffering other, whether of the dead soldier or the famished child, is "regarded only as someone to be seen, not someone (like

18. Jennifer Rubenstein, *Between Samaritans and States: The Political Ethics of Humanitarian INGOs* (Oxford: Oxford University Press, 2015), 56–66.

19. Rubenstein, *Between Samaritans and States*, 54.

20. Rubenstein, *Between Samaritans and States*, 171–206.

21. Susan Sontag, *Regarding the Pain of Others* (New York: Farrar, Straus & Giroux, 2003), 40. However, without a theological frame of reference, Sontag can see the contemplation of the suffering saints or the crucified Christ only as voyeurism (40–42).

us) who also sees."[22] Such depictions diminish the agency and dignity of those portrayed. Moreover, the iconography of suffering, far from making poverty more real, can serve to either numb viewers or generate compassion fatigue rather than call forth sympathy. At its worst, it can make the horrific banal. Yet money must be raised and poverty portrayed to bring it to the attention of those who have resources to share.

The critiques of humanitarianism and its characteristic moral quandaries sketched here pose sharp challenges to churches in the West. First, for many Christians, neighbor love is synonymous with humanitarianism. And within this adopted framework, concern for distant strangers is often seen as superior to concern for more proximate neighbors in distress, as concern for distant strangers is perceived as more neutral, independent, and universal—core commitments of humanitarianism—and thence more *agapē*-like. Second, at a practical level, the adoption of a humanitarian discursive frame by churches and Christian aid agencies mostly replaces theological or ecclesial concerns with technocratic and economic ones. Through processes of isomorphism, these nontheological concerns then drive the form, content, and goal of any actual interventions.[23] Third, humanitarianism emerged in part as a critical intervention within Christianity. It emphasized a shared humanity that transcends religious, ideological, national, and other divides and the moral duties incumbent upon all humans simply by dint of being a human. However, many of these criticisms of humanitarianism call into question the validity and moral status of the solidarity between humans that humanitarian aid and development work embody. Rather than overcoming differences between the privileged and powerless, humanitarianism is seen to subtly reinscribe a sense of distance and superiority that in turn undermines a sense of shared humanity. The suggestion that humanitarianism undermines solidarity is a damning one, as humanitarianism is in part an attempt to articulate what duties of care the rich and powerful have toward the poor and powerless by dint of their shared humanity.

In the light of these concerns, it is imperative for Christians to examine how concern for suffering and impoverished others might be conceptualized theologically outside of a humanitarian discursive framework. Such a nonhumanitarian frame of reference can then be used as a point of contrast to diagnose how humanitarianism, as an assemblage of belief and

---

22. Sontag, *Regarding the Pain*, 72.
23. On this, see Luke Bretherton, *Christianity and Contemporary Politics: The Conditions and Possibilities of Faithful Witness* (Malden, MA: Wiley-Blackwell, 2010), 42-45.

practice, may help or hinder love of neighbor. Moreover, in response to these kinds of concerns, this chapter thinks through the duties of privilege theologically. While in dialogue with liberation theologies, which emphasize a preferential option for the poor and try to see the world from the position of the marginalized and excluded, I begin from a different structural location. Like most readers of this chapter, I am enmeshed in a world of privilege as compared to the lives of those economist Paul Collier calls the "bottom billion." As such, I begin with the question of how to ethically respond when one finds oneself with privilege. Criticism of the structures that produce inequality and the systemic advantages given to some and not others is vital. However, the only word to those who find themselves with power, wealth, and privilege cannot be no. The prophetic no must be premised on some form of eschatological yes. Some redemptive account of what to do with power and wealth is necessary if critique is not to be degraded into a rhetoric of denunciation and removed from the orbit of any proclamation of good news.[24] Nor can the issue be ducked. Most people, at some level, possess a form of privilege, whether based on money, class, education, race, gender, sexuality, seeing, hearing, institutional position, geographical location, intellectual ability, or kinesthetic agility.

In the light of the critiques of humanitarianism as a way of framing concern for and solidarity with the poor sketched here, it is helpful to clarify how poverty is a moral and political problem and thence what kind of response is most fitting by those with resources to help alleviate poverty (i.e., the privileged).

Poverty as a Moral and Political Relation

To name a constellation of phenomena as "poverty" is first and foremost to make a moral and political judgment. The terms "poverty" and "the poor"—like "war," "rape," and "murder"—are moral descriptors. That is to say, "poverty" and "the poor" are not neutral, technical, or impartial terms. They simultaneously name something and make a normative evaluation of it. Analogous to the difference between stating someone has been murdered and stating someone has been killed, calling someone "poor"

---

24. The collapse of revolutions into a politics of denunciation that leads in so many instances to killing from lists points to the tragic implications of divorcing prophecy from any constructive annunciation.

carries a different freighting from saying someone merely lacks food. Attempts to provide wholly technical definitions—for example, as those living below a "poverty line"—fail to grasp the moral claim and dimensions of the phenomenon under inspection. As a moral description, the word "poverty" is laden with a tacit set of claims about what should be valued and what constitutes the right ordering of relations.

Poverty has a range of interrelated meanings that must be located within a broader discursive context and tradition. Within Christianity, and those contexts in which the Bible has been a point of reference for making judgments about what to value and how to order social, political, and economic relations, four broad meanings can be discerned.

1. Drawing on Scripture as a primary point of reference, the first denotation of the term "poverty" is *destitution*. Destitution signifies the material lack of basic needs (food, water, shelter, etc.), a consequence of which is economic, political, and social exclusion or marginality. In the Hebrew Bible/Old Testament (HBOT), the widow, orphan, and stranger are paradigmatic of the destitute, as they lack even the most basic means of sustenance (e.g., Ps. 10:14; Deut. 10:18).

2. Destitution closely aligns with the second denotation of poverty in the HBOT, which is *powerlessness*—a lack of agency and vulnerability to the actions of others, whether rulers, the rich, or foreign powers.[25] Rather than food, shelter, or some other aspect of material provision, what is required are the just and merciful use of power (and thence an end to oppression), the breaking of cycles of dependency, and the reconstitution of the powerless as a people capable of acting for themselves. The most common word for poverty in the HBOT (*'ānî* and *'ānāw*) implies vulnerability to oppression more than material destitution (e.g., Ps. 72). The narrative paradigm of powerlessness is Exodus: God liberates the impoverished, downtrodden, and hovel-dwelling Israelites from the yoke of the wealthy, powerful, and palace-dwelling Pharaoh. The "poor of Yahweh" are those who seek justice from God (e.g., Isa. 42). This sense of poverty as powerlessness dovetails with Greek conceptions of the demos and Roman notions of the *pauperi*, the *plebs*, and the *populus*. They are not destitute but are politically and thence eco-

---

25. Surprisingly, Gustavo Gutiérrez, and Leonard and Clodovis Boff, in their definitions of poverty, do not focus on powerlessness as a form of poverty. Their accounts focus on material lack and poverty of spirit/evangelical poverty. See Gustavo Gutiérrez, *A Theology of Liberation: History, Politics, and Salvation* (Maryknoll, NY: Orbis, 2015 [1973]), 162-71, and Leonardo Boff and Clodovis Boff, *Introducing Liberation Theology*, trans. Paul Burns (Tunbridge Wells, UK: Burns & Oates, 1987), 46-49.

nomically and socially vulnerable. Analogous in the contemporary context are terms such as "the working class" and "the proletariat." A more specific example is the incarcerated: their basic biological needs are catered to, but they lack economic and political agency. As played out in debates between different liberation theologies, the key to shaping the analysis of oppression is the primary analytical lens selected through which to conceptualize the nature of powerlessness. Is race, class, or gender, for example, the primary point of reference? Although powerlessness is defined very differently depending on which form of stratification—class, race, gender, etc.—is in view, a focus on power and agency is a shared point of intersection for many of the disparate concerns and methodologies focused on the need for liberation.[26]

A major form of powerlessness, particularly today, is displacement. The experiences of the unhomed can be wholly different in kind, ranging from the refugee, the exile, the enslaved, and the imprisoned to the vagrant, the émigré, the nomad, the troubadour, and the pilgrim. But what unites them is precariousness—whether temporary or permanent—and the lack of place within their immediate context. This precariousness and lack of place are constituted by an absence within their immediate setting of what constitutes them as persons recognizable in relation to others through time and space. Place understood as our social, economic, political, geographic, and historical location in creation largely constitutes the particularity of creatures. To be unhomed is to lack status and worth within a place and thereby to have a highly diminished agency and be vulnerable and easily exploitable by others who have the right connections or orientations in that place. To put it another way, the unhomed are friendless.

3. The third meaning of poverty is *affliction*. The afflicted or distressed are those who suffer or grieve because of illness, disablement, emergency, demonic possession, an accident, or the loss of a loved one. Whether their need is for solace, pastoral care, emergency aid, healing, or exorcism, the key is to include them within the circle of divine-human relations through the outreach of others who can at least bring comfort, if not relief. In the Bible, the figures of the leper and Job are paradigmatic of the afflicted. By contrast, in medieval Europe, "the beggar" or the one in need of alms represented the afflicted. In the contemporary European and American context, it is victims of war, famine, or natural disaster.[27]

26. The question of whether to focus on cultural or economic agency has been a source of much debate within liberation theologies.

27. Redfield and Bornstein, "An Introduction," 3–34.

4. The final meaning of poverty is *humility*. The poor in spirit/humble are like children ready and open to receive the kingdom of God (Isa. 61; Luke 18:15-17). This is the most ambivalent and problematic point of reference in how poverty is constructed within Christian theology. It is problematic because it can be used to valorize poverty as a moral and political status that is spiritually beneficial for the destitute and powerless. It can thereby serve to mystify and reify structural exclusion. Indeed, it is this aspect of a Christian conception of poverty that seems to have driven Marx's critique of religion as a means to legitimize the deprivations of poverty to the power elite whose interests are served by the system.[28] Marx held that in addition to acting as a narcotic and a mask for, and legitimizer of, oppression, religion enabled elites to reconcile themselves to the system. Conceptions of poverty as a blessed state because it is a humble estate have often operated in this way. Yet Scripture links poverty and humility so that a theological conception of poverty means we cannot avoid this association.

As well as having a range of meanings, the term "poverty" invokes a moral economy of relations between rich and poor, powerful and powerless. Poverty—in all its denotations—is only imaginable in relation to "privilege": some must be rich so that others may be thought of as poor.[29] That

---

28. See, for example, Karl Marx and Friedrich Engels, *The Communist Manifesto*, trans. Samuel Moore (London: Penguin Books, 1967), 92.

29. Privilege denotes the status of having a special right, prerogative, attribute, status, immunity, or benefit that puts the individual or group beyond what is generally available. By way of contrast, not being brutalized or murdered by police on the streets of a North American city is a right, not a privilege. What counts as a privilege varies enormously according to context and culture. It is possible to make a heuristic distinction between what is earned and what is given as a privilege. To say a privilege is given is to recognize that there is an element of something like luck or good fortune in how it came about and to have an agency one did not earn. That agency can be intellectual, moral (some are more self-disciplined and find it easier to be virtuous than others), physical, economic, cultural, or political. This privilege can be combined with other sources of power so that one with privilege has time, space, and relationships over and above those available to others, yet without having to do anything. Their privilege is just a given: one finds that one always already has it (for example, wealth or intellect by dint of birth). Poverty is compounded by how a lack of certain privileges, and thence agency, combines with structural, cultural, and physical barriers to entry into a hegemonic order. Despite one's ability, those without privilege cannot translate their abilities into effective agency because of processes of exclusion that may be geographic, cultural, educational, etc. On this account, privilege is not always linked to injustice. It becomes unjust when it is aligned with other kinds of power. To be privileged is not always in every instance to be *culpable* for the poverty of others. But it is always to have *responsibility* for addressing

is to say, poverty entails stratification and differentiation of one kind or another. You can be starving and without shelter and yet think of yourself as famished and cold rather than poor. To name yourself or be named as poor entails a particular kind of social imaginary, one in which poverty and privilege are forms of recognition that define and coconstruct each other. The Beatitudes exemplify this by connecting and contrasting the blessed and the cursed (Luke 6:20-26). So talk of poverty should always at the same time be a reflection on the meaning of wealth and power. Failure to do this constitutes a failure to reckon with the moral and political implications of poverty. Without locating conceptions of poverty in relation to privilege and the structural dimensions that produce poverty, the poor appear as clients or an interest group to be dealt with by special measures. In the modern period, when poverty is disconnected from reflection on privilege, it ceases to be a shared problem that "we, the people" address together. It becomes instead an anomaly that "experts" manage and govern through "populations" subject to regimes of health, education, welfare, incarceration, and the like.[30] Poverty becomes a stimulus to generate technocratic and anthropocentric interventions in the lives of those "we" think should be more like "us" rather than a provocation to repent and ask questions about the way our lives are structured to exclude the poor and corrode creation.

The interrelationship between poverty and privilege raises a critical question that confronts Western humanitarianism: Is aid a gift, and thus a

---

the poverty of others and ensuring that one's privilege does not exacerbate structures and patterns of domination. Moreover, on a theological reading, privilege always poses an existential temptation that imperils the soul: one takes an entirely contingent and arbitrary aspect of one's life and, instead of understanding it as a gift to be shared, one views it as a personal inheritance or property for one's exclusive benefit or a source of identity and self-worth to be preserved at all costs. We are thereby ensnared in a vicious cycle of false desires and vanity leading to hubris and not merely breaking but actively destroying the bonds of charity. This can be both a personal and a collective dynamic. We have lost many of the spiritual disciplines, most notably that of *memento mori*, which preserve us from such temptations and help us remember that privileges, along with many other aspects of our life, are so much chaff.

30. Michel Foucault's critique of modern regimes of "governmentality" becomes salient at this point (see *Security, Territory, Population: Lectures at the Collège de France, 1977-1978*, trans. Graham Burchell [New York: Picador, 2007]), as does James C. Scott's critique of how modern states come to centralize control over, measure, and tax populations via techniques of scientific management (*Seeing like a State: How Certain Schemes to Improve the Human Condition Have Failed* [New Haven: Yale University Press, 1998]).

gesture of generosity by the privileged to the poor, or is it a form of distributive justice, and so a way that the privileged give what is proportionally due to the poor? I contend that humanitarian aid is a matter of both justice and generosity. The ambiguities and confusions this confluence of justice and generosity in aid and development work sets up complicate any analysis of it. However, to collapse humanitarianism into a species of either justice or gift is to flatten and falsely resolve a complex moral relation. It is also to truncate a full-orbed political theology of humanitarianism that should have as its basis how humanitarianism seeks *tzedakah u'mishpat* (justice and righteousness), the Hebrew term for the complex of obligations that are the basis of the God-given covenantal order.

The four aspects of poverty outlined here have been deployed with regularity and consistency by Christians throughout history. Together they shape how Christians down the ages have defined poverty. However, like many moral terms, the meaning of poverty exhibits both continuity and change over time, with different dimensions coming to prominence and taking on contextually attuned valences in specific times and places. Given that the different dimensions of how poverty is understood theologically vary from one context to another, it is inevitable that the various strands of Christianity contest the primary meaning of poverty. Humanitarianism tends to focus on poverty as destitution to the exclusion of the other three. The most contested of the four is poverty understood as humility, yet it is this meaning that yields the sharpest critical contrast with humanitarianism as an ethical response to privilege.

Poverty of Spirit as a Therapy for Privilege

The "poor in spirit" can be identified as those who, like children, are structurally positioned to be radically dependent on others and lack the agency to secure their place in the world (whether they want to be or not, and whether they are virtuous in their poverty or not). But the poor in spirit can also be identified with those who are *like* children/the materially poor through being humble and who in some cases choose material poverty as a form of spiritual ascesis (for example, monks and nuns). This double identification creates ambiguity about how to interpret the scriptural call to be poor in spirit, making it difficult to avoid conflating humility and affliction, destitution, and powerlessness, or romanticizing them as automatic sources of holiness. Those who are economically poor, physically suffering, or politically lacking in power are often, of necessity, humble, as they are acutely aware of their need for others. Yet, the destitute, powerless, and afflicted can be just as grasping and prideful as the rich, and conditions of material poverty are not inherently a school of virtue. At the same time, if we forget that poverty can also denote humility, poverty as an experience of destitution, affliction, and powerlessness becomes so pathologized that as a condition, poverty justifies and validates positions of privilege. The privileged have nothing to learn from the experiences of the poor, and their privilege remains unchallenged by poverty. Instead of poverty raising fundamental questions about the very system and form of life that produce certain kinds of unjust privilege, poverty is to be eliminated so that everyone is incorporated into the form of life the privileged currently enjoy. Poverty is thereby seen as a glitch in the system rather than as a product of the system, and almost never as a structural location that challenges privileged forms of life. Thence the question of what constitutes justice is never asked, as what is just is taken to be the ability to participate in the status quo.

Pathologizing poverty in a way that leaves unquestioned the structures of privilege is a dynamic humanitarianism tends to exacerbate. Positively, humanitarian organizations such as the International Committee of the Red Cross echo and build on what the church historically called "works of mercy." Humanitarian aid and development work is a way of recognizing another as a human, as one who is the same as me, and thereby communicating to one in distress or peril that he or she is not rejected, abandoned, or forgotten but exists in a common world. This is especially necessary at points of crisis—natural disasters and famine being paradigmatic instances—when others find they are without the necessary resources to act for themselves. In the Christian tradition, following the pattern of Christ's incarnation and crucifixion, such works of mercy may necessitate forms of radical renunciation or *kenosis* on the part of the giver to enable forging a deeper, intimate, and more meaningful relationship. In short, works of mercy require generosity that goes beyond what distributive or commutative justice requires. And this kind of generosity entails cultivating a poverty of spirit. One can see something of this in the witness of monks and nuns down the centuries whose way of life points the broader body politic to the ongoing need to renounce idolatrous ties to property, kinship, comfort, and status if meaningful relationships to God and neighbor are to emerge. However, a kenotic conception of generosity is mostly absent in contemporary notions of humanitarianism. Rather than focus on practices of personal and material renunciation, humanitarianism conceives generosity in terms of *noblesse oblige* and philanthropic donation, both of which emphasize rather than bridge the distance between giver and receiver and too often leave intact structures of economic and political exclusion.

Crucial to understanding poverty as humility within Christianity is its links to the sacramental dimensions of almsgiving and works of mercy. In early Jewish traditions, giving alms was equivalent to an act of worship in the temple.[31] This connection was taken up in the New Testament and the subsequent Christian tradition so that giving to the economically poor had a soteriological dimension: it is a mark of having encountered and responded faithfully to Christ and thereby manifesting appropriate poverty of spirit/humility.[32] Echoing the Jewish connections between the temple and giving, giving alms in the patristic era was linked to the celebration of the Eucharist through the offering taken before Communion. The gift on the altar and the gift to the poor are part of a penitent recognition of God's blessing and what the right ordering of our relationships to those around us entails. Giving to the poor is the appropriate symbolic gesture given who God is. It is also a form of reparation for past wrongs, hence the linkage in Amos 5 or Deuteronomy 12:13-14 between sacrificial offering to God and care for the poor and pursuit of justice. Both are marks of obedience and faithfulness.[33] In the contemporary context, serving the destitute and afflicted through giving alms and volunteering is still a favored way of serving God and considered a diagnostic of faithfulness and holiness, yet it is often shorn of its reparative dimension.[34]

A related aspect of poverty as humility is that humility emerges from the recognition of what it means to be fallen, frail, and finite creatures. True spiritual strength and wisdom come through recognizing our "poverty" as death-bound, perishable bodies in contrast to the resurrected, imperish-

---

31. Gary Anderson, *Charity: The Place of the Poor in the Biblical Tradition* (New Haven: Yale University Press, 2013).

32. A central text in this regard is Matt. 25 and its reception history within the broader tradition.

33. However, as Peter Brown notes, from the third to the sixth century, the "ideal" recipient of Christian almsgiving radically changed from the destitute to monks and nuns, for whom voluntary economic poverty was a mark of humility (*Through the Eye of a Needle: Wealth, the Fall of Rome, and the Making of Christianity in the West, 350-550 AD* [Princeton: Princeton University Press, 2012], 517).

34. A legacy of the Reformation among Protestants is that such giving is mostly shorn of its expiatory, penitential, and atoning dimensions.

able body of Christ (1 Cor. 15; 2 Cor. 12:10). As Augustine and Benedict of Nursia constantly reiterate, humility is necessary to see and hear the truth about ourselves and so be touched by God and neighbor. Poverty of spirit is a necessary condition for the encounter with and proper response to other kinds of poverty and the structural conditions that so often produce them. As those who must cultivate humility, Christians—and especially those who are privileged—are to contemplate Christ so that they might be provoked to repent and to understand both their own "poverty"/sinfulness and their need for a meaningful relationship with the destitute, afflicted, and powerless. Through contemplating the broken body of the suffering servant, the faithful become open to the realization that they have a common life, in and through Christ, with the poor. "We" cannot be healed without "them," nor they without us. Through contemplating Christ, privileged Christians should come to understand the "height and depths of [the] human lot" and so be able to orientate themselves rightly to God and neighbor.[35] When the privileged understand their own poverty of spirit, recognizing their fallenness, frailty, and finitude, and thence their need of others and God, then they not only truly hear, see, smell, taste, and touch the lives of "the poor" but also receive from them, recognizing that "we" need them as much if not more than "they" need us. A complex web of just and generous relations between the privileged and the poor can then emerge.

The first response by the privileged to contemplating Christ's suffering and broken flesh should not be empathy leading to philanthropic action or political activism on behalf of a less fortunate other, but repentance. It is not the privileged human who has something to offer the one suffering. Rather, Christ's situation represents "our" true predicament if only "we," as fallen humans, indelibly benefiting from structures of domination, could see it. It is not the privileged who have a gift to offer the impoverished suffering other but rather the privileged who are the ones who need to contemplate the broken body. Contemplation of Christ crucified, leading to repentance and reparation, helps disrupt and reconfigure all practices of recognition. For example, our gaze should not be conformed to that of either the Western media or the frenzied world of social media, which determines who should appear as the subject of care—this week those made homeless by a tornado, next week those afflicted by famine. Instead, it is

35. Johannes Baptist Metz, *Poverty of Spirit*, trans. John Drury (Glen Rock, NJ: Newman, 1968), 23.

proximity to Christ on the cross that determines who and what we should see. Uncoupled from the contemplation of Christ crucified, the privileged will miscategorize what suffering looks like and who is the stranger to be welcomed. Who does and who does not appear will be determined by fallen and fad-driven standards of what is worthy of attention and sympathy.

Discussions of white privilege and the ethics of how whites should respond to antiblack racism in North America offers a helpful parallel to the discussion of humanitarianism as an ethics of solidarity between the privileged and the poor. Jennifer Harvey identifies what she calls a "reconciliation paradigm" as the predominant framework among white mainline liberal and evangelical Protestants in the United States shaping responses to racism. Reconciliation identifies separation as the primary problem that needs addressing, to which reconciliation is the answer. However, as Harvey points out, "Racial separateness is evidence of the extent to which our differences embody legacies of unjust material structures. Racial separateness is a to-be-expected outcome of the reality that our differences literally contain still painful and violent histories that remain unredressed and unrepaired."[36] For Harvey, if any conception of reconciliation between whites and blacks is to be meaningful, issues of white supremacy, histories of racial oppression, and disparities of power have to be acknowledged and addressed. Division and separateness are not the problem; the nature of the division is. Black separation from whites is a mode of survival and self-determination. White separation from blacks is an articulation of white supremacy. What separation signifies among blacks and whites is very different due to differences of historical experience and the ongoing impact of structures of domination. Failure to understand this will lead to misdiagnosis of what reconciliation must entail. Indeed, as Harvey argues, without a proper appreciation of what whiteness names, the advocacy of reconciliation becomes a way of masking the operations of white supremacy and reinscribing racial disparities and disadvantage between blacks and whites. It is whites who need to embrace racial difference, not blacks. As W. E. B. Du Bois's notion of "double consciousness" points out, blacks have always had to be hyperaware of whites, whereas whites, for the most part, are entirely oblivious both to their whiteness and to how it positions them in relation to "people of color." This is a dynamic I explore further in the next chapter.

36. Jennifer Harvey, *Dear White Christians: For Those Still Longing for Racial Reconciliation* (Grand Rapids: Eerdmans, 2014), 61.

In a parallel way, humanitarianism as a paradigm often masks Western privilege. By identifying destitution as the primary problem, humanitarianism occludes the histories of racial and imperial oppression and disparities of power and access upon which is constructed Western privilege. Humanitarianism thereby fails to address how the West is complicit in creating the suffering, destitution, and powerlessness that humanitarianism seeks to address. Cultivating a poverty of spirit through repentance is the necessary beginning point for reorientating humanitarianism. And it enables humanitarianism to be reconfigured as partly a form of redistribution rather than simply an act of philanthropy. How humanitarianism can forestall the need for repentance while at the same time advocating concern for the poor can be elucidated further by distinguishing between two theo-political ways of imagining relations between the privileged and the poor: beneficence and blessing.

Orders of Beneficence and Blessing

The etymological differences between "beneficence" and "blessing" are significant. "Beneficence" draws on the Latin *beneficium*, meaning to do good or perform kind deeds. It presumes that the locus of agency is the one performing the good action who possesses an advantage or privilege that he or she is sharing. By contrast, "blessing" has a number of sources, notably the Hebrew terms *berakhah*, meaning thanksgiving or praise, and the Old English term *blóedsian/bletsung*, meaning to consecrate, sanctify, or make holy (literally, hallow with blood). Blessing implies the reception of a gift and an acknowledgment of a prior and superordinate source of all blessing that was not created or earned but must be acknowledged with the appropriate gesture. In Scripture, as Ellen Davis notes, "Blessing is essentially the transformative experience of knowing and honoring God as the Giver; it means valuing the steady flow that sustains the world even above the gift of life that each of us receives and in time is constrained to relinquish."[37] By building on these etymological differences, this section proposes a theological distinction between an "order of beneficence" that instrumentalizes the poor in order to justify and glorify itself, and an "order of blessing" that seeks to glorify God and generate healing and

---

37. Ellen Davis, *Scripture, Culture, and Agriculture: An Agrarian Reading of the Bible* (Cambridge: Cambridge University Press, 2009), 164.

nourishment for all, especially the poor. In a paradigmatic instance of the tragic nature of politics in this age, I propose that these two orders tear humanitarianism apart: ideally it seeks the latter, but more often than not it embodies the former.

In an order of beneficence, the privileged think their situation is natural or deserved. Within this justificatory logic, the giving of alms, rather than being either an act of either reparation, redistribution, or the sharing of what some received for the good of all, becomes the noble and private gesture of the privileged toward the poor. The act of beneficence reinscribes the structures of privilege as "natural" rather than as a distortion that needs repenting. Moreover, helping the poor becomes part of the structure of legitimacy through which domination is sanctioned and authorized.[38] One set of people sympathizes, another set suffers; one set judges, another set submits; one set gives, the other accepts. The characteristic difference between the two orders is as follows: an order of beneficence is an order of bestowal where the privileged bestow status on others, whereas an order of blessing is one where the privileged recognize the poor as fellow creatures with whom they share a common life on which everyone depends.[39] An order of beneficence may be generous, but it is fundamentally unjust. By contrast, an order of blessing aims to cultivate a just and loving form of *common* life. In the latter order, mutual sharing (or communion) is the paradigmatic act, whereas, in the former, it is a one-way, philanthropic donation.

The contrast between an order of beneficence and an order of blessing is a theo-political one suggested by Jesus's discussion of the true nature of authority in Luke 22. As the gospel puts it, "Jesus said to them, 'The kings of the Gentiles lord it over them; and those who exercise authority over them call themselves Benefactors'" (Luke 22:25, NIV). This is not just a moral judgment. It is also a description of how those with positions of privilege see themselves and want recognition as in some way benefactors. These dynamics characterized relations between rich and poor in the Roman Empire. The hands of the great, whether of the emperor or a patron, were expected to distribute wealth to others and show largesse. This largesse was part of the legitimatizing structure of wealth and power and

38. Christopher H. Wellman, "Liberalism, Samaritanism, and Political Legitimacy," *Philosophy and Public Affairs* 25, no. 3 (1996): 211-37.

39. As Benedict XVI put it in *Deus Caritas Est*: "Man cannot live by oblative, descending love (agape) alone. He cannot always give, he must also receive" (§7).

the patron-client relations on which the Roman "empire of gifts" rested.[40] Christians built on this but challenged the boundary of care so it included those viewed as "other" and not just those seen as "brothers" (fellow citizens), "mothers" (kith and kin), or "fathers" (patrons).

In contrast to the claims and desires of earthly rulers, the Gospels portray the disciples as being called on to be "servants." But they offer a distinctive vision of service. Disciples are to serve those at a table, that is, those gathered at a messianic banquet, where all may participate, as each has a charism to contribute. What these servants are to offer is not self-aggrandizing and impenitent beneficence but eschatological blessings and participation in the people of God. And what such a meal symbolizes is not simply renewed interpersonal communion but the hallowing and offering up of the fruits of the earth in praise and worship. Food, paradigmatically at the Eucharist, links our common life with the soil, our common life with each other, and our common life with God, and its production, distribution, and consumption inherently involve processes of participation and transformation. After Christ, the difficult discernment is whether configurations of rule and structures of privilege have become self-serving and are masking, through the operations of an order of beneficence, the domination of others.

To see how humanitarianism can function as an order of beneficence, we can compare how Greco-Roman and subsequent Christian political orders conceptualized poverty. As already noted, Greco-Roman political orders had a justificatory structure of bringing a benefit of one kind or another, but this benefit did not revolve around a focused concern for the destitute, afflicted, and powerless.[41] Rather than status and authority being accrued and reinforced through looking after the poor, glory was found primarily in the acclamations of the citizens and civic *euergetism* (that is, the building of temples, holding games, etc., that glorify the *polis*).[42] Peter

---

40. Brown, *Through the Eye*, 56–59.

41. Augustine's *City of God* can be read in part as an attempt to deconstruct the Roman Empire's justificatory argument that it brought peace.

42. Brown, *Through the Eye*, 61–71. Alongside the civic benefaction that resourced the games, built public baths and temples, etc., there were other forms of "welfare" provision. These included hospitality (which was focused on kinship relations or on those of equal status); patronage (which the very poor rarely benefited from, as they had nothing to offer in return); and public grain doles initiated by Augustus and other imperial alimentary schemes (but which did not go to the destitute but to Roman citizens in Rome of the "middling sort"). Also, hospitality and generosity were associated with

Brown argues that, in late antiquity, Christianity instigated a shift whereby a concern for the poor became a measure of an order's legitimacy and a mark of good rule.[43] From this period onward, in European Christian contexts, concern for the poor marked whether a political order was legitimate. At the same time, this justificatory structure for good rule came to be aligned with and used to legitimatize numerous hegemonic forms of domination.[44] For example, Christian justifications of imperialism framed it as a material and spiritual benefit to the colonized and as a sacrifice undertaken by the colonizer on behalf of the weak.[45]

I contend that humanitarianism echoes the same contradictions as Christian orders of beneficence. A contemporary example that illustrates this contradiction (and makes explicit the link between the evisceration of environmental and human flourishing) is the move to forcibly replace agrarian traditions of farming with industrialized forms of agriculture.[46] Such top-down, technocratic schemes are carried out in the name of "development," "modernization," "ending suffering," and "food security." In other words, they are justified as bringing benefit to the poor.[47] Yet they

---

devotion of pagan deities and communicated through stories such as Ovid's *Metamorphoses*. Linked to this was the giving of occasional alms to beggars. See Bruce Longenecker, *Remember the Poor: Paul, Poverty, and the Greco-Roman World* (Grand Rapids: Eerdmans, 2010), 89–107.

43. A central argument of Brown is that a cumulative impact of Christianity was the construction of the category "the poor" as part of a reconfiguration of the social, political, and economic relations of late antiquity.

44. One example is the use of this kind of logic to justify white supremacy. Another aligned project underwritten by a similar justificatory structure is the exceptional status and mission of "America." Yet another is justifications of capitalism that focus on how it is the most effective arrangement for meeting the needs of and efficiently allocating resources to the poor. For an overview of contemporary arguments for and against capitalism as a moral enterprise that brings benefit to the poor, see Marion Fourcade and Kieran Healy, "Moral Views of Market Society," *Annual Review of Sociology* 33 (2007): 285–311.

45. See, for example, Rudyard Kipling's poem "The White Man's Burden: The United States and the Philippine Islands" (1899). In a different vein, the first international advocacy networks—such as those who campaigned to end the slave trade—deployed the lack of benefit to the least, the lost, and the last as a way of bringing accountability and changes to the imperial policies of Britain. See Stamatov, "Activist Religion," 607–28.

46. An example of this in action is what is happening in the Gambella Province of Ethiopia. See Fred Pearce, *The Land Grabbers: The New Fight over Who Owns the Earth* (Boston: Beacon, 2012), 3–16.

47. See, for example, the comments by the Ethiopian prime minister and ambassador regarding the schemes for Gambella (Pearce, *The Land Grabbers*, 16).

concentrate wealth and power and, rather than improve resilience and deepen the agency of the "have-nots" to solve their own problems, exacerbate ecological and human vulnerability.[48]

Humanitarian orders of beneficence operate within a paradox of care. The paradox is that those we don't care about and don't have compassion for we tolerate or leave alone, even if what they are doing is harmful or flies in the face of our moral and political commitments. Those we care about or feel responsible for when we see them doing something wrong or harmful or suffering in some way, we feel compelled to help, even at the expense of their agency. Yet the intervention prompted in such cases is more often than not an attempt to govern lives and is paternalistic or even colonial in orientation. Therefore, while the impulse to rule is often a loving one born out of humanitarian concern for another's welfare, it is distorted by the belief that we think we know better how those in need should live. We then limit their agency so they might conform to our notions of what is good and right and proper in order to be fully human. We direct their *paideia* (education/formation/socialization), and this involves often strict forms of discipline—albeit "pastoral" in nature—to ensure that they live as we determine. Loving concern is then seen to produce modes of domination mediated through practices of governance. This paradox represents a central dilemma in all means of welfare provision and attempts to address poverty and inequality, whether through local, national, or international initiatives. A contrasting approach to a humanitarian order of beneficence is to put people before program. This necessitates the privileged who are seeking to help the poor, whether they are "experts," philanthropists, business leaders, or politicians, attending to the life that already exists among "the poor"—their customary practices, traditions, institutions, leaders, etc.—and beginning from there rather than telling the poor how they should live if they want to enjoy an elite order of beneficence.[49]

Theologically, then, what is the therapy for humanitarianism as an order of beneficence?

---

48. On this, see Scott, *Seeing like a State*.

49. In agricultural terms, this is exemplified in advocacy for "food sovereignty" and the campaigns of the global agrarian movement La Via Campesina (http://viacampesina .org/en/).

Christology as the Basis for an Order of Blessing

Theologically, the symbiosis of poverty and privilege noted earlier can be understood as central to Christology. How does the Lord of lords relate to humans, given the asymmetries of power, status, and nature between us? Conversely, how do humans relate to God, and how is our participation in the people of God mediated by Christ? Our "poverty" (as sinners and finite creatures) needs situating in relation to Christ's, who "though he was rich, yet for your sakes he become poor" (2 Cor. 8:9). A christocentric horizon frames a "preferential option for the poor" as not simply an anthropocentric concern about inequality but also a concern about what it means to participate in Christ's cosmic work faithfully.[50] For the instigators of Latin American liberation theology this was a central concern.[51] Moreover, a theocentric focus makes the primary point of attention not the flourishing of humans alone but the flourishing of all creation. We can thereby connect a preferential option for the poor to the emergence of ecological theologies and the question of how to discover just and loving ways of being alive shared between human and nonhuman life.[52]

In parallel with an emphasis on the kingdom of God, Christology was the beginning point for diverse theological pathways that wrestled with the problem of poverty in early-twentieth-century Europe. The social, political, and economic trauma brought on by industrialized capitalism (and the extremes of destitution and affliction this engendered) and totalitarianism (and the extremes of powerlessness this created) provoked this wrestling. And alongside the destitution, affliction, and powerlessness brought on by processes of modernization, modernity itself seemed to induce a kind of

50. This is a theme in much patristic writings on poverty. See, for example, Gregory of Nyssa, *Fourth Homily on Ecclesiastes* and *Discourses on the Holy Pascha*, and Gregory of Nazianzus, *On Love for the Poor*.

51. See, for example, Leonardo Boff, *Church, Charism, and Power: Liberation Theology and the Institutional Church*, trans. John W. Diercksmeier (New York: Crossroad, 1985). On the origins of the term "a preferential option for the poor" and its use in Catholic social teaching, see Gustavo Gutiérrez, "Option for the Poor," in *Mysterium Liberationis: Fundamental Concepts of Liberation Theology*, ed. Ignacio Ellacuría and Jon Sobrino (Maryknoll, NY: Orbis, 1993), 235-50.

52. See, for example, Leonardo Boff, *Cry of the Earth, Cry of the Poor* (Maryknoll, NY: Orbis, 1997); Larry L. Rasmussen, *Earth Community, Earth Ethics* (Maryknoll, NY: Orbis, 1997)—Rasmussen explicitly links his constructive eco-theology to a critique of anthropocentric conceptions of development; and Ivone Gebara, *Longing for Running Water: Ecofeminism and Liberation* (Minneapolis: Fortress Press, 1999).

impoverished piety that came to be named secularization. One theological response to modernity was the realization that the only real basis for answering the question "what does it mean to be human?" is Jesus Christ.[53] Christ is the true human. Christ and not some revolutionary ideology or bourgeois civilization reveals to us the true nature and telos of our humanity, and our freedom and dignity are secured not through any historically contingent political or economic structure but through our participation in Christ as part of his body. Christ reconciles all things in himself, and so is the only sure foundation for a common world of meaning and action of which the church is to be the first fruit. Neither the state nor the market should be the primary point of mediation for "social" relations. Any attempt to subordinate "society" to the state or the market inevitably led to the undermining and disintegration of forms of covenantal and communal life, whether in the family, the union, civic associations, or vocational institutions. On this account, responding to poverty entails a response to who Jesus Christ is and discerning how human life together enables or disables finite and fallen creatures from participating in both the body of Christ and the body politic. It is the right ordering of divine-human and thence neighbor-to-neighbor relations within the context of the flourishing of creation that is the precondition for addressing poverty and privilege justly and generously.

The ecclesiological implications of a christocentric conception of how to put the last first are manifold as they directly relate to the question of how the body of Christ constitutes a catholic or universal body. Without reordering the whole—not simply in terms of the participation of the poor, but significantly in the character and form of participation evidenced by the privileged—the people of God are not truly a people. They are instead a collectivized mass, a disaggregated crowd, or a constellation of competing interest groups. The overarching goal of a christocentric account of how to address poverty is the constitution of a faithful people in which all have agency and can exercise their charisms and so must be characterized by relations of both justice and generosity of each to all. The fruit of such an order of blessing is thus not welfare but loving justice: everyone giving what they can and getting what they need. This then has enormous implications for the kind of political order and vision of peoplehood the church is to seek and bear witness to in this age.

---

53. The work of Karl Barth, and in dialogue with Barth, James Cone's 1969 *Black Theology and Black Power*, are Protestant examples. Catholic social teaching makes a parallel move. See especially *Redemptor Hominis* (1979) and *Dives in Misericordia* (1980).

A christologically and eschatologically orientated order of blessing follows from an emphasis on what it means to participate in Christ's healing rule. To participate in the rule of Christ does not mean that the privileged exercise rule on behalf of Christ. This would legitimate preexisting forms of, for example, sexist, class-based, and racist structures of authority. Rather, it entails being prepared to dis-identify with unjustly privileged forms of life in order to participate in Christ's cruciform rule. Dis-identification with idolatrous and sinful structures of privilege to enable right participation in Christ's rule entails a double movement of, on the one hand, repentance and, on the other, kenotic generosity that uses privilege to serve others. This double movement marks the pathway through the eye of the needle (Matthew 19:24; Mark 10:25; Luke 18:25).

The connection between participating in the healing rule of Christ, "social action," and responses to poverty is not simply that doing good is a measure of our morality. Neither are "evangelism" and "social action" separable. Rather, the constitution of the people of God and witness to the healing and transfiguring rule of Christ within the body politic (as a human and nonhuman community) are a single movement. A key diagnostic for this simultaneously ecclesiological and missiological movement is the treatment of the poor. By forging a common life with the destitute, powerless, and afflicted in and through Christ, the privileged deconstruct their structural advantage and thereby participate in the extension of God's rule, which brings salvation to a sinful world. In short, the church's response to poverty is a measure of the faithfulness or otherwise of the church's participation in Christ's rule.

Beginning any initiative by putting the last first and calling on the privileged to invest in the kingdom of God ensures that both the body of Christ and the body politic can tell the truth about themselves. Treatment of the poor is a diagnostic of whether power and privilege are exercised justly and lovingly. Scripturally, this is based on the presumption that good leaders should bring blessings to those they rule, including the seeming outer limits of the body politic—the widows, orphans, strangers, and the land (*naḥălâ*) itself.[54] By seeing our common life from the perspective of the poor, what is unveiled is who counts and what is valued. The experience of poverty

---

54. On the centrality of the land to the scriptural envisioning of human flourishing, see Davis, *Scripture, Culture, and Agriculture*. Perhaps the fullest picture of fructifying rule in the Hebrew Bible/Old Testament is the portrayal of the "valorous woman" in Prov. 31:10-31 (Davis, 147-54). At a different scale, another contender is Ps. 72.

should be given epistemological priority, as it is a vital vantage point from which to discern the true order of things. As a truth-telling measure, a preferential option for the poor should be antihegemonic and anti-ideological: if the poor are really to be preferred, then the privileged must listen to and be in a meaningful relationship with them rather than make them subject populations on whom they impose various bureaucratic, colonial, collectivizing, or commodifying programs. Beginning with repentance means presuming one does not speak for all, one does not know everything, and one does not determine the meaning of this time and place. It is to begin from a position of epistemic humility best characterized by a posture of listening. Listening is the first act of any move from an order of beneficence to an order of blessing, as it assumes the poor have something to teach the privileged about how to live and that a common life between them is necessary to the flourishing of each and the flourishing of all.

A Preferential Option for the Demos

We are in the midst of a global conversation about how to address poverty. Old questions, previously thought settled, are being asked again in new contexts. In the Atlantic world, from the late nineteenth century up to and including World War II, basic questions like "How do we care for the old?," "How do we educate children?," "What does good work look like?," "What is the relationship between humans and nature?," and so on were being asked. These were questions driven by massive social dislocations caused by such things as rapid urbanization, mass migration, and changes in the means of production. These kinds of questions are with us again; having been settled, they are now unsettled and in flux. After 1945, the ways both the West and the developing world answered these questions, namely, through either state-centric social democratic welfare regimes or market-centric solutions, are seen to be inadequate or to produce greater inequality. Part of the problem with both solutions is that both see the problem of poverty as one of material scarcity. The state, the market, or combinations of both are then proposed as the most effective, efficient, and just means of distributing scarce resources. But poverty, as already noted, entails a lack of power, not just material scarcity. Both state- and market-centric solutions lead to massive concentrations of power: one in the hands of bureaucrats, the other in the hands of plutocrats. Humanitarian agencies, in the name of being apolitical, tend to reinscribe statecraft and capitalism as the primary way of addressing large-scale human need. The alternative is politics-centric approaches that address inequalities of power through foregrounding the need for highly participatory forms of institutions that distribute and build up the agency of those served to act for themselves. Yet humanitarianism often masks or ignores how democratic politics and economic democracy of various kinds are another route to solving collective problems.

If we are to find innovative ways of addressing shared problems—disease, ignorance, pollution, etc.—and realizing common and public goods—health, education, potable water, etc.—then it is vital that the discovery of these solutions actively involve those affected by the problems in view. If not, then any means of solving them is likely to become a top-down scheme of social engineering. With this concern in mind, democratic politics (and economic democracy) can be understood as forms of collective problem solving. Conversely, aiming to address poverty via participative democratic politics entails ensuring that humanitarian agencies seek to enhance the resilience and capacity of democratic politics and the public life where they are serving. As Rubenstein points out, difficulties arise when humanitarian agencies operate with a strict apolitical principle of "aid based on need alone," as this leads to humanitarian norms being "unconstrained by attention to issues of justice, democracy, and equality."[55] Aid and development decisions are never neutral, nor are they anti-, pre-, or postpolitical. They are always already moral and political judgments about who matters and why.

When the poor are imagined as destitute or afflicted irrespective of whether they are part of or contribute to a body politic, then the relationship between poverty and privilege is depoliticized and a vital reason for why the poor are poor is thereby hidden. Instead, the poor become subjects of humanitarian or pastoral concern, not people enmeshed in and in need of radically transformed political and economic relations.[56]

---

55. Rubenstein, *Between Samaritans and States*, 220.

56. My emphasis on peoplehood counters Arendt's proper concern for how, in the modern period, sympathy for the poor trumps politics and justifies violence and the limitless use of state power to alleviate suffering (Hannah Arendt, *On Revolution* [London: Penguin Books, 2006 (1963)], 49–105).

Conclusion

Humanitarianism is not an explicitly Christian ethic, but neither is it opposed to a Christian ethic. It sits in an ambiguous relation of being a Christ-haunted and Christ-forgetting moral and political vision. Through incorporating and resignifying antecedent forms of political theology, it suffers many of the characteristic deformations that have affected Christian approaches to addressing the interrelationship between poverty and privilege. Primary among these is how humanitarianism generates an order of beneficence rather than an order of blessing. Humanitarianism, as a penultimate and fallen assemblage of belief and practice, is in constant need of reform and, within a theological frame of reference, redirecting to Christ and eschatological ends so that it might contribute to more just and loving forms of common life.

It is tempting to see a neutral, altruistic, and humanitarian concern for the poor as somehow more enlightened or more loving than a Christian one that includes a focus on mission and discipleship. But this misses the ambiguity and complexity of how humanitarianism, divorced from wider political, ecological, ecclesial, and missiological considerations, through its very forms and processes, reinscribes unjust structures of beneficence that make the "haves" feel generous and keep the poor poor. When humanitarianism becomes too self-referential, what is not at stake is changing Western ways of life so that the poor and nonhuman life may be recognized as constituents of it, even if that demands a fundamental transformation of how we live and our order of priorities. Theologically, concern for the poor should be orientated by concern for our common life with our habitat, with each other as neighbors, and with God and the conversion of the privileged that needs to happen to enable this. A political theology of "aid," "development," "welfare," and "pastoral care" should not only focus on the alleviation of affliction or destitution but also seek to build the power of the poor through politics and the participation of all in the body of Christ through mission.

Threshold

This chapter has examined humanitarianism as a political theology born out of the question of how to respond to human suffering and poverty. However, as a political theology, it is an ambiguous legacy of the Atlantic world colonialism forged. In the next chapter, I consider Black Power as a current of political theology that is a legacy of the "black" or "revolutionary" Atlantic world that emerged on the underside of colonial political economies. When it comes to politics, there is a stark contrast between humanitarianism and Black Power. In the name of focusing on pastoral care for other humans imagined as the same, humanitarianism envisions itself as being above or beyond politics. In doing so, it masks ever-present questions about the distribution of power and the role of difference in constituting a common life. Black Power is also a response to suffering and poverty, but one that makes questions of power and politics central and reaches for a common life by beginning with how humans are different.

Suggested Readings for Further Discussion

John Wesley, Sermon 98, "On Visiting the Sick." Available online. Wesley's injunctions to care for the least, the lost, and the last, and his support for the abolition movement were an influential stream of thought feeding into the emergence of modern humanitarianism. This sermon lays out some of Wesley's theological framework for why and how Christians should respond to poverty.

William Lloyd Garrison, "From *The Great Apostate* [1850]," in *American Antislavery Writings: Colonial Beginnings to Emancipation*, ed. James Basker (New York: Library of America, 2012), 558-63. Abolitionism was a precursor to modern humanitarianism, and Garrison is a key figure in the abolitionist movement.

Johannes Baptist Metz, *Poverty of Spirit*, trans. John Drury (Glen Rock, NJ: Newman, 1968). This extended essay articulates a political theology of humility as a form of poverty.

Michael Barnett and Thomas Weiss, "Humanitarianism: A Brief History of the Present," in *Humanitarianism in Question: Politics, Power, Ethics*, ed. Michael Barnett and Thomas Weiss (Ithaca, NY: Cornell University Press, 2008), 1-48. A helpful historical overview of humanitarianism.

Didier Fassin, "Hierarchies of Humanity: Intervening in International Conflicts," in *Humanitarian Reason: A Moral History of the Present Times* (Berkeley: University of California Press, 2012), 223-42. In this chapter, as part of his critical theory of humanitarianism, Fassin explores some of its internal contradictions.

Jennifer Rubenstein, *Between Samaritans and States: The Political Ethics of Humanitarian INGOs* (Oxford: Oxford University Press, 2015), chaps. 4 and 5.

CHAPTER 3

Black Power

The first part of this chapter analyzes the Black Power movement within the context of debates about how black nationalism conceptualized the need to form a people as a response to white supremacy. The second part examines how white supremacy conditions the nature and form of democratic citizenship in the United States and how the formation of a "nation within a nation" is a vital adjunct to dismantling white supremacy as a political system. The third part situates Black Power within a theological conception of poverty understood as powerlessness. Building on James Cone and Cheryl Kirk-Duggan, it closes by suggesting that forming a people as a response to powerlessness constitutes a double movement of healing and exorcism. But let me begin by situating this chapter within a wider set of debates and delimiting what it does and does not try to do.

The long-standing black radical tradition has generated penetrating critiques of democracy in the United States.[1] It seeks, in theory and practice, a form of antiracist, radical democratic politics—or what W. E. B. Du Bois calls "abolition democracy"—while recognizing that such a politics is almost incomprehensible within the existing order of things.[2] For this to be widespread and sustained, the American body politic would need to be radically reconstituted in the face of the cumulative and current impact of systemically racist structures. A recent articulation of this critique is put forward by Ta-Nehisi Coates. For Coates democracy in America is

1. One of the sharpest articulations of this critique is Malcolm X's 1964 "The Ballot or the Bullet" speech. For an account of this tradition, see Cedric Robinson, *Black Marxism: The Making of the Black Radical Tradition* (London: Zed, 1983).

2. W. E. B. Du Bois, *Black Reconstruction in America: An Essay toward a History of the Part Which Black Folk Played in the Attempt to Reconstruct Democracy in America, 1860–1880* (London: Routledge, 2017 [1935]), 165.

founded on racialized conceptions of "the people" even as the realization of its democratic promise is driven, in large part, by constructive responses to racism.[3] In response to this contradictory dynamic, thinkers within the black radical tradition—generating a range of conclusions—reflect on how African Americans can constitute themselves to address both the subjective and objective conditions of domination constructively.

Dominant strands of modern political philosophy—notably, political liberalism—mostly ignore these critiques.[4] In response, Charles Mills calls for an end to the segregation of black political thought from "mainstream" political philosophy.[5] He argues that these two traditions share an important set of concerns. However, these shared concerns cannot be recognized let alone articulated if racism in the United States, which has been judicially backed, morally and theoretically rationalized, and structurally institutionalized, is treated as an anomaly rather than as basic to the construction of the American body politic. When treated as a deviation from an otherwise healthy system, then the remedy that presents itself is to keep doing more of the very things that have historically been part of the problem: the further application of "color-blind" liberal principles and redistributive policies.[6] Mills's critique also applies to political theology generally and to discussions of the relationship between Christianity and democracy in particular.

Beyond Mills's critique is the contention that democracy itself is a "creolized" phenomenon born out of the violent entanglements of Europe, the Middle East, Africa, and the Americas.[7] As noted in the introduction, modern conceptualizations of terms such as "democracy," "sovereignty," and "citizenship" do not emerge pristine from the European context to be exported elsewhere. Rather, a crucible of modern political thought is the "Black Atlantic" and the ways in which political ideas circulated and were

3. Ta-Nehisi Coates, *Between the World and Me* (New York: Spiegel and Grau, 2015), 6.

4. On this see Michael C. Dawson, *Black Visions: The Roots of Contemporary African-American Political Ideologies* (Chicago: University of Chicago Press, 2001), 29-43; Tommie Shelby, *We Who Are Dark: The Philosophical Foundations of Black Solidarity* (Cambridge, MA: Belknap Press of Harvard University Press, 2005), 6-13; and Joel Olson, *The Abolition of White Democracy* (Minneapolis: University of Minnesota Press, 2004).

5. Charles W. Mills, *Blackness Visible: Essays on Philosophy and Race* (Ithaca, NY: Cornell University Press, 1998), 119-37.

6. For a critique of redistributive mechanisms as a means of addressing racism see Olson, *Abolition of White Democracy*, 114-18.

7. Édouard Glissant, *Caribbean Discourse: Selected Essays*, trans. J. Michael Dash (Charlottesville: University Press of Virginia, 1989).

refracted through the relationship between metropole and colony (whether internal or external). Again, Eurocentric political theology and, in particular, discussions of the relationship between Christianity and democracy have largely ignored or concealed the creolized nature of modern political terms and their colonial and racialized formation.

This chapter is an attempt to abide with and learn from the stringent challenge that Mills, Gilroy, and others pose.[8] It is not an attempt to "do" black liberation theology. Rather, it listens to the questions black political thought brings to the fore that should be addressed by any form of political theology and, in particular, attempts to reflect on the relationship between Christianity and democracy. In previous work, I contended that certain kinds of democratic practices are a means through which radically different visions of the good, conflicts of interest, and asymmetries of power can be contested and negotiated in order to generate a more just and compassionate common life. Democratic politics is a means by which antagonistic and sometimes violent friend-enemy relations can be converted into a world of shared meaning and action.[9] But what if the basis and accepted performances of democratic politics constitutively excluded certain kinds of persons or groups? What happens when "we, the people" are defined over and against those not considered a people or even persons (e.g., those defined as not white)? How, then, should the body politic be reconstituted? Is a common-life politics possible when state and market processes are shaped by a structure of power (white supremacy) that inherently advantages one group (whites) in relation to another (blacks) while at the same time actively ensuring the domination, disaggregation, and devaluation of the latter? And is a world of shared meaning and action possible when instances of civil unrest such as what occurred in Ferguson, Missouri, and Baltimore in 2014–2015 generate incommensurable interpretations—when one person's riot is another's uprising?

The questions outlined above have been discussed with an existential urgency and clarity by the Black Power movement of the 1960s and 1970s, and the Black Atlantic diasporic traditions that the movement drew on

8. For a historical account of the emergence of black nationalism prior to the beginning of the Great Migration and some of the key traditions of organizing it drew on, see Steven Hahn, *A Nation under Our Feet: Black Political Struggles in the Rural South, from Slavery to the Great Migration* (Cambridge, MA: Belknap Press of Harvard University Press, 2003).

9. See Luke Bretherton, *Resurrecting Democracy: Faith, Citizenship, and the Politics of a Common Life* (Cambridge: Cambridge University Press, 2015).

and reiterated. This chapter seeks to learn from the critiques of democracy they generated.[10] It examines how debates within and about Black Power help us understand the conditions and possibilities of democratic politics as a means of challenging white supremacy as an oppressive political system when white supremacy is at the same time constitutive of how democratic citizenship and democracy as a mode of statecraft are constructed in North America.[11] In view of these critiques, the chapter also attends to the inherently creolized nature of conceptions of democracy and citizenship by focusing on one historical instance of the violent entanglements of Europe, Africa, and the Americas, namely, the Black Power movement.

Reflecting on the Black Power movement within the fields of political theology and Christian ethics is particularly salient. Alongside the experience of the black churches, Black Power was the catalyst for the work of James Cone and the emergence of black liberation theology.[12] In tandem with Latin American liberation theology, black liberation theology heralded a seismic shift in Protestant social ethics and the use of Christian realism as a dominant framework for thinking about political and social questions.[13] From Cone's work onward, liberationist paradigms of one sort or another became increasingly normative in North American liberal Protestant circles and determinative points of reference and critique in others. Despite its impact, however, Black Power as a social movement has re-

10. Peniel E. Joseph argues that while Black Power activists such as the Black Panther Party rejected any identification with the United States, they embraced its democratic principles and played an important role in shaping, contesting, and transforming the meaning of American democracy. Peniel E. Joseph, "The Black Power Movement: A State of the Field," *Journal of American History* 96, no. 3 (2009): 751-76.

11. More broadly, the relationship between democracy and white supremacy in the United States is a case study of a more generic problem in democratic theory: the majoritarian dimensions of democracy whereby structural injustice against minorities can be reinforced and perpetuated by democratic majorities. Black Power, and black nationalism more generally, can be seen as an attempt to constructively address this more generic problem in a particular context. A parallel case to the situation of African Americans in the United States is that of the Dalits in India. On this, and the historical connections between these two situations, see Gyanendra Pandey, *A History of Prejudice: Race, Caste, and Difference in India and the United States* (Cambridge: Cambridge University Press, 2013).

12. James H. Cone, *Black Theology and Black Power* (Maryknoll, NY: Orbis, 1997 [1969]).

13. Gary J. Dorrien, *Social Ethics in the Making: Interpreting an American Tradition* (Chichester, UK: Wiley-Blackwell, 2008), 390-532.

ceived less attention in Christian ethics and political theology than the civil rights movement. There are numerous reasons for this; one is that the civil rights movement is seen to validate and exemplify core Christian claims. By contrast, Black Power, as Cone discerned, represents a profound challenge to the morality and legitimacy of Christianity as such, and the role of churches in resisting and deconstructing racism. This challenge has been extensively explored in work that examines the interrelationship between Western European strands of theology and white supremacy and the complicity of Western churches in racialized structures of oppression.[14] But while much of this work highlights how racism is a cultural and theological problem, it does not probe in detail how racism conditions the nature and form of democracy. To address this lacuna, this chapter investigates how Black Power unveils the link between democracy and white supremacy, and thus provides clarity about why black and white nationalisms in the United States are *not* morally equivalent—as many today still assume—and debunks the claim that Black Power and, latterly, Black Lives Matter are forms of "reverse racism."

The Black Power movement also challenges anemic and pinched visions of what secularity can entail. Like its heirs, such as Cornel West, and its antecessors, such as the early proponent of black nationalism Martin Delany, Black Power was complexly religious and nonreligious.[15] James Noel argues that within the emergent Atlantic world, from the fifteenth century onward and under the brutalizing and atomizing impact of slavery, the need to be a people and the expression of being a people through the creation of new religious forms and practices were contiguous.[16] Religious symbols, rituals, institutional formations, and discourses have continuously sustained black political activism.[17] Denmark Vesey, Nat Turner, Ida B. Wells, Martin Luther King Jr., and Malcolm X are just a few prominent figures associated with black-led struggles for liberation that interwove politics and religion. More specifically, certain strands

14. See, for example, Willie James Jennings, *The Christian Imagination: Theology and the Origins of Race* (New Haven: Yale University Press, 2010).

15. This contests Eddie Glaude's reading of Black Power as a secularizing movement. Eddie Glaude, *In a Shade of Blue: Pragmatism and the Politics of Black America* (Chicago: University of Chicago Press, 2007), 73.

16. James A. Noel, *Black Religion and the Imagination of Matter in the Atlantic World* (New York: Palgrave Macmillan, 2009).

17. See Gayraud Wilmore, *Black Religion and Black Radicalism: An Interpretation of the Religious History of African Americans* (Maryknoll, NY: Orbis, 1998).

of black nationalism, as exemplified in the work of Marcus Garvey and Albert Cleage Jr., are explicit forms of political theology.[18] The Black Power movement echoed this intersection of religion and politics, even when Christianity was not a primary point of reference and key leaders expressed anticlerical sentiments.[19] Like its forebears, the Black Power movement mixed sacred and profane, public and private, the vernacular and the formal, theory and practice, and refused modern European attempts to separate pursuit of the true, the good, and the beautiful. "Black is beautiful" is a simultaneously political, economic, ethical, spiritual, and aesthetic statement performed in rap and ballet, hairstyles and poetry, political polemics and preaching. Because the Black Power movement, like its antecedents, was complexly religious and nonreligious, it can help envisage ways of understanding contemporary interaction of religion and politics. Or, to go even further, as James Cone and Vincent Lloyd contend, the politics of the Black Power movement points to a form of political theology.[20]

While much of the following is not explicitly theological in focus, I am not thereby setting up a false dichotomy between black political thought and black theology. As already noted, political theory and political theology are intertwined in the black radical tradition and, as per Cone and Lloyd, its politics witnesses to a form of political theology. Rather, for the sake of clarity of exposition, the focus here is on the explicitly political problems black nationalism and Black Power addressed. Shifting key and tempo, the chapter closes by attending to the theological resonances Black Power generated.

18. Cardinal Aswad Walker, "Princes Shall Come out of Egypt: A Theological Comparison of Marcus Garvey and Reverend Albert B. Cleage Jr.," *Journal of Black Studies* 39, no. 2 (2008): 194-251.

19. For an early reflection on the inherently religious nature of the Black Power movement, see Vincent Harding, *The Religion of Black Power* (Boston: Beacon, 1968). For a detailed, place-based historical study, see Kerry Pimblott, *Faith in Black Power: Religion, Race, and Resistance in Cairo, Illinois* (Lexington: University Press of Kentucky, 2017).

20. A central argument of Cone's *Black Theology and Black Power* is that Black Power witnesses to a form of liberation theology, while Vincent Lloyd identifies Black Power as a form of political theology (*Religion of the Field Negro: On Black Secularism and Black Theology* [New York: Fordham University Press, 2018], 183). Lloyd rejects the standard narrative of how the church-led civil rights movement was overturned by atheist Black Power activists.

Black Nationalisms and the Formation of a Demos

The following quotation from Stokely Carmichael and Charles Hamilton's early articulation of what was meant by the term "Black Power" illustrates the tensions within the movement and the issues it sought to address: "The goal of the racists is to keep black people on the bottom, arbitrarily and dictatorially, as they have done in this country for over three hundred years. The goal of black self-determination and black self-identity—Black Power—is full participation in the decision making processes affecting the lives of black people, and recognition of the virtues in themselves as black people."[21] For Carmichael and Hamilton, "black self-identity" and "black self-determination" were intrinsic goods as well as means through which to dismantle racist structures. Combining these goods with the goal of ending racial oppression constituted a means of pursuing another intrinsic good: democratic politics, a definitional feature of which is that people should have a say in decisions that affect their way of life (i.e., have a measure of self-determination). How much weight to accord these goods and means was the object of vehement and sometimes violent contention among Black Power activists: To what extent should self-determination be pursued as an end in itself? Could self-determination be coordinated and consonant with realizing democracy in America? And what were the nature and basis of racism, and thus the best strategy for liberation from its effects? For example, if racial oppression was a symptom of class relations and capitalism, then broader coalitions with revolutionary proletarian movements were the answer.[22] However, if white supremacy was the primary problem, then coalitions with white-led groups such as the Students for a Democratic Society would exacerbate the problem, and the need was for total autonomy. This was exactly the point of contention between the Pan-Africanism of Stokely Carmichael/Kwame Turé and the Marxist-Leninism of an early Black Panther Party leader, Eldridge Cleaver. But for both Turé and Cleaver, democratic citizenship as constituted within Amer-

21. Stokely Carmichael and Charles Hamilton, *Black Power: The Politics of Liberation in America* (New York: Random House, 1967), 47.

22. This was the analysis of the Black Panther Party, which formed alliances with numerous other radical organizations regardless of ethnic background. These included the Young Lords, the Young Patriots, and the Red Guard. It also actively supported the boycotts organized by the United Farm Workers. See Lauren Araiza, "'In Common Struggle against a Common Oppression': The United Farm Workers and the Black Panther Party, 1968-1973," *Journal of African American History* 94, no. 2 (2009): 200-223.

ican liberal democracy was not merely an ineffectual means of pursuing black self-determination, generating democratic freedoms, and ending racial oppression; it was part of the problem that needed overcoming.[23]

Black nationalism was the primary discursive framework through which to debate these issues.[24] Like other modern ideologies that inform aligned social movements—for example, socialism, feminism, and environmentalism—Black Power is a multivalent discourse with local, national, and cosmopolitan variants that intersect and riff off each other. And like all modern social movements, it generated its own internal and external critiques; of note are black feminist and womanist critics that from the outset challenged the role of gender and sexuality in Black Power discourse, some speaking from within the movement's organizations and others by forming independent organizations.[25] Central to debates within all strands of Black Power was the question of how to form a people[26]—for that is the necessary implication of a commitment to self-determination constituted around the axis of "blackness" (whether blackness is conceived in "essentialist" or "pluralist" terms).[27] Michael Dawson distinguishes be-

---

23. Peniel E. Joseph, *Stokely: A Life* (New York: Basic Civitas Books, 2014). This debate directly echoes an earlier debate in Marxist circles in which C. L. R. James was a key protagonist. On this see Grace Lee Boggs, *Living for Change: An Autobiography* (Minneapolis: University of Minnesota Press, 1998), 55–57.

24. Without capitulating to Eddie Glaude's call to abandon the term altogether, the account of black nationalism given here works with the grain of Glaude's more pragmatic conception of black nationalism as a response to a specific set of political problems and heeds his caution that Black Power and black nationalism are a "complicated historical formation with a number of different strands and political outcomes" (Glaude, *In a Shade of Blue*, 121).

25. Ashley Farmer argues that black feminist concerns were constitutive of Black Power from the outset—at the level of both theory and practice—and black nationalist concerns informed the emergence of black feminism. Ashley Farmer, *Remaking Black Power: How Black Women Transformed an Era* (Chapel Hill: University of North Carolina Press, 2017). Moreover, Farmer argues that the internal and external critiques of Black Power by black feminists built on prior positions that combined Garveyite black nationalism with a class- and gender-conscious analysis to address the distinct situation of black women, particularly domestic workers (20–49). These critiques questioned the very nature of political agency, positing a radically different vision of the political subject to that put forward by either liberalism, communism, or separatist and statist visions of black nationalism (28–29).

26. Dawson, *Black Visions*, 85–134.

27. This is to use Paul Gilroy's distinction in *Black Atlantic: Modernity and Double Consciousness* (Cambridge, MA: Harvard University Press, 1993), 32.

tween three overlapping ways of conceptualizing what it means to be "the" black nation: "The first is built on state power and land. The second defines African-Americans as more than 'just another American ethnic group' but as a separate, oppressed people, a nation-within-a-nation, with the right to self-determination. A third, usually less political, conception of 'the' black nation defines it as a community with a defined and unique spiritual and cultural identity. All three definitions of the black nation presume that people of African descent within the borders of the United States have at least some common interests based on their race or their common history of racial subjugation."[28]

Black Power advocates answered variously the question the chapter began with: How could an oppressed group constitute itself to address both the subjective and objective conditions of domination constructively? Cultural nationalists tended to focus more on the subjective conditions of domination whereas revolutionary nationalists mainly focused on the objective, structural conditions of domination. Different critical theorists emphasized different aspects of the problem: Frantz Fanon shows up the intersection of the psychological and political dimensions of the problem; Antonio Gramsci points to how its cultural and economic aspects connect; Malcolm X underscores the confluence of the racial and religious dynamics of being a black nation within a majority white, Christian one. Whatever is made of these analyses, it was vital to have an alternative means of answering Marvin Gaye's question—"What's going on?"—to those given by the dominant, racialized social scripts. And it was imperative to ask Gaye's question before trying to answer Lenin's question—"What is to be done?"—otherwise the prevailing racist hegemony would determine the scope and strategies for action. Yet the different modes of analysis gave rise to different orientations. Within the different strands of Black Power, there is a division between common life and noncommon life-forms. Rather

28. Dawson, *Black Visions*, 91. Marcus Garvey is an example of the first, Martin Delany the second, and LeRoi Jones (before he became Amiri Baraka) the third. For an alternative typology to Dawson's, see John T. McCartney, *Black Power Ideologies: An Essay in African-American Political Thought* (Philadelphia: Temple University Press, 1992), 111–32. What Dawson misses is the "cosmopolitan" dimension of most black nationalisms. For example, revolutionary nationalists located their struggle within broader anticolonial and cross-class struggles elsewhere in the world. The constitution of the black nation/people operated at both a local and a global register. Self-determination was framed in terms of being part of a Muslim *umma*, or Africana diaspora, or worldwide class solidarity.

than "integration," cultural and community forms of Black Power seek to radically reconfigure the polity so that African Americans can be at home where they live while at the same time forging antiracist/abolitionist forms of common or intercommunal life with others outside of state-centric and capitalist structures of determination.[29] As Maulana Karenga puts it, "We can live with whites interdependently once we have Black Power."[30] Over and against the cultural and community forms, separatist forms do not seek a common life; rather, they seek a wholly separate and independent form of existence (which may or may not involve territorial separation).[31]

Even though the analyses drawn on and the form Black Power took varied, the basic goal was the same. The aim was to form a demos/people capable of, in the first instance, surviving; in the second instance, resisting; and, finally, thriving within an oppressive system that refuses to see, hear, or talk about the dehumanizing impact it is having on others and its white beneficiaries. Realizing these goals entails wrestling with two paradoxes central to radical democratic politics in modernity. The first is that democratic citizenship is an expression of individual liberty, but its performance and defense are in great measure dependent on participation in a group. Without being embedded in some form of association, the individual is naked before the power of either the market or the state and lacks a vital means for his or her own self-cultivation. The questions are then what kinds of associations are needed and how are they to be generated. The civil rights movement largely relied on churches for its institutional and associational basis.[32] But spearheaded by the Student Nonviolent Coordinating Committee's (SNCC) development of the Lowndes County Freedom Organization, the Black Power movement experimented with a wide array of sometimes contradictory methods in an attempt to form the kinds of associations and institutions needed to defend and cultivate the individual

29. The term "intercommunal" draws on Huey Newton's work. For an account of the development of his thought, see Judson Jeffries, *Huey P. Newton: The Radical Theorist* (Jackson: University Press of Mississippi, 2002).

30. Clyde Halisi and James Mtume, eds., *The Quotable Karenga* (Los Angeles: US Organization, 1967), 3.

31. For a nonterritorial, separatist vision of black nationalism, see Albert Cleage, *Black Christian Nationalism: New Directions for the Black Church* (New York: William Morrow, 1972).

32. On this, see Aldon D. Morris, *The Origins of the Civil Rights Movement: Black Communities Organizing for Change* (New York: Free Press, 1984), and Kevin Anderson, *Agitations: Ideologies and Strategies in African American Politics* (Fayetteville: University of Arkansas Press, 2010).

liberty and dignity of black people. These included third-party platforms, rifle clubs, community-organizing initiatives, schools, clinics, single-issue campaign groups, cooperatives, entrepreneurial businesses, reading circles, newspapers, and arts organizations.[33] These efforts represented an attempt to create the kinds of associations, institutional forms, and political practices that are the necessary condition for democratic freedoms to be possible but that democratic politics by itself cannot produce.

The second paradox is that democracy presumes the existence of and depends on people and institutions committed to respecting the dignity and agency of each individual, talking and acting together as a means of resolving conflicts, and believing that people should have a say in decisions that affect them. But democratic politics is forged out of immoral people and hierarchal and often authoritarian institutions and is plagued by the despotism of either the one, the few, or the many. As Grace Lee Boggs puts it, "To make a revolution, people must not only struggle against existing institutions. They must make a philosophical/spiritual leap and become more *human* human beings. In order to change/transform the world they must change/transform themselves."[34] Again, the Black Power movement tried to navigate this paradox in various ways.[35] Understanding how black nationalism and Black Power address these two democratic paradoxes renders absurd accusations that they were forms of "reverse racism." Such understanding also, as per Mills, helps delineate some points of shared concern with other strands of political philosophy and political theology.

---

33. Peniel E. Joseph, ed., *Neighborhood Rebels: Black Power at the Local Level* (New York: Palgrave Macmillan, 2010), and Rhonda Williams, *Concrete Demands: The Search for Black Power in the 20th Century* (London: Routledge, 2015). The link with the SNCC is controversial. Wesley Hogan and Charles Payne narrate Black Power as the nadir and betrayal of what SNCC stood for. However, the roles its former members played in the Black Power movement are undeniable, and the influence of the Lowndes County Freedom Organization was enormous. See Wesley C. Hogan, *Many Minds, One Heart: SNCC's Dream for a New America* (Chapel Hill: University of North Carolina Press, 2007), and Charles Payne, *I've Got the Light of Freedom: The Organizing Tradition and the Mississippi Freedom Struggle* (Berkeley: University of California Press, 1995).

34. Grace Lee Boggs, *Living for Change*, 153, and bell hooks, *Salvation: Black People and Love* (New York: HarperCollins, 2001), 4-17.

35. Although it has also been criticized for its failure to do so. For example, Boggs is scathing about the failures of the Black Power activists in Detroit and elsewhere to attend to the moral and personal development of people who became involved as a causal factor in the failure to move from, as she put it, "rebellion to revolution" (Grace Lee Boggs, *Living for Change*, 151-89).

Moreover, it points to a parallel but not equivalent theological question: How are a virtuous and holy people to be formed out of a disaggregated and demoralized crowd shaped by oppressive institutions and structures? This concern is central to the drama of Exodus, a vital scriptural reference point in liberation theologies. I return to this question in the final section.

An aligned problem for black nationalists, one arising directly out of white supremacy as a political system, complicated their ability to navigate these two paradoxes. It is what W. E. B. Du Bois famously called "double consciousness" and relates to the paradoxically insider-outsider status of being African American. Black lives matter in the United States insofar as they are commodities or sources of cheap labor and, latterly, consumers and debtors. This way of valuing black life is a historical and ongoing basis of US economic and political development. Black labor and ways of life are constitutive of the United States as a nation-state; however, as Du Bois puts it, "I have been in the world, but not of it."[36] While black bodies are a vital means of life for the system, they are simultaneously and consistently constituted as paradigmatic outsiders (as are Native Americans), those through and against whom the political, cultural, and economic structures come to be defined.

Whiteness is a constitutive part of how North America constructs normalcy. However, whiteness is neither an ethnic identity nor a clearly demarcated property. Rather, as George Yancy puts it, whiteness is "a historical process that continues to express its hegemony and privilege through various cultural, political, interpersonal, and institutional practices, and that forces bodies of color to the margins and politically and ontologically positions them as sub-persons."[37] The practices converge over time to create white supremacy, which is here taken to mean "a political, economic and cultural system in which whites overwhelmingly control power and material resources, conscious and unconscious ideas of white superiority and entitlement are widespread, and relations of white dominance and nonwhite subordination are daily reenacted across a broad array of insti-

36. W. E. B. Du Bois, *Darkwater: Voices from within the Veil* (New York: Harcourt, Brace & Howe, 1920), vii. As Reggie Williams points out, this is a direct scriptural reference to John 15:19. The line both identifies Du Bois/black folk with Jesus and locates this standpoint as a privileged one from which to understand the wider dynamics of a white-centered, Eurocentric worldview (*Bonhoeffer's Black Jesus: Harlem Renaissance Theology and an Ethic of Resistance* [Waco, TX: Baylor University Press, 2014], 55).

37. George Yancy, introduction to *Christology and Whiteness: What Would Jesus Do?* (London: Routledge, 2012), 5.

tutions and social settings."[38] On this account, white supremacy becomes a self-perpetuating part of the political system that is veiled behind a desire to benefit from existing, supposedly neutral structures of privilege and "rational" forms of self-interest and group interest.[39] Thus, white nationalists, rather than seeking to defend an embattled minority—as they claim—are instead seeking to perpetuate a system of injustice that directly benefits them.

Within black nationalism, the trope of being a nation (however conceived) is a way to develop an alternative, positive construction of identity to that determined by being the opposite of what is white and therefore abnormal. But as Paul Gilroy argues, the use of the term "nation" is problematic, as it takes up a trope central to modern European political discourse and often falls prey to an "ethnic absolutism."[40] True. But there is another dimension to the use of the term "nation" that Gilroy misses but which comes to the fore in the later development of the Black Power movement and can be separated from "ethnic absolutism": it was a ready-to-hand discursive framework through which to challenge the insider-outsider status of being a racialized other in the United States. As Dawson notes, this challenge operated on two fronts simultaneously: the claim to be a nation was a way of demanding entry to and recognition within white channels of public discourse (whether mainstream, such as universities, or subaltern, such as the labor and women's movement) *and* a way of developing an alternative counterpublic, providing a space for critical reflection and self-cultivation, a form of life within which to live and move more freely.[41] The claim to be a nation within a nation is a claim to be all that being a nation invokes as a "social imaginary": belonging, sense of place, self-determination, citizenship, and a history, future, and distinctive culture.[42] It is a claim to possess a way of being in the world that lives an alternative to and refuses

---

38. Frances Lee Ansley, "Stirring the Ashes: Race, Class and the Future of Civil Rights Scholarship," *Cornell Law Review* 74, no. 6 (1989): 993-1077, here 1024n129.

39. On this see Mills, *Blackness Visible*, 139-66.

40. Gilroy, *Black Atlantic*, 3-5. See also Dawson, *Black Visions*, 91.

41. Dawson, *Black Visions*, 27-28. On the dual role of counterpublics as means of incorporation, see Jeffrey C. Alexander, *The Civil Sphere* (New York: Oxford University Press, 2006), 275-77.

42. For a definition and discussion of the broader category of a "social imaginary," see Charles Taylor, *Modern Social Imaginaries* (Durham, NC: Duke University Press, 2004), and Graham Ward, *Cultural Transformation and Religious Practice* (Cambridge: Cambridge University Press, 2005), 119-47.

racialized constructions of blackness as a form of nonbeing and an antitype of the good citizen. Such a claim is a precursor to generating abolitionist and genuinely shared ways of imagining citizenship. By contrast, white nationalism, in the name of self-defense, intentionally seeks to subvert and destroy attempts to move toward shared ways of imagining citizenship and forming a genuinely common life. As argued here, black nationalism can contribute to the intensification of a democratic common life, whereas white nationalism, even though it shares many of the discursive tropes of black nationalism, because of the structural location of its participants and its aims, is inherently antidemocratic.

Black Power addressed the insider-outsider problem in numerous ways. For example, some separatist strands resolved it by seeking a territorially defined sovereign polity, whereas community-orientated, cultural, and some revolutionary and separatist forms sought to create enclaves of self-determination within the existing structures where blacks constituted either a majority or a large, concentrated minority.[43] One example of this latter strategy was the 1968-1971 mayoralty of Carl Stokes in Cleveland.[44] Stokes's campaign heralded a turn to the Democratic Party as a means of gaining power. Another example is Rev. Albert Cleage Jr., who represents a very different modus operandi to achieve similar ends. Cleage argued there was a need for full citizenship (which he viewed as using "enemy institutions" to serve black people) and a need to struggle for self-determination via separate "counterinstitutions," as blacks needed an independent economic base and should never be reliant on the government for protection or the provision of welfare.[45] Cleage practiced what he preached: he ran for governor of Michigan in 1964 as part of the Freedom Now Party and founded the Black Christian National Movement in 1967 along with a wide range of independent institutions. What is at stake in these different forms of praxis is the problem of how to form a people: Is peoplehood based on some prepolitical basis, often imagined in either familial (brother/sister) or cultural terms?[46] Or is it formed by economic agency, whether capitalist or

43. An important early statement articulating this position was James Boggs and Grace Lee Boggs, "The City Is the Black Man's Land," *Monthly Review* 17, no. 11 (1966).

44. On this see Leonard Moore, *Carl B. Stokes and the Rise of Black Political Power* (Urbana: University of Illinois Press, 2003).

45. Cleage, *Black Christian Nationalism*, especially 123-70.

46. "Prepolitical" denotes a basis for identity or community that is posited as existing prior to any actual process of talking or acting together politically (e.g., blood, race, or culture).

socialist?[47] Or as necessitating a sovereign, bounded territory? Black Power was a response to the need to honor existing yet demeaned forms of life and construct a basis of power in a context where democratic citizenship is indexed to whiteness yet its primary discursive framework, liberalism, proclaims itself color-blind.[48] Proclamation of nationhood is a way to make the blind see, of rendering the invisible visible.

Arguably, before the Black Power movement, proclamations of nationhood operated inside of what Zora Neale Hurston called the "bell jar" of black experience. They were out of sight and out of mind for most whites. The civil rights movement had generated a huge amount of media exposure, on which Black Power activists built. Yet the kinds of claims, discourses, and stances of Black Power appeared to whites as a rupture from the civil rights movement because they were mostly oblivious to earlier black political movements and the kinds of debates that had been going on for a long, long time within the "bell jar." Television and consolidated, nationwide media outlets brought to white public consciousness awareness of Black Power activities. Very few whites contemporaneous with Marcus Garvey would have known about his work. Most whites were aware of and had an opinion about Stokely Carmichael. Rather than any innovation of political position, the potency of Black Power rested on white awareness via a white-controlled and racially prejudiced media.[49] What was innovative was the use of the white-controlled media as an instrument of political communication. Carmichael, Bobby Searle, and others experimented

47. For example, despite their ideological differences, the Black Panthers, the Congress of Afrikan Peoples, and the League of Revolutionary Black Workers all rejected a separate, bounded territory and instead posited socialist forms of economic production and ownership as a key basis for achieving black liberation (Dawson, *Black Visions*, 217). In contrast, Floyd McKissick's failed venture, "Soul City" in North Carolina, envisaged an enclave of self-determination based on capitalist enterprise (Williams, *Concrete Demands*, 167). On the broader history of democratic self-determination through forms of cooperative economic development, see Jessica Gordon Nembhard, *Collective Courage: A History of African American Cooperative Economic Thought and Practice* (University Park: Pennsylvania State University Press, 2014).

48. For a critique of how color-blind policies reinforce racism, see Olson, *Abolition of White Democracy*, 100-105. For an account of how the discourse of color-blindness has been used to dismantle the gains of the civil rights movement, see Jim Rutenberg, "A Dream Undone: Disenfranchised," *New York Times*, July 29, 2015. For a classic statement on the neutrality of liberalism, see John Rawls's treatment of the "veil of ignorance" in *A Theory of Justice*, rev. ed. (Oxford: Oxford University Press, 1999), 118-21.

49. William L. Van Deburg, *New Day in Babylon: The Black Power Movement and American Culture, 1965-1975* (Chicago: University of Chicago Press, 1992), 11-16.

with the relatively new cultural form of media-generated celebrity. They intuited the power and importance of the sound bite, image, and notoriety as part of political communication in the age of television. However, the resort to the media, and the celebrity it generated, was questioned and contested within groups such as the SNCC. For example, SNCC activist Fay Bellamy questioned the engagement of Carmichael and others with a white-controlled media that systematically misrepresented their position. In her "Little Old Report" she states: "It makes me wonder if we are addicted to the press." She called for greater attention paid to the needs and demands of local people they worked with, saying, "I would argue for a little more talking to black people and less talking to the press."[50] Yet, as never before, the media visibility of certain Black Power activists staged the claims of black nationalism in the majority white public sphere. It was a demand for recognition in categories and forms inassimilable and undetermined by the prevailing hegemony.

Herrenvolk Democracy and Citizenship as the Performance of White Supremacy

Let me substantiate the assertion that white supremacy, understood as a political system, partly structures democratic citizenship in the United States. Citizenship, and the benefits and protections that came with it, was historically limited to "white" immigrants.[51] The most obvious instantiation of this was the denial of civic and political status to kidnapped and enslaved Africans. Even after the emancipation of slaves in the 1860s, the racialization of citizenship continued. For example, immigrants from Asia were excluded from being full citizens through legislation in 1882 aimed at those from China; in 1917, from India; in 1924, from Japan; and in 1934, from the Philippines.[52] Processes of racialization also deeply shaped who received social rights from the New Deal era onward. For example, the National Labor Relations (Wagner) Act, which guaranteed the right of employees to organize or join a union, and the Social Security Act, both passed

---

50. Quoted in Williams, *Concrete Demands*, 143.

51. George Lipsitz, *The Possessive Investment in Whiteness: How White People Profit from Identity Politics* (Philadelphia: Temple University Press, 2009), 2.

52. Lipsitz, *Possessive Investment in Whiteness*, 2. For an account of the political and ideological backdrop to these policies, see Gary Gerstle, *American Crucible: Race and Nation in the Twentieth Century* (Princeton: Princeton University Press, 2001), 44-127.

in 1935, did not apply to farm and domestic workers, thus denying these disproportionately minority sectors of the workforce the protections and benefits now legally afforded other, predominantly white workers. In 1934 the Federal Housing Act was implemented through overtly racist categories in the Federal Housing Agency's city surveys and appraisers' manuals that directed the overwhelming majority of loan money toward whites and away from communities of color. These social policies, and many more besides, widened the gap between the resources available to those judged white and the resources available to nonwhite, predominantly black communities.[53] The cumulative social, economic, and political impact of these policies in disadvantaging nonwhites is immeasurable. Alongside all this, from the 1890s onward, urban and social policies stigmatized blackness by identifying it with criminality.[54] This process of stigmatization has continued apace with the contemporary reinscription of systemic disadvantage through the "New Jim Crow."[55] The New Jim Crow combines the long-term socially and politically marginalizing effects of mass incarceration with the punitive management and criminalization of poverty through regimes of indebtedness, workfare, and conditions of social and spatial precariousness.[56] Yet most whites are entirely oblivious to this history and how the social, economic, and political structures of the United States bake in white privilege. Ignored are long-standing policies of affirmative action for whites, while black poverty is blamed on a dearth of collective virtue and a lack of individual vigor in pursuing the American Dream.

It is on the basis of this history and contemporary practices of systemic exclusion, a history that reaches back to 1619, that some argue that the United States is a *Herrenvolk* democracy.[57] What is meant by this term is

53. For a detailed account of the ways in which, from the New Deal through to the GI Bill, social policy privileged whites, see Ira Katznelson, *When Affirmative Action Was White: An Untold History of Racial Inequality in Twentieth-Century America* (New York: Norton, 2005).

54. See, for example, Khalil Gibran Muhammad, *The Condemnation of Blackness: Race, Crime, and the Making of Modern Urban America* (Cambridge, MA: Harvard University Press, 2011).

55. Michelle Alexander, *The New Jim Crow: Mass Incarceration in the Age of Colorblindness* (New York: New Press, 2010).

56. Loïc Wacquant, *Punishing the Poor: The Neoliberal Government of Social Insecurity* (Durham, NC: Duke University Press, 2009); Loïc Wacquant, *Deadly Symbiosis: Race and the Rise of Neoliberal Penalty* (London: Polity, 2009); and Matthew Desmond, *Evicted: Poverty and Profit in the American City* (New York: Crown, 2016).

57. David R. Roediger, *The Wages of Whiteness: Race and the Making of the American*

that white supremacy partly constitutes the basis of the demos. Citizenship is not indexed to a singular *ethnos* or *Volk*, as in German legal conceptions of *jus sanguinis*. There never was a singular *Volk* or ethnicity in the United States, white Anglo-Saxon Protestant or otherwise. Rather, citizenship was indexed to whiteness politically constructed and theoretically rationalized as a caste; that is, whiteness entails stratification not just by class and race but also on a scale of purity and moral worth.[58] As David Roediger contends, "blackness" became identified with dependency and servility, which were antithetical to the virtues that republican citizenship demanded.[59] Mills argues that underlying this prejudice were the ways whiteness functioned as an ontological category as much as a racial and class-based one.[60] Alongside other registers, most notably Protestantism, property ownership, militarism, and masculinity, democratic citizenship was imagined and idealized as white. This is articulated in the following quote from a white Alabaman in 1860: "Your fathers and my fathers built this government on two ideas; the first is that the white race is the citizen and the master race, and the white man is the equal of every other white

---

Working Class, rev. ed. (New York: Verso, 1999); Mills, *Blackness Visible*; Olson, *The Abolition of White Democracy*. Building on the work of Roediger, Gerstle nuances this account, arguing that, from the 1890s on, there were two overlapping traditions: one based on a "racial nationalist ideal" and the other on a racialized form of civic nationalism that was more capacious. As his account makes clear, while the civic national ideal could incorporate nonwhite ethnic and religious minorities, African Americans were consistently excluded from it. It was, however, mobilized to argue for civil rights by the likes of Martin Luther King Jr. in the 1950s and 1960s. Gerstle suggests there was a gradual shift of emphasis through the course of the twentieth century from a racial to a civic, melting-pot ideal. Black Power challenged both and catalyzed the rise of "hard" and "soft" forms of multiculturalism that rejected any notion of the nation as a coherent, morally uplifting project. The contemporary political landscape on Gerstle's account contains an unstable and divisive mix of racial, civic, and multicultural visions of nationhood. See Gerstle, *American Crucible*.

58. Caste is derived from the Latin (*castus*) and Spanish (*casta*), and in both instances it carries connotations of racial hierarchy, degrees of purity, and divisions of socioeconomic status and function. For an account of the ambiguous yet explicitly racialized character of the "melting pot" or civic nationalist vision of US citizenship, see Gerstle, *American Crucible*, 44–127.

59. Roediger, *The Wages of Whiteness*, 172. An example of this attitude is the figure of Theodore Roosevelt; see Gerstle, *American Crucible*, 14–43.

60. Mills, *Blackness Visible*, 67–118. Mills argues also that "white supremacy" is itself a political discourse that is equivalent to and often aligned with liberalism, capitalism, and nationalism, yet it is a system almost wholly ignored within the canons of political philosophy.

man. The second idea is that the Negro is the inferior race."[61] As Mills points out, this view was not idiosyncratic. Rather, the 1857 *Dred Scott* decision enshrined it in law.

In the light of this history, we can contextualize the shrill and vindictive reaction that Black Power provoked as a symptom of a systemic problem. The converse of trying to form a black people/nation in a context where "we, the people" is structured in part by white supremacy is that any attempt to do so will inevitably be seen as an attempt to undermine the existing system: black self-determination and self-affirmation become by definition acts of sedition. Members of the Black Power movement constantly confronted the vindictive reaction that their apostasy from faith in the American Dream generated. For example, while the Black Panther Party in Oakland, California, set up educational initiatives and a free breakfast program, the FBI publicly labeled the Panthers a threat to national security and secretly licensed a series of counterintelligence operations against them.[62]

The civil rights movement addressed the formal exclusion of blacks from citizenship. However, its apogee—the Voting Rights Act of 1965— only addressed two dimensions of citizenship. The primary use of the term "citizenship" is to denote a legal status with certain civil, political, and social rights as granted and distributed by the institutions of a national government whose sovereignty is derived from the citizens themselves. The second use of the term "citizenship" refers to participation in a system for representing, communicating, and legitimating the relationship between governed and government. In large-scale nation-states, a popular assembly cannot undertake this process of authorizing. Therefore, it involves a system of representation. To be a citizen is to be designated as someone who can participate in these kinds of mechanisms, whether as a voter or a representative or both. Democratic citizenship demarcates who is authorized to govern and the processes by which his or her authority is legitimized. The civil rights movement powerfully addressed these two dimensions of citizenship, which up to that point had largely excluded blacks. The 1965 Voting Rights Act was in effect the end of the *Herrenvolk* democracy as a formal, de jure system. However, as a de facto system, it has continued to undergird three other dimensions of citizenship.

---

61. Quoted in Mills, *Blackness Visible*, 109.

62. Peniel E. Joseph, *Waiting 'Til the Midnight Hour: A Narrative History of Black Power in America* (New York: Holt, 2006), 229.

Alongside the juridical and governmental dimensions of citizenship is a third dimension, identity. To be a citizen of a polity is to identify or be identified with an "imagined community."[63] As a political identity that co-inheres with an imagined community, "citizenship" is not just a legal term; it has an affective and subjective dimension that is the result of cultural processes. Key questions to be asked about this aspect of citizenship are as follows: What does a citizen look like, and who counts as included in the body politic or as a "normal" member of it? In relation to these questions, issues of belief, race, gender, class, physical ability, and sexuality come to the fore. In a *Herrenvolk* democracy, a central way in which the community is imagined is as normatively white. Blacks by definition cannot be full citizens except by passing as white.[64]

The fourth dimension is how citizenship necessarily includes the performance of a vision of politics. In this guise, citizenship involves doing certain things. However, the performance of citizenship is not reducible to formal mechanisms of representation or involvement with the apparatus of the state. Rather, it entails a much broader assemblage of beliefs, narratives, practices, bodily proprieties, habits, and rituals reiterated and enacted in contexts as diverse as the workplace, social media, the football stadium, and the mall. Together these constitute a social imaginary of what good and bad politics entail and, thus, what the good citizen should do. Again, in America's *Herrenvolk* democracy, whiteness constitutes a key regulative performance of good citizenship. To perform well as a citizen—that is, to be considered respectable—is to perform as or in a way analogous to being white.[65] Failure to do so provokes suspicion of being anti-American.

Finally, citizenship names a political and moral rationality through which a "common sense" is forged and reproduced; that is, it constitutes

63. On the term "imagined community" and its relationship to identification with a nation-state, see Benedict Anderson, *Imagined Communities: Reflections on the Origin and Spread of Nationalism*, rev. ed. (London: Verso, 2006).

64. A recent articulation of such a view is given in Samuel P. Huntington's *Who Are We? The Challenges to America's National Identity* (New York: Simon & Schuster, 2004). For Huntington, American identity is normatively English (i.e., white) and Protestant. Lack of conformity to a white Protestant outlook threatens to undermine and dissolve what Huntingdon calls "the American Creed." This is a direct echo of Theodore Roosevelt's racialized vision of civic nationalism.

65. On this see Theodore Allen, *The Invention of the White Race* (New York: Verso, 1994); Noel Ignatiev, *How the Irish Became White* (New York: Routledge, 1995); and David R. Roediger, *Working toward Whiteness: How America's Immigrants Became White* (New York: Basic Books, 2005).

a way of discerning and deliberating about goods in common and a vision of the good life through which "we, the people" come to decide how we shall live. In relation to this denotation of citizenship, the question is how citizens should talk and deliberate together and on what basis they can make shared judgments about what to do and how to do it. The construction of citizenship involves an ongoing debate about what constitutes the requisite kinds of moral and political rationality that make one capable of talking and acting with others in ways that build up the common life of a polity. As Dawson notes, within liberal conceptions of citizenship, "rational dialogue among reasonable citizens is problematic when those with power determine both who is reasonable and with what weight their dialogue is accepted."[66] When nonwhites are deemed irrational, their voices are not just excluded but demeaned.

The civil rights movement targeted the juridical and governmental dimensions of citizenship. By contrast, Black Power's political, cultural, religious, and economic interventions focused on how white supremacy is a key way in which citizenship as an identity, performance, and rationality is structured. What Black Power activists discerned was that "integration" on terms set by the existing third, fourth, and fifth dimensions of citizenship was self-negating. The terms and conditions of citizenship needed fundamental recalibrating and resignifying. The aim could not be recognition in the existing *Herrenvolk* system. Rather, the need was and still is to change the means and criteria by which to produce and evaluate the identity, performance, and rationality of citizenship.

Arguably, from the 1970s onward, black feminist and womanist authors such as Audre Lorde, bell hooks, and Angela Davis and organizations such as the Black Women's Liberation Committee, the Third World Women's Alliance, and the Combahee River Collective catalyzed a re-visioning of Black Power that laid the groundwork for the emergence of contemporary movements such as Black Lives Matter. They drew attention to the often-conflicting sources of identity that race, class, gender, and sexuality generate and how one identity marker does not exhaust a person's way of being in the world.[67] Some called for a more coalitional approach—what is

66. Dawson, *Black Visions*, 246.

67. Combahee River Collective, "The Combahee River Collective Statement," in *Home Girls: A Black Feminist Anthology*, ed. Barbara Smith (New Brunswick, NJ: Rutgers University Press, 2000), 264-74, and Angela Davis and Lisa Lowe, "Reflections on Race, Class and Gender in the USA," in *The Angela Y. Davis Reader*, ed. Joy James (Malden, MA: Blackwell, 1998), 307-25, here 313. An example of the conflict

now referred to as intersectional—to addressing injustice, one that could encompass multiple loyalties and avoid illusions of innocence.[68] In the following statement from James Cone we hear an echo of this call for a revision in approach to confronting white supremacy: "The ideals of integration and nationalism are insufficient for the problems we now face and for the issues with which we will have to deal in the future. We need to do more than try to be assimilated into white American society or to separate ourselves from it. Neither alternative is possible or even desirable. We need a broader perspective, one that includes the creative values of both but also moves beyond them to an entirely new vision of the future."[69]

Contemporary conceptions of black nationalism take the view that black solidarity does not require territorial separation, a homogenous identity, or even a shared consciousness. For example, Tommie Shelby questions whether these are morally justifiable, politically fruitful, or even empirically possible.[70] In their stead, he argues for a "pragmatic" vision of black nationalism as an alternative way to conceptualize the need for black political solidarity.[71] Shelby contends that "Blacks can and should agree, in the present, to collectively resist racial injustice, not only because it is the morally responsible thing to do but also because it negatively affects them all, albeit to varying degrees and in different ways. Mobilizing and coordinating this effort will be difficult enough without adding the unnecessary and divisive requirement that blacks embrace and preserve a distinctive

---

womanism represented is staged in James Baldwin and Audre Lorde, "Revolutionary Hope: A Conversation between James Baldwin and Audre Lorde," *Essence Magazine*, 1984, http://mocada-museum.tumblr.com/post/73421979421/revolutionary-hope-a -conversation-between-james.

68. Bernice Johnson Reagon, "Coalition Politics: Turning the Century," in Smith, *Home Girls*, 343–55, and Audre Lorde, *Sister/Outsider: Essays and Speeches* (Trumansburg, NY: Crossing, 1984), 138.

69. James Cone, *For My People: Black Theology and the Black Church* (Maryknoll, NY: Orbis, 1984), 193. The thesis of this statement by Cone is explored at length in James Cone, *Martin and Malcolm and America: A Dream or a Nightmare?* (Maryknoll, NY: Orbis, 1991). Cone revised his position in the light of criticism he received from black feminist and womanist theologians. And whether consciously or not, Cone is here echoing the position of Claudia Jones from the 1940s. See Farmer, *Remaking Black Power*, 28–29.

70. Shelby does not advocate for color-blind policies and is very concerned to uphold the need for distinctive forms of black political solidarity. It is just that he is equally concerned to conceptualize an alternative basis for this solidarity to those generally put forward within the different strands of black nationalism.

71. Shelby, *We Who Are Dark*.

ethnocultural identity."[72] Shelby goes on to argue that rather than being measured in terms of the "thickness" of someone's identity, a "political mode of blackness" entails "loyalty to the collective struggle" and particular kinds of civic engagement.[73] His argument echoes that of Angela Davis, who calls for a consciousness that is "politically rather than racially grounded and at the same time anchored in a more complex antiracist consciousness."[74] This argument can be extended to say that an abolitionist politics, whether black nationalist or multiracial in form, requires a commitment and contribution to shared democratic practices that generate antiracist forms of civic identity, performance, and rationality, and that reckon with the realities of mutual dependence.[75]

But what might such a form of solidarity look like in practice? Especially one that meets the need, as West sees it, for "any serious form of black resistance" to build alliances and coalitions with latino/a, asian, first nation, and white people committed to transforming capitalist, patriarchal, and racist America.[76] Or what Angela Davis calls "basing the identity on politics rather than the politics on identity."[77] I want to suggest that community organizing represents an example of a form of politics that is amenable to the kind of political solidarity that, among others, Shelby, West, hooks, Davis, Boggs, and Lani Guinier envisage.[78] My claim is not

72. Shelby, *We Who Are Dark*, 229.

73. Shelby, *We Who Are Dark*, 246-47. Shelby does not propose the deconstruction of loyalty to the black nation but a redefinition of the object of loyalty. For a discussion of the virtue of loyalty in the context of emancipatory struggles where identity is a key site of mobilization, see Lisa Tessman, *Burdened Virtues: Virtue Ethics for Liberatory Struggles* (New York: Oxford University Press, 2005), 133-57.

74. Davis, in James, *Angela Y. Davis Reader*, 323.

75. As James Baldwin puts it, any attempt to transform the current situation has to reckon with how African Americans have been "formed by this nation [i.e., America], for better or worse, and do not belong to any other—not to Africa, and certainly not to Islam" (*Collected Essays*, ed. Toni Morrison [New York: Library of America, 1998], 133).

76. Cornel West, "The Paradox of the African American Rebellion," in *Is It Nation Time? Contemporary Essays on Black Power and Black Nationalism*, ed. Eddie S. Glaude Jr. (Chicago: University of Chicago Press, 2002), 38. West's scathing analysis of the class basis of "pork-chop" black nationalism is an important immanent critique that is not directly addressed here. However, West's insightful class analysis misses its own paradox: that an emphasis on class undermines the formation of a demos, as it sublates all other potential points of solidarity to a superordinate fracture, that of class. That said, while not explicitly named, West's actual narrative is attentive to this problem.

77. Davis, in James, *Angela Y. Davis Reader*, 320.

78. For Shelby's constructive conception of black political solidarity, see *We Who Are*

that community organizing inevitably or necessarily generates antiracist forms of democratic politics, but that it is constitutively open to and has historically been a vehicle for this kind of democratic politics and that the reasons for this are instructive.[79]

Community organizing takes the need for distinctive corporate life and institutional independence as basic, but in a way that allows for multiple identities and loyalties to intersect.[80] And it makes central the constructive role of power, anger, and conflict.[81] With its emphasis on participation and agency, it also represents a very different framework to either political liberalism (which emphasizes equality but leaves untouched asymmetries of power) or multiculturalism (which emphasizes recognition by existing institutional formations rather than the need to change the power structure as such).[82] Crucially, community organizing, with its iron rule to never do for others what they can do for themselves, takes seriously Grace Lee Boggs's admonition that "In order to change/transform the world [people] must change/transform themselves."[83] Broad-based forms of community organizing are not compatible with essentialist and noncommon life-forms of black nationalism. However, as a mode of praxis, community organizing has been a vehicle for community-based and cultural forms of black nationalism in so far as they are orientated

---

Dark, 136–60. Shelby's proposals for action are diffuse, but his definition of black self-determination is not merely compatible with but would seem to require something like a consociational account of democracy and community organizing in particular (248–54). For a different account that explicitly advocates forms of community organizing, see Grace Lee Boggs, *Living for Change*, 143–89. See also Lani Guinier and Gerald Torres, *The Miner's Canary: Enlisting Race, Resisting Power, Transforming Democracy* (Cambridge, MA: Harvard University Press, 2002).

79. For a quantitative analysis of the racial and ethnic demography of broad-based community organizing, see Richard Wood and Brad Fulton, *A Shared Future: Faith-Based Organizing for Racial Equity and Ethical Democracy* (Chicago: University of Chicago Press, 2015). In response to the data, Wood and Fulton note that community organizing, as a field, is "significantly more diverse on racial/ethnic lines" than other areas of civil society, and as such, "swims against the tide of deep trends in American civil society in which voluntary associations tend toward racial homogeneity" (69). Their book documents how, under particular circumstances, community organizing can help "exorcise" the "demons" of "racial injustice that is bound up with economic inequality" (196).

80. Bretherton, *Resurrecting Democracy*, 219–42.

81. Bretherton, *Resurrecting Democracy*, 123–26, 136–41.

82. Bretherton, *Resurrecting Democracy*, 179–218.

83. Grace Lee Boggs, *Living for Change*, 153.

to forging forms of common life that proactively seek to dismantle white supremacy.[84]

In his 1969 book *Black Self-Determination*, the Reverend Arthur Brazier, pastor of the Apostolic Church of God in Chicago, details the work of the Woodlawn Organization (TWO).[85] TWO was a community-organizing coalition of churches, businesses, and civic associations situated in a poor, majority black neighborhood on the South Side of Chicago. It was affiliated with the Industrial Areas Foundation (IAF), set up by Saul Alinsky in 1940 to develop community-organizing initiatives around the country. Brazier, who was president of TWO, explicitly envisages its work as embodying a form of Black Power: "Black people must always remember that equality and freedom are two things that will never be handed to them on a silver platter. These things will not come as an act of charity or as an act of good will. When they have the strength to take them, and by the very act of taking them, black people will achieve personal dignity, self-respect, and pride of color. It is to this end that The Woodlawn Organization came into being."[86]

Minister Franklin Florence in Rochester, New York, echoed Brazier's understanding of community organizing as a way to achieve meaningful black self-determination and black political solidarity. Florence was president of FIGHT (Freedom, Independence, God, Honor, Today) in Rochester at its founding in 1965.[87] FIGHT was another affiliate of the IAF that Alinsky helped organize, explicitly establishing it as a blacks-only coalition of institutions. FIGHT's slogan, Self-determination through Community Power, was a clear expression of a key concept of Black Power. Or as Florence once put it: "When you say 'black power' in Rochester, it's spelled F-I-G-H-T."[88] Stokely Carmichael echoed this sentiment, stating in 1967:

84. Conversely, community organizing can also be a way for whites to dis-identify with white supremacy. On this see Mark R. Warren, *Fire in the Heart: How White Activists Embrace Racial Justice* (Oxford: Oxford University Press, 2010); James Perkinson, *White Theology: Outing Supremacy in Modernity* (New York: Palgrave Macmillan, 2004), 233-37; and L. A. Kauffman, *Direct Action: Protest and the Reinvention of American Radicalism* (London: Verso, 2017), 179-87.

85. Arthur Brazier, *Black Self-Determination: The Story of the Woodlawn Organization* (Grand Rapids: Eerdmans, 1969).

86. Brazier, *Black Self-Determination*, 21.

87. "Independence" was subsequently changed to "integration."

88. Mike Miller, "The Student Movement and Saul Alinsky: An Alliance That Never Happened," in *Too Many Martyrs: Student Massacres at Orangeburg, Kent, and Jackson State during the Vietnam War Era*, ed. Susie Erenrich (forthcoming). Miller notes that

"If you want an example of black power, look at FIGHT." Even though white IAF organizers played a role in FIGHT and TWO, both black participants and external observers saw community organizing, as a form of praxis and, I would argue, by extension, a pluralistic conception of democratic politics, as compatible with Black Power and some expressions of black nationalism.[89]

Exorcising Democracy: Rome Dethroned Is Not Israel Empowered

Here I want to pick up a theological trail signposted earlier. When James Cone says Jesus is black and "Christianity is not alien to Black Power; it is Black Power," he is making a theological statement about how the revelation of who God is cannot be understood apart from Jesus's identification with the poor and oppressed.[90] For Cone, Black Power was a contingent but concrete manifestation of divine action in the history of North America. What follows is a theological consideration of the Black Power movement and the various forms of praxis through which it sought to generate a sense of peoplehood and address constructively poverty understood as powerlessness. This consideration brings to the fore the ways in which the political problems Black Power addressed connect to the scriptural portrayal of divine action in history and how this portrayal is taken up in black liberation and womanist theology.

Within Scripture, powerlessness is the predominant way in which poverty is understood. The most common words for poverty in the Hebrew Bible/Old Testament (*'ānî* and *'ānāw*) imply vulnerability to oppression more

---

when Florence asked Malcolm X about whether he should become involved with a white man to organize a black community, Malcolm X told him Alinsky was the best organizer in the country. For more on FIGHT, see Sanford D. Horwitt, *Let Them Call Me Rebel: Saul Alinsky, His Life and Legacy* (New York: Random House, 1989), 450-505.

89. For a parallel but different account of how black-led, faith-based community organizing is a form of praxis through which to pursue black political solidarity and faithful and hopeful witness in the world, see Lloyd, *Religion of the Field Negro*, 113-30. While I am broadly sympathetic to his critique of broad-based community organizing, his sweeping condemnation of it as a form of "neoliberal multiculturalism" (121) that perpetuates secularism (138) is too reductive. I maintain that broad-based community organizing can, at times, be a form of "faithfully secular" politics that actively contests what Lloyd calls "neoliberal multiculturalism" (Bretherton, *Resurrecting Democracy*, 76-110).

90. James Cone, *Black Theology and Black Power*, 38, and *God of the Oppressed*, rev. ed. (Maryknoll, NY: Orbis, 1997), 122-26.

than material destitution. The biblical sense of poverty as powerlessness dovetails with Greek conceptions of the demos and Roman notions of the *pauperi*, the *plebs*, and the *populus*. They are not destitute, but they are politically and therefore economically and socially vulnerable. The analogy in the contemporary context is with terms such as "the working class," "the proletariat," and, I suggest, "the black nation." Rather than philanthropy or social welfare programs, poverty as powerlessness demands the formation of a people. Part of how God addresses poverty as powerlessness is by forming a people. However, the process of forming a demos/people matters.

The narrative paradigm of God addressing powerlessness by forming a people is Exodus.[91] Exodus opens with Pharaoh claiming to control the bodies and discipline the biological processes of the Israelites. As Zora Neale Hurston parses it, "The Hebrew womb had fallen under the heel of Pharaoh."[92] Fleeing after killing an Egyptian overseer, Moses eventually returns as a thaumaturge who performs miraculous "biopolitical" wonders in contrast to the counterfeit magic of Pharaoh's priests. The contrast here is between Moses's attempt to address the plight of the Israelites by merely taking life, which is shown to reproduce the problem, and his subsequent ability to liberate the people by drawing on new sources of power in excess of and undetermined by the prevailing system. The conflict depicted between Moses and Pharaoh is over who has the power to fructify creation or render it desolate.[93] The flourishing of creation is intertwined with and

91. Although as womanist and Palestinian liberation theologians have rightly pointed out, this paradigm can mask "the oppressed of the oppressed." See, for example, Delores Williams, *Sisters in the Wilderness: The Challenge of Womanist God-Talk* (Maryknoll, NY: Orbis, 1993).

92. Zora Neale Hurston, *Moses, Man of the Mountain: A Novel* (New York: Harper-Collins, 2009 [1939]), 1.

93. The word "eviscerate" is used, as it means to disembowel, that is, to destroy from the inside out. Rule that eviscerates hollows out or guts the social, political, and economic patterns of relationship and identity through which solidarity and compassionate action on behalf of others is sustained. The Good Samaritan parable captures something of this dynamic. Unlike the privileged priest and Levite, who pass by on the other side of the road, the Samaritan responds to the destitute, powerless, and afflicted stranger he encounters. Rather than being empty of a sense of solidarity and compassion and thus unable to act on behalf of someone in need, the Samaritan is moved by *esplanchnisthē*, from the verb *splanchnizomai*, meaning to be moved from inside or from the entrails. By contrast, the vocation and vision of the priest and Levite have been eviscerated, literally emptied out of meaning and purpose, rendering them incapable of responding appropriately when confronted with poverty.

represented by whether the one who claims to rule sees the Israelites as humans capable of being a people or a mere population to be exploited for the good of those with a monopoly of power.

The movement from liberation to the formation of a people who inhabit creation in shalom-like ways is the central drama of Exodus, and it is a drama that runs through the course of the Scriptures. Following Moses, the messianic figure, the ultimate measure of righteous political agency, is to bring not mere justice but healing and a new form of common life in which human and nonhuman life flourish together.[94] The primary achievement of healing is not simply the restoration of sight or the ability to walk; it is the restoration of the ability of those currently excluded to be involved in the formation of a common world. Walking and seeing symbolize active participation in the people of God.[95] Mirroring Moses's actions, Christ's miracles of healing and exorcism, on the one hand, enable the oppressed to discover new forms of agency so they can act for themselves (forms that are not reducible to immanent, material means) and, on the other hand, show up the impotent (and merely immanent) nature of Roman power.

As enactments of new forms of power that reestablish the agency of the oppressed, exorcism and healing generate conflict. Exorcism involves convulsion and struggle and is sometimes achieved against the conscious desire of the one being exorcised. The story of the Gerasene demoniac is paradigmatic in this respect (Mark 5:1–20).[96] In this episode, the one in need of exorcism does not realize he is possessed, despite being driven to extreme, unrestrainable violence that harms himself and others. Demon possession makes those possessed immune to help and incapacitates their ability to act freely. The nameless demoniac thereby sees the prospect of release as a form of torment and resists his own healing and deliverance (v. 7). As one possessed, he stands in a domain between life and death, subjecting himself and those around him to the threat of death.

---

94. A key text in this regard is Isa. 65.

95. As N. T. Wright puts it: "Jesus' healing miracles must be seen clearly as bestowing the gift of *shalom*, wholeness, to those who lacked it, bringing not only physical health but renewed membership in the people of YHWH" (*Jesus and the Victory of God* [London: SPCK, 1996], 192). See also Bruce Longenecker, *Remember the Poor: Paul, Poverty, and the Greco-Roman World* (Grand Rapids: Eerdmans, 2010), 121.

96. This incident extends Jesus's practice of exorcism into non-Jewish contexts, pointing to how his healing and exorcism are for all people, not just those identified as belonging to the people of God, while at the same time reinforcing how healing and exorcism are central to Jesus's ministry.

The demoniac is possessed by a militaristic, colonial, and death-dealing power, as indicated by the demon's name—Legion—and the location of the episode—a graveyard. The demonic spirits stand metonymically for Roman military might, whose power derives from the threat of death. This incident can be read as a symbolic and thaumaturgic battle with the Roman colonial political economy wherein Jesus exposes how Roman power is an out-of-control, demonic, shameful, and self-destructive force at once alien and oppressive.[97] The location of the battle reveals the impotence of Roman rule: the possessing spirits have made their *oikos*—that is, their household and place of economic production—in the land of the dead, a dwelling place that is absurd because it is lifeless and yet also produces fear and shame. Not only is the one possessed tormented, but he spreads anxiety, fear, and powerlessness among others. Jesus challenges this formation of living death from the inside out, liberating the demoniac from physical and psychic enslavement and purifying the land from imperial forms of mass production that exploit and defile it and the people who live there: a herd of pigs is not only an abomination but is also a near-industrial level of agricultural production. Yet exorcism, as a form of liberation from an individually and collectively traumatizing power, involves dispossession and so is encountered by those invested in the status quo as a source of terror. Those who see the formerly demon-possessed man standing clothed and in his right mind are not grateful but afraid, and they demand that Jesus leave them alone (vv. 15-17). In short, exorcism horrifies those who benefit from the status quo (as it does white nationalists and their allies in the contemporary context). Exorcism is a public promulgation of God's apocalyptic judgment against the principalities and powers that feed off the oppression and torment of the powerless and the self-destructive collusion of those with power.[98] Thus, those whose way of life depends on visible and hidden forms of oppression cannot but hear this judgment as condemnation and threat. In an analogous way, rather than being receptive to the possibility of a more just and loving form of life in which everyone could flourish, many whites could only hear the claims of both the civil rights

97. For readings of Mark 5 that draw out the theo-political dimensions of the episode, see Ched Myers, *Binding the Strong Man: A Political Reading of Mark's Story of Jesus* (Maryknoll, NY: Orbis, 1988), 190-94, and Michael Welker, *God the Spirit*, trans. John F. Hoffmeyer (Minneapolis: Fortress, 1994), 197-203.

98. Or, as Cone puts it: "In Jesus' exorcisms . . . he was pointing to the new age that was breaking into the present, disrupting the order of injustice" (*God of the Oppressed*, 205).

movement and Black Power as a fundamental threat to their existing way of life, a way of life that disfigured both whites and blacks.

Jesus's act of exorcism points beyond itself to how merely changing the immanent structures of power is never enough: disempowering Rome does not of itself generate the empowerment of Israel.[99] The people of God need reconstituting, and the broader body politic needs a new animating spirit. To accomplish this, Jesus embodies and mediates a new source of power—the power of the Spirit—unavailable to those who oppress.[100] Jesus's acts of power serve to reconstitute an atomized people so that they may be capable of acting together in pursuit of life-giving, eschatological ends. But this covenantal community is unassimilable by the existing religious and political structures, and its formation is at the same time an act of exorcism of the wider body politic that generates attempts to banish or suppress it.

Echoing Scripture, James Cone and Cheryl Kirk-Duggan use exorcism as a way of framing divine action within history. In Cone's early statement of black liberation theology, racism is identified as a demonic force and Black Power a form of exorcism.[101] This emphasis on exorcism forms part of Cone's wider thesis that "To resist evil is to participate in God's redemption of the world."[102] On Cone's account, as well as a means of survival, black nationalist and Black Power efforts to form a nation within a nation are theo-political gestures of exorcism within the wider body politic. He states:

> First, the work of Christ is essentially a liberating work, directed toward and by the oppressed. Black Power embraces that very task. Second, Christ in liberating the wretched of the earth also liberates those responsible for the wretchedness. The oppressor is also freed of his peculiar demons. Black Power in shouting Yes to black humanness

99. Oliver O'Donovan, *The Desire of the Nations: Rediscovering the Roots of Political Theology* (Cambridge: Cambridge University Press, 1996), 95.

100. For a review of the emphasis on and role of pneumatology in black theology, see William C. Turner, "Pneumatology: Contributions from African American Christian Thought to the Pentecostal Theological Task," in *Afro-Pentecostalism: Black Pentecostal and Charismatic Christianity in History and Culture*, ed. Amos Yong and Estrelda Alexander (New York: NYU Press, 2011), 169-89.

101. Cone, *Black Theology and Black Power*, 41-42. See also Perkinson, *White Theology*, 237-39.

102. Cone, *God of the Oppressed*, xviii.

and No to white oppression is exorcizing demons on both sides of the conflict. Third, mature freedom is burdensome and risky, producing anxiety and conflict for free men and for the brittle structures they challenge. The call for Black Power is precisely the call to shoulder the burden of liberty in Christ, risking everything to live not as slaves but as free men.[103]

Like Cone, Kirk-Duggan uses exorcism as a way of framing a theo-political vision of liberation. She identifies racism and slavery as forms of "collective possession," stating: "The treatment for collective possession is a collective exorcism."[104] She identifies the abolitionist and civil rights movements as forms of collective exorcism that seek to expel structural evil. Unlike Cone but in keeping with other womanist theologians, Kirk-Duggan emphasizes the self-loving, solidaristic, and mutually upbuilding dimensions of the ongoing work of liberation and the need for new forms of personal agency undetermined by white supremacy.[105] Womanist theology explores this process of formation through the leitmotif of individual and communal healing.[106] In the light of Kirk-Duggan's work and the analysis given above, Black Power can be framed not only as a means of exorcism, addressing the objective conditions of domination, but also as a source of healing that helps form a people, thereby addressing the inter-subjective conditions of domination.[107]

103. Cone, *Black Theology and Black Power*, 42–43.

104. Cheryl Kirk-Duggan, *Exorcizing Evil: A Womanist Perspective on the Spirituals* (Maryknoll, NY: Orbis, 1997), 132.

105. See also Katie Cannon, *Black Womanist Ethics* (Atlanta: Scholars Press, 1988); Marcia Y. Riggs, *Awake, Arise and Act: A Womanist Call for Black Liberation* (Cleveland: Pilgrim, 1994); and Melanie Harris, *Gifts of Virtue: Alice Walker and Womanist Ethics* (New York: Palgrave Macmillan, 2010). In his critique of Cone's pneumatology, William Turner argues that the need for a unity between an "outward thrust for liberation with inward holiness and spiritual empowerment bound with the person of the Spirit" is entirely absent in Cone's theology ("Contributions," 176).

106. See, for example, Emilie M. Townes, *Breaking the Fine Rain of Death: African American Health Issues and a Womanist Ethic of Care* (New York: Continuum, 2001); Stephanie Mitchem, "Healing Hearts and Broken Bodies: An African American Women's Spirituality of Healing," in *Faith, Health, and Healing in African American Life*, ed. Stephanie Mitchem and Emilie M. Townes (Westport, CT: Praeger, 2008), 181–91; and Shawn M. Copeland, *Enfleshing Freedom: Body, Race, and Being* (Minneapolis: Fortress, 2010).

107. Kirk-Duggan, *Exorcizing Evil*, 160–68. Cone, like Kirk-Duggan, also sees the spirituals as a paradigmatic instance of community formation and transformation.

Drawing on Cone, Kirk-Duggan, and others, the Black Power movement can be understood as a way of forming a people as a response to pervasive conditions of systemic powerlessness.[108] It sought to address the objective and subjective conditions of powerlessness through attending to and recalibrating existing forms of community and patterns of belief and practice. I contend that different forms of democratic politics were a vital means through which to accomplish this. That said, and as will be explored further in chapter 13, forming a sense of peoplehood through democratic politics is an inherently ambiguous task since the identity of the people is itself ambiguous. On the one hand, there is the aspirational sense of the term "people" as denoting the whole or common; on the other, there is its factionalist use as a term for one section of the whole, the "have-nots." Black nationalism emphasized the latter while the civil rights movement (and more recently, community organizing) emphasized the former.

One way to coordinate these divergent emphases is by understanding how the aspirational use of the term "the people" can denote heterogeneity rather than homogeneity. The people as a whole are not monolithic and should not necessarily be equated with a nation-state. Rather, the people can be an intricate, differentiated, intercommunal, or "consociational" body.[109] An emphasis on the common life of the people understood in either intercommunal or consociational terms, rather than as denoting oneness or integration, encourages a vision of peoplehood as about mutual exchanges between different parts that together make up the commonwealth. This point is clarified by Marcia Riggs in relation to the church understood as the people of God: "People of different racial-ethnic groups organizing themselves into separate movements and structures within and outside of the church are not in and of themselves signs of failure in the quest for unity in the body of Christ. Such separation is, however, a sign of moral failure when its sole purpose is exclusion, and differences are used

---

108. This was also a theme developed by both Albert Cleage in *Black Christian Nationalism* and James Baldwin. See James Baldwin, "No Name in the Street," in Morrison, *Collected Essays*, 455–58. On this account, Black Power is the exact opposite of being a form of blackness that whiteness creates, as it is premised on a struggle to form a way of being in the world not wholly determined by white supremacy and which shows forth the barrenness of white supremacy through the birth of a people with power to act for themselves.

109. A consociational (or confederal) polity is made up of a plurality of interdependent, self-organized associations. For a full discussion of consociationalism, see chap. 12.

to set us over and against one another. Exclusionary separation is divisive; functional separation recognizes differences as meaningful for interrelationship between groups."[110]

Politically, an intercommunal or consociational body politic is not one where everyone is the same but one where all may be recognized as having gifts to bring. But for such a body politic to stand, there is a need to identify and pursue goods in common, and democratic politics (that is, a politics that aims at forming a people through ensuring that political agency is distributed as widely as possible) is the ongoing way to do this. At the same time, the witness of Black Power points to how any such project of intercommunalism or consociationalism in the United States has to take as a *sine qua non* the dispossession/exorcism of white supremacy and the healing of others through the formation of independent and self-organized forms of black political, social, economic, and spiritual agency.

Conclusion

I have tried to suggest that, against the atomizing impact of white supremacy, the affirmation of personhood through the formation of a people is best achieved not via recognition of individual rights (as liberalism supposes), nor via changes in the means of production (as scientific Marxism suggests), nor via the redistribution of resources by the state (as in social democratic visions), nor via identity recognition as a mode of incorporation into a wider system (as multicultural accounts envisage). Each of these approaches tends to ignore the specific history and experience of African Americans and thus fails to reckon with how integration into the political economy as currently structured reinscribes white normativity into the identity, performance, and rationality of democratic citizenship. These approaches, tacitly or otherwise, thereby treat white supremacy as an accidental rather than a formal feature of political order in the United States. What the Black Power movement points to, even in its failures, is how a prerequisite for reconstituting the polity and democratic citizenship to address the subjective and objective dimensions of racial injustice as a formal feature of the political system entails some way of being a "nation within a nation" (i.e., independent and self-organized forms of communal political, social, economic, and spiritual agency).

110. Riggs, *Awake, Arise and Act*, 95-96.

The need to enable dominated people to form a "nation within a nation" is a vital insight that political theology can learn from in conceptualizing the relationship between Christianity and democracy. And it connects to a central thematic of modern theological anthropology, namely, that humans are not isolated, autonomous, self-reflexive subjects but persons constituted through relations with others, and ultimately through communion with God. Consequently, personhood involves being embedded in some form of life, culture, or people. The formation of a people, whether ecclesial or civic, involves questions of love, politics, and power. In Augustinian terms, the common object of its loves defines a people. The pursuit of these loves necessitates action in time (power) and making judgments about when, where, and with whom to act, and what to do and how to do it in order to forge and sustain some kind of shared life (politics). The Black Power movement represents but one iteration of attempts to form a people/nation, through the pursuit of power via democratic politics, and how what it means to be a people/nation comes to be understood in nonessentialist terms. The formation of this people inherently unveils the self-negating ways in which the United States—despite its constitutional commitments—is "under the dominion of its very lust for domination." Indeed, what Augustine said of Rome can be said of the United States: "that republic never actually existed, because there was no true justice in it."[111] Rather, Black Power unveils how the peace and order of the United States are what the twelfth-century prelate Rufinus of Sorrento called "the sleep of Behemoth." When disturbed, Behemoth reveals its beastly nature by turning on those with the temerity to challenge its disordered and unjust tranquillity.[112] However, the formation of even a modestly just earthly peace requires agitating the monster rather than leaving undisturbed a subjugated quiescence that dresses up compliance as harmony. The formation of a nation within a nation can be one means of agitation through which the body politic is shriven and purged, purgation taking the form of healing for some and exorcism for others, depending on one's structural location within the polity as a whole. It can also contribute to the discovery of shalom-like, eschatological anticipations that embody forms of common life that point beyond social, political, and economic systems shaped by white supremacy.

111. Augustine, *The City of God*, trans. William Babcock (New York: New City Press, 2012), 59.
112. Rufinus of Sorrento, *De Bono Pacis* (Hannover, Germany: Hahn, 1997).

Threshold

Black nationalism, Black Power, and black liberation theology emerge from the "Black Atlantic" world across which the middle passage cuts like a gaping, festering wound. Pentecostalism emerges from this same world, as do the Holiness movements, revivals, and entrepreneurial energies that shaped its demotic religious cultures. The leader of the Azusa Street Revival, William J. Seymour (1870-1922), the son of former slaves and a founding figure of Pentecostalism, represents the interaction between the traditions feeding into black liberation theology and the antecedents of Pentecostalism. It is a connection that black Holiness traditions still foster within Pentecostalism.[113] The Pentecostal theologian Leonard Lovett says these traditions represent a "pneumatological liberation theology."[114] And the pioneer historian of Pentecostalism, Walter Hollenweger, draws a direct parallel between Black Power and black Pentecostalism as movements of social transformation.[115] An argument can be made that black Holiness traditions were an antecedent to Black Power. It is a connection that is also marked by the division along racial lines of the earliest North American Pentecostals. Despite the "color line" being "washed away" in the initial services and leadership team at Azusa Street, racism divided Pentecostals from the outset, and despite efforts at reconciliation, it still haunts Pentecostalism to this day.[116]

Outside of the historical connections of black Holiness Pentecostalism, the political theology of Pentecostalism has many parallels to that of black liberation theology. But it generally operates in a different register and with a different kind of analysis of problems. Black liberation theology makes a

113. Cheryl Sanders, *Saints in Exile: The Holiness-Pentecostal Experience in African American Religion and Culture* (Oxford: Oxford University Press, 1996), and Estrelda Alexander, *Black Fire: One Hundred Years of African American Pentecostalism* (Downers Grove, IL: IVP Academic, 2011).

114. Quoted in Amos Yong, *The Spirit Poured Out on All Flesh: Pentecostalism and the Possibility of Global Theology* (Grand Rapids: Baker Academic, 2005), 77.

115. Walter Hollenweger, *Pentecostalism: Origins and Developments Worldwide* (Peabody, MA: Hendrickson, 1997), 34-37.

116. On the racial divisions shaping early Pentecostalism, see Gastón Espinosa, *William J. Seymour and the Origins of Global Pentecostalism* (Durham, NC: Duke University Press, 2014), 126-42. On the radically egalitarian and interracial character of events such as Asuza Street, see Harvey Cox, *Fire from Heaven: The Rise of Pentecostal Spirituality and the Reshaping of Religion in the Twenty-First Century* (Reading, MA: Addison-Wesley, 1995), 58-59, and Estrelda Alexander, *Black Fire*, 121-23.

distinctive set of experiences and culture the basis of forming a people so as to address powerlessness, thereby emphasizing difference rather than sameness. Pentecostalism also emphasizes difference, but the primary difference in view is between church and world. So while both identify the need to form a people to address powerlessness, for Pentecostals the people in question is the church. However, there are points of overlap. Like black liberation theology, Pentecostalism makes the need for healing and deliverance from oppression a central part of its soteriology. But again, the nature of the oppression is framed somewhat differently. Black liberation theology emphasizes social, economic, and political forces such as white supremacy and sexism and the suffering and subjugation these cause, yet their operation is hidden and needs to be exposed. By contrast, Pentecostals emphasize unseen spiritual forces such as demons and the affliction and the oppression these generate. Both Pentecostals and Black Power advocates see conflict as an inevitable part of politics, but for the former, the source of the conflict is primarily spiritual, whereas for the latter it is structural. Likewise, both call for the radical reconfiguration of the identity, performance, and rationality of democratic citizenship to address the inheritance of historical evils and current social inequities. However, Pentecostals prioritize spiritual warfare and personal conversion as the precursor to the transformation of the social, political, and economic basis of a common life. I am not thereby claiming Black Power and Pentecostalism are antithetical. As will be argued in the next chapter, and as the traditions of black Holiness Pentecostalism bear witness, a synthesis is both necessary and possible.

Suggested Readings for Further Discussion

Martin Delany, *On the Condition, Elevation, Emigration, and Destiny of the Colored People of the United States* (1852). Available online. An early statement of black nationalism as a political theology.

Malcolm X, "The Ballot or the Bullet" (speech delivered on April 12, 1964, Detroit). Available online. This speech articulates a stringent critique of American democracy.

Martin Luther King Jr., "Black Power," from *Where Do We Go From Here: Chaos or Community?* (1967) in *A Testament of Hope: The Essential Writings and Speeches of Martin Luther King Jr.*, ed. James M. Washington (New York: HarperOne, 1986), 569-97. King's constructive and critical response to Black Power and how it both aligns with and departs from his own approach.

James Cone, *Black Theology and Black Power* (Maryknoll, NY: Orbis, 1997 [1969]), chaps. 1 and 2.

Albert Cleage, *Black Christian Nationalism: New Directions for the Black Church* (New York: William Morrow, 1972), chaps. 1, 3, 11, and 12.

Emilie M. Townes, "Living in the New Jerusalem: The Rhetoric and Movement of Liberation in the House of Evil," in *A Troubling in My Soul: Womanist Perspectives on Evil and Suffering*, ed. Emilie M. Townes (Maryknoll, NY: Orbis, 1993), 78–91.

Cheryl Kirk-Duggan, "African-American Spirituals: Confronting and Exorcising Evil through Song," in *A Troubling in My Soul: Womanist Perspectives on Evil and Suffering*, ed. Emilie M. Townes (Maryknoll, NY: Orbis, 1993), 150–71.

CHAPTER 4

Pentecostalism

Like all forms of Christianity, the Pentecostal and charismatic movement is a response to a particular event—the life, death, resurrection, and ascension of Jesus Christ—and the question of how to inhabit a particular time, the time between Christ's ascension and his return. The primacy of the Christ event within Christianity and its reorientation of believers to their surrounding context demand that Christians distance themselves from the present order of things. "The present form of this world is passing away" (1 Cor. 7:31), so it cannot be wholly determinative of what is true, good, and beautiful. It also contains the possibility and moments of its own inversion and dissolution; it can become worldly. That is, the world is coterminous with forms of life turned away from God in active pursuit of sinful and idolatrous ends (what Augustine called the "earthly city").[1] But even as a form of the earthly city, the world cannot be wholly rejected, resigned to, or treated with indifference. Christianity is dependent on the discursive, symbolic, and institutional forms of the world. And the world is constituted by genuine, albeit penultimate, goods (e.g., health, family, and education), even if sin cankers the human desire for and pursuit of them. Moreover, God is present and active in and through history and within penultimate, worldly structures, so these cannot be ignored or avowed. In addition, even worldly forms of life contain the possibility of the Spirit's natality—resurrection joy and the birthing of new ways of being alive. So not only must the world be valued in some way, but the possibility of radical change or newness within the world must be witnessed to and anticipated. This chapter examines what it means for the church to inhabit the time between Christ's

---

1. A fuller account of what I mean by the terms "world" and "worldly" is given in chap. 8.

ascension and his return by reflecting on how Pentecostalism negotiates a basic question of political theology—what is the relationship between the church and the world? Or to put it differently, in what ways is the church simultaneously an "insider" and an "outsider," constituted by *and* acting upon the world?

This question is central to any consideration of how to form and sustain a common life, as it frames both the question of responses to cultural and religious others and the status and role of the church within any process of cultural and political change in this age before Christ's return. I focus on the relationship between Pentecostal/charismatic forms of Christianity (hereafter Pentecostalism), democracy, and capitalism, as this intersection represents a generative case study for thinking through the ambiguities and tensions of church-world relations.[2] I argue that Pentecostalism witnesses to how, paradoxically, attempts to separate the church from the world (because it is judged polluting or demonic) end up revalorizing sinful and idolatrous patterns of life, whereas when Pentecostals form a common life with non-Pentecostal others, they radically resignify and reorientate the earthly city (i.e., sinful and idolatrous patterns of life) toward Christ through the power of the Spirit. Pentecostalism thereby displays, both positively and negatively, how the duality of the church-world relation is dyadic (both/and), not binary (either/or). The combination and pairing in a dyad co-construct something greater than the sum of the parts. As in the dyads left/right or up/down, each term makes no sense without the other. Each is both constitutive and regulative of the other. Church cannot be church without the world, and vice versa (the constitutive relation). And the church becomes something it is not (idolatrous, worldly, anti-Christic, etc.) if it fails to be rightly ordered

---

2. I use "Pentecostalism" as a catchall term for the multifarious strands of the Pentecostal and charismatic movement. This is to follow, among others, Amos Yong, *In the Days of Caesar: Pentecostalism and Political Theology* (Grand Rapids: Eerdmans, 2010), xviii. Following the lead of Walter Hollenweger, "Pentecostalism" as a catchall term includes "classical Pentecostalism," which stems from its initial emergence and includes denominations such as the Assemblies of God and the Church of God in Christ; the charismatic movement, dating from the 1960s, which occurred in mainline Protestant, Roman Catholic, and Orthodox churches; and neo-Pentecostal, nondenominational churches, often associated with prosperity teachings. Another catchall term is "renewal." For a taxonomy of different "Pentecostalisms" and an account of how to define the term, see Allan Anderson, "Varieties, Taxonomies and Definitions," in *Studying Global Pentecostalism: Theories and Methods*, ed. Allan Anderson et al. (Berkeley: University of California Press, 2016), 13-29.

in relation to and disciplined by the world, and vice versa (the regulative relation). By contrast, in a binary, each pairing is perpetually divided into two and opposed to each other in a zero-sum game so that more of one equals less of the other.[3] Dyads can, however, collapse into binaries. Part of what I address in this chapter is how Pentecostalism shifts between dyadic and binary constructions of the church-world relation by conflating the world with what is worldly.

The chapter unfolds as follows. First, it situates the emergence of Pentecostal political theology as a formal discourse in the context of empirically based assessments of Pentecostalism as a global social movement. Second, it identifies the methods and resources Pentecostal political theology draws on to develop normative proposals for how Pentecostals should imagine and narrate politics. The third, fourth, and fifth parts examine pneumatology, eschatology, and soteriology as the three central doctrinal reference points through which church-world relations, and by extension politics, are understood. The sixth part draws on the constructive, normative framework developed in the previous sections, to critically examine how Pentecostalism reconfigures democratic citizenship. The final section then assesses the relationship between Pentecostalism and capitalism. These last two sections constitute case studies in how a constructive, normative Pentecostal political theology might provide an immanent critique of how Pentecostals navigate the church-world distinction in political and economic terms.

Pentecostalism is a multifarious, mercurial, intercultural, and global phenomenon that lacks a clear canon, an identifiable set of key thinkers, and specific institutional expressions and sociopolitical forms.[4] Its protean nature means my arguments point to tendencies and patterns of thought within Pentecostalism rather than a definitive, all-encompassing, and stable set of commitments and institutional configurations. Moreover, there is an inevitable tension and distance between the formal theologies I discuss and the lived theologies of many Pentecostals, something I try to address in the two case studies.

3. A dyad can also be contrasted with a dialectic. In a dyadic relation, the elements of the dyad can conflict or exist in tension with each other even as they are mutually constitutive, but one does not cancel out or supersede the other. In a dialectical relation, conflict is also present, but it is resolved by each new element superseding or sublating the other.

4. This comment should not be construed as a criticism. The lack thereof may well enable the rapid cross-cultural transmission of Pentecostalism.

Before proceeding further, let me locate myself in relation to this topic. While a cradle and still-confessing Anglican, I write as one suckled on exorcisms, baptized in the Holy Spirit, and for whom prophetic words, healing, and glossolalia have been, from childhood, a catalytic part of my Christian formation. As well as immersing me in the networks and practices of the Pentecostal and charismatic movement, my parents were actively engaged in addressing issues of inequity and poverty such as slum housing.[5] Rather than having a sense of disjuncture, my mother and father narrated their social and civic engagement as born out of and sustained by their Christian commitments. That said, their engagement was never framed in terms of justice or liberation, even though much of what they did directly addressed the need for both. I also write as one who has been actively involved in various forms of democratic politics and who discovered there a kind of quickening often absent in the church. And finally, I am someone who is skeptical (to say the least) about the unalloyed benefits of capitalism, seeing in democratic politics a way to remediate the often-destructive impact of economic globalization. This chapter is born out of the attempt to bring these experiences into conversation in order to determine whether they cohere or clash.

Situating Pentecostalism

The 1906 revival on Azusa Street, Los Angeles, is often identified as the birthplace of Pentecostalism. A founding figure was William J. Seymour (1870–1922), the son of former slaves, who drew on black Holiness traditions and African American spirituality in his theology and practice. These have had a profound impact on Pentecostalism worldwide. However, while Azusa Street is the most prominent and significant point of origin, it was not the only one. Pentecostalism emerges simultaneously from multiple places, including Wales, Korea, and India.[6] As an ecclesial movement, Pentecostalism drew on prior revivalist movements around the world, foremost among these being Wesleyan Holiness movements.[7] David Martin,

---

5. On this see Luke Bretherton, *Christianity and Contemporary Politics: The Conditions and Possibilities of Faithful Witness* (Malden, MA: Wiley-Blackwell, 2010), x–xii.

6. Allan Anderson, *An Introduction to Pentecostalism: Global Charismatic Christianity*, 2nd ed. (Cambridge: Cambridge University Press, 2014), 36–39, 206–10, and Ogbu Kalu, *African Pentecostalism: An Introduction* (Oxford: Oxford University Press, 2008), 20.

7. Anderson, *Introduction to Pentecostalism*, 25–30; Wolfgang Vondey, *Pentecostal The-*

a leading sociologist of Pentecostalism, situates it as a continuation and expansion of the "unsponsored mobilizations of *laissez-faire* lay religion" circulating throughout the Atlantic world that began with eighteenth-century revivalism.[8] Far from being an export of North America, Pentecostalism built on existing translocal networks; as an ecclesial movement, it was a "glocal" phenomenon from the outset.[9] Furthermore, a backdrop to its adoption around the world included indigenous attempts to generate vernacular expressions of Christianity as alternatives to those introduced by Western missionaries. Overall, the size and scale of the movement are staggering. Only emerging at the beginning of the twentieth century, Pentecostals (broadly understood) were, as of 2011, estimated to number over 584 million, constituting 8.5 percent of the world's total population.[10]

Pentecostal and charismatic churches do not have a good reputation when it comes to politics. Criticisms frequently leveled at them are that they legitimate and collude with neoliberal ideologies and represent a form of capitalism-friendly Christianity; are quietist and inward-looking, being so heavenly focused that they are no earthly good; are naïve and easily co-opted by authoritarian regimes as a counterbalance to more socially and politically critical churches; and have an emphasis on spiritual warfare that lends itself to demonizing and scapegoating political opponents, thereby transforming economic and political conflicts of interest into cosmic struggles between good and evil.[11] Countering the negative assessments of Pentecostalism are studies that point to the transformative impact of Pentecostals on poverty. For example, Martin's studies of Pentecostalism in Latin America suggest that Pentecostal churches are transforming the barrios of Latin America for the better.[12] Donald Miller and Tetsunao Ya-

---

ology: Living the Full Gospel (London: Bloomsbury, 2017), 182; Donald Dayton, *Theological Roots of Pentecostalism* (Grand Rapids: Francis Asbury, 1987), 35-60.

8. David Martin, *Pentecostalism: The World Their Parish* (Oxford: Blackwell, 2002), 5.

9. For example, see Heather Curtis's account—"The Global Character of Nineteenth-Century Divine Healing," in *Global Pentecostal and Charismatic Healing*, ed. Candy Gunther Brown (Oxford: Oxford University Press, 2011), 29-45—of how healing practices drew on transatlantic and then global alliances and networks and the latest technologies and means of communication to cultivate translocal connections from the nineteenth century onward.

10. Pew Forum of Religion and Public Life, *Global Christianity: A Report on the Size and Distribution of the World's Christian Population* (Washington, DC: Pew Research Center, 2011), 17.

11. For some examples of this, see Yong, *In the Days of Caesar*, 131-34.

12. Martin, *Pentecostalism*.

mamori echo this assessment, arguing that "progressive Pentecostalism" is a vibrant movement of social transformation among the poorest and most marginalized communities around the world.[13]

Beyond empirical studies of the positive or negative impact of Pentecostalism is how it challenges the ways politics is imagined and narrated. I contend that the ways Pentecostals address political and economic life reveal the inadequacy of analytical frameworks that assume that politics and economics are constituted by rational, self-interested individuals who, in the process of becoming modern, become nonreligious. Pentecostals refuse deterministic and secularizing demarcations of public from private and the rendering of politics as a disenchanted sphere. Contrary to the secularization thesis that assumes processes of modernization such as urbanization and bureaucratization generate the decline in the public significance of religion, Pentecostalism points to how modernization can generate the revitalization of religion and an increase in its public significance.[14] In doing so, Pentecostalism resignifies the nature of what is political, envisaging the material as spiritual, the mundane as miraculous, and worship as an act of citizenship. Pentecostalism thereby contests Western rationalist epistemologies.[15]

Interpretations of Pentecostalism that view it as apolitical or politically quietist reflect constricted conceptions of what is political. Like Black Power, but in a different register, Pentecostalism challenges constructions of citizenship and what form political agency can take. This is not to baptize Pentecostal political judgments—which are as prone to injustice and careless unconcern as anyone else's—but rather to recognize that Pentecostals construct politics in a distinctive way. They put less focus on statecraft and more emphasis on how unseen powers are the condition for the possibility of peaceable economic and political relations. The way they do democratic politics may not conform to standard scripts of what democracy entails, but that does not make them antidemocratic. Rather, it points to how democratic citizenship can be imagined and performed in radically different ways. In this chapter I reflect on how Pentecostalism challenges the dominant conception of what is and what is not political. More controversially, I entertain the idea that the real focus of emancipatory agency should not be capture of the state or control of economic resources. That dual focus

13. Donald E. Miller and Tetsunao Yamamori, *Global Pentecostalism: The New Face of Christian Social Engagement* (Berkeley: University of California Press, 2007).

14. A critique of the secularization thesis is set out in chap. 8.

15. Nimi Wariboko, *Nigerian Pentecostalism* (Rochester, NY: University of Rochester Press, 2014), 263.

generated the technocratic and totalitarian catastrophes of genocide, social engineering, and ecological devastation that overshadow modern history. Likewise, in the face of either nuclear annihilation or human-made ecological desolation that threatens the existence of life on earth, being radical cannot mean simply instituting better or more efficient versions of the existing political economy on the assumption that things will only get better. Reflection on Pentecostalism suggests that it is the resignification of everyday life; the interruption of the present by an alternative eschatological, spatiotemporal register; and the introduction of a new source of power—the power of the Spirit—that represent the truly emancipatory locus of political agency, one that opens up new ways of being alive with and for others, including nonhuman others.

As already noted, many think Pentecostalism reinforces capitalism and is a manifestation of rather than a check on economic globalization. It is true that as a populist, entrepreneurial social movement it cannot be understood without situating it in relation to capitalism and globalization.[16] However, as Nigerian Pentecostal theologian Nimi Wariboko notes, Pentecostals should not view economic globalization as providential even though it has facilitated the spread of the movement. Rather, for Wariboko, globalization is a crucible of Christian witness that, alongside the need to challenge the depredations globalization brings, also provides opportunities for cultural innovation and forming new kinds of community.[17] A focus of this chapter is the ambiguities of the relationship between Pentecostalism and capitalistic forms of economic globalization that Wariboko draws attention to. I contend that Pentecostalism challenges Manichaean accounts of the relationship between Christianity and capitalism that assume the relationship should, normatively, be oppositional. Rather, Pentecostalism points to how forms of faithful witness might be generated in and through capitalism, provoking the question of whether Pentecostalism displays something of the possibilities for converting capitalism.

16. Even positive appraisals of Pentecostalism point to its inherent linkages with capitalism and a neoliberal form of globalization. See, for example, Mark Gornik's study of the advent of Nigerian diaspora and missionary churches in New York. Gornik points to the importance of economic migration and the dynamics of New York as a center of economic globalization as key factors in the emergence of Nigerian Pentecostalism there. Mark R. Gornik, *Word Made Global: Stories of African Christianity in New York City* (Grand Rapids: Eerdmans, 2011).

17. Nimi Wariboko, *The Charismatic City and the Resurgence of Religion: A Pentecostal Social Ethics of Cosmopolitan Urban Life* (New York: Palgrave Macmillan, 2014), 52–54.

Resourcing Pentecostal Political Theology

Since the 1990s Pentecostals have become significantly more involved in politics across sub-Saharan Africa as well as in South and Central America, North America, and countries with sizable Pentecostal populations such as Korea and the Philippines.[18] This is in tandem with the emergence of more formal Pentecostal political theologies. Theologians laboring to articulate a Pentecostal political theology adopt a number of strategies. Some engage in *ressourcement* (i.e., retrieval and renewal) through readings of early Pentecostal figures to draw out liberative themes and nascent political theologies from the formative stages of the movement. In North America, black Holiness traditions are vital in this regard.[19] Such a move follows the trail set by Leonard Lovett and James Forbes, who saw early on that black Pentecostalism possessed a latent liberation theology.[20] In a similar vein, other theologians focus on Pentecostals seen to exemplify constructive forms of political engagement. In the United States, Arthur Brazier (1921–2010), Herbert Daughtry (1931–), Reiss López Tijerina (1926–2015), and John McConnell Jr. (1915–2012), the founder of Earth Day, are cases in point.[21] Brazier and Daughtry drew on Black Power and black nationalist discourses in their involvement in the civil rights movement and other forms of radical democracy.[22] Tijerina was involved in the

18. Anderson, *Introduction to Pentecostalism*, 284–90.

19. Cheryl Townsend Gilkes, "'You've Got a Right to the Tree of Life': The Biblical Foundations of an Empowered Attitude among Black Women in the Sanctified Church," in *Philip's Daughters: Women in Pentecostal-Charismatic Leadership*, ed. Estrelda Alexander and Amos Yong (Eugene, OR: Wipf & Stock, 2009), 152–69; Estrelda Alexander, "Recovering Black Theological Thought in the Writings of Early African-American Holiness-Pentecostal Leaders: Liberation Motifs in Early African-American Pentecostalism," in *A Liberating Spirit: Pentecostals and Social Action in North America*, ed. Michael Wilkinson and Steven Studebaker (Eugene, OR: Wipf & Stock, 2010), 23–52; Paul Alexander, ed., *Pentecostals and Nonviolence: Reclaiming a Heritage* (Eugene, OR: Wipf & Stock, 2012); and Dale Coulter, "Toward a Pentecostal Theology of Black Consciousness," *Journal of Pentecostal Theology* 25, no. 1 (2016): 74–89.

20. See James Forbes, "A Pentecostal Approach to Black Liberation" (PhD diss., Colgate-Rochester, 1975), and Leonard Lovett, "Black Holiness-Pentecostalism: Implication for Ethical and Social Transformation" (PhD diss., Emory University, 1979). I am grateful to Eric Williams for pointing me to the work of James Forbes.

21. On McConnell, see Darrin Rodgers and Nicole Sparks, "Pentecostal Pioneer of Earth Day: John McConnell, Jr.," in *Blood Cries Out: Pentecostals, Ecology, and the Groans of Creation*, ed. A. J. Swoboda (Eugene, OR: Pickwick, 2014), 3–21.

22. Arthur Brazier, *Black Self-Determination: The Story of the Woodlawn Organization*

land rights and farmworker movements, drawing on a mix of Pentecostal theology and apocalyptic visions to develop his evolving framework.[23] Brazier, Daughtry, Tijerina, and others contrast with more well-known figures, most notably Pat Robertson (b. 1930), a charismatic Baptist and controversial onetime contender for the Republican presidential nomination. In the European context, an example is Lewi Pethrus (1884–1974), who helped found the Christian Democratic Party in Sweden in 1964.[24] And in South Africa, there is Frank Chikane (b. 1951), a leader in the anti-apartheid movement. Another strategy is to interrogate Pentecostal theological commitments and practice in dialogue with a broad range of other political theologies, whether premodern such as that of Augustine, or contemporary such as Catholic social teaching, Latin American liberation theology, black liberation theology, and womanism.[25] Again, along similar lines, when embedded in other traditions, charismatics draw on the methods and resources of the "host" tradition to generate political theology attentive to Pentecostal concerns. For myself, the charismatic dimensions of my faith generate a heightened appreciation for pneumatology, eschatology, healing, exorcism, embodied experience, and a populist impulse as key loci of reflection. Another strategy is to frame political theology within the fivefold "full gospel" that some see as the theological heart of Pentecostalism,[26] which focuses on Jesus as savior/

(Grand Rapids: Eerdmans, 1969), and Herbert D. Daughtry, *My Beloved Community: Sermons, Speeches, and Lectures of Rev. Daughtry* (Trenton, NJ: Africa World, 2001).

23. Rudy Busto, *King Tiger: The Religious Vision of Reiss López Tijerina* (Albuquerque: University of New Mexico Press, 2005), and Gastón Espinosa, *Latino Pentecostals in America: Faith and Politics in Action* (Cambridge, MA: Harvard University Press, 2014), 329–34.

24. Joel Halldorf, "Lewi Pethrus and the Creation of a Christian Counterculture," *Pneuma* 32, no. 3 (2010): 354–68.

25. See, for example, Leonard Lovett, "Liberation: A Dual-Edged Sword," *Pneuma: The Journal of the Society for Pentecostal Studies* 9, no. 2 (1987): 155–77; Cheryl Sanders, *Empowerment Ethics for a Liberated People: A Path to African American Social Transformation* (Minneapolis: Fortress, 1995); Veli-Matti Kärkkäinen, "Are Pentecostals Oblivious to Social Justice? Theological and Ecumenical Perspectives," *Missiology: An International Review* 29, no. 4 (2001): 417–31; Yong, *In the Days of Caesar*; and Steven Studebaker, *A Pentecostal Political Theology for American Renewal: Spirit of the Kingdoms, Citizens of the Cities* (New York: Palgrave Macmillan, 2016), 109–40.

26. Yong, *In the Days of Caesar*, 95–98; Vondey, *Pentecostal Theology*, 199–253. Dayton makes the case that it is a fourfold or foursquare pattern of Jesus as savior, baptizer with the Holy Spirit, healer, and coming king that is the distinctive theological framework of Pentecostalism. Dayton, *Theological Roots of Pentecostalism*, 15–33, 173–80.

deliverer, sanctifier, Spirit baptizer, healer, and coming king. Whether it is revisionist readings of the early movement, attending to exemplary figures, dialogue with other political theologies, or drawing on the doctrinal topoi of the full gospel, all these strategies share a common move: they openly reject or simply bypass a central tenet of "classical" Pentecostalism—premillennialism—looking to alternative eschatological frameworks instead.[27] In what follows I draw on all these approaches, beginning with a consideration of the doctrinal topoi that most formal Pentecostal political theologies engage, either tacitly or explicitly, namely, pneumatology, eschatology, and soteriology. A further point of reference is how Pentecostal theology situates political theology within missiology.[28] I examine how these doctrinal topoi and the focus on missiology might be drawn on to think about the relationship between church and world and thence the nature and proper form of Christian political witness.

A Pneumatological Political Theology

Most modern confessional political theologies make Christology the Archimedean point of reference. As is clear from their emphasis on the full gospel, Christology is still central to Pentecostalism. But Pentecostal political theologies make pneumatology pivotal for conceptualizing a rightly ordered form of politics and the relationship between church and world.[29] To understand this move, it is important to account for the work of the Spirit in creation and redemption. Following the lead of numerous Pentecostal

27. Murray Dempster, "Christian Social Concern in Pentecostal Perspective: Reformulating Pentecostal Eschatology," *Journal of Pentecostal Theology* 2 (1993): 51-64, and Frederick Ware, "On the Compatibility/Incompatibility of Pentecostal Premillennialism with Black Liberation Theology," in *Afro-Pentecostalism: Black Pentecostal and Charismatic Christianity in History and Culture*, ed. Amos Yong and Estrelda Alexander (New York: New York University Press, 2011), 191-208. Biblical scholars George Eldon Ladd and Gordon Fee are influential in driving a move away from premillennialism. It should also be noted that not all early Pentecostals subscribed to premillennialism.

28. See, for example, Kenneth Archer and Richard Waldrop, "Liberating Hermeneutics: Toward a Holistic Pentecostal Mission of Peace and Justice," *Journal of the European Pentecostal Theological Association* 31, no. 1 (2011): 65-80, and Kirsteen Kim, *Joining In with the Spirit: Connecting World Church and Local Mission* (London: SCM, 2012). I am grateful to Creighton Coleman for helping me clarify this point.

29. See, for example, Lovett, "Liberation," 165-67, and Studebaker, *A Pentecostal Political Theology*, 5-7, 141-73.

theologians, I will sketch a pneumatological basis to political theology by drawing on resources both within and beyond Pentecostalism.

In Scripture, it is the Spirit who hovers over the formless void, bringing forth each kind of thing to be itself and ordering it in relation to every other kind of thing.[30] It is the Spirit who animates creaturely life; brings deliverance to an enslaved people; and anoints judges, prophets, and leaders to call forth new capacity among the people for shared and faithful action in the face of either idolatry or oppression.[31] It is the Spirit who overshadows Mary, bringing forth Jesus, enabling him to be fully human and fully divine.[32] In turn, Jesus breathes on the disciples the Spirit, who then empowers them to be witnesses to the ends of the earth (John 20:21-23; Acts 2).

Through the scriptural narrations of the Spirit's action, a threefold synergistic work of the Spirit can be discerned. First, the Spirit enables creation to be itself through animating, healing, and delivering it (in the double sense of bringing life to birth and liberation). Second, the Spirit comes alongside what exists, fructifying it so as to generate an unexpected excess.[33] This superfluity is not against nature. Nor is it a protological extension of nature, as in a notion of grace perfecting nature.[34] The transforma-

---

30. As Moltmann puts it: "Remembering the analogy of breath and voice, we might even say that the words of creation specify and define, but that they are spoken in the same breath, so that all creatures come to life through the one same *ruach*; and it is this that constitutes the community of creation." Jürgen Moltmann, *The Spirit of Life: A Universal Affirmation*, trans. Margaret Kohl (Minneapolis: Fortress, 1992), 42.

31. Michael Welker, *God the Spirit*, trans. John F. Hoffmeyer (Minneapolis: Fortress, 1994), 52-65.

32. On how Jesus's humanity is empowered by the Spirit, see Colin Gunton, *Father, Son, and Holy Spirit: Toward a Fully Trinitarian Theology* (London: T&T Clark, 2003), 153-58.

33. Eugene Rogers, *After the Spirit: A Constructive Pneumatology from Resources outside the Modern West* (Grand Rapids: Eerdmans, 2005), 99-103.

34. As Oliver O'Donovan notes: "This is what is meant by describing the Christian view of history as 'eschatological' and not merely as 'teleological.' The destined end is not immanently present in the beginning or in the course of the movement through time" (*Resurrection and Moral Order: An Outline for Evangelical Ethics* [Grand Rapids: Eerdmans, 1986], 64). Michael Wyschogrod draws the same kind of contrast, noting that the transformation of nature God brings about is not evolutionary but apocalyptic. He states: "It is a transformation that is discontinuous with nature as it has been. It envisages a break with the autonomy of nature brought about by God's intervention and not by working itself out of the *telos* of nature" (*The Body of Faith: God in the People of Israel* [San Francisco: Harper & Row, 1983], 226). See also John Zizioulas, *Being as Communion: Studies in Personhood and the Church* (New York: St. Vladimir's Seminary Press, 1985), 180.

tional newness is eschatological. Even as the Spirit builds on and intensifies what already exists, there is a surprising departure, a rupture even. The Spirit adds to nature more than is expected or seems possible, generating new and joyful ways of being alive. A wandering Aramaean couple can be a source of blessing to all peoples, swords can become plowshares, Jebus can become Jerusalem, the Word can become frail flesh, bread and wine can become the body and blood of Christ, gentiles can become part of the people of God, and what is a source of shame or foolishness can reveal divine wisdom and glory (1 Cor. 1:20–31). Third, the Spirit draws creation into its eschatological fulfillment through enabling participation in the triune life of God. A paradigmatic form of this threefold pattern is the work of the Spirit in Christ's resurrection and ascension. In Christ's resurrection, the Spirit heals and delivers creation from sin and death. In Christ's ascension and glorification, the Spirit enacts the eschatological transformation and consummation of creation as a new creation. And as a work of Father, Son, and Spirit in and through creation, resurrection and ascension mark the participation of creation in the triune life. With the resurrection and ascension, the Spirit is poured out on all flesh (Joel 2:28; Acts 2:17–18), so that all may now participate in the work of healing and blessing creation, thereby recapitulating the work of Christ in this age before Christ's return.

A pneumatological political theology envisages the Spirit as an active person undertaking this dynamic, threefold work of animating and healing, generating new life, and consummation, both in the church and in the world.[35] As the personal presence of God in creation, the Spirit mediates the world to the church and mediates the church to the world. Understood pneumatologically, the church-world relation is dyadic, not binary, each needing the other to be truly itself. Conversely, both church and world can be worldly—that is, creation turned against itself and God in death-dealing idolatry and sin. Insofar as the *kosmos*/world is oriented to and captivated by death, the Spirit acts to convert it. Conversely, insofar as the church is orientated to death, the Spirit moves to convert the church. Insofar as the church is attuned to and participating in the Spirit's work, it will be rejected by what is worldly (rather than of itself being world denying). Such participation can thereby generate a sharp church-world distinction, and at other times the church can look very much like the world or the world can look and feel more church-like than the church.

---

35. On the personhood of the Spirit understood in narrative terms rather than as a post-Cartesian center of consciousness, see Rogers, *After the Spirit*, 52–54.

Discerning the work of the Spirit requires attending to how the Spirit enables connection and differentiation. As part of restoring and blessing creation, the Spirit reweaves what is frayed or pulled apart and cuts loose what is oppressively bound together or ensnared.[36] A paradigmatic example of this binding and loosing is Pentecost: an event of communion in which each hears the good news in his or her native tongue and many tongues speak forth God's praise. As part of generating commonality through plurality, the Spirit does not generate new ways of being alive, like an alien spaceship arriving out of nowhere. Its shape and form are determined by what it means for creation qua creation to be renewed and fulfill its eschatological possibilities. In fructifying material life, the Spirit gestates joyful and surprising newness from the womb of specific social, economic, and political milieus. The work of the Spirit is thereby always contingent and contextual. Healing and newness are generated among these people, at this time, in this place. At another time and place, something different may be generated. But what is generated is not random; it follows the threefold work of healing and bringing to birth new life in creation, in all its diversity and abundance, so that creation may be eschatologically fulfilled through participating in the Trinitarian life of God.[37]

Following the pattern of binding and loosing, healing and blessing do not necessarily mean repair. They can mean release or deliverance of something to become itself in new ways, ways that are unexpected and in excess of current arrangements. For example, rather than making the deaf hear, the work of the Spirit may be to change social, economic, and political relations so that what is considered disablement is understood to be a different way of being alive. Some need healed hearts, others need their hearts broken; some need lifting up, others need to be brought low. The Spirit brings to Sabbath rest or shalom or fullness each person in the distinct way each person needs renewing and blessing so as to participate in the consummation of creation in and through Christ. In doing so, the Spirit does not generate homogeneity but pluriformity. A mark of the Spir-

36. The church is commissioned by Jesus to participate in this work of binding and loosing (Matt. 16:19; 18:18).

37. For a parallel account to mine, see Studebaker, *A Pentecostal Political Theology*, 141-73. Studebaker strongly emphasizes the continuity between creation and new creation and instead of newness, he accents restoration. His lack of a sense of the need for the conversion of cultural and political processes generates an at-times too quick identification of large-scale, state-centric projects of beneficence—notably, "American global leadership"—as works of the Spirit (225-51).

it's work is therefore vibrant, diverse forms of embodied existence in harmonious differentiation. However, to sinful and finite creatures used to listening to a narrow spectrum of sounds, the fruit of the Spirit can seem discordant, arrhythmic, and threatening. This, in turn, provokes rejection and scandal. Yet, whatever the sound, the bass line underlying all these many works is how the Spirit makes possible participation in the Trinity.[38]

Acts of healing and exorcism are a mark of the Spirit's threefold activity. In Scripture, Jesus's acts of healing, which include exorcism, represent a new source of power, one greater and more generative than that available to earthly political authorities.[39] This power is dependent on God, not on humans. To modern eyes, Jesus's ministry can look like a refusal of power. But it is better seen as a refusal of the spectacular but vacuous power that Satan offers.[40] It is also a refusal to exercise the unilateral, coercive power of institutionalized means of command and control (power over). But in refusing power over, Jesus affirms relational power (power with). At Pentecost, Spirit-animated relational power is made available to everyone. It is a power that generates rules written on hearts, not laws backed up by coercion. It is a power that blesses, bringing new, joyful life in the face of despair and death. To echo the account of healing and exorcism developed in chapter 3, healings are acts of power that relativize earthly forms of political power, revealing their impotence by showing forth a form of power that animates and heals, generates newness, and brings life to fullness.

Attention to the work of the Spirit opens up a very different form of theological reasoning about politics. Many political theologies deploy an analogical form of reasoning. In effect, if it is good, "this" works like "that." For example, economic relations are good insofar as they are like eucharistic relations of communion.[41] Or an attribute or action of Christ is

38. Crucially, *pace* Eugene Rogers, participation is not a case of moving from the Son to the Spirit or from the Spirit to the Son on a hierarchal model of ascent. Rather, the move is to participate in the perichoretic relationship between Son and Spirit experienced as both a journey through time and as kairotic events in time. This is what it means to be participants in the divine nature (2 Pet. 1:4).

39. For a parallel reading in relation to exorcism, see Richard A. Horsley, *Jesus and Empire: The Kingdom of God and the New World Disorder* (Minneapolis: Fortress, 2002).

40. Welker, *God the Spirit*, 187.

41. Sacramental frameworks can also deploy mediation rather than analogy. See, for example, William Cavanaugh, *Theopolitical Imagination: Discovering the Liturgy as a Political Act in an Age of Global Consumerism* (London: T&T Clark, 2002). However, a monolithic focus on sacraments as the anchor point of mediation tends to produce an ecclesiocentric and clerical approach that makes the church the dispenser of the Spirit

paradigmatic, and then a human action is judged good or bad to the extent that it is analogous to the action of Christ. For example, Karl Barth justifies freedom of speech by analogy to how the Word of God is free for humans.[42] Analogy is a vital form of theological reasoning. But it is not the only one. In a pneumatological political theology, the focus is on mediation and the ways in which the Spirit enables frail flesh to both be itself and become something more than itself. And in contrast to the liturgical invocation "Come, Holy Spirit" at the Eucharist, which is episodic and routinized, in Pentecostalism calling on the Holy Spirit to rest upon and transform mundane matter is an everyday cry.

The transformative ways the Spirit mediates divine-human relations within a community are through gifts of speech, action, and patterns of sociality. For example, free speech is an extension of how the Spirit empowers particular kinds of speech, speech directed to the building up of the common good of this community in this place (1 Cor. 12:7). Shared speech, action, and relation are not just modes of apprehension but also means of mediation through which the Spirit generates forms of perichoretic divine-human agency.[43] There are gifts of speech for forming a just and loving common life (e.g., prayer and prophecy); there are gifts of character or virtue—notably, faith, hope, and love—that sustain the fragile ecology of relationships essential to the hard work of building a common life; and there are gifts of transformative action that herald unexpected or seemingly impossible new beginnings for existing forms of dispirited and despairing common life (e.g., forgiveness, reconciliation, healing, and deliverance).[44] When combined, these gifts can generate new practices and patterns of interpersonal relationship characterized by communion/*koinōnia* in any given culture, which in turn reverberates throughout that culture.

---

rather than a witness to the prior and superordinate actions of the Spirit. As illustrated in the work of Stanley Hauerwas and Cavanaugh, it also tends to frame church-world relations in terms of a binary. For a Pentecostal critique of Hauerwas and Cavanaugh along these lines, see Studebaker, *A Pentecostal Political Theology*, 123–35.

42. Karl Barth, "The Christian Community and the Civil Community," in *Community, State, and Church: Three Essays* (Eugene, OR: Wipf & Stock, 2004), 176–77.

43. On this, see Mark Cartledge, *The Mediation of the Spirit: Interventions in Practical Theology* (Grand Rapids: Eerdmans, 2015), 60–87.

44. See Mark Cartledge, "Renewal Theology and the 'Common Good,'" *Journal of Pentecostal Studies* 25, no. 1 (2016): 103–5; Vondey, *Pentecostal Theology*, 185–88. Studebaker also focuses on the mediation of the Spirit, but through imaging God rather than through gifts (*A Pentecostal Political Theology*, 175–98).

Commonality across different communities is also understood to be mediated by the Spirit. Spirit-mediated pluriformity or differentiated unity is an alternative approach to framing points of connection and shared communication between cultures in terms of either a shared rationality, as in natural-law approaches; a notion of common grace; the status of being a creature; or the commonality of being made in the image of God. It is the need to discern the active work of the Spirit beyond the church that drives attention to and the ability to hallow the speech and action of non-Christian and cultural others. A need to discern where the Spirit is blowing affirms the church as a site of discernment, naming, and witness, *and* values both nonecclesial and unfamiliar forms of life as crucibles of divine disclosure. In Pentecostal political theology, how the Spirit generates newness within the particularity of a given culture means that political theology understood as an extension of missiology is tied to debates about contextualization and cross-cultural transmission: what faithful witness to and participation in the work of the Spirit entail in Lagos is different from what that involves in London. At the same time, the two are connected, and one can pollinate the other.[45] Moreover, if the Spirit is mediating God's presence in all creation, then political theology is, at least in part, about discerning whether and how the Holy Spirit is at work forming and sustaining a common life in this place among these people, or whether what is at work is some other kind of animating spirit, principality, or power that generates distorting and oppressive forms of commonality.[46] Political theology as a "discernment of spirits" is itself a gift of and a way of participating in the work of the Spirit (1 Cor. 12:10).[47]

45. On the centrality of mission, contextualization, and cross-cultural transmission to Pentecostalism, see Anderson, *Introduction to Pentecostalism*, 198–221, 234–41.

46. Welker, *God the Spirit*, 280–83; Amos Yong, *Discerning the Spirit(s): A Pentecostal-Charismatic Contribution to Christian Theology of Religions* (Sheffield: Sheffield Academic, 2000), 243–55; Kirsteen Kim, *The Holy Spirit in the World: A Global Conversation* (Maryknoll, NY: Orbis, 2007), 164–69. Yong and Kim are primarily focused on discernment in relation to other religions, but in keeping with the ways Pentecostalism situates political theology within missiology, their frameworks also relate to navigating cultural and political differences.

47. Kim, *Holy Spirit*, 169.

An Eschatological Political Theology

Ogbu Kalu notes that "Pentecostal political theology has a very strong eschatological emphasis."[48] And as Waldo César contends, "The blending of everyday time and millennial time reveals in many ways the very ethos of Pentecostalism, bringing into the daily timeframe the experience of the glorious promise of a thousand years in the kingdom of Christ."[49] For some Pentecostals, this emphasis can mean deferring any expectation of social and political change to the end times, which in turn generates indifference to politics. But for others, it can have direct social, political, and economic ramifications for how Christians act now.[50] Whatever form it takes, the emphasis on eschatology in Pentecostalism brings to the fore a question central to all political theology: What is the relationship between history and eschatology, this age and the age to come? This question is central because it determines how to value politics as such.

If this time is all there is, then politics has no limits, as it has to bear the full weight of human meaning and possibilities. The problem that then ensues is the totalization of politics, which leads either to an overinvestment in political projects as programs of salvation or to an underinvestment that despairs of any meaningful yet chastened political activity being possible. By contrast, an eschatological horizon to history—meaning there is a time beyond this time—disqualifies any absolute claims of a political or economic system to either shape human life or determine the history and significance of everything and everyone. A theological vision of time as history, as open to healing and redemption, and as fulfilled in the eschaton undergirds the possibility of politics as a finite, contingent, yet meaningful activity. The time we live in is limited, but it also has significance beyond the immediate needs and vicissitudes of the moment. When we understand politics as situated between Christ's ascension and his return, it is freed to be about enabling a penultimate peaceableness.[51] As those

---

48. Ogbu Kalu, *African Pentecostalism: An Introduction* (Oxford: Oxford University Press, 2008), 221.

49. Waldo César, "From Babel to Pentecost: A Social-Historical-Theological Study of the Growth of Pentecostalism," in *Between Babel and Pentecost: Transnational Pentecostalism in Africa and Latin America*, ed. André Corten and Ruth Marshall (Bloomington: Indiana University Press, 2001), 35-36.

50. See, for example, Wariboko, *Nigerian Pentecostalism*.

51. This arguably more "Augustinian" orientation contrasts with Moltmann's eschatology, which, in parallel with some streams of Pentecostalism, can overfreight

intentionally living into this in-between time, Christians do not have to establish regimes to control the time so as to determine the outcome of history. Rather, they can live without control because the resurrection and ascension of Jesus Christ already inaugurated the fulfillment of history, even as its consummation awaits Christ's return. Time is therefore neither cyclical nor linear; it vibrates and dances with eschatological possibilities made present by the Spirit.[52] Thus, for example, in the Sacrament, bread and wine can become a memory of the future. For Pentecostal political theologians, Christians are to cultivate forms of life in this age that bear witness to these eschatological possibilities even as they stand in solidarity with those still suffering.[53]

Contrary to overrealized eschatologies apparent in some Pentecostal churches, formal Pentecostal political theology draws attention to how living within the eschatological "now–not yet" tension means addressing ongoing suffering and oppression. Amos Yong identifies this as a need to "pathically live out a political theology of suffering and hope."[54] Yong is not advocating passive acceptance or resignation. Rather, pathos involves active contemplation of, abiding with, and waiting on, in order to encounter the truth about the world as it is and thereby act fittingly in response to reality. Yong's call for suffering love as a way of living out a Pentecostal political theology is a call to engage with what we fear, don't understand, or find difficult (death, illness, tragic circumstance, injustice) through *pathos/passio*: that is, a fierce desire and orientation to participate in and bear witness to reality as determined by the loving presence of God in a world of suffering. In the context of the Fall, such passionate engagement may well entail pain, struggle, and great difficulty. This passionate or pathic witness contrasts with how we tend to understand compassion or sympathy as an altruistic sentiment that, as noted in chapter 2, triggers forms of

---

immanent and penultimate political projects with eschatological and salvific import. Moltmann's cosmic eschatology lacks Augustine's sense of the ambiguity of all human political endeavors.

52. Jürgen Moltmann, *The Coming of God: Christian Eschatology*, trans. Margaret Kohl (Minneapolis: Fortress, 2004 [1996]), 138.

53. See, for example, Vondey, *Pentecostal Theology*, 193-97; Kalu, *African Pentecostalism*, 213-23; Yong, *In the Days of Caesar*, 347-58; Daniela Augustine, *Pentecost, Hospitality, and Transfiguration: Toward a Spirit-Inspired Vision of Social Transformation* (Cleveland, TN: CPT, 2012), 111-38.

54. Yong, *In the Days of Caesar*, 358. See also, Steven Land, *Pentecostal Spirituality: A Passion for the Kingdom* (Sheffield: Sheffield Academic, 1993), 218-19, and Moltmann, *The Spirit of Life*, 188-92.

beneficence rather than blessing.[55] Passionate engagement as defined here seeks loving justice, not philanthropic concern.

A Missiological Political Theology

In Pentecostal political theology, the emphasis on pneumatology and eschatology situates the church as both a witness to the work of the Spirit in this age and a participant in that work. The political work of the church is therefore understood in terms of mission. Given the missiological framing of political theology, salvation and sanctification—doctrines central to the "full gospel"—take on a political valence, no longer being understood in either ethereal or pietistic terms. As Pentecostal theologian Steve Land contends: "The church, where possible, must work to make structures more adequate to the life as righteously ordered and intended by God. Structures cannot be sanctified in the same way as individuals, but, since the Spirit is at work in all creation, discerning action of the church can bear witness to and participate in those activities which more nearly embody righteousness, dignity and love for people."[56]

The pathway of salvation and sanctification neither leads away from life in the body nor is it an interior journey of self-actualization. Rather, it generates flourishing in the here and now, not just eternal life in the hereafter. A mark of this flourishing is movement toward the fulfillment of one's personhood in and through life with others, including nonhuman others.[57] Salvation can thereby bring bodily healing and material blessings, as sanctification entails the ongoing transformation of both the body of Christ and the body politic, as each refracts the other.[58] This "holistic soteriology" generates a view of mission that sees the church being a blessing to all peoples by participating in the Spirit's threefold synergistic work of healing, generating newness, and bringing creation to eschatological fulfillment. Tacit within this soteriology is a nondualistic cosmology. As Wolfgang Vondey notes, Pentecostal soteriology rejects a division between "the natural and supernatural, or the natural and spiritual, as opposite and

55. For a discussion of the distinction between beneficence and blessing and a definition of both, see chap. 2.

56. Land, *Pentecostal Spirituality*, 206.

57. Land, *Pentecostal Spirituality*, 122–81; Moltmann, *The Spirit of Life*, 94–98; Welker, *God the Spirit*, 331–41.

58. Wariboko, *Nigerian Pentecostalism*, 118–22.

unrelated dimensions of human existence. Instead, the outpouring of the Spirit on all flesh demands a holistic soteriology that resonates with the unity of the physical, material, spiritual, psychological, behavioral, and relational needs of human life."[59]

An emphasis on prosperity is a common way Pentecostals articulate their holistic soteriology. This emphasis takes myriad forms.[60] However, prosperity teachings often equate prosperity with God's shalom, the Hebrew word that denotes wholeness, flourishing, prosperity, peace, well-being, and a state of blessing. As Katherine Attanasi outlines it, prosperity teachings about shalom take it to mean "psychological, social, spiritual, and physical wholeness; peace with the natural world, ancestors, God, and fellow human beings; and inner satisfaction, contentment and peace. The prosperity gospel emphasizes that as part of God's covenant, Christians enjoy unassailable claims to certain blessings as well as to right relationship with God, other humans, and nature."[61]

Concern for prosperity and abundance speaks to a vision of salvation that includes social, political, economic, and ecological flourishing, but only when such a vision incorporates the good life as being one lived with and on behalf of others and a shalom-like vision of health and wealth.[62] When unhooked from concerns for a flourishing common life, prosperity teachings align sanctification with the ascetic disciplines demanded by capitalist forms of production, distribution, and consumption. Divine-human relations are understood not in covenantal terms but in contractual, mechanistic ones: so much "faithful" action produces a requisite amount of God's "blessing." Conversely, lack of such action is the cause of impoverishment. For example, as historian Kate Bowler argues, in North America, the prosperity gospel's confidence in the possibility of human trans-

---

59. Vondey, *Pentecostal Theology*, 189.

60. On prosperity theologies, see Amos Yong, "A Typology of Prosperity Theology: A Religious Economy of Global Renewal or a Renewal Economics?" in *Pentecostalism and Prosperity: The Socio-Economics of the Global Charismatic Movement*, ed. Katherine Attanasi and Amos Yong (New York: Palgrave Macmillan, 2012), 15-32.

61. Katherine Attanasi, "Introduction: The Plurality of Prosperity Theologies and Pentecostalisms," in Attanasi and Yong, *Pentecostalism and Prosperity*, 4-5.

62. See, for example, Wariboko, *Nigerian Pentecostalism*, 234-38; Afe Adogame, "Reconfiguring the Global Religious Economy," in *Spirit and Power: The Growth and Global Impact of Pentecostalism*, ed. Donald Miller, Kimon Sargeant, and Richard Flory (Oxford: Oxford University Press, 2013), 194-97; and Miroslav Volf, "Materiality of Salvation: An Investigation in the Soteriologies of Liberation and Pentecostal Theologies," *Journal of Ecumenical Studies* 26, no. 3 (1989): 447-67.

formation, when allied with a belief that Christian virtues are the same as market virtues, affirms the basic economic structures of capitalism. North American prosperity teaching encourages congregants to trust that within the providential equilibrium of the market the faith-filled and hardworking sheep will be separated from the lazy and unrighteous goats.[63] This version of the prosperity gospel reduces prosperity to economic success understood in consumerist terms, reinforces an unjust status quo, and generates an overinvestment in capitalism as a this-worldly yet providential project of beneficence. In terms of normative Pentecostal political theology, this form of prosperity teaching represents a failure to exercise a true discernment of spirits.

Alongside an emphasis on prosperity is a commitment to healing understood as an outworking of a holistic soteriology and a missiological political theology.[64] Healing is a way of seeking the peace and prosperity of a polity. Yong argues that for Pentecostals, Jesus's healing ministry is an extension of soteriology, because if "the work of Christ reversed the effects of the fall with regard to the nature of sin, then it did so with regard to the nature of sickness and disease."[65] A central claim of Pentecostal theology is that the same Spirit who healed through Jesus continues to work today. But healing is not just personal and physical. It is also a theo-political act.[66] Healing challenges injustice through enacting God's shalom and promulgating God's judgment against the principalities and powers.[67] As a theo-political act, healing points to the ongoing reordering of the principalities

---

63. Kate Bowler, *Blessed: A History of the American Prosperity Gospel* (New York: Oxford University Press, 2013).

64. Candy Gunther Brown identifies healing as a defining feature of contemporary Pentecostalism (introduction to *Global Pentecostal and Charismatic Healing*, ed. Candy Gunther Brown [Oxford: Oxford University Press, 2011], 3-21).

65. Yong, *In the Days of Caesar*, 259.

66. Luke Bretherton, "Pneumatology, Healing and Political Power: Sketching a Pentecostal Political Theology," in *The Holy Spirit in the World Today*, ed. Jane Williams (Oxford: Lion, 2011), 130-50.

67. There is not the space to rehearse debates about the nature of the principalities and powers. This debate centers on two questions: Do the principalities and powers refer solely to material structural dynamics or to cosmic, extramaterial forces? And are the powers redeemable or not? For a review of this debate in biblical studies and political theology, see Yong, *In the Days of Caesar*, 129-51. I take the view that the principalities and powers mentioned in Luke-Acts and the Pauline epistles are both spiritual and sociopolitical and are created good, presently fallen, judged in the Christ event, and open to redemption at the eschatological fulfillment of all things. They are not to be equated with the demonic.

and powers in the present age and the possibility of their ultimate renovation in the age to come.[68]

Another aspect of Pentecostal soteriology and the pursuit of the peace and prosperity of a polity is exorcism and deliverance.[69] I take exorcism and deliverance to be specific forms of healing, which, like other forms of healing, are theo-political acts.[70] As Yong puts it, "Central to the Pentecostal notion of salvation, especially in the global south, is the idea of deliverance understood in socio-cultural terms."[71] Exorcism and deliverance are a manifestation of the fulfillment of God's purposes, a mark of faithfulness, and a sign that what is preached is true. If exorcism is the expulsion of demonic activity and the abolition of oppressive forces, then deliverance is their replacement by a new animating spirit and direction, one orientated to flourishing, not to harm.[72] Like other forms of healing, they are a way the church participates in the Spirit's work of binding and loosing. Laying on of hands and anointing with oil are a part of deliverance, as they are a way the Holy Spirit mediates divine presence. The emphasis on exorcism and deliverance acts as a destabilizing, critical current within Pentecostal missiology by identifying existing social, economic, and political arrangements as potentially a source of oppression and manifestation of demonic activity from which everyone needs liberating.[73] Mission, therefore, in-

68. Oliver O'Donovan, *The Desire of the Nations: Rediscovering the Roots of Political Theology* (Cambridge: Cambridge University Press, 1996), 93.

69. Vondey, *Pentecostal Theology*, 201–6.

70. This is to follow the depiction in Matthew and Luke-Acts and subsequent early church traditions of exorcism as a healing activity.

71. Yong, *In the Days of Caesar*, 124.

72. Kalu, *African Pentecostalism*, 172, 217. This distinction is somewhat arbitrary. Exorcism is a sacramental practice of ancient origin. "Deliverance," as a generic term, originates in Pentecostal and charismatic circles.

73. The demonic can be understood variously. For some it is a malignant agentic force that can be personified. For others it is a mythic and metaphorical way of framing either structural evils or psychological struggles. More recent theological accounts build on the work of Karl Barth and Walter Wink to identify the demonic as an empty vacuum generated by human sinfulness—what Barth called "hypostases of nothingness." As a vacuum, the demonic possesses a negative energy of its own that supersedes or possesses human agency, sucking life and light out of what exists and distorting human relations. Spiritual warfare is replacing that negative, life-destroying energy—which nevertheless attracts humans like moths to a flame—with virtuous forms of action and practices through which the Spirit mediates creative, life-giving power that fills up and therefore closes down the vacuous, chaos-generating forms of nonbeing that have taken root. As per the previous chapter, within this nonontological but realist theology of de-

volves witnessing to and participating in the deliverance of politics and culture, which necessarily includes discernment of spirits. Spiritual warfare, as a form of discernment, witness, and participation, is thus a form of mission. It is exemplified in such actions as the symbolic contestation of territory through prayer walks, fasting, and worship services that fight the occult forces that are believed to be parasitic on and further distort forms of political and economic life turned away from God.[74]

For Pentecostals, exorcism and spiritual warfare are a praxis of democratic citizenship. With reference to the Guatemalan churches like El Shaddai that Kevin O'Neill researched, he contends: "El Shaddai's efforts at warring against demons to change Guatemala, no matter how off-putting those efforts are, reinforce one of democracy's central assumptions: democracy's ideal citizen is active, responsible, and willing to participate for the greater good. This ideal citizen owns societal problems and works to solve those problems. This vision of the citizen is the very one that Alexis de Tocqueville notes in his foundational work, *Democracy in America*, and one that neo-pentecostal mega-churches, such as El Shaddai, actively cultivate through the logic and practice of spiritual warfare."[75]

Democratic politics seeks to make unseen and oppressive structures of power visible and publicly accountable. Pentecostal democratic citizenship also seeks to make unseen and oppressive power accountable, but, rather than the public square, it prioritizes a different space of appearing—the heavenlies. On a Pentecostal account of how power operates, this is a more significant space of appearing.[76] It renders power—visible and invisible—accountable to the true sovereign, Jesus Christ. Lack of accountability to Jesus Christ is the precursor to a lack of accountability for use of state or economic resources.[77] Political imaginaries locked into an immanent, Weberian framework view spiritual warfare as irrational and

---

mons, something like racism is a hypostatized form of nothingness that has taken on a life of its own and needs exorcising.

74. Wariboko, *Nigerian Pentecostalism*, 279-84; Yong, *In the Days of Caesar*, 155-65.

75. Kevin O'Neill, *City of God: Christian Citizenship in Postwar Guatemala* (Berkeley: University of California Press, 2009), 101.

76. Kalu, *African Pentecostalism*, 218-21.

77. Troublingly, the obverse can also be true. If politicians are seen to make themselves spiritually accountable and transparent—they repent and confess the name of Jesus Christ—then they can be forgiven a lack of transparency (e.g., not making their tax returns public when running for office) and corruption or sin in other areas (e.g., sexually predatory behavior).

bizarre. But this is a failure to see how, whether in Nigeria or North America, politics and economics are themselves irrational and grotesque when such things as abject poverty, lack of public investment in basic amenities, mountaintop removal, toxic waste dumping, exploitative lending, and abandonment of the old are routine outcomes of "rational" policies. Rather than a sociological or psychological framework, exorcism and spiritual warfare need situating within a populist, enchanted, apocalyptic vision of democratic citizenship, one struggling to cope with a surreal world of corruption, systemic exploitation, and the hidden forces shaping an increasingly precarious social and economic life.[78] Its forebears are Gerrard Winstanley, William Blake, and Sojourner Truth, not John Locke, Immanuel Kant, and John Stuart Mill.

Spiritual warfare—and deliverance more generally—can serve and be tied to visions of material transformation. As Vondey contends, conceptions of exorcism and deliverance address the person as someone embedded in a broad range of cultural, economic, and political practices that need converting if the person is to experience peace and prosperity.[79] He states, "The solidarity of the Spirit with the oppressed and ostracized elements of society, echoing the ministry of Jesus (Acts 10:38), shows that deliverance is not exclusively the separation of individuals from the injustices of society but also the transformation of the institutions, structures, symbols, logics, systems and power dynamics in which they participate."[80] However, in the contemporary context, where capitalism and post-Enlightenment rationalities dominate the formal economy and public life, healing, exorcism, and spiritual warfare are part of the informal economy and a contraband worldview. Their practice is unofficial, unregulated, untaxed, highly entrepreneurial, and dependent on social networks and mutual solidarity. Like other parts of this outlaw world, such as prostitution and drug trafficking, they exist separate from the bureaucratized and managed sectors so that exploitation and racketeering are endemic to their practice. However, at the same time, as Yong suggests, participation "in the informal economy serves as a protest against the self-interested greed, consumerist materialism, and rampant hedonism that perennially threaten to undermine the market economy."[81] Joel Robbins echoes Yong, pointing to how most

---

78. On my use of the term "populist," see chap. 13.
79. Vondey, *Pentecostal Theology*, 202–4. See also Kalu, *African Pentecostalism*, 213–23.
80. Vondey, *Pentecostal Theology*, 207.
81. Yong, *In the Days of Caesar*, 308.

Pentecostals stress ways of coping with and avoiding extreme poverty and political corruption.[82]

In what follows, I draw on the normative framework of Pentecostal political theology developed thus far to evaluate two interrelated case studies in how Pentecostals navigate the church-world distinction: the relationship between Pentecostalism and democratic citizenship, and that between Pentecostalism and capitalism. I begin with the former.

Pentecostalizing Democracy

As should be clear, to demand that Pentecostals conform to democratic politics as conventionally understood is a failure of analysis. If Black Power calls for the reconfiguration of citizenship to address white supremacy and thereby generates a community unassimilable by the existent order of things, Pentecostalism also reconfigures the performance, rationality, and identity of democratic citizenship in ways that are at odds with established institutional patterns. Instead, Pentecostalism seeks to transform those patterns.

Many scholars identify the centrality of transformation in Pentecostal belief and practice.[83] And as noted above, this transformation is not just personal but also looks to social, economic, and political changes as a sign of divine activity. But transformation is not understood in emergent, progressive, or developmental ways. It entails both renewal of what exists and radical discontinuity.[84] Ruth Marshall and Kevin O'Neill, in their ethnographic work on Pentecostals, see the combination of renewal and rupture in Pentecostal beliefs and practices as formative of a new political subjectivity. It is a process that, as both Marshall and O'Neill suggest, me-

82. Joel Robbins, "The Globalization of Pentecostal and Charismatic Christianity," *Annual Review of Anthropology* 33, no. 1 (2004): 117–43.

83. See, for example, David Martin, *Tongues of Fire: The Explosion of Protestantism in Latin America* (Oxford: Blackwell, 1990), 163.

84. Herein lies a key contrast between Jürgen Moltmann and his Pentecostal interlocutors. While a number of Pentecostal theologians note the crucial and generative influence of Moltmann's work on the development of more formal and academic genres of Pentecostal theology, his panentheistic and more developmental view of cosmic eschatology stands in tension with approaches within "real existing" Pentecostalism and with the theological visions articulated by prominent Pentecostal theologians. On this see Peter Althouse, *Spirit of the Last Days: Pentecostal Eschatology in Conversation with Jürgen Moltmann* (London: T&T Clark, 2003), 186–92.

diates between and integrates globalized and local repertoires of identity formation, fashioning moral and political subjects who make sense of the world around them in new ways. Marshall notes that this process of formation is in keeping with long-standing Christian eschatological traditions. In her view, Pentecostal discourses articulate a "revolutionary program of redemption in which the future appears both as the possible overcoming of what has gone before and as the fulfillment of an original promise."[85]

As part of a process of renewal, Pentecostal democratic citizenship is an ongoing and learned project situated within a particular context. Marshall notes that the process of learning involves the "gradual acquisition and enactment of a series of bodily techniques (fasting, speaking in tongues), narrative forms (testimony, prayer, song), and an aesthetics (dress, comportment). Through this process the convert gradually learns, with heart, soul, and body how to experience the truth of revelation and the power of the Holy Spirit."[86] But alongside renewal through a process of *paideia*, Pentecostal discourse is "littered with images of rupture and discontinuity."[87] This emphasis on rupture manifests itself in a variety of ways. These include the rupture of historical time through the expected rapture at the second coming of Christ; the ritualization of discontinuity through baptism and exorcisms that deliver the individual from sin and the negative influence of his or her past life; the dualisms between the saved and unbelievers or between the Christlike and the demonic; the resignification of a given culture as worldly and governed by territorial spirits through spiritual

85. Ruth Marshall, *Political Spiritualities: The Pentecostal Revolution in Nigeria* (Chicago: University of Chicago Press, 2009), 65. Conceptualizing how the emphasis in Pentecostalism on eschatology might inform democratic and emancipatory forms of political engagement has been a key motive for Pentecostal theologians' dialogue with Moltmann's work, as he explicitly makes these connections. On this see Althouse, *Spirit of the Last Days*. For Moltmann's own account of the relationship between pneumatology, eschatology, and political theology, see especially the following from Jürgen Moltmann: *The Trinity and the Kingdom of God: The Doctrine of God*, trans. Margaret Kohl (London: SCM, 1981), 191-222; *The Spirit of Life: A Universal Affirmation*, trans. Margaret Kohl (Minneapolis: Fortress, 1992), 99-122; and *The Coming of God: Christian Eschatology*, trans. Margaret Kohl (Minneapolis: Fortress, 2004 [1996]), 129-202.

86. Marshall, *Political Spiritualities*, 132. For a parallel analysis, see O'Neill, *City of God*; Joel Robbins, "Pentecostal Networks and the Spirit of Globalization: On the Social Productivity of Ritual Forms," *Social Analysis* 53, no. 1 (2009): 55-66; and Thomas J. Csordas, *The Sacred Self: A Cultural Phenomenology of Charismatic Healing* (Berkeley: University of California Press, 1994).

87. Robbins, "Globalization," 127.

warfare; and lastly, the separation of the individual from other forms of cultural production and personal formation through strict ascetic codes and an all-encompassing church life.

Democratic citizenship as a form of political spirituality entails the intense cultivation of virtue often explicitly linked to pursuing the peace and prosperity of the nation. However, as O'Neill argues in relation to Guatemalan Pentecostals, this vision of citizenship can be uncoupled from any broader collective initiatives to bring about change. It is the lone citizen-soldier, engaging in spiritual warfare, living righteously, and proselytizing, who constitutes the primary agent of change.[88] Within this performance of citizenship, initiatives such as community organizing, trade unionism, or more conventional social movements appear insufficient as means of generating societal and political transformation.[89] But this does not make such a performance of citizenship any less orientated to political change, aligned as it is with the "steadfast conviction that the spiritual world affects the material world and that the Christian soldier, by praying and fasting, can manipulate the material world."[90] What we have instead are rival performances of what democratic citizenship entails. Some Pentecostal performances construct democratic politics within a different register and mode of signification—one of political spirituality—so that other kinds of performance and practice can appear at best secondary and at worst irrelevant.

That Pentecostalism often constitutes an alternative performance of democratic citizenship is not of itself problematic, and it rules out simplistic judgments against Pentecostalism as somehow inherently antidemocratic. The primary problem is theological and relates to how certain Pentecostal

---

88. A parallel account to that of O'Neill is given regarding Nigerian Pentecostals in Richard Burgess, *Nigeria's Christian Revolution: The Civil War and Its Pentecostal Progeny (1967-2006)* (Oxford: Regnum Books, 2008), 284-88.

89. As O'Neill notes, "The citizen-soldier tradition now coincides with neo-pentecostalism in a way that asks each Christian citizen to fulfill his or her responsibility by fighting Satan for the soul of the nation." But, as O'Neill goes on to say: "An increasing number of neo-pentecostals . . . enlist in God's army, surrounding themselves with fellow soldiers, but the missions that they are sent on—the battles that they are expected to win—are so remarkably singular, so deeply heroic, as to make one question the place of community even in postwar Guatemala City's largest of congregations" (*City of God*, 89-90). A contrasting view from a different context is given by Joseph Quayesi-Amakye, who argues for how Ghanaian Pentecostals advocate for more conventional forms of civic engagement as ways of addressing evil and suffering as part of a "responsible spirituality" (*Christology and Evil in Ghana: Towards a Pentecostal Public Theology* [Amsterdam: Rodopi, 2013], 169-239).

90. O'Neill, *City of God*, 95.

performances of democratic citizenship construct neighbor love.[91] What need critique and condemnation are the ways Pentecostals refuse to listen to, learn from, and build reciprocal relations with their neighbors. Pentecostal performances of democratic citizenship often result in the other appearing as an enemy to be defeated through spiritual warfare rather than a neighbor to be loved and cared for as part of a shared common life.[92] Instead of the church being open to the work of the Spirit among all peoples (so requiring the church to listen to and learn from its neighbors), many Pentecostals become locked in a mimetic rivalry with other groups who are seen as subject to demonic powers.[93]

Chantal Mouffe's account of agonistic democracy helps open up why Pentecostal approaches to democratic citizenship can be problematic. In Mouffe's diagnosis, some religious groups convert material, political differences into Manichaean conflicts between good and evil. For Mouffe, participation in a pluralistic democratic politics necessitates seeing one's opponent not as an enemy to be destroyed but as an adversary whose existence is legitimate and must be tolerated. She identifies the need to move from "antagonism" between enemies—that is, "persons who have no common symbolic space"—to "agonism" between adversaries or "friendly enemies"—that is, "persons who are friends because they share a common symbolic space but also enemies because they want to organize this common symbolic space in a different way."[94] As Mouffe puts it, "We could say that the aim of democratic politics is to transform an 'antagonism' into an 'agonism.'"[95] Such a process of conversion entails the difficult and time-consuming work of democratic politics. Many Pentecostals operate with an antagonistic rather than an agonistic framework that in turn militates against involvement in conventional forms of democratic politics. What makes "unbelievers" legible in a spiritual register of demons and spiritual warfare makes them illegible in a civic register of conventional democratic politics.

91. On the theological roots of separateness and an antagonistic attitude to others, see Yong, *In the Days of Caesar*, 27-28.

92. For example, Marshall notes the growing intolerance and hostility that have emerged between Muslims and Pentecostals in Nigeria since the 1990s. Marshall, *Political Spiritualities*, 214-30.

93. Yong, *In the Days of Caesar*, 126-34.

94. Chantal Mouffe, *The Democratic Paradox* (London: Verso, 2000), 13.

95. Chantal Mouffe, "Religion, Liberal Democracy, and Citizenship," in *Political Theologies: Public Religions in a Post-secular World*, ed. Hent de Vries and Lawrence E. Sullivan (New York: Fordham University Press, 2006), 324.

Within an antagonistic framework, it is felt to be vital to have divinely appointed figures in positions of "worldly" power. This theo-political vision opens the door to support for authoritarian figures who use Pentecostal—or prosperity gospel—sounding rhetoric but whose political practice is corrupt or antidemocratic. Instead of holding up to scrutiny whether or not the practice of a political leader is just and loving as part of a discernment of spirits, what matters to antagonistic Pentecostals is the way political leaders are perceived as an anointed presence within a system portrayed as under the sway of demonic powers. As an anointed presence, such a figure can channel, in a drain-like way, the power of the Holy Spirit within the political system, thereby countering demonic influences. Within an antagonistic framework of democratization through individual conversion, anointed presence, and spiritual warfare, the church qua church is wholly subordinated to and leaves untouched both the institutions and processes of statecraft and the agonistic and dialogic practices of a democratic common life. The irony here is that for all the emphasis in Pentecostalism on moving in the power of the Holy Spirit, within antagonistic frameworks the Spirit is reduced to a creature of the church, and openness to the movement of the Spirit outside and beyond those who self-identify as Pentecostal Christians is unfaithfully refused.[96] The church thereby becomes deaf both to its sinfulness and to its need of others if it is to be faithful, hopeful, and loving and thereby witness to Jesus Christ.

At a formal level, Pentecostal political theology addresses the problem of antagonistic friend-enemy relations in politics through emphasizing the possibilities of friendship across difference and the practice of hospitality as a constructive way of navigating difference.[97] Extending friendship beyond the bounds of the church is a way to convert an antagonism that absolutizes difference into an agonism that recognizes that conflicts between church and world exist, but that there are also possibilities of conciliation and the discovery of shared meaning and action. For example, Wariboko envisages friendship as "a route to the common."[98] He goes on to say: "Friendship is between the private and the public, family and state; it is indeed in the common, a civil *ecclesia.* . . . [The common] is an in-between platform that is not beholden to biology or nation-state sovereignty. It is a space between denominations, nations, and sovereignties; it is a conso-

---

96. This is an example of what Cartledge identifies as the problem of conflating divine and human agency; see Cartledge, *Mediation of the Spirit*, 83.

97. Wariboko, *Nigerian Pentecostalism*, 201-17, and *The Charismatic City*, 119-35.

98. Wariboko, *Nigerian Pentecostalism*, 212.

ciation of voluntary associations, networks of friendship, which creates a social space not subject to blood, race, ethnicity (genetic connection), special interest, or central political control by force."[99] Hospitality as a civic, cross-cultural, and interfaith practice is another, nonstate-centric way Pentecostal political theology frames constructive possibilities for encounter with others and generating a common life between strangers.[100] Hospitality is explored in detail in chapter 9.

Relations with various non-Pentecostal others can generate antagonistic friend-enemy relations. However, a different problem attends how Pentecostals relate to broader economic systems within which those relations are embedded. If the problem that needs addressing in the relationship between Pentecostalism and democracy is too much conflict and a lack of conciliation, the problem in the relationship between Pentecostalism and capitalism is too little conflict and a tendency to assimilation. But as with democracy, the remedy is not becoming less Pentecostal, but more fully living into the promise of Pentecostal political theology and its pneumatological, eschatological, and missiological orientation.

Pentecostalizing Capitalism

Echoing John Wesley's famous remark, Pentecostals see the world as their parish. And like their Wesleyan-Holiness antecedents, Pentecostal entrepreneurs embody the possibilities of globalized capitalism with their confident transmission of faith through freedom of travel, their independent learning (setting up their own colleges, Bible courses, etc.), their pragmatism, and their innovative and independent expression through information technology. They are at the vanguard of the revolution in cultural agency afforded ordinary people by capitalism, one that enables them to create and fund their own religious and cultural identities.[101] In short, Pentecostalism makes use of capitalism to generate and spread its populist ecclesial practices and theological discourses.

99. Wariboko, *Nigerian Pentecostalism*, 212.

100. Vondey, *Pentecostal Theology*, 233–38; Augustine, *Pentecost, Hospitality, and Transfiguration*, 43–70; Amos Yong, *Hospitality and the Other: Pentecost, Christian Practices, and the Neighbor* (Maryknoll, NY: Orbis, 2008).

101. On how consumerism enables an increase in the cultural agency of lay Christians, see Vincent J. Miller, *Consuming Religion: Christian Faith and Practice in a Consumer Culture* (London: Continuum, 2004).

Pentecostals do not have a fixed form of ecclesial polity. Given the emphasis on mission and contextualization, Pentecostals follow in the footsteps of William Carey, founder of the Baptist Mission Society in 1792. In the eyes of many, Carey is the initiator of the modern missionary movement.[102] Abandoning established ecclesial forms—congregational, episcopal, etc.—Carey modeled the mission society on the joint-stock trading company.[103] It was a response determined by practical rather than theological considerations: what worked was deemed to be what was faithful. As the historian of missions Andrew Walls notes, "There never was a theology of the voluntary society."[104] Capitalist institutions and processes, based on the individualistic anthropology of voluntarism, and driven by pragmatism, generated the institutional form of the mission society. In effect, the market rather than the monastery or the church becomes the school for the Lord's service. Walls celebrates Carey's initiative as an act of contextualization, while the missiologist David Bosch suggests that all Protestant churches are now in effect modeled on mission societies.[105] It is an open question whether Carey's initiative is a daring act of prophetic appropriation or a heretical act of complicity and collaboration with the spread of capitalism and colonialism. But in the light of the subsequent rise to preeminence of non-European Christianity and the collapse of many Christian institutions in Europe, we must at least entertain the view that Carey engaged in a radical and imaginative act of *paradosis*.[106] As such, this enabled Christianity to be transmitted to different contexts and new

102. For example, Lamin Sanneh describes Carey's arrival in India as "a watershed in the history of Christian mission" (*Translating the Message: The Missionary Impact on Culture* [Maryknoll, NY: Orbis, 1989], 137).

103. Stephen B. Bevans and Roger Schroeder, *Constants in Context: A Theology of Mission for Today* (Maryknoll, NY: Orbis, 2004), 211. Carey's action continues to reverberate in current Pentecostal practices, which, as Marshall and others note, often model the organization of the church on a small or large private enterprise (see Marshall, *Political Spiritualities*, 182).

104. Andrew F. Walls, "Missionary Societies and the Fortunate Subversion of the Church," in *The Missionary Movement in Christian History: Studies in the Transmission of Faith* (Edinburgh: T&T Clark, 1996), 246.

105. Walls, "Missionary Societies," 241-54. Bosch points out that the differences between Protestant denominations conceived of as voluntary societies and mission organizations are minimal; in effect, all churches became voluntary societies. See David J. Bosch, *Transforming Mission: Paradigm Shifts in the Theology of Mission* (Maryknoll, NY: Orbis, 2011), 328-29.

106. *Paradosis* has a double meaning, denoting both the dogmatic or apostolic content of faith and the dynamic process of passing that content on.

settings and to flourish in them even in the face of its disorientation and reconfiguration within the emergence of European modernity.[107] And it is a form of *paradosis* that Pentecostals continue today through their own pragmatic, entrepreneurial initiatives.[108]

While many of the beliefs, practices, and institutional forms of Pentecostalism owe a debt to capitalism, Pentecostalism is also a response to its ravages and dislocations. Pentecostalism creates what Martin calls "islands of social care."[109] These islands constitute a protected enclave in which Pentecostals can forge their own identity and practices through experimenting with egalitarian social relations and, like their Methodist forebears, developing new skills in leadership, literacy, public speaking, and self-organization. The assumption is that in contexts such as Latin America and Africa, such experimental enclaves are a precursor to more democratic forms of civic life.[110] Whether that assumption is correct is another matter. However, while it is up for debate whether Pentecostalism is the vanguard of democratization, Pentecostal churches do function to create new forms of social solidarity. Omar McRoberts, in his ethnographic study of black Pentecostal churches in Boston, suggests that ecstatic worship and healing are a way in which marginalized and poor groups build up a social body. This constructive social labor counteracts how participants are constantly broken down as individuals and disaggregated and disorganized as a community by the power of the market and state acting upon them. The flow of the Spirit counters the demand that families and

107. Without being committed to some version of the secularization thesis, we can still point to the deinstitutionalization of Christianity in Europe. On this see Grace Davie, *Europe: The Exceptional Case; Parameters of Faith in the Modern World* (London: Darton, Longman & Todd, 2002).

108. On pragmatism as a central feature of Pentecostalism, see Grant Wacker, *Heaven Below: Early Pentecostals and American Culture* (Cambridge, MA: Harvard University Press, 2001).

109. Martin, *Pentecostalism*; David Martin, *Tongues of Fire: The Explosion of Protestantism in Latin America* (Oxford: Blackwell, 1990). Numerous other scholars echo this insight. For example, Marshall points to how Nigerian Pentecostal churches provide rudimentary social security via reciprocal relations and "self-help" activities (*Political Spiritualities*, 115). This self-care is now internationalized through such things as remittances. See Gornik, *Word Made Global*, 210-13.

110. For an example of this kind of account, see Robert Woodberry, "Pentecostalism and Democracy: Is There a Relationship?" in *Spirit and Power: The Growth and Global Impact of Pentecostalism*, ed. Donald Miller, Kimon Sargeant, and Richard Flory (Oxford: Oxford University Press, 2013), 119-37.

neighborhoods be broken up and migrate in order to serve the flows of capital, goods, and services. The work of the Spirit is to reconstitute a social body in particular places that can act together for its own good—in the first instance through "inreach"—and then in pursuit of the welfare of others through "outreach."[111]

How are we to make sense of Pentecostalism's ambiguous relationship to capitalism?[112] Sociologically, one way is to borrow from Karl Polanyi's analysis of capitalism and draw an analogy between Pentecostalism and trade unionism, both of which are simultaneously creatures of and countermovements to capitalism. Polanyi argued that the formation of a global market system inherently led to spontaneous countermovements to re-embed market relations within social and political relations as populations and governments struggled to cope with the deleterious impact of an unregulated market on society and nature. Ruth Marshall's description of the advent of petrodollars in Nigeria captures something of the deleterious and all-encompassing nature of the rupture capitalism poses. She describes the chaotic liquefaction of existing patterns of political and social order that followed the pouring of oil money into Nigeria. Political leaders then utilized the resulting corruption and crisis as a formal mode of governance.[113] As one of her interviewees puts it:

> All our people are now caught in this intense craze for money. Money and women. People are terribly mean to each other now. The old trust, the open handshake is gone. There is so much hatred now, a lot of hatred and a lot of bitterness and a lot of greed and a lot of jealousy, in short, a lot of everything that is bad. And the reason is that everyone wants to be rich. So they steal from each other and plunder the nation's coffers and use the people carelessly and shamelessly.[114]

Countermovements seek to reembed labor, land, and money within a wider social and political matrix and thereby inhibit the destructive effects

111. Omar M. McRoberts, *Streets of Glory: Church and Community in a Black Urban Neighborhood* (Chicago: University of Chicago Press, 2003).

112. On the ambiguous relationship between Pentecostalism and capitalism, see Elaine Padilla and Dale Irvin, "Where Are the Pentecostals in an Age of Empire?" in *Evangelicals and Empire: Christian Alternatives to the Political Status Quo*, ed. Bruce Ellis Benson and Peter Goodwin Heltzel (Grand Rapids: Brazos, 2008), 183.

113. Marshall, *Political Spiritualities*, 99-107.

114. Marshall, *Political Spiritualities*, 95.

of commodification on political and social life. Part of the ambiguous relationship between Pentecostalism and capitalism lies in how Pentecostalism is both a form of acculturation to capitalism and a resignification of capitalism from within, thereby contextualizing and particularizing the supposedly universal "logic" of capital.[115] The Pentecostalization of capitalism (and thus its resignification) represents one instance of the inability of capitalism to subsume everyone and everything to a supposedly universal historical process of European origin.[116]

To draw an analogy, Pentecostalism is a kind of squatter's encampment within the structures and discursive registers of capitalism: capitalism determines its conditions but doesn't limit its possibilities. Like the barrios around cities such as Lagos and São Paulo, or the populist movements that reclaim land and factories in South America, Pentecostalism is occupying territory that does not belong to it while at the same time fully participating in the very structures that render it vulnerable. Yet it seeks to repurpose and resignify those very same structures. Its occupation is inherently unstable, temporary, adaptive, and precarious, and the faithfulness of its witness is systemically vulnerable to dissolution—whether by political and economic processes or by the internal irruptions of chaos and corruption. Nevertheless, as an occupation of capitalist space and time, it creates openings within that space and time to new possibilities.

We can speculate that part of the felt need for the political spirituality of Pentecostalism is to address the epistemic crisis and rupture that processes of capitalist modernization represent to traditional patterns of belief and practice. Social scientists have frequently envisaged the rise of Pentecostalism as a constructive response to the anomie induced by the structural and social deprivations capitalism brings.[117] However, framing the emergence of Pentecostalism as, on the one hand, a coping mechanism

115. For a parallel account of Pentecostalism along these lines, see Shane Clifton, "Pentecostal Approaches to Economics," in *The Oxford Handbook of Christianity and Economics*, ed. Paul Oslington (Oxford: Oxford University Press, 2014), 263–81.

116. For a critique of accounts of capitalism along these lines, see Dipesh Chakrabarty, *Provincializing Europe: Postcolonial Thought and Historical Difference* (Princeton: Princeton University Press, 2000).

117. See, for example, André Droogers, "Globalisation and Pentecostal Success," in *Between Babel and Pentecost: Transnational Pentecostalism in Africa and Latin America*, ed. André Corten and Ruth Marshall-Fratani (Bloomington: Indiana University Press, 2001), 49. See also, Robbins, "Globalization," 123. Robbins values such arguments but recognizes that they are not the whole story.

and, on the other hand, a form of exotic "time discipline" that prepares the "underdeveloped" to be ready for working within a capitalist economy is too reductive. It also wholly subsumes the history of Pentecostalism into the history of capitalism. Moreover, it misses the theological heart of the matter. For this, we must focus on the differing conceptions of time and space in Christianity and capitalism and how Pentecostalism mediates between them.

On any theological account of time, Christ's life, death, and resurrection are central. *Kairos* is one term used to name the kind of time the Christ event represents. Kairotic time is "systolic" in form: that is, like a moment of inhalation, kairotic time is contracted, enfolded, and tensely gathered into the Christ event awaiting its exhalation in renewed life-giving possibility.[118] Through Christ's life, death, and resurrection and the outpouring of the Holy Spirit, each moment is open to this life-giving possibility and capable of anticipating the eschatological consummation of all creation. In becoming enfolded in the Christ event, all time is liberated from its entropic movement toward nothingness and can be breathed out in infinite, fructifying variations. Subsequent kairotic events of the Spirit's action create further possibilities and variations. By contrast, chronological time is linear, regular, monotonous, and measurable.[119] It is also time devastated by the Fall. For it is time that leads inexorably to death—whether it is the duration and deaths of plankton, persons, or planets. By contrast, the kairotic time of Christ, through the work of the Spirit, opens chronological time to and suffuses it with eternal life.[120] And unlike chronological time, which can only be experienced by those existing at this moment, the kairotic time of Christ is a gift open to enjoyment by anyone at any time: hence talk of the communion of saints as a transtemporal and coinhering reality. We can thus experience two times or two histories simultaneously in the same place: kairotic time and its aftershocks, and chronological time and its duress.

Given the symbiotic relationship between our experience of time and our experience of space, we must attend to how a Christian view of time

118. On this see Paul J. Griffiths, *Decreation: The Last Things of All Creatures* (Waco, TX: Baylor University Press, 2014), 95-98. Systole refers to the moment when the heart is contracted, ready to drive the blood out from itself.

119. Griffiths, *Decreation*, 89-93.

120. For Moltmann's parallel but different conception of the healing and fulfillment of creation through the interplay of the eschatologically orientated Sabbath nature of creation and its consummation in the "Shekinah" glory of God that indwells creation, see *The Coming of God*, 261-67.

reconfigures a sense of place. Pentecostal constructions of place generate a subjectivity that is simultaneously local *and* attuned to and participating in globalized flows of people and products (e.g., music, social media, conference speakers, books, etc.).[121] Arguably, this Pentecostal subjectivity resonates with a theological view of place, which is hallowed not by means of a sacred geography—for example, by dint of its distance from Jerusalem or its relation to a division between spaces such as that between the *Dar al-Islam* and the *Dar al-harb*. Instead, it is hallowed by means of its participation in a particular time: the time of the Christ event. Through the Spirit, all places can participate in the Christ event, and our citizenship is in heaven—a spatiotemporal realm to which all times and spaces are present. Moreover, salvation is not from Rome (or, latterly, New York, Tokyo, Shanghai, or London). That is to say, salvation cannot come from any earthly political and economic project like capitalism for ordering, controlling, and stabilizing time and space. Rather it is eschatological: that is, it comes from "outside" of chronological time and beyond human agency and is inaugurated not by an earthly rule but by the cosmic rule of Christ.[122]

To foreshadow what I argue at greater length in chapter 13, the Spirit-empowered, Christ-orientated social relations of the *ekklēsia* should produce a distinctive sense of place. Paul's statement that the community is the "temple of the living God" points to how holiness is, in the first instance, socially rather than spatially manifested. Such things as ascetic practices, collective worship, patterns of gift relation, and shared experience, memories, and narratives construct holiness. These combine to form the constitutive elements of a "holy nation." This holy nation is, paradoxically, a people who are "resident aliens"; that is, they do not require a single, sovereign, bounded territory to be a people. This eschatological, relational, and temporally defined conception of place reconfigures attempts to sacralize one place or form of life as all-determinative. For example, in her study of Nigerian Pentecostals, Marshall points to how a simultaneously global and local sensibility involves the resignification of both the inheritance of the European missionaries *and* traditional, place-based religions. Theologically this entails reconfiguring sacralized geographies through an act of

121. In this respect Pentecostalism contrasts with Orthodox and mainline Protestant churches, which are prone to the heresy of phyletism. On this see chap. 13.

122. For an example of a pneumatological, relational conception of place attentive to conditions of globalization and the nature of Pentecostalism as a "glocal" ecclesial movement, see Wariboko, *The Charismatic City*, 99–117.

dual conversion: the conversion of the missionary constructions of Jesus as a European tribal deity and of local cosmologies into a Christian one.[123]

Capitalism, theologically understood, is, among other things, the idolatry of chronological time: it renders the time of death into the means of life. Capitalism represents in part the mystification of chronological time's death-dealing nature through the commodification of time itself. It is premised not only on a progressive view of time that attempts to manage and order time minutely through scientific, bureaucratic, and industrial forms of production but also makes buying and selling time a requirement to live. Marx pointed to the role of primitive accumulation in the form of the enclosure of common lands and the enslavement of colonized peoples in the emergence of industrial capitalism. Michael Hardt and Antonio Negri draw on this insight to argue that capitalism can only sustain itself through repeated acts of enclosure (contemporary examples include the gene pool or language itself).[124] However, what neither Marx nor Hardt and Negri address is how the enclosure of time through usury precedes the enclosure of common-pool resources and the commodification of people.[125] Charging interest on a loan came to be seen as an attempt to buy and sell time, which, as a gift of God, was to be shared by all (this was a key part of, for example, the Scholastic prohibition against usury).[126] Yet the buying and selling of time through charging interest is now axiomatic of contemporary finance capitalism, and other than in a diminishing slice of western Europe, the ability of most people to sustain a life through acquiring housing, education, and health care increasingly requires buying and selling time in the form of usury.

123. O'Neill observes a parallel process of rupture in relation to Maya spirituality and Roman Catholicism in his ethnographic work on Pentecostalism in Guatemala. O'Neill, *City of God*, 96–101.

124. Michael Hardt and Antonio Negri, *Commonwealth* (Cambridge, MA: Belknap Press of Harvard University Press, 2009).

125. It could be argued that Marx does include an account of the enclosure of time within his labor theory of value. Marx's account of capitalism is largely built on the coercive extraction of surplus time from the producing classes and the use of technology to make ever more efficient use of time and thereby extract greater value from labor. The homogenization of time and the overcoming of time as a limit are thereby central to Marx's critique of capitalism. On this see William James Booth, "Economies of Time: On the Idea of Time in Marx's Political Economy," *Political Theory* 19, no. 1 (1991): 7–27. However, Marx does not discuss the temporal dimensions of usury in his analysis of it.

126. John T. Noonan, *The Scholastic Analysis of Usury* (Cambridge, MA: Harvard University Press, 1957).

The commodification and financialization of time within capitalism represent the refusal of a church-world distinction because it is a refusal of an eschatological horizon marked in some way by a form of life orientated to and organized around that horizon. As the idolatry of chronological time, capitalism contends that chronological time is the only time that matters. In response, what is needed is the reclamation of time and space as a commonwealth free for all and the reopening of time to an eschatological horizon. Part of what any project of reclamation and reopening entails is the formation of a people and a sense of place that bear witness to the possibilities of kairotic time within the strictures that capitalist time disciplines demand.[127] Pentecostalism, at its best, witnesses to kairotic time amid the earthly city. Pentecostalism is not merely a countermovement analogous to trade unionism. It can also be a counterperformance of capitalist constructions of time and space within the institutional, symbolic, and representational forms of capitalism itself, a counterperformance that reverses the enclosure of time, redirecting it to its true end—Jesus Christ—thereby reopening chronological time to an eschatological horizon.

It is in the light of the above that we can ask whether Pentecostalism is a converted form of capitalism. The formation of a people who embody an eschatological or messianic horizon to history within the terms and conditions of history is vital if we are to challenge the absolutist claims of capitalism to shape human life and be the determinative end of history. Pentecostalism can be read as a way of forming such a people out of the ways and means of capitalism. It is at least theologically plausible that something like this is going on in Pentecostalism, framed as a diastolic moment or exhalation of the Spirit within capitalism, which itself is understood as an idolatrous construction of time and space.

Theologically, following the Spirit might well mean mimicking social realities not characteristically identified with the people of God. For example, Christ commends the faith of the pagan centurion against the faithlessness of Israel (Matt. 8:5-13).[128] Furthermore, the reconfiguring work of the Spirit enables the unholy possibilities of sinful and idolatrous forms of social,

127. The classic statement on time discipline is E. P. Thompson, "Time, Work-Discipline, and Industrial Capitalism," *Past and Present* 38 (1967): 56-97. Thompson argues that social movements such as Methodism and various nationalisms lead workers to "internalize" time discipline and so prepare an incipient working class to be fit for the logic of capital.

128. On this see Luke Bretherton, *Hospitality as Holiness: Christian Witness amid Moral Diversity* (Aldershot, UK: Ashgate, 2006), 105-14.

political, and economic life to become generative, proleptic disclosures of eschatological patterns of human sociality. A paradigmatic example of this transfiguring process at work is David's act of using a city (created by Cain and, as Augustine and others have argued, the paradigmatic embodiment of human alienation from God), and moreover, a pagan city, Jebus, as the basis of Jerusalem, a place where God's glory resided.[129] It is at least worth considering whether Pentecostalism points to how the Jebus of capitalism might be reconfigured to anticipate the new Jerusalem. What it might mean to convert capitalism is a theme explored more fully in chapter 11.

Conclusion

Making pneumatology, eschatology, and soteriology foundation stones of political theology gives a distinctive shape and orientation to how Pentecostals situate the church in relation to politics and economics. Both in its vernacular and formal modes, Pentecostal political theology contests modern, rationalistic frameworks for determining the meaning, purpose, and nature of political and economic life. For Pentecostals, political and economic relations are crucibles of divine activity within which the church comes to discern and participate in the ongoing work of the Holy Spirit in animating, healing, delivering, and generating new life, and bringing creation to consummation. In both theory and practice, church-world relations are dynamic and dyadic, dependent on the action of the Spirit to determine their character and form. A dyadic framework contrasts with those that see the church-world relation in terms of either a binary, where the church is always opposed to the world, or a dialectic, where the church supersedes the world. In Pentecostal political theology, it is not given to the church to define its relationship to the world. Rather, the primary agent in any such determination is the Spirit. The role of the church is to witness to and participate in the work of the Spirit, which can mean acting at times in continuity with the world and at other times in radical discontinuity with it. Moreover, acting freely in relationship with and for the neighbor does not mean looking to the state or the market as the primary or only locus of

129. Ezek. 16. Wariboko riffs on a parallel idea with his conception of how the secular city becomes the charismatic city, his term for anticipations of the new Jerusalem in history (*The Charismatic City*, 7-12). See also Jacques Ellul, *The Meaning of the City* (Carlisle, UK: Paternoster, 1997), 94-97.

political or economic agency. Ultimately, such means lack the necessary power to transform this present age, and more often than not, they create new or even worse problems. Real transformation is born out of attunement to and participation in the ongoing work of the Holy Spirit.

Threshold

Catholic social teaching, the topic of the next chapter, has a direct connection to Pentecostalism through the adoption of the charismatic movement within Catholicism (particularly by its vibrant, lay-led movements), while, as already noted, Pentecostal theologians draw on Catholic social teaching. An institutional expression of this engagement was the ecumenical dialogue between Pentecostals and the Roman Catholic Church, especially its fourth phase, between 1990 and 1997, which focused on mission and social justice.[130] However, the contrast between the two is instructive.

Pentecostalism is developing a political theology that is populist, eclectic, and polycentric in its constitution, emerging as it does from multiple points around the globe and having no fixed site of institutional authority. By contrast, Catholic social teaching is the result of a formally institutionalized process that draws on voices from many nations, but which radiates out from a single place—Rome—and source of authority—the magisterium of the papacy. A further contrast with Pentecostal political theology is that it is less apocalyptic in orientation and has less of a sharply drawn sense of the church-world distinction, presuming as it does upon the possibility of a shared rationality existing across cultures and between different faiths.

Suggested Readings for Further Discussion

Murray Dempster, "Christian Social Concern in Pentecostal Perspective: Reformulating Pentecostal Eschatology," *Journal of Pentecostal Theology* 2 (1993): 51-64.
Eldin Villafañe, "Toward an Hispanic American Pentecostal Social Ethic," in *The Liberating Spirit: Toward an Hispanic American Pentecostal Social Ethic* (Grand Rapids: Eerdmans, 1993), 193-222.

---

130. Kärkkäinen, "Are Pentecostals Oblivious to Social Justice?," 421-26.

Ogbu Kalu, *African Pentecostalism: An Introduction* (Oxford: Oxford University Press, 2008), chaps. 10 and 11.

Amos Yong, *In the Days of Caesar: Pentecostalism and Political Theology* (Grand Rapids: Eerdmans, 2010), chaps. 1 and 4.

Estrelda Alexander, "Recovering Black Theological Thought in the Writings of Early African-American Holiness-Pentecostal Leaders: Liberation Motifs in Early African-American Pentecostalism," in *A Liberating Spirit: Pentecostals and Social Action in North America*, ed. Michael Wilkinson and Steven Studebaker (Eugene, OR: Wipf & Stock, 2010), 23–52.

Nimi Wariboko, "Pentecostalism and Nigerian Society," in *Nigerian Pentecostalism* (Rochester, NY: University of Rochester Press, 2014), 278–97. Wariboko develops an account of sovereignty and how Pentecostal political theology operates on an axis of visibility and invisibility.

Wolfgang Vondey, *Pentecostal Theology: Living the Full Gospel* (London: Bloomsbury, 2017), chap. 9.

CHAPTER 5

Catholic Social Teaching

My focus in this chapter is the relationship between democracy and Catholic social teaching, and more specifically, how and why democracy became the normative form of political order advocated by the magisterium of the Roman Catholic Church. This focus provides a lens through which to understand Catholic social teaching (CST) as a form of political theology. My analysis differs from most other summary accounts of how Catholic social teaching developed. These accounts address what led to justifications for religious freedom and human rights, consider debates about church-state relations, and examine the distinctive concepts of CST, notably "subsidiarity," "solidarity," "social justice," and the "common good."[1]

In contrast to other accounts, I examine a number of the less obvious but more theological dimensions to the development of CST. The first is the emergence of a theological and sociopolitical conception of the role of the laity. The conception CST develops stands in contrast to, on the one hand, an anticlerical and secularizing *laïcité*, and on the other hand, a clericalism that accompanied reactionary and authoritarian "throne and altar"

1. Russell Hittinger, introduction to *The Teachings of Modern Roman Catholicism on Law, Politics, and Human Nature*, ed. John Witte and Frank Alexander (New York: Columbia University Press, 2006); Martin Rhonheimer, *The Common Good of Constitutional Democracy* (Washington, DC: Catholic University of America Press, 2013); Michael Schooyans, "Democracy in the Teachings of the Popes," *Proceedings of the Workshop on Democracy*, December 12-13, 1996, Pontificiae Academiae Scientiarum Socialum, 11-40; Paul E. Sigmund, "Catholicism and Liberal Democracy," in *Catholicism and Liberalism: Contributions to American Public Philosophy*, ed. R. Bruce Douglass and David Hollenbach (New York: Cambridge University Press, 1994), 217-41; J. Bryan Hehir, "The Modern Catholic Church and Human Rights: The Impact of the Second Vatican Council," in *Christianity and Human Rights: An Introduction*, ed. John Witte Jr. and Franklin S. Alexander (Cambridge: Cambridge University Press, 2010), 113-34.

political theologies. The work of Joseph de Maistre (1753–1821), Louis de Bonald (1754–1840), and the nationalistic and antidemocratic organization Action Française (founded in 1899) exemplifies the latter. Second is the role of theological anthropology and, in particular, the question of how humans participate in Christ's rule. Third is the development of a pluralistic— or what I will call "consociational"—vision of sovereignty and how such a vision differs from top-down, monistic, and transcendent conceptions of sovereignty. Fourth is the importance of labor to a proper understanding of human dignity. And last is the discovery of "society," as distinct from the market and the state, at the very moment of witnessing its perversion and collapse into a mass of atomized individuals brought on by either industrialized capitalism or totalitarianism. I shall briefly examine each of these to develop an account of why, in the contemporary context, Catholic social teaching comes to see democratic politics as a means of telling the truth about what it means to be human. And in the process of setting out this argument, I will provide an overview and introduction to Catholic social teaching as a form of political theology.

The Consecration of the Laity

Catholic social teaching emerged in part through the need to steer a path between the Scylla of revolutionary ideologies that would destroy the church and the Charybdis of reaction that would instrumentalize it as part of a toxic mix of autocracy and nationalism. Central to navigating this narrow path was reckoning with the role of the laity in Christian witness. As Leo XIII told his curial cardinals in 1892, the church's temporal mission needed to center upon "faith embodied in the conscience of peoples rather than restoration of medieval institutions."[2]

Like all paths, it had two sides. The question of how to reconfigure the relationship between clergy and laity marked one side. The question of how to renegotiate the relationship between church and state marked the other. As it turned out, the pathway by which to navigate both relationships was the same. "Society" became the point of mediation between clergy and laity and between church and state. A lexical shift heralded the emphasis on society as a core focus of concern. As Russell Hittinger notes, "After the

2. Quoted in Hittinger, introduction to *The Teachings of Modern Roman Catholicism*, 10.

pontificate of Leo XIII (1878-1903), *doctrina civilis* became *doctrina socialis*; for its part, *iustitia legalis* [legal justice] became *iustitia socialis* [social justice]."[3]

Evidenced in the birth of *socio*logy and *social*ism, the development of Catholic *social* teaching is part of a broader "discovery" of society in nineteenth-century thought. Society came to be seen as something distinct from the market, the state, and the church, and was understood to be the creature of none. Society was also distinct from nature. Part of the emphasis on society was in resistance to forms of naturalism, exemplified in social Darwinism, that saw social and political relations as subject to physical and biological laws. Unlike nature understood in deterministic ways, society could be subject to moral regulation rather than biological determination.

As the fruit of debates within Catholic political theology, a new emphasis on the laity as having a distinctive role formed the foundation of the emphasis on society in Catholic social teaching. Rather than a division between "throne" and "altar" wherein the laity were entirely subordinated to a role of obedience to and legitimation of church and state, the laity were seen to have their own agency and charism.[4] The vocation and offices of the laity needed valuing as part of their contribution to the formation of the people of God and the witness of the church in the world. In turn the laity became the means through which ecclesial authority could have "indirect" influence and avoid the twin problems of either the subordination of the church to political ends or the instrumentalizing of the state for ecclesial ends—a set of problems that had long bedeviled Christianity, from Constantine through to the Investiture Controversy, *Unam Sanctam* (1302), and beyond.[5] At the same time, hallowing the laity needed to be distinguishable from regimes of *laïcité* that would entirely privatize and marginalize

3. Russell Hittinger, "The Coherence of the Four Basic Principles of Catholic Social Doctrine—an Interpretation," in *Pursuing the Common Good: How Solidarity and Subsidiarity Can Work Together, Proceedings of the 14th Plenary Session, 2-6 May 2008*, ed. Margaret S. Archer and Pierpaolo Donati (Vatican City: Pontifical Academy of Sciences, 2008), 3.

4. There is an argument to be made that the "discovery" of the laity as a point of mediation between "throne" and "altar" is an extension and elaboration of a more ancient configuration of the crown and miter as types and vicars of Christ who are coresponsible for the good ordering of society. Alongside the offices of the clergy and the king, the laity could now take their place as exemplars and vicars of Christ within the body politic.

5. In the modern period, concern about the subordination of the church to immanent political ends underlies the Vatican's condemnation of Action Française in 1926, workerpriests in 1954, and liberation theology in 1984.

Christian belief and practice.[6] The task of illuminating the temporal order came to be entrusted to the laity so that not only would the church respect the "legitimate autonomy of the democratic order" but also that that order might respect the legitimate autonomy of the church.[7] The fruit of this process is visible in *Lumen Gentium*, which emphasized the *consecratio mundi* and the notion of specifically Christian service in the temporal sphere.[8] Catholic Action (a prodemocratic movement originating in Belgium) and, after 1945, such lay movements as Communion and Liberation, St. Egidio, and Focolare embody this consecration of the world via the laity.[9] An emphasis on "lay apostolic movements," the central role of the laity in the mission of the church, and the relationship between "the people" and the "people of God" were also a central concern of Latin American liberation theology.[10] And it is a constitutive feature of Pope Francis's teaching.[11]

The growing appreciation of the laity was driven in part by a response to facts on the ground. The involvement of figures such as Cardinal Manning in the 1889 London Dock Strike and the involvement of Catholics in trade unions and popular parties across late-nineteenth-century Europe were key catalysts for the thinking that went into *Rerum Novarum* (1891). Later, the experiences of both lay leaders and theologians, such as Henri de Lubac, during World War II became an important factor in generating deeper reflection on and involvement in democratic politics.

6. Emile Perreau-Saussine, *Catholicism and Democracy: An Essay in the History of Political Thought*, trans. Richard Rex (Princeton: Princeton University Press, 2012), 91–99, 109–27.

7. *Centesimus annus*, §47. Hugues-Félicité Lamennais had begun developing this distinction in the nineteenth century. But it was Yves Congar who articulated the first full-blown theology of the laity through his conception of a distinction of planes, a distinction that was later criticized by Latin American liberation theologians such as Gustavo Gutiérrez. See Yves Congar, *Lay People in the Church: A Study for a Theology of Laity* (Westminster, MD: Newman, 1965).

8. *Lumen Gentium*, IV, "The Laity." Picking up on themes first enunciated by John Paul II, Pope Francis links this temporal service explicitly to evangelization in his encyclical *Evangelii Gaudium*.

9. See Bradford Hinze, *Prophetic Obedience: Ecclesiology for a Dialogical Church* (Maryknoll, NY: Orbis, 2016), 7–9, 193–97.

10. See, for example, Gustavo Gutiérrez, *A Theology of Liberation: History, Politics, and Salvation*, rev. ed. (Maryknoll, NY: Orbis, 1988), 39–46, 59–60, and articles by Enrique Dussel, Pedro Ribeiro De Oliveira, and Leonardo Boff in *Concilium* 6, no. 176 (1984), focusing on "La Iglesia Popular: Between Fear and Hope."

11. Paul Vallely, *Pope Francis: Untying the Knots* (London: Bloomsbury, 2013). On the influence of *teología del pueblo* on Pope Francis, see chap. 13.

For example, the experience of cooperation with "secular" politicians as part of resistance movements or through being imprisoned together in concentration camps gave birth to a remarkable degree of cooperation between Social Democratic and Christian Democratic parties across Europe after 1945.[12] Christian Democracy as a political movement was born out of a rejection of both revolution and reaction and came to power after 1945 in Italy, Germany, and elsewhere in the ashes of fascism and in resistance to communism. Unlike the parties of revolution and reaction, postwar Christian Democratic parties, alongside Social Democratic parties, sought to be broad-based, drawing together the working and middle classes, Protestants and Catholics, socialists and capitalists. They refused an apocalyptic politics of fear, hate, and paranoia—which communism and fascism thrived on—and called for a politics of the common good.[13] It was this vision of politics that lay behind the formation of the Common Market (now the European Union) by, among others, Jean Monnet, and generated support for the United Nations by the likes of Jacques Maritain.

An emphasis on the public mission of the laity, however, presented its own set of problems. First was the question of how to avoid simply swapping the absolutist claims of a monarchy for those of popular sovereignty. Second was the problem of what it meant to be a people rather than a crowd or mass. The underlying issue is how the body of Christ and the body politic constitute a "catholic" or universal body in which all may participate and fulfill their respective vocations. Without reordering the whole to enable the full participation of the poor/the people, neither the people of God nor the demos is truly a people. It is instead a collectivized mass, a disaggregated crowd, or a constellation of competing interest groups. While the nature and basis of the body politic and the role of the body of Christ within it were contested and negotiated over millennia, industrialization and totalitarianism were the earthquakes that brought these questions into

12. James Chappel, *Catholic Modern: The Challenge of Totalitarianism and the Remaking of the Church* (Cambridge, MA: Harvard University Press, 2018), 144–81.

13. For overviews of the development of Christian Democracy as a political movement, see Michael P. Fogarty, *Christian Democracy in Western Europe, 1820–1953* (London: Routledge, 1957); Thomas A. Kselman and Joseph A. Buttigieg, *European Christian Democracy: Historical Legacies and Comparative Perspectives* (Notre Dame: University of Notre Dame Press, 2003); Wolfram Kaiser, *Christian Democracy and the Origins of the European Union* (Cambridge: Cambridge University Press, 2007); Stathis Kalyvas, *The Rise of Christian Democracy in Europe* (Ithaca, NY: Cornell University Press, 1996); and Chappel, *Catholic Modern*, 14–226.

focus in new and frightening ways.[14] Again, attention to the nature of society became the means of providing answers. Society was not amorphous but a multitude made up of distinct parts. Understanding what it meant to be a people or demos rather than a mass or crowd of individuals led to specific conceptions of, first, what it meant to be human, second, the nature of sovereignty, and third, the dignity of labor. These developments fed into and helped drive a broader *ressourcement* of Roman Catholic belief and practice that entailed a turn to doctrine and the Bible.

Participating in Christ's Offices

Intellectual and material processes of modernization presented a crisis to settled ways of understanding what it means to be human and how to order rightly social, economic, and political life. Modern "realists" on the left and right, who defined politics in amoral terms and focused on the exercise of unilateral power, tended to reduce what it means to be human to material concerns alone.[15] Catholic social teaching sought other kinds of answers, ones committed to the proposition that, as *Centesimus Annus* puts it, "there can be no genuine solution of the 'social question' apart from the Gospel."[16] Consequently, central to the development of Catholic social teach-

14. If *Rerum Novarum* can be read as an initial response to the problems raised by industrialization, the response to totalitarianism comes to fruition with Pius XII, who in the space of fourteen days in March 1937 issued encyclicals against fascism in Germany, communism in the Soviet Union, and atheistic liberalism in Mexico. As Hittinger notes, "Totalitarianism prompted Catholic thinkers to support democratic government, to call for domestic and international authorities to be bound by justiciable natural or human rights, and more generally to develop what can be called a bottom-up model of legal, political, and social thought" (introduction to *The Teachings of Modern Roman Catholicism*, 16). See also James Chappel, "The Catholic Origins of Totalitarianism Theory in Interwar Europe," *Modern Intellectual History* 8, no. 3 (2011): 561-90.

15. Charles Curran notes that for John Paul II both capitalism and Marxism share the same root problem—materialism. He states: "Wojtyla's philosophical personalism opposes the materialism of both Marxism and capitalism. *Laborem exercens*, the first social encyclical of the Wojtyla papacy continues the same approach by showing that capitalism and Marxism are based on what the pope calls 'materialistic economism,' a form of materialism that gives priority to the objective rather than the subjective aspects of work" (*The Moral Theology of Pope John Paul II* [Washington, DC: Georgetown University Press, 2005], 219).

16. *Centesimus Annus*, §5. The interrelationship between truth and freedom and how these are grounded in the gospel was a central theme in many of John Paul II's encycli-

ing was the realization that the only real basis for answering the question "what is a human?" was Jesus Christ.[17] Christ is the true human; Christ, and not some revolutionary ideology or bourgeois civilization, reveals the true nature and telos of humanity, and freedom and dignity are secured not through any historically contingent political or economic structure or power but through our participation in Christ as part of his body.

John Paul II's Apostolic Exhortation *Christifidelis Laici* (1988) is a meditation on the linkage between human participation in Christ, the constitution of the church as the people of God, and the role of the laity. It emphasizes again and again how the teachings of the Second Vatican Council envisage everyone who is part of the people of God sharing in Christ's threefold mission as prophet, priest, and king. The lay faithful in particular are called to be involved in "ordering creation to the authentic well-being of humanity" as part of their sharing "in the exercise of the power with which the Risen Christ draws all things to himself and subjects them along with himself to the Father, so that God might be everything to everyone (cf. 1 Corinthians 15:28; John 12:32)."[18]

Russell Hittinger argues that at the heart of the development of Catholic social teaching is the recovery of a notion of the *munus regale* as a way of understanding what it means to participate in Christ. In the Latin of the encyclicals, the word translated as "function" is *munus*, meaning service, office, gift, or vocation.[19] Pius XI introduces it to contrast with contractual notions of recognizing the dignity of individuals and associations. The vocations, or *munera*, of the laity are the means by which they participate in the offices/*munera* of Christ. This connection is articulated by Paul VI in the *Decree on the Apostolate of the Laity* (1965): "In the Church there is a diversity of ministry but a oneness of mission. Christ

cals; see especially *Redemptor Hominis* (1979), *Veritatis Splendor* (1993), and *Evangelium Vitae* (1995). Likewise, Benedict XVI's *Deus Caritas Est*, with its emphasis on the centrality of the love of God and neighbor to authentic charitable service, can be read as a profound reaffirmation of John Paul II's link between the gospel and the "social question" (see in particular *Deus Caritas Est*, §§33-38). This linkage was developed further in *Caritas in Veritate* (2009).

17. *Redemptor Hominis* (1979); *Dives in Misericordia* (1980).

18. *Christifidelis Laici*, §14. See also *Lumen Gentium*, §31 and §36.

19. Russell Hittinger, "Social Roles and Ruling Virtues in Catholic Social Doctrine," *Annales Theologici* 16, no. 2 (2002): 385-408, and "The Coherence of the Four Basic Principles of Catholic Social Doctrine—an Interpretation." On the definition of *munus*, see Émile Benveniste, *Indo-European Language and Society*, trans. Elizabeth Palmer (Coral Gables, FL: University of Miami Press, 1973), 150.

conferred on the Apostles and their successors the duty of teaching, sanctifying, and ruling in His name and power. But the laity likewise share in the priestly, prophetic, and royal office of Christ and therefore have their own share in the mission of the whole people of God in the Church and in the world."[20]

Inherent in the use of *munus* is an ontology that values a multiplicity and diversity of social forms, primarily the family, but also trade unions, professional societies, political parties, universities, and the like, as the means and outworking of our participation in the *munera* of Christ. In terms of political theology, the implication is that the state does not devolve, delegate, concede, or grant rights to persons; rather it is to facilitate the development of persons and their respective *munera* as these take shape in multiple forms of corporate and vocational life.[21] A condition of lay participation in Christ's offices is an active civil society and vibrant democratic politics, as they provide a space through which different vocations, offices, and social forms are lived out in practice. To embody the truth about what it means to be humans, the laity must have the opportunity for participation in the ordering of social, political, and economic life. Attempts to subordinate this social life to the state or the market are anti-Christic attempts to pervert the faithful ordering of creation. Likewise, a failure by clergy to value the integrity and autonomy of these temporal vocations is a failure to honor what it means for the church to be the people of God. The danger with such an approach is that the church as a *res publica* can disappear while "society"—under the aegis of either the market or the state—becomes the primary means through which the formation of the laity occurs. To counter such an implication, it is vital to understand the conception of sovereignty underlying an emphasis on the lay participation in the *munera* of Christ.

A Consociational Vision of Sovereignty

Directly related to a conception of the participation of the laity in the rule of Christ through a vibrant associational life is a "consociational" vision of sovereignty. "Consociation" is a term derived from the work of the seventeenth-century Protestant political thinker Johannes Althusius and

---

20. *Apostolicam Actuositatem*, §2.
21. See, for example, *Divini Redemptoris*, §31, and *Pacem in Terris*, §68 and §77.

means the art of living together.[22] It draws on the rich scriptural and theological trope of covenant. Largely mediated via the work of the German legal scholar Otto von Gierke (1841–1921), Althusius's work was a key point of reference in the debates that helped shape Catholic social teaching.

A consociational vision rejects a unitary, hierarchically determined understanding of the state and a top-down, transcendent, monistic conception of sovereignty.[23] Rather, a consociational (or confederal) polity is made up of a plurality of interdependent, self-organized associations. In such a compound commonwealth, rather than reducing federalism to a division of powers between different branches of government, federalism entails social and political plurality and the distribution of power among numerous forms of covenantal association. In a consociational vision of sovereignty, sovereignty arises from the bottom up, constituted as it is from multiple consociations. Sovereignty is an assemblage that emerges through and is grounded upon a process of mutual communication between consociations and their reciprocal pursuit of common goods. Rather than securing unity by legislative procedures, the transcendent nature of sovereign authority, or a centralized monopoly of governmental power, the quality of cooperation and relationship building is its basis. Sovereign authorities discover rather than impose order, while political judgment is about discerning and weighing up goods in common. These goods emerge through the complex weave of social and economic relations, customary practices, and institutional exchanges that constitute the body politic. Political judgment involves adjudicating what to do in order to fulfill these goods.

In a consociational account of sovereignty, the individual is not subordinated to a collective vision of peoplehood, as in nationalist, fascist, state socialist, and state communist regimes. As I will explore more extensively in chapter 13, polities characterized by one or another of these regimes may include democratic elements, but the foundation of the demos is a supposedly prepolitical species of peoplehood such as an *ethnos* or a *Volk*. In contrast to such conceptions of peoplehood, a consociational account begins with the formation of the people through families, trade unions, congregations, and the like. CST's emphasis on social, economic, and political plurality challenges collectivist, homogenous, and monistic conceptions of peoplehood and popular sovereignty. Understanding "the peo-

22. Johannes Althusius, *Politica*, ed. and trans. Frederick Carney (Indianapolis: Liberty Fund, 1995 [1964]), 17.

23. A consociational account of sovereignty is set out in more detail in chap. 12.

ple" as being made up of many parts prioritizes the relationship between distinct but reciprocally related consociations or forms of life. In Catholic social teaching, such an approach is seen as the best way of generating the collective self-rule of a people.

Maritain's influential personalist and pluralist vision of social, economic, and political life exemplifies such a consociational account.[24] He describes the plurality of society as "an organic heterogeneity" and envisages it as being constituted by multiple yet overlapping "political fraternities" that are independent of the state.[25] Maritain distinguishes his account of a consociational political society and economic life from fascist and communist ones that collapse market, state, and civil society into a single entity *and* from collectivist and individualistic conceptions of economic relations.[26] Pius XI makes a parallel distinction in *Quadragesimo Anno* (1931), §§ 94-96, as a way of distinguishing a Catholic corporatist vision of politics from fascist ones.[27] Crucially, for Maritain, society constitutes a sphere of "fraternal" relations that has its own integrity and telos. Nevertheless, society also serves the defensive function of preventing either the market or the state from establishing a monopoly of power. It thereby counteracts the instrumentalizing of social relations for the sake of the political order or commodifying them for the sake of the economy. Within the sphere of society there can exist multiple overlapping and—on the basis of subsidiar-

24. Jacques Maritain, *Man and the State* (Washington, DC: Catholic University of America Press, 1998 [1951]), and Maritain, *Integral Humanism: Temporal and Spiritual Problems of a New Christendom*, trans. Joseph Evans (New York: Scribner's Sons, 1968), 162-76.

25. Maritain, *Integral Humanism*, 163 and 171.

26. Maritain, *Integral Humanism*, 169-71, 186-95.

27. In CST, corporatist and personalist forms of civic association and economic organization are precisely a means of preventing the subsuming of all social relations to the political order. However, a variety of criticisms are made of the approach Catholic social teaching developed. John Milbank criticizes *Quadragesimo Anno* as giving too much ground to fascism and calls on CST to pay far closer attention both to socialism and to medieval forms of gothic or complex space (*The Word Made Strange: Theory, Language, Culture* [Oxford: Blackwell, 1997], 268-92). Oliver O'Donovan goes further and criticizes the very concept of subsidiarity. He argues that when it is understood as a way of protecting the integrity and relative autonomy of parts in relation to an overarching and integrating whole, then the totality of the whole always assumes an overriding, or even totalizing, claim in its movement toward an all-embracing unity (*The Ways of Judgment* [Grand Rapids: Eerdmans, 2005], 259). For O'Donovan, the need for CST to distinguish itself from fascism on this score is not incidental, but a problem intrinsic to the conceptualization of subsidiarity itself.

ity—semiautonomous forms of institutional life and association, forms that are not reducible to either a private or a voluntary association. However, as William Cavanaugh contends, Maritain's broader framework implies that the church ceases to be a body politic in its own right. By implication, the church thereby relinquishes to the modern nation-state the formation and socialization of human bodies even as it tends their souls.[28]

Even given Cavanaugh's critique, Maritain—and CST more generally—came to see that authoritarian and totalitarian forms of political order are not simply political problems but forms of idolatry that distort basic patterns of human life by subordinating them to the state.[29] The consociational form of sovereignty advocated by CST allows for the freedom of association that is an expression and condition of living a human life in fellowship with others. It also allows for the freedom of worship and conscience that Catholic social teaching has come to see as necessary to maintain a horizon of reference beyond wholly materialistic and political concerns. It is these freedoms that guard against the totalizing of political and economic life.

The Dignity of Labor

Determining the nature of sovereignty entails perceiving what it means to participate in Christ's rule while standing at the church door looking out. In contrast, valuing the dignity of work is to view the matter from the

28. As William Cavanaugh puts it: "The key difficulty with Maritain's project is that he makes the Christian community the repository of purely supernatural virtues which stands outside of time, and thus interiorizes and individualizes the Gospel. Because he has sequestered political virtue from any direct habituation in Christian community, the state becomes that community of habituation, the pedagogue of virtue" (*Torture and Eucharist: Theology, Politics, and the Body of Christ* [Oxford: Blackwell, 1998], 195). This critique can be extended to Christian Democratic parties, which eventually became aligned with a turn to the nation-state as both the sole keeper of the common good and the primary or only means of addressing social and economic ills via legal regulation and welfare programs. On the rejection of Maritain's nonstate-centric democratic vision by Christian Democratic parties, see Chappel, *Catholic Modern*, 144-81.

29. Like Maritain, Pius XII declared that the state is an instrument rather than an end. Its role is to facilitate the "natural perfection of man"; the purpose of a juridical order "is not to dominate but to serve, to help the development and increase of society's vitality in the rich multiplicity of its ends" (Pius XII, *Christmas Address*, 1942, http://w2.vatican.va).

perspective of the street. Whether in the home, the factory, or the office, work is the central means through which humans exercise their vocations and giftedness. CST contends that beyond questions about the material conditions of work is its moral status—work is constitutive of person-hood.[30] It is the moral and spiritual status of labor that undergirds notions of alienation, proletarianization, commodification, and other critiques of the indignity of modern work. As the Catholic Church reiterates again and again, the principle of the priority of labor—and thence the person—over capital is a necessary postulate of any moral vision.[31] *Laborem Exercens* summarizes this insight as follows: "Since work in its subjective aspect is always a personal action, an *actus personae*, it follows that the whole per-son, body and spirit, participates in it, whether it is manual or intellectual work."[32] To make labor serve and be subject to capital is to invert the moral order by making persons serve money. For CST, work, of whatever kind and in whatever field, is not only toil but also gift. Like all gifts, the fruit of human labor is a way in which the person is symbolically present to and recognizes others. Work, worker, and the objects and services produced are profoundly related. As part of the circulation of gifts that constitute life together, in all its dimensions, work generates a *habitus* or form of life. To make work degrading is to desecrate the personhood of the workers and demean a way of life. Conceptualized as part of how humans exercise their giftedness/*munus*, work points beyond class-based analyses that posit an inherent conflict between "labor" and "capital" to an understanding of work as constitutive of how humans forge a common world of meaning and action. Work can never be merely economic or reducible to a utility. It is always social, political, and spiritual as well. In CST, support for the labor movement and other forms of economic democracy is a necessary corollary of upholding the dignity of labor as part of human participation in Christ's rule.[33]

---

30. A contrast can be drawn here with the work of Hannah Arendt, and her distinc-tions between "work," "labor," and "action" in the generation of a common life and the realization of personhood in relation to others. See Hannah Arendt, *The Human Condition* (Chicago: University of Chicago Press, 1998 [1958]).

31. This is set out explicitly in John Paul II's encyclical *Laborem Exercens* (1981), which sees the nature and purpose of human work as the key to what it calls "the social ques-tion," that is, how, in the modern period, to make life more human. For an early state-ment along these lines, see John Ryan, *Distributive Justice* (New York: Arno, 1978 [1916]).

32. *Laborem Exercens*, §V.24.

33. Christian Democratic parties across Europe understood this well, if not theologi-

Democratic Politics as a Condition of Telling the Truth

The role of the laity in the witness of the church, a consociational vision of sovereignty, a pluriform understanding of society, and upholding the dignity of labor all entail putting people before program. We must take seriously the history, customary practices, and ordinary life of a people if the laity are to be hallowed, if a common life is to emerge through the interaction of consociations, and if the fruits of human labor and thence interpersonal and fulfilling forms of life are not to be subordinated to the state or the market. The life of a people is the conduit for humans partic- ipating in the *munus* of Christ and the means for generating the practical wisdom necessary for judgments about how to live well. Yet it is precisely this ordinary, customary, and common life of the people that is, in the mod- ern period, constantly subordinated to various legal, bureaucratic, tech- nocratic, or market-based procedures and principles. Sadly, what passes for democracy too often reproduces the corrosion of a common life, and Catholic social teaching is increasingly critical of what is seen as inauthen- tic forms of democracy. In contrast to the largely technocratic, managerial, and consumerist procedures for aggregating choices that take place under the mantle of democracy, participatory, relational, and grassroots forms of democratic organizing and association have emerged as a crucial way to protect society from its subordination to both market and state and thereby preserve the conditions for living a truthful and faithful life. The United Farm Workers union led by Cesar Chavez and Dolores Huerta, the Solidar- ity movement in Poland that overthrew communism, and the People Power Revolution in the Philippines that overthrew the Marcos dictatorship are but three historical examples of the requisite kind of democratic politics. Broad-based community organizing is another.[34]

---

cally, then in practice. Instead of either complete laissez-faire economics or the nation- alization of industry and the formation of command economies, they advocated for the codetermination of the firm by workers and management. This could entail a variety of means of ownership ranging from shareholder to cooperative and mutual owner- ship. Codetermination and economic democracy were the new "third way" between "Manchester" and "Moscow," allowing for both the independence of the firm and the participation of the worker within the firm's management, without involving the state as an overseer. See Chappel, *Catholic Modern*, 200–214, and Maurice Glasman, *Unnecessary Suffering: Managing Market Utopia* (London: Verso, 1996).

34. On how broad-based community organizing expresses key aspects of Catholic social teaching, see Austen Ivereigh, *Faithful Citizens: A Practical Guide to Catholic Social*

At this point, as well as distinguishing "authentic" from "inauthentic" democracy, we must distinguish democratic politics from electoral party politics and a parliamentary system of government. Catholic social teaching is officially agnostic about specific constitutional forms, holding an "accidentalist" view that Christianity is compatible with any number of governmental regimes. As *Pacem in Terris* puts it: "It is impossible to determine, once and for all, what is the most suitable form of government, or how civil authorities can most effectively fulfil their respective functions, i.e., the legislative, judicial and executive functions of the State."[35] However, the internal logic of Catholic social teaching commits it to the rule of law and a self-limiting state (i.e., something like a liberal polity), and the pursuit of a democratic body politic as distinct from a democratic system of government.[36] John Paul II outlines the conditions to be met by democracy if it is to be "authentic": "Authentic democracy is possible only in a State ruled by law, and on the basis of a correct conception of the human person. It requires that the necessary conditions be present for the advancement both of the individual through education and formation in true ideals, and of the 'subjectivity' of society through the creation of structures of participation and shared responsibility."[37] A participatory democratic society, as exemplified in relational and place-based forms of political and economic association such as community organizing, unions, and cooperatives, is a vital means through which the "structures of participation and shared responsibility" can be both upheld and performed.[38]

My argument here intersects with Bradford Hinze's parallel account of the connection between democracy and CST. Hinze contends that the

---

Teaching and Community Organising (London: Darton, Longman & Todd, 2010), and Hinze, *Prophetic Obedience*, 151-64

35. *Pacem in Terris*, §67.

36. *Centesimus Annus*, §46, frames support for a democratic system of government in the following terms: "The Church values the democratic system inasmuch as it ensures the participation of citizens in making political choices, guarantees to the governed the possibility of both electing and holding accountable those who govern them, and of replacing them through peaceful means when appropriate."

37. *Centesimus Annus*, §46.

38. Broadly stated, a democratic body politic/civil society serves three interrelated roles: it is protective (securing space for the development of different forms of consociation), integrative (enabling the integration and communication between different associations), and transformative (generating critique, resistance, and new ideas and inclusions).

church only fulfills what it means to be the people of God when it is in dialogue intramurally through synods and councils that include the laity in the deliberative and decision-making processes of the church. This intramural process is matched extramurally through participation in forms of democratic politics that enable the church to hear the laments of its neighbors and so respond faithfully. These intramural and extramural processes of listening and shared deliberation go alongside listening to tradition and Scripture.[39] Such a process of double listening enables mutual "accountability and transparency" between officeholders, community leaders, and the faithful as well as those outside the church. This process is a constitutive element of what Hinze calls "prophetic obedience." As he summarizes it: "The prophetic character of the people of God is realized in and through synodality in the church, and in and through democracy in civil society."[40]

Conclusion

In Catholic social teaching, democratic politics is a vital means by which to build up a truthful and humble politics and a faithful, penitent church. First, participatory and grassroots democratic politics and economic democracy ensure that the state and market recognize that humans have ends and vocations beyond political and economic life and that the role of the market and the state is to serve humans, not vice versa. A vibrant, pluralistic civil society, alongside a commitment to truth and the dignity of the person, helps prevent democracy from becoming a "thinly disguised totalitarianism."[41] Second, a consociational, democratic body politic or civil society provides a context through which the church learns to listen to and love others and for humans to exercise their *munus regale*. Lastly, democratic politics is an important way in which the church learns to tell the truth about itself. As a means of listening, democracy is a therapy for the self-love or pride that is the attempt to secure oneself outside of relationship with God and pursue illusions of self-sufficiency in relation to both God and neighbor. When I listen to someone, I encounter that person nei-

39. For my own, prior account of "double listening" as the basis of faithful politics, see Bretherton, *Christianity and Contemporary Politics* (Malden, MA: Wiley-Blackwell, 2010), 213–15.

40. Hinze, *Prophetic Obedience*, 38.

41. *Centesimus Annus*, §46.

ther as a statistic nor a stereotype but as a human being, as one who bears the image of God with all the density and complexity being human entails. In sum, listening is vital to deepening our moral conversion in relation to God and others and thus our ability to reason rightly about what is the just and truthful judgment to be made with these people, at this time, in this place. To know what is true, we must first listen. In certain configurations, democratic politics is one such way of listening well.

Threshold

Alongside Pentecostalism, Roman Catholicism is the largest current in Christianity worldwide. Rhizome-like, Pentecostal political theology grows and extends along multiple interconnected nodal points around the world. As a formal body of thought, Catholic social teaching is more radial in form, issuing from a central authority. The next chapter deals with Anglican political theology. Anglicanism is also a worldwide church, but rather than being rhizomatic or radial, its political theology is fluvial in form. Many streams feed into a main river from which numerous tributaries emerge. It is less institutionalized and more eclectic in form and genre than Catholic social teaching, but less populist and more formalized than Pentecostal political theology.

CST is a vital interlocutor for Anglican political theology, which envisages itself as Catholic and Reformed. And while having a very different set of theological rationales and conclusions, they share a number of concerns: for example, how to conceive the relationship between plurality and commonality in political order; how to respond to capitalism and secularizing forms of liberalism; the reception of Marxism; the compatibility of Christianity and socialism; and how to address poverty worldwide.

Suggested Readings for Further Discussion

Leo XIII, *Rerum Novarum* (1891). All encyclicals are available online from vatican.va.

Jacques Maritain, *Christianity and Democracy*, trans. Doris C. Anson (New York: Scribner's Sons, 1944).

Jacques Maritain, *Man and the State* (Washington, DC: Catholic University of America Press, 1998 [1951]).

John XXIII, *Pacem in Terris* (1963).

Second Vatican Council, *Gaudium et Spes: Pastoral Constitution on the Church in the Modern World* (1965).

John Paul II, *Centesimus Annus* (1991).

Francis, *Laudato Si'* (2015). This encyclical articulates how economic relations should serve ecological as well as human flourishing.

CHAPTER 6

Anglicanism

Anglican political theology (APT) is a diffuse and multifaceted tradition.[1] Sketched here is a constructive account that recognizes divergence and convergence while drawing on a deliberately eclectic range of sources to illustrate the full scope of the tradition. A central premise of the chapter is that all political theologies, either explicitly or implicitly, work with a determinate conception of how to situate humans in time and space. This premise provides the central thread in my account of the historical development of APT. The first section outlines APT's characteristic political rationality. This provides a backdrop to a consideration of the relationship between three distinct yet interrelated phenomena—church, nation, and state—and how they were understood as together constituting a polity. A central theme of the chapter is how APT sought to coordinate these different elements within a coherent vision of good order and how that order was understood to be related to and a vehicle for the work of God in history. The focus on the right ordering of church, nation, and state generates an absent presence in APT: it tends to avoid any explicit discussion of power as, in contrast to Black Power and Pentecostalism, it assumes the possession of power. Given this assumption, the primary focus is the right ordering of power rather than the problem of how to get power, thereby muting the need to ask questions about who has power and why.

The second half situates APT in the context of how Anglicanism is in part a response to processes of modernization. It then outlines how key concerns of APT emphasize a way of imagining the role of church and nation within history, with providence as an important doctrinal point of

---

1. While used here generically, "Anglicanism" was only coined as a term by John Henry Newman in the 1830s.

reference. Given its historical provenance, there is an unavoidable emphasis on the Church of England. That said, the Church of England serves as a case study of dynamics shared by all parts of the Anglican Communion.

As mentioned in the introduction, alongside the chapter on Pentecostal/charismatic political theology, this chapter is also a way to make sense of the strengths and weaknesses of a tradition central to my own formation.

What It Is Not

APT is not a defined system of thought. Unlike Catholic social teaching, Anglicanism has no formal body of encyclicals. Nor does it refer to a distinct confession or creed: the Thirty-Nine Articles rarely, if ever, appear as a reference point in APT.[2] In contrast to Lutheran and Calvinist traditions of moral and political thought, there is no single foundational figure whose body of work serves as a constant reference point for further reflection. And unlike those churches emerging from the Radical Reformation, such as the Mennonites, there are no distinctive practices—for example, adult baptism and pacifism—that undergird a correlative set of political commitments (such as freedom of conscience, church-state separation, and nonviolence). APT's characteristic thinkers are essayists and writers of ad hoc treatises, rather than creators of formal, internally consistent systems of thought. Reflecting its dual nature as Catholic and Reformed, Anglicanism draws on numerous traditions and approaches to social and political reflection. But for all its ecumenical and philosophical bricolage, APT tends to favor practical over theoretical forms of rationality and is orientated to questions of political order in a distinctive way: it is a church for a particular place and history rather than for a gathered people.

Anglicanism shares with other Protestant traditions a commitment to the primacy of Scripture—a point foregrounded in its evangelical streams. However, the form political theology takes within it has many genres: history, art, and literature can all be vital conduits for its articulation. Poets and novelists such as George Herbert (1593–1633), Jonathan Swift (1667–1745), Anthony Trollope (1815–1882), and Dorothy L. Sayers (1893–1957), alongside historians such as Thomas Macaulay (1800–1859), R. H. Tawney (1880–1962), and Maurice Cowling (1926–2005), represent the political

---

2. The exception that proves the rule is Oliver O'Donovan, *On the 39 Articles: A Conversation with Tudor Christianity* (Carlisle, UK: Paternoster, 1986).

imagination of Anglicanism as much as its theologians or political thinkers. Some figures, notably Samuel Taylor Coleridge (1772-1834), combine the role of theologian, political thinker, and poet. Indeed, Coleridge's work illustrates a central feature of APT.

Contemplative Pragmatism

Coleridge exemplifies an emphasis on practical reason as the basis of political judgments in APT and inaugurates a focus on history and forms of life as the primary loci of inquiry. Natural law, doctrine, Scripture, and philosophy may well be vital elements in the subsequent development of a moral or political position, but attention to ways of imagining life together is what initiates and provides an essential reference point for Coleridge, and by extension, APT. Later in the nineteenth century, the educator and historian Thomas Arnold (1795-1842), the theologian and one of the founders of Christian socialism F. D. Maurice (1805-72), and liberal politician and prime minister William Gladstone (1809-1898) further developed Coleridge's ideas, and they, in turn, influenced Christian socialists and liberals. In the contemporary context, we can discern the watermark of Coleridge's concerns, particularly his emphasis on the role of culture, history, and the imagination in shaping the good life, in figures such as Desmond Tutu, Sarah Coakley, Kathryn Tanner, Graham Ward, and Elaine Graham. Even Oliver O'Donovan, for whom Scripture and doctrine are central to the articulation of his political theology, still makes history (notably, intellectual history) and contextually situated prudential judgments a constitutive feature of his methodology. Indeed, O'Donovan's understanding of creation in many ways echoes that developed by Coleridge.[3]

In a gesture that has since become characteristic of Anglican theology, Coleridge rejected a notion of natural law as that which can be excavated by reason alone. Instead, he saw creation as an open yet unfinished cosmos, the value of which is not objectively given but depends on the human capacity to participate in it via symbolic processes of meaning making. That is to say, the human self stands in an interpretative and constantly evolving relationship to creation.[4] Thus, overly abstract kinds of reasoning

3. See Oliver O'Donovan, *Self, World, and Time* (Grand Rapids: Eerdmans, 2013).
4. Thomas Pfau, *Minding the Modern: Human Agency, Intellectual Traditions, and Responsible Knowledge* (Notre Dame: University of Notre Dame Press, 2013), 489.

render humans not only mere spectators but also spectral beings alienated from any actual form of life. By contrast, close attention to, participation in, and openhearted wonder about the world around us can generate imaginative visions for inhabiting creation in more nourishing, concrete, and profound ways. The world as it is can then be brought into conversation with and reimagined through the life, death, and resurrection of Jesus Christ as narrated in Scripture.

On this approach, it is neither reason nor nature, but culture and history, that connect and divide humans from each other, and it is not simply better ideas or principles that are needed but a conversion of our imagination and a change of practice. Coleridge, abhorring Jacobin and anti-Jacobin tendencies alike, held that a humane culture must have an interplay between "permanence"—the tending of our inherited customs and traditions—and "progression"—innovation and development of new approaches.[5] And specifically echoing the theologian Richard Hooker (1554-1600)—a founding figure of APT—Coleridge sees custom as able to embody reason, leading to a preference for what is already established as that which is reasonable rather than for innovation, which must be carefully scrutinized and tested. However, Coleridge was alive to how we are always caught between continuity and change and so must learn to live and act as frail, time-bound creatures in need of shared forms of life that can adapt and innovate. As will be seen, however, APT consistently struggles to hold the creative and necessary tension Coleridge established between continuity and change.

Echoing Coleridge, APT does not posit a nature/culture binary. Rather, in contrast to natural-law approaches to moral and political theology, it recognizes that a specific cultural-historical form of life is the beginning point and primary focus for political reflection. Thus, for example, Desmond Tutu's homiletic reflections on South Africa are informed by the need to evaluate a particular context within its cultural-historical situation as well as in relation to its conformity to Christ.[6] Instead of focusing on nature, which tends to de-historicize and mystify what is contingent and fallen, APT's focus on culture and history recognizes that contingency, and thence revisability, is a constitutive feature of all forms of life. Such a view is not against a notion of nature per se; rather it recognizes that our

5. *The Collected Works of Samuel Taylor Coleridge*, vol. 10, *On the Constitution of the Church and the State*, ed. John Colmer (Princeton: Princeton University Press, 1976 [1839]).

6. Desmond Tutu, *Hope and Suffering: Sermons and Speeches* (Grand Rapids: Eerdmans, 1984).

experience of nature is always already historical and cultural and thereby fallen and finite. To name nature requires poetic, historical, and cultural insight, along with forms of practical reasoning, not adherence to formal laws or speculative and abstract rationalizations.[7] Rowan Williams calls such an approach "contemplative pragmatism" and sees it as a hallmark of Anglican thought. He traces it back to Hooker, of whom he states: "He is pragmatist to the degree that the accumulation of historical precedent has real intellectual weight, in the light of our ineradicable folly, selfishness and slowness as human thinkers, and he is contemplative to the degree that his guiding principles are seen by him as received, not invented, as the uncovering of a pattern of 'wisdom' in the universe, focused in and through the Word incarnate."[8]

APT's political rationality is focused not on blueprints for how to live but on proposing settlements for how the church, nation, and state might be properly related within existing historical conditions.

Sociality and Plurality

Hooker developed an early and influential view of the church-nation relationship and how to articulate it within state structures. He assumed that the populace of the commonwealth and the laity were one and the same, with Parliament being a synod of the laity.[9] In Hooker, this paradigm is aligned with a conception of the ideal polity as being modeled on the "Hebrew Commonwealth" and constituted by one people, one religion, and one law under God. This is a form of *integralism*. The danger with it is that it converts a contingent relation into a providential necessity by presuming that there should be an organic unity between the people of God and the

---

7. The emphasis on practical reason given here contrasts with the "middle axioms" approach as developed by the likes of the liberal Anglican Ronald Preston. Preston's approach deduces abstract principles from theology and then applies them to particular contexts or areas of specialist knowledge. It favors theoretical and technical over practical reasoning. Yet, arguably, as understood by their progenitor, J. H. Oldham, middle axioms can be more like rules of thumb that aid contextually situated practical reason. See, for example, Willem Adolph Visser 't Hooft and Joseph Houldsworth Oldham, *The Church and Its Function in Society* (London: Allen & Unwin, 1937).

8. Rowan Williams, *Anglican Identities* (Cambridge, MA: Cowley, 2003), 38-39.

9. Richard Hooker, *Of the Laws of Ecclesiastical Polity*, vol. 3, ed. P. G. Stanwood (Cambridge, MA: Belknap Press of Harvard University Press, 1981), 316-31.

English people. Yet when the *ekklēsia* and the *ethnos* are so closely identified, then dissent from what is considered orthodoxy is heard as sedition
and rebellion becomes a form of blasphemy. Jews, Catholics, Dissenters,
and atheists are not merely nonconformists who contest the status of ecclesial authority and the normativity of certain beliefs, they are potential
enemies of the people, and their very existence calls into question the basis of the political order. Crises in the body politic are not mere signs of
decrepitude and sin but are keenly felt as wounds in the body of Christ.
A muted version of integralism was revived with Tractarian ideas about
the "confessional state" in the nineteenth century, leading John Keble
(1792-1866) to preach that failure to uphold the integral union of church
and state was a form of "national apostasy."[10] Within an integralist configuration, what is secular is that which is not directly ecclesial, but the nation
is normatively understood as Christian even if non-Christian others are
tolerated as part of it.

One alternative to integralist visions of the interrelationship of church,
nation, and state is a *comprehensive* view in which the church should care for
the nation as a whole but does not claim to be coterminous with the whole.
On this account, partly inspired by Coleridge but further developed by F. D.
Maurice, the church is the bearer of the nation's traditions and upholder of
a truly national faith, but this does not require uniformity of confession in
public life. Neither does the church have a merely contractual relationship
with the state, as William Warburton (1698-1779) argued in *The Alliance
between Church and State* (1736). Rather, there is a covenant between the
established church and the nation that gives historical expression to the
nation's underlying spiritual unity in Christ.

Colonial developments, notably the creation of the Episcopal Church in
the United States as an independent church in 1789, instigated the need to
reimagine plurality and commonality in the public sphere. The Episcopal
Church became one denomination among many, and unlike the Church
of England, could not look to state structures as a point of connection between church and nation. While the nation remained the fundamental unit
of political order, the Episcopal Church and then subsequent Anglican
churches had to imagine different, less state-centric kinds of relationships
to the nations they served. For some, such as Kenyan bishop David Gitari
(1937-2013), South African bishop Desmond Tutu (b. 1931), and Palestinian

---

10. "National Apostasy" is the name of a sermon preached by John Keble on July 14,
1833. It is often cited as a point of initiation for the Oxford Movement.

priest Naim Stifan Ateek (b. 1937), this could take an oppositional stance toward state officials in defense of the integrity of the nation.[11] For others, such as the black Episcopal abolitionist Peter Williams Jr., this could mean a call to transcend the nation in the name of humanity while pointing to the barbarity of Europeans involved in the slave trade, with their "adamantine heart of avarice, dead to every sensation of pity."[12] Contrary to British strands of APT, many non-European strands had to confront situations of systemic oppression and powerlessness (e.g., apartheid in South Africa). Therefore, rather than focus on how best to order existent forms of power, they have had to make explicit questions about the conditions of agency (and thus, how the powerless can get power) and the justice of the political system as such. More recently, internal debates within the Anglican Communion over issues such as same-sex marriage have generated questions about the constitution and distribution of power within the communion. In terms of ecclesial polity, the rootedness of Anglican churches in national contexts means the communion as it has emerged is consociational in structure: it is a communion of communions rather than an indivisible whole directed from a single monarchical center.

Post-Holocaust and with the rapid loss of empire after 1945, Britain saw a move away from a providential view of the relationship between church and nation. This shift, combined with an intensification of ethnic and religious diversity due to inward migration from former colonies, pressed the question of what it means for the church to negotiate a common life with various Christian and non-Christian others, while at the same time negotiating a constructive but critical relationship to the state and the market.[13] Should the state still be the point of unity with the nation? And what makes a nation? These questions came to be aligned with a critique of secularism. Rather than accepting a determination of the secular as that-which-is-not-religious, a more theological and historically attuned one

11. David Gitari, *In Season and out of Season: Sermons to a Nation* (Carlisle, UK: Regnum, 1996), and "'You Are in the World but Not of It,'" in *Christian Political Witness*, ed. George Kalantzis and Gregory Lee (Downers Grove, IL: IVP Academic, 2014), 214-31; Tutu, *Hope and Suffering*; Naim Stifan Ateek, *Justice and Only Justice: A Palestinian Theology of Liberation* (Maryknoll, NY: Orbis, 1989).

12. Peter Williams Jr., "An Oration on the Abolition of the Slave Trade; Delivered in the African Church in the City of New York, January 1, 1808," University of Nebraska-Lincoln, https://digitalcommons.unl.edu/etas/16/.

13. These developments are generating more explicit reflections on power. See, for example, Stephen Sykes, *Power and Christian Theology* (London: Continuum, 2006).

emerged.[14] This defined the secular as that-which-is-not-eschatological. The secular thereby becomes identified as an ambivalent space and time constructed through the interaction of multiple forms of belief and unbelief. The church is neither for nor against what is secular (understood as that-which-is-not-eschatological), neither is the church reducible to a separate (and private) "religious" sphere.[15] Rather, state and nation should be "faithfully secular," such that theological beliefs and ecclesial practices coconstruct and are interwoven with other patterns of belief and practice to constitute a common life through genuine plurality, albeit one bounded by the conditions and possibilities of life in the earthly city.[16]

Finally, a *consociational* position was built on the work of John Neville Figgis (1866–1919) to develop an alternative to an integralist and comprehensive view.[17] Such a position draws on early modern "ancient constitutionalism" exemplified in a figure such as Robert Molesworth (1656–1725) and represents an alternative to the social contract tradition represented by John Locke (1632–1704).[18] Following Augustine, Figgis posits a disjuncture between the church and broader social realities and does not view the nation in organic terms as an expression of some prepolitical *ethnos* or ideal: the nation is a historically constructed and irreducibly plural body politic. Christianity neither has to be nor should be the foundation of political order, but neither should Christians exclude themselves from contributing to national life. National life itself is more than just the sum of individual choices or the outcome of conflicting group interests: it is a common life constituted by multiple forms of overlapping association. The interaction of these associations, the ad hoc commensurability between their different visions of the good, and the common objects of love they discover together generate the contingent moral consensus on which a common life is based. The role of the state is to uphold a rule-bound, accountable, and equitable

14. On the history of the changing historiography, see Jeremy Morris, "Secularization and Religious Experience: Arguments in the Historiography of Modern British Religion," *Historical Journal* 15, no. 1 (2012): 195–219.

15. For example, Oliver O'Donovan and Rowan Williams both develop accounts along these lines.

16. See chap. 8 for my exposition of such an account.

17. As noted in the previous chapter, the term "consociation" means a mutual fellowship among distinct institutions or groups that are federated together for a common purpose. For a broader discussion of the term, see chap. 12.

18. See Jacob Levy, *Rationalism, Pluralism, and Freedom* (Oxford: Oxford University Press, 2015), 106–40.

arena of earthly peace that enables the negotiation of a just and merciful common life between diverse communities. The primary good the state itself seeks is the good of political association/commonwealth/common life and the structures and programs that uphold this good. Pursuing the good of association sustains the concrete conditions of freedom, as freedom is in great measure dependent on participation in both proximate and broader forms of association. Without being embedded in some form of group or institution, the individual citizen is naked before the power of either the market or the state and lacks a vital means for his or her own self-cultivation. For freedom to be possible and an associational life to flourish, a plural and "complex" political space, one with myriad institutional configurations, is needed to preserve the space of negotiation and interaction.[19]

On this consociational account there can be a mutually disciplining yet critically constructive relationship between the church and the broader body politic/nation. The church is distinct from yet also a constituent element of the consociational body politic. In joint action in pursuit of common goods, the church has to listen to and learn from its neighbors (and perhaps, thereby, encounter the fresh work of the Spirit). Conversely, Anglicanism, as a moral tradition with an eschatological vision of the good, brings a wider horizon of reference and relationship to bear upon the immediate needs and demands of the body politic. This mutual disciplining helps ensure that when it comes to earthly politics, both state and body politic remain directed toward penultimate ends while still being open to recognizing that humans don't live by bread alone (i.e., there are purposes, meanings, and loyalties beyond the realm of politics and economics that must be given space and time).[20]

Williams calls this approach "interactive pluralism" and grounds it christologically. Contrary to Coleridge and Maurice, for Williams the incarnation is not brought to expression through culture and history. Rather, the incarnation of Jesus Christ challenges and contests any culture's sense of itself. At the same time, humans can only know the truth about God and what it means to be a creature through finitude and risking negotiated historical relations with others (including nonhuman others). Through partic-

---

19. John Milbank, "On Complex Space," in *The Word Made Strange: Theology, Language, Culture* (Oxford: Blackwell, 1997), 268-92.

20. Part of what my work is doing is contributing to the development of a consociational approach.

ipation in the world around us, humans may discover and then make sense of who we are in relation to God and others. This requires attentiveness to and reception of a world we did not make and others we do not control yet with whom we must order our social, economic, and political relationships. Attentiveness and reception—characterized by a posture of listening or contemplation—are the precursor of shared speech and action and thence the coming into being of a common life.

Following Coleridge, APT cannot be divorced from history and the concrete particulars of life. Therefore, any understanding of APT today necessitates an understanding of the ways in which the Church of England was never hermetically sealed within the bell jar of the British Isles and then, at a certain point, exported elsewhere. It came to be within the interactions shaping the Atlantic world from the fifteenth century onward. This was the beginning of a world that saw the creation, destruction, and re-formation of whole cultures across the Atlantic basin.

Anglicanism as a Modern Social Imaginary

An early instantiation of how the nation is imagined in the context of the emerging Atlantic world is the "Ditchley portrait" of Elizabeth I (1592). The painting shows Elizabeth standing on a map of England with her feet in Oxfordshire, physically facing the Atlantic and continental Europe. Ships travel to and fro from the four corners of the earth. Behind her are dark stormy skies and before her, the clouds are clearing to reveal sunshine.[21] It is a piece of political theology that inscribes English royal rule in cosmic terms. The picture depicts a correspondence between the cosmic order, Elizabeth's sovereignty, and her possession of land, trade, and sea power. From Elizabeth's reign onward, the development of England and the commercial and naval preeminence of Britain became seen as providential for the worldwide spread of the gospel.

The life and writings of John Locke exemplify the connection between APT, the Atlantic world, and colonial rule. As secretary to the Council of Trade and Plantations (1673-1674) and, later, a member of the Board of Trade (1696-1700), Locke was a well-informed observer of the interactions shaping the Atlantic world of the late seventeenth century. And as a

21. Elizabeth is depicted both as the goddess Fortuna—Renaissance art and literature's ruling deity of politics—and as one favored by fortune.

shareholder in the Royal African Company, a key catalyst in the formation of the Atlantic slave trade, he actively invested in this world. Intellectually, Locke's defense of individual rights and liberties is correctly hailed as a fountainhead of liberalism. Yet, as exemplified in the Fundamental Constitutions of the Carolinas, adopted in 1669, he was part of a milieu that sought to legitimize, philosophically and in practice, patrician rule throughout the emerging colonies. And, as James Tully argues, Locke's work came to serve as an ideological justification for the expropriation of lands from America's indigenous peoples.[22]

Many subsequent figures in the tradition wrestled with the worldwide mission of the church, the civic responsibilities of Christians within that mission, and the role of political authorities not just within a national context but also in a capitalist, colonial, and then postcolonial one. By the time the British Empire covered its greatest landmass in 1922, this consciousness of a broader responsibility to the world at large had reached a similarly expansive scope. As symbolically represented by Greenwich mean time, Britain had come to stand at the center of the world, with everything else classified and ordered in relation to this center. The ambiguities and tensions of this self-consciousness are illustrated by missionary J. H. Oldham's (1874-1969) role in labor and education issues in Kenya and India through the 1920s and '30s and his critique of what he called "white settler civilization" in his 1924 book *Christianity and the Race Problem*. The self-consciousness can be overheard in William Temple's (1881-1944) declaration two years later that in the British Empire "we cannot doubt that we have found something fashioned in the providence of God for the fulfillment of his purpose,"[23] while in the same year he opined that God is Father to "the unemployed at home, to the refugees from oppression in the near East, to the 'untouchable' outcasts of India . . . [and so i]f we are to say 'Our Father' with full right, it must be in union with all these; it must be for the satisfaction of their needs as truly as our own that we pray."[24] Evangelical strands of Anglicanism also display this consciousness of a global responsibility. John Stott's (1921-2011) role in evangelicalism worldwide exemplifies this, and in particular his involvement in drafting the 1974 Lausanne Covenant. The covenant directed evangelicals to affirm

22. James Tully, *Strange Multiplicity: Constitutionalism in an Age of Diversity* (Cambridge: Cambridge University Press, 1995).

23. William Temple, "Christianity and the Empire," *Pilgrim* 6 (1926): 447-57.

24. William Temple, *Personal Religion and the Life of Fellowship* (London: Longmans, Green, 1926), 38.

that "The message of salvation implies also a message of judgment upon every form of alienation, oppression and discrimination, and we should not be afraid to denounce evil and injustice wherever they exist."[25] It drives Archbishop George Carey's partnership with the World Bank to initiate the World Faiths Development Dialogue in 1998 in order to strengthen connections between religious leaders and development institutions to address poverty around the world.[26] All these moments suggest a certain orientation to history, an unquestioned assumption that one possesses power to change things, and a sense that the church has a responsibility to stabilize and improve the world as it is.

Throughout the history of Anglicanism, and in the various places where it took root around the globe, debates about the proper shape and character of political order were at the same time debates about the role of the churches within it and the theological basis of that order. Contrary to a secularization narrative of a fall from medieval sacrality to a modern, religionless form of secularity, these theological debates helped birth crucial elements of what we recognize as distinctly modern social, political, and economic institutions. These include limited government, universal suffrage, parliamentary democracy, the nation-state, capitalism, publicly funded welfare structures, national educational and health systems, international humanitarian movements, and a morally and religiously plural public life. Imbricated in each of these institutional configurations, and the debates and movements that shaped them, were constructive theopolitical responses to modern processes such as industrialization and urbanization, and the disruptions that came in their wake. Temple's role in conceptualizing and legitimizing the British welfare state serves as a case in point.[27] It is not hyperbolic to say that Anglicanism, from its very origins, has been a pathway into imagining what it means to be modern, but one that does not require rupture with or a disavowal of the past as a criterion for being modern. Indeed, an emphasis on tradition and history is one of the hallmarks of Anglican theology.

---

25. "The Lausanne Covenant," Lausanne Movement, August 1, 1974, https://www.lausanne.org/content/covenant/lausanne-covenant

26. On this see Katherine Marshall and Marisa Van Saanen, *Development and Faith: Where Mind, Heart, and Soul Work Together* (Washington, DC: World Bank, 2007).

27. See William Temple, *Christianity and Social Order* (New York: Penguin Books, 1942).

Providence and History

An understanding of God's action in history is foundational to any theological account of the legitimacy of a political order. Questions about what God has done in the past, what God is doing for us now, what we should do in response, and how the last things affect the present age are the backdrop against which to make judgments about the role of church, nation, and state in human life. They are also questions about where to invest hope. In APT, nation, church, state, and universal ideals each at times provided more viscerally satisfying vehicles of hope than Christ and the work of the Spirit.

In imagining church and nation as having a role in world history, Anglicans have leaned toward providential rather than apocalyptic readings of their historical situation.[28] Apocalyptic readings of history emphasize that the world does not have to be as it is and envisage a fundamental division between church and world. They also assume a certain powerlessness to control events. In providential theologies of history, however, wisdom may be found in the world such that Christians should examine the status quo and existing institutional configurations sympathetically. The emphasis on history and culture seen in Coleridge was part of this providential orientation, although such an orientation generated two contradictory readings of history—one conservative, the other progressive.

A dominant strand in the eighteenth century was *conservative providentialism*. Hannah More's *Village Politics* (1792), written as a counter to Thomas Paine's *Rights of Man* (1791-1792), exemplifies this. The example of More (1745-1833), and the Clapham Sect generally, demonstrates that a conservative view can foster a commitment to social reform and generate conservative critiques of slavery and empire. More's 1788 poem *Slavery* declares that its participation in the slave trade shamed Britain, and it challenged the nation to abandon its hypocrisy: "Shall Britain, where the soul of Freedom reigns / Forge chains for others she herself disdains?" A further example is Edmund Burke's (1729-1797) repeated stress on the need to counteract imperial power's tendency to abuse by having in place structures of accountability, legal protections of subjects, and restraint in the exercise of power. Michael Oakeshott (1901-1990), following in the footsteps of Burke, argued that a conservative approach is more reliably

---

28. In the contemporary context, a more apocalyptic approach is the domain of Anglican biblical scholars, most notably, Christopher Rowland and Richard Bauckham.

humane, for conservatives "prefer the tried to the untried, fact to mystery, the actual to the possible, the limited to the unbounded, the near to the distant, the sufficient to the superabundant, the convenient to the perfect, present laughter to utopian bliss."[29] Yet conservativism is also slower to acknowledge the arbitrariness and injustice of who does and who does not have power, and quicker to conflate penultimate and prudential ends with providential ones.

For the likes of More and Wilberforce, humanitarian grounds were the basis for legitimizing imperial rule. Slavery undermined this legitimacy and corrupted the nation. By the end of the nineteenth century, this same humanitarian logic came to justify the expansion of empire: Britain was fulfilling its providential calling of extending liberty and civilization to the unfortunate of the world. The social vision of conservative providentialism can caustically—but not inaccurately—be summarized thus: the rich should set a good example and act benevolently to those less fortunate than themselves, while the poor (whether at home or abroad) "should remain poor, but suffer less, worship more, and behave better."[30] That said, its paternalist interventionism contrasts with those who, following the lead of William Paley (1743–1805) and Thomas Malthus (1766–1834), aligned Christian notions of providence with laissez-faire economics, and held that only the "deserving poor" should receive charity.

The conservative providentialist view entails the interdependence of a good society with "vital religion." William Wilberforce's *A Practical View* (1797) forcefully expresses this idea. For Wilberforce, church and nation stand or fall together, and both are under the judgment of God. In his view, Christianity is the essential basis for social harmony and good government. By contrast, the loss of "vital religion" leads to loss of respect for authority and chaos. This is a common trope in conservative providentialist views: the abandonment of Christianity leads to immorality, nihilism, and the collapse of the social order, and brings God's judgment on the nation for failing to fulfill its vocation. At such a time, what is required are well-educated, faithful men of character—and it is gendered—who are called by God to take up positions of authority and lead the country back to holiness. This kind of approach is alive and well in conservative evangelical streams of Anglicanism.

---

29. Michael Oakeshott, "On Being Conservative," in *Rationalism in Politics and Other Essays* (New York: Basic Books, 1962), 169.

30. Christopher Leslie Brown, *Moral Capital: Foundations of British Abolitionism* (Chapel Hill: University of North Carolina Press, 2006), 346.

If a providentialist view can sacralize the status quo, it can equally sacralize a view of progress. *Progressive providentialism* comes to prominence under the influence of idealism in the nineteenth century. As with the conservative Wilberforce, progressive providentialists were equally concerned about the moral development of individuals and social harmony. However, in contrast to Wilberforce and the evangelicals who followed in his wake, they emphasized the need for structural reform to enable these goods to emerge. Yet structural changes were only ever secondary to a primary ideal of spiritual fellowship. A more fundamental point of contrast with Wilberforce and his ilk was an emphasis on the immanent work of God through social life rather than through individual conversion and responsibility. The individual is envisaged as part of a larger whole, with freedom being attained through social cooperation, which in turn embodied the divine purpose in history. Theologically, a strong emphasis on the incarnation undergirded their idealism. As Henry Scott Holland (1847-1918) put it in his 1911 Christian Social Union pamphlet *Our Neighbors*: "If we believe in the Incarnation, then we certainly believe in the entry of God into the very thick of human affairs. That is just what our faith means. It is, itself, the assertion that God and man cannot be kept apart in separate compartments."[31] As exemplified in the work of Charles Gore (1853-1932) in Britain and Vida Scudder (1861-1954) in the United States, Christian socialism and its derivative, sacramental socialism, were a primary expression of this approach.[32] Although initially skeptical, Christian socialists came to support such things as trade unions, unemployment benefits, and a welfare state as a means to enable full participation in society so that individuals could realize their freedom, that is, fellowship with and service of others through shared social, economic, and political enterprises. This linkage is laid out by Temple in 1934 as follows:

> It cannot be too strongly emphasized that the help for the unemployed which has proved really redemptive and recreative of character is that which has enabled them to realize themselves and fulfil their function

31. Henry Scott Holland, *Our Neighbours* (London: A. R. Mowbray, 1911), 145.

32. Charles Gore, *Christ and Society* (London: Allen & Unwin, 1928); Vida Scudder, *Socialism and Spiritual Progress: A Speculation* (Boston: Church Social Union, 1896), and Scudder, *Socialism and Character* (Boston: Houghton Mifflin, 1912). For a history of Christian socialism as a progenitor of modern political theology and its roots in Anglicanism see Gary Dorrien, *Imagining Democratic Socialism: Political Theology, Marxism, and Social Democracy* (New Haven: Yale University Press, 2019).

as members of the community, of whom the community has need. The greatest evil and bitterest injury of their state is not the animal grievance of hunger or discomfort, nor even the mental grievance of vacuity and boredom; it is the spiritual grievance of being allowed no opportunity of contributing to the general life and welfare of the community. All efforts for their assistance should therefore look towards the provision of that opportunity.[33]

An influential philosophical current for this view came from T. H. Green (1836-1882), who saw progress toward the ideal of a universal harmonious fellowship as an inevitable corollary of the progressive evolution of the divine in history.

The danger with this kind of account is that salvation becomes merely a historical process and there is a loss of tension between being a Christian and being a citizen. The church may function at times as an institution of critique, but this is in service of its role as handmaiden to the unfolding of a progressive society, with the nation and statecraft the primary vehicles for the realization of freedom in history. As exemplified by Samuel Barnett (1844-1913), a founder of the Settlement House movement, this view easily slipped into Erastianism, whereby the church was subordinated to the state. Barnett saw the church as a department of the state that existed to serve the interests of the nation. The purpose of the church was "to make men friends, to unite all classes in common aims, to give them open minds."[34] However, in parallel with conservatives, progressives saw a nation and state without the leaven of the church as quickly losing its way. Yet, the threat to the cohesion of society came not from personal immorality but from atomistic and mechanistic social forces unleashed by the malign influence of laissez-faire economics that defined society as nothing more than an aggregation of self-interested choices.

An alternative position to conservative and progressive approaches emerged through a turn to Augustine's amillennial theology of history. Figgis's work exemplifies this turn. One of his key concerns was how to maintain the freedom, specificity, and self-development of all forms of association, particularly churches and trade unions. In contrast to the

---

33. F. A. Iremonger, *William Temple, Archbishop of Canterbury: His Life and Letters* (New York: Oxford University Press, 1948), 440.

34. David Nicholls, *Deity and Domination: Images of God and the State in the Nineteenth and Twentieth Centuries* (London: Routledge, 1994), 71.

progressive providentialists, he rejected an overreliance on the reforming powers of the centralized state. And in contrast to conservatives, he argued for a pluralistic conception of sovereignty.

Contrary to the political theology of the Ditchley portrait, Augustine's amillennialism renders political and institutional arrangements as historical achievements rather than direct reflections of the cosmic order. For Augustine, political authority is not neutral (it is either directed toward or away from God); rather, in this age before Christ's return, it is ambivalent. There cannot be an expectation of progress, nor is history orientated toward regress or a movement away from God. Within Augustine's framework, human history is secular (rather than neutral); that is, it neither promises nor sets at risk the kingdom of God. The church can reside in this age regarding its structures and patterns of life as relativized and rendered contingent by what is to come.

For Augustine, politics in this age is about enabling a limited peace. On the one hand, the peace is shorn of messianic pretensions, but on the other, it is not given over to demonic despair. Humans can and should act to ensure that a tolerable civic peace exists within which to preach the gospel and that the city of God can make use of for a time. Conversely, any project of salvation or human fulfillment through an earthly order is to be condemned. Given conditions of finitude and fallenness, all political formations are provisional and tend toward oppression. At the same time, whether it be a democracy or a monarchy, any polity may display just judgments and enable the limited good of an earthly peace through the pursuit of common objects of love. Parallel to Catholic social teaching, this framework generates an "accidentalist" view that Christianity is compatible with any number of governmental regimes. As T. S. Eliot (1888–1965) put it: "To identify any particular form of government with Christianity is a dangerous error for it confounds the permanent with the transitory, the absolute with the contingent."[35]

Building on Augustine, Figgis and others envisaged the role of political institutions as being to serve and defend prior and more basic forms of associational life from the overweening power of either the market or the state. C. S. Lewis (1898–1963) captures the spirit of this approach: "The state exists simply to promote and to protect the ordinary happiness of human beings in this life. A husband and wife chatting over a fire, a couple of friends having a game of darts in a pub, a man reading a book in his own

---

35. T. S. Eliot, *The Idea of a Christian Society* (London: Faber & Faber, 1939), 57.

room or digging in his own garden—that is what the state is there for. And unless they are helping to increase and prolong and protect such moments, all the laws, parliaments, armies, courts, police, economics etc. are simply a waste of time."[36] Yet the way Anglicans continued to imagine the church and the nation as having a world historical role stood in tension with Augustine's emphasis on the inscrutability of divine action in history. And as with conservative and progressive providentialists, English Pluralists like Figgis continued to see Christianity as the necessary basis of civilization.

From Figgis on there is a consistent move to pose an Augustinian moral and political vision as the last redoubt against a Nietzschean future of domination and depravity.[37] John Milbank is but one example of such a stance.[38] For Figgis (and Milbank), modernity is not a problem because it produces this or that instance of injustice, it is a problem because it inverts the moral order and makes the *libido dominandi* a point of virtue. However, the modernity-critical stream of Augustinianism Figgis helps initiate contradicts Augustine, for whom this noneschatological age was a field of wheat and tares. It works with and reifies an epochal division between modernity and prior ages, and through this division introduces a dangerous nostalgia that sacralizes the past (often an idealized medieval era) and demonizes the present. On this kind of account, Christianity either becomes an endangered species to be protected on special reservations or a weapon to defend Western culture from internal collapse and external attack. At the same time, it forgets that the Spirit makes Christ present in modernity, just as Christ was made present to other times and places.

A turn to Augustine does not necessitate making Christianity a defensive civilizational project. Combining Augustine with contemplative pragmatism emphasizes that just and loving forms of life in the earthly city are still discoverable in the modern world. And of necessity, if this process of discovery is to be faithful, it entails rendering ourselves vulnerable to God and neighbor. An approach that predetermines what is to be discovered by overidentifying Christianity with either a prior cultural-historical form or a fixed set of ideals is a refusal to inductively discover and bear witness to what Christ and the Spirit are doing among these people in this place. Such

36. C. S. Lewis, *Mere Christianity* (New York: HarperOne, 2001 [1952]), 199.

37. John Neville Figgis, *Will to Freedom or the Gospel of Nietzsche and the Gospel of Christ* (New York: Scribner's Sons, 1917).

38. John Milbank, *Theology and Social Theory: Beyond Secular Reason* (Oxford: Blackwell, 1990), 389-34.

a move also denies how loss, vulnerability, and lack of control are central to the experience of acting faithfully, lovingly, and hopefully with and for others. Indeed, as Williams argues, the most intense moment of divine presence and agency in human history is one in which "the sheer historical vulnerability of the human is most starkly shown, where unfinishedness, tension, the rejection of meaning and community are displayed in the figure of a man simultaneously denied voice and identity by the religious and political rationalities of his day."[39]

The life, death, resurrection, and ascension of Jesus, rather than culture or history per se, are the condition for the possibility of movement into new kinds of relationship with God and neighbor. Any such journey of conversion demands that as humans we orient ourselves in specific ways to living in time and the experience of flux and transition that is constitutive of being temporal creatures. The emphasis on culture and history in APT is right, but only insofar as it enables a reckoning with human frailty, finitude, and fallenness. Becoming church is about discovering—with these people, in this place, at this time—how unity in Christ amid and through our differences might be experienced and lived into through reception of the gifts of the Spirit. It should rule out a nostalgic division that poses the past as good and the present as intrinsically bad, as well as making judgments about who is and who is not on the "right side of history." Rather, ways must be found to identify with Christ and thereby dis-identify with the historical idols and cultural systems of domination within which human life is always and already entangled. Understood as action in time through which to cultivate forms of peaceable common life, politics is a necessary part of any such process of discovery. However, as Donald MacKinnon (1913-1994) cautions, the tragic dimensions of social and political life cannot be avoided, and failure is often the result. Yet faith, hope, and love demand that the risk still be taken.[40]

The temptation of a providential reading of history is to make either the nation or the institutions of the church the center and subject of history rather than Jesus Christ. It is then what serves the nation or church rather than what witnesses to Jesus Christ that becomes the locus of judgments about what and who is true, good, and beautiful. The antidote to a top-

39. Rowan Williams, "Hegel and the Gods of Postmodernity," in *Wrestling with Angels: Conversations in Modern Theology*, ed. Mike Higton (Grand Rapids: Eerdmans, 2007), 32.

40. Donald M. MacKinnon, "Tragedy and Ethics," in *Explorations in Theology 5* (London: SCM, 1979), 182-95.

down reading is to interpret history from a christological center outward and, at the same time, to exegete it from the bottom up, giving priority to the testimony of those on the underside of history. Some evangelicals did try to listen to the cries of those on the underside of history, notably slaves, but, perhaps counterintuitively, they made either themselves or the nation rather than Christ the subject of history. Conversely, Christian socialists, with the emphasis on the incarnation, put Christ at the center of history but did not start from the actual experiences of the poor when generating social and political programs. Rather, they pursued universalized ideals of fellowship through patrician and then technocratic means that generated action *for* rather than *with* the poor. The top-down programs of Toynbee Hall are but one example of this process. In the latter half of the twentieth century, through the influence of Karl Barth, Christ displaces the nation as the subject of history. And through the impact of liberation theologies, APT is beginning to place much greater emphasis on learning from the marginalized. In relation to the latter, a vital means of its *ressourcement* is attending to voices such as those of Peter Williams Jr. (1786–1840), Anna Julia Cooper (1858–1964), and Pauli Murray (1910–1985) within the Anglican tradition. Finally, the influence of the Pentecostal/charismatic movement on Anglicanism worldwide calls for attention to the pneumatological dimensions of political theology along the lines set out in chapter 4. Connecting Christology, pneumatology, and a preferential option for the poor are questions related to power: Who has it? What is its character? How is it constituted? And when, where, and for whom is it used? Going forward, these questions must be central to the development of APT.

Conclusion

The pragmatic political settlements that APT reflected on and sought to interpret contain numerous contradictions and unresolved conflicts of theory and practice. What they point to is how Christians necessarily begin *in via*, responding to an already and a not yet. The next chapter of APT must take this as wisdom, not failure. Learning to live betwixt and between different ages, rather than at the center or end of history, enables political engagement that is open to being both a guest, ready to listen and learn, and a host, ready to shelter and share. Such a guest/host orientation enables Anglicans, working alongside others, to figure out what kind of life together is possible here and now in which the flourishing of each, including the least, the lost, and the last, is recognized as dependent on the flourishing of all, while we wait for the coming of the Lord Jesus Christ, who alone is the first and the last word.

Threshold

Part 1 examined an interlinked series of influential political theologies each of which wrestles with the central problem of politics: how to create and sustain a common life amid suffering, difference, and asymmetries of power. Part 2 picks up on key themes and issues that have emerged over the course of part 1, notably how the church is implicated in and yet seeks to address structural inequalities and social conflicts; the role of the church in a pluralistic society (and aligned with that, the nature and basis of secularity); and how to navigate sameness and difference, whether understood in cultural, ideological, or ecclesial terms. These issues are addressed in chapters 7, 8, and 9, respectively.

The next chapter takes its cue from an influential framework within Anglican political theology—sacramental socialism—in order to analyze how worship is both a way of addressing unjust divisions of class and a replication of them. This analysis provides a route by which to assess how the church, as a body politic, constitutes a key point of reference in political theology and the primary locus of political witness.

Suggested Readings for Further Discussion

Richard Hooker, "From *Laws of Ecclesiastical Polity*," in *From Irenaeus to Grotius: A Sourcebook in Christian Political Thought, 100-1625*, ed. Oliver O'Donovan and Joan Lockwood O'Donovan (Grand Rapids: Eerdmans, 1999), 743-56.

Hannah More, *Village Politics* (1792), http://ota.ox.ac.uk/text/4612.html.

Peter Williams Jr., "An Oration on the Abolition of the Slave Trade; Delivered in the African Church in the City of New York, January 1, 1808," University of Nebraska–Lincoln, https://digitalcommons.unl.edu/etas/16/.

Samuel Taylor Coleridge, *On the Constitution of the Church and State, according to the Idea of Each* (London: J. M. Dent & Sons, 1972 [1830]), chaps. 1-9.

John Keble, "National Apostasy" (1833), http://anglicanhistory.org/keble/keble1.html.

Anthony Trollope, *Barchester Towers* (1857), various editions.

Vida Scudder, "A Plea for Social Intercession," in *The Church and the Hour: Reflections of a Socialist Churchwoman* (1917), http://anglicanhistory.org/socialism/scudder/hour/05.html.

William Temple, *Christianity and Social Order* (New York: Penguin Books, 1942).

Desmond Tutu, "Fortieth Anniversary of the Republic?" and "The Role of the Church in South Africa," in *Hope and Suffering: Sermons and Speeches* (Grand Rapids: Eerdmans, 1984), 43-47, 74-87.

Rowan Williams, "Incarnation and the Renewal of Community," in *On Christian Theology* (Oxford: Blackwell, 2000), 225-38.

John Stott, "Our Changing World: Is Christian Involvement Necessary?" *Issues Facing Christians Today*, 4th ed. (Grand Rapids: Zondervan, 2006), 23-47.

PART TWO

Sustaining a Common Life

CHAPTER 7

Communion and Class

Scripture repeatedly enjoins its readers to "Greet one another with a holy kiss."[1] When congregants offer each other this or a similar sign of peace, the following question is posed: What is the basis of Christian relations? Or to put it another way: What binds and looses those who congregate in church, and how does congregating to worship God contrast with other ways humans gather together? And in giving and receiving a sign of Christ's peace, what kinds of social, political, or economic order are thereby challenged or confirmed?

Intrinsic in the theological conception of Christ's peace is the notion of a time and place beyond human conflict, when the basis of what leads to human tears and suffering will be transcended and God will establish a harmonious communion with humans and all creation. The shorthand we use for this time and place includes the phrases the "peaceable kingdom," the "city of God," and the "new creation." In its life together, the church is to bear witness to this time and place. One way of pointing to and anticipating this coming communion is by sharing the peace through a kiss, handshake, or some other gesture. As a physical gesture, sharing the peace makes a

---

1. Rom. 16:16; 1 Cor. 16:20; 2 Cor. 13:12; 1 Thess. 5:26; 1 Pet. 5:14. Though restricted to family members, kissing was a standard greeting in the ancient Mediterranean world. Sharing a kiss with those outside one's kinship networks, but who were now brothers and sisters in Christ, enacted the changed social boundaries that membership in the church entailed. The third-century theologian Lactantius expresses both the radical nature of social relations reconfigured in and through Christ and the anxiety it provoked when he says: "Somebody will ask, 'Are there not among you differences between poor and rich, between slave and master? Do you not have social distinctions?' Not at all! Nor would we be able to use the term 'brother' to one another if we did not believe that we are all equal" (*Divine Institutes* 5.16).

claim about how reality can and should be structured, thereby signifying how the church embodies rather than merely has a political theology, its practices constituting a form of political witness. Or at least that is part of what I will argue here.

It is all very well saying sharing Christ's peace embodies a political theology, but how are we to relate the perfect and harmonious communion established by Christ it represents to the conflictual and unjust form of the earthly peace that we encounter in this age, before Christ's return? And following on from this, how are we to seek the welfare of this selfsame earthly city, even though it be "Babylon"? These are perennial questions that confront Christian moral and political reflection and that we have encountered already in this book. In part 3, I examine humanity, sovereignty, and peoplehood as ways of addressing these questions in the modern period. In this chapter, I reflect on these questions through an analysis of class. Class conflict, born out of asymmetries of power, is a paradigmatic challenge that corrodes a common life over time. Here I review debates about class and how these inform political theology, while assessing whether or not practices of worship (e.g., sharing the peace)—and, through them, the church—are a means of constructively addressing such conflict.

An assessment of class in a consideration of political theology is important for three reasons. First, accounts of class inherently make normative moral claims about the right ordering of social relations. As a sociological term, "class" is assumed to be neutral. However, in modern accounts of class, class-based hierarchies are presumed to be wrong, primarily because they involve inequality. This inequality is a form of injustice because it arises out of the unequal distribution of the resources that form the basis of human flourishing. The ideal is to move beyond a class-based society, and the conflict inherently generated by competition between different classes for control of scarce resources, to a classless society characterized by the equal distribution of resources. This change may be brought about through revolutionary means, as in Marxist accounts; through the interventions of the state and redistributive policies, as in social democratic accounts; or even through the mechanisms of a truly free and properly functioning market, as in some neoliberal/libertarian accounts. Each of these approaches is a tacit theodicy that explains why there is suffering in the world and what needs to happen to resolve the causes of that suffering. Discerning whether such accounts correlate with or are analogous to the peace Christ inaugurates and fulfills or whether they constitute its parody is one motivation for discussing class in relation to political theology.

Second, an analysis of class is relevant because it allows for discussion of the basis and order of contemporary economic life. Here the question of class confronts Christian moral and political reflection about how we treat those we meet in the market and workplace. How the rich treat the poor and vulnerable is a constant theme in the Bible and subsequent theological reflection. Arguably, it is central to understanding salvation itself. Here the parables of Dives and Lazarus (Luke 16:19-31) and the rich fool (Luke 12:16-20) are instructive. These parables indicate that the wealthy who hoard their riches, using them for their aggrandizement and benefit instead of giving and lending to others in need, are not only foolish but damned. Along with a host of other texts, these parables suggest that there is no true worship of God outside of loving and just relations with our neighbors, especially those poorer and less powerful than ourselves. An analysis of class gives insights into the peculiar circumstances of modern economic relations and the condition and possibilities of neighbor love within them.

Third, an analysis of class is directly relevant to developing an account of the relationship between worship and political theology. As I argue in chapter 13, the people of God are necessarily heterogeneous. Yet this heterogeneity is not all good. While some arises from created and Spirit-inspired differences, much grows out of sinful and idolatrous patterns of relationship. Class provides a lens through which to assess how sin and idolatry shape the quality and character of the relations of those assembled to worship God. As a phenomenon, class directly affects common worship. It determines the form, timing, order, language, and aesthetic of worship in often unacknowledged ways. Class thereby affects who we do or don't gather with on a Sunday and therefore what kind of common life is witnessed to in formal acts of worship.

The background political question I address in this chapter is, what are the conditions of agency? Class relations, whether in a congregation or elsewhere, are an important factor that structure the ability to act. They shape who has more or less power. As a background condition, class as a means of agency is often invisible and therefore unaccountable. It works in unconscious ways to shape judgments about what to do and what not to do. Worship is also a means of agency, both in divine-human relations and between humans. In what follows, I map how worship and class interact, both positively and negatively, to construct or diminish the ability to act with and for others in sustaining a common life. The interaction of class and worship provides a window on how the church qua church both counters and perpetuates unjust social, political, and economic hierarchies.

I do not, however, argue that class is the matrix from which all other points of social conflict and injustice emerge. Rather, my claim is that an analysis of class sheds light on the dynamics shaping other systemic yet often tacit or hidden forms of injustice and conflict, notably, those related to gender, race, sexuality, and physical ability. Class was one of the earliest and most systematically developed frameworks of critical social theory. Part of what this chapter tries to model is how social and critical theories—in this case, of class—can illuminate, critique, and help repair ecclesial life and, conversely, how theological conceptions of what it means to be church may illuminate, critique, and provide resources for the repair of social and critical theories. In doing this, I attend to how both ecclesial frameworks and critical social theories are pluralistic, are internally contested, and change over time. The crude version of my argument is that when it comes to social and political problems, neither liturgy nor critical social theory provides a complete solution, but both can help diagnose and describe the nature of the problems we face even as they mutually discipline each other.[2]

I begin by locating class as a category of analysis within broader debates in social theory and political theology. I do so by drawing a contrast between class-based conceptions of social order and that performed in Christian worship. Second, through examining two classical theorists of class, Max Weber and Karl Marx, I assess how an analysis of class helps shine a light on the social effects of capitalism as a form of political economy. This section sketches the influence of this kind of analysis on a significant stream of political theology—Latin American liberation theology—and how, in response to Latin American liberation theology, other theologians looked to the church as itself a source of social theory and a counterperformance to destructive social conflicts exemplified in class relations. Third, against the background of social theories of class, I examine worship as a mode of production, distribution, and exchange. However, against idealized accounts of worship as a counterperformance of class conflict, this section draws on Pierre Bourdieu's account of class as a form of status acquisition to reflect on how worship itself can reproduce and sacralize unjust social and economic hierarchies. Fourth, in dialogue with Durkheim's

---

2. More broadly, I take the relationship between theology and critical social theory to exist on a spectrum from the oppositional (some critical social theories constituting a form of antitheology), through dialectical, to dialogical and analogical relations, with each fertilizing new insights in the other.

conception of class formation, I examine how communion, as the fruit of worship, is analogous and disanalogous to class-based forms of solidarity. Lastly, in dialogue with black feminist and womanist conceptions of intersectionality, I discuss the insufficiency of class as a mode of analysis and how assessments of what fractures and corrodes a just and loving common life must deploy a multitude of lenses.

Class, Power, and Inequality

The notion of class is a way of conceptualizing the ordering of human relations. At its most basic level, "class" refers to divisions in social hierarchy and how these relate to power relations within a body politic. For example, while there are always exceptions, an aristocracy, as a class, has more power to act socially, economically, and politically than peasants as a class have. The division of society into different levels or strata, arranged in a hierarchy of wealth, status, and other forms of power, is a nearly universal feature of social and political life. However, the origin, basis, and structure of these hierarchies, how they are interpreted and legitimated, and how their moral significance is understood, vary so widely that we must be cautious about whether we are comparing the same kind of thing.

From the eighteenth century onward, with the advent of industrialization, increased attention was given to social hierarchy and the processes that generated new forms of social order. There was a wide range of responses to the question of whether money and what it could buy were replacing older forms of distinction such as birth and profession, and whether a new "industrial aristocracy," which would be an aristocracy without honor, might emerge to replace the existing one. These responses were shaped by the different experiences across the Atlantic world, particularly in Germany, France, Britain, and North America. By the early nineteenth century, class emerged as a way of talking about changing patterns of social, economic, and political hierarchy and their legitimation.

There are two distinctive features to class as a modern way of thinking about stratification among humans. The first is that it represents an attempt to self-consciously identify and reflect upon the existence of inequality in a systematic way. Hierarchy, instead of being accepted as "natural" and immutable, is understood to be historically contingent and open to change. For example, in contrast to the Hindu caste system, modern accounts of class do not accept hierarchy as a necessary feature of the cosmic order.

This is not to say that class-based analyses see all hierarchy as wrong. Following Rousseau, there can be distinctions between a hierarchy based on an inequality of opportunity and one based on the inequality of ability.[3] However, equality has become an a priori good and is a central evaluative criterion of modern social and political theory. However, as the distinction made by Rousseau suggests, we cannot escape hierarchy and hence inequality of some kind. The question is, what is the basis and character of any human hierarchy and its attendant form of inequality?

Augustine distinguished between what he saw as the natural hierarchies that Scripture validates, such as those between parents and children, and those it questions and points to as historical, postlapsarian developments. For Augustine, all political relations were of this latter kind. As he puts it: "[God] did not wish the rational beings, made in his own image, to have dominion over any but irrational creatures, not man over man, but man over beasts. Hence the first just men were set up as shepherds of flocks, rather than as kings of men."[4]

For Augustine, formal political hierarchy inherently involves relations of domination resulting from social relations ordered by self-love. This contrasts with the city of God where there is a perfect form of society ordered harmoniously by the love of God. The modern debate about class follows on from the Augustinian sense that all political orders are both contingent on and riven by unjust hierarchies. Attention to class helps denaturalize and desacralize human social orders and unveil the oppressive power structure at work within them. At the same time, Augustine's insight that even the earthly city enjoys a kind of peace can be said to find its analogue in the stream of thinking about class that emphasizes how class constitutes a mode of solidarity.

Class and Political Economy

Most modern accounts of class incorporate three elements, placing different emphases on each. The first element is how hierarchy is constructed through people's relationship to the means of *production*. The second is the construction of hierarchy through people's location in relation to the

---

3. Jean-Jacques Rousseau, "A Discourse on the Origin of Inequality," in *The Social Contract and Discourses* (London: Everyman, 1993), 49.
4. *City of God* 19.16.

distribution of resources, be this education, capital, social networks, or oc-cupation. The third element attends to the formation and maintenance of hierarchy through how people participate in patterns of *consumption* (what they buy, wear, or eat).

The work of Max Weber illustrates a conception of class that integrates how production, distribution, and consumption create a hierarchy. His work also points to how analysis of class oscillates between determining it by focusing on an economic relation (e.g., working class) and determining it by focusing on a relation of status or rank (e.g., middle class).[5] Weber explicitly distinguishes between class and status, both of which are "phe-nomena of the distribution of power within a community."[6] Weber sees class as defined by economic interests and wealth that is determined by conditions of labor and position in the market. This aspect of his analysis focuses on the means of production. "Property" and "lack of property" are for Weber "the basic categories of all class situations."[7] It is property (which may take many different forms, from land to products) that gives one class an advantage in the market over others and allows that class to accumulate resources that in turn result in different standards of living. Status is a separate and more subjective source of stratification than the more objectively defined class. Status is not defined by one's situation in the market or by one's ownership or nonownership of property. Rather, it depends on the honor accorded certain groups and occupations. Distinc-tions of prestige are forged and maintained through patterns of distribution and consumption, notably, lifestyle, education, and relational ties (e.g., only marrying people from a similar background). Thus, one can be ma-terially poor but have a high status (e.g., a bankrupt aristocrat). However, wealth is a key determinant of one's ability to sustain a high-status position. For Weber, status and class are two competing modes of group formation in relation to the distribution of power in society, and their interaction leads to a more plural and dynamic conception of social hierarchy than that of other classical theorists of class, notably Karl Marx.

While theories of class share a common focus on production, distri-bution, and consumption, within modern analyses of class there are two broad trajectories. One emphasizes the conflictual dynamic of class forma-

---

5. Raymond Williams, "Class," in *Keywords: A Vocabulary of Culture and Society* (Ox-ford: Oxford University Press, 1976), 51-59.

6. *From Max Weber: Essays in Sociology* (London: Routledge & Kegan Paul, 1948), 181.

7. *From Max Weber*, 182.

tion (represented by Karl Marx and Max Weber), and the other emphasizes how class formation is a feature of consensus and social cohesion (represented by Émile Durkheim). As will be seen, to each of these modes of class formation, we find the church performing a contradictory mode of social formation in its ongoing worship life.

A contrast between caste and class points to the second distinctive feature of class as a modern way of understanding human hierarchy and social order: its emphasis on economic and material relations as against legal, political, or religious divisions. Most influential in this regard is the work of Karl Marx. Marx located the divisions between classes in their differing relationship to the means of production. On Marx's reading, a distinctive feature of modern society is the formation of two distinct classes: the proletariat and the bourgeoisie. These classes emerge due to changes in the means of production, most notably those brought about by the Industrial Revolution. The proletariat neither possess capital nor own the means of production and so have to sell their labor in the market to earn a living. The bourgeoisie own property and surplus capital/money, which form the basis of their ability to expropriate the surplus generated from the labor of the proletariat. Ranged between them are various forms of "transitional" classes (e.g., petit bourgeoisie) who would eventually form part of either the proletariat or the bourgeoisie. For Marx, feudal society had classes, but these were more properly called "estates," the relationship between them not being governed solely by their relationship to the means of production and property. For Marx, what distinguishes modern classes is their relationship to the means of production and the money economy.[8] The underlying moral import of Marx's analysis is made explicit by the messianic role he ascribes to the proletariat. The proletariat is a revolutionary element in society because through them the transcendence (rather than the destruction) of the whole class system is made possible.

Part of the importance of Marx's insight is how his analysis of class relations points not merely to conflict between different class interests but to how that conflict is a sign of exploitation. Like slave owners and feudal lords, the owners of capital can expropriate the surplus labor of others. But ideological mystifications of the real nature and form of the relation mask its illegitimacy and coercive nature. An analysis of class relations reveals a site of suffering, injustice, and idolatry the church must prophetically call

---

8. Despite its prominence in his work, Marx never set out a systematic analysis of class, and in places, he takes contradictory views.

attention to even while it seeks to identify its complicity in either reproducing or mystifying these structures of exploitation. It was this aspect of Marxism that was taken up by Latin American liberation theology.

In his seminal book *A Theology of Liberation* (1971), Gustavo Gutiérrez speaks of theology's "direct and fruitful confrontation with Marxism." He goes on to say that "it is to a large extent due to Marxism's influence that theological thought, searching for its own sources, has begun to reflect on the meaning of the transformation of this world and human action in history."[9] Gutiérrez and other liberation theologians, in their initial formulations, attempted to use a Marxist conception of class as a way to give an account of the unjust social order in South and Central America. As Gutiérrez put it in 1983: "Only class analysis will show what is really at stake in the opposition between oppressed lands and dominant peoples."[10] Liberation theology drew on particular streams of nondeterministic Marxist analysis as tools for articulating how and why faithful Christian witness entailed solidarity with the poor.[11] For Latin American liberation theology, the church and its forms of worship perpetuate the dominance of elite groups and reinforce social divisions if they fail to confront injustice, of which the class system is a symptom.[12] Hence its most influential insight: God has a preferential option for the poor, and we encounter God most fully in solidarity with the poor.[13] Alongside Marx, this insight draws on (and is now explicitly incorporated into) Catholic social teaching.[14] The episte-

9. Gustavo Gutiérrez, *A Theology of Liberation: History, Politics, and Salvation*, rev. ed. (Maryknoll, NY: Orbis, 1988), 8.

10. Gustavo Gutiérrez, *The Power of the Poor in History* (Maryknoll, NY: Orbis, 1983), 46.

11. Gustavo Gutiérrez, *The Truth Shall Make You Free: Confrontations*, trans. Matthew O'Connell (Maryknoll, NY: Orbis, 1990), 75-78, and Enrique Dussel, "Theology of Liberation and Marxism," in *Mysterium Liberationis: Fundamental Concepts of Liberation Theology*, ed. Ignacio Ellacuría and Jon Sobrino (Maryknoll, NY: Orbis, 1993), 85-102.

12. Gutiérrez, *Theology of Liberation*, 145-61, and Enrique Dussel, *Beyond Philosophy: Ethics, History, Marxism, and Liberation Theology*, ed. Eduardo Mendieta (New York: Rowman & Littlefield, 2003), 41-52.

13. Subsequent waves of Latin American liberation theology have emphasized culture rather than class, and thence gender, sexuality, and race as prisms through which to identify and analyze the fundamental structures of injustice the church must address, both within itself and externally. For example, Marcella Althaus Reid challenges the exclusive focus on the economic basis of oppression by contending that the sexual ordering of social relations is coterminous with if not prior to its economic ordering and so must be addressed as a primary issue. See Marcella Althaus Reid, *Indecent Theology* (London: Routledge, 2000), 11-23.

14. See, for example, Francis, *Evangelii Gaudium*, §198.

mological implication of this insight for political theology is that the initial step toward right reflection on politics is solidarity with and involvement in the struggles of the poor, and dialogue with the experience and knowledge about their situation that the poor produce of and for themselves.[15] But this dialogue can mean rejecting ideologies that, as Jorge Bergoglio puts it, "act for the people but never with the people" in order to truly learn from the poor as people.[16]

Some went beyond Gutiérrez's cautious use of a Marxist analysis of class as a tool situated within a broader theologically grounded methodology.[17] They insisted that faithful witness must take (rather than might take) the form of involvement in the class struggle to establish socialism (whether by revolutionary or other means), and a commitment to the social ownership of the means of production, as the primary way of moving beyond exploitative class relations. For example, Clodovis Boff, writing in 1979, states: "Liberation is the social emancipation of the oppressed. Our concrete task is to replace the capitalist system and move toward a new society—a society of a socialist type."[18] For the Colombian priest Camilo Torres, who died as a guerrilla, being faithful necessitated taking off his cassock and no longer celebrating the Mass in order to become involved in revolutionary politics so as to—in his view—more authentically fulfill his priestly vocation. More generally, while they came to recognize many forms of oppression, including those based on gender, sexuality, and race, for the first wave of Latin American liberation theologians, socioeconomic class was the primary and paradigmatic form of oppression.

In response to Latin American liberation theology, some theologians, notably John Milbank and William Cavanaugh, criticized any overreliance on Marxism, and the social sciences more generally, as tools of analysis. Their constructive move was to restate how the church itself is a *polis* and theology is itself a social theory.[19] Cavanaugh, in his critique of liberation theology, proposes that the liturgy constitutes a counterperformance to

15. Clodovis Boff, "Epistemology and Method of the Theology of Liberation," in Ellacuría and Sobrino, *Mysterium Liberationis*, 57–84.

16. Quoted in Thomas Rourke, *The Roots of Pope Francis's Social and Political Thought: From Argentina to the Vatican* (Lanham, MD: Rowman & Littlefield, 2016), 77.

17. Gustavo Gutiérrez, "Theology and the Social Sciences," in *The Truth Shall Make You Free*, 58–67.

18. Clodovis Boff, *Salvation and Liberation* (Maryknoll, NY: Orbis, 1984), 116.

19. John Milbank, *Theology and Social Theory: Beyond Secular Reason* (Oxford: Blackwell, 1990).

the politics of domination and oppression in Latin America.[20] For Cavanaugh, to stop saying the Mass in the name of revolutionary politics is an act not of faithful witness but of capitulation to and co-option by systems of domination. The paradigmatic contrast for Cavanaugh is not between state socialism and capitalism but between torture and Eucharist. Torture as a practice disaggregates and disciplines bodies so that society becomes subject to the control and manipulation of the state. The Eucharist, by contrast, congregates and forms an alternative physical regime that liberates bodies for communion with each other.[21] As he puts it: "The liturgy does more than generate interior motivations to be better citizens. The liturgy generates a body, the Body of Christ . . . which is itself a *sui generis* social body, a public presence irreducible to a voluntary association of civil society."[22] For Cavanaugh, the Catholic Church, through its worship practices, constitutes a body politic that witnesses to a distinctive vision of political life. Milbank uses a parallel framework to situate Anglican political witness. And Amos Yong, Nimi Wariboko, and other Pentecostal theologians have drawn on Cavanaugh and Milbank's approach to interpret the political theology tacit within Pentecostalism.[23]

For Cavanaugh and Milbank, Latin American liberation theology uncritically accepted the role of the state in delivering social justice and failed to take seriously enough the church and its practices as both sources of social analysis and sites of political witness. For these theologians, the church is a polity or *res publica* that forms and socializes human bodies in ways that are very different from those of the modern nation-state and either a capitalist or a centrally planned economy. At this point, the influence of Augustine on their work is visible. For Augustine, the ends or loves of the polity form the basis of its common life. Thus the difference between the earthly city and the City of God rests in their different ends

20. There was a parallel turn to liturgy in the early 1990s among those carrying the mantle of liberation theology in Brazil, but not for reasons of preserving theological orthodoxy. It was born out of a move toward inculturation and the use of liturgy to address racism in the church. See John Burdick, *Legacies of Liberation: The Progressive Catholic Church in Brazil at the Start of a New Millennium* (Aldershot, UK: Ashgate, 2004), 24-32.

21. William Cavanaugh, *Torture and Eucharist: Theology, Politics, and the Body of Christ* (Oxford: Blackwell, 1998).

22. William Cavanaugh, *Theopolitical Imagination: Discovering the Liturgy as a Political Act in an Age of Global Consumerism* (London: T&T Clark, 2002), 83.

23. Amos Yong, *In the Days of Caesar: Pentecostalism and Political Theology* (Grand Rapids: Eerdmans, 2010), 155-61, 230-38, and Nimi Wariboko, *Nigerian Pentecostalism* (Rochester, NY: University of Rochester Press, 2014), 172-74, 211.

or objects of love.[24] An earthly city cannot be a true *res publica* because the nature of its loves means that it can never be a truly harmonious society; rather, it always involves individual and group competition and hostility. This framework does not necessarily lead to a binary between either relying on earthly means to engage with the world or passively withdrawing to an enclave. For Milbank and Cavanaugh, instead of drawing on an atheistic ideology, social scientific analysis, or earthly means of power, the church can embody an alternative to the oppressive dynamics of structural power.[25] Where what it means to be human is threatened or undermined, it is the vocation of the church to witness to its proper form, that is, its form as established by and reconciled to God in Christ. And, on their view, it is in the practices of worship that we see this witness most fully articulated and performed. It is to worship as a contradiction of class conflict that I now turn in order to excavate further Milbank's and Cavanaugh's constructive assessment of worship as a form of political witness—an assessment that is shared by later streams of liberation theology.

Worship as a Mode of Production, Distribution, and Consumption

Theologically, the sign of peace (whether enacted in an actual kiss or some other verbal or physical gesture), and the performance of worship more generally (whether formal or informal), contains the potential to constitute an alternative pattern of social order and hierarchy to those based on class and its largely economic determination. The performance of this alternative social order takes place within and through a local and catholic body that is at the same time profoundly distorted and divided around issues of gender, race, sexuality, and class. Thus, the liturgical sign of peace is an address to both the church and the world. Etymologically, "liturgy" is a political term drawn from the Greek word *leitourgia*, meaning a public work of service or duty undertaken by the citizen and done for the benefit of the people or wider community.[26] As a work of service, an act of Chris-

24. *City of God* 14.28

25. Cavanaugh, *Torture and Eucharist*, 264-81; Milbank, *Theology and Social Theory*, 398-434.

26. On the inherently political nature of liturgy, see Erik Peterson, "The Book on the Angels: Their Place and Meaning in the Liturgy" and "Christ as Imperator," in *Theological Tractates*, trans. Michael J. Hollerich (Stanford, CA: Stanford University Press, 2011), 106-42 and 143-50.

tian *leitourgia* is both a political act that builds up and restores the people of God and a Spirit-filled act that mediates the work of God in the world. As a public work of the people of God and a work of the Spirit within the world (of which the church is a part), liturgy is a mode of nonalienated work born out of the mutual or common labor of God and humans. The fruits of this work are distributed and consumed both by the participants, as each has need, and by the world, which the working people represent before God in their prayers, songs, and words. Within this economy of worship, there is an asymmetric dynamic of exchange—some give more than others—but it is one where all are dependent on each other.

Within the doxological economy of *leitourgia*, there is a hierarchy, but it is one based on covenant, vocation, and gifting, not kinship, social origin, or ownership of the means of production. Within this hierarchy, one's status is determined not by wealth, degrees of property ownership, or taste, but by a complex interaction of moral dispositions/virtues and the work of the Spirit. Within the church, it is a hierarchy of moral and spiritual excellence that is normatively valued, not a hierarchy of status. There is an elite—the saints—but their status is not based on material and social privilege. And, unlike fallen hierarchies of status, their excellence in piety does not create unjust divisions and exclusions. Rather, through what they practice and model, their excellence inspires and invokes ever-richer forms of just and loving communion.

Normatively, worship as *leitourgia* represents a nonmonetized, noncompetitive form of work outside of the capitalist economy. As a way of inhabiting divine-human relations, it is work that is paradoxically a form of Sabbath rest that relativizes all other forms of work. In its catholicity and representativeness, worship is both local—it is work among these people in this place at this time—and universal—it participates in a work for everyone (we pray for the world), and across past, present, and future (it participates in the common worship of the communion of saints). As a mode of production, it entails nonproprietorial, nonmonetized exchange: we exchange the peace, prayers, sermons, and words as gifts from God given for building up the body politic of the church but which, by their very nature, cannot be expropriated by one set of people for exclusive use. An act of worship, as both an event and a generic activity, is a nonfungible, unique activity that cannot be commodified and thence exchanged for cheese or bread in the monetary economy. It can exist only as an event and network of relationships rather than as an object to be bought and sold. Conversely, Christian worship should be the antithesis of a priestly class that extracts tokens of sacrifice from the surplus of ordinary people in order to sustain a cultic system of religious production and that sacralizes inequality. It is just such a corrupt system that the story of the "scoundrel" sons of Eli, who "treated the offerings of the LORD with contempt," portrays (1 Sam. 2:12-17). They were exploiting their position for their private benefit and not serving the commonwealth. Similar judgments should be leveled at any Christian leader who commodifies the pastoral and liturgical relation, as these are to be based on trust and covenant, not money and contract. It is this insight that lies behind the seemingly arcane formulation in the Anglican Church whereby clergy are paid a stipend to ensure that their liturgical and pastoral labor is free and that they do not have to charge for their services.

As an event, true worship is constituted not by the aggregation of individual self-interests but as an expression of the participants' shared love for God and neighbor. It is thus something in which the flourishing of each is intertwined with the flourishing of all: if I don't contribute my charism to the proceedings, or am excluded from doing so, then both I and the body are impoverished. Or as Paul puts it in 1 Corinthians 12:7: "To each is given the manifestation of the Spirit for the common good." And so while there are differences of role (some are teachers, evangelists, etc.), the form of social order established in worship entails no essential conflict of interest between these roles (even though the actual distribution of these roles may be unjustly determined by false criteria based on gender, race, sexuality, or class).

Theologically, the social order of worship is analogous to a choir in which individual differences work in harmony to produce a common and mutually enhancing output of sound. The choir contrasts with the factory and bureaucracy, in which the system rests on competing interests (e.g., between owners and workers, or managers and managed); the mass or crowd, which leaves the individual utterly alone and is blind to real differences (everyone is the same, simply part of the mass); and a class, which subsumes individuality to the interests of the collective. As a mode of production, liturgy represents a far more profound crisis to capitalism than the crises of overproduction and market failures that Marx identified. It represents a crisis of the kind Karl Barth spoke of: it is a judgment on the world insofar as it is idolatrous and overdetermined by the things of this age. Through providing a contradiction, worship shows up capitalism's historically contingent and unnatural form (this is not the way the world always is or has to be) and unveils how the premise of capitalism is the *libido dominandi* of the earthly city.

The above may be an appropriate *theological* description of worship. However, returning to the insights of Latin American liberation theology, reflection upon modern conceptions of class introduces a proper moment of suspicion about any act of "real-existing" worship. It is to social theories of class that I now turn to rebalance an overly positive assessment of the role of liturgy in political witness that characterizes the "ecclesial turn" in political theology as articulated in the work of Milbank, Cavanaugh, and Stanley Hauerwas.

As well as constituting an alternative mode of production to that which dominates contemporary forms of social order, liturgy has the potential to reproduce and reinforce class conflict. Pierre Bourdieu's conception of class formation brings critical insight to this dynamic. Bourdieu argues that classes form out of the interaction between the unequal distribution and consumption of cultural, economic, and social capital within different "fields." Fields are arenas such as politics, science, and the arts. One's location in a field, combined with one's formation in a "habitus"—one's socialization to think, feel, and act in certain ways—determines how individuals are situated in and adapted to the world around them. For Bourdieu, the ruling class maintains itself across generations by mobilizing different forms of capital and inducting its young into certain dispositions, primarily aesthetic, that subsequently guide them toward behaviors and tastes that reinforce their status and distinguish them from other, lower classes. These are often highly nuanced differences, such as differences in grammar, physical bearing, or diet. For Bourdieu, social origins and taste are more important in determining class position than a relationship to the means of production. Following the insights of Bourdieu, we can posit that how we sit, talk, dress, and comport ourselves, as well as what and where we sing, read, and speak in worship, can express and reproduce class relations and thereby reinscribe social divisions and class conflict into the heart of the worshiping community.[27] Thus liturgy can do the work of interrupting capitalistic modes of production through such practices as Sabbath keeping while at the same time reinforcing stratification based on status and class as an identity through the dress, bodily proprieties, behavioral codes, etc., that accompany a practice such as Sabbath keeping. The reproduction of inequitable and unjust social divisions in worship is a perennial problem

27. In Bourdieu's emphasis on social distinction, we encounter the difference between class as relationship to production and class as a feature of distribution and consumption.

that Paul had to deal with when writing to the Corinthian church about how they ate and worshiped together (1 Cor. 11:17–34). The sign of the peace is addressed to this very issue.

Many liturgies follow the pattern of Justin Martyr's *Apology* and locate the sign of peace before the offertory prayer during the Eucharist. This timing echoes Jesus's injunction in Matthew 5:23–24: "So when you are offering your gift at the altar, if you remember that your brother or sister has something against you, leave your gift there before the altar and go; first be reconciled to your brother or sister, and then come and offer your gift."

Liturgically, the sign of peace is there to insert a conciliatory gesture. On the one hand, this gesture recognizes the reality of ongoing divisions and unjust inequalities and thence the need to become enemies reconciled. On the other hand, it embodies the need to ritually enact and conform to the group's primary identity as brothers and sisters in Christ and thereby relativize class or other earthly divisions. The sign of peace makes visible the otherwise hidden divisions of class while simultaneously gesturing toward the possibility of their transfiguration. In making the invisible visible, the sign of peace ritually unveils the hidden powers still at work in the congregation, making them subject to the authority and judgment of God's Word.[28] To the hidden acts of faithlessness and idolatry that ongoing class divisions embody within the worshiping community, the sign of peace enacts a gesture of faith that we are members of one another in Christ. Whether we then live according to that which we gesture is another matter.

In this time between the times, worship as an event is a paradoxical one. In worship, we encounter the sharpest divisions within the church as a participant in the earthly city *and* convergence of the church with the communion of saints. In modern worship, all those in attendance participate in the competitive, conflictual patterns of capitalism and state administration, and yet they are also part of God's body politic and subjects of God's peaceable rule. However, we cannot know ourselves as sinful members of worldly systems of idolatry and domination until we gather as the church

28. Luther's rejection of the kiss of peace can be read as a radicalization of this point. In remembering Judas's kiss of betrayal, the absence of the kiss of peace during the celebration of the Mass during Holy Week was common practice in Luther's time. Craig Koslofsky contends that the year-round rejection of the *Pax* to the laity in the 1520s "suggested liturgically that all kisses of peace were in fact Judas kisses. The human inability to perform good works such as peacemaking without divine grace was underscored by the omission of the *Pax*" ("The Kiss of Peace in the German Reformation," in *The Kiss in History*, ed. Karen Harvey [Manchester: Manchester University Press, 2005], 26).

and therein encounter each other as members of God's covenantal order. Class as a lens of analysis can help identify what needs converting if the pilgrim people of God are to not overidentify with the earthly city and are to help rather than hinder sustaining a more just and loving common life.

Conflict, Solidarity, and Communion

Milbank and Cavanaugh bring to the fore the centrality of worship in shaping a Christian conception of peace, and worship as a potential counterperformance of class conflict. Roman Catholic social teaching develops a different set of concerns in response to Marxist analyses of class. Marxist accounts tend to subordinate social relations to material ones, seeing them as epiphenomena of material processes. Herein lies an important aspect of the magisterial critique of recourse to Marxist modes of analysis.[29] Pope John Paul II argued that civil society, and society more generally, has priority over politics and economics as that which drives historical change and is the true sphere of human freedom.[30] For John Paul II, it is through our shared social/cultural life that humans become persons through the pursuit of transcendent, nonmaterial goods. The contrast here is with political ideologies on the left *and* right that wish to define what it means to be human in solely material terms. Christian theological appropriations of Marxism need to question therefore the materialist and deterministic view of social relations that characterizes Marxism and much of the social sciences more generally.

At this point, another account of class formation comes into view, that of Durkheim. A theological emphasis on the priority of society over politics and economics fits very well with Durkheim's conception of class formation. Like Weber and Marx, Durkheim saw industrialization and capitalism as generating distinctively new patterns of social order. However, instead of it inevitably leading to class conflict, for Durkheim, it could lead to new forms of solidarity. Durkheim contrasted "mechanical" solidarity with

---

29. See *Laborem Exercens* (1981), §11; Congregation of the Doctrine of the Faith, *Libertatis Nuntius* (1984); and *Libertatis Conscientia* (1986). Gutiérrez makes clear that he entirely rejects this aspect of Marxist analysis and concurs with the magisterial critique of it (*Truth Shall Make You*, 76-77); likewise, Enrique Dussel agrees with the magisterial critique of historical materialism but contends that this was never an aspect of Marxism that liberation theology drew on ("Theology of Liberation," 85-102).

30. John Paul II, *Centesimus Annus* (1991).

modern, "organic" solidarity. The former existed in premodern societies and involved both the subordination of the individual to a collective consciousness and a high degree of homogeneity. The latter entails increasing division of labor leading to greater differentiation and autonomy combined with interdependence. Involvement in specialist occupations would, for Durkheim, spontaneously lead to new forms of cooperative activity and the generation of shared social norms and rules as workers became increasingly aware of their dependence on each other. If sameness was the foundation of mechanical solidarity, organic solidarity arose because of differentiation and the complementarity between workers engaged in different tasks. However, Durkheim recognized that there was a "pathological" transition stage between mechanical and organic solidarity as people adjusted to the new forms of society. He went so far as to say that "A society made up of an extremely large mass of unorganized individuals, which an overgrown state attempts to limit and restrain, constitutes a veritable sociological monstrosity."[31]

For Durkheim the problems of modern society arose not because of alienation from ownership of the means of production, as for Marx, but because of anomie. Anomie is a lack of solidarity and a breakdown in moral formation brought about through under- or overregulation by external authorities and institutions, most notably the state. His solution was the creation of more cooperative institutions that could bind people together within common occupations, represent the collective interests of these professions, and generate the social norms and rules to guide people in their work and relations with each other. A corporatist system of interlocking institutions, analogous to the old Roman *collegium* and medieval guilds, would fill the vacuum of social significance, integrate people into larger sets of communal relations, and forge new moral rules and social norms in a way that neither the state, a reliance on legal contract, nor the isolated individual could ever achieve.

The parallels between Catholic social thought, with its emphasis on solidarity and fraternal conceptions of political life, and the work of Durkheim are not coincidental.[32] Conversely, Durkheim's work is the root of many interpretations of the church as an institution that integrates otherwise

---

31. Émile Durkheim, *The Division of Labour in Society*, trans. W. D. Halls (Basingstoke, UK: Palgrave, 1984), liv.

32. Milbank notes that the genealogy of Durkheim's thinking and that of certain strands of Catholic social thought overlap (*Theology and Social Theory*, 61-66).

isolated individuals and generates social cohesion and norms through its beliefs and practices. It is true that gathered worship, and in particular, the sign of peace, asserts the primacy of society or a unitary social body of which all are a part. The very act of worship thence upholds the possibility of a common life as against the refusal of such a life in conflict-based models of class formation (Marxist or otherwise). Conflict-based approaches see social conflict as primordial and, for some, irresolvable. By contrast, in worship, conflict is recognized as ever present in this age (hence the need for a kiss of peace). However, conflict is neither the first nor the last nor the most important thing to know about social reality. Worship mediates the possibility of another, eschatological social order in which the proud are laid low and the lowly raised up. However, pursuit of this order through communion with Jesus Christ in the power of the Holy Spirit generates a genuinely common good that both the privileged and the poor can identify with and participate in. Thus, on a Christian account, it is communion, not conflict, that is primordial.

In and through worship we encounter an alternative story through which to make sense of our lives. It is one that contrasts with that offered by both the "American dream," with its accompanying status anxiety, and class war, with its accompanying class envy, antagonisms, and snobbery. However, the church should not be reduced to one of Durkheim's mediating institutions within civil society, standing between the individual and the state. The very term the early church adopted to name their gatherings suggests this: they did not choose the language of a guild or association that would indicate that the church was gathered around particular interests. Instead, they used the term *ekklēsia*, meaning an assembly of the whole city in which the interests of all were to be represented and deliberated upon together. Likewise, the performance of Christian worship should contradict all forms of single issue, corporatist, and group-identity politics.

In worship, relations of class are to be superseded by relations of fellowship: we are brothers and sisters in Christ, not rich and poor, slave and free, or bourgeoisie and proletariat. In worship we are not merely in solidarity, nor is worship a temporary alliance. Rather, worship enacts how, through Christ, Christians are members of one another. Hence Paul uses the image of a body made up of many parts. Within this body, the *koinōnia* or fellowship established is to transcend the friend-enemy distinctions of class, the occupational divisions of labor, and the hierarchal divisions of cultural status, and in their place forge a catholic community that anticipates the gathering of all classes into a single body. However, this does not mean that social divisions, whether economic, racial, or cultural, or of gender and sexuality, are ignored or replaced. Rather, they are transfigured. For fallen creatures, transfiguration entails a threefold movement of conversion involving healing, exorcism/deliverance (which can entail abolition of systemically evil practices and institutions), and the formation of new, eschatologically anticipative ways of being alive with and for others—a framework I expand on in chapter 11.

More Than Class

Contrary to Durkheim's predictions, the division of labor did not lead to occupational solidarity and the formation of cohesive classes. Durkheim failed to account for how the structure of class is never static but responds to changing economic and cultural conditions. For example, Geoffrey Ingham sees class-based inequality continuing but no longer determined by social status or the material conditions of labor, but by who has access to and control of credit. Ingham sees contemporary society divided between the "relatively poor majority of debtor 'classes' that borrows from the minority of net creditors and the owners and controllers of the means of producing credit-money."[33] On this account, power over credit-debt relations is key, with the expropriating class being the moneylenders, not the bourgeoisie. Credit and risk rating constitute the real class system and reveal the structure of inequality. It is the banks, not the factory owners, who hold real power, and the highest class are low-risk, "high-net-worth" individuals who receive favorable terms for borrowing money. The lowest class are the financially excluded, who are considered high-risk borrowers and do not have access to bank accounts or credit cards, locked as they are into a cash economy. A particularly egregious source of financial exclusion is the racially discriminatory practice of "redlining" whole districts, thereby denying those who live there access to banking, insurance, and investment. For the financially excluded, lack of access to credit means the following: they pay more for utilities or household items because they miss out on the discounts available to those who pay direct from a bank account or by credit card; they pay more for loans, as they have to resort to high-interest, subprime lenders such as payday lenders; and they become locked

33. Geoffrey Ingham, "Class Inequality and the Social Production of Money," in *Renewing Class Analysis*, ed. Rosemary Crompton et al. (Oxford: Blackwell, 2000), 73.

into impoverished localities because they cannot borrow money to cover a move to where better work is available or draw in investment to start new businesses. However, unlike in a factory system, where class consciousness could develop and collective action was possible through unionization, the underclass of the financially excluded are individually isolated with few means of social organization. The result is that they lack political agency and struggle to establish forms of mutual aid and alternative provision such as a credit union. In this context, religious congregations are one of the few means of social and nonpecuniary, self-governing organization still available to the lowest classes.

Ingham's account points to the difficulty of generating forms of solidarity and mobilizing people along class lines in the contemporary context. The sociologist Anthony Giddens, in his revisionist account of class, sees this as intrinsic to the nature of class-based politics. He argues that a class is not a cohesive political actor but the aggregation of individual interests without any clear identity.[34] Giddens focuses on the middle classes and the contradictions they experience between the need for autonomous control over their work (e.g., as an academic, accountant, or engineer) and the bureaucratic exigencies and manipulation of the organizations to which they are subject. However, the lack of class identity and an inability to act together are even more acute among groups such as undocumented migrant workers and casual, often low-paid female workers such as cleaners and caregivers. An analysis such as that by Giddens and the realities of the atomizing and precarious state of work in a globalized economy raise a broader question: Is class still a relevant category of analysis? Black feminist and womanist accounts of class make the point that attention to class dynamics is still salient for understanding contemporary social and political life even while it is insufficient as a starting point for political action.

Absent from Giddens's early analysis is how inequality correlates with discrimination based on race and gender. He is not alone in this respect. The inattention of all the class-based analysis sketched so far to such factors is drawn out with immense force and clarity by black feminist and womanist thinkers.[35] Black feminist bell hooks articulates the problem thus:

34. Anthony Giddens, *The Class Structure of the Advanced Societies* (London: Hutchinson, 1973), 192.

35. An earlier generation of scholars—for example, Oliver C. Cox in his *Caste, Class, and Race* (1948)—analyzed the parallels between and coemergence of racial and class-based hierarchies and how capitalism was central to race-based antagonism. Black feminists added gender and sexuality to this kind of analysis. An early formulation of this

As a group, black women are in an unusual position in this society, for not only are we collectively at the bottom of the occupational ladder, but our overall social status is lower than that of any other group. Occupying such a position, we bear the brunt of sexist, racist, and classist oppression. At the same time, we are the group that has not been socialized to assume the role of exploiter/oppressor in that we are allowed no institutionalized "other" that we can exploit or oppress. . . . White women and black men have it both ways. They can act as oppressor or be oppressed. Black men may be victimized by racism, but sexism allows them to act as exploiters and oppressors of women. White women may be victimized by sexism, but racism enables them to act as exploiters and oppressors of black people. Both groups have led liberation movements that favor their interests and support the continued oppression of other groups. Black male sexism has undermined struggles to eradicate racism just as white female racism undermines feminist struggle. As long as these two groups or any group defines liberation as gaining social equality with ruling class white men, they have a vested interest in the continued exploitation and oppression of others. Black women with no institutionalized "other" that we may discriminate against, exploit, or oppress often have a lived experience that directly challenges the prevailing classist, sexist, racist social structure and its concomitant ideology. This lived experience may shape our consciousness in such a way that our worldview differs from those who have a degree of privilege (however relative within the existing system). It is essential for continued feminist struggle that black women recognize the special vantage point our marginality gives us and make use of this perspective to criticize the dominant racist, classist, sexist hegemony as well as to envision and create a counter-hegemony.[36]

The experience of black women displays the interconnections among a mutually constitutive set of oppressions that have a multiplying effect on each other.[37] Moreover, the intersection of gender, class, and race shows

position was the 1974 "Combahee River Collective Statement," in *Home Girls: A Black Feminist Anthology*, ed. Barbara Smith (New Brunswick, NJ: Rutgers University Press, 2000), 264-74.

36. bell hooks, *Feminist Theory: From Margin to Center* (Cambridge, MA: South End, 1984), 14-15.

37. See Kimberle Crenshaw, "Mapping the Margins: Intersectionality, Identity

up the need for a holistic vision of change that integrates the interpersonal as well as the structural, the subjective as well as the objective, dimensions of oppression.[38] Black feminist and womanist analysis thereby points to the need to move beyond an exclusive focus on class. Coming to the fore in womanist approaches, and in contrast to the other class-based analyses detailed so far, is a refusal to idealize science, technology, and a technical rationality as liberating forces. These forces and modes of rationality are often means of exploiting black women. In their stead, quotidian and communal wisdom, and attention to intimacy, spirituality, and ecology, are vital resources for learning how to survive and thrive amid multiple interwoven and systemic oppressions that form the background conditions that diminish the agency of some even as they enhance the agency of others.[39]

Womanist theologians such as Katie Cannon, Delores Williams, Jacqueline Grant, Cheryl Townsend Gilkes, and Emilie M. Townes recognized that neither feminist theology, which problematized gender, nor black liberation theology, which problematized race, nor Latin American liberation theology, which problematized class, provided all the categories needed to make sense of the world as they and other black women, particularly poor black women, experienced it. Echoing hooks, they argue that a separate approach is needed to make sense of the situation of black women who live at the intersection of three systems of oppression: one economic (class), one racial (white supremacy), and another gendered (patriarchy).[40] Of late, a new generation of womanist theologians has added sexuality as a point of reference and argued for the need to include heterosexism among these structures of oppression. For example, Keri Day, who draws on Audre Lorde to raise up the importance of the erotic as a dimension of

---

Politics, and Violence against Women of Color," *Stanford Law Review* 43, no. 6 (1991): 1241-99.

38. See, for example, Keri Day's assessment of how affirmative action policies address racial disparity but fail to address class disparities and so do not provide the support structures needed, in *Religious Resistance to Neoliberalism: Womanist and Black Feminist Perspectives* (Basingstoke, UK: Palgrave Macmillan, 2016), 122-23.

39. See Alice Walker's definition of womanism in *In Search of Our Mother's Gardens: Womanist Prose* (San Diego: Harcourt Brace Jovanovich, 1983), xi-xii. See also bell hooks, *Feminism Is for Everybody: Passionate Politics* (Cambridge, MA: South End, 2000), 105-9, and Delores Williams, "Sin, Nature, and Black Women's Bodies," in *Ecofeminism and the Sacred*, ed. Carol J. Adams (New York: Continuum, 1993), 24-29.

40. For a case study in this kind of multidimensional analysis, see Marcia Y. Riggs's account of the black women's club movement in *Awake, Arise and Act: A Womanist Call for Black Liberation* (Cleveland: Pilgrim, 1994).

transformational love, points to how capitalism diminishes our ability to experience the erotic in creative and healing ways and instead constantly reduces the erotic to the pornographic. Day attends to the erotic as a source of political and economic knowledge and energy that can challenge existing structures and systems.[41] Womanist social ethics, read as a form of political theology, seeks to uncover and resist the way assemblages of class, race, gender, and sexuality assign negative value. As part of this, womanists reject any notion that suffering brought on by these oppressions is God's will. Rather, God's will is for the liberation of black women and, in concert with them, the liberation of all people.

Womanism attempts to awaken humanity to the possibility of richer visions of social relations and enable a way beyond conditions of alienation and anomie; we are not just economic monads but living, desiring, social, and embodied creatures whose form of life should enable all people to thrive. Discerning what thriving means entails critically investigating "the conditions and circumstances of daily life." However, as Emilie Townes contends, such investigation and analysis must go beyond disenchanted, materialist critical theories and attend to how theology both colludes with and reinforces hegemonic discourses while, at the same time, identifying how theology can be a source of contesting and overturning them.[42] Focusing on how constructions of class, gender, sexuality, and race deny and distort creative and life-affirming forms of common life, both within and without the church, womanists seek ways toward love and justice for all people. As Townes puts it: "Because God loves humanity, God gives all peoples the opportunity to embrace the victory of the resurrection. The resurrection moves the oppressed past suffering to pain and struggle and from pain and struggle to new life and wholeness."[43]

Conclusion

In congregating for worship, people do not, at least ostensibly, gather for commercial, occupational, or state-directed transactions. They gather to worship God and care for each other. The relational power derived from

41. Day, *Religious Resistance to Neoliberalism*, 77–104.

42. Emilie M. Townes, "Living in the New Jerusalem: The Rhetoric and Movement of Liberation in the House of Evil," in *A Troubling in My Soul: Womanist Perspectives on Evil and Suffering*, ed. Emilie M. Townes (Maryknoll, NY: Orbis, 1993), 88–89.

43. Townes, "Living in the New Jerusalem," 85.

this ability to act in concert comes not from property ownership, mastery of a knowledge regime, social status, or kinship relations but from associating together in the name of Christ for common action. At a normative level, the interaction between the worshipers and the power of God circulated among them through the Holy Spirit grounds the production of this new social order. This relational power is then recirculated and reproduced in the earthly city to the degree that the worshipers are attuned to and participate in God's economy of healing and exorcising the world and breaking forth eschatological anticipations of the world to come. The institutional basis of common worship is crucial, for institutions provide a legal, organizational, financial, moral, social, and physical place to stand. Such institutions are the building blocks of a more complex space that inhibit the totalizing, monopolistic thrust of economic and state processes that instrumentalize persons and the relationships among them (thereby denying the primacy of the social over the economic and political). These processes can also subordinate all other interests to a single, dominant interest: the power of money or the power of the state. Thus, worship itself can be a means of pursuing the peace of the earthly city and mitigating its unjust and unstable social order as it inserts into the modern earthly city noninstrumental, nonpecuniary, reciprocal relations. These doxologically grounded relations are reperformed and recirculated through myriad pastoral and political endeavors. Worship can thereby be a counter to the dynamics of class conflict and injustice that distort and fracture a common life. However, worship can also reproduce class and other conflicts and injustices in its very forms and practices. Worship as a work of love must attend to both its generative and sinful dynamics so as to sustain a truly common life both within and without the church.

Threshold

Political theology, in giving an account of the nature and form of political order, must attend to the social, economic, and political hierarchies that help structure a common life and the conditions of agency. This chapter examined class as one such hierarchy. As seen in the discussion of worship in this chapter, another way to structure political order and the conditions of agency is through constellations of belief and practice. But if hierarchies of one kind or another can create and perpetuate divisions and conflict, then so can differences of belief and practice. So political theology must also attend to how different, often rival visions of what it means to be human—some designated religious, others not—are ordered in relation to each other. A key way in which differences of belief and practice are negotiated to generate a peaceable common life is through a notion of secularity. It is to debates about this term and a theological account of the secular that I turn in the next chapter.

Suggested Readings for Further Discussion

Scriptural texts: Genesis 16:1-16 and 21:1-21, Deuteronomy 24:6-22, Matthew 20:20-28, Luke 16:19-31, 1 Corinthians 11:17-34, Colossians 3, Philemon, and James 2.

Jean-Jacques Rousseau, "Discourse on the Origins and Foundations of Inequality among Men" (1755). Various editions.

Erik Peterson, "The Book on the Angels: Their Place and Meaning in the Liturgy," in *Theological Tractates*, trans. Michael J. Hollerich (Stanford, CA: Stanford University Press, 2011), 106-42. Explores how early Christian liturgies were also political visions.

Gustavo Gutiérrez, "Option for the Poor," in *Mysterium Liberationis: Fundamental Concepts of Liberation Theology*, ed. Ignacio Ellacuría and Jon Sobrino (Maryknoll, NY: Orbis, 1993), 235-50. Gives an account of the origins and meaning of a preferential option for the poor.

Emilie M. Townes, "Vanishing into Limbo: The Moral Dilemma of Identity as Property and Commodity," in *Womanist Ethics and the Cultural Production of Evil* (New York: Palgrave Macmillan, 2006), 29-55.

Stanley Hauerwas and Samuel Wells, "Christian Ethics as Informed Prayer" and "The Gift of the Church and the Gifts God Gives It," in *The Blackwell Companion to Christian Ethics*, ed. Stanley Hauerwas and Samuel Wells, 2nd ed. (Chichester, UK: Wiley-Blackwell, 2011), 3-27. These two intersecting essays articulate how liturgy, ethics, and politics interrelate to form a distinctive community of witness.

CHAPTER 8

Secularity, Not Secularism

Sustaining a common life requires commitment to a vision of human flourishing. In complex societies, numerous accounts of the meaning and purpose of life emerge—which may or may not be religious—and some way of both accommodating and coordinating these accounts must be found. Failure to do so leads to either civil strife or an oppressive hegemony whereby one account overdetermines others. The constructive way to frame this dilemma in the West is to say our common life is secular yet open to multiple substantive claims. But when we call something secular, what do we mean? The answer depends on whether we are using a notion of the secular to frame a theological or philosophical commitment, a sociological description, or a mode of statecraft used for controlling and managing religious groups. Confusions abound because these frames of reference are often conflated.

Against the view that the secular constitutes a neutral realm stripped of the false accretions of religion, I make two arguments. First, that talk of "the secular" inherently mixes up talk of God and talk of politics, so that formations of the secular are as much a religious as a nonreligious process. And second, that different sets of metaphysical, political, and moral commitments produce different forms of secularity, each of which enshrines normative assumptions about what it means to be human and how to order differences of belief and practice in relation to each other.[1]

1. José Casanova argues that processes of secularization are reiterations of developments within all axial religions that posit a duality between transcendent and mundane orders of space and time. Following Shmuel Eisenstadt, different axial religions give rise to "multiple modernities," each with its own construction of secularity that now, under conditions of globalization, contests and interacts with the others. See José Casanova, "Rethinking Secularization: A Global Comparative Perspective," in

In the course of making these arguments, I examine several uses of the term "secular" that inform debates in political theology. What I don't do is address questions relating to toleration and freedom of conscience. I discuss these in chapter 9. Instead, I contend that the status of what does and does not count as secular and the relationship between politics and secularity are distinct from and prior to questions about religious liberty, toleration, and the treatment of religious minorities. Avowedly atheist (e.g., the Soviet Union) and militantly secularist regimes (e.g., France) can be just as intolerant if not more so than those with an established religion. In both these cases, what is and is not tolerated depends on a prior conception of what being secular is understood to demand.

In what follows, I review debates about the nature of the secular, and in doing so describe how secularity is a factor shaping the conditions of political judgment and the formation of a common life in the contemporary context. I also offer a theological take on how secularity should be understood and constructed to optimize the conditions for making faithful and wise political judgments and negotiating sameness and difference constructively. I begin this task of evaluative description and prudential prescription by setting out a theological understanding of secularity. A primary focus of this first section is how a theological conception of the place of humanity in the cosmos contrasts with anthropocentric and materialist conceptions of the universe. I also attend to the role of a series of dyads—church and world, eschatology and history, religious and secular, and church and state—the interactions of which generate different constructions of secularity.[2] Second, I assess accounts of secularity as historical and sociological phenomena, paying particular attention to the validity or otherwise of the "secularization thesis" that religion will necessarily decline in public significance due to its fundamental incompatibility with processes of modernization. Such an assessment entails discussing whether secularity is a specifically Christian or even Protestant phenomenon, or whether there can be multiple forms of secularity, each born out of the interaction between differing constellations of modernity and multiple traditions of belief and practice.

Religion, Globalization, and Culture, ed. Peter Beyer and Lori Beaman (Leiden: Brill, 2007), 101-20.

2. As noted in chapter 4, a dyad is not a binary, even though dyads can collapse into binaries. For example, in the medieval era church/state had a dyadic relation, but in modernity it can take the form of a binary whereby the state is opposed to and seeks to abolish the church.

Third, I contrast *secularization* as a regime of liberal statecraft with *secularity* as a political good. The former is antagonistic toward religious traditions, while the latter enables the formation and preservation of a common life among members of multiple traditions—both religious and nonreligious—amid ongoing difference, disagreement, and asymmetries of power. Different modes of statecraft can either serve or hinder patterns of secularity as a political good. I argue that constructions of a common life as secular result from the interplay of religious beliefs and practices with numerous philosophies, state procedures, and modern processes such as industrialization. Regarding political theology, secularity is a way to talk about the need to coordinate with non-Christian others the pursuit of the kingdom of God with pursuit of penultimate goods. To coordinate these dual foci demands constructing a common life that is not dominated by the church yet which is open to transcendent claims. As a contingent assemblage, subject to multiple iterations, formations of the secular should be judged good or bad not by whether they are religiously neutral or not, but by the extent to which they enable the possibility of a just and loving common life amid difference, disagreement, and asymmetries of power.

Before proceeding, it is necessary to say a prefatory word about my use of the term "religion." While there are analogues for the modern use of the term in the ancient world, there is a shift from the seventeenth century onward whereby "religion" ceases to mean piety and becomes a generic term marking specific kinds of belief and practice.[3] Some argue that religion is a Eurocentric, colonial category that subsumes radically different phenomena within a largely Protestant framework.[4] This framework was born out of interactions between metropole and colony that generated a

---

3. One of the roots for the word "religion" is the Latin verb *religo*, which means "to bind" or "fasten up"—an action that brings to the fore the social and political work that has always been a part of religious practice. This is a consistent feature of all uses of the term and points to its inherently divisive nature; like the demos, just as it binds some together, religion separates them from others.

4. Talal Asad, "The Construction of Religion as an Anthropological Category," in *Genealogies of Religion: Discipline and Reasons of Power in Christianity and Islam* (Baltimore: Johns Hopkins University Press, 1993), 27-54; Peter van der Veer, *Imperial Encounters: Religion and Modernity in India and Britain* (Princeton: Princeton University Press, 2001); and Brent Nongbri, *Before Religion: A History of a Modern Concept* (New Haven: Yale University Press, 2013). On modernization as a mode of Protestantization, see Hans Joas, *Faith as an Option: Possible Futures for Christianity*, trans. Alex Skinner (Stanford, CA: Stanford University Press, 2014), 50-62.

progressive and hierarchal view of religions, a view exemplified in David Hume's *Natural History of Religion* (1757). In Britain, Germany, and the United States, Protestantism (and its offshoots, including Deism) was the standard used to measure all other religions. That which did not conform to a tacitly Protestant conception of true religion was labeled primitive or in need of reform. Such a view can still be heard in contemporary de-bates about the need for Islam to undergo a "reformation": that is, be-come more Protestant and therefore "better." Haunted by free-floating fragments of Protestantism, modern sociological concepts of religion took as definitional that religion is an assemblage of propositional beliefs, in-terior experiences, and social practices. Traces of this kind of approach are found in Robert Bellah's recent definition of religion as "a system of beliefs and practices relative to the sacred that unite those who adhere to them in a moral community."[5] Yet this definition could be applied as much to a graduation ceremony or political rally as to a worship service, so why it demarcates something called "religion" is not clear. Bellah is well aware of the problems of this definition and proceeds to question it. Nevertheless, it shapes his monumental analysis of the role of religion in human evolution. Such an account of religion is not neutral. And it can be questioned whether it is even an accurate account of congregational life in the multifarious strands of Protestantism. What it does do, however, is homogenize disparate and arguably incommensurable phenomena, re-making different traditions into versions of the same kind of this-worldly thing called religion.[6] In recognition of this narrow conception, there are moves in sociology to incorporate how religion is as much a sensorium of sounds, smells, and sights as it is a set of beliefs, as much a sensibility and set of bodily proprieties and affects as it is a set of distinct practices and interior experiences.[7] It would probably be better to talk of philosophies or schools of life and catalogue whether or not these had a transcendent

5. Robert Bellah, *Religion in Human Evolution: From the Paleolithic to the Axial Age* (Cambridge, MA: Belknap Press of Harvard University Press, 2011), 1.

6. The refusal to take the particularity of different traditions seriously generates di-rect political effects. Failure to evaluate different traditions in terms of their own frames of reference leads to misinterpretation and misunderstanding, which in turn generate ill-judged action on the part of "outsiders." For example, government officials confusing Sikhs with Muslims, or Reformed Jews not being distinguished from ultra-Orthodox ones.

7. For one such account, see Miguel Vásquez, *More Than Belief: A Materialist Theory of Religion* (Oxford: Oxford University Press, 2011).

dimension. However, for the purposes of this chapter, I will use the term "religion," but only as a kind of pidgin English, acknowledging its imprecision, contestability, and vagueness.

The Secular as a Theological Commitment

As a theological term, the secular is that which is not eternity. What is secular can be open to and transfigured in eternity, but its primary point of focus is the things of this age rather than the age to come. The demarcation of the current age as secular is a Christian innovation that breaks open divisions between sacred and profane. If something is secular, it can be both sacred and profane, rather than sacred or profane, concerned with both the immanent and the transcendent, able to participate simultaneously in the penultimate and the ultimate. Secular time is thereby ambiguous and contingent. And therein lies the problem. Like a pile of Lego bricks, the concept of the secular can be taken up and put together in multiple ways; this is what the philosopher Charles Taylor calls the "polysemy of the secular."[8] In the process, each iteration is taken to be the definitive one, and fights then ensue over whether it is or not. Lost in the quarrel and confusion between rival versions is that the secular, like pieces of Lego, is supposed to enable free and imaginative play. No one shape is definitive or determinative. Theologically, the secular is a time for the church to improvise forms of witness in response to the prior work of Christ and the Spirit, who are drawing creation into its eschatological fulfillment.

Historically, the theological conception of secular time gave rise to a series of dyads. These included the distinctions between secular and religious and between temporal and spiritual. Until the twentieth century, these dyads mostly framed how the secular was understood. As the 1880 *Oxford English Dictionary* defined it, the secular meant "Of or belonging to the present or visible world as distinguished from the eternal or spiritual world; temporal, worldly. Belonging to the world and its affairs as distinguished from the church and religion; civil, lay, temporal." Priests who served parishes were secular, while those that served in monasteries were religious. Secularization could refer to the transfer of a priest from being religious to being secular. The priest was still a priest, but the context of his

8. Charles Taylor, "The Polysemy of the Secular," *Social Research* 76, no. 4 (2009): 1143–66.

ministry changed. It became a legal term used for the transfer of property or institutional control from spiritual to temporal power. Monarchs and the "lords temporal" wielded temporal power (the sword), while popes and bishops wielded spiritual power. How ecclesial and temporal power were related was subject to much debate. Responses included calls for the separation of "church" and "state," the primacy of ecclesial over temporal authorities (sacerdotalism/clericalism), the subordination of ecclesial to temporal authorities (caesaropapism/Erastianism), and a symphony between ecclesial and temporal authorities.[9] But both ecclesial and temporal authorities were political, and both served the right ordering of this time before Christ's return.[10]

Contemporary understandings of the secular and secularization draw on this theological framework. However, the secular comes to mean reality stripped of religion, while secularization, from roughly the eighteenth century onward, comes to refer to the decline and potential disappearance of Christianity.[11] These shifts translate the secular from being situated in a dyadic relationship with what is eternal to a binary between what is modern and what is not. In the process the temporality of the secular shifts from a nonlinear, christological conception (all times are equidistant from Christ, who is the point of origin, the center, and the end of history) to a linear and progressive temporality (all time is inexorably moving forward, finding its apogee in a religion-free modernity). In the former, past and present are judged good or bad to the extent that they display Christlike ways of being alive. In the latter, what is modern is always better than what is past. Religion is judged to be of the past and thereby incompatible with what is modern.

Within modern understandings of secularization, the inevitable fate of religion in the modern world is to disappear or be subject to conversion (or more properly, de-conversion) so that it serves rather than challenges the present. Insofar as religions serve present concerns (human autonomy, economic growth, social cohesion, etc.), they are good, insofar as they do not, they are bad. When religions contest what is taken to be modern, they are said to be antimodern or reactionary. The worst kind of this reactionary

9. Modern political philosophy did not invent arguments for the separation of church and state. In the West, earlier advocates include Dante's *De Monarchia* (c. 1312), Marsilius of Padua's *Defensor Pacis* (1324), and, in the case of John Wyclif's *On Lordship* (c. 1373), the effective subordination of the church to temporal authority.

10. See the discussion of the Gelasian doctrine of the two in chap. 12.

11. Joas, *Faith as an Option*, 13.

religion is labeled fundamentalism and thereby stigmatized.[12] Within the modern framework of secularization, what is religious is epiphenomenal, whereas what is secular is reality stripped of its superstitious, irrational, and exotic garb. For all intents and purposes, eternity ceases to exist. Religion can be tolerated if it confines itself to what takes place between consenting adults in private. Religions exposing themselves in public are inherently suspicious and probably up to no good. The violent absurdity of this position is illustrated by the 2016 incident when armed French policemen in Nice forced a Muslim woman relaxing on a beach wearing a headscarf and long-sleeved shirt to disrobe and thereby cease to be so provocative in her public display of religion.

A theological conception of secularity stands in stark contrast to modern ideas of secularization. It is rooted in conceptions of time and space that build on New Testament understandings of the cosmos and the place of humans within it. In the New Testament, the term "world" (*kosmos/* κόσμος) is a synonym for the universal order of things.[13] Before the day of judgment, this order is coterminous with a worldly system opposed to

---

12. Many scholarly identifications of fundamentalism see it as a negative or defensive reaction *against* modernity. For example, Manuel Castells envisages the political role of "fundamentalist" religious expressions as a form of what he calls "resistance identities" that build "trenches of resistance and survival on the basis of principles different from, or opposed to, those permeating the institutions of society" (*The Power of Identity* [Malden, MA: Blackwell, 1997], 8). The "Fundamentalist Project," a ten-year academic study of fundamentalism around the world, was key in developing this kind of perspective. While recognizing that fundamentalism was a diverse phenomenon, the project identified enough "family resemblances" to deploy it to describe different kinds of things as versions of the same. See Martin E. Marty and R. Scott Appleby, eds., *Fundamentalisms Observed* (Chicago: University of Chicago Press, 1991). Others question whether there is such a thing as "fundamentalism," suggesting that the term is an unhelpful academic construct that functions in the same way as the term "Oriental" did; that is, it is used to delegitimize and stigmatize certain forms of discourse.

13. In the New Testament, the term "world" (*kosmos*) denotes either the unified order of created things, understood as a neutral description (John 17:5, 24; Rom. 1:20; 1 Cor. 4:9), or the worldly system that is hostile to God's good order (John 15:18-19; 17:14-16; 1 Cor. 1:20; 5:10). In New Testament Greek a number of variations on these two basic connotations can be discerned. For example, Paul Ellingworth identifies six variations: the universe, the earth, human beings and angels, humanity as a whole, humanity as organized in opposition to God, and particular groups of human beings ("Translating Kosmos 'World' in Paul," *Bible Translator* 53, no. 4 [2002]: 414-21). See also David J. Clark, "The Word Kosmos 'World' in John 17," *Bible Translator* 50, no. 4 (1999): 401-6.

God's ordering of creation, what Augustine calls the "earthly city."[14] New Testament usages of the term *kosmos* resist a strict dualism between order and chaos, thus contrasting with prior philosophical and largely Platonic usages of *kosmos* to mean a wholly harmonious order, the antinomy and limit of which was chaos.[15] In the New Testament, the *kosmos* is envisioned as a single creation that is at once good but corrupted and subject to chaotic, nihilistic forces yet open to its healing and participation in God, and thence open to change.

For Christians, Christ is Pantocrator (ruler) over the *kosmos*. How his rule is understood varies, but I take it to be neither about Christianizing the world nor turning the world into the church (both temptations to which the church repeatedly falls prey). Rather, Christ's rule liberates the *kosmos* to be the world (an arena of human flourishing to which the church can contribute) rather than worldly (the world turned in on itself so that social, political, and economic relations diminish our humanity and desecrate our dignity). As noted in chapter 4, the church-world relation should therefore be dyadic, not binary. As the world, history does not bear within itself its own resolution and there is no inherent direction to history: things will not always get better (or worse). To be faithful, Christians should resist ascension and declension narratives about the direction of history. An eschatological view of history challenges both cyclical and declensionist views. It also challenges progressivist ones. The nonprogressive nature of history means that a perfect or true order of things is not realizable within history, so any human system or ideology that claims to provide the means of bringing about this order is a denial of the fallen and contingent nature of historical existence.

God in Jesus Christ deals with the world as it is, and, in the light of the incarnation, history constitutes the crucible of divine-human relations, and the eschaton is the only true fulfillment of these relations.[16] Political en-

---

14. I favor use of the New Testament conception of *kosmos* (κόσμος) as distinct from Augustine's term, the *saeculum*, because, as the wide-ranging exegetical debates that surround Augustine's use of the term *saeculum* reveal, Augustine is much more ambiguous than the New Testament is about the possibility of common objects of love being forged between Christians and non-Christians in the noneschatological order.

15. For a comparison of Plato's influential conceptualization of cosmos in the *Timaeus* and how it contrasts with the Pauline use of the term, see Edward Adams, *Constructing the World: A Study in Paul's Cosmological Language* (Edinburgh: T&T Clark, 2000).

16. Axial age theory posits a similar account of how Judaism and thence Christianity come to delineate a gulf between a true and good order and the order realized concretely

deavors, Christian or otherwise, should seek to approximate more closely the world as it could or should be, but in doing so, they must work from historical experience and existing patterns of life. Attempts to overturn a political system in the name of an ideological blueprint or set of abstract principles will be inherently destructive, as they are attempts to circumvent historical conditions. They thereby deny the goodness and the limits of creation reaffirmed in the incarnation and seek to realize an ersatz eschaton by sinful means. Change and redemption are always possibilities, and good and bad are present in all political systems.[17] To use Dietrich Bonhoeffer's categories, faithful political witness involves neither straightforward "radicalism" (which sees only the world as it should be and with legalistic zeal opposes working within the limits of a good but fallen creation) nor "compromise" (which places the ultimate beyond the bounds of daily life and reconciles itself to unjust worldly systems).[18]

Theologically understood, the secular, noneschatological order is a deeply ambiguous and paradoxical one in which the world is complexly faithful and unfaithful, loving and idolatrous, in which political authorities may both participate in the reordering of creation to its true end and be anti-Christic (i.e., utterly opposed to God's good order). The protean nature of the secular understood theologically is captured in the following quote from Karl Barth. He is discussing how the church is fashioned out of the world, and hence is like the world, yet is also fashioned in response to the Word of God, and therefore, is unlike the world.

---

by any given society. The distinction then serves to provide a horizon against which a real-existing political order can be criticized. On this see Armando Salvatore, *The Public Sphere: Liberal Modernity, Catholicism, Islam* (New York: Palgrave Macmillan, 2007), 53-67. Salvatore goes on to outline how the tension between a transcendent vision of the good and concrete political order shapes overlapping notions of the public sphere in Islam, Judaism, and Christianity.

17. Totalitarian political systems would seem to be the obvious exception to this claim. Even here, a distinction must be made between the evil of the system as such and the political life present within it, which is not monolithically evil throughout. As Scripture testifies, within the total depravity of Sodom and Gomorrah, good was a possibility and good people existed. Beyond even that, Nineveh is capable of repentance. We must not be like Jonah and suffer a failure of imagination and sympathy by first limiting the sovereignty, power, and mercy of God; and second, refusing to believe repentance is possible even in the most unlikely candidates.

18. As Bonhoeffer points out, both constitute forms of hatred of the world because both refuse the possibility of change and redemption. *Dietrich Bonhoeffer Works*, vol. 6, *Ethics*, ed. Clifford Green, trans. Reinhard Krauss et al. (Minneapolis: Fortress, 2005), 153-57.

[God's omnipotent Word] cannot be hindered by the obvious secularity of all human forms of society from creating within these a society
which in the first instance is not distinct from them, yet which is still
this specific society, the people of God, the Christian community, nor
can it be prevented from maintaining, accompanying and ruling this
society as such. And, as it can use the secular possibilities of human
speech, to establish this particular society it can use the secular possibilities of social structuring, not changing them essentially nor di-
vesting them of their secularism, but giving to them as they are a new
meaning and determination. . . . This is what actually takes place in
the power of this Word. Intrinsically unholy possibilities in the structuring of man's life in society are sanctified and made serviceable to
the gathering and upbuilding of the people of God in the service of its
commission and for the purpose of its election and calling.[19]

On Barth's account, the secular may now respond to the Word of God and
be sanctified. In the process, the worldly can become both church and
world. As church, the secular confesses the name of Christ. As world, it
can speak of Christ in what Barth calls "secular parables."[20] But any such
process of sanctification is always subject to attack.

The New Testament language of "empire," "anti-Christ," and the "principalities and powers" reckons with the capacity of political, ecclesial, or
any other authorities to act in wholly malevolent ways that destroy processes of sanctification. They articulate how idolatrous cultural patterns
and political systems are something more than simply a distortion of a gift:
they are evil. A Christian conceptualization of the world as *kosmos*—a moral
order that simultaneously contains the possibility and moments of its own
inversion and dissolution—helps capture the ambiguity of our participation
in this order.[21] It allows us to see Babylon (and its contemporary iterations
in something like capitalism) as mediating things of value. Babylon constitutes part of the noneschatological order of things in which we can perform
the gift and vocation of being human. At the same time, we cannot be naïve
about how Babylon is also an instantiation of a worldly system that can
utterly desecrate that gift and vocation. To enable the worldly city to be a

19. Karl Barth, *Church Dogmatics* IV/3.2, trans. A. T. Mackay et al. (Edinburgh: T&T
Clark, 1961), 740-41.

20. Karl Barth, *Church Dogmatics* IV/3.1, trans. A. T. Mackay et al. (Edinburgh: T&T
Clark, 1961), 115.

21. Stanley Marrow, "κοσμος in John," *Catholic Biblical Quarterly* 64 (2002): 90-102.

place where this gift and vocation can flourish rather than be desecrated, the prevailing social, political, and economic orders must neither be made to bear the full weight of humanity's meaning and purpose nor nihilistically divested of all meaning and purpose. What is required instead is—paradoxically—a faithfully secular politics.

As set out in chapters 6 and 13, Augustine's framework of the two cities is an influential attempt to systematize this New Testament cosmology. Augustine wrestles with how to integrate a Platonic conception of what it meant to participate in the *kosmos* understood as a harmonious order and Christian understandings of the *kosmos* as created yet fallen and redeemed. He also sought to create an alternative to both Eusebian triumphalism (marked by an expectation of progress until the church would overcome the world and universally display heaven's glory in history) and radical Donatist views that advocated separatism from the world (wherein history is orientated toward regress or a movement away from God). In place of both of these polarities, Augustine (influenced by the moderate Donatist, Tyconius) reestablishes a Pauline eschatological perspective through his conception of the two cities.[22] For Augustine, the city of God is an alternative yet co-terminus society to the earthly city. These two cities are two political entities coexistent in time and space and thus part of this noneternal age or *saeculum*. Within this framework, human history is "secular" (rather than neutral); that is, it neither promises nor sets at risk the kingdom of God. The kingdom of God is established, if not fully manifest, and the "end" of history is already achieved and fulfilled in Christ. The church can reside in this age regarding its structures and patterns of life as relativized by what is to come and therefore see them as contingent and provisional. Within an Augustinian framework, the secular is a synonym for the noneternal age before Christ's return.

From the thirteenth century onward, another way to read the secular emerged within a very different strand of theologizing about the dyadic relationships between history and eschatology and church and world. Joachim of Fiore (c. 1135-1202) broke with the Augustinian view in a number of ways, one of which was that he saw human history as the arena through which the new Jerusalem would be made fully manifest through immanent developments. Joachim divided history into three ages: the age of the

---

22. For how Augustine's eschatology directly draws on Paul's eschatology, especially the Pauline account of the "principalities and powers," see Robert A. Markus, *Christianity and the Secular* (Notre Dame: University of Notre Dame Press, 2006), 14-17, 55-56.

Father, which refers to the period of the old covenant; the age of the Son, which began with the period of the New Testament; and the final age, the age of the Holy Spirit, which was imminent. The reign of the antichrist and a period of persecution would precede this last age. At the same time, an outburst of renewal would anticipate the age of the Spirit. In his context, Joachim identified various forms of monasticism as the renewal that presaged the age of the Spirit.[23] Within Joachim's framework, his realized eschatology subsumes the secular.

A Joachimite view of history has inspired a variety of millenarian or apocalyptic movements that identify themselves with the age of the Spirit and call all who oppose them agents of the antichrist. Some of these have taken a direct political form. The sixteenth-century Radical Reformation preacher Thomas Müntzer (c. 1489-1525) represents one example. He helped lead a peasant's revolt in Germany, a revolt that he saw as ushering in a new age of the Spirit. The attempt by Anabaptists and others to establish the new Jerusalem in Münster, Germany (1532-1535)—an episode that ended in its violent collapse and suppression—echoed the earlier revolt. The contemporary equivalents of Müntzer and the citizens of Münster are less the pacifist Anabaptists influenced by Menno Simons (1496-1561) than groups such as the Branch Davidians in Waco, Texas (an offshoot of the apocalyptic-focused Seventh-day Adventists). In the eighteenth century, Gotthold Ephraim Lessing appealed to Joachim of Fiore to argue that humanity had come of age, while Kant drew on a millenarian schema to frame what he saw as a transition of ecclesiastical faith into the universal religion of reason.[24] In the nineteenth century, this Joachite tradition informed the postmillennialism of Walter Rauschenbusch (1861-1918), who advocated a "Social Gospel" and saw in modern scientific, economic, and political developments, and the reform they enabled, the heralds of the last age. In the twentieth century, the German Marxist philosopher Ernst Bloch and the theologian Jürgen Moltmann both claim Joachim as an ally. The political philosopher Eric Voegelin interprets modern political phenomena such as Marxism and Nazism as gnostic political religions that draw on Joachimite impulses in their attempts to build the new Jerusalem now.[25] Echoing this

23. For a discussion of Joachim of Fiore's theology of history, see Bernard McGinn, *The Calabrian Abbot: Joachim of Fiore in the History of Western Thought* (London: Macmillan, 1985).

24. Jürgen Moltmann, *The Coming of God: Christian Eschatology*, trans. Margaret Kohl (Minneapolis: Fortress, 2004 [1996]), 187-89.

25. Eric Voegelin, *The New Science of Politics: An Introduction* (Chicago: University of

thesis, Roland Robertson suggests that the concept of secularization is itself a transvaluation of Christian millennial categories.[26]

In Christianity, a Joachimite approach tends to hold that the new Jerusalem can be experienced in human history and that the direction of history and the legibility of divine action in history are clear if one has the right spiritual insight and way of reading the Bible. It is on this basis that such approaches are ready to pass definitive judgment on the worth or otherwise of present political arrangements. By contrast, a more Augustinian approach holds that the new Jerusalem is an irruption of the divine from outside human history, an act of grace that surpasses all that precedes it and changes the terms and conditions of the politics and social life that follow it. The paradigmatic and definitive event is the resurrection and ascension of Jesus Christ, but it does not follow that just because Christ has ascended, God ceases to act in human history. Precisely because Christ now sits at the right hand of the Father, the Spirit can break open the kingdom of God in any place at any time in ways that are over and beyond human construction and developments within history. By implication, we can never be certain what direction history is going in, and so an Augustinian approach is more open-ended and less absolutist in its judgments on present political arrangements. The Augustinian tradition is ready to see both good and bad in any polity, yet at the same time pursue change and be open to the Spirit's work here and now. By contrast, the Joachimite tradition tends to be more radical and revolutionary: a polity is either for or against the end of history it confidently predicts. However, both see a direct link between eschatology and present secular political arrangements.

There is a third approach that is more Joachimite than Augustinian but tends to wholly spiritualize the new Jerusalem, decoupling eschatology and politics by rendering the new Jerusalem either an inner-worldly or otherworldly reality. Some mystics, for example, envisage the coming of the new Jerusalem as a renewal of the inner spiritual life. In the modern period, many premillennial eschatologies, such as those influenced by John Nelson Darby (1800–1882), tend to make the new Jerusalem a wholly otherworldly reality so that it becomes "pie in the sky when you die." Statecraft and party

---

Chicago Press, 1952). For a more detailed and nuanced study of how various modern political ideologies echo or draw on Joachite impulses, see Marjorie Reeves, *Joachim of Fiore and the Prophetic Future* (London: SPCK, 1976).

26. Roland Robertson, "Global Millennialism: A Postmortem on Secularization," in *Religion, Globalization, and Culture*, ed. Peter Beyer and Lori Beaman (Leiden: Brill, 2007), 9–34.

politics are something to be avoided, for at their best they are a pointless activity for those who will enjoy the "rapture," and at worst, they are vehicles of the antichrist. The secular is identified as not merely of this world but worldly, and thereby a realm of pollution to be feared. The popular Left Behind novels articulate this view. While a premillennial eschatology often sponsors evangelistic activism, it tends to breed political quietism.[27]

These theological debates about secularity differ in kind from modern philosophical understandings of secularization, aligned as these often are with ideological rejections of religion. That said, these modern philosophical conceptions themselves emerged out of the theological debates just outlined. It is to these philosophical frameworks that we now turn.

The Secular as a Philosophical Commitment

Charles Taylor notes that a significant shift into the modern period was the loss of a "cosmic imaginary." This shift entailed the loss of what it meant to participate in and collaborate with a preexisting order, understood theologically or otherwise, and the emergence of a view of order as imposed *ab extra* on nature by the human will.[28] Taylor calls this the shift from cosmos to universe, and it entails a change in how to imagine the world.[29] His account of this shift makes clear that in debates about different conceptions of secularity, rival metaphysical constructions of order are also at stake. The conception of order in axial religions (which include Christianity and classical philosophies) entails a sense that the cosmos provides meaning and purpose to those who participate in it and the sense that this meaning can be discerned through the right kinds of participation. Part of the shift into the modern period is a move to disengagement and disenchantment such that the cosmic order becomes understood as mechanistic and morally neutral: it cannot disclose to us any sense of how we should live. As Taylor puts it, "The move to mechanism neutralizes this whole domain. It

27. For a systematic overview of the relationship between different combinations of millennialism, eschatology, and apocalypticism, and how these frame the nature of political order, see Moltmann, *The Coming of God*, 131-92.

28. Charles Taylor, *A Secular Age* (Cambridge, MA: Harvard University Press, 2007), 123-30. Although Taylor refers to the term "cosmos," he does not pay sufficient heed to the important differences between the Christian and Platonic conceptions, neither does he account for the range of uses of the term in the New Testament (158).

29. Taylor, *A Secular Age*, 323.

no longer sets norms for us, or defines crucial life meanings."[30] However, Taylor also notes how the emergence of a "modern cosmic imaginary" from the eighteenth century onward reintroduces a sense of mystery, meaning, and moral significance through our participation in and kinship with nature and the "dark genesis" of human being out of immeasurable time.[31] The environmental movement is but one expression of such a sensibility.[32] Taylor's account is incisive, but what it misses is the continuing force of a mechanistic view of the universe in the realm of politics and economics, where "Weberian" notions of politics as a rational-legal order articulate the dominant political imaginary in the West, whether it takes a liberal, libertarian, or social democratic form.[33]

In the shift from cosmos to universe, the ground of philosophy changes. Philosophy used to be pagan but is now secular. To name a philosophy secular—as in "secular humanism"—is to name how some modern, post-Christian philosophies are committed to a closed or wholly immanent conception of the universe. By contrast, "pagan" or non-Christian philosophies/religions may be nontheistic and primarily immanent in focus (e.g., Confucianism and some strands of Buddhism) or transcendent in orientation (e.g., Platonism, Islam, and Hinduism). But in either case, they are open to extramaterial dimensions to reality: love, for instance, is more than an electrical and chemical reaction between one's synapses. In contrast to cosmic imaginaries, modern, secular philosophies and schools of life are deterministic and naturalistic: they deny, as a point of faith, any nonempirical dimension to reality. From this perspective, love is nothing but a biomechanical response. Truly secular philosophy demands living without the illusion of any metaphysical basis for meaning and morality. Nietzsche was the great prophet of such a vision.[34] The irony is that modern secular

30. Taylor, *A Secular Age*, 284.

31. Taylor, *A Secular Age*, 349.

32. Taylor notes: "the striking fact about the modern cosmic imaginary is that it is uncapturable by any one range of views. It has moved people in a whole range of directions, from (almost) the hardest materialism through to Christian orthodoxy; passing by a whole range of intermediate positions" (*A Secular Age*, 351).

33. The irony is that Weber was sensitive to the interrelationship between the construction of political and economic orders and religious traditions of belief and practice, as is evidenced in his account of the relationship between Protestantism and capitalism. That said, the impact of Weber's teleological account of processes of modernization, rationalization, and disenchantment is to close off the contemporary context from experiencing a parallel symbiosis.

34. John Gray articulates a contemporary version of a nonfoundationalist, material-

philosophy—with its tacit atheism—is itself a fruit of Christianity.[35] What radical skepticism produces depends on the prior patterns of belief and practice it responds to and emerges out of. Thus, radical skepticism in response to monotheism produces atheism, whereas skepticism in response to an animist or polytheist context produces something different.

If secular philosophy frames religion as a form of irrationality, another stream of thinking rejects religion as a form of fantasy. Exemplified in the work of Ludwig Feuerbach and, more ambiguously, Sigmund Freud, on this line of thought, to become secular is to move from magical, wishful, enchanted, or mythical thinking to reality. Reality is posited as a realm of thought and practice liberated from religious commitments. But these accounts fail to see that religion is not reducible to wish fulfillment or projection. Moreover, discerning and articulating reality require a combination of mythos and logos, imaginative and empirical analysis, symbol and facts, mundane and transcendent registers, time as event and as chronology, and a sense of existing between ordinary and nonordinary realities, whether of ecstasy, horror, wonder, dream states, play, or whatever. A cosmic imaginary combines these while the reductive (and dreary) insistence that empirical description is the only truth misses how science depends on analogy, metaphor, and symbol and, tacitly and explicitly, trades in religious beliefs and practices.[36] Even if one brackets theological or metaphysical considerations and treats what is identified as religion as a set of purely sociological and anthropological phenomena, it is still the case that what we now call religion is a way to navigate the multivalent, kaleidoscopic nature of reality and how, as ultrasocial animals, we must sustain shared meanings across generations to survive and thrive. This requires telling stories, creating rituals, mimesis, imagining other possibilities, and developing enduring symbolic and figurative frames of reference.[37] And these are just as needed today as they have ever been.

---

ist philosophy in *Straw Dogs: Thoughts on Humans and Other Animals* (London: Granta, 2002). There are also the popular versions peddled by Richard Dawkins, Sam Harris, and others.

35. On the theological genealogy of modern atheism, see Michael Buckley, *At the Origins of Modern Atheism*, rev. ed. (New Haven: Yale University Press, 1990).

36. For example, see Mary Midgley's *Evolution as a Religion: Strange Hopes and Stranger Fears* (London: Routledge, 2002)—an account of the inherent overlap between theories of evolution and religion, and how evolutionary theories can function in religious ways.

37. For a systematic account of the role of religion in human evolution, see Bellah, *Religion in Human Evolution*.

It is important at this point to distinguish between skepticism and suspicion. Skepticism questions the validity of belief. Suspicion questions why we value belief rather than what we believe. The former is a feature of secular philosophy, while the latter is a proper fruit of a theological commitment to secularity rather than secularism. Secularism as a governmental project demands that citizens adopt a skeptical attitude to their belief as a condition of public discourse and favors education that fosters such skepticism to generate a more cohesive nation-state. For example, Amy Gutmann, Dennis Thompson, and other deliberative democratic theorists call for skeptical and morally tentative citizens who are "uncertain about the truth or their own position" and who "should not be dogmatic about their view."[38] Such skepticism is very different from a prudential suspicion born out of a theological commitment to the secularity (and thus contingency) of all fallen and finite social, economic, and political structures.[39] The Bible preaches that the faithful should exercise a judicious measure of suspicion (rather than paranoia) so they can identify the sacralization of injustice, the normalization of idolatry, false worship, and the hypocrisy of religious and political leaders. Such suspicion is the wellspring of prophetic critique, a species of loyal opposition. Long before the modern "masters of suspicion"—Nietzsche, Freud, and Marx—questioned whether the order of things was what it seemed, the prophets recognized suspicion and demystification as necessary adjuncts to true faithfulness and maintenance of a just and merciful polity (e.g., Amos 5:21-24). The Gospels build on this precedent to critique "whitewashed sepulchers" (Mathew 23:27-28), while the book of Revelation reveals the brutality undergirding the *Pax Romana*. Suspicion is necessary to keep in play the tensional relationship between belief and practice, appearance and reality, knowledge and being, and the works of the flesh and those of the Spirit. Suspicion is a move in the delicate dance between confession of sin and confession of belief that keeps faith faithful. In summary, if skepticism refuses the plausibility of religious faith but generates credulity toward the things of this world, suspicion is an ascesis that helps foster

38. Amy Gutmann and Dennis F. Thompson, *Democracy and Disagreement* (Cambridge, MA: Harvard University Press, 1996), 77.

39. I say prudential suspicion because a hermeneutics of suspicion and the use of critique are themselves problematic when they become the only mode of inquiry. Suspicion is but one among a number of ways of paying attention to and interpreting the world. On the limits of suspicion and critique, see Rita Felski, *The Limits of Critique* (Chicago: University of Chicago Press, 2015).

authentic faithfulness, the pursuit of justice, and a critical stance toward all worldly authorities.

While the distinction between theological and philosophical understandings of what it means to be secular should now be clear, both of these understandings need distinguishing from sociological accounts of the secular, which draw on the theological dyad of "secular" and "religious" but repurpose it.

Secularization as a Sociological Description

Secularization used to be a problem for the church. It is now a problem for sociology. The assumptions driving a sociological conception of secularization turn out to be wrong. The classic secularization thesis identifies modernization with secularization and sees secularization as both a subprocess of modernization—like industrialization and bureaucratization—and an inevitable outcome of modernization. Secularization names the process whereby, as Bryan Wilson puts it, "religious institutions, actions and consciousness, lose their social significance."[40] The thesis came to imply three interrelated dynamics: the decline of religious adherence, the privatization of religion, and the differentiation of religion into a separate sphere with the consequent result that other spheres such as the economy, art, and politics cease to be motivated and shaped by religious beliefs and practices.

While the secularization thesis seems to be an immovable point of faith among Western political and economic elites, the past decade or more witnessed a massive shift in academic thinking about the fate of religion in modernity.[41] Of the three dynamics outlined above, the first two proved wrong, while the third is contested. In place of assumptions about the inevitable decline in the public significance of religion, a more nuanced account is emerging of how religious and nonreligious commitments and practices interact over time and across cultures and continents. This inter-

---

40. Bryan Wilson, *Religion in Sociological Perspective* (Oxford: Oxford University Press, 1982), 49.

41. Central figures in developing this academic shift include David Martin, José Casanova, Talal Asad, Grace Davie, Danièle Hervieu-Leger, Saba Mahmood, Charles Taylor, and Peter van der Veer. While there are differences and arguments among them (for example, Asad has been highly critical of the approach developed by Casanova), their combined questioning and cumulative deconstruction of the secularization thesis warrant grouping them together.

action generates different and varying formations of secularity. Constructions of the public sphere as secular can be as much a creation of religious
beliefs and practices as of anticlerical ideologies and modern processes
such as industrialization.[42] For example, conflicts between Dissenters
and the established church in Great Britain helped produce one kind of
secularity—a defanged and porous form of establishment. By contrast, in
France, the conflict between anticlerical movements and a "throne and
altar" form of Roman Catholicism that aligned itself with an authoritarian
ancien régime produced a radically different form, that of *laïcité*. The shift in
academic understanding has generated calls for "postsecular," "asecular,"
or "religio-secular" forms of analysis that identify how religious beliefs and
practices coconstruct and interweave other forms of belief and practice,
how religious and secular formations exist on a continuum, and how combinations of these constitute multiple patterns of secularity.

The original secularization thesis was based on an interpretation of developments in Europe and then was universalized to the rest of the world.
It paid little attention to what was happening elsewhere, shoehorning what
was going on outside of Europe into the European paradigm. This framework also ignored the history and impact of Christian mission over the
course of two millennia. A more granular and global historical account
would have revealed that a distinctive feature of Christianity is its serial nature and how, throughout its history, Christianity has undergone periods
of decline and revitalization, recession as well as advance, spurred for the
most part by cross-cultural transmission.[43] These recessions take place in
the Christian heartlands just as the faith is passed on at the periphery. Despite the claims of Jerusalem and Rome, Christianity has no fixed homeland
or center. There is no Mecca that Christianity radiates out from or sacred language through which to hear revelation. It is polycentric and polyglot, with
an ever-changing center of gravity. In the contemporary moment, this center
is shifting from the North Atlantic world to Africa, Asia, and Latin America.

Sociological uses of the term "secular" and the secularization thesis
need distinguishing from both philosophical skepticism about the validity

42. For an account of the secularization thesis as itself a product of this kind of interaction, such that it should be understood less as a scientific paradigm and more as
a form of "epistemological anti-Catholicism," see Christopher Clark, "From 1848 to
Christian Democracy," in *Religion and the Political Imagination*, ed. Ira Katznelson and
Gareth Stedman Jones (Cambridge: Cambridge University Press, 2007), 190-213.

43. Andrew F. Walls, *The Missionary Movement in Christian History: Studies in the
Transmission of Faith* (Edinburgh: T&T Clark, 1996).

of religious belief and ideological critiques of religion as "the opiate of the people." The sociological account was meant to be a descriptive and empirical claim rather than a philosophical and critical one. It posited a fundamental incompatibility between modernity and religious adherence supposedly based on evidence. However, rather than an empirical and contingent claim subject to variation and change, the thesis was premised on a teleological belief in a progressive view of history. This can be overhead in the following quote from the influential American sociologist C. Wright Mills. Writing in 1959, he stated: "Once the world was filled with the sacred—in thought, practice, and institutional form. After the Reformation and the Renaissance, the forces of modernization swept across the globe and secularization, a corollary historical process, loosened the dominance of the sacred. In due course, the sacred shall disappear altogether, except possibly, in the private realm."[44]

This statement is manifestly false, most obviously in the United States, where religion was and is of huge public significance. Processes of modernization, whether in Indonesia, Iran, or India, can generate the revitalization of religion and increase its public significance. For example, India is the largest secular democracy in the world and used to be directed by the secularist Indian National Congress party, but it is now the Bharatiya Janata Party (BJP), a Hindu nationalist party, that dominates the political process. And in what were the atheist states of the former Soviet Union, which brutally repressed all religions in the name of an emancipated, nonreligious future, religion is once more a political influence.

Even in Europe, the situation of religion is subject to debate. For example, Danièle Hervieu-Léger argues that in Europe what is seen is not a straightforward decline in the public significance of religion but its deinstitutionalization and, aligned with that, a pluralization of religious forms. This process leads to new patterns of religious practice (e.g., twelve-step programs), the revitalization of older forms (e.g., pilgrimages), and a resurgence of the sacred unmediated by institutional forms of religious beliefs and practices (e.g., the rise of the spiritual but not religious, and new religious movements).[45] Fewer people are sitting in churches each week, but that does not mean religion per se is disappearing. We just need

44. C. Wright Mills, *The Sociological Imagination* (Oxford: Oxford University Press, 1959), 32–33.

45. Danièle Hervieu-Léger, *Religion as a Chain of Memory* (New Brunswick, NJ: Rutgers University Press, 2000).

to look in different ways and in different places to understand what is going on. José Casanova points out that the most interesting thing about secularization in Europe is not whether it is an empirical reality, but that the secularization thesis became so internalized by both the nonreligious and religious that it became a matter of shared faith. As he puts it:

We need to entertain seriously the proposition that secularization became a self-fulfilling prophecy in Europe, once large sectors of the population of Western European societies, including the Christian churches, accepted the basic premises of the theory of secularization: that secularization is a teleological process of modern social change; that the more modern a society the more secular it becomes; that "secularity" is "a *sign of the times.*" If such a proposition is correct, then the secularization of Western European societies can be explained better in terms of the triumph of the knowledge regime of secularism, than in terms of structural processes of socio-economic development such as urbanization, education, rationalization and so on.[46]

As a regime of knowledge shaping governance and self-governance, the secularization thesis has direct material and political effects. For example, church leaders and faith-based organizations self-censor their use of theological language and adopt managerial modes of speech and action as if these make the church more contemporary or help it fit in with assumed historical realities. Conversely, political and intellectual elites entirely ignore religious considerations in policy and practice, assuming they are irrelevant or will disappear in due course.

Responding to sociological debates about the place of religion in the modern world, Charles Taylor identifies a change that does signify a profound sociological shift. Taylor outlines the conditions of belief whereby belief in God moves from being a given to becoming "one option among others."[47] This shift entails neither a necessary decline in religious belief nor an incompatibility between religion and modernity. However, before the modern period, some form of religious belief and practice was felt by most people to be existentially necessary: one could not make sense of

46. José Casanova, "Immigration and the New Religious Pluralism: A European Union/United States Comparison," in *Democracy and the New Religious Pluralism*, ed. Thomas F. Banchoff (Oxford: Oxford University Press, 2007), 63.

47. Taylor, *A Secular Age*, 2-3.

life without it. In modernity, religion does not disappear, but it does become avoidable for some, while for others it becomes a totalizing, tightly bounded identity. This latter point is not one Taylor makes. Yet it is the flip side of religion becoming avoidable. Its role as a totalizing identity (a preferable term to fundamentalism) was largely unworkable prior to the modern period or, at the least, restricted to religious virtuosos. Prior to modernity, kinship, social status, occupation, and locality intersected with and interrupted religious beliefs and practices to form fuller yet porous, less bounded, and oftentimes less literalist patterns of religious life.

Taylor contends that what characterizes the contemporary context is a plurality of forms of belief and unbelief, which are themselves constantly interacting. In the light of Taylor's thesis, the contemporary condition is one where everyone, including the agnostic and the atheist, must be self-reflexive and critical about his or her commitments. Rather than a process of *secularization*, it is better to think about this shift in terms of ongoing and ever-changing patterns of *secularity* that emerge as part of the complex interactions modernization generates around the world.[48] Constructions of secularity vary according to cultural, historical, and religious context and institutional domain. Secularity is not like Jell-O—the same stuff poured into different molds. It is like the category "rainforest"—it is recognizably the same kind of thing in Liberia, Brazil, and Indonesia but the flora and fauna vary radically, and there can be different ecosystems existing within the same forest. Thus, the form secularity takes in health care is different from its outworking in prisons or the military. Likewise, how it emerges and develops in Britain is different from its construction in the United States, Australia, China, Nigeria, Egypt, or India.[49] In the West, the secularity of both specific institutions, such as universities or hospitals, and a society in general is as much the result of dynamics and discourses within Christianity as the fruit of external pressures. What is generated is a switch from a plurality of political forms and a singularity of religion (Christianity), albeit one with plural expressions, to a singularity of political forms (the nation-state) and a plurality of religions. What comes next is an open question.

48. My use of the term "secularity" harks back to an earlier English usage given in Samuel Johnson's *Dictionary of the English Language* (1755): "Secularity, n. s. [from secular.] Worldliness; attention to the things of the present life."

49. For a review of different constructions of secularity both within and beyond the West, including countries such as Thailand, Lebanon, and Taiwan, see Bruce J. Berman, Rajeev Bhargava, and André Laliberté, eds., *Secular States and Religious Diversity* (Vancouver, BC: UBC Press, 2013).

Modernity did not slay religion. But it did help reconstitute and recompose religion in a field of possibilities that ranges from self-conscious reassertions of orthodoxy at one pole to militant unbelief at the other. The spectrum between these poles is occupied by myriad combinations and formations of lived religion, some old, some new. The secularization thesis presumed a progressive model of change, where history was moving in one uniform direction and society would gradually fill up with secular ways of doing things, so displacing religious beliefs and practices.[50] The inevitable result of this process is that modern men and women would emerge as enlightened, rational individuals washed clean of the foul accretions of their atavistic beliefs and practices. The reality is very different. It turns out that the modern world is like a Jacuzzi in which belief and unbelief are bubbling up from everywhere and contesting each other in a dynamic, constantly changing, and not very hygienic environment. But the change is not necessarily in place, quantity, or substance. It is one of quality and character. No one, from the confessional Darwinist to the so-called fundamentalist, can assume that his or her view is "normal" or simply the way things will be.[51] Instead of a linear march from faith to rationality, we have the more intuitive recognition that cross-pressures are pulling at one moment toward religion and at another away from it, resulting in the mutual fragilization of all patterns of belief and practice, including those of radical skepticism.[52] These cross-pressures can generate a wide range of responses, of which an exclusivist total identity (whether religious or not) is one. The defining feature of the contemporary religious situation is thus plurality, *not* secularization.

Theologically, secularity as plurality is not a problem. Nostalgia for Christendom and a more culturally homogenous society when Christianity was a hegemonic power should have no place in faithful responses to the contemporary context. There are substantive theological reasons

50. As the anthropologist Talal Asad argues, the secular "should not be thought of as the space in which *real* human life gradually emancipates itself from the controlling power of 'religion' and thus achieves that latter's relocation" (*Formations of the Secular: Christianity, Islam, Modernity* [Stanford, CA: Stanford University Press, 2003], 191).

51. The increasing vehemence and vigor of certain antireligious exponents of Darwinism can be understood as a growing self-awareness and felt need to argue their corner as against the previous assumption that their view would inevitably prevail.

52. An example of this process is how secular humanism is refashioning itself as a "religious" movement.

for welcoming conditions of secularity. First, faithfulness demands self-reflexivity, so to the extent that plurality calls this forth, it is a good thing. Part of becoming faithful is learning to live with heterogeneity, ambiguity, and tension by resisting the temptation to reduce Christianity to a legalistic procedure, moralistic code, institutional program, or cultural anchor. Ongoing conversion requires that Christians attend to and receive from those perceived as poor, strange, or scandalous, and so ultimately be open to the otherness of God, who troubles our boundaries and categories. Plurality can and should agitate Christians to unwrap tightly bound and fiercely grasped packages of belief and practice and rediscover them as gifts to share rather than possessions to defend.

Second, concern about the fate of religion in modernity is a distraction. Following Karl Barth, "religion" can be understood as a human attempt to construct a life apart from the revelation of God. For Barth, the critique of religion as a form of idolatry is the precursor to openness to the otherness of God.[53] On his account, human religion—including Christianity, insofar as it ceases to be dependent on the grace and revelation of God—is prone to idolatry even while any religion may mediate the revelation of God. The nub of Barth's critique of religion is that the real division to be overcome is not between church and world but between humans and God. An age that renders human constructions of religion fragile is at least potentially more open to revelation than a context in which a pallid, cultural Christianity has inoculated people against richer, more holistic embodiments of Christian belief and practice. Building on Barth's insight, I contend that the primary challenge of modern patterns of secularity is one that is ever before the church: that of mission and how mission incorporates the need to form and sustain a just and loving common life with strangers, enemies, and the rest of creation. And, following on from this, the more nearly attuned to God, the greater the felt need for forms of common life with others as part of faithful witness, and the more developed the virtues necessary to create and sustain one.

Politically, plurality does present problems, as it makes it harder to form, norm, and sustain a common life. But this is not a problem with religion, nor is religion specifically the problem. Yet again and again, whether by anti-immigrant groups targeting Islam or governmental regimes of *laïcité*, religion is framed as the thorn in the flesh of the liberal

---

53. Karl Barth, *Church Dogmatics* I/2, *The Doctrine of the Word of God*, trans. G. T. Thomson and Harold Knight (Edinburgh: T&T Clark, 1956), 280-325.

body politic and secularism, the tweezers that will remove the problem. It is to an assessment of secularism as this type of political project that I now turn.

Secularism as a Regime of Governance

There is a question whether secularity as a concept is a solely Christian construct. I contend that a distinction is needed between *secularity* and *secularism*. Secularity entails the commitment to, and institutional configuration of, a religiously plural and morally diverse common life, the construction and conceptualization of which vary by historical and cultural context. Indian configurations of secularity, for example, are different from those that emerge within a predominantly Christian, Western setting. Secularity takes account of the fact that convivial ways of living with others evolved in many different religious traditions and are neither the monopoly of a modern, Western binary between the religious and the secular nor dependent on metaphysical skepticism or empiricism.[54] Secularity is a fruit of the entangled histories that shape processes of modernization around the world. But the combination of divergent pathways into modernity with different cultural-historical-religious contexts of formation generates enormous variation in the form and structure of secularity. In contrast to secularity, however, secularism should be understood as a singular—and highly problematic—phenomenon.[55] Secularism becomes the basis of a post-Christendom, liberal regime of governance often imposed beyond the West through colonial means.[56] Secularism as a governmental and hegemonic project generates specific configurations of divisions between public and private, depends on a monistic and centralized conception of political sovereignty, and looks to the nation-state as both the normative

54. Ashis Nandy, "The Politics of Secularism and the Recovery of Religious Tolerance," in *Time Warps: The Insistent Politics of Silent and Evasive Pasts* (Delhi: Permanent Black, 2001), 61–88, and Charles Taylor, "Can Secularism Travel?" in *Beyond the Secular West*, ed. Akeel Bilgrami (New York: Columbia University Press, 2016), 1–27.

55. "Secularism" as a term comes to prominence in the work of George Jacob Holyoake (1817–1906), founder of the British Secular Union. He used it first in 1851, but his fullest expression of secularism as a moral and political project is set out in *The Origin and Nature of Secularism* (1896). While not atheist, Holyoake did see secularism as entailing the active removal of religion from moral and political life.

56. As in the case of Kemalist Turkey, it can be imposed by indigenous elites.

form of polity and the primary focus of identity.[57] At heart, it seeks the active removal and exclusion of religious considerations from shared moral and political judgments.

As a mode of statecraft, secularism endeavors to reorder religion and relations between different religious communities. Following Saba Mahmood, secularism as a regime for governing religion can be conceptualized as "the modern state's sovereign power to reorganize substantive features of religious life, stipulating what religion is or ought to be, assigning its proper content, and disseminating concomitant subjectivities, ethical frameworks, and quotidian practices. Secularism, in this understanding, is not simply the organizing structure for what are regularly taken to be a priori elements of social organization—public, private, political, religious—but a discursive operation of power that generates these very spheres, establishes their boundaries, and suffuses them with content, such that they come to acquire a natural quality for those living within its terms."[58]

As a way of governing religion, secularism steps beyond the principle of state impartiality or the separation of church and state. It reorders and remakes religious life and relations between different religions in accord with norms and procedures alien to the forms of life of the religious communities themselves.[59] Secularism, justified as the enforcement of neutrality and a means of leveling religious differences in the public sphere, generates increasing amounts of state regulation and management of religious life, including intervention in substantive issues of doctrine and practice.[60] This intervention consequently exacerbates religious polarization and inequality as state procedures—laced as they are with often unacknowledged conceptions of what constitutes good and bad religion—inevitably favor some and stigmatize others.[61] Religious groups' intervention in and

57. Mahmood raises a parallel critique but conflates secularity and secularism.

58. Saba Mahmood, *Religious Difference in a Secular Age: A Minority Report* (Princeton: Princeton University Press, 2016), 3. See also Nandy, "Politics of Secularism," 61–88.

59. Mahmood, *Religious Difference*, 20–21. Mahmood concludes that secularism, by making the state the sole arbiter of religious equality, colonizes and often undercuts the very aspiration to religious equality it is meant to uphold (211). I make a parallel case in *Christianity and Contemporary Politics: The Conditions and Possibilities of Faithful Witness* (Malden, MA: Wiley-Blackwell, 2010), 31–70.

60. This intervention operates not just nationally but also internationally. See Saba Mahmood, "Secularism, Hermeneutics, and Empire: The Politics of Islamic Reformation," *Public Culture* 18, no. 2 (2006): 323–47.

61. An example of secularism determining modes of both external and internalized governance is the dynamics of institutional isomorphism. Institutional isomorphism is

incorporation of state policy, on conditions set by secularism, close down nonstate spaces that religious belief and practice hold open and that have, historically, been important contributors to moral and political life and the formation of civil society. We should never forget what Lenin, Stalin, and Hitler understood only too well, that the liquidation or co-option of civil society is the precursor of totalitarianism.

A commitment to the rule of law, religious liberty, and the equitable treatment of all religions by the state does not necessitate a commitment to secularism as a governmental project for managing religion. There are many ways to structure the state so it sustains and fosters *secularity*, without enforcing a program of *secularism*. At a formal level, the First Amendment to the US Constitution, which stipulates that the state should not interfere in matters of religion, is one. The "principled distance" and context-sensitive secularity of the Indian state is another.[62] Neither necessitates a commitment to secularism, which is arguably antithetical to both frameworks. The role of the state should be to uphold a rule-bound, accountable, and equitable arena that enables a just and merciful common life between diverse communities to be negotiated. Religion is not untouchable, nor are all religions the same. Rather, different religious communities can receive symmetric and proportional treatment by state authorities, which seek to be self-reflexive about and sensitive to the different needs of each religious group.[63]

A primary good the liberal state seeks (rather than liberalism) is the good of political association and the structures and policies that enable the upholding of this good. Pursuing this good entails sustaining the concrete conditions of freedom. Freedom is in part dependent on participation in a proximate form of association. Without being embedded in some form of group or institution, the modern citizen is naked before the collective

---

a process where religious organizations reshape themselves to fit government policy and thereby lose their unique characteristics while taking on the same institutional shape and processes as state agencies. For a discussion of how institutional isomorphism reshapes religions, see Bretherton, *Christianity and Contemporary Politics*, 41–45.

62. For a discussion of how the Indian state models the kinds of statecraft required to sustain secularity (as defined here), see Rajeev Bhargava, "Indian Secularism: An Alternative, Trans-cultural Ideal," in *The Promise of India's Secular Democracy* (Oxford: Oxford University Press, 2010), 63–105. However, in Bhargava's terms, what I call secularity he identifies as a specific form of pluralistic and porous secularism that appreciates the public contribution of religious communities.

63. Bhargava, "Indian Secularism," 87–96.

power of either the market or the state and lacks a vital means for his or her own self-cultivation. For freedom to be possible and an associational life to flourish, a complex political space, one with myriad institutional configurations and visions of the good, is needed to preserve the space of politics.[64] Religious institutions are a vital component of this complex space. A commitment by the state to secularity entails a commitment to plurality (and modes of statecraft that can sustain it). By contrast, a commitment to secularism entails a commitment to secularization, that is, the exclusion of and decline in the public significance of religious beliefs and practices and their aligned institutions.

Secularity as a Political Good

Constructively and prescriptively I take secularity to be a political good that serves the formation and sustaining of a common life amid difference, disagreement, and asymmetries of power. It entails a commitment to the formation of *mutual* rather than *neutral* ground. This requires practices that enable such mutual ground to be discovered together with others with whom one disagrees or finds objectionable. Democratic politics is one such means, as it allows for multiple traditions to identify and pursue goods in common while recognizing that these common objects of love are provisional and penultimate. Conversely, the sustaining of a provisional and plural mutual ground requires commitments to something more than politics and economics. Without a commitment to a cosmic imaginary, either the state or the market (or some combination thereof) is all that exists to connect and order life together. If state and market are the only public realities, then they have no limits and quickly metastasize into antipolitical and totalizing systems of control.

Diverse religious traditions in the same polity may have radically different conceptualizations of the cosmic order, but they share a sense that, as humans, we participate in a cosmos that is meaningful, that political ends require moral means, and that humans are not reducible to administrative units or commodities. In my view, a plurality of cosmic imagi-

---

64. Sustaining meaningful material conditions of plurality can involve funding religiously based schools, hospitals, and the like. Although if processes of institutional isomorphism and co-option are to be avoided, something like endowment is a better form than direct grants.

naries is the basis of a genuinely plural and provisional—that is, faithfully secular—democratic politics. A faithful and democratic form of secularity challenges both state and market-centric ways of ordering life together. In doing so, faithful secularity disrupts totalizing, secularist systems that demand uniformity, disaggregate and dissolve any form of common life, and deny that there is either meaning to history or a moral life because the only thing that matters are wholly immanent political or economic goals. By contrast, a faithful and democratic secularity allows for the public recognition and interplay of the myriad obligations and commitments that citizens keep faith with (whether transcendent, immanent, or whatever) and that must be coordinated and negotiated to generate mutual ground.

The problem at the heart of debates about the secular is not religion per se but plurality. This is also the problem at the heart of how to sustain politics as a good. Both secularity and politics need a genuine institutional plurality within the body politic. Both, therefore, require taking seriously how forms of covenantal association/consociation—and the faithfulness or loyalty these entail—make a constructive contribution to democratic politics. Hence my emphasis in this book on consociational democracy, which entails living into the paradox that institutional plurality is a condition for a just and compassionate common life. For a complexly religious and nonreligious form of politics to be possible, the following are required: faith in a cosmic imaginary (whether transcendent or immanent) in which material needs, violence, and unilateral power neither exhaust nor define all that politics entails; an openness to a variety of forms of rationality, wisdom, and sources of knowledge informing political judgments other than the empirical; and acknowledgment of religious forms of life as having public significance, thereby establishing boundaries to state action and commodification.

Conclusion

I have argued for a capacious understanding of secularity, one that is complexly religious and nonreligious, born out of plurality, and established and sustained through democratic politics. We tend to equate democracy with one rather pinched and anemic form of political secularism that, as a mode of statecraft, excludes religious beliefs and practices from the public sphere. Rarely acknowledged is how secularism, as a hegemonic governmental project, reinforces the dominance of state and market as the only public realities that shape life together. Contrary to secular philosophies, which view religion as the enemy of forming a common life, it is traditions with a cosmic imaginary that have the requisite resources for fostering the plurality and sense of contingency that is necessary for a faithfully secular, democratic, common-life politics. Without them, the state and market have no epistemic, social, or institutional limits.

Theologically, the secular is that-which-is-not-eschatological and not that-which-is-not-religious. As a penultimate good determined by its relation to eschatology, secularity enables political and economic structures to be contingent, and it enables a plurality of forms of life to emerge within which what it means to be human may be explored. The secular may be a form of "the world" rather than inherently worldly. As a penultimate good, secularity is an aid to discipleship, providing a time within which to form a common life with others and thereby learn virtues such as humility, love, courage, hope, and patience. Before Christ's return, Christians are always having to navigate one form of secularity or another. This is as it should be. In the contemporary context, this navigation entails complex negotiations, as patterns of secularity shift and change around the world. These patterns emerge out of dynamic relations between processes of modernization and the religious history and demography of a context, which includes how Christianity was mediated to that context and how it is currently lived out.

Threshold

This chapter analyzed how conceptions and institutionalizations of secularity set the terms and conditions of both church-state and interfaith relations. It looked at the question of how to navigate religious diversity from a bird's-eye view and thereby generate a common life amid differences of belief and practice. The next chapter looks at the same issue from the ground up. It examines how toleration and hospitality enable the just and merciful negotiation of not just religious but also moral, cultural, and ideological differences between friends, strangers, enemies, and the friendless as they seek to form, norm, and sustain a common life.

Suggested Readings for Further Discussion

Scriptural texts: Jeremiah 29:4-14, Matthew 22:15-22, Acts 17:10-34.

Augustine, *City of God*, book 19. Various editions.

Marsilius of Padua, "From *Defensor Pacis*," in *From Irenaeus to Grotius: A Sourcebook in Christian Political Thought, 100-1625*, ed. Oliver O'Donovan and Joan Lockwood O'Donovan (Grand Rapids: Eerdmans, 1999), 423-52. This is a medieval argument for the separation of church and state and for "secular" (i.e., nonecclesial) authorities having priority over ecclesial authorities.

Martin Luther, *On Secular Authority*. Various editions. Luther sets out an influential version of the "doctrine of the two" that draws a sharp line of separation between church and state.

George Jacob Holyoake, *The Origin and Nature of Secularism* (London: Watts, 1896). Available online. The book offers one of the first, if not the first, formulations of a modern conception of secularism.

Charles Taylor, "The Immanent Frame," in *A Secular Age* (Cambridge, MA: Harvard University Press, 2007), 539-93.

José Casanova, "Rethinking Secularization: A Global Comparative Perspective," in *Religion, Globalization, and Culture*, ed. Peter Beyer and Lori Beaman (Leiden: Brill, 2007), 101-20.

William Cavanaugh, *The Myth of Religious Violence: Secular Ideology and the Roots of Modern Conflict* (Oxford: Oxford University Press, 2009), chaps. 3 and 4.

Saba Mahmood, "Religious Reason and Secular Affect: An Incommensurable Divide?" *Critical Inquiry* 35, no. 4 (2009): 836-62.

CHAPTER 9

Toleration with Hospitality

What are some of the virtues that help us sustain the politics of a common life amid asymmetries of power, competing loyalties, conflicting interests, rival visions of human flourishing, and incommensurable patterns of belief and practice? In a Christian account, love and justice must rank as primary. But these need further specification if we are to move beyond abstract admonitions and sustain a common life over time. This chapter examines toleration and hospitality as two such virtues that help maintain a common life in the midst of difference and disagreement, particularly of a moral and religious kind. Toleration names a form that justice takes in a plural society, while hospitality specifies how to love strangers in practice. Each constructively addresses disparities of agency without necessarily challenging structures of power. The central contrast between them is that while toleration presumes a common life already in existence, hospitality does not, seeking as it does to generate one between strangers.

The chapter recognizes the importance of toleration as a way of navigating plurality even as it criticizes certain understandings of toleration and points beyond toleration to hospitality as an alternative way of approaching those we find strange or objectionable. I begin by defining toleration and situating its contemporary emphasis in a broader historical context. I then examine several theological and philosophical justifications for toleration, outlining some of its key characteristics and presuppositions. Arguing that toleration is a necessary but insufficient civic virtue for navigating difference and disagreement, I go on to define hospitality and discuss three modern philosophical uses of hospitality as an alternative to toleration. The theological basis of hospitality is then set out and used as a framework through which to approach interfaith relations. I close the chapter by contrasting toleration and hospitality, drawing out why hospitality is necessary as a practice within democratic politics. Again, like toleration, hospitality is found to be a necessary but insufficient virtue. Both need situating within a web of virtues and practices that when combined sustain the politics of a common life.

Numerous issues could be used to examine toleration and hospitality. In some contexts, issues of gender and sexuality will be lightning rods, generating fraught contestation. My own experience has been working in the area of interfaith relations. I take such relations to be a paradigmatic instance of the need to navigate difference and disagreement construc-tively if we are to foster some form of common life. Historically, conflict over religious beliefs and practices is a key site at which thinking about toleration and hospitality is produced. And, whether in regions as diverse as West Africa, Europe, the Middle East, central Asia, or the Indian subcon-tinent, such conflict is still a fissure shaping political dynamics that directly affect the lives of millions of people around the world. So my primary point of reference in discussing tolerance and hospitality will be the navigation of religious plurality.

Toleration Defined

A primary way in which contemporary debates address the question of how to cope with moral and religious plurality and relate to those with whom one disagrees is through the concept of toleration. It is used not just for society in general but also within many religious communities. A common assumption in the literature relating to toleration is that toleration and the willingness to live with difference are a phenomenon that emerged in the West from the seventeenth century onward.[1] Its prominence is nar-rated as a direct reaction against the so-called religious wars of the post-Reformation era.[2] However, the framing of toleration as an invention of

1. One of the most influential accounts of the view that toleration and acceptance of diversity are recent historical phenomena is given in John Rawls's introduction to *Political Liberalism* (New York: Columbia University Press, 1993), xxiii-xxvii. See also John Horton, "Toleration," in *The Routledge Encyclopedia of Philosophy*, vol. 9, ed. Ed-ward Craig (London: Routledge, 1998), 429-33. For a critique of Rawls's historical and conceptual reconstruction of toleration, see Will Kymlicka, "Two Models of Pluralism and Tolerance," in *Toleration: An Elusive Virtue*, ed. David Heyd (Princeton: Princeton University Press, 1996), 81-105.

2. For example, see John Horton and Susan Mendus, introduction to *Aspects of Tol-*

modern Western civilization is mistaken.[3] It was through the search for a neutral arbiter between competing truth claims and a growing emphasis on individual autonomy that the notion of toleration acquired increasing prominence. Acceptance of difference and the advocacy of toleration as a good are now the preeminent ways of thinking about how to live with those we find strange or objectionable. Indicative of its prominence is the United Nations's annual International Day for Tolerance on November 16.[4]

Colloquially, toleration invokes a sense of live and let live. But in terms of moral philosophy, toleration involves the willingness to accept differences (whether religious, moral, or cultural) which one might, as an individual or community, find objectionable or which conflict with one's own beliefs and practices.[5] Formally, three conditions must be met for a person or group to be considered tolerant. First, there must be some conduct about which one disapproves, even if only minimally or potentially. Second, although such a person or group has the power to act coercively against, or interfere to prevent, that of which they disapprove, they do not. Inherent, therefore, to toleration are questions about the distribution of power: the tolerated are rarely those with more power, such as a majority or an elite. Third, not interfering must result from more than acquiescence, resignation, indifference, apathy, or a balance of power. One does not tolerate that which one is not concerned about; nor is it tolerance merely to accept what one cannot, or is not willing to, change (either because one lacks the power to effect change or because, for whatever reason, one fears to use one's power). Toleration involves a principled refusal to prohibit or seek to prohibit conduct believed to be wrong or harmful. As John Horton notes, "This gives rise to the so-called 'paradox of toleration' according to which toleration requires that it is right to permit that which

---

eration: Philosophical Studies, ed. John Horton and Susan Mendus (London: Methuen, 1985), 1-15. I say allegedly, as these wars are better understood as wars centered on the formation of modern nation-states in which the conflicts took on a religious valence.

3. Cary Nederman and John Laursen point out that the conventional picture of how the principle of toleration emerged in the West has been challenged by a considerable body of historical scholarship that demonstrates both the longevity and diversity of approaches to toleration. Cary Nederman and John Laursen, eds., *Difference and Dissent: Theories of Toleration in Medieval and Early Modern Europe* (London: Rowman & Littlefield, 1996), 1-16.

4. It was inaugurated after the 1995 "Year for Tolerance." The day forms part of the UN's efforts to promote human rights, mutual understanding between cultures, and social and economic development. See http://www.un.org/en/events/toleranceday/.

5. It is related to, but distinct from, notions of freedom of belief.

is wrong."[6] However, rather than a *refusal* to judge, toleration entails a *suspension* of judgment about one thing—prosecution of the truth as one sees it here and now—in favor of a judgment for maintaining an ongoing relationship. Toleration thereby hangs precariously between power, morality, community, and truth.

Against standard narratives, toleration is not inherently "secular," Western, or modern.[7] Scriptural warrants for toleration and freedom of conscience are given, for example, in Romans 14:1-23, 1 Corinthians 8:1-12, and 2 Corinthians 1:6.[8] The primary identification of toleration in Scripture is with the virtue of patient endurance in the face of either suffering or disagreement for the sake of faithful witness to Christ. Two early Christian advocates of toleration are Lactantius and Tertullian.[9] Medieval proponents of toleration as a form of political forbearance include John of Salisbury, William of Rubruck, and Marsilius of Padua.[10] Beyond the Christian tradition, arguments for toleration and freedom of conscience are a theme in numerous religious and philosophical traditions.[11] Toleration is seen by some as a virtue that can occur in any form of social life.[12] It is fair to say, however, that from the Reformation onward, interest in the concept of toleration intensified in the West, especially as it related to difference and disagreement about the question of religious belief and practice.[13] In the modern period, the increase of relations between Western Christianity and other faith traditions, initially as a result

6. Horton, "Toleration," 431.

7. On the premodern, theological roots of toleration in the Christian tradition, see Rainer Forst, *Toleration in Conflict: Past and Present* (Cambridge: Cambridge University Press, 2013), 36-137. For an assessment of the five main historical "regimes of toleration" and what they do not tolerate, see Michael Walzer, *On Toleration* (New Haven: Yale University Press, 1997), 14-36.

8. Forst, *Toleration in Conflict*, 39-42.

9. Lactantius, *The Divine Institutes* 5.19-21, and Tertullian's "The Apology" and "Letter to Scapula."

10. Cary Nederman, *Worlds of Difference: European Discourses of Toleration, c. 1100-c. 1550* (University Park: Pennsylvania State University Press, 2000). For a general treatment of medieval conceptions of *tolerantia*, see István Bejczy, "Tolerantia: A Medieval Concept," *Journal of the History of Ideas* 58, no. 3 (1997): 365-84.

11. See, for example, Jacob Neusner and Bruce Chilton, eds., *Religious Tolerance in World Religions* (West Conshohocken, PA: Templeton Foundation, 2008), and Khaled Abou El Fadl, *The Place of Tolerance in Islam* (Boston: Beacon, 2002).

12. Forst, *Toleration in Conflict*, 502-17, and John Bowlin, *Tolerance among the Virtues* (Princeton: Princeton University Press, 2016).

13. On this see Wilbur Jordan, *The Development of Religious Toleration in England*, 4 vols. (Cambridge: Cambridge University Press, 1932-1940).

of colonial expansion and then as a result of increased immigration, gave a renewed impetus to the question of religious toleration.[14] Subsequently, the increasing cultural diversity in democratic societies and substantive moral disagreement among Christians and then between Christians and non-Christians—for example, over abortion and same-sex relations—have led to assessments of toleration as a means of navigating ethical disputes.

Post-Reformation theological justifications for toleration are varied, and who or what is tolerated changes. For example, John Milton (1608–1674) presents arguments for toleration throughout his work, some drawn from his anti-Trinitarian theology, although he is consistently and vehemently opposed to any toleration of Roman Catholics.[15] By resorting to a minimalist doctrinal framework, some justifications of toleration are more expansive than others. One such is given by Sebastian Castellio, a contemporary of Calvin, in his *De haereticis* (1554). Castellio presents a selection of quotes from a range of authors, including Augustine and Luther, which speak in favor of toleration. Alongside an argument that the persecution of heretics is inconsistent with the example of Christ, his core argument is that all can agree that there is one God, including Jews and "Turks," but all other doctrines are secondary and open to dispute. These grounds provide the basis for tolerating religious differences. Other Protestants developed a very different justification, envisaging toleration as a precondition for the preaching and reception of the gospel.[16] Foremost among these was Roger Williams (1603–1683). For Williams, a commitment to conversion entails a commitment to toleration. Faithful confession is of necessity uncoerced (unwilling piety being no piety at all), and so freedom of conscience is a condition of true belief. Echoing a conception of toleration as a condition of evangelical witness, the Anglican Mandell Creighton (1843–1901) reflects on the need for toleration to have a robust theological foundation, without which its exercise could easily become distorted.[17] In Creighton's

---

14. See, for example, Reinhold Niebuhr, *The Children of Light and the Children of Darkness* (London: Nisbet, 1945), 84–104, and John Courtney Murray, *The Problem of Religious Freedom* (London: Geoffrey Chapman, 1965).

15. Arguments for toleration are evident in his early divorce tracts (1643–1645) and *Aeropagitica* (1644) and continue to the preface of his unpublished *De Doctrina Christiana*. Even up to his final pamphlet, *Of True Religion* (1673), Milton inveighed against toleration of Roman Catholics.

16. Teresa Bejan, "Evangelical Toleration," *Journal of Politics* 77, no. 4 (2015): 1103–14.

17. Mandell Creighton, *Persecution and Tolerance* (London: Longmans, Green, 1895), 115–16.

view, toleration is part of the faithful witness of the church to the truth it has received from God.[18]

For the most part, theological justifications ground toleration in some combination of the following rationales:

- the inherent capacity of humans as created in the image of God, the expression of which must be respected even if the form it takes is sinful (for example, free will);
- the fallibility and finitude of humans resulting from humans being created and fallen, and thus generating the need for epistemic humility and a plurality of views, as no one person or group holds a monopoly of truth;
- final judgment as to who is saved as lying with God, not humans, so both wheat and weeds should be allowed to grow up together; and
- the application of the golden rule to do unto others as you would have them do unto you.

There is a prudential dimension to this last argument: one cannot presume that the rulers of the day will share one's commitments.[19] The situation of Christians around the world testifies to this, for in some places Christians are the cultural majority, and in others Christians are a persecuted minority.

The four main modern defenses of toleration echo these theological rationales. The first argument centers on concern about human fallibility and the limits to human knowledge. However, the concern about human fallibility is not of itself a form of relativism. Neither does concern about human fallibility imply that the tolerant person is completely skeptical about the possibility of knowing the truth about a question or issue. As Rainer Forst notes, "The difficulty of toleration, which so many authors have wrestled with, is precisely to justify toleration *without* calling for the abandonment of ethical or religious claims to truth."[20] Moreover, a certain kind of relativist is opposed to the concept of toleration.[21] Arguments from fallibility imply

---

18. Creighton, *Persecution and Tolerance*, 135.

19. Connected to this point is a further argument that is less to do with toleration per se and more to do with the nature and limits of political authority in relation to matters of doctrine and morality. Such arguments are mostly based on some variation of the separation of temporal and spiritual powers, often referred to as either the two-swords or two-kingdoms doctrine.

20. Forst, *Toleration in Conflict*, 94.

21. Jay Newman, *Foundations of Religious Tolerance* (Toronto: University of Toronto Press, 1982), 22.

the need for epistemic humility that maintains belief in an ultimate horizon of truth on which differing positions may shed light. Such justifications may be epistemologically relativist (truth is difficult to know, and no one possesses a monopoly of it) while being ontologically realist (there really is a truth to know). For example, Reinhold Niebuhr, for whom "complete scepticism represents the abyss of meaninglessness,"[22] contends, in relation to religious toleration, that while each religion should seek to proclaim its "highest insights," it should preserve a "humble and contrite recognition of the fact that all actual expressions of religious faith are subject to historical contingency and relativity."[23] In his view, "Such a recognition creates a spirit of tolerance."[24] Arguments for toleration on the prudential grounds of human fallibility can take a variety of forms.[25] These include the view that neither party has complete possession of the truth, truth will benefit from free investigation (and thence dissent), and certainty in theological or philosophical questions is difficult to achieve. This approach to toleration operates horizontally between parallel groups or persons.

A second way of approaching the issue of toleration is by seeking toleration through creating "neutral" procedures. Arguments for limits to intervention and coercion are invoked when someone has the power to change another's behavior that is found to be objectionable. John Locke's *Essay on Toleration* (1667) exemplifies this approach.[26] Procedural arguments are mostly advocated in vertical relations where the exercise of judicial and political authority is held by one group (for example, a majority) over another (a minority). Bernard Williams identifies a procedural approach as central to what he calls "liberal pluralism" and describes it thus: "On the one hand, there are deeply held and differing convictions about moral or religious matters, held by various groups within society. On the other hand, there is a supposedly impartial state, which affirms the rights of all citizens to equal consideration, including an equal right to form and express their convictions."[27]

22. Reinhold Niebuhr, "The Test of Tolerance," in *Religious Pluralism in the West*, ed. David Mullan (Malden, MA: Blackwell, 1998), 293.

23. Niebuhr, *Children of Light*, 88.

24. Niebuhr, *Children of Light*, 88.

25. An earlier justification of tolerance on the grounds of the fallibility of human knowledge appears in Pierre Bayle, *Treatise on Universal Tolerance* (1686).

26. *Locke: Political Essays*, ed. Mark Goldie (Cambridge: Cambridge University Press, 1997), 134-59.

27. Bernard Williams, "Toleration: An Impossible Virtue," in Heyd, *Toleration*, 22.

A problem with this approach, exemplified in the modern liberal state, is that the state is never neutral. It has very definite commitments that it prosecutes vigorously and often violently. As Alasdair MacIntyre notes: "The modern state is never merely a neutral arbiter of conflicts, but is always to some degree itself a party to social conflict, and . . . acts in the interests of particular and highly contestable conceptions of liberty and property."[28] The basis of modern notions of and policies regarding toleration is substantive moral commitments that inevitably conflict with those who do not share these commitments. The nonneutrality of the state in relation to rival conceptions of the good is a separate issue from the nonneutrality of the liberal state toward that which is judged intolerable.

The good of ongoing association depends on making a distinction between what is objectionable, but tolerable, and what is intolerable and thus prohibited through recourse to a legal (and thereby coercive) process. The liberal state can aim to be impartial regarding rival conceptions of the good, but it is obliged to prosecute that which is judged intolerable as a crime or to censor it in some way. For example, dog fighting as a sport and paedophilic sexual practice are crimes, while speech that is seen to threaten national security is censored. The liberal state, like ecclesial authorities, places limits on toleration and displays toleration's underside once that limit is reached; that is, it is intolerant of that which lies beyond the bounds of what is considered tolerable. Only now it is the liberal state rather than the church that has the power and resources to "persecute" that which is judged intolerable.

The third approach seeks to argue for toleration as a substantive good. The arguments for toleration in *On Liberty* (1859) by John Stuart Mill are an example of this approach. However, framing analyses of how one should live with difference in terms of toleration as a substantive good is conceptually problematic. As Bernard Williams comments: "The difficulty with toleration is that it seems to be at once necessary and impossible."[29] He points out that there is a difference between pragmatic toleration and toleration as a substantive value. The good of individual autonomy is the substantive value that grounds modern notions of toleration. This leads to the following problem: "The practice of toleration cannot be based on a value

28. Alasdair MacIntyre, "Toleration and the Goods of Conflict," in *The Politics of Toleration: Tolerance and Intolerance in Modern Life*, ed. Susan Mendus (Edinburgh: Edinburgh University Press, 1999), 138-39.

29. Bernard Williams, "Tolerating the Intolerable," in Mendus, *The Politics of Toleration*, 65.

such as that of individual autonomy, and also hope to escape from substantive disagreements about the good."[30] Those who disagree with the liberal conception of the good will necessarily reject liberal conceptions of toleration, just as they reject liberal conceptions of rationality deployed to justify toleration as a good. There is a further conceptual problem with arguments for toleration as a substantive good based on voluntaristic notions of human autonomy. As Susan Mendus puts it: "We need to understand how people are *inter*dependent as well as *in*dependent. We need to explain how autonomy is formed, not solely from the internal nature of individuals, but also from the nature of the society in which they find themselves."[31] To ground arguments for toleration solely on individual autonomy ignores how no one is an island unto himself or herself.

The fourth justification for toleration directly addresses the above critique of toleration by positing toleration as a virtue. On this account, while toleration intends to respect and enable autonomy, it also seeks to enable the good of sustaining a shared life. Toleration presumes and depends on a prior form of common life, which benefits both the one who tolerates and the one tolerated. In intending to perpetuate this common life, despite finding what a fellow member is doing objectionable, toleration recognizes that membership of a relatively just and merciful common life is a condition and possibility of purposeful agency that goes beyond mere survival. "Autonomy" understood as purposeful agency is not reducible to choice and is not necessarily voluntaristic. Independent action always exists within certain conditions and possibilities (economic, social, political, environmental, physical, psychological, etc.) that make that purposeful agency possible. Therefore, our choices inevitably have limits. The boundaries of what is considered tolerable by the customs, mores, and laws of the polity are one primary set of limits. Given different histories and cultures, what is licit/tolerated in some societies is more varied than what is licit/tolerated in others. But limits are inevitable, even as these boundaries are always contested. However, alternative forms of life and worldviews are needed if autonomy (understood as independent and purposeful agency) is to have any meaning: if there is no choice, then autonomy is an entirely abstract proposition. So rather than autonomy per

30. Williams, "Tolerating the Intolerable," 73. See also Thomas Nagel, *Equality and Partiality* (Oxford: Oxford University Press, 1991), 154-68.

31. Susan Mendus, *Toleration and the Limits of Liberalism* (London: Macmillan, 1989), 67-68.

se, toleration aims at maintaining plurality as a condition of purposeful agency amid commonality.[32]

John Bowlin develops a sustained philosophical and theological account of toleration as a virtue. Building on the work of Thomas Aquinas, he envisages toleration as a "natural virtue" that occurs in all forms of complex society. After distinguishing toleration from its distortions and semblances, he defines it as "the patient endurance of another's objectionable difference."[33] Those with the virtue of toleration neither resent enduring what they find objectionable or scandalous nor welcome it; nevertheless, they tolerate it without effort or reserve, as this is the right or just response to objectionable difference.[34] Revision or abandonment of what is found objectionable might be hoped for, but desire for renunciation cannot be a condition of toleration if the act is to be virtuous. As an act, toleration is both a good in itself and a means to achieve other goods. These other goods are a well-ordered and peaceable society characterized by a high degree of personal and communal autonomy. One tolerates the objectionable out of love for those goods that are a condition of human flourishing. The goods that the virtue of toleration intends are therefore shared between the tolerant and the tolerated: "The tolerant want to secure the common goods of that society, but they also want the person they tolerate to enjoy those goods and share in that society."[35]

On Bowlin's account, toleration is a species of justice, as it seeks what is due to a fellow member of a common life if the good of the whole and the goods of association are to be maintained.[36] As a form of justice, the limits of toleration, and thereby judgments about what is objectionable but tolerable and what is intolerable, are set by what is identified as morally evil, that is, acts that constitute a total inversion of the moral order. This

---

32. John Bowlin, *Tolerance among the Virtues* (Princeton: Princeton University Press, 2016), 188–93.

33. Bowlin, *Tolerance among the Virtues*, 118, 147, 164. Bowlin's Christian conception contrasts with the earliest philosophical treatments of tolerance as a virtue by Cicero and Seneca, both of whom saw tolerance as a form of bravery that involved dignified or steadfast endurance in the face of suffering, injustice, or the twists and turns of fate. This Stoic conception sees *tolerantia* as a self-directed virtue that enables self-control. This contrasts with a Christian conception that sees *tolerantia* as a virtue orientated to sustaining right relationship with God and others. Bowlin's account echoes this other-oriented form first developed by patristic writers building on scriptural precedent.

34. Bowlin, *Tolerance among the Virtues*, 145–47.

35. Bowlin, *Tolerance among the Virtues*, 119.

36. As does Forst (*Toleration in Conflict*, 510). However, Forst and Bowlin have radically different conceptions of justice.

can include things that don't merely fracture but poison the good of the whole by perpetuating systemic injustice—racism and sexism being two cases in point. However, in practice, this is often exactly when toleration is required. Judgments about what is objectionable and what is intolerable will differ and be contested within societies and between societies. What Muslims, Christians, and atheists find intolerable will differ within each group and between them as well. For example, some will find wearing the hijab objectionable but tolerable while others will argue that it is an unjust, patriarchal imposition on women and so should not be tolerated. Or while two people judge sexism to be intolerable, one might find sexist jokes objectionable while the other sees them as intolerable, arguing in turn that there is a need to limit the autonomy of those intent on making such jokes through coercively censoring them in some way.[37] Moreover, not everything that is intolerable can be prohibited and so must, to some degree, be tolerated, lest, as Aquinas puts it, "certain goods be impeded or greater evils incurred."[38] For example, some Christians judge abortion to be a moral evil and thereby intolerable but argue that it should be legally licit, albeit quarantined within certain limits, to avoid greater evils.

Part of sustaining a political life is making prudential judgments about what is objectionable but tolerable and what is intolerable and must be actively opposed or reconfigured through either democratic politics or a legal process. Navigating these different judgments takes us beyond toleration to politics as defined in the first chapter. For example, for theological reasons, I find living in a state that possesses nuclear weapons intolerable and something to be endured whereas others, with justifiable, nontheological reasons, see possessing nuclear weapons as rational and necessary to defend our common life against domination or destruction by an oppressive foreign power. They view my call for getting rid of nuclear weapons as intolerable and dangerous. Navigating these differences requires politics,

37. For an example of why, in certain contexts, making judgments about the licitness or otherwise of sexist humor can be complex, see Kimberle Crenshaw's intersectional analysis of 2 Live Crew's album *As Nasty as They Wanna Be* ("Mapping the Margins: Intersectionality, Identity Politics, and Violence against Women of Color," *Stanford Law Review* 43, no. 6 [1991]: 1283–95).

38. Aquinas, *Summa theologiae* II-II.10.11. For a study of how a Thomistic account of tolerance was applied to the extreme cases of human sacrifice and cannibalism by Bartolomé de Las Casas and Francisco de Vitoria, see Edgardo Colón-Emeric, "Human Sacrifice: Religious Act or Vicious Desire? Testing the Limits of Tolerance with Vitoria and Las Casas," *Journal of Early Modern Christianity* 4, no. 2 (2017): 227-61.

not just toleration. But for politics to be possible, I am required to endure those who advocate for the need for nuclear weapons and the apathy of my fellow citizens who have never thought about the issue even as I actively try to persuade them of their error.

As already noted, some things that are intolerable (because identified as a moral evil) must still be endured because coercively prohibiting them would create havoc or greater oppression. Other things that are intolerable must be endured because they are systemic and not easily changed. Rather than patient endurance, they must be endured *impatiently* as we engage in a democratic process to dismantle them at a structural and cultural level.[39] I am positing impatient endurance as a political virtue that stands beyond toleration but alongside other virtues such as perseverance, hope, and courage. In theological terms, it is a concrete form of hope. Impatient endurance entails "cold" or "righteous" anger, which points to God's wrath against sin and idolatry. Such anger is born out of grief for the gap between the world as it is and the world as it should be and hope that things can change.[40] For example, racism is an intolerable moral evil, yet it is baked into the forms of life and structures of the West. Therefore, even as it must actively be dismantled through civil resistance and agitation as expressions of righteous anger, the reality is that it has to be impatiently endured even as its abolition is hoped for and actively sought. But this is *not* to tolerate it. Likewise, patriarchy, debt slavery, and ecological devastation, to name but three systemic, "wicked" problems, are all intolerable. They need opposing in the strongest terms possible, yet they are not about to disappear, so must be impatiently endured.

To clarify what I mean by impatient endurance, a brief excursus on the distinction between problems and issues is helpful. Problems are systemic, long-term injustices that take a shift of social imaginary and structure of feeling, not just policy, to change. A problem is an amorphous, multifac-

---

39. This is to build on but also depart from Bowlin. That said, Bowlin does argue that some combination of contestation and tolerance is a central feature of democratic politics. Bowlin, *Tolerance among the Virtues*, 171.

40. It is important to distinguish between wrath as blind fury that is vindictive and seeks revenge, and wrath as the urgent pursuit of retributive justice, respect, and reparation. The latter is anger tempered by perseverance, orientated to hope, and yet it maintains a sense of urgency. For a constructive political theology of wrath, see Willa Boesak, *God's Wrathful Children: Political Oppression and Christian Ethics* (Grand Rapids: Eerdmans, 1995). For an account of "cold anger," see Mary Beth Rogers, *Cold Anger: A Story of Faith and Power Politics* (Denton, TX: University of North Texas Press, 1990), 188-92, and Jeffrey Stout, *Blessed Are the Organized: Grassroots Democracy in America* (Princeton: Princeton University Press, 2010), 64-69.

eted, and generalized structural condition such as crime or poverty. To focus on problems can be antipolitical because it generates apathy and fatalism and so drains energy for change, directing people away from public action and toward making the best of their situation for themselves and their family. In contrast to a problem, an issue is a specific and potentially "winnable" course of action or proposal targeted at identifiable people and institutions. As Saul Alinsky succinctly defines it: "An issue is something you can do something about."[41] If climate change is a problem, mountaintop removal is an issue. If sexism is a problem, ending pay disparities based on gender is an issue. The focus on issues is a turn from structure to agency. People cannot choose the problems that afflict them, but they can choose the solutions they think might help alleviate those problems. Political action involves motivating and mobilizing people to act together for change through identifying the possibilities for agency through breaking structural problems down into winnable issues. Impatient endurance means addressing issues even while we endure problems.[42]

What is tolerable relates to a prior set of commitments about the goods of a common life and conceptions of justice. A difficult case is those who, in bad faith, would use the goods of a democratic common life to destroy or subvert it. The crucial distinction is the *intentional* commitment to subvert and destroy the rule of law, the equality and dignity of all persons regardless of belief or identity, basic freedoms (of speech, belief, and association), and democratic politics as a primary way of solving collective problems and addressing social conflicts.[43] Since World War II there have been various "political heretics," including Marxist-Leninists, fascists/white nationalists, and certain Wahhabist/Salafist Sunni Muslims.[44] Members of such groups are intolerable because, rather than either forming separatist enclaves or dissenting from and critiquing liberal democracy, they seek to destroy it through taking advantage of its goods in bad faith to

41. Saul Alinsky, *Rules for Radicals: A Practical Primer for Realistic Radicals* (New York: Vintage Books, 1989 [1971]), 119.

42. This will sound insufficiently radical or revolutionary to some. However, actual revolutions—as distinct from utopian fantasies—only ever address a cluster of issues, and no revolution to date has solved problems like poverty or patriarchy.

43. Aquinas treats this problem under the heading of sedition, defined as that which is opposed to and seeks to disturb justice and the common good (see *Summa theologiae* II.II. q. 42).

44. "Political heretics" is a term coined by Jacques Maritain in *Man and the State* (Washington, DC: Catholic University of America Press, 1998 [1951]), 114-19.

actively undermine the bonds of trust and cooperation necessary to sustain a common life.[45] This subversion tries to demolish democratic politics and establish what those committed to liberal democracy see as a tyrannous regime of domination. Again, differences will occur as to judgments about who is acting in bad faith and whose approach will subvert democratic life.[46] Populists argue that plutocrats fall into this category, and libertarians see democratic socialists in this light, while democratic socialists see libertarians in the same way. There is a clear and uncontroversial mandate to use rule-bound coercive power to police political heretics who commit crimes to achieve political ends (murder, kidnapping, bombing, etc.), but what about the recruitment and grooming of new adherents? And should antidemocratic ideologies be considered intolerable speech and thereby censored or banned? How to address political heretics acting in bad faith without in turn destroying the conditions for the possibility of a democratic common life—the rule of law, freedom of association, freedom of speech, etc.—is a vexed matter only addressable by contextual political judgments. There can be no one-size-fits-all approach, and toleration on its own is inadequate as a framework for developing policy, as any coherent response demands an unequivocal and explicit commitment to substantive moral goods.

Toleration is a necessary virtue in democratic politics but not a sufficient one. And while toleration is a species of justice, theologically, neighbor love, as well as justice, must form part of the response to both objectionable and intolerable difference. Bowlin focuses on forbearance as a form

---

45. This echoes core arguments in Locke's *Essay on Toleration*. Locke sees as intolerable those who, by dint of their commitments, cannot be trusted to act in good faith (for Locke this was atheists), and those who are subject to a hostile foreign power and so, likewise, cannot be trusted to act for the commonwealth (for Locke this was Roman Catholics).

46. As indicated in the discussions in this book of Augustine, class, and Black Power, there are judgments to be made about whether a liberal capitalist order is a basically just regime acting unjustly or a fundamentally unjust regime that needs to be overturned (a key distinction in Protestant resistance theory). However, even if the current political order is judged fundamentally unjust, if such a judgment entails a commitment to a more just and compassionate form of democracy pursued through democratic means, it is entirely different in kind from one that makes the same judgment against the system but then intends to replace democracy itself with a totalitarian or tyrannous form of political order. While the latter sits within the moral terrain of *sedition* and renders its proponents intolerable, the former sits within the moral terrain of *civil disobedience*, and its proponents' views must be judged as to whether they are objectionable or not.

love takes as it endures.[47] In contrast, I will focus on hospitality as another form love takes, particularly as it pertains to how to approach religious differences lovingly. The focus on hospitality provides a corrective to the narrow focus on toleration that to many seems insufficient as the horizon of thought about the current context of religious plurality. As Nederman and Laursen point out, "One stimulus to enlarging the horizons of current toleration theorists may well be a careful examination and appreciation of how earlier thinkers dealt with similar issues concerning the diversity of human conviction and action."[48] The analysis and assessment of hospitality given here constitute precisely the kind of exercise for which Nederman and Laursen have called.

Hospitality and Receiving the Stranger

As a way of framing relations between Christians and non-Christians (understood as ideal-typical categories), hospitality is political. It is a way of conceptualizing how to forge a common life with others with whom we disagree or who are, at some level, either strangers to us or friendless. Although it can appear to be one-way and nonreciprocal, it is *not* a form of *agapē* or grace, that is, a one-way giving without the expectation of a return. Hospitality as a penultimate virtue operates with the expectation that there will be an appropriate response: the guest will be a guest and not an enemy who harms me.[49] Hospitality aims at forging a common world of meaning and action between giver and receiver while recognizing actual or latent conflict and difference. Existing or potential hostility is converted into hospitality, even if only for a while. Thus the other, who may or may not be an enemy, is treated as a stranger to be welcomed.

Hospitality can entail enormous asymmetry between the gifts received and what is offered in return. What is offered may only be a symbolic gesture such as a song or a word of gratitude. Yet the exchanges are tokens of recognition or esteem that mark both guest and host as having standing in relation to each other. The gift of hospitality both signals respect and

47. Bowlin, *Tolerance among the Virtues*, 206–41.

48. Nederman and Laursen, *Difference and Dissent*, 12.

49. On the inherently reciprocal nature of hospitality and the etymological connection between enemy, guest, and gift in the word *hostis*, see Émile Benveniste, *Indo-European Language and Society*, trans. Elizabeth Palmer (Coral Gables, FL: University of Miami Press, 1973), 71–83.

demands reciprocal recognition from the other, a demand that presumes and intends the possibility of a common life. Ultimately, hospitality is a gift of oneself. It demonstrates that, first, you are someone who can participate in reciprocal relations over time, and second, you recognize you (and your household) are not self-sufficient but need others.[50]

The demand for and offer of reciprocal recognition via hospitality entails a simultaneous challenging of and compassionate reaching out to another. It also entails the interplay of freedom, equality, and association constitutive of all generative human agency. As the philosopher Marcel Hénaff contends: "Above all, [gift exchange] remains governed by the triple obligation to give, to receive, and to reciprocate the gift. This is a paradoxical obligation, not only because it is at the same time free and required but also because for the partners it constitutes the reciprocal recognition of their freedom. The giver recognizes the other's freedom by honoring him, but he also claims his own freedom through his offer of munificent gifts, which amounts to a challenge for the other to do the same. This agonistic relation is first and foremost an equal one."[51]

The sociologist Marcel Mauss suggests that ceremonial and public gift exchange is an agonistic yet peaceful means of generating mutual recognition between distinct groups in contexts where there is no centralized, sovereign state. With the advent of the modern state, public and mutual recognition between strangers becomes increasingly mediated and guaranteed through law and bureaucracy—with toleration replacing hospitality as the primary virtue governing relations with strangers. The intolerable is that which is policed in some way by the state; the tolerated, that which is legally licit even if it is socially condemned. Libel is an example of the former, being crude is an example of the latter. Where to draw the line between them is not always clear and often contested. Although hospitality now operates in the shadow cast by the modern state, it is a nonstate-centric form of relation. It involves offering gifts from one's customs and traditions as a way of calling forth reciprocal recognition from others. Without the kind of public recognition generated by gift exchange, exemplified in hospitality, the kinds of social bonds such gift exchange can generate between diverse and potentially hostile groups are absent. In their stead, political and social

50. Marcel Mauss, *The Gift: Forms and Functions of Exchange in Archaic Societies* (New York: Norton, 1967), 46.

51. Marcel Hénaff, *The Price of Truth: Gift, Money, and Philosophy* (Stanford, CA: Stanford University Press, 2010), 397.

existence becomes entirely determined (and thus dominated) by administrative and commodified ways of organizing and constituting social relations. The result is that persons become treated as things, and the dynamic interplay of freedom, equality, and mutual association becomes brittle and shatters. This is not to say that hospitality is without its deformations. The corruption of hospitality results in forms of paternalism and clientelism (and the injustices these reinscribe) or can trigger a degenerative cycle of mimetic rivalry leading to processes of scapegoating and victimization.[52]

Some philosophers conceptualize hospitality as an essential political practice for negotiating life with strangers. Foremost among them is Immanuel Kant. Kant accords hospitality a central significance in his account of how people from different cultures can "enter into mutual relations which may eventually be regulated by public laws, thus bringing the human race nearer and nearer to a cosmopolitan constitution." Kant sees hospitality as a "natural right" possessed of all humans "by virtue of their right to communal possession of the earth's surface." He distinguishes the "natural right of hospitality" from the "right of a guest." The guest makes a claim to "become a member of the native household for a certain time." By contrast, a stranger may only claim a "right of resort," that is, the right to enter into relations with other inhabitants of the land or community. The converse of this is that the visitor may *only* attempt to enter into relations. It is on this basis that Kant critiques the inhospitable and oppressive behavior of the "commercial states" that conquered, rather than merely entered into relations with, foreign countries and peoples—for example, the British in India.[53]

Alasdair MacIntyre, like Kant, envisages hospitality of strangers as required if society is to be maintained and humans are to flourish.[54] Echoing Kant, MacIntyre sees hospitality as a universal practice.[55] However, instead of grounding hospitality in notions of a universal possession as Kant does,

---

52. This draws on the work of René Girard. The implication of his account of mimetic rivalry is to highlight the ambiguity of sacrifice—which I take to be a form of ceremonial gift exchange—as a means of resolving or forestalling violent conflicts but through processes of scapegoating and victimization leading to violence being visited upon the one rather than erupting between the many.

53. Immanuel Kant, "Perpetual Peace: A Philosophical Sketch," in *Kant: Political Writings*, ed. Hans Reiss (Cambridge: Cambridge University Press, 1991), 106.

54. Alasdair MacIntyre, *Dependent Rational Animals: Why Human Beings Need the Virtues* (London: Duckworth, 1999), 122–28.

55. MacIntyre, *Dependent Rational Animals*, 123.

MacIntyre grounds it in a universal capacity: the virtue of *misericordia*. He understands *misericordia* to denote the capacity for grief or sorrow over someone else's distress just insofar as one understands the other's distress as one's own. It is not mere sentiment; instead, it is sentiment guided by reason. Following Aquinas's definition of the term, he states, "*Misericordia* is that aspect of charity whereby we supply what is needed by our neighbour and among the virtues that relate us to our neighbour *misericordia* is the greatest."[56] For MacIntyre, to understand another's distress as one's own is to recognize that other as a neighbor, whether the other is family, a friend, or a stranger. Thus, *misericordia* directs one to include the stranger within one's communal relationships. It is thus the basis for extending the bounds of one's communal obligations and thereby including the other in one's relations of giving and receiving characterized by just generosity. In contrast to toleration as a virtue, which presumes an already existent common life, *misericordia*, as the virtue that undergirds the practice of hospitality, intends to create a common life where there may be none.

MacIntyre's conception of hospitality fits within his broader account of how different traditions of belief and practice can, over time, come to adjudicate between their rival accounts of the good life. This adjudication involves a process wherein each tradition plays guest and host to the other. This interweaving of guest-host relations comprises three steps.[57] The first is that protagonists from each tradition must learn the language of their rivals' tradition, enriching their own vocabulary where necessary. By inhabiting both standpoints, they will be able to recognize what is and what is not translatable from one language to the other. MacIntyre cites the examples of Cicero translating between Greek philosophy and Latin and the Jesuits translating between Christianity and Confucianism as instances of this process. Translatability and the consequent option of rejection make possible the second stage, which involves each protagonist giving an account or history of the other in the other's terms, thus demonstrating that she properly understands the *other's* point of view. MacIntyre then asks: "To what might the construction of such histories lead?"[58] He answers

---

56. MacIntyre, *Dependent Rational Animals*, 125.

57. For an account of this process, see Alasdair MacIntyre, "Incommensurability, Truth and the Conversation between Confucians and Aristotelians about the Virtues," in *Culture and Modernity: East-West Philosophical Perspectives*, ed. Eliot Deutsch (Honolulu: University of Hawaii Press, 1991), 104-22, and MacIntyre, "Moral Relativism, Truth and Justification," in *The Macintyre Reader*, ed. Kelvin Knight (London: Polity, 1998), 202-20.

58. MacIntyre, "Incommensurability," 117.

this question by setting out the third step in his theory of how different traditions may negotiate their differences. This involves each tradition evaluating itself in the light of the other tradition and judging whether its account of the truth is inferior to that offered by the other. For MacIntyre, if each tradition gives an account of the other and irresolvable problems are seen in either of the traditions that the rival can explain, or give a solution to, then it is rational for the "loser," within the terms of reference of their own tradition, to accept their rival's criteria of evaluation. MacIntyre's account of tradition-constituted deliberation about the good helpfully points beyond the binary of tolerance/intolerance. It exemplifies a way of being committed to a distinctive position yet engaged with others for reasons intrinsic to one's own position. To put this another way, it suggests a way to put roots down into one's own tradition while at the same time taking down the defensive walls between one's tradition and that of another so as to engage in dialogue.

The force of MacIntyre's account is underscored when situated in contexts of hyperdiversity. MacIntyre envisages the renewal of contemporary social, economic, and political structures as emerging from local reflection and local political structures. It is only in the context of local communities that goods in common can be rationally deliberated upon and embodied. Anything from a congregation, to household farms, to schools, to businesses can embody particular conceptions of human flourishing. However, to construct such embodiments requires engaging in cooperative enterprises with those whose point of view is very different. Thus, disagreements will be formulated in concrete terms as people make and remake schools, clinics, workplaces, and other institutions. The resolution of such disputes is worked out through something like the process of intertradition conversation outlined above. For MacIntyre, and in contrast to the first argument for toleration, far from being something to avoid, conflict is a necessary part of the process of deliberation. But it is conflict set within a dance of conflict and conciliation navigated through dialogue. On his approach, and in contrast to the second argument for toleration, religious reasons are not to be left at the door so that dialogue occurs in a space governed by supposedly neutral procedures. Rather, "thick" language and clarifying what we disagree about are a precondition of rational deliberation about goods in common.

As should be clear from the above, MacIntyre neither advocates withdrawal into sectarian ghettos nor seeks to establish a single tradition that suppresses all dissenting voices. MacIntyre is sometimes criticized for having an idealistic account of tradition, yet he sees traditions as inherently contested, fissiparous entities that—through their history of interaction and encounter—incorporate and build on bits and pieces of other traditions. While he gives a formal account of traditions, his conception can accommodate a vision of traditions as loose-leaf folders rather than tightly bound books. He can thus envisage relations between traditions not as defined by incommensurability but as characterized by ad hoc commensurability. However, a significant problem in MacIntyre's approach is that he gives no account of how his process of conversation between traditions is possible in a context where power is distributed unequally; for example, where one tradition is dominant and another is an immigrant tradition. Asymmetric relations between traditions are the reality of diversity in Western societies, even in the United States, where immigrant communities have to define themselves in relation to a prevailing Protestantism. It is precisely this reality of unequal relations in plural societies and the mutually constitutive nature of intertradition relations that hospitality addresses.

Jacques Derrida develops a very different conception of hospitality to that of either Kant or MacIntyre.[59] Derrida's account connects hospitality to democracy and its inherently exclusionary or sectarian nature. For Derrida, democracy involves drawing some and not others together in a circle that thereby excludes those on the outside. We call the circle "the people," and democratic government is said to be of, by, and for, and therefore entirely enclosed within, this circle of people. A generalized form of familial relation—namely, fraternity—is then taken as the sign or figure that is paradigmatic for political relations within the circle.[60] Linking the political relation with the blood relation renders the imagined and constructed political community natural and necessary.

Derrida's strategy for opening up and pluralizing the circle is to contend that the circle constitutes only one pole of democracy. Its other pole is the absolute value placed on the equality and singularity of everyone. These two poles are in tragic relation to each other. As Derrida puts it: "There is no democracy without respect for irreducible singularity or alterity, but there is no democracy without the 'community of friends' (*koína ta philōn*), without the calculation of majorities, without identifiable, stabilizable,

59. For example, Jacques Derrida and Anne Dufourmantelle, *Of Hospitality*, trans. Rachel Bowlby (Stanford, CA: Stanford University Press, 2000).

60. Jacques Derrida, *Politics of Friendship*, trans. George Collins (London: Verso, 1997), 93-99, 197-98.

representable subjects, all equal. These two laws are irreducible one to the other. Tragically irreconcilable and forever wounding."[61] It is the "forever wounding" quality of the relations between these two poles that opens the way for a more pluralistic democracy "yet to come." The value placed on the irreducible singularity of everyone, and the universal horizon this opens up, means democratic politics can include others outside the circle. It is hospitality that enables us to be receptive to the singularity of others. Derrida calls for a radical, kenotic, and unconditional grace as the basis for a form of hospitality in which guest and host both recognize and mutually learn from each other. For Derrida, hospitality that is unconditional and involves self-dispossession (which on my account is not hospitality but a form of agapic love) is the key to opening the closed circle of friends. As such, it stands in a dynamic and deconstructive tension with the kinds of social and political patterns of sociality necessary to build stable and ongoing relationships. Derrida explicitly recognizes this tension:

> Pure hospitality consists in leaving one's house open to the unforeseeable arrival, which can be an intrusion, even a dangerous intrusion, liable eventually to cause harm. This pure or unconditional hospitality is not a political or juridical concept. Indeed, for an organized society that upholds its laws and wants to maintain the sovereign mastery of its territory, its culture, its language, its nation, for a family or for a nation concerned with controlling its practices of hospitality, it is indeed necessary to limit and to condition hospitality. This can be done with the best intentions in the world, since unconditional hospitality can also have perverse effects.[62]

Derrida's work highlights the paradox that to be hospitable we must come from somewhere—we must have a home/circle of friends—yet such a circle depends on acts of exclusion. Self-dispossession is one way through which to open this circle.[63]

---

61. Derrida, *Politics of Friendship*, 22.

62. Jacques Derrida and Elisabeth Roudinesco, *For What Tomorrow . . . : A Dialogue*, trans. Jeff Fort (Stanford, CA: Stanford University Press, 2004), 59. See also Jacques Derrida and Jean-Luc Marion, "On the Gift: A Discussion between Jacques Derrida and Jean-Luc Marion," in *God, the Gift, and Postmodernism*, ed. John D. Caputo and Michael J. Scanlon (Bloomington: Indiana University Press, 1999), 72.

63. It should be noted that it is not the only way, and it too is problematic. John Milbank criticizes Derrida's "other-regarding" ethics for reintroducing forms of self-

Following the analysis of Kant's, MacIntyre's, and Derrida's differing conceptions of hospitality, we can see that while hospitality may be a practice central to most cultures, it can be conceptualized (and practiced) in very different ways. Thus, living with those who are different, and framing relations with those who are different in terms of hospitality (rather than toleration), entails understanding hospitality in the light of one tradition, and then bringing this conception into dialogue with understandings from other traditions. What follows is an assessment of hospitality within Christianity.

Interfaith Relations and Christian Hospitality

In some contexts, it is the church that has a cultural-historical, and in parts of Europe, legal, priority. Their structural location means churches are not struggling to make sense of a new situation. They have established institutions, educational and representational processes, wide-ranging relational networks, and affective and symbolic resonance in the broader culture. Those outside such religious communities tend to understand this within a framework of discrimination and seek ways to use legislation to create equality between all faiths, whether minority faith traditions want it or not. From the perspective of minority faith traditions, such a process of equalization can be perceived not as one of leveling up but as one of leveling down and eventually excluding religion from the public sphere.[64] Such exclusion is often justified in terms of a commitment to toleration (understood as a policy rather than a virtue), when in fact it is the attempt to establish secularism as a hegemonic ideology and regime of governance.[65]

Regarding interfaith relations, there are many instances where the Christian church is the host and other traditions are the guest. Rabbi Jonathan Sacks portrays this negatively as the "country-house" model that demands assimilation.[66] Outlined here is a more generous and generative

---

possession and invulnerability and refusing the contingent and therefore open-ended and uncertain nature of the moral life. See John Milbank, *Being Reconciled: Ontology and Pardon* (London: Routledge, 2003), 138-61.

64. Tariq Modood, "Establishment, Multiculturalism, and British Citizenship," *Political Quarterly* 65, no. 1 (1994): 53-73.

65. For a discussion of secularism and a distinction between secularity and secularism, see chap. 8.

66. Jonathan Sacks, *The Home We Build Together: Recreating Society* (London: Continuum, 2007), 15-18.

reading of hospitality that sees it as a constructive way of framing the re-lationship between "established" and "immigrant" traditions. While the account of hospitality given here is explicitly Christian, most traditions have beliefs and customary practices deeply embedded within them re-lating to hospitality. So while hospitality must always take a determinate form depending on which tradition is the host, it need not be an exclusively Christian approach to interfaith relations.

Within Christianity, hospitality as a virtue and practice is part of the church's witness to the life, death, and resurrection of Jesus Christ and the hospitality that weak and sinful humans have received from God.[67] We who bring nothing to our relationship with God echo this in our reception of others. Consonant with the nature of divine-human relations, within Christianity, there is a normative concern for the friendless: for example, the poor, the sick, and the refugee. Moreover, the focus on the weakest and the vulnerable stranger will, on occasion, mean that the church finds itself actively opposed by those who would be, by Christian criteria of evalua-tion, inhospitable to the vulnerable stranger. Thus the Christian practice of hospitality can be—because of its priorities—prophetic, calling into ques-tion the prevailing economic, social, or political settlement. Conversely, because of its understanding of what hospitality requires, the church is not uncritically welcoming: evaluations are necessarily made of who, in any particular instance, is the vulnerable stranger to be welcomed. The obli-gation to be hospitable thereby provides the resources for the immanent critique of "real-existing" Christianity when Christians fail to be faithful.[68]

For Christians, welcoming the vulnerable stranger involves a process of decentering and reorientation to God and neighbor. Openness to such a process entails accepting that all human constructions of life are under God's judgment. Welcoming the other as other is a means by which we respond to God's judgment of human constructions of God and our sinful perceptions of our neighbors. Welcoming the stranger reorientates us to ourselves, to our neighbor, and to God by raising a question mark over the "way we do things around here." Stories of faithful Roman soldiers and faithless disciples, of heretic women recognizing Jesus as the Son of God

67. For a more extensive reflection on the scriptural and theological basis of hos-pitality as a Christian virtue and practice, see Luke Bretherton, *Hospitality as Holiness: Christian Witness amid Moral Diversity* (Aldershot, UK: Ashgate, 2006), 128-46.

68. See, for example, Letty Russell's feminist and postcolonial "hermeneutics of hospitality," in *Just Hospitality: God's Welcome in a World of Difference* (Louisville: West-minster John Knox, 2009).

while the male, religiously orthodox authorities fail to see and hear should alert Christians to how God is often a stranger and so to the possibility that strangers may well be the bearers of God's presence to us. Taking account of the sinful and yet-to-be fully realized nature of all relations this side of the eschaton means there is a heavily provisional dimension to all relations in this age. This provisionality involves a *deferral* of both meaning and full-ness of relationship (the full significance and the fulfillment of all relations are yet to be disclosed), and it also involves a *breakdown* of meaning and relationship (in this age, all our relationships are fractured by sin). Thus, before Christ's return, there is always something more to be known and en-countered. Christians should never absolutize or fix their judgments about other traditions. Hospitality is always required, as the other is always, at some level, a stranger.

A Christian conception of hospitality can involve forms of radical change, and certainly involves listening to and learning from strangers, as this entails forming a relationship with those not like us that we disagree with or find scandalous. Practices of hospitality are thereby a means by which we encounter strangers—sometimes as their guest and at other times as their host. This is to follow after Christ, who is the *journeying guest/host*. Encapsulated in the Emmaus road encounter, Luke's Gospel portrays Jesus as the rejected guest who in turn becomes the gracious, crucified host.[69] Jesus journeys with Cleopas and his friend on the road they are traveling, and is in dialogue with them about the kingdom of God. As two or three gathered together on the road, they form a peripatetic assembly. Jesus is then a guest at their home, and becomes their host at the meal. At this meal strangers see each other in a new light, enjoy fellowship, and Jesus is un-derstood to be the risen Lord—something new has emerged that ruptures their existing beliefs and practices. In response to this event of communion, the two disciples go out, leaving their home, and journey to the very heart of their social, political, and economic world—Jerusalem—to begin a new life-bearing witness, with others, to the risen Christ. As a pilgrim people, the people of God are likewise to be a journeying teaching fellowship of guest/hosts who both give to and receive from the world around them.

The encounter with strangers, whether as guest (receiving from) or host (providing for), is at the heart of how we encounter God—the ulti-mate stranger—in new ways. In Hebrews, amid an exhortation to lead a

---

69. David Moessner, *Lord of the Banquet: The Literary and Theological Significance of the Lukan Travel Narrative* (Minneapolis: Fortress, 1989), 184.

righteous life, we are told not to "neglect to show hospitality to strangers, for by doing that some have entertained angels without knowing it" (Heb. 13:2). There is the suggestion here that strangers may be the bearers of God's presence to us. But angels are scary, off-putting, and threatening, and entertaining them involves demands on our time and resources (e.g., Abraham, Gen. 18:2-15), and may involve threats to our family and livelihood (e.g., Lot, Gen. 19), deep personal struggle (e.g., Jacob, Gen. 32:24-30), incomprehension or shock (e.g., Mary, Luke 1:26-38), and we will not necessarily agree with what they have to teach us (e.g., Zechariah, Luke 1:8-20). Nevertheless, such troublesome encounters are often the primary arena of our encounter with God. To shy away from them, as if proclaiming the gospel has nothing to do with learning from strangers, is to turn our backs on transformative encounters with God. Engaging strangers is also a way we learn to love our neighbors. Having to build relationship and listen to others through hospitable, community-building ventures is a vital way in which Christians learn the humility and penitence necessary to hear from and love God and neighbor. Listening to and learning from others is a therapy for the self-love or pride that is the attempt to secure oneself outside of a relationship with God and pursue illusions of self-sufficiency in relation to both God and neighbor.

The kinds of mutual transformation that just and loving hospitality involves necessarily entail loss, as the familiar and what counts as "home" are renegotiated. For new forms of common life to emerge, a process of grieving is necessary, as both guest and host emigrate from the familiar. Such grieving is the prelude to the formation of shared memories, an interdependent identity narrative, and a new place emerging that both guest and host can call home. I am thinking here of changing demographics in a neighborhood or town. But without any account of loss and grief, the promise of hospitality is never fulfilled as a racist politics and an exclusionary nostalgia gain legitimacy.

Some argue that hospitality, whereby one makes room for another, is an inherently patronizing way of organizing relations between strangers. This is the nub of Sacks's objection to it. Drawing on what I have said so far, the following are responses to this criticism. First, hospitality, as outlined here, is precisely a way of countering patronizing or excluding relations between strangers because it demands that the hosts become decentered and transform their understanding of themselves in order to make room for encounter with others. We could draw a contrast with toleration, which demands no such process, and generosity, which may give abundantly but does not necessitate any form of shared life. Second, hospitality refuses the fantasy of neutral ground on which all may meet as equals: one tradition or another already fills all places, and so an account is needed of how to cope constructively with asymmetry between "established" and "immigrant" traditions if a common life is to emerge. Hospitality is a way of framing how to forge mutual ground in a context where the space—be it geographic, cultural, or political—is already occupied and no neutral, uncontested place is available. To be hospitable is not simply to accommodate another, but, on a Christian account at least, it involves a process of reconfiguring/conversion wherein both oneself and the other change in order that all may encounter God and each other in new ways.

More generally, it is necessary to distinguish between hospitable action in which the church—for a variety of reasons, some good, some bad—is the initiator and lead, and common action that is a negotiated, multilateral endeavor. In the former, it is Christian beliefs and practices that set the terms and conditions of shared action (e.g., a hospice), while in the latter, negotiations between many parties constitute the basis of shared action (e.g., interfaith community work). However, rather than an opposition between a politics of hospitality and a common life politics, the latter simply involves multiple points of hospitality as part of a guest/host dynamic. Moreover, a multifaith, common life politics is subsistent on *temples*—authoritative traditions of interpretation and practice—and *houses*—local, contextually alert places of worship and formation (such as a congregation). But as a form of democratic politics, it is itself a *tent*: that is, a mobile, provisional place where faithful witness is lived in conversation with other faiths and those of no faith. Such a politics is a form of tent making where hospitality given and received between multiple traditions creates a shared place. Many issues can be heard in the tent, some of which can be collectively acted upon and some of which cannot, but the encounter with others and their stories informs the sense of what it is like to live on this mutual (not neutral) ground, to dwell together as part of a common life. The hearing of others' interests and concerns in the context of ongoing relationship and the recognition that everyone in the tent occupies the same mutual ground foster the sense that in each other's welfare we find our own. One of the best examples of this kind of politics in practice is broad-based community organizing.[70]

---

70. See Luke Bretherton, *Resurrecting Democracy: Faith, Citizenship, and the Politics of a Common Life* (Cambridge: Cambridge University Press, 2015), 76-110.

Hospitality and Toleration Contrasted

In contrast to the kind of hospitable politics sketched above, toleration is conservative. It presumes and seeks to maintain an existing form of life shared by the tolerant and the tolerated. As important and worthwhile as that is, hospitality intends something different. It seeks constructive movement toward a different or new form of common life. Thus, unlike toleration, hospitality does not presume the preexistence of a shared society and does not know in advance whether the differences encountered will be intolerable; that is, whether the guest will be an enemy. Rather, it intends to create a shared society, and it is only in the context of that shared society that knowledge of the differences between oneself and another can emerge. Because the intention of hospitality is the formation of society, it fails if relations remain locked in the form of guest and host. Over time there should be movement into an ongoing and reciprocal form of common life where there is increasing equality of agency and equal regard. But without the initial act of hospitality, a common life cannot emerge. The host acts in faith that the gift will be received, and the guest acts in trust that he or she will not be dominated, while both act with forbearance regarding the strange ways they encounter in each other.

As has already been noted, toleration intends to uphold the good of autonomy.[71] But in doing so, it presumes that a high degree of agency is already available, and that the tolerated participate in a shared form of life they can already navigate and negotiate. Hospitality makes no such assumption. It is orientated to seek the good of the stranger, not one with whom one already shares a common life, and to provide what is lacking for someone to survive and thrive. Moreover, within the Christian practice of hospitality, it is imperative to enter into relationship with and accommodate not only those who are different but also those who are friendless: that is, vulnerable strangers whose agency is impaired or threatened.

For Christians, making room for the other, particularly the friendless, is a command. The imperative to welcome the weak and the vulnerable serves as a constant reminder to see and hear those members of society who are most easily marginalized, oppressed, and rendered invisible. Welcoming the "least of these" may mean dis-identifying with hegemonic frames of reference, giving up privileges and respectability, and enduring suffering as a result of offering hospitality. While often ignored, the Chris-

71. Williams, "Tolerating the Intolerable," 73.

tian commitment to hospitality has also been consistently invoked and acted upon in relation to the treatment of the socially excluded. Moreover, the diverse and wide-ranging legacy of its practice, for example, in hospitals, hospices, and the provision of asylum, demonstrates how hospitality has inspired a wide variety of community-building ventures. Toleration involves no equivalent imperative to attend to and actively help those without a place or a voice in society; indeed, a tolerant society can be socially and economically oppressive for many of its members. That said, toleration also entails a kind of suffering: enduring what one finds objectionable.

The issue of exclusion comes to the fore in instances where a high degree of asymmetry is involved. Some hospitality is reciprocal: each hosts the other in turn. However, a situation of asymmetry often determines the practice of hospitality: one party is in a position of strength and the other is vulnerable or weak. An emphasis on asymmetry rather than foreignness points to the insight of Georg Simmel, who in his essay "The Stranger" noted that the stranger is not geographically distant from us; the geographically distant other is rather in a situation of nonrelation.[72] Strangers are those with whom we share the same space but who are different from us. A coordination of simultaneous nearness and distance constitutes their social position. Hence, as Simmel points out, the European Jews were a paradigmatic stranger. However, this is now the situation of many in hyperdiverse polities. We encounter those of other faiths not only on our doorstep but also in our schools, hospitals, political institutions, and households. A temptation that besets members of liberal polities when they meet the stranger is the desire to objectify the other, creating a form of abstract relationship by which to manage and coordinate relations between generalized others so that we never really meet them. A Christian account of hospitality, while often not practiced, directly addresses this temptation by generating meaningful encounter. Unlike toleration, hospitality, as an outworking of neighbor love, demands actively building a relationship with those judged strange.

---

72. Georg Simmel, *The Sociology of Georg Simmel*, trans. Kurt H. Wolff (New York: Free Press, 1950), 402-8.

Conclusion

No one likes to be tolerated. As Goethe observed, "to tolerate is to insult." Toleration casts the tolerated as an outsider or a deviant, and hanging over it is the suspicion that toleration trades in charitable contempt. But under conditions of fallenness and finitude, amid the uneven distribution of cultural, economic, and political power, and where we fear what we don't know but often lack the motivation to know better what we fear, then to be tolerated is better than to be persecuted. Toleration as both a policy and a virtue is part of navigating difference to sustain a more just form of common life amid deep disagreement about basic questions such as those to do with the ordering of sexuality, gender, or religious belief and practice. Despite feelings of contempt or disgust, toleration calls on everyone to exercise conscientious courtesy. But toleration and mere civility are not sufficient, and at times can be part of the problem. It is a *reductio ad absurdum* to imply that a public philosophy built around toleration aims to get people to stop talking and acting together. Yet, toleration, understood as enduring positions others hold that one finds objectionable, can reduce us to silence and inactivity out of fear that to seek to change what others think is, by definition, intolerant. Conversely, the demand for civility can be a mode of censoring certain kinds of speech by excluding behaviors and speech deemed rude. Other community-creating modes of interaction are needed for navigating the objectionable and contesting what is judged intolerable, both by those with power and by those with little power or position. Hospitality as a practice and a virtue is one such means for creating new worlds of shared meaning and action, especially in the face of unequal agency. When transfigured by the love of God in the power of the Holy Spirit, hospitality directs attention to the friendless, seeking to foster conditions where those without power may, over time, develop the means to act for themselves in relationship with others. However, to ensure movement toward a more loving and just common life that seeks the flourishing of all, not just the majority or those with power, toleration and hospitality need embedding in ongoing forms of political life and the dance of conflict and conciliation that politics entails.

Threshold

Part 2 has examined endemic problems the church must navigate faithfully, hopefully, and lovingly if it is to sustain any penultimate form of just and merciful common life with others. More specifically, it has addressed issues that are confronted when forming, norming, and sustaining a democratic form of common life. Part 3 will excavate the foundations of such a life by interrogating key concepts, terms, and dynamics that shape how we imagine and narrate the nature and basis of democracy. It begins with a chapter on humanity that picks up on a theme central to this chapter: namely, how to constructively navigate commonality and plurality amid asymmetries of power. But it situates this problematic within the broader landscape of how to understand what it means to be human, as a notion of shared humanity is central to all conceptions of democracy.

Suggested Readings for Further Discussion

On Toleration

Scriptures: Deuteronomy 13; Matthew 13:24-30, 36-43; Luke 9:51-56; Acts 5:33-39; Romans 14:1-23; 1 Corinthians 8:1-13.

Tertullian, "The Apology" and "To Scapula," in *The Ante-Nicene Fathers*, vol. 3, ed. Alexander Roberts, James Donaldson, and A. Cleveland Coxe (Edinburgh: T&T Clark, 1994). Also available online at newadvent.org.

Lactantius, "The Divine Institutes," in *The Ante-Nicene Fathers*, vol. 7, ed. Alexander Roberts, James Donaldson, and A. Cleveland Coxe (Edinburgh: T&T Clark, 1994), bk. 5, chaps. 20 and 21. Also available online at newadvent.org.

John Locke, "Letter concerning Toleration" (translated by William Popple and published in 1689). Various editions and available online.

Roger Williams, "The Bloody Tenet of Persecution for Cause of Conscience [1644]," in *On Religious Liberty: Selections from the Works of Roger Williams*, ed. James Calvin Davis (Cambridge, MA: Belknap Press at Harvard University Press, 2008), 85-156.

John Courtney Murray, "The Problem of Religious Freedom [1965]," in *Religious Liberty: Catholic Struggles with Pluralism*, ed. J. Leon Hooper (Louisville: Westminster John Knox, 1993), 127-97. Also available online. This is a modern philosophical and theological defense of tolera-

tion and freedom of conscience as Christian commitments that influenced key shifts in Catholic social teaching.

On Hospitality

Scriptures: Genesis 18:1-15; Deuteronomy 4:41-43; Joshua 2; 1 Kings 17:8-
   24; Matthew 25:31-46; Luke 14:1-24; 24:13-53; Acts 10.
John Chrysostom, "Homily 45 on the Act of the Apostles." Available online
   at newadvent.org.
Benedict, *Rule of St Benedict*, chap. 36, "Of the Sick Brethren," and chap.
   53, "Of the Reception of Guests." Various editions and available online.
Dorothy Day, *House of Hospitality* (New York: Sheed & Ward, 1939).
Philip Hallie, *Lest Innocent Blood Be Shed: The Story of the Village of Le Chambon and How Goodness Happened There* (New York: HarperCollins, 1979).
   This is a narrative exposition of hospitality as a prophetic practice. Le
   Chambon provided sanctuary to Jews fleeing persecution by Nazis and
   helped them escape to safety.
Jean Vanier, "Welcome," in *Community and Growth*, rev. ed. (London: Darton, Longman & Todd, 1989), 265-83. Vanier is a founder of L'Arche, a
   movement that builds community between people with and without intellectual disabilities. L'Arche embodies a vision of Christian hospitality.
   In L'Arche communities, despite asymmetric relations between different
   members, hospitality is understood to involve reciprocity, where everyone gives and receives. This text offers Vanier's own reflections on what
   it means to welcome someone.
Miroslav Volf, *Exclusion and Embrace: A Theological Exploration of Identity,
   Otherness, and Reconciliation* (Nashville: Abingdon, 1996), chaps. 2 and
   3. Volf outlines a Trinitarian account of welcoming others—what he calls
   "embrace"—that provides one way of framing hospitality as a central
   Christian practice.
Christine Pohl, *Making Room: Recovering Hospitality as a Christianity Tradition* (Grand Rapids: Eerdmans, 1999), chaps. 6 and 7. Pohl has done
   much to popularize hospitality as a Christian ethical and social practice.
   Here she sets out key dynamics and tensions important for understanding a Christian vision of hospitality.
Alasdair MacIntyre, "The Virtues of Acknowledged Dependence," in *De-
   pendent Rational Animals: Why Human Beings Need the Virtues* (London:
   Duckworth, 1999), 119-28.

PART THREE

Forming a Common Life

CHAPTER 10

Humanity

Some notion of a shared humanity is central to any conception of a common life that extends beyond parochial boundaries of kinship or locality. However, the boundaries of who counts as human, and thence whose moral and political agency deserves recognition, along with the question of how to distinguish humans from other kinds of being, are always vehemently contested. In previous eras, distinguishing humans from animals and the gods was a matter of debate. Today, the lines of dispute are somewhat different.

In the contemporary context, the concept of humanity itself is in question even as the need for it grows more acute. The ability to edit human DNA, the capacity to merge humans and machines at a cellular level, and the prospect of artificial intelligence that shares characteristics of human consciousness lead some to ask whether there will emerge different kinds of humans, or even posthumans. Conversely, attention to how humans are not self-sufficient as a species, but biologically symbiotic with other forms of life, particularly the microbiome, and how the quality of these symbiotic relations directly affects what are taken to be specifically human capacities, notably higher-level reasoning, blurs the sense of humanity as a singular phenomenon. For example, in biocentric frameworks, humanity is merely a knot in a broader assemblage of life, and it is the whole assemblage, not humanity, that is the center of value.

If, on the one hand, there are moves toward the dissolution of humanity as a thinkable entity, there is, on the other hand, an ever-greater impetus to use humanity as a category for delineating moral and political responsibilities. One speculative example of this dynamic is how space exploration and the possibilities of relations with life on other planets ask questions about the moral and political responsibilities of humanity as a species. A more pressing example is the concept of the anthropocene, whereby humans are seen to impact the geological formation of the planet, and the negative manifestations of this impact in such things as climate change and mass-level extinctions. Folded within ethical and political reflections on anthropogenic climate change are concerns about how economic globalization unequally distributes costs and benefits and produces structural inequalities at a global level, even as globalization connects humans more intricately and enables a consciousness of all humans as participants in a shared time and space. These interplanetary, planetary, and global concerns connect to more established foci in which humanity is the primary locus of moral and political concern, namely, the legitimacy and efficacy of human rights, and aligned notions such as crimes against humanity, genocide, global citizenship, and humanitarianism.

This chapter reviews recurrent ways in which humanity as a moral and political concept is understood and how humanity can be imagined and narrated theologically. First, I distinguish humanity as a biological claim from humanity as a moral and political one. Second, I identify two basic moves through which a notion of a shared humanity can be arrived at, namely, either beginning with what humans share or beginning with how humans are different. Third, I compare the way these starting points generate anthropocentric approaches to conceptualizing humanity with a theocentric way of grounding a moral and political commitment to a shared humanity. Lastly, I reflect on how humanity can function as a moral and political judgment in a way that attends to the tensions and paradoxes explored over the course of the chapter.

Natality, Mortality, and the Teleological Nature of Being Human

There are claims about humanity as a biological species that are proper to science. For example, humans share 99.9 percent of their DNA.[1] But it is not the mere fact of shared biology that is salient morally and politically. To meet another *homo sapiens* is not to encounter one who necessarily makes a claim on me or "us." It is in encountering someone with a need that a moral

---

1. On how to interpret scientific data regarding the genetic similarity of humans, the genetic similarity of humans to other species, and the genetic variation between human populations, see Jonathan Marks, *What It Means to Be 98% Chimpanzee: Apes, People, and Their Genes* (Berkeley: University of California Press, 2002).

and potentially political claim is made upon me or "us." But, conversely, the sense that this other human is in need depends on a sense that he or she is indeed another human. It is that person's humanity rather than that person's need that I must deny if I am to ignore or discount the moral claim that human in need makes upon me (i.e., this is not a human, or at least, not the same kind of human as me, and so the person's need for food, water, comfort, liberation, etc., makes no claim upon me). National, ethnic, and religious identities can function to discount the needs of whole classes of humans. Conversely, humanitarianism is a paradigmatic example of how a shared sense of humanity and a sense that this person or group is in need are the basis of moral and political claims. The enduring and widespread appeal of the good Samaritan parable turns on the recognition of a fellow human as the basis of recognizing one in need of help.

The use of "humanity" as both a biological and moral term obscures what prior conceptual frameworks separated. The ancient Greeks distinguished between *zōē*—the biological or physical life that plants, animals, and humans share (and which can be a divine gift)—and *bios*—the manner, form, and means of life (which is a moral and political construct). We hear echoes of this distinction in the difference between "zoology" and "biography" rather than between "zoology" and "biology." There is a parallel distinction in Scripture, although it operates with a different cosmology and anthropology. To be human/*adam* is to be made of the soil/*adamah*, that is, the ground that all animate life and inanimate things share. But to be this kind of creature is also to be Spirit-breathed soil (*nephesh ḥayyah*), a condition shared with all animate life (Gen. 2:17, 19; Ps. 104:27-30; Eccles. 3:18-21).[2] But the pneumatological and biological conditions of life do not exhaust and define what it means to be human. When alone with other forms of animate life, Adam cannot realize the plenitude of human being. It is only in and through communion with another human that what it means to be *human* can be named and lived out. Ultimately, human per-

---

2. In origin *nephesh* denotes breath and appetite; that is, that which is the seat of physical and social vitality and desire. It is used variously in ways that signify the complex of will, desire, and agency, hence it is usually translated as "soul." One way of understanding *nephesh ḥayyah* is to see it as situating humans among the animals. But the broader interpretation given here is more likely. Within the agrarian context from which the text emerges, the soil is known to be teeming with life and is the crucible through which life and death are metabolized. Humans are the fruit of this Spirit-breathed soil and depend on it, and so share creaturely standing with all animate life, not just animals. I am grateful to Norman Wirzba for this insight.

sonhood can only be fulfilled in and through communion with Christ. This is marked at Pentecost, which is not solely about the birth of the church; it also reiterates the act of genesis (Joel 2:20-29; John 20:19-23; Acts 2:1-21). Pentecost recapitulates an event of cosmogenesis when the Spirit breathes on *adamah*: creation is renewed through the transfiguration of earthly distinctions and the exorcism and healing of a common life wrecked by sin and idolatry (symbolized in ancient rites of baptism by the exorcism of the water). This renewal is mediated and symbolized by the formation of a new communion of persons that represents the firstfruits of the new creation (Rom. 8:22-23).

The specific ways in which humans are animate creatures need attention. Any account of human being as an assemblage of life entails moral claims about the distinction between animate life and being a person, between being alive and being someone situated within a meaningful and purposeful moral and political community that is open to and always already called into a specific kind of relationship with God.[3] To be human, on this account, is to be goal directed. The questions then are: what goals or visions of the good life do we desire and pursue? And what are the qualities and kinds of relationships needed to fulfill such an end? The further implication of this interpersonal and covenantal delineation of what is a human being is that to become human is to be embedded in relations of care, even when these cause toil, grief, and pain. This pushes against individualistic and competitive conceptions of humanity. It is not our essential condition but a failure of humanity when, as per Hobbes, we are "wolves" to each other. As in the story of Cain and Abel, to deny how we are constituted through mutually responsible, cooperative fellowship with others that must be ordered in relationship to God is to deny and diminish our humanity. Love of God and love of neighbor (which includes nonhuman creation) are the ground and fulfillment of what it means to be human.

On a theological reading, to be human is to exist within a shared realm of human and divine meaning and agency. Such a realm comes to be through divine action—paradigmatically, through the incarnation of Jesus Christ—and is always already a cultural, political formation in which we live and move and have our being. Claims about humanity, theological or otherwise, cannot be separated from determinate forms of life and their

---

3. On the distinctiveness of humans from nonhumans as residing in their vocation, see David Clough, *On Animals*, vol. 1 of *Systematic Theology* (London: Bloomsbury, 2012), 64-76, 89-103.

ecological-cultural-historical practices. In evolutionary terms, humans are what are called "ultrasocial" animals, with no clear boundary between humans and other-than-human-animals. What is specifically human is not that we are rational, or use tools, or have language, or culture and animals do not.[4] None of these distinctions hold up. Rather, it is the practices through which we become human that mark humanity as a distinctive kind of animal. It is the specific ways humans depend on, care for, and cooperate with each other that account for what differences there are between humans and, for example, our primate cousins.[5] The first of these practices is that humans cook and need to cook their food, and animals do not.[6] I contend that beginning with cooking, the specific ways in which humans are precarious and thereby dependent on the care of others to live mean that it is constellations of practices of care that constitute humanity as a moral and political entity.[7] By beginning with cooking, I am emphasizing that practices of care mark our natality—that which creates life, energy, joy, and intimacy—and thereby mark the beginning of identifiably human forms of life together. But practices of care also mark our mortality—that is, our finitude, frailty, and suffering.

Arguably, something else uniquely human is an awareness of mortality and the sense of finitude attendant on such an orientation in the world. Again, this generates practices of care. As Judith Butler notes: "Precisely because a living being may die, it is necessary to care for that being so that it may live. Only under conditions in which the loss would matter does the value of the life appear. Thus, grievability is a presupposition of

---

4. For an overview of attempts—theological or otherwise—to distinguish between humans and animals, see Clough, *On Animals*, 45-77.

5. There are obvious resonances with an "ethics of care." Initiated by Carol Gilligan and Nel Noddings, this is an influential strand of feminist ethics. See Virginia Held, *The Ethics of Care: Personal, Political, and Global* (Oxford: Oxford University Press, 2006). It also resonates with contemporary restatements of virtue ethics. See, for example, Alasdair MacIntyre, *Dependent Rational Animals: Why Human Beings Need the Virtues* (London: Duckworth, 1999). For a synthesis of a feminist ethics of care with virtue ethics, see, for example, Raja Halwani, "Care Ethics and Virtue Ethics," *Hypatia* 18, no. 3 (2003): 161-92.

6. See, for example, Sonia Ragir, "Diet and Food Preparation: Rethinking Early Hominid Behavior," *Evolutionary Anthropology* 8 (2000): 153-55.

7. An "ethics of care" underlies Johannes Althusius's conception of politics as inherently consociational: humans depend on determinate forms of life together with others if they are to survive, let alone thrive. Johannes Althusius, *Politica*, ed. and trans. Frederick Carney (Indianapolis: Liberty Fund, 1995 [1964]), 17-18.

the life that matters."[8] Mythopoetically, humans mark lives that matter through mortuary and funerary practices that locate us as neither gods (who, as immortal, do not need burial) nor beasts (who do not bury).[9] Theologically, humans are those who live in between heaven and earth, this world and the next, animals and angels, biological kinship and a communion of saints. Phenomenologically, marking death and the dead gives birth to community as existing through time.[10] The remembrance and marking of the dead is, paradoxically, a stake in a future and ongoing life together, a life together in which the dead can be remembered as a past to our future. Our way of life stands in continuity with and builds on the life of our ancestors but also reaches beyond both the past and our present moment to a horizon beyond the burial mound. This is taken up in the birth of philosophy and axial religions (Confucianism, Judaism, Buddhism, Hinduism, Zoroastrianism, and classical Greek philosophy and theater). Axial religions posit a duality between transcendent and mundane orders of space and time. The premise of this duality is the ability to both reach back and reach beyond what is seen and heard and posit a relationship between bodily life and a deeper/transcendent horizon of meaning and action.

As a relational practice that situates humans in relations of proximity and natality, cooking points to how a notion of humanity must include all those who currently exist at this moment (i.e., be synchronic). Care for the dead, which situates humans as having a past and a future and as finite, points to how conceptions of humanity must incorporate not just those humans who are currently alive but also the dead and the unborn, ancestors and generations to come (i.e., be diachronic). Thus, as a moral claim, humanity carries tacit commitments to the honoring of those who came before us as well as a commitment to the tending and handing on of what

8. Judith Butler, *Frames of War: When Is Life Grievable?* (London: Verso, 2010), 14. Butler's account of mortality, for understandable reasons, does not distinguish between mortality as a feature of finitude and mortality under conditions of sin, whereas in recent Christian theology, this distinction is central to debates about the meaning and purpose of death.

9. The *ur*-text in this "mortalist" conception of what it means to be human is Sophocles's play *Antigone*. On this see Bonnie Honig, *Antigone, Interrupted* (Cambridge: Cambridge University Press, 2013), 1-35. Honig critiques a mortalist conception, not to dismiss it, but to extend it to what she calls an "agonistic humanism."

10. Françoise Dastur, *How Are We to Confront Death?* trans. Robert Vallier (New York: Fordham University Press, 2012), and Robert Pogue Harrison, *The Dominion of the Dead* (Chicago: University of Chicago Press, 2003).

we have received, which is to say, it incorporates relations of reception and transgenerational transmission. The semantic registers of debt and gift are near-universal points of reference for framing such relations. For example, conceptualizing human being in terms of debt is at the root of classical Greek philosophy. The pre-Socratic philosopher Anaximander of Miletus posited that everything comes from something, so that every being owes an ontological debt to that which came before it. Inhumanity is the refusal to engage in or the willingness to intentionally destroy and violate the kinds of practices that receive, tend, and pass on the ability to participate in the work of becoming human.[11] There are the obvious brutal forms of this, such as enslavement, conquest, and genocide, but there are also more subtle forms, such as the debasement and distortion of language itself through propaganda and systematic lying. As evidenced in totalitarian regimes and dictatorships, this latter form of inhumanity deprives humans of the ability to trust each other, thereby dissolving the capacity to generate shared meaning and action.[12]

To recognize another as human and to claim that there is a humanity all share is not just to claim that there is a common realm of meaning and action, it is also to make a teleological claim. Humanity presumes a movement from biological life to personhood and thence from alienation to flourishing, indignity to dignity. But as a teleological notion, humanity entails some normative measure of what it means to be human. It is at this point that problems arise: Who or what constitutes that normative measure? Babylonian elites? The gnostic elect? White European men? The proletariat? Those made in the image of God? In which case, who and what determine what that image consists of? Or is there a necessary apophaticism when it comes to defining what it means to be human—its grasp eluding any final, normative conceptualization?

11. Again, Sophocles's *Antigone* is a classic text addressing the inhumanity of this kind of refusal. The play is a meditation on how statecraft and democratic politics can be both a source of such refusal, designating some enemies who cannot be grieved or remembered, *and* a way to contest such refusals. In the play, this refusal is marked by grieving in public what is deemed private; by not accepting the terms of what is considered reasonable or socially acceptable; by insisting on the singularity of the one grieved as against his or her substitution, so that the needs and status of one person are honored over those of the *polis* and its priorities; and by blurring lines of loyalty (whether to kin, city, outsiders, or the gods), so that settled ways of assigning value, status, and responsibility are disrupted and established boundaries and obligations fissured. Honig, *Antigone, Interrupted*.

12. George Orwell's *1984* is a study in this latter form of inhumanity.

Given the inherent cultural and historical dimensions of humanity as a moral and political claim, there is a paradox at the heart of it. It is a claim that is diachronically and synchronically universal in scope but which can only be understood and realized through determinate forms of life and their correlative practices of care. We come to what is common through the specific. The knowledge and realization of humanity only come by means of historically mediated particularity.[13] As I shall argue in due course, acquisition of this knowledge necessarily entails politics.

Knowledge of another as human is always personal and cultural.[14] It is not speculative knowledge but knowledge that connects our affective response and self-reflexive sense of self to a concrete other or group of others. Raimond Gaita makes the point that when we recognize another as vulnerable or in need, we do not recognize a rational agent or rights-bearing subject. We recognize a person who comes from somewhere. Failure to notice the person's particularity as constitutive of our shared humanity is a form of moral failure. Conversely, being moved to act with this person, in this place, at this time, is never simply a movement to help Jamie or Jasmine, it is simultaneously an affirmation of sharing something common with Jamie or Jasmine, of being a fellow human. The philosopher Jean-Paul Sartre captures this coconstitutive relation between universality and particularity in his caustic critique of the "democrat" or liberal cosmopolitan who sees the individual as "only an ensemble of universal traits" and thereby, "in his defense of the Jew saves the latter as man and annihilates him as Jew."[15] The paradox of humanity is that we need modes of attending to particularity to establish what is shared by all and modes of attending to what is common to safeguard our particularity. But the need to attend to particularity to establish what is shared by all inevitably sets up divisions between who does and who does not count as fully human. Linguistically and conceptually, we must name people within bounded categories or as types so that they might be intelligible, but our classificatory systems are inherently exclusionary frameworks: they exclude recog-

13. Schillebeeckx develops an extended reflection on this dynamic and implications for Christology. Edward Schillebeeckx, *Jesus: An Experiment in Christology*, trans. Hubert Hoskins (New York: Seabury, 1979), 591–612.

14. Raimond Gaita, *A Common Humanity: Thinking about Love and Truth and Justice* (London: Routledge, 2000), 259–85.

15. Jean-Paul Sartre, *Anti-Semite and Jew: An Exploration of the Etiology of Hate*, trans. George Becker (New York: Schocken Books, 1948), 56.

nition of those who don't fit the categories and types we use to apprehend another as human.[16]

One way to understand the necessary symbiosis of particularity and universality in humanity as a moral and political category is identifying how the form and content of humanity emerge together.[17] The form of a human life is inseparable from the content. But the content of a life is always specific to each person and nonfungible. Full recognition demands comprehension of each of these dimensions simultaneously and how they are in dynamic interplay. Enumerations of shared characteristics or capacities (language, rationality, etc.) don't do this. Nor do philosophical axioms or principles. Such approaches separate the form from the content. Modes that keep form and content together are stories, poems, photos, films, and ritual processes (e.g., a marriage or funeral) that call us to attend to a sense of what it is to live a human life through this specific person's life. Gaita notes that the Book of Common Prayer exemplifies a ritual mode of attending to a specific person as the basis for generating a shared sense of the human condition: "Man, that is born of a woman, hath but a short time to live, and is full of misery. He cometh up, and is cut down, like a flower; he fleeth as it were a shadow, and never continueth in one stay."[18] In scriptural terms, we hear in this prayer the conjoining of humans as *nephesh*—spirit-breathed soil—and a human life as a breath—frail, ephemeral, mortal, or in the harsher words of the King James translation of Ecclesiastes, vanity.

The way invocations of humanity are always particular points to a problem that humanity as a moral category seeks to address, namely, how to respond to the other, the one not like me, the stranger. This problem is central to the formation of all social and political orders. Determinations of who is a friend and who is a stranger, who is "inside" and who is "outside" the boundaries of the community, shape and form the identity and practices of a polity. The word "humanity" is a placeholder for the commitment to discover a shared way of being alive with outsiders. Talk of humanity is an invitation to extend the reach of who to include in the common life rather than limit who is judged to be human to one group. Talk of humanity is thereby also a refusal to absolutize friend-enemy relations. It is a way to

16. On the distinction between apprehension and intelligibility, see Butler, *Frames of War*, 6-7. On the problem of the inherently exclusionary nature of claims to define humanity, see Anne Phillips, *The Politics of the Human* (Cambridge: Cambridge University Press, 2015), 1-46.

17. Gaita, *A Common Humanity*, 285.

18. Gaita, *A Common Humanity*, 283.

keep open the possibility of discovering with strangers (and enemies) a shared realm of meaning and action rather than either killing or dominating them so they don't appear, don't have to be recognized, and are neither listened to nor learned from. But contrary to what many humanists have argued, talk of humanity is not thereby pre-, post-, or antipolitical. It is inherently political talk. It entails a commitment to contesting the hierarchal significance often attached to differences, conciliating conflicts over the nature of the good, and creating and sustaining a common life amid disagreement. As the feminist political theorist Anne Philips notes: "Recognizing others as equals is a political not a cognitive matter."[19] In short, there is no knowledge of humanity beyond or beneath politics.[20]

As political talk, talk of humanity contests the boundaries of citizenship. In doing so, it functions first and foremost as a form of dissent, contesting definitions of what it means to be human derived solely from what is inherited and familiar. This has been a central theme of cosmopolitan thought in the West from Diogenes the Cynic onward; his claim to be a "citizen of the cosmos" was a way to question the institutions and conventions of his polity. In the contemporary context, claims to humanity have often functioned to agitate those reasonably secure in their status as equals to recognize those still struggling to achieve such equality.[21] Talk of humanity thereby pushes against closed or totalizing systems of thought, insisting on the open-ended nature of who or what defines humanity. As will be seen, talk of humanity must account for and work with the grain of finitude (the temporal and spatial limits of human being), but in doing so, it pushes against the deformation of particularity into parochialism, communalism, and the sacralization of contingent and unjust hierarchies.

Babylonians, Egyptians, and Sumerians—to name but a few of our antecedents—all envisaged themselves as civilized in contrast to various "barbarian" others. Their creation myths inscribed this distinction into the cosmos. The civilized were children of the gods—and so masters by divine inheritance whose social and political order was an analogue of the cosmic divine order—while those outside its boundaries were savages who were either natural slaves or existed in a realm of chaos. Such a framework is completely uninterested either in understanding the other as the same

---

19. Phillips, *Politics of the Human*, 44.

20. I am echoing here Bonnie Honig's conception of "agonistic humanism" (*Antigone, Interrupted*, 19).

21. Phillips, *Politics of the Human*, 133–35.

as me or in understanding how the other is not like me. The other is *not* a focus of moral and political concern. This contrasts with axial religions and philosophies and their canonical texts. In these traditions, we see two moves for framing those not like us, both of which generate problems, but which also need understanding as moral gestures of concern for those we find strange.

The first move is to posit that all humans are the same (the common humanity frame), the second is to begin moral and political reflection on humanity from how humans are different (the ethnographic frame).[22] Both moves are born out of concern for justice, that is, how to give strangers what is due to them.[23] Common humanity frames are generally aspirational and based on theoretical reason. They seek to establish normative conditions for the recognition of a shared world of meaning and action. Ethnographic frameworks presume interaction and knowledge of others. They are attempts to name the stranger in dialogue with the stranger's own terms of reference based on inductive, practical reason, seeking to aid prudential judgments about how to act fittingly in relationship with a stranger. Scripturally these two moves are marked, and to a certain extent coordinated, by two distinct but related covenants. The first is the Noachian covenant, which calls all humans to be a specific kind of creature. The second is the Abrahamic covenant, which calls the people of God to bear witness to who God is amidst the nations through a distinctive pattern of life.

To summarize, talk of humanity needs to account for how such talk is never simply a biological claim; it is always already a claim about a shared realm of meaning and action, and so is a cultural, political, and philosophical or theological claim. Humanity can thereby only be made sense of and experienced within a determinate form of life; that is, it cannot be separated from attention to biography. As a moral and political claim, humanity is necessarily a teleological claim with a specific vision of what human flourishing consists in, as it entails a movement from the merely biological to becoming human.[24] It is also a historical claim that has a dia-

22. This distinction draws on Siep Stuurman, "Common Humanity and Cultural Difference on the Sedentary-Nomadic Frontier: Herodotus, Sima Qian, and Ibn Khaldun," in *Global Intellectual History*, ed. Samuel Moyn and Andrew Sartori (New York: Columbia University Press, 2013), 33-58.

23. Kwame Anthony Appiah seeks to combine both moves in what he calls a "partial cosmopolitanism." See his *Cosmopolitanism: Ethics in a World of Strangers* (New York: Norton, 2007).

24. It is this movement that connects humanity, humanism, and the humanities.

chronic and synchronic dimension. In what follows I examine variations of the common humanity and ethnographic frames as ways of coming to make judgments about who or what is human. However, as will be seen, problems arise when one aspect of how humanity constitutes a moral and political category of judgment is emphasized to the exclusion of others.

Common Humanity, or Beginning with How Humans Are the Same

Common humanity frameworks are philosophical or theological moves that speculate that, despite different forms of life, underneath it all, the other is like "us." Often involving a high level of abstraction, such frameworks appeal to what are presumed to be universal sets of values and human commonalities while bracketing cultural differences. As a moral discourse, frameworks that focus on our common humanity transform a stranger into a fellow human being. Such frameworks emerge from within the intellectual resources of a particular tradition.[25] Versions of this move in the contemporary context include human rights (broadly built off a deontological form of moral reasoning) and humanitarianism. Within Christianity, Judaism, and Islam, some version of natural law is a primary instantiation of such a framework.[26]

Epistemically, common humanity frames too easily slip into claiming a false transparency that obfuscates how others are different. A primary way this manifests itself is through the creation of categories that predetermine how to interpret others. In doing so, moral concern, combined with an asymmetry of power, becomes a colonial imposition that forces others to conform to an account of what it means to be human that is at a minimum alien to them but often destructive of their own way of life.[27] Im-

Humanism and the humanities are "civilizing" projects or ways of becoming "cultured," thus, they are a means through which humanity comes to be articulated and, so the claim goes, fulfilled. On the problems with humanism as a way of articulating and fulfilling our humanity, see Philips, *Politics of the Human*, 107-11.

25. Stuurman, "Common Humanity," 36-37.

26. The most obvious historical exemplars are Maimonides, Ibn Sina, and Thomas Aquinas. But, within Christianity, more significant for the purposes of this essay are Bartolomé de las Casas's response to the indigenous peoples of the Americas and Matteo Ricci's response to Confucianism, both of which drew on natural law to argue for the shared humanity of non-European others.

27. An example of this problem within an Aristotelian-Thomistic conception of natural law thinking is José de Acosta Porres. See Willie James Jennings, *The Christian*

manuel Kant represents an example of liberal cosmopolitanism displaying this problem. Kant critiqued colonialism, but he was an early proponent of scientific racism.[28] However, alongside his justifications of white supremacy and his pointed silence regarding chattel slavery, even his conception of cosmopolitanism, which might be presumed to contradict the racial hierarchy he advocated, reveals a decided Eurocentrism that imposes itself as a universal standard of adjudication. For Kant, "Since the earth's surface is not unlimited but closed, the concepts of the right of a state and of a right of nations lead inevitably to the idea of a right for all nations (*ius gentium*) or cosmopolitan right (*ius cosmopoliticium*)."[29] There is a difference, however, between a concept of *ius gentium* in which each people is recognized as having its own law and Kant's cosmopolitan vision in which the laws of European peoples become the laws of all peoples. Kant follows a trajectory of thought away from explicitly theological formulations of natural law and toward the extension of a Westphalian model of cooperation between nation-states as the model for "perpetual peace" in all places. While deeply problematic, the self-awareness of Christian legal orders as contrasted with other "infidel" forms of order marked a more pluralistic and contingent conception of *ius gentium*. Forerunners of Kant such as Ábbe de Saint Pierre's *Project for Perpetual Peace* (1713) and the hugely influential *Law of Nations* (1787) by Emer de Vattel saw religious differences as irrelevant and an avowed nonreligious, European conception of international law as universal.[30] The United Nations embodies this secularist vision of a shared humanity and peaceable global order. Such

---

Imagination: Theology and the Origins of Race (New Haven: Yale University Press, 2010), 65–116.

28. Robert Bernasconi, "Kant as an Unfamiliar Source of Racism," in *Philosophers on Race: Critical Essays*, ed. Julie Ward and Tommy Lott (Oxford: Blackwell, 2002), 145–66. Without attempting to excuse or explain away the racist dimensions of Kant's work, Jon Mikkelsen does situate them within the broader dynamics of Kant's overall system. See Jon Mikkelsen, "Translator's Introduction," in *Kant and the Concept of Race: Late Eighteenth-Century Writings*, ed. and trans. Jon M. Mikkelsen (New York: State University of New York Press, 2013), 1–40.

29. Immanuel Kant, *The Metaphysics of Morals*, trans. Mary Gregor (Cambridge: Cambridge University Press, 1996), 89.

30. Jennifer Pitts,"Empire and Legal Universalisms in the Eighteenth Century," *American Historical Review* 117, no. 1 (2012): 96–99. Notable exceptions Pitts points to include Edmund Burke and Abraham Hyacinthe Antquetil (105–14). On my account, Burke represents a common humanity frame that is nevertheless pluralistic rather than hegemonic.

an order is arrived at through the negotiation of relations between nation-states in which a monistic European standard of what a nation-state looks like determines what constitutes a legitimate sovereign power. While such a liberal cosmopolitan vision proposes that all nations are free and equal, it hides how some nation-states, by dint of access to resources, setting legal norms, military power, and historical precedent, are more equal than others.[31] As Jennifer Pitts notes, the narrative in which other polities are incorporated into a universal state system once they become decolonized or independent ignores the Eurocentric and imperial contexts and sources for international law.[32] It is this false universalism, and the work it does to legitimize a racialized hierarchy of humans, that Du Bois lambasts with such force in "The Souls of White Folks."[33]

If Kant represents the attempt to conceptualize humanity in terms of a shared territory, which nevertheless places Europeans as the ideal of that nature most fitted to rule over all other "races," Hegel represents the attempt to conceptualize common humanity as derived from humans existing within a shared history. For Hegel, there is a single history, and this history has a teleologically ordered purpose, which is to unfold the spirit of freedom and authentic humanity. Hegel envisages European modernity as the zenith and crowning achievement of this history. His *Lectures on the Philosophy of World History* portrays humanity as finding its center and fulfillment in Europe (specifically, Germany, France, and Britain), such that all other times and spaces are judged in relation to Europe understood as the telos of world history. Hegel's philosophy of history does not simply sacralize history and humanity, it sacralizes *European* humanity as the true end toward which history progresses.[34]

31. On the intersections of liberalism and imperialism, see Bhikhu Parekh, "Liberalism and Colonialism: A Critique of Locke and Mill," in *The Decolonization of Imagination: Culture, Knowledge, and Power*, ed. Jan Nederveen Pieterse and Bhikhu Parekh (Delhi: Oxford University Press, 1997), 81-98; Uday Mehta, *Liberalism and Empire: A Study in Nineteenth-Century British Liberal Thought* (Chicago: University of Chicago Press, 1999); Jennifer Pitts, *A Turn to Empire: The Rise of Imperial Liberalism in Britain and France* (Princeton: Princeton University Press, 2005); and Jeanne Morefield, *Covenants without Swords: Idealist Liberalism and the Spirit of Empire* (Princeton: Princeton University Press, 2005).

32. Pitts, "Empire and Legal Universalisms," 93.

33. W. E. B. Du Bois, *Darkwater: Voices from within the Veil* (New York: Harcourt, Brace & Howe, 1920), 29-52.

34. Matthew Jantzen, "Hermeneutics of Providence: Theology, Race, and Divine Action in History" (ThD diss., Duke University, 2017), and Robert Bernasconi, "'The

Karl Marx turns Hegel on his head but continues to work with the same logic. In place of Western European man, Marx substitutes the proletariat as the subject of history. Only the experience and consciousness of the proletariat are the authentically human consciousness (i.e., their experience, structural location, and material conditions mean only they can rightly interpret reality). Anything else is false consciousness. After Marx, in the wake of Gramsci, and the shift from economic to cultural production as the primary generator of an authentically human and emancipated way of experiencing and understanding the world, numerous other subjects of history replace the proletariat. Maoism posits the Chinese peasant; some strands of feminism, women's consciousness; and certain strands of Black Power, black consciousness. Each of these represents a different subject of history who possesses the key to understanding reality and living out a truly emancipated, authentically human form of life. The problem with such approaches is twofold. First, like Hegel, they absolutize the friend-enemy distinction through dividing up the world between those who are on the right and wrong side of history (the friend-enemy distinction thereby operating on a temporal rather than spatial division). Second, they totalize one set of experiences (this time of the oppressed rather than the privileged) as all-determinative of what it means to be human.

The challenge is to recognize the reality of friend-enemy relations without absolutizing or ontologizing them. In the same breath, experiences of oppression must be recognized as epistemologically prior (they give a better read on what is really going on) without slipping into a view that says the oppressed are ontologically privileged and their experience is infallible (i.e., they can do no wrong because their structural location makes them a better kind of human and their experience is all-determinative). The argument running through the course of this book is that the way to thread this needle is through democratic politics—the difficult and risk-laden negotiation of a common life through a dance of conflict and conciliation in pursuit of goods in common on which the flourishing of all depends. The rest of part 3 lays out frameworks for understanding democratic politics as a risk-laden dance.

With Hegel in mind, we must ask whether positing a subject of history (whether of the privileged or the oppressed) takes on an ersatz christologi-

---

Ruling Categories of the World': The Trinity in Hegel's Philosophy of History and the Rise and Fall of Peoples," in *A Companion to Hegel*, ed. Stephen Houlgate and Michael Baur (Oxford: Wiley-Blackwell, 2016), 315-31.

cal and eschatological form. Theologically, it is only Jesus Christ who is the true subject of history, in whom and through whom humans might come to experience true liberation and a nonalienated form of life. The life, death, resurrection, and ascension of Jesus, rather than earthly forms of culture or history, are the condition for the possibility of movement into new and fulfilling ways of being alive. But in this age, any such movement is paradoxical rather than progressive; it entails both recollection and rupture, honoring our mothers and fathers and being born again.

Kant, Hegel, and humanitarianism are instances of using the common humanity frame from a position of strength and their alignment with colonialist projects of one kind or another. But a common humanity frame can also be used to resist domination "from below." Human rights discourses are one obvious example. Another is what Vincent Lloyd calls the black natural law (BNL) tradition. Lloyd's account also represents an example of threading the needle through politics that I outline above. For Lloyd, black natural law emerges from reflection on human nature as experienced within conditions of systemic oppression and the work of organizing done to end this oppression. He argues that the oppressed, of which, in the context of the United States, African Americans are the paradigmatic instance, have an epistemic priority in determinations of human nature.[35] Failure to grant this epistemic priority leads to mystified and false constructions of human nature that reinscribe unjust systems and oppressive forms of life. As a form of natural law thinking, BNL has a normative conception of what it means to be human, one grounded in theistic conceptions of all humans as made in the image of God, which can be appealed to as part of challenging idolatrous, hegemonic constructions of what it means to be human that privilege some and exclude others. White supremacy, and its manifestation in such systemic injustices as mass incarceration, is one such idolatrous construction of human nature that BNL seeks to dismantle in thought and modes of political action. For Lloyd, figures who exemplify this approach include Frederick Douglass, Anna Julia Cooper, W. E. B. Du Bois, and Martin Luther King Jr.[36]

35. Vincent Lloyd, *Black Natural Law* (Oxford: Oxford University Press, 2016), ix.

36. A parallel "bottom-up," particularistic conception of natural law is developed in David Novak, *Natural Law in Judaism* (Cambridge: Cambridge University Press, 1998).

Ethnography, or Beginning with Difference, Not Sameness

Ethnographic frameworks presume that others are not like us, but "we" must try to understand them in relation to their own customs and language if they are to be given what is their due. In contrast to the common humanity frame, epistemically, an ethnographic starting point begins with the recognition of a certain opacity to the lives of others. However, at the same time, the ways of the other are not seen as random, outlandish, or incomprehensible (i.e., others do not live in chaos). Rather, their form of life has an intelligible order that must be understood in its own terms of reference if we are to understand them and how they might see us. Without such an attempt at understanding, no realm of shared meaning and action can emerge. An ethnographic framework entails an act of moral imagination rather than speculative reasoning. As a framework, it most often emerges at close quarters, when negotiating a common life amid a sense of difference and thus the need to make sense of others is existentially pressing. Siep Stuurman notes that whereas common humanity is expressed mainly in the languages of theology and philosophy, the primary discourses of ethnographic frameworks are history, geography, and anthropology.[37] Stuurman gives the examples of Herodotus's analysis of the Scythians in his *Histories*, Sima Qian's discussion of the Xiongnu in his *Records of the Historian*, and Ibn Khaldun's treatment of the nomadic Berbers in his *Muqaddimah*. To these, we might add the travelogues of Muhammad Ibn Battuta and Marco Polo, and the ethnographic reports of numerous missionaries.[38]

Still, ethnography is not automatically the panacea for overcoming abstract and alien categories in the interpretation of others. Ethnographies can exoticize strangers, rendering them objects rather than those with whom we might share a reciprocal common life. Edward Said names one example of this dynamic "Orientalism."[39] The other becomes simultaneously a source of fear and fascination. The other is portrayed as both a

37. Siep Stuurman, "Herodotus and Sima Qian: History and the Anthropological Turn in Ancient Greece and Han China," *Journal of World History* 19, no. 1 (2008): 1–40, and Stuurman, "Common Humanity and Cultural Difference on the Sedentary-Nomadic Frontier."

38. A modern classic of the missionary genre is Vincent J. Donovan's missiological reflections about the Masai in his 1978 book *Christianity Rediscovered: An Epistle from the Masai* (London: SCM, 2001).

39. Edward Said, *Orientalism* (New York: Vintage Books, 1979).

source of vitality, authenticity, and strength, and in contrast to the decadent and corrupt ways of "our" civilization, the other represents a way to reconnect to what is real and true. At the same time, the other represents a form of life that is less than or a potential threat to "our" civilized way of life.

As with common humanity frames, there are ways ethnographic frames can be deployed "from below." If Orientalism represents an ethnographic frame "from above," then black nationalism and its subsequent iteration in Black Power represent an ethnographic claim "from below." To echo what I argued in chapter 3, the claim to be a nation within a nation is a claim to be all that being a nation invokes as a "social imaginary": belonging, sense of place, a history, a future, self-determination, citizenship, and a distinctive culture. Rather than "integration," black nationalism seeks to radically reconfigure a polity so that those of African descent (whether in the United States, the United Kingdom, or Brazil) can be at home where they live while at the same time forging antiracist forms of "intercommunal" life with others.[40] As Vincent Harding puts it in his discussion of Black Power: "Perhaps we were urged towards an identification with mankind-at-large (often meaning white mankind) before we had learned to identify with our black neighbors. It is likely that our humanity really begins in the black ghetto and cannot be rejected there for an easier, sentimental, white orientated acceptance elsewhere."[41] That said, some strands of black nationalism, for example, the Nation of Islam, can absolutize friend-enemy relations and thereby refuse the possibility of a shared humanity, at least between blacks and whites.

For a nonhegemonic, pluralistic conception of humanity to emerge, whether at an interpersonal, intercommunal, or structural level, change is necessary. If either a common humanity or ethnographic framework is to generate change through enabling wisdom and insight about others, it must orientate us toward discovering ways of interpreting and experiencing reality that decenter our own experience and history and open up the terms and conditions of life together.

40. The term "intercommunal" draws on Huey Newton's work. For an account of the development of his thought, see Judson Jeffries, *Huey P. Newton: The Radical Theorist* (Jackson: University Press of Mississippi, 2002).

41. Vincent Harding, *The Religion of Black Power* (Boston: Beacon, 1968), 10.

Theological Anthropology, or Beginning with God

As already indicated, Christianity has sponsored variations on both the common humanity and the ethnographic frames and their characteristic pathologies. I turn now to examine theological ways of conceptualizing humanity. A (political) theology of humanity is necessary, as any talk of humanity builds on a metaphysical conception of human being, so Christian usages of the term "humanity" need to be consonant with theological understandings of who God is and who humans are in relation to God. Theologically, knowledge of what it means to be human and what kind of thing humanity is comes through reflection on the relationship God cultivates with creation and with humans as creatures. In other words, the discovery of who, how, and what a human being is comes through participating in and reflecting on how God relates to human beings and calls them to relate to one another and to nonhuman life.[42] And this cannot be done apart from reflection on the self-revelation of God in Israel and in Jesus Christ. It is this starting point that generates Paul's conception of redeemed humanity in terms of a differentiated unity of Jews and gentiles in Christ rather than an abstract humanity that supersedes the particular histories of each.[43]

On a theological account, the status of being a human is not something other humans can grant or remove. The intrinsic value of every human is determined through how each human is always already situated in and open to relation with God. By implication, one's humanity is not owned like a piece of property, and so it cannot be revoked or alienated. Nor can it be reduced to some inherent essence or substance. Rather, our humanity resides in a set of dependent and interdependent relations. Sin is the shattering of the finite and historically contingent meshwork of relations on which the flourishing of human and nonhuman life depends. It occurs when humans either overdetermine or fail to cultivate the kinds and character of relations that enable this meshwork to be fruitful and humans to fulfill their vocation to be a specific kind of creature that is blessed by and blesses nonhuman life. Christ's work of redemption is both the healing

42. Christoph Schwöbel, "Recovering Human Dignity," in *God and Human Dignity*, ed. R. Kendall Soulen and Linda Woodhead (Grand Rapids: Eerdmans, 2006), 48. As Schwöbel notes, this way of determining what humanity is avoids establishing a prior metaphysical framework, as it depends on attending to the Bible and its descriptions and narratives of divine-human relations.

43. Eugene Rogers, *After the Spirit: A Constructive Pneumatology from Resources outside the Modern West* (Grand Rapids: Eerdmans, 2005), 86-88.

of this meshwork and the bringing of it to fulfillment so that all creation may fruitfully participate in communion with God. The paradox for humanity is that to fulfill what it means to be human, to bring to blossom the vocation given to us as creatures, we must grow into and become like that which we are not, namely, God.[44] To become like an invisible God whose paradigmatic way of relating to us as creatures is incarnation, crucifixion, and Pentecost renders contingent and relativizes any attempt to identify a single class, gender, or *ethnos* as defining and fulfilling what it means to be human. All peoples and any person may be a vital part of the meshwork through which we come to participate in human being, and humans fulfill their vocation through being priests and gardeners of creation.

A central Christian confession is that each person has an inviolable dignity born out of an equality of status in relation to God and all other humans.[45] There are various ways to ground this confession. These range from all humans being created by God; all humans being generated from a single point of origin (Adam/Eve) and so being of the same kind, substance, and form; all humans being made in the image of God; all humans being subjects of Christ's redemptive work; and, lastly, all humans sharing a common eschatological destiny. Often missed, however, is the threefold structure of creaturely personhood necessary to realizing human dignity. While we are the same as all other persons, we are more like some persons than others, and we are also like no other person; each person is unique. To put this another way, there are the person, the person-in-relation-to-other-persons-and-non-human-life situated in a specific time and place, and the person-in-relation-to-the-whole-of-humanity-and-the-whole-of-creation. This basic structure of human being is at once assumed and affirmed in the incarnation of Jesus Christ. Jesus is unique; Jesus, as a historical person, is more like some than others; and Jesus is human.[46] And as Logos and

44. Kathryn Tanner, *Christ the Key* (Cambridge: Cambridge University Press, 2010), 28–57.

45. For a comparison of Christian conceptions of human nature with Jewish, Islamic, Hindu, and Buddhist conceptions, see Veli-Matti Kärkkäinen, *Creation and Humanity* (Grand Rapids: Eerdmans, 2015), 269–305, 369–86.

46. A fully developed, systematic christological basis for the account of humanity set out here is needed but beyond the scope of this chapter. However, I deliberately did not *begin* with one because, in the context of doing political theology rather than systematic theology, I am wary of Christology being used as a rigid ideological blueprint through which to read diverse forms of life. Echoing what was said in the introduction, beginning a political theology of humanity with Christology can operate with a fallacy that if we get the theory right, then good practice will follow. Rejecting such a move, I argue

Pantocrator, Jesus is the one through whom the whole cosmos is created and fulfilled. Encounter with and reception of strangers, if it is to be fruitful and respect the dignity of each, must attend to this threefold pattern of interpersonal and intracreational relationships. To welcome the other is to recognize one who is the same as me (common humanity frame). Yet to welcome the other is to be in a place of welcome, to be at home, and thus in a relationship with others who are more like me than the stranger welcomed, and thereby recognize that the stranger comes from a different form of life than me (ethnographic frame). However, to truly welcome another is to welcome someone who is like nobody else, affording them the attention and respect that communicates recognition of their uniqueness.

Contrasting humans with the status of animals and plants is frequently a way of formulating human dignity. A central feature of such contrasts is the mistaken account of humans having dominion over/ownership of the rest of creation. The character of this dominion is then said to mirror God's rule, understood in monarchical or patriarchal terms: God as king or *paterfamilias*. But when God's relationship to the cosmos is properly understood as a gardener cultivating life or an artisan crafting creation who calls humans to participate in this cultivation, then the analogies and metaphorical frameworks change. Humans are gardeners or artisans of life who are not just psychosomatic, cultural-political persons but also biospiritual creatures, whose own cultivation and flourishing are interconnected with the cultivation and flourishing of other ways of being alive.[47] Transcendence is not to rise above the body, our forms of human sociality, or our animality and biology, as dualistic accounts of human nature suppose. Rather, transcendence is better understood as becoming fully alive, that is, attuned to, resonating with, and fulfilling the relations within which we are enmeshed and through which we live and breathe and have our being. As Irenaeus

---

here that we discover our shared humanity, and what that means in practice, through politics, a politics within which christological and other theological commitments are circulating. For formal, Chalcedonian Christologies that the account set out here resonates with, see Karl Barth, *Church Dogmatics* III/2, ed. and trans. G. W. Bromiley and T. F. Torrance (Edinburgh: T&T Clark, 1960), 223-86; Tanner, *Christ the Key*; and Brian Bantum, *Redeeming Mulatto: A Theology of Race and Christian Hybridity* (Waco, TX: Baylor University Press, 2010), 87-138.

47. Stewardship within this framework is not about dominion understood as mastership or management. Rather, the steward is one who receives an endowment or role in trust, primarily related to the provision of food, which is to be tended so as to ensure the flourishing of all.

puts it: "The Glory of God is a human fully alive."[48] Being fully alive entails the flourishing of the microbiome in our gut, with which we have a symbiotic relation, through to the flourishing of the wider ecosystems on which all animate life depends. Right relations with God are the condition and possibility of loving and just (i.e., fruitful) intersubjective human relations and loving and just relations with nonhuman ways of being alive. Thus, we must ask how "nature" should participate in human society, how human society should participate in nonhuman forms of life, and how both, symbiotically, may participate in the triune life.

We are neither masters nor sovereigns of creation (i.e., treating creation as if we have total control over it), nor are we custodians or parents (i.e., creation is not dependent on us). But the alternative to these patterns of relationships is not to preserve creation as pristine. The idea that humans should work to keep the world in a "natural" state is not just contradictory, it is not Christian. Human activity understood as the cultivation of a garden should seek to fructify creation, and so enable the wonder and goodness of what God has created to shine forth as part of fostering reciprocal relations of praise and thanksgiving with creation. As exemplified in the preparation of food and wine, such priestly activity enables opportunities for human fellowship. This priestly activity is affirmed and fulfilled in the Eucharist: Christ did not take grain and grape, but the products of human labor and creativity, and used them as an anticipation of the coming eschatological fulfillment of all creation.[49] What is received is freely and joyously offered back as thanksgiving and praise within an ecology of blessing.

East of Eden, however, the groaning of creation and the blood of Abel that cries out from the soil are one and the same cry for justice and deliverance. All interpersonal and political problems are also ecological problems, and vice versa. "Am I my brother's keeper?" we ask as we extract and exploit what we can from land, sea, and air, and in that process enslave our brothers and sisters for material gain. We cannot separate the conversion of the soul from the cultivation of the soil and the cure of the city. They are intertwined. What and how we eat are shaped by what and how we produce and consume, and both shape how we relate to God, other humans, and the rest of creation. What is cooked, how it is prepared, who does and does

48. "The glory of God is a human fully alive, and the life of a human is the vision of God. If the revelation of God through creation already brings life to all living beings on the earth, how much more will the manifestation of the Father by the Word bring life to those who see God" (Irenaeus, *Against Heresies* 4.20.7).

49. Luke 22:16, 19.

not cook, and how and when food is eaten are a window to the soul of a society. A political economy is always already a political ecology, a culture a form of cultivation.

The picture of the fulfillment of all things in Christ is one of cosmic eschatology where there is not a separation out of human and nonhuman creation but their *perichōrēsis* as the presence of God transfigures them. The people of God are to bear witness to a messianic banquet (i.e., the priesting of creation in feasting and fellowship) and the new Jerusalem (i.e., a garden-city that signifies the healed and harmonious interrelationship between human political economy and nonhuman life).[50] Irrespective of whether one agrees with the data on anthropogenic climate change, it is always incumbent upon Christians to forge just and loving relations with nonhuman life. Theologically, any account of human flourishing must entail concern for the flourishing of all creation, and conversely, no conception of what a flourishing environment might entail can be a true account if it excludes an account of human flourishing.

Humanity as a Moral and Political Judgment

Talk of humanity is political talk because it is talk about the conditions and possibilities of a shared world of meaning and action with those we find strange. It is a recognition that to be who we are we need others, and this entails negotiating some form of common life with them, either through positing a common humanity or through bringing difference/alterity into fruitful relationship. And this entails a political process of conflict and conciliation through which a just and compassionate common life might be discovered. War, alongside forms of structural domination, is a refusal of politics and represents the absolutizing of friend-enemy relations. As exemplified in the work of Herodotus, Sima Qian, and Ibn Khaldun, for most of human history, reflection on humanity as a whole was done in response to the interaction between two or more forms of life. However, in response to globalization and planetary-level problems such as climate change, reflection is needed on what it means to pursue the good of *all* humanity at the same time (including, the transgenerational dimensions).

50. Jürgen Moltmann, *The Coming of God: Christian Eschatology*, trans. Margaret Kohl (Minneapolis: Fortress, 2004 [1996]), 313-15.

The need to make global, transtemporal political judgments related to the good of humanity raises the question of whether meaningful conditions for making such judgments are possible. As already noted, humanity as a moral and political category is inherently universal in scope. However, within finite and fallen historical conditions, such a judgment can only be made between one community and another. Whether or not something eventuates in war or domination has historically depended on a relative symmetry of power. Too great an asymmetry, and the frequent move is to determine the other as subject to "our" categories, because "we" can use these categories to control "them." In the contemporary context, global social movements—such as the alter-globalization movement—embody a vision of humanity as a moral and political category in such a way as to attend to both its historical conditions and asymmetries of power.[51] Such movements and their political practices constitute performances of humanity that take seriously how humanity is a moral and political claim. However, such social movements, which include reformist and revitalizing globalized religious movements within Islam and Christianity, represent contending universalisms: each particular movement claims to best represent the full realization of humanity to which everyone should conform. Therefore, they run into the problems that the common humanity and ethnographic frameworks display.

Humanity Is *Nepantla*

To be human is to find oneself in between putting down roots and being en route, between stranger and friend, resident and alien. Humans are not from nowhere, nor are we reducible to being defined as coming from somewhere. We are not from no time nor only from this time. Nor is being human to be in a permanent state of liminality. We shift back and forth from the settled to the unsettled. And while we are, in some ways, the same, there are always an opacity and difference between oneself and another that must be honored. The account of humanity developed here pushes against sacralizing local, regional, or national identities that overvalue a

51. On this see Donatella della Porta et al., *Globalization from Below: Transnational Activists and Protest Networks* (Minneapolis: University of Minnesota Press, 2006), and Geoffrey Pleyers, *Alter-Globalization: Becoming Actors in a Global Age* (Cambridge: Polity, 2010).

sense of place *and* cosmopolitanisms that value no place because humanity is understood as existing in an undifferentiated time and space. Rather, I have tried to situate humanity as a claim that values intimate and proximate communities while at the same time locating human being within a broader set of relations that coordinate fruitfully what it means to always already be in a relationship with near and distant neighbors.

Confronted with the rise of fascism and a bourgeois cosmopolitanism, Karl Barth reflected on the question of how to order the love of near and distant neighbors. He concluded that "To unite loyalty towards those who are historically near with openness towards those who are historically distant will always involve the enduring of a tension and overcoming of an antithesis within which the individual practical decisions may be very different. The man who is obedient to the command of God will always be summoned and ready to endure this tension and to seek to overcome this antithesis."[52] He goes on to say: "And so the command of God does not see and meet him either at the one point or the other, as a member of his own people and then perhaps as a participant in its relationships with other peoples, but always as one who is on the way from the one to the other."[53]

Barth understands cultural-political communities as a necessary condition for human flourishing, but he understands them as always in a state of flux and converging with other communities. To fulfill what it means to be human is to live in cultural-political communities of some kind. These are where we build relationships and create ongoing forms of life together. But such communities are only ever a beginning point for a movement beyond the inherent boundaries of intimacy and proximity. The movement leads us relentlessly from a narrower to a wider sphere, from our own people to other human peoples. Barth's position reflects a deep theo-logic within the Christian tradition, which orders the good of a community as being fulfilled in the good of humanity, which is itself fulfilled in communion with God. We live in concentric circles, so rather than, on the one hand, proclaiming a love of humanity at the expense of any regard for local relationships, or on the other hand, proclaiming a love of the local, regional, or national leading to disregard, fear, and hatred of outsiders, we are, as Barth puts it, "always on the way from one point to another."

---

52. Karl Barth, *Church Dogmatics* III/4, *The Doctrine of Creation*, trans. A. T. Mackay et al. (Edinburgh: T&T Clark, 1961), 297-98.

53. *Church Dogmatics* III/4, 298.

One way of moving beyond myopic, self-limiting spatial and temporal frames of the kind Kant and Hegel exemplify is through a theological imaginary in which the local is not absolutized or made an end in itself; instead, it is the necessary beginning point for the pilgrim's journey that culminates in communion with God. Within a Christian, dialogical, *and* agonistic cosmopolitan vision, a sense of place— that is, our social, economic, political, and historical location in creation—helps constitute human particularity. But our humanity is also partly constituted by how our sense of place is related to other places. Politics within a Christian, dialogical, and agonistic cosmopolitan vision involves the formation of a common world of meaning and action within and between different places. It also requires situating one's own sense of place within concentric circles of human sociality that culminate, via historical relations of conflict and conciliation, in an eschatological, christologically shaped horizon of fulfillment. This horizon of fulfillment both draws in and constantly interrupts all attempts to make any place or scale of human interaction idolatrously self-sufficient or totally encompassing in terms of economic, political, and social relationships. On this account, various forms of localism, nationalism, and identity politics radically overvalue the particularity of a place or culture or history, while many cosmopolitan and global conceptions of citizenship and a neoliberal vision of economic globalization radically undervalue it.

The Latino/a *theological* use of the term *mestizaje* points toward a dialogical and agonistic cosmopolitanism, both pushing back on and opening a way toward the constructive development of Barth's account of near and distant neighbors. It draws on the experience of peoples living in the Americas as those whose identity and history are a confluence of multiple ethnicities.[54] That said, *mestizaje* has proven problematic. Its nontheological uses include being deployed to support racist constructions of national identities that direct attention away from histories of slavery, and render invisible African and indigenous contributions to Central American and Caribbean history.[55] However, as a theo-political and intercul-

---

54. Virgil Elizondo, "*Mestizaje* as a Locus of Theological Reflection," in *Mestizo Christianity: Theology from the Latino Perspective*, ed. Arturo J. Bañuelas (Maryknoll, NY: Orbis, 1995), 7-27, and Benjamín Valentín, "Mestizaje," in *Hispanic American Religious Cultures*, ed. Miguel de la Torre (Santa Barbara, CA: ABC-CLIO, 2009), 351-56.

55. Néstor Medina, *Mestizaje: (Re)Mapping Race, Culture, and Faith in Latino/a Catholicism* (Maryknoll, NY: Orbis, 2009), 48-49. It is also a term that is posed negatively as a contrast to notions of indigeneity. Stefanie Wickstrom and Philip Young, *Mestizaje*

tural category, *mestizaje* (or *mestizaje-mulatez* and *mezcolanza*) refuses any attempt to create binary or essentialist identities: black/white, Hispanic/non-Hispanic, etc.[56] As Ada María Isasi-Díaz puts it, *mestizaje* and *mulatez* refer not only to ethnic and racial diversity but also to the "ability to sustain a sense of community in spite of religious and political differences, to identify and maintain similarities without ignoring specificities and particularities, to insist on a continuum of differences that not only permits diversity but actually welcomes it."[57] It is also suggestive of what it might mean to have a sense of shared humanity while recognizing that any sense of a shared humanity is born out of tragic and brutal histories of domination.[58] Ruben Rosario-Rodriguez frames *mestizaje* theologically in terms of Pentecost: "The miracle of Pentecost is that everyone is able to hear God's word in their own tongue. Rather than coercing a false sense of community through domination and social control, or simply breaking off into small enclaves of like-minded others, the new community born from Christ's saving work embraces difference and strives to build bridges between different cultures because in Christ we find an all-inclusive common ground that does not dissolve our cultural particularities. . . . In other words, in Christ and through the Spirit we find a genuine *mestizaje*."[59]

It is not the case that humanity only entails a sense of being on our way from and to some place. The formation of a sense of humanity is also and always an intermixture, containing seeds of hope amidst grotesque exploitation and misery. In this respect, the specific Nahautl term *nepantla*, meaning "to be between" or "torn between ways," draws this out even more sharply and is used by some as an alternative to *mestizaje*.[60]

---

and Globalization: Transformations of Identity and Power (Tucson: University of Arizona Press, 2014), 6–10.

56. For an overview of different uses and formulations of *mestizaje* as a constructive theological and ethical category, see Ruben Rosario-Rodriguez, *Racism and God-Talk: A Latino/a Perspective* (New York: New York University Press, 2008), 69–110.

57. Ada María Isasi-Díaz, "Strangers No Longer," in *Hispanic/Latino Theology: Challenge and Promise*, ed. Ada María Isasi-Díaz and Fernando F. Segovia (Minneapolis: Fortress, 1996), 370.

58. Rosario-Rodriguez, *Racism and God-Talk*, 108–10. Other terms, deployed in parallel ways, are "creole" and "mulatto." See Barnor Hesse, "Symptomatically Black: A Creolization of the Political," in *The Creolization of Theory*, ed. Françoise Lionnet and Shu-mei Shih (Durham, NC: Duke University Press, 2011), 37–61, and Bantum, *Redeeming Mulatto*.

59. Rosario-Rodriguez, *Racism and God-Talk*, 210.

60. Lara Medina, "Nepantla," in *Hispanic American Religious Cultures*, ed. Miguel de la Torre (Santa Barbara, CA: ABC-CLIO, 2009), 403–8.

It denotes a middle ground that is made up of bits and pieces of various traditions and recognizes that people have multiple loyalties. As a category, it calls for attention to different histories, geographical situations, and ongoing conflicts through which a sense of shared humanity emerges. In Gloria Anzaldúa's use of the term, it suggests that we cannot simply react to what is oppressive but must forge a habitable way of life out of what is there by passing on what is valuable from our histories amid the contradictions of what is cruel and coercive.[61] She calls this "the great alchemical work" of "morphogenesis" that unfolds a new way of being in the world.[62] As Romand Coles puts it: "The task is to work history in this way in an effort creatively to forge better modes of coexistence while resisting those tendencies and forces that would congeal into a new, tensionless, unreceptive totality."[63] Unlike the concepts of hybridity, nomadism, or fugitivity—which suggest that we can live anywhere, come from nowhere, and have no duty of care to tend and pass on the means of generating some kind of common life with others—*mestizaje-mulatez* and *nepantla* recognize the possibilities of a common life or *convivencia* while contending that one voice or culture cannot determine it, and any form of shared life must attend to the brutal histories that inevitably form its backdrop.[64]

Barth's conception and terms such as *mestizaje-mulatez* and *nepantla*, while helpful, are still anthropocentric in focus. The southern African term *ubuntu* has an analogous emphasis on relationality and in-betweenness but more clearly situates humanity within a cosmic and ecological framework. Michael Onyebuchi Eze contends that *ubuntu* is a modern term that draws on multiple southern African traditions to generate a conception of humanity as a single moral community. In one maxim, it means *umuntu ngumuntu*

61. Gloria Anzaldúa, *Borderlands: The New Mestiza = La frontera* (San Francisco: Aunt Lute Books, 1987), 77–82.

62. Anzaldúa, *Borderlands*, 81.

63. Romand Coles, *Beyond Gates Politics: Reflections for the Possibility of Democracy* (Minneapolis: University of Minnesota Press, 2005), xv.

64. *Nepantla* points us to a problem with notions of hybridity, nomadism, and some uses of fugitivity in the context of contemporary economic globalization. As ways of framing humanity as an ethical-political orientation, they too easily disconnect themselves from particular traditions and real histories. In the contemporary context, their use conforms to the spirit of capitalism that precisely demands the dissolution of particularity and the formation of liquid identities to aid capital flows. Hybridity and nomadism are ways in which we can all come from nowhere and so be moved anywhere the market requires, and by which any effective and affective political and social alternatives to the logic of capital may be dissolved.

ngabantu—a person is a person through other people.[65] According to another take on this maxim, *ubuntu* means the following: a human being is a human being through the otherness of other human beings.[66] Eze calls *ubuntu* a "bold conjecture" that, despite its often romanticized and reified use, provides a basis to move beyond particularism through "creative dialogue."[67] He states: "In theory, ubuntu is a hermeneutic process that remains inclusive but allows one to dialogue with people from other historical cultures while being sensitive to differences in context and other historical cultures and traditions."[68] As a conceptuality, it emphasizes how humanity is a creative convergence that emerges through a process that can involve conflict but also cross-pollination and reconciliation. As Eze puts it:

> *A person is a person through other people* strikes an affirmation of one's humanity through recognition of an "other" in his or her uniqueness and difference. . . . This idealism suggests to us that humanity is not embedded in my person solely as an individual; my humanity is co-substantively bestowed upon the other and me. Humanity is a quality we owe to each other. We create each other and need to sustain this *otherness* creation. And if we belong to each other, we participate in our creations: *we are because you are, and since you are, definitely I am.*[69]

The dialogical and agonistic constitution of humanity across generations and between places is not just between humans, it also entails the encounter with the divine and nonhuman forms of life.[70] As Leonard Chuwa puts it: "In Ubuntu the physical and the spiritual, the living and the non-living, the human and the non-human are perceived as necessary in sustenance of human life. Human life comes from, and is sustained by both organic and inorganic cosmos."[71]

---

65. Michael Onyebuchi Eze, *Intellectual History in Contemporary South Africa* (New York: Palgrave Macmillan, 2010), 155. See also Leonard Chuwa, *African Indigenous Ethics in Global Bioethics: Interpreting Ubuntu* (New York: Springer, 2014), 12, and Michael Battle, *Reconciliation: The Ubuntu Theology of Desmond Tutu* (Cleveland: Pilgrim, 1997), 39.
66. Chuwa, *African Indigenous Ethics*, 15.
67. Eze, *Intellectual History*, 154.
68. Eze, *Intellectual History*, 160.
69. Eze, *Intellectual History*, 190-91.
70. Chuwa, *African Indigenous Ethics*, 13-17.
71. Chuwa, *African Indigenous Ethics*, 14.

Conclusion

The use of the terms *mestizaje-mulatez, nepantla,* and *ubuntu* points to possibilities for reframing how we imagine humanity within non-Eurocentric conceptualities that can encompass a sense of humanity as simultaneously shared (community humanity frame) and emerging from distinctive forms of life (ethnographic frame). Western European conceptions of humanity have been tested and found gravely wanting due to how they fed into colonialist projects. This does not necessarily mean that notions such as human rights or natural law should be dismissed since they may prove to be, as Dipesh Chakrabarty puts it, indispensable but inadequate.[72] Their inadequacy points to the need for other kinds of conceptual frameworks, which both provincialize European ways of understanding humanity and provide nonanthropocentric, dialogical, and agonistic ways of formulating humanity as a moral and political category. Reaching beyond Western conceptual frameworks is itself a performance of humanity and the need for others in the realization of a shared humanity. At the same time, no language that connects humans beyond small-scale kinship structures is innocent of inhumanity. I write this in a Latin alphabet with words inflected with the blood of conquest by Romans, Vikings, and Normans and those cut from peoples the English conquered in turn. To imagine there is such a thing as humanity and attempt to deploy humanity as a moral and political category of evaluation is to draw on words and concepts torn and shredded by brutality. Seeking out words such as *neplanta* and *ubuntu* could be just another case of the West, yet again, cannibalizing other cultures for its own benefit. But while the conditions of conceptualizing and speaking about humanity are never innocent, the challenge of imagining and narrating humanity as a moral and political category is as urgent now as it ever was, if not more so.

Threshold

Conceptualizing an understanding of what it means to be human and how, as humans, we share a common humanity necessarily entails politics. It also entails economics. It is to economics as both an adjunct of and a po-

---

72. Dipesh Chakrabarty, *Provincializing Europe: Postcolonial Thought and Historical Difference* (Princeton: Princeton University Press, 2000), 16.

tential threat to politics and the formation and sustaining of a common life that I now turn.

Suggested Readings for Further Discussion

Scriptures: Genesis 1–2; 8:1–9:17; 11:1–9; and 15; Isaiah 25:6–10; Luke 10:25–37; Acts 2; Revelation 5.

Gregory of Nyssa, "Fourth Homily on Ecclesiastes," in *Homilies on Ecclesiastes: An English Version with Supporting Studies*, ed. Stuart George Hall (Berlin: de Gruyter, 1993), 73–75. Gregory offers a theological critique of slavery and a vision of the equal status of all humans before God.

Francisco de Vitoria, "On the American Indians (*De Indis*)," in *Vitoria: Political Writings*, ed. Anthony Pagden and Jeremy Lawrance (Cambridge: Cambridge University Press, 1991), 231–92. The essay is a vision of shared humanity grounded on natural law, one born out of the encounter between Europe and the "New World."

Olaudah Equino, *The Interesting Narrative of the Life of Olaudah Equino, or Gustavus Vassa, the African. Written by Himself* (1789), chaps. 1–5. Various editions. An ethnographic and narrative approach to articulating a theologically grounded vision of a shared humanity, but one in which a European way of life is observed from the perspective of a slave. The account inverts the then-expected order of who is the civilized and who is the savage. The account also illustrates the violent entanglements of the Atlantic world, which is a key context out of which modern political theology emerges.

Immanuel Kant, "Perpetual Peace: A Philosophical Sketch," in *Kant: Political Writings* (Cambridge: Cambridge University Press, 1970), 93–130, and also available in other editions. This is the classic statement of liberal cosmopolitanism.

David Walker, *Appeal to the Colored Citizens of the World* (1829). Available online. The book is an example of a theologically grounded, agonistic account of common humanity set in the context of a call for the abolition of slavery.

Universal Declaration of Human Rights (1948). Available at https://www.un.org/en/universal-declaration-human-rights/index.html.

Karl Barth, "Near and Distant Neighbors," in *Church Dogmatics: The Doctrine of Creation* III/4, trans. A. T. Mackay et al. (Edinburgh: T&T Clark, 1961), 285–305.

Ruben Rosario-Rodriguez, "Exploring Mestizaje as a Theological Metaphor," in *Racism and God-Talk: A Latino/a Perspective* (New York: New York University Press, 2008), 69–110.

Norman Wirzba, "The Human Art of Creaturely Life," in *From Nature to Creation: A Christian Vision for Understanding and Loving Our World* (Grand Rapids: Baker Academic, 2015), 95–129. A theological account of humans as creatures who share a common life with nonhuman ways of being alive.

CHAPTER 11

Economy

Any theological vision of a just and loving common life must include an account of our economic life together. This raises the question of how to understand the relationship between theology and economics. Given the primary forms of contemporary economic life, this question inevitably leads to a further question about the relationship between Christianity and capitalism. To answer these questions, I open this chapter by showing how divine-human relations are framed in economic terms and the ways this may hinder or help a theological assessment of economic life. The first section focuses on the interplay between theological and economic language through situating earthly human economies within God's providential "economy." The second explores this interplay further through a case study of how salvation is portrayed using economic terms. The third, fourth, fifth, and sixth sections develop critical, theological assessments of money as a form of memory, debt as situated in reciprocal relations, property as a communicative good, and markets as a social practice. The seventh builds on the discussion of these terms to analyze capitalism theologically. Within this assessment, I describe and critique libertarianism as a widespread ideological justification of capitalism. A critique of libertarianism is important because many Christians adopt it as an ideological framework, either consciously or tacitly, to justify a positive stance toward capitalism. Yet libertarianism is a utopian project of social engineering that opposes a more realistic and theological understanding of contemporary economic life as finite, fallen, and prone to idolatry. I close the chapter by turning to concrete forms of practice that can be used to inhibit some of the sinful and idolatrous dynamics of capitalism and to ensure that money, debt, property, and markets serve rather than undermine the symbiosis of human and ecological flourishing.

Divine and Human Economies

The term "economy" derives from the management of a household as the basic unit of production, distribution, and consumption of things necessary to survive and thrive. Historically, the household was not a solely human entity. It incorporated the livestock with whom the humans of the household shared a common life. The things managed could be material, but also what we now designate as religious, interpersonal, and cultural. "Economy," in origin, is not a neutral term, but one that carries with it a sense of how to properly use and order things so that they might enable the household to thrive.[1] And while it involves technical and theoretical knowledge to order things properly, the knowledge of economy is more craft-like than scientific. The analogue in political life is government: the right ordering and administration of things so that the polity might prosper.

In ancient Greece, economy serves a vision of the good life. The management of the household as a site of flourishing is situated within concentric circles of moral and spiritual relations extending outward to the whole cosmos. The kinds of conduct that are fitting in the household are different from those appropriate in the *polis* or the temple, but all three are integrally related.[2] Attempts to make money for its own sake (what Aristotle called chrematistics) are immoral, as they are attempts to enrich oneself without regard for the use and ordering of things so that they contribute to wider patterns of thriving. While hierarchies of one kind or another determined the distribution of resources, wealth was social, not private. Underlying this normative conception of economy, and in stark contrast to modern economics, was an ontology of abundance rather than scarcity: while everyone was subject to the vagaries of fate, the cosmos provided all that was needed to live well, materially and otherwise, if wisely participated in through virtuous economy.[3] By implication, ill-managed excess was more

1. See, for example, Xenophon, *Oikonomikos*.

2. Contrary to the characterization of the *oikos* as a realm of despotic rule in which virtue was not required, more recent treatments demonstrate that many kinds of relation were expected in the household, including virtuous ones between different members. Judith Ann Swanson, *The Public and the Private in Aristotle's Political Philosophy* (Ithaca, NY: Cornell University Press, 1992).

3. Karl Polanyi, "Aristotle Discovers the Economy," in *Primitive, Archaic, and Modern Economies: Essays of Karl Polanyi*, ed. George Dalton (Garden City, NY: Doubleday, 1968), 78–115, and Dotan Leshem, "Oikonomia Redefined," *Journal of the History of Economic Thought* 35, no. 1 (2013): 43–61.

morally troubling than coping with dearth. Leisure time enabled by a surplus was to be used to pursue either a political or philosophical form of the good life, not gluttony, luxury, or private interests. That said, slaves were the foundation of the system. They generated the surplus that enabled others to live well, while themselves existing in what Orlando Patterson calls a state of "social death."[4]

Theology draws on but also radically contests this holistic, noncompartmentalized understanding of economy to frame God's providential administration of the cosmos, referred to as God's *oikonomia*. Its use in this way intersects with a whole range of scriptural and theological metaphors for divine-human relations: the shepherd caring for a flock, the vigneron tending a vineyard, the farmer cultivating the land, the teacher educating students, and the physician attending to the health of a patient. Likewise, the Gospels portray Jesus along these lines. Rather than administration or management in the modern, bureaucratic sense of that term, each of these metaphors involves an element of cultivating things to create and sustain conditions in which what is tended might grow. The sheep, vines, field, etc., have a form and nature beyond human control or designation that, nevertheless, require nurturing if they are to flourish. In the formative period of Christian theology, God's *oikonomia* referred to God's cultivation of salvation throughout creation, coming to a head in the incarnation of Jesus Christ (e.g., Eph. 1:7-14).[5] Christ was both the means of cultivation and the embodiment of flourishing.

The theological conception of God's *oikonomia* developed an innovative understanding of God's action in history. It represents a movement out of a cyclical view of history, with its cycles of growth and decay, to one of historical development and eschatological fulfillment beyond the iterative cycles of nature.[6] This innovation emerged by combining a diachronic con-

---

4. Orlando Patterson, *Slavery and Social Death: A Comparative Study* (Cambridge, MA: Harvard University Press, 1982).

5. The primary focus was not divine-human relations so much as the relation between the Father and the Son, within which all other relations were situated.

6. It could be argued that this shift is the conceptual backdrop to modern ideas of progress and aligned notions of economic growth without limits. A cyclical view of history has a notion of limits built in whereas some eschatological conceptions of history can lead to either the material world not mattering (as in premillennial accounts) or a sense of ever-unfolding progress (as in postmillennial accounts). The Irenaean view outlined here stands as a critique of both a gnostic undervaluing of creation and materiality and a wholly immanent protological and progressive view of God's action in history.

ception of divine action as evolving through history with a synchronic one of divine action as occurring in particular events or moments. Irenaeus of Lyon (c. 120-202) systematizes this development in his doctrine of recapitulation. His was an antignostic way of framing how history is the soil of salvation. For Irenaeus, creation is good but unfulfilled: it does not arrive *ex nihilo* in full bloom but must grow up and mature so that it might then receive its perfection in Christ. The Fall constitutes a turn away from growth into maturity and results in humans walking backward into chaos and nothingness. Jesus Christ redeems creation by restoring creation to its original goodness (first movement), and then enabling creation, through the perfecting actions of the Spirit, to once more move into its fulfillment (second movement). This double movement involves both action through time (*chronos*) and action in time (*kairos*). The perfection of creation is not immanent to itself—it is not an outworking of what was present at the beginning—so there is no need to return to the point of origin. Rather, God gives fulfillment eschatologically. Therefore, there is no movement back to an original state or Edenic condition—as Origen argues—but a movement *forward*, through time, to perfection, a perfection inaugurated by the actions of Christ and the Spirit at the ascension wherein God takes up the material creation into the triune life. In Irenaeus's eschatology, the emphasis is not on *space* (that is, a move beyond creation) but on *time*: the advent of the kingdom of God involves a movement to a new time through the existing creation.[7] Based on this theological vision, Irenaeus understood asceticism, or the spiritual life, not as an escape from or overcoming of the bodily life, but as the life of God lived in all dimensions of the body.[8] For Irenaeus, a holy, spiritual, and healed human life anticipates its eschatological perfection now.

God's *oikonomia*, whether conceived in Irenaean terms or according to some other framework, conditions and renders possible all other economies. Conversely, all other economies are good or bad to the extent to which they are attuned to and participate in God's *oikonomia*. To borrow a distinction from Wendell Berry, if these "little" economies are to be rightly ordered, then it is participation in God's "great" *oikonomia* that must be prioritized (or as the Gospel of Matthew puts it: "seek first the kingdom of God

---

7. The pneumatological framework I set out in chapter 4 intentionally parallels and echoes Irenaeus's doctrine of recapitulation.

8. John Behr, *Asceticism and Anthropology in Irenaeus and Clement* (Oxford: Clarendon, 2000), 209.

and his righteousness, and all these things will be given unto you").[9] Human economies make, exchange, distribute, and consume things, but such activity must work from the basis that humans are first and foremost members of God's *oikonomia* and that the things manufactured, exchanged, distributed, and consumed are first received as gifts to be shared and not objects entirely under human control. When economic life ceases to serve right participation in God's *oikonomia*, and instead serves the perpetuation of little economies divorced from membership of a cosmic economy, then these little economies have become idolatrous and self-destructive. Little economies turned in on themselves are manifested in, for example, the idea that the sole purpose of economic activity is profit maximization and the competitive pursuit of private interests.

Building on scriptural precedent, Christian theology did not create a hard-and-fast division between the *oikos* and the *polis*. Blurring the boundaries between politics and economics was in keeping with and amplified broader, already existing understandings of good rule, notably that the good ruler exercise pastoral care for the people.[10] The bishop was the *oikonomos* who cultivated right participation in God's *oikonomia* through pastoral care, preaching, and administering the sacraments. The fellowship or *koinōnia* church members were exhorted to cultivate was said to be at once familial and civic in character. The church, as a hybrid of *oikos* and *polis,* creates a new social-political space that stands between political and kinship structures, what we now call civil society. The church, as a new form of life, does not have an economic ethic but rather seeks to embody a "little" economy rightly attuned to its participation in God's *oikonomia*. It is

9. Wendell Berry, "Two Economies (1983)," in *The Art of the Commonplace: The Agrarian Essays of Wendell Berry,* ed. Norman Wirzba (Washington, DC: Counterpoint, 2003), 219-35.

10. Contrary to Michel Foucault and Giorgio Agamben, Christianity did not invent pastoral care as a primary trope of good rule, neither did it herald a shift to biopolitical forms of government. A common image of the good ruler in the ancient world was that of a shepherd, and alongside a crown, the most ancient symbol of authority is a scepter, symbolic of the ruler as one who secures fertility and who possesses thaumaturgic or wonder-working powers. As Richard Corney notes, there are many portraits of ancient Near Eastern monarchs with scepter and/or staff that symbolize pastoral and thaumaturgic power. See Richard Corney, "'Rod and Staff' (Psalm 23:4): A Double Image?" in *On the Way to Nineveh: Studies in Honor of George M. Landes,* ed. Stephen Cook and S. C. Winter (Atlanta: Scholars Press, 1999), 28-41. The origins of the scepter can partly be located in representations of female deities. Othmar Keel and Christoph Uehlinger, *Gods, Goddesses, and Images of God in Ancient Israel,* trans. Thomas Trapp (Minneapolis: Fortress, 1998).

within this context that the consideration of distinct moral questions about usury, treatment of the poor, and the like take place. What is in view is not the regulation of economic behavior per se but the material conditions and form of faithful, hopeful, and loving discipleship.

Soteriology, Morality, and the Coinherence of Economics and Theology

The relationship between theology and economics is complex, characterized as it is by circuits of resonance and resistance connecting them so that each refracts the other. Theology can never rid itself of economic language and concepts. This is as undesirable as it is implausible. Any such attempt would herald a disincarnate and gnostic attempt to speak theologically outside of any actual form of material life, which necessarily has an economic dimension. An illustration of this is the relationship between, on the one hand, notions of economic exchange and debt language, and on the other, theologies of salvation. From the very outset, economic exchange and debt relations are crucial semantic registers within scriptural and subsequent conceptions of salvation.[11] For example, the book of Genesis closes with the story of Joseph, in which we see the Israelites, along with everyone else in Egypt, saved from famine, but in the process, reduced to debt slavery. The book of Exodus opens with a new pharaoh who takes advantage of the Israelites' debt slavery to exploit them. The Israelites were not prisoners of war or chattel slaves; they were debt slaves undertaking forced labor on behalf of the ruling elite.[12] It is this condition from which the Israelites are delivered. The primal vision of salvation as deliverance from debt slavery is then picked up in the law and the prophets and used in the Gospels to frame the life, death, and resurrection of Jesus Christ.

11. In modern theology, while critiques of capitalism abound, there has been little investigation of the semantic register of economics in theology. Notable exceptions are Marion Grau, *Of Divine Economy: Refinancing Redemption* (New York: T&T Clark, 2004); M. Douglas Meeks, *God the Economist: The Doctrine of God and Political Economy* (Minneapolis: Fortress, 1989); and Philip Goodchild, *Theology of Money* (Durham, NC: Duke University Press, 2009).

12. Gregory Chirichigno, *Debt-Slavery in Israel and the Ancient Near East* (Sheffield: Sheffield Academic, 1993), and Isaac Mendelsohn, *Slavery in the Ancient Near East: A Comparative Study of Slavery in Babylonia, Assyria, Syria, and Palestine from the Middle of the Third Millennium to the End of the First Millennium* (New York: Oxford University Press, 1949).

The notion of redemption, or Jesus paying with his life to deliver humans from our debt of sin, is a leitmotif in the New Testament (Mark 10:45; Rom. 6:21–23; Col. 3:5–6). In parallel to this motif, the declaration of Jubilee—that is, the release from debt bondage—forms the basis of how Luke frames Jesus's announcement of his purpose and mission (Luke 4:18–19). And what Luke then depicts in Acts 2 as a direct fruit of the outpouring of the Holy Spirit is the enactment of the Jubilee community in which no one is oppressed by debt-bondage because "all who believed were together and had all things in common; they would sell their possessions and goods and distribute the proceeds to all, as any had need" (Acts 2:44–45). Thus, the admonition that we cannot serve both God and Mammon (Matthew 6:19–24) is not merely a moral matter—it is a matter of salvation. To put the pursuit of money before the welfare of people, and to use money to dominate and exploit people, especially the poor and vulnerable, rejects God's salvation and denies in practice God's self-revelation given in Scripture.

The language of debt is central to many atonement theologies and pervades patristic and subsequent ways of framing salvation. For example, Polycarp's early-second-century *Epistle to the Philippians* envisages all believers being "in debt with respect to sin" (6:1). Likewise, Justin Martyr's *Second Apology* sees "death" as a "debt due by every human that is born" (chap. 11). *The Epistle to Diognetus* describes the Father paying the "wages of unrighteousness" by giving "his own Son as a ransom for us," while the work of God in Christ is a "sweet exchange" (9.2; 9.5). In his sixth clause of *On Prayer*, Tertullian sets out in detail how Christians are in "debt" to Christ. And throughout his *On the Flesh of Christ*, Tertullian uses the language of "payment" and "wages" to describe Christ's payment of our "debt." Such themes come to the fore in Origen, and in the evolution of a ransom theory of atonement. They continue on into the medieval period in Bernard of Clairvaux, Peter Abelard, and Anselm. Within the ransom metaphor, Christ is the living currency/slave through which sinful humanity is bought back from the devil.[13]

Amid the diversity of approaches to atonement, there is a consistent recourse to economic and debt language. And as exemplified in the Lord's Prayer, debt and property relations are often understood as synonyms for sin. We cannot, nor should we, expunge such language from our theologies of salvation. Debt and economic exchange are inevitably constitutive of the forms of life from which language about divine-human relations is

---

13. Grau, *Of Divine Economy*, 136.

cast. Attempts to purge economic frames of reference from theology are a gnostic attempt to flee material forms of life.

The coinherence of theological and economic semantic registers raises two questions. The first is whether our "little" economies, whatever form they take—capitalist, socialist, etc.—serve God's *oikonomia*. To this end, is it the life, death, and resurrection of Jesus Christ that mold our understandings of economy, or vice versa? Can the biblical stories, metaphors, and language of redemption from debt slavery, as well as the patterns of relationship envisioned in Jubilee, Sabbath rest, covenant, and *koinōnia*, be drawn on to reimagine what economic life amid our salvation means? And through a process of reimagining economics, can we convert rather than conform to our little earthly economies? The second question follows on from this initial set of questions. It asks how faith, hope, and love can embed and order economic relations even as they circulate through them. Implicit within this question is a refusal to establish false binaries between, say, love and money, or gift and debt. Rather than seeing money or debt as inherently immoral or polluting, what is important is the right ordering of their use. This is not to say that money and debt are neutral or uncomplicated; even their right use sets up numerous moral hazards.

Crucial to understanding the relationship between theological and economic semantic registers is keeping in view the analogies and disanalogies between them. This can be illustrated by contrasting Christ and money as means of exchange, conversion, and substitution. Money can be a metaphor for atonement, because it is a universal medium of exchange that can convert one kind of thing into a different kind of thing, without remainder. It also enables value to be ascribed to things that are worthless in one context but richly prized in another, thereby reframing how that thing is related to and perceived. Within this metaphorical equation, Jesus is money. To unpack this equation and keep to the fore the disanalogy alongside the analogy, we must revisit what we mean by conversion and how Jesus's life, death, and resurrection constitute a form of exchange. Conversion into being in Christ has a double aspect: it entails both the recovery or recollection of one's created and true way of being in the world that is lost because of sin *and* being "born again" through undergoing a fundamental rupture and reorientation in one's relationship with God, self, and others so as to embark on a new way of being alive. In contrast to Jesus, who acts as a medium of exchange through incarnation, money extracts and abstracts us from our histories and forms of life.[14]

14. For a parallel discussion of the analogy between Jesus and money, see Karl Marx,

In relation to *recollection/restoration*, money as a means of conversion does not recover or display a thing's true or original value; indeed, it operates by turning something into an abstract, exchangeable commodity. Neither does it enable *newness*: rather than new birth on the pattern of resurrection, where there is a paradoxical relation of continuity and change, money demands the complete discarding of a thing's prior material and affective life. For example, money as a means of conversion renders who we are, our relationships, and history as irrelevant, alienating what we do (our labor that can be exchanged in the marketplace) from who we are as persons. Even more significantly, money converts everything into the same and so sublates difference (everything becomes a commodity). In this regard, Jesus is the opposite of money: in Christ, through the Spirit, each part of creation is both healed and redirected to its consummation. The result is that it is enabled to be its own unique and specific kind of thing, so that its original value can be appreciated and can enter into communion with every other kind of created thing in its own particular way. This involves not the discarding of materiality or the forgetting of history, but their transfiguration.

Recently, several theologians have explored connections between conceptions of gift and economic and political relations.[15] However, they tend to replicate a false dichotomy between gifts (seen as inherently moral) and money (envisaged as either amoral or immoral). By contrast, for medieval rabbinic scholars and scholastic theologians, money could be both gift and commodity simultaneously. And while money always had a moral valence, the real problem was not money per se but "filthy lucre," that is, social relationships subordinated to and instrumentalized for the making of money.[16] Similarly, debt and commerce were not bad per se. Commercial and credit-debt relations become immoral when they cease to be rooted in prior and superordinate relations of mutuality. When relations of interdependence

---

"Comments on James Mill, *Éléments D'Économie Politique*" (1844), Marxists Internet Archive, https://www.marxists.org/archive/marx/works/1844/james-mill/.

15. See, for example, John Milbank, *Being Reconciled: Ontology and Pardon* (London: Routledge, 2003), and Kathryn Tanner, *Economy of Grace* (Minneapolis: Fortress, 2005). The most prominent theological account that brings together love, gift, and an integrated narrative of economic and political relations in the contemporary context is that given in Catholic social teaching. This is particularly apparent in the 2009 papal encyclical *Caritas in Veritate*.

16. Julie L. Mell, "Cultural Meanings of Money in Medieval Ashkenaz: On Gift, Profit, and Value in Medieval Judaism and Christianity," *Jewish History* 28, no. 2 (2014): 125–58.

they articulate are exploited to extract more than is owed, both morally and economically, debt and commerce become unjust. This is the problem with usury as a sinful and idolatrous form of debt relation. Again, the decisive issue is not debt per se, but the quality and character of the relationship between lender and borrower. Usury (the extortionate charging of interest) converts relations of mutuality, which credit-debt relations can be constitutive of, and converts them into relations of exploitative extraction. In what follows I will explore the positive and negative aspects of money, debt, property, and markets along the lines just outlined.

The Moral Hazards of Money

The medieval rabbinic and scholastic understanding of money built on Aristotle's critique of the pursuit of money as an end in itself. For Aristotle, when divorced from any involvement in a social and political community, the pursuit of money (or profit maximization) for its own sake led to a disturbed form of desire: *pleonexia* or insatiable acquisitiveness.[17] Money is prone to generate *pleonexia* because it has no natural limit. It can be pursued without end, and in the process, everything else is subordinated to its accumulation. For Aristotle, the pursuit of money as an end in itself tended to instrumentalize and commodify all other relationships and arts, even philosophy.[18] While money is necessary as either a medium of exchange, a store of value, or a means of accounting, the practice of chrematistics or moneymaking (as distinct from its use for production and trade) threatens the *polis* because it makes the pursuit of profit an end in itself, and in doing so not only turns money from its proper end but also, through *pleonexia*, becomes the enemy of citizenship because it undermines the pursuit of civic virtue and justice. The pursuit of money/profit/capital as an end rather than as a means of exchange or an aid to further production or trade undermines the virtues of courage and justice necessary to pursue the truly good

17. To quote Aristotle: "And the avarice of mankind is insatiable . . . men always want more and more without end; for it is of the nature of desire to be unlimited, and most men live only for the gratification of it" (*The Politics, and The Constitution of Athens,* ed. Stephen Everson [Cambridge: Cambridge University Press, 1996], 45 [1267b.1]). In the New Testament, the figure of the goat is the picture of *pleonexia*—an animal that tramples over anyone and ignores the most vulnerable in order to get what it wants (Matt. 25:31-46).

18. Scott Meikle, "Aristotle on Money," *Phronesis* 39, no. 1 (1994): 26-44.

life and sustain the freedom of the body politic that is the condition of the pursuit of such a life. The collective liberty of self-governing citizens and their virtuous pursuit of common goods are undermined by commercial and competitive values that prioritize the self-interested pursuit of private property and consumer goods.[19]

As to what kind of thing money is, that is another matter. Among myriad theories about the origins and meaning of money, there are three dominant approaches: a "fiat" or "chartalist" theory of money, in which money is a creature of the law; "metallism" or a commodity theory, wherein money contains or represents something of equivalent value (as in the gold standard); and that of credit money, where money is a form of memory or mode of accounting. In the latter account, money emerges from ways of keeping records of who owes what to whom in the circulation of goods and services. For example, in medieval China and early medieval Europe, credit and debt relations were tracked via tally sticks. Historically there is a shift back and forth between virtual or credit money and commodity money: tokens of exchange such as gold and silver that were taken not simply to be a record of the exchange but as tokens with intrinsic value equivalent to what was received. Arguably, credit money emerges in relatively stable, high-trust contexts, while commodity money becomes desirable in unstable, often violent low-trust contexts where wealth needs to be easily transportable and exchangeable. For Geoffrey Ingham, the key shift to a modern capitalist economy comes when signifiers of debt (e.g., a bill of exchange) could be anonymously transferred to third parties (i.e., the circulation of paper money). The depersonalization of debt and the formation of an abstract monetary space emerge in Europe from the seventeenth century onward and involve a coalescence of commercial and monarchical interest as well as a delicate balance of power between them.[20] Ingham suggests that in the shift from credit to commodity money or cash, centralizing sovereign and often imperial authorities play a crucial role: they monopolize the issuing and production of money for the purposes of taxation and the provisioning of armies. Money moves from being a way of tracking credit and debt relations between persons (and thereby interpersonal) to becoming a way for sovereigns to manage what subjects are said to owe the state, backed

19. Contemporary philosophers like Michael Sandel and Alasdair MacIntyre reiterate this critique, using it to question the moral basis of liberalism and capitalism. See, for example, Alasdair MacIntyre, *Ethics in the Conflicts of Modernity: An Essay on Desire, Practical Reasoning, and Narrative* (Cambridge: Cambridge University Press, 2016).

20. Geoffrey Ingham, *The Nature of Money* (Cambridge: Polity, 2004).

up by coercive measures if necessary.[21] While Ingham is right regarding the modern development of money, arguably, the same applied in ancient imperial economies as well. Whatever the historical context, however, the moral and political issue is not money per se, but its right use and the ends to which it is directed.

Debt and Citizenship

A parallel set of concerns to those that surround money is found in the treatment of credit-debt relations by medieval rabbinic and scholastic scholars. These thinkers drew a distinction between noncoercive and commercial lending on the one hand, and forms of extortionate and exploitative lending on the other.[22] The fundamental issue was whether the lending relationship involves reciprocity, equitable relations, and shared risk.[23] On this account, the charging of interest is licit when it is noncoercive and involves just relations and mutual benefit rather than selfish gain. When it becomes coercive and fundamentally alters the relationship between lender and borrower, then it pertains to the public order of a polity

21. Ingham, *The Nature of Money*, 97–101; see also Keith Hart, *The Memory Bank: Money in an Unequal World* (London: Profile Books, 1999), 233–72.

22. For developments in the theological analysis of usury and its treatment in Scholastic and Reformation thought, see John T. Noonan, *The Scholastic Analysis of Usury* (Cambridge, MA: Harvard University Press, 1957); Odd Langholm, *Legacy of Scholasticism in Economic Thought: Antecedents of Choice and Power* (Cambridge: Cambridge University Press, 1998); Diane Wood, *Medieval Economic Thought* (Cambridge: Cambridge University Press, 2002), 159–205; Jacques Le Goff, *Your Money or Your Life: Economy and Religion in the Middle Ages*, trans. Patricia Ranum (New York: Zone Books, 1990); Eric Kerridge, *Usury, Interest, and the Reformation* (Aldershot, UK: Ashgate, 2002); and Joan Lockwood O'Donovan, "The Theological Economics of Medieval Usury," *Studies in Christian Ethics* 14, no. 1 (2001): 48–64. Against those who argue for a radical disjuncture between the Reformers and the Scholastic view of usury, such as R. H. Tawney and Max Weber, Kerridge and O'Donovan are right in arguing for consistency between the two. For a summary of the changes in rabbinic teaching on charging interest, see David Novak, "Economics and Justice: A Jewish Example," in *Jewish Social Ethics* (Oxford: Oxford University Press, 1992), 223–24.

23. This concern has an ancient lineage. According to Émile Benveniste, in Indo-European languages the moral and economic conception of both credit and debt is linked to a notion of reciprocity. See Émile Benveniste, *Indo-European Language and Society*, trans. Elizabeth Palmer (Coral Gables, FL: University of Miami Press, 1973), 138–58.

and the question of who legitimately can exercise coercive force. At this point, legislation is required to protect the weaker party in the exchange. The most consistent and long-standing example of this kind of protection is a cap on interest rates (such legislation dates back to the oldest legal code archeology has discovered, the Laws of Hammurabi). Legislative limits on interest rates are necessary to stop the conversion of indebtedness into debt bondage, thereby dissolving the conditions for equitable relations between members of the same body politic.

In debates about usury, up to and including the time of the Reformation, the linkage between debt and the ability to sustain citizenship as a form of *koinōnia* (fellowship) was well understood. However, with the emergence of the social contract tradition of modern political thought, there was a shift away from a view of citizenship as a form of *koinōnia*. This shift entailed moving away from seeing property as a communicative good toward a contractual view in which notions of absolute and exclusive ownership determine conceptions of property. Citizenship eventually becomes located within a vision of "possessive individualism" in which freedom is a zero-sum game, with individual freedom no longer premised on interdependent relations that seek fulfillment in mutual flourishing.[24]

With the advent of the authentic and liberated human envisaged as an autonomous, self-directed subject, we find it hard to imagine owing anything to anyone but ourselves as anything other than an imposition. In a prevalent American form of this ideological construct, the individual is said to be a "self-made man" (the gendered nature of this invocation is not incidental). This self-imagining underwrites vast swathes of the American political economy and stigmatizes the poor as immoral and feckless. Another term for it is "meritocracy." To the meritocratic mind, framing success as incorporating a debt that is owed to society becomes incomprehensible at best and reprehensible at worst. Economically, the freely choosing, self-interested *homo economicus* is posited as existing prior to and independent of relations of credit and debt to god(s), nature, country, and ancestors, all of which are taken to be extrinsic rather than interior to and the condition of economic relations. To take but one example, we do not view human life as inherently indebted to nature, but instead, nature becomes raw material out of which we fashion a human life: our life is something we choose according to values we create and impose on the

---

24. The term "possessive individualism" is drawn from C. B. Macpherson, *The Political Theory of Possessive Individualism: Hobbes to Locke* (Oxford: Clarendon, 1962).

ecology within which we are enmeshed. But as this example illustrates, even as we create a world that abhors the idea of owing nature anything, we cannot escape our ecological debts: with the ensuing environmental devastation, human life becomes in turn more precarious and the pillars of economic growth turn to dust.

Atomized conceptions of independence and voluntaristic conceptions of autonomy undergird numerous modern projects of emancipation, whether cultural, political, philosophical, or economic, giving rise to a false binary between debt and freedom. This is a symptom of a wider problem: the sundering of autonomy from association. However, like a gift, debt entails a tangled interplay of freedom and obligation. Yet such a view of debt only makes sense within a relational anthropology that envisages humans as always already participating in a meshwork of relations—human, ecological, and divine. When understood as purposeful agency, autonomy is not reducible to choice and is not necessarily voluntaristic. As noted in chapter 9, independent action always exists within certain conditions and possibilities (economic, social, political, environmental, physical, psychological, etc.) that make such purposeful agency possible. These relations are also directed to goals that surpass the satisfaction of material needs alone. Independence understood as purposeful agency directed to various ends is, paradoxically, a fruit of reciprocal relations—not that which is in opposition to them. Such a view can encompass a notion of debt as a positive moral category as well as a necessary economic one.

Debt is, however, profoundly tricky, existing as it does on two axes. The first is the axis of ontological and economic debt (ontological debt being what we owe to God, nature, ancestors, etc.). The second is the axis of debt as an expression of mutuality and debt as a mode of domination. It is the way in which debt relations circulate around these two axes that makes debt such an ambiguous phenomenon. Debt can be *simultaneously* ontological and economic as well as bond forming and exclusionary. Thus, like a drug (*pharmakon*), debt can be both a poison and a remedy.[25] It both expresses and enables cooperation and exchange across mundane and transcendent registers, yet debt can also be used as a means of bondage and exploitation in these same registers. Modern Western thinking about

---

25. Derrida points to the ambiguity in the word *pharmakon* in his study of Plato's *Phaedrus*. He notes how the term *pharmakon*—meaning a drug—can signify both a remedy and a poison. A *pharmakon* can be—alternately or simultaneously—beneficent and maleficent. Jacques Derrida, *Dissémination*, trans. Barbara Johnson (London: Athlone Press, 1981), 70.

debt has generally lost the ability to think about debt along these axes, generating instead a simplistic way of framing debt as either exclusively positive or exclusively negative rather than both positive and negative.

With the shift to a contractual basis for political order and a view of the individual as an autonomous, freely choosing subject, the need to place limits on debt so that it serves reciprocity, not exploitation, wanes as a primary public concern.[26] For example, the founder of utilitarianism, Jeremy Bentham, writing in the 1780s, expounded the influential view that anti-usury measures are unnecessary and irrational.[27] In the contemporary context, good citizenship and political order are not seen to be threatened by usurious forms of personal and national debt. Yet, because debt is said to be voluntarily chosen, the liberal social contract tradition cannot recognize how debt can be a means of domination. Within the context of finance-centric forms of capitalism, debt is divorced from mutuality and used to subjugate, command, manage, order, and normalize particular behaviors.[28] For example, student debts direct graduates "voluntarily" into certain streams of employment and away from lower-paying yet more vocational and politicized forms of work. The social means of citizenship (public housing, education, health care, and so on) are ceasing to be provided by the state and funded by tax revenues. Instead, they are outsourced to the "private" sector and paid for by taking on debt (individually, or at the municipal or national level). Rather than the state providing the means of agency so that citizens may act with political and economic parity in relation to others, public and common goods such as housing, education, and health care provided by regimes of indebtedness create dependency and vulnerability, concentrating power in the hands of those who control the means of credit. For example, in the realm of education and training, rather than the state investing in educa-

26. While contesting Macpherson's dating and genealogy of the emergence of notions of "possessive individualism," J. G. A. Pocock narrates the importance of speculative finance capitalism and national debt to the emergence of contractual concepts of citizenship. As Pocock points out, contractual conceptions were initially partly developed as a negative reaction to the emergence of financial speculation and public credit. See J. G. A. Pocock, *Virtue, Commerce, and History: Essays on Political Thought and History, Chiefly in the Eighteenth Century* (Cambridge: Cambridge University Press, 1985), 51-71, 91-102, 103-24, and 193-212. For an account of the importance of debt to the emergence of the modern state, see Ingham, *The Nature of Money*, 69-85.

27. Jeremy Bentham, "Defence of Usury," in *Economic Writings*, vol. 1, ed. Werner Stark (London: Allen & Unwin, 1952), 123-207.

28. As noted in chapter 7, some see access to credit as the new determiner of class relations and basic to the structures of socioeconomic inequality.

tion and training as a public good that provides the means for all citizens to have agency to act economically and politically with parity, the state is disinvesting from training and educating workers through free or subsidized education. In parallel with such disinvestment, companies are decreasing the number and type of apprenticeships. Education and training are now increasingly paid for by the individual through debt so that training and education are themselves commodities and framed as private rather than public goods. Rather than serving the nurture of a common life, education is increasingly a means of private profit, with all the liability taken on by the individual rather than the state or firm.

A linguistic inversion hides the real structure of power: instead of being understood as the condition for the possibility of shared political and economic agency, welfare and government "entitlement" programs are said to create dependency. Conversely, instead of making explicit how providing these public goods through regimes of indebtedness concentrates power in the hands of the financial services industry, providing them through forms of debt bondage is said to give freedom of choice. The shadowy brilliance of this move is that the means of alleviating political and economic oppression are converted into the means of oppression by transforming the means for citizens *not* to be dependent on others into means by which dependency is generated. But this is always how unilateral, nonreciprocal debt operates as a means of domination. Exploitative debt relations are like digging a well for much-needed water, only to have the sides collapse as one digs so that one is buried alive by the very means of seeking alleviation. Every time you turn on the light, buy food or clothes, ride the bus, or heat the house, you exacerbate the debt and make matters worse. One's means of living and existing socially becomes the means through which one is dominated and isolated. And all of this occurs "voluntarily" and legally and thereby conforms to liberal norms.

Indebtedness as a regime of statecraft does not operate solely through objective conditions of oppression; it also trades on subjective conditions of domination. This subjective dimension of domination operates by inducing feelings of shame, guilt, and inferiority: to be moral, righteous, and just is to be responsible and pay back what you owe. But when we are increasingly burdened with an infinite series of debts, whether at the personal level (payday lenders, mortgages, and the like) or in our public life (sovereign debt), then we are constantly made to feel morally suspect. Our credit score becomes a placeholder for our character. Yet in another inversion, those we are made responsible for and to are the banks and the "masters of the universe" who themselves constantly act irresponsibly with other people's money, privatize profits while socializing costs, reward risky behavior, are dependent on benefits and bailouts they did not earn, and straightforwardly steal from and betray those they have a fiduciary responsibility to serve.

Against the faux morality of finance capitalism, the potency of a story about a God who forgives debts can be heard afresh. Rather than the story about an oppressive system to which there is no alternative (which economics as a discipline tells), the church must proclaim a story about a God who comes to a people in debt bondage and makes a way where there is no way; who lavishes credit on those the world considers subprime; who riskily invests, to the point of emptying himself, in those who cannot repay; and who seeks a dividend of love and Sabbath fruitfulness, not of material prosperity.

Property as a Communicative Good

Avoiding false binaries between theology and economics and between gift and money helps make sense of property as neither an unadulterated blessing nor an unequivocal curse. Ownership withdraws a good from the wider community, but that does not mean the wider community ceases to have any claim to its use. Moreover, the claim to own something depends on a prior common life and the legitimization of any claim to ownership by a wider community. For the most part, within Christianity, property is morally licit and is seen as enabling the pursuit of important goods and virtues (e.g., responsibility). However, it can only do so when situated within and serving the development of a common life and goods held in common. There is, though, a deep ambivalence within Christianity toward possessions. Raising a permanent question mark over the moral worth of any notion of ownership are, first and foremost, Jesus's renunciation of property, his teaching about earthly riches, and his instructions to his disciples (e.g., Matt. 19:21-30; Luke 9:3; 21:1-4; Mark 6:7-9). There are then the subsequent early church, monastic, and radical Protestant traditions of communism, and groups such as the Franciscans advocating voluntary poverty. However, the need for ambivalence about property should not give way to Manichaean conceptions of property ownership as inherently immoral and in need of abolition. Rather, what is needed are normative conceptions of right use. For this, New Testament disavowals of property must be situated in relationship to the Hebrew Bible/Old Testament conceptions of property as a communicative good.

In ancient Israel, possession of land did not entitle the holder to exclusive use; rather, it was a nonexclusive leasehold. Human ownership and use of created goods were limited because ultimately the territory and its fruit—like creation itself—was God's homeland: humans are trustees and priests of what they have received from God. To convert land or people into fungible goods of no greater value than anything else is not only to instrumentalize them for our own benefit, and so place our own welfare above the good of all, it is to usurp God. In modern parlance, we call such a process "commodification": the treating of that which is not for sale as a commodity to be bought and sold. The extensive manumission laws of Exodus, Leviticus, and Deuteronomy relating to debt slavery are measures to keep in check such a process of commodification of land and people, ensuring that treatment of land and people serves covenantal rather than idolatrous relations.

Treatment of the poor is a touchstone that marks whether property relations are properly situated within and orientated to covenantal relations of faithful, mutual responsibility. The turning of people and land into commodities capable of being traded within a monetary economy is a direct threat to the proper ordering of economic, social, and political relations and the concrete ability of all the people to participate in the covenantal order as members of equal dignity. Neither land nor people were to be expropriated for personal gain or monetized as commodities to be bought and sold. The Jubilee legislation (whether historically enacted or not) serves as an imperative that disrupts any justification for expropriating land permanently through debt. Land/property was to be used to provide the means of life and build up the commonwealth, not converted through exploitation or monopolization into a means for either the death or the enslavement of one's neighbor. Within this theo-political vision of land, property was a communicative and not an absolute good. This communicative vision of property relations as the basis for a shared life premised on the ability of each having agency within the whole contrasts with both privatized and nationalized (i.e., state-centric forms of socialization) conceptions of property. In the former, the use of property is solely determined by the sovereign individual or corporate owner, whereas in the latter its use is determined by the sovereign state.

Alongside privatized and nationalized conceptions of property, property envisaged as a communicative good contrasts with some recent reconceptions of the commons. For example, the influential post-Marxist thinkers Michael Hardt and Antonio Negri view both capitalism and state socialism as related systems that enclose and expropriate the commons. Moreover, rather than either private or public ownership constituting the basis of freedom, it is the relational basis of the commons and the inter-actions of nature and culture in the production of a commonwealth that are the locus of freedom and innovation.[29] The basis of the "biopolitical" commons—knowledge, language, scientific techniques, community re-lations, etc.—is produced through social, cooperative processes that are autonomous in relation to and in excess of public or private ownership and material means of production. For Hardt and Negri, public and private means of management and production increasingly threaten and under-mine the kinds of encounter, cooperation, and communication necessary for innovation within and the reproduction of the commons—and it is the commons rather than property relations that is the basis of economic flourishing. A case in point is contests over the patenting of genetic infor-mation and whether it should be possible to claim specific DNA of wheat that evolved through innumerable human interactions over millennia as the "intellectual property" of a single company. Such a claim to ownership of what is the fruit of the commons threatens the livelihoods and indepen-dence of millions of farmers.

The commons, however, cannot be wholly separated from forms of public and private ownership. Rather, following the economist Elinor Os-trom's more empirical account, the commons as a cultural-political con-struct is the fruit of a negotiation between and interweaving of public au-thorities, market processes, and nonpecuniary forms of organization and association based on customary practice and tradition. Each actor involved must exercise prudence about how to tend (rather than manage/control) the commons so that it and those who depend on it might flourish. Part of the problem with Hardt and Negri's conception of the commons and their critique of property is that they never countenance that there may be noncapitalistic conceptions of property that prioritize the communica-bility and sharing of goods rather than their private or exclusive use. One such alternative conception is Thomistic. Aquinas's social conception of property derives from a notion of the prior common gift of the earth to all humanity; the contingent status of ownership arrangements as the result of

29. Michael Hardt and Antonio Negri, *Commonwealth* (Cambridge, MA: Belknap Press of Harvard University Press, 2009), 282.

historical, human, legal developments; and the telos of property in serving the "common good."[30] It is a tradition of conceptualizing property that finds clear expression in later strands of Catholic social teaching, encapsulated in the following statement from the encyclical *Laborem Exercens* (1981): "Christian tradition has never upheld this right [to private property] as absolute and untouchable. On the contrary, it has always understood this right within the broader context of the right common to all to use the goods of the whole of creation: *the right to private property is subordinated to the right to common use*, to the fact that goods are meant for everyone."[31]

Thomistic conceptions of property, unlike Hardt and Negri's conception, do not establish a dualistic opposition between property ownership and the cultivation of civic and economic virtue. Rather, they envisage property ownership as able to contribute to the development of moral and civic responsibility and the building of a common life. Furthermore, the opposition Hardt and Negri establish between the commons and property relations seems to close down the space for an account of the relationship between forms of social and personal ownership and the commons as mutually constitutive: ownership and the production of the commons are not *necessarily* opposed to each other.[32] A vision of property as a com-

30. Thomas Aquinas, *Political Writings*, trans. R. W. Dyson (Cambridge: Cambridge University Press, 2002), 205-20 (*Summa theologiae* IIa-IIae, q. 66). See also John Finnis, *Aquinas: Moral, Political, and Legal Theory* (Oxford: Oxford University Press, 1998), 187-210. A parallel account of property as a communicable and shared good can be found in the work of John Wesley and early Methodism. Wesley, while in many respects a Tory, rejected an account of property as an inviolable right. On this see Randy L. Maddox, "'Visit the Poor': John Wesley, the Poor, and the Sanctification of Believers," in *The Poor and the People Called Methodists, 1729-1999*, ed. Richard P. Heitzenrater (Nashville: Kingswood, 2002), 59-81.

31. John Paul II, *Laborem Exercens*, §14. See also John Paul II, *Centesimus Annus*, §43. Although it is modified in subsequent encyclicals (see, for example, *Quadragesimo Anno*, §§44-49), *Rerum Novarum* grounds private property in nature. However, the prior common gift and orientation of property to common use are still emphasized (Leo XIII, *Rerum Novarum*, §§8-9). For an account of the twin currents in Catholic social teaching—one Lockean, emphasizing an absolute right to private property, and the other Thomistic—and the gradual eclipse of the former and the reassertion of the latter, see A. M. C. Waterman, *Political Economy and Christian Theology Since the Enlightenment: Essays in Intellectual History* (New York: Palgrave Macmillan, 2004), 169-74.

32. David Harvey, *Rebel Cities: From the Right to the City to the Urban Revolution* (London: Verso, 2012), 67-88. Building on Ostrom's and Hardt and Negri's work, Harvey comes close to a social conception of property with his account of the constructive interaction between enclosure and the building of the commons.

municative good is necessary to make sense of the actual practice of such initiatives as Creative Commons licensing.[33]

Markets as a Social Practice

As with property, an account of right use rather than total rejection is needed when it comes to markets. Markets are a social practice with intrinsic goods that should serve broader patterns of communal flourishing. Yet markets can be overidealized as the means of solving all human problems or condemned as having only negative consequences. On the negative side, critics accuse markets of operating with only an instrumental rationality and thereby failing to respect the internal goods of human practices and moral motivations to act with and for others. Therefore, markets are complicit in an assault on virtue and on human well-being.[34] While markets can operate in this way, they need not. Against how academic economics often portrays them, some humanistic and natural law traditions of thinking about markets envisage them as a social practice with intrinsic goods and accompanying virtues. Luigino Bruni and Robert Sugden argue that even in mainstream modern economic thought, from Adam Smith to Milton Friedman, there is a consistent response to what good or end the market should serve: that of mutual assistance by means of trade.[35] This in turn can serve wider moral goods. For example, one of the founders of economic neoliberalism, Friedrich Hayek, developed the concept of "catallaxy": the coordination and reconciliation of divergent and conflicting interests through market exchanges. It is premised on the notion that market exchange can transform enemies into friends through trade.[36] On this account, the market ceases to be a market when it serves a different end, as it contradicts its

33. Creative Commons, http://creativecommons.org.

34. Luigino Bruni and Robert Sugden, "Reclaiming Virtue Ethics for Economics," *Journal of Economic Perspectives* 27, no. 4 (2013): 141-64.

35. Bruni and Sugden, "Reclaiming Virtue Ethics," 151-53.

36. Hayek defines "catallaxy" as the order "brought about by the mutual adjustment of many individual economies in a market. A catallaxy is thus the special kind of spontaneous order produced by the market through people acting within the rules of the law of property, tort and contract." Friedrich A. von Hayek, *Law Legislation and Liberty*, vol. 2, *The Mirage of Social Justice* (Chicago: University of Chicago Press, 1978), 107-8. For Hayek, the market represents the means of overcoming the political as defined by the friend-enemy distinction.

own telos. But what many mainstream economists ignore is that markets can only operate as a constructive social practice when rooted within a wider and prior set of moral and political practices.

Foregrounding how markets are a social practice with intrinsic moral ends the fulfillment of which entails the practice of certain virtues provides criteria for evaluating when a market is not a market and has become a mode of domination. And it highlights how markets depend on prior forms of social life to function properly. The production, exchange, distribution, and consumption of goods and services emerge out of prior, place-based networks of interpersonal and ecological relationships. This is a point made with great force by feminist economists.[37] Breakdowns in reciprocity, trust, and cooperation, as exemplified in civil strife or war, directly affect the ability of markets to function. Conversely, improvements in them improve the efficiency and productivity of market transactions.[38]

Part of the reason we cannot see markets as a social practice dependent on and situated within other practices is that the vast majority of modern economics styles itself as a neutral science.[39] The very concepts and language we are furnished with to talk about our life together as producers and consumers, creditors and debtors, owners and leasers, etc., are disenchanted and anemic, with normative moral, spiritual, social, and political questions routinely banished from economics as a discipline. Responses to ethical questions (for example, in relation to market failures) are framed within a strict fact-value distinction and operate with a sense that we live in an amoral universe on which "I" bestow value. Within this framework, modern economics makes subjective value primary and so inherently fosters a relativistic worldview. Talk of markets that accept the terms and conditions laid upon them by mainstream modern economic thought—whether of the left or the right—will struggle to articulate a vision that constructively coordinates economic life and human flourishing.[40] It is like trying to box with a punctured lung: one is out of breath and enfeebled before the fight has even begun. It is incumbent upon theology to

---

37. See, for example, Julie Nelson, *Economics for Humans* (Chicago: University of Chicago Press, 2006), and J. K. Gibson-Graham, *A Postcapitalist Politics* (Minneapolis: University of Minnesota Press, 2006).

38. Luigino Bruni and Stefano Zamagni, *Civil Economy: Efficiency, Equity, Public Happiness* (Bern: Lang, 2007).

39. Christina McRorie, "The Emptiness of Modern Economics: Why the Dismal Science Needs a Richer Moral Anthropology," *Hedgehog Review* 16, no. 3 (2014): 120-29.

40. See MacIntyre, *Ethics in the Conflicts*, 70-105.

discover, or more accurately, rediscover, ways of thinking and talking about our common life unbounded either by the mores of academic economics or by capitalism as an all-determining frame of reference.

Uncritically accepting the terms and conditions of modern economic discourse also generates an inability to set limits on what should and what should not be subjected to market exchanges. Understanding economics as amoral or neutral undermines and delegitimizes the need for judgments about what should and what should not be up for sale. For example, should we be able to sell a kidney or our citizenship status or a child, and if not, why not? To make such judgments, we must understand economic reasoning as intrinsically bound up with moral deliberation, processes of cultural formation, and questions about political order. Some economists do recognize this.[41] Failure to include moral and political considerations is not being neutral; it is a sin of omission that fundamentally distorts one's analysis. Economic decisions can be more or less moral, but they are never wholly neutral or asocial. At the very least, putting a price on something alters its meaning, for better or worse. At a maximal level, if everything is for sale, then nothing is sacred. In short, markets have a place, but they must know their place, and that place is necessarily and rightly determined by moral and political considerations.

Distinguishing Markets from Capitalism

At this point, it is necessary to distinguish markets as a common social practice from capitalism as a historically contingent way of structuring production, distribution, and exchange. My concern here is not to define and explain capitalism economically. As already indicated, that is problematic given the refusal of modern economics as a discipline to countenance moral considerations. My concern here is to give an account of it in terms of *political theology*. To this end, the difference between markets and capitalism is analogous to the difference between a desire for food (a good thing) and gluttony (a vice). Only this is too mild an analogy. Capitalism is a metastasized, at times cancerous, mode of the market as a social practice. The shift from markets to capitalism is what Karl Polanyi calls

41. For an account of one such approach spearheaded by Robert Dorfman, see Spencer Banzhaf, "Objective or Multi-objective? Two Historically Competing Visions for Benefit-Cost Analysis," *Land Economics* 85, no. 1 (2009): 3-23.

"the Great Transformation." In Polanyi's account of this process, markets per se are not the problem. Rather the problem emerges when markets are no longer subordinated to and embedded within social and political relationships and instead subordinate human flourishing to the demands of the market.[42] In theological terms, this inversion means capitalism is an instantiation of Babylon. Central to understanding why capitalism is a Babylonian regime of life is that it inherently seeks to subordinate social and political life to market exchanges. Instead of the market knowing its place, it is market transactions that try to determine the place of everything else. That said, following Jeremiah 29, the welfare of the church is, at a penultimate level, bound up with the welfare of capitalism. Nevertheless, the song capitalism should call forth is one of lament, not praise.

In contrast to markets, capitalism is idolatrous because it prioritizes love of things and profit over love of God and neighbor. It thereby distorts how we should desire creation, multiplying desire for ephemeral rather than substantive goods and hollowing out the social practices and institutional forms through which a common life is sustained. A telling example is the fate of British football clubs. Formerly they were institutions that combined civic, social, and economic dimensions and contributed to the formation of a neighborly common life. Market transactions and making a profit were a vital part of sustaining the institution, but these were held in tension with the pursuit of a range of noncommercial, nonprofit-maximizing goals. This is now abandoned. The owners of football clubs understand identification with a club as a voluntaristic consumer choice expressed through buying branded merchandise. Instead of market transactions and commercial considerations serving the flourishing of the institution, the institution itself is an abstracted commodity traded on financial markets and a piece of collateral used as a debt-leverage instrument. Any notion that a football club has meaning or civic purpose or generates noncontractual relations

---

42. As Karl Polanyi summarizes it: "Instead of economy being embedded in social relations, social relations are embedded in the economic system" (*The Great Transformation: The Political and Economic Origins of Our Time*, 2nd ed. [Boston: Beacon, 2001], 60). Polanyi initially argued that prior to the nineteenth century, no market existed that was not embedded within or subservient to social and political relations. Arguably, Polanyi is right in his normative account of the embedded nature of markets but wrong in his assertion that no disembedded markets existed prior to the modern period. For an account of how Polanyi came to nuance his own position and distinguish between capitalistic markets (which existed prior to the modern period) and capitalism per se, see Gareth Dale, *Karl Polanyi: The Limits of the Market* (Cambridge: Polity, 2010), 137-87.

that demand loyalty and respect is entirely subordinated to and undermined by the demands of profit maximization. Framing all relations as contractual intensifies commodification so that the use value (and sacral/ social value) of something is separated from its exchange value. As a result, the only thing recognized as having value is what can be exchanged. Schools, universities, hospitals, libraries, your home, your parks, and myriad other institutional forms that make and sustain a common life have gone the same way as British football clubs. Yet sustaining a common world of meaning and action depends on maintaining a connection between a thing's symbolic use (and the practices of remembrance and covenanting in which it participates) and its exchange value. Capitalism, particularly finance capitalism, as an economic system depends on separating sign and signifier, separating the meaning and moral value of a thing from its exchange value.

The benefits of capitalism, and its sponsorship by sovereign nation-states, are said to outweigh its costs, with capitalism portrayed as liberating humans from the accidents of nature.[43] The tragic irony of capitalism, however, is that the very means through which humans sought liberation from "the accidents of nature" (e.g., carbon-based energy production) now present the greatest threat to human survival and could generate mass-extinction-level events (e.g., severe climate change). Moreover, the idea that capitalism liberated humanity ignores how its emergence depended on the Atlantic slave trade and colonialism as forms of primary accumulation. It also renders invisible how the racialized legacies of this history still shape the basic form of social and economic life in the United States and elsewhere. In short, capitalism, both historically and now, produces order and prosperity for some by generating disorder and destruction for others (especially nonhuman others and those judged less than human by the owners of capital and their state sponsors).

To understand capitalism theologically, it is important to realize that it is not one kind of thing. Yet both its detractors and its supporters paint a picture without shade or hue.[44] Capitalism can take multiple and overlap-

43. Such accounts of capitalism rest on a kind of immanent theology of providence. On this see Johnathan Sheehan and Dror Wahrman, *Invisible Hands: Self-Organization and the Eighteenth Century* (Chicago: University of Chicago Press, 2015).

44. Again, feminist economics pioneered approaches to capitalism that refuse monolithic interpretative frameworks. See Laura Bear et al., "Gens: A Feminist Manifesto for the Study of Capitalism," *Cultural Anthropology*, March 30, 2015, https://culanth.org /fieldsights/652-gens-a-feminist-manifesto-for-the-study-of-capitalism.

ping forms, ranging from liberal democratic (e.g., the United States and the United Kingdom), to socialized (e.g., Germany), to statist (e.g., China and Japan), to oligarchic (e.g., Russia and Saudi Arabia). However, there is a historical teleology assumed within accounts of capitalism, from Adam Smith through Marx and on through Hayek, whereby all local histories are subsumed within the one universal history of capitalism so that it is thought to convert everything and everyone into the same kind of time and space. This conversion narrative is told as either a story of salvation (Hayek) or a theodicy (Marx). Now undoubtedly there have been parallel false salvation histories in Christianity, most notably, the assumed sublation of all cultures and histories into a normatively white and European way of being in the world. Indeed, it is plausible to argue that it is precisely out of European Christianity, and its prevalent supersessionist theologies, that monolithic, totalizing, and universal conceptions of history have been born. On this kind of account, the secularizing of Providence as the invisible hand of the market veils bad theology.[45] However, a properly christological, pneumatological, and eschatological view of history should help us historicize capitalism (it is neither natural nor inevitable nor the way things should be); recognize that it is not a singular phenomenon and is capable of generating radically divergent effects; and acknowledge that it is as much a moral and spiritual phenomenon as it is a set of procedures and processes for the production, exchange, and distribution of scarce resources. Within a christocentric view of history, salvation is not from Babylon (or, latterly, New York, Shanghai, or London as command points of the contemporary manifestation of Babylon), for salvation cannot come from any earthly political and economic project for ordering, controlling, and stabilizing time and space. Rather, as noted in chapter 4, salvation comes from "outside" this age, is beyond human agency, and is inaugurated not by an earthly rule but by the cosmic rule of Christ.

Within contemporary approaches to capitalism, libertarianism (and aligned terms such as "neoliberalism" and "laissez-faire capitalism") is a name for an influential set of justifications for a specific form of capitalism.[46] As an ideology, it displays the following characteristics. It is based

45. On the secularization of Providence, see Amos Funkenstein, *Theology and the Scientific Imagination: From the Middle Ages to the Seventeenth Century* (Princeton: Princeton University Press, 1986), 202–89.

46. I am referring to "right libertarianism." There are forms of "left libertarianism" that include "socialist libertarianism" and "libertarian communism." I take forms of left libertarianism to be better named as forms of anarchism. However, as I outline in

on a voluntaristic, atomized anthropology and holds a view of the economy as the sphere of free relations. It sees markets as natural, spontaneous, self-regulating, efficient, and neutral mechanisms that best enable freedom of choice and the equal distribution of resources. Libertarianism conceptualizes the state as a guarantor of property rights but as a poor mechanism for social justice, welfare provision, or the redistribution of wealth, all of which are best achieved through market-based processes and entrepreneurial, philanthropic interventions.

Libertarianism/neoliberalism looks back, reacting against the formation of welfare states, nationalized industries, and the dominance of Keynesian economic policies, and so is an ideology that deploys a rhetorical repertoire of being a "conservative" corrective to a pendulum that has swung too far toward the state. This corrective takes the form of the remarketization of nationalized industries, utilities, and social services (notably, health, education, and welfare provision). But libertarianism is two-faced. It also looks forward, wearing the mantle of an emancipatory and progressive project that liberates individuals from both state policies and customary practices, rhetorically constructed as overbearing, inefficient, and outdated. However, at its heart, libertarianism enshrines a utopian project. It claims to know best how to order our common life through refusing the possibility that there can be goods in common that determine and shape what should be done. Instead, there are only individuals and their self-interested choices, and the aggregation of these determines what is good or bad, desirable and undesirable. This utopian core belief is constantly obscured and mystified by the positioning of libertarianism as *Realpolitik*. Rather than making explicit how libertarianism is a revolutionary ideology, advocates position it as merely realistic, framing attempts to contest its plausibility as idealistic. In reality, libertarianism is itself a highly idealistic program of social engineering. In the face of this kind of mystification and inversion, the language of left and right is scrambled: libertarianism can position itself as both revolutionary and reactionary—at the same time.

The plausibility of libertarianism as a simultaneously "conservative" and progressive project is sustained through posing a false dichotomy: the choice between the state or the market as a way of ordering life together. It is a false dichotomy that cannot countenance the possibility of a common life; such a possibility is simply implausible within a libertarian framework

---

chapter 12, both left and right libertarianism tend to share a voluntaristic anthropology and a vision of spontaneous order.

because it entails countenancing something other than the individual and the state as social, economic, and political realities and something more than choice as a source of value. As a political project that constantly seeks to monopolize state processes to achieve its aims, libertarianism sponsors specific policies for governing, notably, privatization, outsourcing government provision, "individual responsibilization," casualization of work, economic zoning, and differentiated legal regimes affecting different zones in terms of tax and labor laws. Such policies, in the name of free markets, justify and institute corporate authoritarianism. To resist these policies and reimagine economic life in ways that foster a just and compassionate common life, what is needed is an explicitly moral language that refuses the terms and conditions of Manichaean divisions between left and right and market and state. What is more, it needs to be a robustly theological language fully alive to the reality that we do not live by bread alone.

There is a wide spectrum of responses to capitalism by political theologies of various stripes. A frequent approach takes an economist's view and sees capitalism as a neutral/amoral system Christians can make use of in a way informed by Christian commitments.[47] By contrast, others view capitalism as a rival and opposing system, which positions Christianity as somehow external to capitalism. On this account, capitalism needs abolition. European Christian socialism and Latin American liberation theology are variants of this approach. An oppositional approach also feeds into an understanding of capitalism as another religion.[48] Rather than viewing the relationship as oppositional, some see Christianity as sitting within capitalism, which leads to either accommodation or attempts to reshape it from the inside out. The chapters on Pentecostalism and Catholic social teaching discuss variations of this kind of response. Others see capitalism as a product of Christianity. An influential basis for such a view was developed by the sociologist Max Weber, who envisaged Protestantism as providing the necessary cultural basis and ethos for capitalism to emerge. For Weber, capitalism subsequently undermined the plausibility of Christian

47. See Rebecca M. Blank, "Viewing the Market Economy through the Lens of Faith," in *Is the Market Moral? A Dialogue on Religion, Economics, and Justice*, ed. Rebecca M. Blank and William McGurn (Washington, DC: Brookings Institution Press, 2004), 11–56.

48. See David Loy, "Religion of the Market," *Journal of the American Academy of Religion* 65, no. 2 (1997): 275–90, and Robert Nelson, *Economics as Religion: From Samuelson to Chicago and Beyond* (University Park: Pennsylvania State University Press, 2002).

beliefs and practices, leading to them being hollowed out.[49] Conceiving of capitalism as an outgrowth of Christianity (and Christianity as thereby both internal and external to capitalism) can generate positive or negative responses. For example, Michael Novak, a neoconservative, sees capitalism as a legitimate expression of Christian values; whereas Vincent Miller views it as a cultural system and structure of desire that trades off Christian impulses while at the same time inverting and distorting them; while Emilie Townes envisages Christianity as complicit in the cultural production of racism and sexism through uncritical collusion with consumer and capitalist processes.[50] A variation of this view is to see capitalism and Christianity as mutually imbricated in each other, a relationship that sets off shockwaves of resonance and resistance that, alongside a need to muddle along, open up fissures for the abolition of some parts and reforming of others.[51]

One can view Christianity and capitalism as ultimately antithetical to each other—capitalism being the latest iteration of Babylon—while still seeing scope for ad hoc cooperation in the here and now to achieve penultimate goods. But the plausibility of this approach depends on realizing that capitalism is neither monolithic nor all-embracing.[52] Capitalism is best conceived of as a domineering power that takes multiple forms, some better and some worse. Like Babylon, capitalism is a symbol, structure, and culture of rule that stands apocalyptically under judgment. As with the

49. Max Weber, *The Protestant Ethic and the Spirit of Capitalism*, trans. Stephen Kalberg (Oxford: Oxford University Press, 2010 [1904]). The empirical validity of Weber's thesis is quite another matter.

50. Michael Novak, *The Spirit of Democratic Capitalism* (New York: Simon & Schuster, 1982); Daniel Bell, *Liberation Theology after the End of History: The Refusal to Cease Suffering* (London: Routledge, 2001); Vincent J. Miller, *Consuming Religion: Christian Faith and Practice in a Consumer Culture* (London: Continuum, 2004); and Emilie M. Townes, *Womanist Ethics and the Cultural Production of Evil* (New York: Palgrave Macmillan, 2006).

51. For a case study of such an approach, see my treatment of fair trade as a form of political consumerism in Luke Bretherton, *Christianity and Contemporary Politics: The Conditions and Possibilities of Faithful Witness* (Malden, MA: Wiley-Blackwell, 2010), 175–209.

52. For a theological evaluation, it is vital to resist the allure of monothematic, totalizing analyses that posit an epochal rupture between "tradition" and "modernity," and which operate with either a progressive or an evolutionary temporality and thereby deny contingency. One of the most influential of these is put forward by Marx, who predicted that capitalism would melt all that was solid into air, causing everything from the family to religion to the nation-state to disappear. They did not. Powerful as it is, capitalism is not all-pervasive and does not determine the form and nature of everything else.

depiction of Babylon/Rome given in Revelation, capitalism stands for and produces a whole system of domination and degradation. And yet, like all forms of empire, alongside the decadent and the damned, it is capable of producing things of great scientific merit and technological sophistication, as well as precious artifacts of immense beauty. As a regime, it can take very different forms around the world, even as each of these forms has a tentacular global reach. These different forms of capitalism are present at different concentrations in different places. In some contexts, they are an enveloping smog that chokes and pollutes everything; in others, they are a trace element one hardly notices. What capitalism is not is all-determining. That claims too much on its behalf. When assessing systems of domination, it is important to recognize that there is always an interplay of structure and agency, and these structures are never stable, involving as they do complex and shifting configurations of multiple institutions and processes. In terms of agency, capitalist processes diminish certain kinds of agency even as they make possible new kinds of social and political relations, which in turn undermine or challenge these same processes: for example, trade unions.[53]

Christianity posits the need to resist rendering contingent social, political, or economic orders immutable and determinative of what it means to be human. Part of this resistance is refraining from according any earthly order too much significance—for good or ill. Today, this means unveiling how capitalism is a contingent and mutable reality rather than a natural and inevitable one. At the same time, following Paul and Augustine, it means also recognizing that, as with the Roman Empire, we cannot extract ourselves from its influence or overthrow it by a revolutionary event or act of will. This side of Christ's return, capitalism, like any imperial system of domination, will not suddenly disappear because of a revolutionary moment that comes from "outside" the system, nor can we posit an untainted or wholly innocent subcultural politics of resistance "from below." Both postures presume forms of human speech and action capable of operating from a spatial and temporal register unconditioned by sin and prior patterns of domination. We must also resist the attempt to clothe a single, immanent ideological program in messianic robes; neither socialism nor anarcho-communism nor any other one-size-fits-all human program will

---

53. Catastrophizing (rather than apocalyptic) views of dominatory systems tend to condemn these new forms of agency as colluding or compromising. For example, Marxist-Leninist ideologies tend to see trade unionism as a non-revolutionary means of propping up the existing system by reforming it.

save us. Theologically, a sober and simultaneously radical hope for change in this age is to seek the conversion of capitalism, that is, its reconfiguration from within and without by redirecting its discursive and structural apparatus to different, God-given ends. This entails both recollection and rupture, being salt and light, conservative and radical, continuity and change, prophetic critique of what is and was as well as messianic hope for what will be but is beyond human control or determination.

Building on all I have said so far, I take the sociopolitical conversion of capitalism to involve three simultaneous movements that incorporate intense events as well as ongoing processes of change. The first is events and processes of healing achieved through recalling capitalist structures back to being merely a market operating as a social practice and serving rather than dominating human sociality. This work of healing or reform entails establishing such things as legislative limits, strengthening economic democracy, and generating new modes of production (e.g., wind and solar power), distribution (e.g., smaller-scale networks for distributing power derived from less-centralized means of energy production), and consumption (e.g., energy-efficient, longer-lasting appliances). The second is events and processes of deliverance that abolish the idolatrous and evil practices and institutions capitalism manifests, such as exploitative labor and lending practices; environmentally destructive forms of production, distribution, and consumption; monopolization of resources and production; the dominance and centralized nature of the financial services industry; and pay inequalities and wage theft. These first and second acts will generate great opposition because, as in the story of the Gerasene demoniac outlined in chapter 3, those possessed of the spirit of capitalism seek immunity from healing and exorcism, while those who most benefit from it can only encounter the prospect of healing and exorcism as a threat.

The third movement is events and processes that embody eschatological anticipations that draw capitalism through the cross and resurrection so as to transfigure its fallen and idolatrous forms. Like turning swords into plowshares, these eschatological anticipations mold new, Spirit-empowered possibilities out of unholy realities. These proleptic disclosures of the eschaton emerge through inventive tinkering and "mustard-seed"-like improvisations across innumerable locations at various scales, which when combined, germinate something new within and through the old.[54]

---

54. Peter Brown's magisterial study of the gradual shift in conceptions of poverty under the influence of Christianity is a case study of such radical yet incremental change

Embodiments of surprising newness cannot be proceduralized into a one-size-fits-all program, as they only make sense in the light of how we experience cross, resurrection, and the work of the Spirit in particular communities and contexts. Yet they can be recognized. And some initiatives can embody all three movements at once. In my judgment, one small example in the North American context is community-supported agriculture. It reforms the production and distribution of food, works to abolish cruel practices of animal husbandry and monopolistic modes of agricultural production, and embodies more shalom-like patterns of economic life. However, these three movements will not make Babylon/capitalism disappear—that is to deny history and the inevitable afterlife of capitalism. They can, however, fragilize, temper, and catalyze the transformation of Babylon/capitalism. But the long-term results of any process of transformation cannot be known, and within the tragic ironies of life before Christ's return, it could generate something worse. But then movements of healing, deliverance, and eschatological anticipation are to be undertaken not because of their utility (although these may be manifold). They are to be pursued because of their intrinsic worth, and this is what it means in practice to faithfully, hopefully, and lovingly witness to and participate in the work of the Spirit among these people, in this place, at this time.

On a theological account, real change must also involve the conversion of the self and not just the material conditions of human relationships; cure of the soul is profoundly interrelated with the cure of the *oikos* and *polis*. Thus, any meaningful change entails a conversion of self and others through time-intensive means of building relationships one person at a time and the cultivation of ascetic and liturgical practices that redirect us to desire God first. Such interpersonal events and processes help foster a profound transformation of imagination and subjectivity so that we learn to touch, see, hear, taste, and smell temptations and idolatries for what they are and can turn instead to bear witness to the transformative actions of the Spirit, who is the only one with the comprehensive agency to irrupt a transfigured spatiotemporal register (a new heaven and a new earth) within the bounds of the old.

---

over time. Peter Brown, *Through the Eye of a Needle: Wealth, the Fall of Rome, and the Making of Christianity in the West, 350-550 AD* (Princeton: Princeton University Press, 2012).

Economic Democracy and the Formation of a Common Life

Let me close by laying out some of the concrete implications of what can seem like an abstract and abstruse position. As argued here, markets and money are not neutral. Within a capitalist economy, they tend to crowd out nonmarket values and considerations, which can lead to traumatic social and political consequences. The state cannot be the only means to either prevent or alleviate these consequences. Indeed, it is often part of the problem. Instead, alongside state action, forms of participatory and economic democracy are needed to ensure that more decentralized and agency-centered ways of coming to moral and political judgment are embedded within the means of production, distribution, and exchange (whether in the "private" or "public" sector). Economic democracy helps modulate capitalist economic processes by directing them to contribute, first, to the commonwealth and not just the wealth of the few; second, to a more even distribution of power; and third, to the provision of efficient and accurate accountability at the appropriate location. For this to be possible, contractual property relations backed by the state urgently need supplementing with the institutionalization of the means for producing relational power, that is, covenantal or consociational organizations that embody relations of mutuality. Without countervailing forms of democratic association, judgment making, and the means of communication to signal both variations in context and points of social and political conflict, the market will metastasize and dominate all aspects of life. The institutional apparatus of economic democracy is a vital but neglected part of constituting the people or the body politic. Moreover, legal limits, a participatory democratic politics, upholding the dignity of labor, and the reembedding of market relations in social and political relations of reciprocity are needed if money, economic debt, markets, and property are to serve rather than diminish human and ecological flourishing.

My prescriptive judgment is that economic democracy needs massive extension. This extension is possible through such measures as the representation of workers on pension remuneration boards; active trade union and shareholder involvement in corporate governance; alternative and local financial institutions such as credit unions, regional banks, and Local Exchange Trading Schemes (LETS); and other forms of economic democracy such as community-supported agriculture and fisheries, community land trusts, fair trade schemes, guilds and professional associations, and consumer associations. Such measures depend on maintaining reciprocal relations and enable sharing profits, distributing power, and prioritizing social over political and economic relations. This latter "mark" reflects the self-ascribed names such ventures adopt in the modern period: *friendly* societies, *cooperatives*, *mutuals*, credit *unions*, and *social* insurance. These ways of structuring the production, distribution, and exchange of goods and the distribution of assets provide an alternative to capitalistic forms. They feed into and emerge out of the traditions of modern political theology that developed the most extensive accounts of economic democracy: European Christian socialism, particularly in its non-statist currents such as guild socialism, and Christian Democracy. A central insight of both Christian socialism and Christian Democracy was that economic democracy is a vital means through which Christians might come to understand and enact a common life that enmeshes markets, economic debt, and property relations in prior and superordinate forms of moral and political life, thereby inhibiting the subordination of human well-being to the demands of Mammon (that is, the use of money and markets to determine the value and use of everything and everyone).

Conclusion

There are three underlying themes in this chapter. The first is the coinherence of talk of God and talk of economics. The second is the inadequacy of modern talk of economics that treats economics as a neutral science and economic life as amoral. The third is that the economy is not an autonomous sphere. I have argued that our life together as producers and consumers, borrowers and lenders, etc., necessarily entails moral and political judgments and that economic life, if it is to serve rather than destroy a just and loving common life, must always be understood as dependent on prior forms of life together with God, other humans, and the rest of creation. Only when the moral and political dimensions of economic life are front and center can a true account of the uses and ends of property, debt, money, and markets be given. Understanding markets as a social practice with internal goods that serve and are subordinate to the pursuit of other kinds of goods provides a way of distinguishing markets from capitalism, with capitalism understood as a "Babylonian" way of structuring the production, distribution, and consumption of material things. In the light of a theological conception that our little economies are always already housed within divine-human relations, economic democracy offers an embodied response to capitalism, helping to ensure that property, debt, money, and markets serve rather than diminish the symbiosis of human and ecological flourishing.

Threshold

As part of the reflection on how economic relations are both a condition of and conditioned by politics, this chapter suggested that the state has a place in ensuring that economic relations serve human and ecological flourishing. But this begs the question of how to understand the nature and form of sovereignty, and thus the role of the state in structuring social, economic, and political life. Different conceptions of sovereignty generate different accounts of what the remit of the state is in shaping life together. It is to a consideration of sovereignty that I turn in the next chapter.

Suggested Readings for Further Discussion

Scriptural texts: Deuteronomy 5; Leviticus 25; Psalm 15; Amos 8; Luke 4; 12:16-20; 19:1-10; Acts 2:44-47; James 5:1-11; 1 Timothy 6:8-10; and Revelation 18.

Gregory of Nazianzus, "Oration 14: On Love for the Poor," in *St. Gregory of Nazianzus: Select Orations*, trans. Martha Vinson (Washington, DC: Catholic University of America Press, 2003), 39-71. This is a classic statement of how care for the poor (understood variously) is a primary Christian obligation and outworking of love of God that reshapes how Christians are situated in the world.

Thomas Aquinas, *Summa theologiae* II-II, q. 61 and qq. 77-78. Various editions. Develops a social view of property as a communicative good.

Gustavo Gutiérrez, *A Theology of Liberation: History, Politics, Salvation* (Maryknoll, NY: Orbis, 1973), chaps 2 and 9. Gutiérrez offers a critique of economic growth as the only measure of human development and a statement of how economic and political liberation are part and parcel of a theology of salvation.

Michael Novak, "A Theology of Democratic Capitalism," in *The Spirit of Democratic Capitalism* (New York: Simon & Schuster, 1982), 333-60. Defends capitalism as expressive of Christian commitments.

Wendell Berry, "Two Economies (1983)," in *The Art of the Commonplace:*

The Agrarian Essays of Wendell Berry, ed. Norman Wirzba (Berkeley, CA: Counterpoint, 2003), 219-35.

Katie G. Cannon, "Racism and Economics: The Perspective of Oliver C. Cox," in *Katie's Canon: Womanism and the Soul of the Black Community* (New York: Continuum, 1995), 144-61. Cannon draws on the work of Oliver Cox to argue that capitalism is bound up with and reinscribes racism. Cox analyzed the parallels between and coemergence of racial and class-based hierarchies and how capitalism was central to race-based antagonism.

Benedict XVI, *Caritas in Veritate* (2009). Available online from vatican.va. Here Benedict puts forward a constructive theological vision of economic relations as serving civic and interpersonal flourishing as well as sustaining human dignity and creativity.

CHAPTER 12

Sovereignty

The nature and basis of sovereignty are a central concern of political theology. This chapter examines debates about sovereignty while at the same
time making a case for a particular, pluralistic conception of sovereignty
as having normative value. In doing so it rejects what I take to be a false
dichotomy between top-down, centralizing ways of structuring sovereignty
that legitimize forms of domination and the denial of any need for a public
authority to coordinate and adjudicate between competing and conflicting claims, as if any such authority is inherently illegitimate. The rejection
of any form of sovereignty—and thence the need for some kind of public
authority—is born out of a suspicion that all claims to sovereignty are attempts to suppress difference in the name of a homogeneous political order
and unjust social hierarchy. This suspicion is not without warrant.

Integralist visions of political order, in which the individual, the household, and political structures cohere into a uniform and seamless hierarchy,
are more often than not tied to absolutist and top-down conceptions of
sovereignty. Integralist visions draw an analogy between soul, polity, and
universe that emphasizes uniformity over plurality. While exemplified in
Plato's *Republic*, it is an analogy that is common within the Christian tradition, one often derived from a doctrine of God that emphasizes the oneness, omnipotence, sovereignty, and transcendent lordship of God over the
universe. By extension, there is said to be but one king governing the polity,
one father governing the family, and each human governing his or her actions. God is the archetypal sovereign, and human sovereignty—in all its
forms—takes on the various attributes ascribed to God's nature. Eusebius
(c. 260-340 CE), in his panegyric to the emperor Constantine, articulates
this theo-political logic. He envisages the emperor as an icon of the divine
Sovereign, and government as a reflection of the divine order: "Invested as

[the emperor] is with a semblance of heavenly sovereignty, he directs his gaze above, and frames his earthly government according to the pattern of that Divine original, feeling strength in its conformity to the monarchy of God. And this conformity is granted by the universal Sovereign to man alone of the creatures of this earth: for he only is the author of sovereign power, who decrees that all should be subject to the rule of one."[1]

On one reading, modernity is a revolution against this way of conceptualizing sovereignty and the hierarchal and homogenizing schema supposedly legitimized by it. Modernity is said to represent the dethronement of God, monarchs, and all patriarchal and patrician authorities, replacing them with human reason, constitutional democracy, and an egalitarian social structure in which power rises from the bottom up. This reading of history assumes that the further back in time one goes, the greater the unconstrained power of rulers. This chapter contests the idea that modernity represents a revolution against top-down, hierarchal, and homogenizing schemas of sovereignty previously legitimized by Christianity. In doing so, it runs in parallel to, intersects with, and complicates the next chapter on the people as the basis of democratic sovereignty. My first contention is that, despite an emphasis on popular sovereignty, the modern period witnessed the untrammeled centralization and expansion of political sovereignty, both conceptually and in practice. This concentration of power drew on the notion that divine sovereignty is indivisible—a notion that came to prominence in early modern theological and political thought. My second contention is that far from rejecting theological notions of sovereignty, modern notions of sovereignty have a theological pedigree that in turn produces a theological counterreaction.

Modern Euro-American thought on sovereignty sees itself as replacing earlier medieval understandings of political authority. On closer inspection, however, it traces over and reproduces many aspects of earlier conceptions. Against overly disjunctive readings of the relationship, Quentin Skinner and other historians of political thought point to how we cannot understand modern political concepts without understanding their foundations in the medieval and early modern period. Carl Schmitt goes beyond making a point about intellectual history, contending that modern political ideas are secularized theological concepts and so continue to carry a trace of their original imprint. In the wake of Schmitt, other theorists, notably, Jacques Derrida and Giorgio Agamben, have done much to

1. Eusebius, *Oration in Praise of the Emperor Constantine* 3.5.

foreground the theological imprint in modern Western notions of political sovereignty. For Derrida, there is always "some unavowed theologeme" at work in even the most secularized societies, and when it comes to claims to sovereignty, we cannot escape the inherently theological dimension of such claims.[2] On Derrida's account, we have not replaced God with something new; rather, we have simply displaced God but left the structural analogy intact so that in God's place is put an autonomous, sovereign individual with an indivisible will who issues laws to himself or herself. Parallel to notions of God's sovereignty and nature, what is sovereign is taken to be what is legitimate and moral. The paradox is that just when the self-governing individual gains supreme sovereignty, the individual is seen to be subject to what Michel Foucault calls "biopower." Biopower names the control of entire populations through numerous and diverse techniques for achieving the subjugation and regimentation of human bodies. Paradigmatic examples include medicine and prisons. Building on and responding to these insights, theologians have offered theological critiques of modern liberalism. For example, Oliver O'Donovan sees liberalism as doomed to incoherence unless it understands itself as the apostate child of Christianity, repents, and regrounds its claims in the Christ event.[3] In the spirit of such concerns, we need to see the relationship between theology and modern Western conceptions of political sovereignty not as a wholly new or disjunctive relationship but as an iteration of earlier developments.

This chapter begins by excavating the premodern and early modern developments out of which modern, Western notions of political sovereignty emerge. Second, it examines the intertwined theological and philosophical development of a view of sovereignty as indivisible in dialogue with the work of Hobbes, Rousseau, Locke, and Hegel and their reception. This section ends by mapping the countermovement in modern theology that critiques indivisible notions of sovereignty by drawing on a Trinitarian doctrine of God and Pauline eschatology. Interwoven with the first and second sections are assessments of the alternative political imaginaries inherent

2. Giovanna Borradori, *Philosophy in a Time of Terror: Dialogues with Jürgen Habermas and Jacques Derrida* (Chicago: University of Chicago Press, 2003), 113, and Jacques Derrida, *Voyous* (Paris: Galilée, 2003), 155. Derrida's insight is not without precedent in the modern period. For example, one of the founding figures of anarchism, Pierre-Joseph Proudhon, remarks in his *Confessions of a Revolutionary* (1849), "at the basis of our politics we always find theology."

3. Oliver O'Donovan, *The Desire of the Nations: Rediscovering the Roots of Political Theology* (Cambridge: Cambridge University Press, 1996), 275.

in such notions as a messianic age, Cockaigne, Arcadia, and utopia, all of which dissolve any need of a single sovereign power in the name of some form of spontaneous order. Correlations are also drawn between these alternative political imaginaries and modern attempts to conceptualize a social order that does not need a single sovereign power: namely, Marxism, anarchism, and technocracy. Lastly, the chapter sketches a countertradition of thinking about sovereignty as neither indivisible nor in need of dissolution but as inherently distributed through various powers and as more thoroughly democratic. In political theology, this countertradition is given voice in the work of Johannes Althusius, the Guild Socialists, notions of sphere sovereignty, and Catholic social teaching, and involves the recovery of a conception of humans as political animals.

Medieval and Early Modern Trajectories

To make sense of the continuing theological imprint in modern conceptions of sovereignty, some theologians and political theorists point to the emergence of voluntarism and nominalism.[4] The theologians John Duns Scotus (c. 1265-1308) and William of Ockham (c. 1288-1348) are critical to the shift from a participatory metaphysics to one in which God's sovereign will is the ultimate principle of being (voluntarism), and the separation of being and thinking such that mental concepts are not taken to refer to real things directly (nominalism). As progenitors of voluntarism and nominalism, Scotus and Ockham are identified as a point of origin for modern notions of individual and state sovereignty. The shift to voluntarism and nominalism is a shift from seeing God as Logos (that is, as loving, relational, and Trinitarian divine presence in whose order humans can participate creatively through reason) to seeing God primarily as a sovereign whose omnipotent will is unbounded, absolute, and indivisible. In the former, good order comes through right participation within the limits of creation and patterns of social relations, the goal of which is communion with God mediated through participation in Christ's body, the church. In the latter view, order and social peace come through obedience and subordination to the sovereign and indivisible will of God and those who represent God

4. See Michael Gillespie, *The Theological Origins of Modernity* (Chicago: University of Chicago Press, 2008), and John Milbank, *Theology and Social Theory: Beyond Secular Reason* (Oxford: Blackwell, 1990).

on earth, whether popes or emperors. The latter view gives rise to a conflict between ecclesial and political authority over who is the primary vicar of Christ on earth, a conflict that shapes all subsequent conceptions of sovereignty.[5]

Whether Scotus and Ockham are the progenitors of more voluntaristic conceptions of sovereignty is open to debate.[6] However, what can be said is that when God is primarily understood as a willing agent whose authority is delegated to a human representative, various solutions present themselves as to how to resolve the conflict between ecclesial and political authorities over whose sovereignty is supreme. One solution is to create not two swords, each of which has a coequal and reciprocal role in shaping the political order, but two distinct domains—spiritual and secular—within which ecclesial and political authorities exercise sovereign power without threatening each other. This solution is not without precedent. In *The Bond of Anathema*, Pope Gelasius I (492-496) distinguishes between a realm of spiritual activity governed by the church and a realm of secular affairs over which the church had no control. However, Gelasius envisaged the church as able to decide its own affairs and as having a dual responsibility with political authorities for fostering good order. The dual responsibility and division between the two authorities were to safeguard the modesty of both: only Christ could be both priest and king. However, as noted in chapter 8, in the modern period the spiritual becomes private and interior, while the secular pertains to what is public and material (i.e., social, economic, and political). The body is thereby ruled by the state while what happens to the soul is a religious and immaterial matter.

The shift to a more voluntaristic conception of God eclipses Trinitarian theology, and there emerge in its stead Deist, Unitarian, and rationalist conceptions of God. Immanuel Kant (1724-1804) both exemplifies and intensifies the marginalization of Trinitarian theology. For Kant, reason

---

5. For the genealogy of this conflict over who is the anointed and supreme representative of Christ on earth, see Ernst Kantorowicz, *The King's Two Bodies: A Study in Mediaeval Political Theology* (Princeton: Princeton University Press, 1957).

6. Against Milbank and Gillespie, Agamben sees an emphasis on the sovereign will of God in the creation and rule of the cosmos as a basic development in the emergence of patristic Trinitarian theology born out of the fracturing of the being and acting of God (*The Kingdom and the Glory: For a Theological Genealogy of Economy and Government*, trans. Lorenzo Chiesa and Matteo Mandarini [Stanford, CA: Stanford University Press, 2011], 56-57. Chapter 11 on the economy should be read as a critique and rejection of Agamben's view).

and law govern what should be said and done in public, not revelation. There is a God, but parallel to the development of Deism in Britain, Kant conceived of God as a supremely perfect being, immutable, indivisible, and timeless. The right political order of perpetual peace is the corollary of the right ontological order of a rule-governed, rational deity. The church, its liturgies, rituals, and institutional form, is to be tolerated but can have no public presence in the rationally administered state. The move from Trinitarian to monarchical, voluntarist, and rationalist doctrines of God generates a process of mimesis in the political realm. Political sovereignty becomes understood as being of one substance, indivisible, set apart, non-participative, and defined by the exercise of a single will, the sole function of which is to secure an immanent rational mechanism.

In the wake of nominalism and voluntarism came a shift from complex to simple space.[7] After the French Revolution, the paradigmatic modern polity was taken to be the republican nation-state whose citizens determine their laws. This paradigm has its origin in the conception of the ideal polity as constituted by one people, one religion, and one law under God.[8] The bounded nation-state with a single law and indivisible source of rule is unbounded in the exercise of its sovereign will within its own borders. This type of polity contrasts with the complex and overlapping jurisdictions of medieval Christendom, in which the sovereign authorities of popes, emperors, kings, abbots, bishops, dukes, doges, and various forms of self-governing corporations (e.g., universities and cities) were interwoven with each other and spanned disjunctive or noncontiguous territories and overlapping times (the eschatological and the *saeculum*).[9] These patchwork polities were situated within an overarching, providential order. What was divided on earth was unified in heaven, with each authority contributing to the governance of the single economy of God's kingdom.[10] The analogues of complex spaces were customary forms of measurement, evaluation, and practical reasoning that were "decidedly local, interested, contextual and

---

7. John Milbank, "On Complex Space," in *The Word Made Strange: Theology, Language, Culture* (Oxford: Blackwell, 1997), 268-92.

8. See Adrian Hastings, *The Construction of Nationhood: Ethnicity, Religion, and Nationalism* (Cambridge: Cambridge University Press, 1997), and Eric Nelson, *The Hebrew Republic: Jewish Sources and the Transformation of European Political Thought* (Cambridge, MA: Harvard University Press, 2010).

9. For an overview of the form of the medieval polity, see Jacob Levy, *Rationalism, Pluralism, and Freedom* (Oxford: Oxford University Press, 2015), 87-105.

10. Agamben, *Kingdom and the Glory*, 109-42.

historically specific" and were thereby highly resistant to centralized forms of either state administration and taxation or commercial exploitation.[11] But modern political thinkers began to view this mixed economy of political forms and customary practices with increasing incomprehension. In its stead, as Benjamin Constant observed when reflecting on Napoleon, "the conquerors of our days, peoples or princes, want their empires to possess a unified surface over which the superb eye of power can wander without encountering any inequality which hurts or limits its view. The same code of law, the same measures, the same rules, and if we could gradually get there, the same language; that is what is proclaimed as the perfection of the social organization. . . . The great slogan of the day is *uniformity*."[12] The standardization of political space, time, law, and measurement was the prelude to homogenized conceptions of citizenship.[13]

In the shift to the nation-state as a singular and simple space with an indivisible and transcendent sovereign authority (whether monarchical or democratic), a key debating point was the legitimacy or otherwise of constitutional pluralism. Of particular concern in these debates was the status of the Holy Roman Empire, formed in the late tenth century, but which, after the Diet of Cologne in 1512, became the Holy Roman Empire of the Germanic Nation and consisted of most of central Europe. As a commitment to singular constitutional forms gained preeminence, the Germanic Imperial Constitution comes to be seen as a problematic exception rather than a norm. In this regard, the rejection of the Germanic Imperial Constitution mirrors the suppression of all forms of political order that derive their authority from assemblages of custom, tradition, and common law, whether they be the indigenous structures of the Americas, Africa, and Australasia or the medieval forms of Europe. Behind the shift in the European context lies the rejection of Aristotelian political thought, which saw constitutional pluralism as the ideal: the idea that the best form of govern-

---

11. James C. Scott, *Seeing like a State: How Certain Schemes to Improve the Human Condition Have Failed* (New Haven: Yale University Press, 1998), 27. Scott explains: "If we imagine a state that has no reliable means of enumerating and locating its population, gauging its wealth, and mapping its land, resources, and settlements, we are imagining a state whose interventions in that society are necessarily crude. A society that is relatively opaque to the state is thereby insulated from some forms of finely tuned state interventions" (77).

12. Benjamin Constant, *De l'esprit de conquête* (1815), quoted in Scott, *Seeing like a State*, 30.

13. Scott, *Seeing like a State*, 32.

ment involved monarchical, aristocratic, and democratic elements.[14] Jean Bodin's *Les Six Livres de la République* (1578) is the prototype of and catalyst for a rejection of Aristotle and the development of a conception of sovereignty as indivisible, transcendent, and monistic.[15] Bodin directly attacks the Germanic Imperial Constitution. For Bodin, sovereignty is absolute, by which he means that the sovereign must not be subject in any way to the commands of someone else.[16] Bodin can locate sovereignty in a single person, in the people, or in a fraction of the people. However, to combine these elements in a mixed constitution is "impossible and contradictory, and cannot even be imagined. For if sovereignty is indivisible . . . how could it be shared by a prince, the nobles, and the people at the same time."[17] Thus sovereignty, which is indivisible, must be distinguished from governmental power, which can be divided and distributed to many parts—a distinction that flows into many streams of modern political thought. But, as Jacques Maritain noted in his critique of modern conceptions of sovereignty:

When Jean Bodin says that the sovereign Prince is the image of God, this phrase must be understood in its full force, and means that the Sovereign—submitted to God, but accountable only to Him—transcends the political whole just as God transcends the cosmos. Either Sovereignty means nothing, or it means supreme power separate and

14. Prior to Rousseau, Thomas Paine, and Immanuel Kant were John Milton, James Harrington, and a host of Protestant political thinkers who viewed monarchy as idolatrous and sinful. This republican position was in turn opposed by the assertion of the divine right of kings: an equally simple and singular early modern conception of political space. As Hannah Arendt notes, both republicanism and absolute monarchy prepared the way for the rise of the "secular" nation-state (see *On Revolution* [London: Penguin Books, 2006 (1963)], 149-56). For both "Hebrew Commonwealthsmen" and the proponents of absolute monarchy, the key texts were Deut. 17:14 and 1 Sam. 8, and the question of whether Scripture marks kingship as inherently wicked or positively required (Nelson, *The Hebrew Republic*, 23-56). What neither side would countenance was a mixed constitutional order. Agamben, in his discussion of the place of monarchy and *oikonomia* in political theology in *Kingdom and the Glory*, completely misses both the significance of this early modern debate and the role of Scripture in the development of political theology.

15. See Julian Franklin, "Sovereignty and the Mixed Constitution: Bodin and His Critics," in *The Cambridge History of Political Thought: 1450-1700*, ed. J. H. Burns and M. Goldie (Cambridge: Cambridge University Press, 1991), 298-344.

16. Jean Bodin, *On Sovereignty: Four Chapters from "The Six Books of the Commonwealth,"* trans. Julian Franklin (Cambridge: Cambridge University Press, 1992), 11.

17. Bodin, *On Sovereignty*, 92.

transcendent—not at the peak but above the peak—and ruling the entire body politic *from above*. That is why this power is absolute (absolute, that is non-bound, separate) and consequently unlimited, as to its extension as well as to its duration, and unaccountable to anything on earth.[18]

In contrast to Maritain, Carl Schmitt celebrates an indivisible, monistic, and transcendent conception of sovereignty.[19]

A countervoice to Bodin is that of the early-seventeenth-century Dutch Protestant political thinker Johannes Althusius (1563-1638). Althusius systemizes the medieval constitutional view and catalyzes the emergence of modern confederal or consociational accounts of sovereignty as constituted by the whole body politic and not derived from a monistic source of sovereignty whose authority stands over and above the people and their forms of association.[20] For Althusius, it is the body politic that delegates authority "up" to the sovereign, and not vice versa. However, with the defeat of absolutist monarchies and the passing of the *ancien régime*, republican and democratic self-government is increasingly seen as the only form of legitimate (and God-given) rule. Such a form of rule could involve a separation of legislative, judicial, and executive elements, but sovereignty is still taken to be indivisible and derived from a monistic, Olympian source (e.g., the "general will" or the "nation"). Bodin rather than Althusius sets the course for understanding the sovereignty of the people. The theory of sovereignty and the political form of the nation-state come to mirror and justify each other. By contrast, for medieval constitutionalists, sovereignty was shared among all the estates in proportion to their contribution to the body politic, which, as a body, was necessarily made up of many parts and could be one and many or, echoing the eucharistic body, catholic and distributed simultaneously.

Alongside the formal inheritance of medieval and early modern political thought, we must attend to the informal legacy of popular piety

18. Jacques Maritain, "The Concept of Sovereignty," *American Political Science Review* 44, no. 2 (1950): 346.

19. Carl Schmitt, *The Concept of the Political*, trans. George Schwab (Chicago: University of Chicago Press, 2007).

20. See Thomas Hueglin, *Early Modern Concepts for a Late Modern World: Althusius on Community and Federalism* (Waterloo, ON: Wilfrid Laurier University Press, 1999). Althusius can be situated within the development of "ancient constitutionalism" as an early modern political theory. On this see Levy, *Rationalism, Pluralism, and Freedom*, 106-40.

in which millennialism, Cockaigne, and Arcadia suggested alternative visions of political order. For Renaissance humanists and Puritan republicans, the well-ordered commonwealth required the overcoming of sin and the vicissitudes of *fortuna* through the exercise of personal virtue, a disciplined society, well-crafted laws, and strong government. However, from the Brethren of the Free Spirit and the Taborites through to the Anabaptists of Münster, those seized with populist expectation of an imminent millennium rejected programs of reform.[21] For example, the millenarian Anabaptist Thomas Müntzer (1489-1525) understood that he and his followers were already living in the end of days when earthly sovereigns were overthrown and all things were to be held in common.

Numerous modern revolutionary programs echo these millennial expectations. These reject the existing liberal capitalist system *tout court* and envisage themselves as vanguards ushering in a new time. For some the connection is explicit: in *The Peasant War in Germany* (1850), Friedrich Engels interprets Müntzer as a protocommunist revolutionary; likewise, in *Thomas Müntzer als Theologe der Revolution* (1921), Ernst Bloch envisages Müntzer as embodying an anticipatory utopian consciousness that finally comes to expression in Marxism. An alternative form of millennial expectation can be overheard in Walter Benjamin (1892-1940), who combined Marxism with Jewish mysticism and for whom the messianic provides a critical horizon that interrupts and calls into question all historical political projects. These appropriations provoked a theological response. Martin Buber saw them as forms of "dispossessed Messianism."[22] Henri de Lubac, in his two-volume work *La Posterité Spirituelle de Joachim de Flore* (1979-1981), explored in detail the connections between medieval millennialism and modern political thought. Jürgen Moltmann, in his extensive analysis of the interaction of Christian millennialism and politics, reads modernity itself as a form of millennialism.[23] De Lubac's and Moltmann's studies point to a key theological issue at stake in the modern appropriation of millennialism: Is the church the primary meditator of divine revelation, or can it be superseded in a new age of the Spirit by a revolutionary social movement?

The zealous fervor of medieval and early modern reform and millennial movements, which at times converge and then separate like crosscutting

---

21. Norman Cohn, *The Pursuit of the Millennium: Revolutionary Millenarians and Mystical Anarchists of the Middle Ages* (Oxford: Oxford University Press, 1970).

22. Martin Buber, *Paths in Utopia* (New York: Macmillan, 1950).

23. Jürgen Moltmann, *The Coming of God: Christian Eschatology*, trans. Margaret Kohl (Minneapolis: Fortress, 2004 [1996]), 184-92.

tidal flows, must be set against those who dreamed of Cockaigne. Cockaigne was a paradisiacal land in which all social, political, and economic problems dissolved because every individual was satisfied and every need was met.[24] Pieter Bruegel the Elder's *Land of Cockaigne* (1567) depicts such a dreamworld in which eggs have legs and walk to you, roasted pigs amble around with carving knives strapped to their backs, and fowl lie down on a silver platter ready to be eaten. The point of interest here is not that Cockaigne is a land without labor, production, or conflict, but that it requires no governing authority: it is a spontaneous order of plenty. Libertarian economics echoes the notion that the best of all possible worlds is an apolitical socioeconomic realm that spontaneously organizes itself. It envisages material prosperity as flowing spontaneously out of the free decisions of individuals. Johann Kaspar Schmidt (whose *nom de plume* was Max Stirner [1806–1856]) explored these themes. He was a onetime associate of Engels and a so-called individualist anarchist. A former student of Ludwig von Mises, Murray Rothbard (1926–1995) also elaborates these ideas. He coined the term "anarcho-capitalism." The analogue of this *pro*capitalist, antistatist, libertarian vision is the *anti*capitalist and antistatist vision that rested on a parallel notion of spontaneous order and an equally voluntaristic anthropology. It is a position exemplified in the anarcho-syndicalism of Pierre-Joseph Proudhon (1809–1865) and Georges Sorel (1847–1922). They looked to the abolition of the state, as any need for coercive power and centralized coordination would disappear within a decentralized and federal organization of *syndicats* or occupational associations, which in turn would give rise to a spontaneous order of transactions and exchanges. The administration of things would replace the government of persons, and a new polity, one founded on the workshop, not the state, would be created. In such a polity, the advent of technocratic self-government would eradicate the need for any kind of coercive political order. Myths of spontaneous order continue to reverberate through contemporary radical political theories that posit forms of polity without sovereignty, ways of life without order or hierarchy, modes of organization without structure, and autonomy without association (and the time-bound, place-based patterns of loyalty, trust, and cooperation just and compassionate association entails).[25]

24. Herman Pleij, *Dreaming of Cockaigne: Medieval Fantasies of the Perfect Life*, trans. Diane Webb (New York: Columbia University Press, 2001).

25. Strains of these can be seen in "transhumanism," "accelerationism," "fully automated luxury communism," and the work of Michael Hardt and Antonio Negri. On this

Cockaigne, Arcadia, and millennialism are pre- or postpolitical visions that presume a world without sin. The negotiation of a common life in the face of immorality, competing and conflicting interests, different visions of human flourishing, and the unequal distribution of resources is dissolved because either all needs are satisfied (Cockaigne), all citizens exist in a state of pastoral innocence uncorrupted by civilization (Arcadia),[26] or justice is achieved through the return of the true king who vindicates the virtuous and removes the vicious, turning the existent world upside down in order to establish what is true and good (millennialism). However, we do not have the agency to achieve these forms of spontaneous order, and they exist beyond any actual spatiotemporal realm. They are either sheer fantasy, an unrecoverable golden age, or the result of an apocalyptic event. What changes in the modern period is the emergence of a revolutionary ideal whereby humans believe they can remake the world. As I noted in chapter 8, a critical feature of the modern period was the loss of a sense of what it meant to participate in and collaborate with a preexisting order, understood theologically or otherwise, and the emergence of a view of order as imposed *ab extra* on nature by the human will.[27] This loss entails a move to disengagement and disenchantment such that the cosmic order is now understood as mechanistic and morally neutral: it cannot disclose to us any sense of how we should live. In the shift from cosmos to universe, political sovereignty becomes unbounded by moral limits while sovereign individuals can remake the world as they please.

Thomas More's *Utopia* (1516) reflects the shift to the centrality of the unbounded sovereign will. It is premised neither on a notion of spontaneous order irrupting through an apocalyptic event nor on an alternative reality through which to render contingent and satirize present conditions. Rather than existing outside of or beyond history, More's utopia is designed as a blueprint and intended as a guide to action in history. Unlike his republican peers, More's ideal commonwealth issued not from the actions of a prince or parliament but from technocratic procedures. Its founder, Utopus, is not a lawgiver after the model of Solon or Moses, but a systems designer and bureaucrat. Neither revelation, nature, nor immemorial custom forms the

---

see F. H. Pitts and A. C. Dinerstein, "Corbynism's Conveyor Belt of Ideas: Postcapitalism and the Politics of Social Reproduction," *Capital and Class* 41, no. 3 (2017): 423–34.

26. Other formulations of this trope frame it in relation to the figure of the noble savage.

27. Charles Taylor, *A Secular Age* (Cambridge, MA: Harvard University Press, 2007), 123–30.

basis of his laws. They are a work of technique. More's utopia is entirely different from an Arcadia or a Cockaigne where the lawgiver is unnecessary because everyone is a law unto himself or herself; or the millennium, where the law is divinely inspired and written on the heart rather than coercively imposed.[28] *Utopia* presents a postpolitical regime in which we see foreshadowed all attempts to supersede the need for a sovereign political ruler through a rationally and scientifically administered state.

What I hope is clear from this brief sketch of developments in conceptions of political sovereignty is that it is at once a theological and secular story. But also, it is a story in which corporate forms of life other than the nation-state inherently emerge as problematic. The problem is not religion per se. Rather, the problem is one of how, when sovereignty is understood as indivisible and monistic, intermediate and autonomous groups must necessarily appear as a threat or rival. To excavate this dynamic further, I turn to three thinkers who have shaped modern conceptions of the relationship between sovereignty and citizenship: Thomas Hobbes (1588–1679), Jean-Jacques Rousseau (1712–1778), and Georg Wilhelm Friedrich Hegel (1770–1831).

Hobbes, Schmitt, and the Indivisible Sovereignty of the One

Modern discussions of sovereignty operate in the shadow of Hobbes. Debates about the exegesis and context of Hobbes's writing continue. However, I will not focus on the specifics of what Hobbes did or did not mean and the seventeenth-century context of his work. More relevant to the concerns of this book is the reception of Hobbes in contemporary political theology. For this purpose, the work of Carl Schmitt (1888–1985) stands as a crucial interlocutor. Schmitt both looks back to the constitutional debates of the sixteenth and seventeenth centuries, out of which Hobbes emerged, and stimulates a renewed attention to Hobbes in contemporary political theology and critical theory.

On Schmitt's reading, the core purpose of the state for Hobbes is to protect its citizens. Conversely, the primary duty of the citizen is to obey the sovereign. As Schmitt puts it: "The *protego ergo obligo* is the *cogito ergo sum* of the state. . . . Human nature as well as divine right demands its in-

28. J. C. Davies, "Utopianism," in Burns and Goldie, *The Cambridge History of Political Thought*, 341–42.

violable observation."[29] Thus, the relationship between citizens and the sovereign is a reciprocal one: the citizen gives obedience and receives protection in return. The obedience is given to an abstract sovereign who can be monarchical, democratic, or aristocratic in form but whose sovereignty is absolute and indivisible, and transcends the immanent political order. For Schmitt, the mark of sovereignty is the ability to decide the exception. He contends that for Hobbes, "The sovereign is not the *Defensor Pacis* of a peace traceable to God; he is the creator of none other than an earthly peace. He is *Creator Pacis*."[30] In contradistinction to the divine right of kings theory, in this account sovereignty is not derived from God above. Its omnipotence flows up from below because it is based on a covenant entered into between individuals. Echoing my earlier distinction between cosmos and universe, Schmitt argues that "The decisive element of the intellectual construction resides in the fact that this covenant does not accord with mediaeval conceptions of an existing commonwealth forged by God and of a preexistent natural order. The state as order and commonwealth is the product of human reason and human inventiveness and comes about by virtue of the covenant. This covenant is conceived in an entirely individualistic manner. All ties and groupings have been dissolved. Fear brings atomised individuals together."[31]

Here we encounter the anti-Aristotelian element of Hobbes. Humans are not inherently political animals, and there are no "natural" intermediate elements between the individual and the state. All groups, especially the church, must be made to serve the state and are subsidiary to or incorporated under state sovereignty. In Rousseau's estimation, "Of all Christian Authors the philosopher Hobbes is the only one who clearly saw the evil and the remedy, who dared to propose reuniting the two heads of the eagle, and to return everything to political unity, without which no State or Government will ever be well constituted."[32]

In individualist-contractualist theories of sovereignty, from Hobbes onward, the church is the primal enemy, as it is the paradigmatic form of an alternative source of sovereign authority that relativizes the claims of

29. Schmitt, *Concept of the Political*, 52.

30. Schmitt, *The Leviathan in the State Theory of Thomas Hobbes: Meaning and Failure of a Political Symbol*, trans. George Schwab and Erna Hilfstein (Westport, CT: Greenwood, 1996), 33.

31. Schmitt, *The Leviathan*, 33.

32. Jean-Jacques Rousseau, *The Social Contract and Other Later Political Writings*, ed. Victor Gourevitch (Cambridge: Cambridge University Press, 1997), 146.

the political sovereign. For all his espoused Catholicism, Schmitt sees this clearly and is adamant about the need to "de-anarchize" Christianity (i.e., counter the ways Christianity relativizes all forms of political order and radically questions all social and political hierarchies).

For Hobbes, obedience to the sovereign is conditional. If the sovereign does not protect its citizens, then any duty to obey is dissolved: citizens cannot swap the fear of the state of nature for fear of a Moloch. It is the latent right of resistance in Hobbes's account of sovereignty, combined with Hobbes's distinction between public and private belief, that led the political theorist Leo Strauss to postulate that Hobbes vindicated limited government, rendering him a liberal rather than a prophet of authoritarianism. Schmitt agrees, but for Schmitt this is the pathos of Hobbes. Schmitt argues that Hobbes fatally undermined his political philosophy by incorporating the right of freedom of thought and belief into his political system. As Schmitt contends, Hobbes's thought "contained the seed of death that destroyed the mighty leviathan from within and brought about the end of the mortal god" because it created a whole area of independent activity over which the state had no authority.[33] Revealing his anti-Semitism, Schmitt says the Jewish thinkers Baruch Spinoza, Moses Mendelssohn, and Johann Georg Hamann saw this opening and turned it from a crack into a fatal fissure. Schmitt objects to the distinction between inner freedom of faith and outer conformity of behavior and sees the division between them as the conceptual flaw destabilizing Hobbes's theory of state. However, the primary practical problem to be overcome is the "indirect" powers of the church. In Schmitt's view, these powers are reiterated in the nineteenth century in the form of political parties, trade unions, social organizations, and what he calls the "forces of society" acting independently of the state under the banner of freedom of conscience. These "forces of society" threaten the indivisible and transcendent sovereignty of the state.[34] By way of contrast, where Schmitt sees the emasculation of Leviathan, Foucault and Agamben see its triumph. On their account, the constitutional liberal state turns out to be the "biopolitical" state. It no longer needs external threats because, far from constituting a realm set apart from state power, conscience constitutes the extension of state power into the heart, mind, and habits of citizens. Consequently, we no longer need a sovereign Leviathan because we have internalized its ways.

33. Schmitt, *The Leviathan*, 57.
34. Schmitt, *The Leviathan*, 73.

For Schmitt, there is a paradoxical relationship between the mythic symbol of the Leviathan and the Prussian and French process of state building. Hobbes's sea monster becomes the trope for European land powers whose absolutist monarchies, positivist law state, standing armies, and bureaucracies contrast with the seafaring, mercantilist power, and mixed, parliamentary constitution, of England. For Schmitt: "[Hobbes's] concepts contradicted England's concrete political reality."[35] Like Schmitt, Karl Barth sees Hobbes's Leviathan as the mythic embodiment of modern European "political absolutism," from the sun-king Louis XIV to the fascism and Stalinism of his day.[36] In contrast, C. B. Macpherson (1911–1987), who connects the reception of Hobbes with post–World War II developments in European Marxism, takes exactly the opposite view: Hobbes's political philosophy was the ideological articulation of England's seafaring, protocapitalist state. On Macpherson's reading, Hobbes is observing the emergence of a "possessive market society" where everyone is taken to be an autonomous, self-directing individual and not as Aristotle would have it, an animal that can only thrive in some form of sociopolitical fellowship. The need for society is not to realize one's freedom and potential through relationships with others, but to secure one's individual and atomized self-interest.

Critics of Macpherson accused him of giving an anachronistic reading of Hobbes. However, whatever his failings as an interpreter, Macpherson anticipates the connection between centralized political sovereignty and the reemergence of laissez-faire economics under Ronald Reagan and Margaret Thatcher. Drawing on Marx, he pointed to how the state, far from being opposed to the market, is used to buttress property relations and serves the interests of capital. Conversely, he uses Hobbes to unveil the need capitalism has for a strong sovereign authority, something Marx viewed as epiphenomenal.

Rousseau and the Sovereignty of the Many

We find in Rousseau an alternative to Hobbes's attempt to resolve the question of sovereignty. Instead of resolving the rivalry of independent, individual wills by postulating the renunciation of their independence and

35. Schmitt, *The Leviathan*, 85.
36. Karl Barth, *The Christian Life: Church Dogmatics* IV/4, *Lecture Fragments*, trans. Geoffrey Bromiley (Edinburgh: T&T Clark, 1981), 221.

subjection to the one indivisible will of the sovereign, Rousseau envisaged each indivisible will as directed to choose the general will. Rousseau rejected Hobbes because Hobbes's conception of the protection-obligation of the social contract leads not to sovereignty but to despotism: just because the Leviathan produces peace does not make it legitimate. As Rousseau says, there is peace in a dungeon, but that does not make it inviting.[37] For Rousseau: "To renounce one's freedom is to renounce one's quality as man, the rights of humanity, and even its duties. There can be no possible compensation for someone who renounces everything. Such a renunciation is incompatible with the nature of man, and to deprive one's will of all freedom is to deprive one's actions of all morality."[38]

While Rousseau shared Hobbes's conception of sovereignty as inherently indivisible and transcendent, he sought an account of sovereignty that maintained the freedom of the individual and a foundation for political order on something other than egoistic self-interest. Rousseau conceived of sovereignty as a property of a people rather than as an aggregate of individual wills. The unified *volonté générale* expresses the transcendent and indivisible sovereignty of the many. As Rousseau puts it: "Each of us puts his person and his full power in common under the supreme direction of the general will; and in a body we receive each member as an indivisible part of the whole."[39] Each one becomes subsumed within the monistic will of the many.

To make sense of the concept of the general will, it is necessary to locate it within a specific set of theological debates. Rousseau, drawing on a distinctively French contribution to moral and political thought, developed the notion of "generality" as a point midway between particularity and universality. The general interest is good, whereas particular interests are sectional and therefore bad. Justice is linked to generality and opposed to particular exceptions and interests. The backdrop to Rousseau's notion of generality is seventeenth-century debates about predestination.[40] Blaise

37. Rousseau, *Social Contract*, 45.
38. Rousseau, *Social Contract*, 45.
39. Rousseau, *Social Contract*, 50.
40. The original theological problem, beginning with the dispute between Augustine and Pelagius, related to the Pauline assertion in 1 Tim. 2:4 that "God wills that all men be saved." The theological question was how could a general will for universal salvation be related to the election of particular humans for salvation? On this see Patrick Riley, *The General Will before Rousseau: The Transformation of the Divine into the Civic* (Princeton: Princeton University Press, 1986), and Christopher Brooke, "Rousseau's Political

Pascal subsequently developed the theological notion of the general will. He envisaged the particular as leading to disorder and self-love (*amour propre*) and maintained that failure to incline toward *le général* was unjust and depraved.[41] Rousseau transmutes a theological and then moral distinction into a political one. The general will of the citizen to place the good of the republic above his or her particular will becomes the basis not only of good political order but also of the "salvation" of egoistic individuals through converting *amour propre* (self-regarding concern) into *amour de soi* (appropriate concern for oneself). In the process, the church becomes identified as a particular interest that threatens to divide the sovereign, general will of the people. In place of the church, Rousseau promotes the need for a civil religion that bolsters the general will.[42] As with Hobbes, what threatened the indivisibility and transcendence of sovereignty was the public pursuit of private interests, and this is exactly the danger the church represented when conceptualized as a private and particularistic interest.

Hegel and the Sovereignty of the State

Hegel was an avid reader of Rousseau during his seminary education in Tübingen. As it did Hobbes and Rousseau, the question of how to overcome the division of the political community—and, in particular, the role of the church in fostering that division—haunted Hegel. He found Christianity problematic and in his early writings contrasted it with an idealized Greek *Volksreligion* that enabled integration of and harmony between political, cultural, and religious life rather than creating a disjuncture and compartmentalization between a private, otherworldly, and individualistic belief and practice and the obligations of citizenship. Hegel held that Christianity had politically enervating effects, envisaging these as a symptom of a fundamental lack of freedom that only the formation of a rationally administered and socially unified nation-state could overcome.

For Hegel, Christianity teaches people to look to heaven for their fulfillment, and this, in turn, trains them to accommodate themselves to their

---

Philosophy: Stoic and Augustinian Origins," in *The Cambridge Companion to Rousseau*, ed. Patrick Riley (Cambridge: Cambridge University Press, 2001), 94–123.

41. Riley, *General Will before Rousseau*, 19.

42. Rousseau's advocacy of civil religion was itself deeply ambiguous and contradictory. See Ronald Beiner, *Civil Religion: A Dialogue in the History of Political Philosophy* (Cambridge: Cambridge University Press, 2011), 73–83.

political and economic alienation. Thus an otherworldly eschatology is the enemy of political and economic freedom, a theme picked up by Marx. Hegel blamed religion for the rupture of the Holy Roman Empire of the Germanic Nation—a rupture that manifested the more basic problem of the assertion of particularity against universality. In contrast to the unified nation-states of France and Britain, the Holy Roman Empire of Hegel's day was a mosaic of three hundred more-or-less sovereign territories. There were the monarchies of Prussia and Austria, several prince-electors, ninety-four princes (both ecclesiastical and secular), 103 barons, forty prelates, and fifty-one free towns.[43] This gothic constitution that so troubled Bodin and other early modern constitutionalists was still in operation, only now these overlapping and intersecting sites of sovereignty were viewed by Hegel not as a constitutional anomaly but as an anomaly to the spirit of the age. The problem was not conceptual and legal but absolute; it should no longer exist and was an obstacle to the realization of human freedom, and what was needed was a unified nation under a supreme sovereign. For Hegel, the state as a unity is alone the bearer of sovereignty. The medieval society, as a mere conglomeration of factions, does not possess the harmony and unity of functions characteristic of the state.[44]

By way of contrast, those contemporary thinkers who advocate complex space over simple space take a very different view from Hegel's. After the historical experience of totalitarianism, the complex sovereignty of the Holy Roman Empire, where ecclesial and secular rulers limited each other's sovereignty, looks attractive. It is the unified and sacralized nation-state that appears to be the problem, not the solution. In the wake of gulags and death camps, the concerns of Hobbes, Rousseau, and Hegel for a monistic and transcendent sovereign authority with the power to secure and guarantee order against the disorder and chaos of particular interests (whether of the individual or the group) have been reversed. The transcendent sovereign is now the wolf who threatens us. Agamben's work illustrates this inversion. He turns Schmitt on his head so that, far from the sovereign deciding the exception being the answer to the problem of lawlessness, the lawless state of exception—the paradigmatic form of which is

---

43. Bernard Cullen, *Hegel's Social and Political Thought* (Dublin: Gill & Macmillan, 1979), 42.

44. This is not to say that there was an absolute rejection of the medieval inheritance. As Cary Nederman argues, traces of the gothic constitution were incorporated into Hegel's political theory ("Sovereignty, War and the Corporation: Hegel on the Medieval Foundations of the Modern State," *Journal of Politics* 49, no. 2 [1987]: 500-520).

the death camp—has become the true *nomos* of the modern state.[45] Given a state where this kind of exception is the norm, multiplicity and diversity are no longer problems but the solution.

For Hegel, different constitutional forms—monarchy, aristocracy, and democracy—must be understood as historically contingent.[46] Given the evolution of history, these forms are inevitably subsumed within and superseded by the modern state and its realization of universality in historical existence. Divisions based on substantive difference are converted into internal differentiation within the state. Hegel divides the powers of the state into three: legislature, executive, and crown. However, this division is one of functional differentiation and does not represent any division of sovereignty. It is not so much a separation of powers as a division of labor. As Hegel puts it: "Where there is an *organic* relation subsisting between members, not parts, then each member by fulfilling the function of its own sphere is *eo ipso* maintaining the others; what each fundamentally aims at and achieves in maintaining itself is the maintenance of the others."[47] The state is now the substantive unity, and all particular powers are simply moments and different manifestations of its univocal nature.

For Hegel, the hereditary monarch is the personification of the constitutional state's indivisible and organic unity. On one reading, Hegel's account of hereditary monarchy is christological in shape and origin: to manifest its universal presence in history and move beyond an abstract idea to objective realization, the unity of the state needs realizing in a particular individual.[48] The monarch is a kind of god-human; through the monarch, the implicit unity of the universal spirit and the particular natures and interests of civil society become real and assume a definite existence. The monarch, being hereditary, had an unfounded, noncontractual basis to her sovereignty, and so the authority of the sovereign transcended the immanent political order.

If the monarch is the personification of the divine will, it is the nation-state that sublates religion because it becomes the vehicle for fulfilling the universal element in the human spirit. Within Hegel's overall schema, the state replaces the church as the bearer of salvation wherein a people can re-

---

45. Giorgio Agamben, *State of Exception*, trans. Kevin Attell (Chicago: University of Chicago Press, 2005).

46. G. W. F. Hegel, *Hegel's Philosophy of Right*, trans. T. M. Knox (Oxford: Oxford University Press, 1967), 177 (#273).

47. Hegel, *Hegel's Philosophy of Right*, 188 (#286).

48. Hegel, *Hegel's Philosophy of Right*, 185 (#280).

alize their freedom and catholicity/universality. For Hegel, "The state is the divine will."[49] Christianity is but one stage along the way in the realization of freedom in history. The organic unity of the state and its actualization of freedom is the fulfillment of the divine will. It is a manifestation of the kingdom of God within history, as opposed to an eschatological kingdom that interrupts history.[50] The unity of the state overcomes the division of space and time. Rejecting the "two swords" tradition that stems from Gelasius, Hegel is highly critical of the view of the church as the vestibule of the kingdom of God and the state representing the earthly kingdom. For Hegel, this is a false dichotomy. Church and state should not stand in opposition to each other. While there is a proper difference of form, truth and rationality are the content of both.[51] The state, of which the church is a part, is not a mere "mechanism" or a means to an end. Rather, to participate in the state is to participate in the rational life of self-conscious freedom. Beyond Hegel stands the political theology of Metz, Moltmann, Sölle, and some liberation theologies. They propose a commitment to praxis within history as a means of anticipating the universal kingdom of God in specific social, economic, and political forms of order. This framework owes as much to Hegel as it does to Marx and Ernst Bloch.[52]

Regarding political theory, Hegel looks backward and forward. He looks back toward Hobbes and Rousseau and the assertion of a transcendent sovereign authority, and forward toward the division of governmental powers. For Hegel, the state is both one and sovereign. Each of its parts contributes to the whole, with no need for a single transcendent sovereign authority to hold together particular interests. The rationally and juridically administered state enables particular interests to be transcended. That said, the political system Hegel envisages builds in and accepts a plurality of interests, though they are subsumed within a unified public sphere. This public sphere represents the arena of free and universal action within which to realize authentic human being. However, Hegel's sovereign political system can also be seen to contain the seeds of Foucault's panoptical state.

49. Hegel, *Hegel's Philosophy of Right*, 166 (#270).

50. Paul Lakeland, *The Politics of Salvation: The Hegelian Idea of the State* (Albany: State University of New York Press, 1984), 53.

51. Hegel, *Hegel's Philosophy of Right*, 170-71 (#270).

52. The church does not disappear for Hegel; instead, it is divided into state churches, which support the state and provide an integrating function, and voluntary sects, such as Quakers, who are reduced to being part of civil society and tolerated by the state (Hegel, *Hegel's Philosophy of Right*, 168 [#270]).

The sovereignty of a single public authority (such as a monarch) remains, but this sovereignty disperses within a field of relations, discourses, and technologies such that the sovereign state exercises its authority over all aspects of a population's life. In doing so, it habituates those within the state to conform to its order. Power is no longer exercised over the body by an external authority but becomes "biopower" exercised within, through, and around the body such that sovereignty becomes an internalized and self-administered regime of "governmentality."[53]

More directly, Hegel anticipates much of what emerges in the post–World War II European nation-state. While some interpret Hegel as the progenitor of the communist and fascist totalitarian state, a better way of seeing him is as anticipating that all-encompassing hybrid, the liberal-capitalist/social-democratic nation-state. Political parties; a single public and administrative authority (*Polizei*); a two-chamber legislature; public opinion; a constitutional ruler; organized corporate/professional interest groups (*Korporationen*); *Stände*/class interests (although notoriously, Hegel did not include the working class among these); a nonpartisan, merito-cratic, and well-educated civil service; public education; and public office as a site of rule-bound and accountable obligation rather than personal fiat—all these contribute to and constitute but are sublated within the rational political order that represents the guarantor and objectification of universal human freedom.

Custom and the Mediation of Consent

Hobbes, Rousseau, and Hegel do not represent the only voices in modern political thought, and the interpretations of them given here are contestable. However, their work does illustrate how corporate forms of life—of which the church is paradigmatic—become problematic when sovereignty is understood as indivisible, monistic, and transcendent. At the same time, this is as much a theological problem as it is a problem of political philosophy. There are other theological and philosophical resources available for thinking about this problem, ones in which the church—or any corporate or culturally distinct entity—appears not as anathema but as a legitimate and proper part of a political order. These other resources tend to begin not

---

53. Nikolas Rose, *Governing the Soul: The Shaping of the Private Self*, 2nd ed. (London: Free Association Books, 1999).

with a Trinitarian doctrine of God but with human nature and, more specifically, with the recovery of an Aristotelian sense of humans as political animals and attention to customary practices, gift relations, *phronēsis*, and the traditions necessary to secure a common life. Such a beginning point is in stark contrast to most modern political thought—particularly in its "right-wing" and libertarian strands—that not only begins with the individual as the primary point of reference but also sees tradition, custom, practical reason, and gift relations as of the past and in conflict with what is new or modern. The Weberian rationalist-legal order that is the dominant political imaginary shaping both "left" and "right" banishes tradition, custom, and gift relations to the realm of the private. In doing so, it simultaneously renders practical reasoning an illegitimate and illegible means of public deliberation. What the modern state requires are universal and uniform modes of rationality on which to base standardized and centralized forms of measurement, taxation, policy, and administration.

For medieval constitutionalists, custom-mediated consent and established historical practices—such as the use of common land or sanctuary practices—set limits on what could or could not be done by a sovereign authority.[54] Tacit within the medieval view was a right of resistance if customary rights were violated. This view carried over into the early modern period: a case in point is debates in Stuart England about the "ancient constitution" and the demand for the king to recognize and respect the liberties and privileges corporate bodies (e.g., chartered cities, guilds, universities, and ecclesial institutions) enjoyed by custom and precedent. These customary practices were not set in stone, but rather, following the pattern of common law, they constituted arenas of negotiation and discretionary judgment. The capacity to make appropriate, prudential judgment depended on apprenticeship into particular habits of action and contexts of application. Customary rights allowed for the recognition of distinct forms of self-governing association (i.e., political associations that could claim rights without claiming a full measure of autonomy). As political theorist James Tully notes: "The convention of the continuity of a people's

---

54. Medieval constitutionalists were building on distinctions in Roman law between *ius scriptum* and *ius non scriptum*. The principal text that justified custom as legally binding was taken to be *Digest* 1.3.32.1, which was ascribed to the emperor Julian. See P. G. Stein, "Roman Law," in *The Cambridge History of Medieval Political Thought, c. 350–c. 1450*, ed. J. H. Burns (Cambridge: Cambridge University Press, 1988), 45. See also Howell Lloyd, "Constitutionalism," in Burns, *The Cambridge History of Medieval Political Thought, c. 350–c. 1450*, 267–68.

customary ways and forms of government into new forms of constitutional associations with others is the oldest in Western jurisprudence. . . .
It is the spirit of ancient constitutionalism, expressing the view that customs and ways of people are the manifestation of their free agreement.
To discontinue them without their explicit consent would thus breach the
convention of consent."[55] In Tully's view, Hobbes, Locke, and Kant—and,
we might add, Rousseau and Hegel—represent theories and justifications
of discontinuity.

The "convention of consent" was partly derived from the principle of
Roman law *Quod omnes similiter tangit ab omnibus comprobetur* (Justin-
ian's Code VI.59.5.2), or *quod omnes tangit* for short: what touches all ought
to be tested or approved by all. In practice, this meant that all those who
have legal rights at stake in a decision are entitled to be consulted in the
decision, or at the very least, be present.[56] The modern disability rights
movement's parsing of this principle captures its spirit: "nothing about
us without us." In early medieval Europe, the principle was particularly
applied to taxpayers, and formed the basis of both houses of Parliament
in England. From the thirteenth century onward, when the monarch
needed to raise money, he gathered both the aristocracy, in what became
the House of Lords, and the gentry and freehold commoners, in what became the House of Commons, to consult them on the uses to which their
money was put. Just decisions, particularly about the use of money for
things that affected everyone, required the representation and consent
of all the relevant interests in the decision-making process. The modern
form of the British parliamentary system emerges from a fierce debate in
the seventeenth century, mainly led by Puritans, which radicalized the
principle into a demand that what touched all required the direct consent
of all.[57] It was this principle that formed part of the legal status of the people as the basis of sovereignty discussed in the next chapter. The upshot
of its radicalization was that government by law for the people became
government of and by the people through law. This same principle lay

55. James Tully, *Strange Multiplicity: Constitutionalism in an Age of Diversity* (Cambridge: Cambridge University Press, 1995), 125.

56. Gaines Post, "A Roman Legal Theory of Consent, *Quod Omnes Tangit*, in Medieval Representation," *Wisconsin Law Review* 1 (1950): 66–78, and Arthur Monahan, *Consent, Coercion, and Limit: The Medieval Origins of Parliamentary Democracy* (Montreal:
McGill-Queen's University Press, 1987), 97–111.

57. Danielle Allen, *Talking to Strangers: Anxieties of Citizenship Since Brown v. Board
of Education* (Chicago: University of Chicago Press, 2004), 7–75.

behind the rallying cry of the American Revolution: "no taxation without representation." As we shall see, there is a grotesque irony in the demand by American colonists that this principle of consent be applied to them but was then denied by these same colonists to the indigenous peoples, the sovereignty of which the British Crown had already recognized through a series of treaties.[58]

Indivisibility and Imperialism

As just noted, Western conceptions of political order that build on rather than reject medieval conceptions of sovereignty take time, gift relations, place, tradition, practical reason, and customary practices as having public force. They thereby create greater scope for dialogue and ad hoc commensurability with non-Eurocentric and aboriginal conceptions of political order and so create the possibility of forging more diverse, "glocal" enactments of citizenship.[59] This claim may seem outlandish, but to illustrate its basis, we can observe a curious parallel between the conquest of Italian city-states by Napoleon Bonaparte and the perception of the status of Native American "republics" during the process of US nation building and westward expansion. Part of the justification given by supporters of Napoleon for his conquest of the millennia-old republic of Venice in 1797 was that it was primitive, brutal, and in need of dismantling so it could be incorporated into a modern, rational political order that accorded with historical progress. Likewise, the autochthonous peoples in North America were taken to be a relic of an earlier, "savage" stage in human development in need of "liberation" by modernization and assimilation into a singular constitutional order. This kind of view contrasts with the pre-1776 approach established in law by the British Crown through numerous treaties with indigenous peoples.[60] The approach the British Crown took derived from one developed by Bartolus of Saxoferrato for the recognition of the Italian city-states as sovereign entities by the Holy Roman Empire in the fourteenth century.[61] In the Bartolian approach (which, alongside Roman

58. Jedediah Purdy, *The Meaning of Property: Freedom, Community, and the Legal Imagination* (New Haven: Yale University Press, 2011), 70–71.

59. James Tully, *Public Philosophy in a New Key*, vol. 2, *Imperialism and Civic Freedom* (Cambridge: Cambridge University Press, 2008), 243–309.

60. Tully, *Strange Multiplicity*, 118.

61. Tully, *Strange Multiplicity*, 120.

law, can be traced back to Augustine and Aquinas), customary practices of self-government had the status of common law and needed recognition as having continuing validity.[62]

The dismissive attitude toward earlier forms of political order, whether medieval European or aboriginal, was of a piece with notions of constitutional order as singular and sovereignty as transcendent and indivisible. Tully draws out how the rejection of constitutional pluralism and an emanatory and distributed vision of sovereignty had its analogue in the rejection of customary practices and traditions as means of mediating consent in processes of colonialism. He states: "The vision of modern constitutionalism legitimates the modernizing processes of discipline, rationalization and state building that are designed to create in practice the cultural and institutional uniformity identified as modern in theory. These processes include the construction of centralized and uniform constitutional systems over the legal and political pluralism of early modern Europe, the implementation of similar systems by European colonization, the extension of these by post-colonial states over Indigenous populations and customary law, the imposition of linguistic and cultural uniformity, and countless programmes of naturalization, assimilation and eugenics to construct modern states and subjects."[63]

On this account, the internal colonization of regional, religious, and other forms of association and self-government in modern projects of nation building was the analogue of external programs of colonial subjugation. Tully argues that from Locke to Kant and onward, aboriginal and medieval political orders were the "other" against which modern social contract theories of political order defined themselves. The delegitimization and dismantling of both were perceived as a morally and historically necessary project so that "mankind" might progress in "manners" toward a universal vision of cosmopolitan citizenship. They were also necessary to dispossess those whose claims to the use and title of common land and other common-pool resources derived from customary practices and traditions rather than a written legal contract. The post-Marxist theorists Michael Hardt and Antonio Negri argue that the expropriation of the commons, the imposition and defense of an absolutist conception of private property, and what they call the "modernity-coloniality-racist complex" constitute the basis of modern liberal republicanism and cosmopolitan

---

62. See especially, Aquinas, *Summa Theologiae* I-II, Question 97.
63. Tully, *Strange Multiplicity*, 82.

conceptions of citizenship.[64] While Hardt and Negri direct their critique primarily toward capitalist forms of modernity, Martin Buber presents a trenchant critique of state communist and state socialist forms of modernization, arguing that the destruction of the customary and traditional basis of common ownership such as the Russian *mir* was intrinsic to the development of such forms.[65]

The work of John Locke (1632-1704) illustrates and exemplifies the broader connections between visions of modernization as progress, regimes of private property, and justifications of colonialism. In his case, a protoliberal vision of modernization is put forward.[66] In contrast to those who recognized indigenous peoples as having jurisdiction over the territories Europeans came to settle, in his *Two Treatises on Government* Locke developed arguments to reject these claims.[67] In the first place, Locke locates the aboriginal peoples as existing in a "state of nature" and thus at a primitive stage of human history in contrast to "civilized" Europeans. Such a condition had political and economic implications. Politically, rather than existing as self-governing, sovereign peoples, they lived as individuals, in nonpolitical forms of association. Economically, their only property rights related to what they hunted and gathered and not the land on which this activity took place. As Tully notes, two hugely significant consequences follow from Locke's conception of the state of nature. First, Europeans do not need to form treaties with the aboriginal peoples, as there is no sovereign authority with which to deal. Moreover, there could be no objection to European settlement, and if there was, then the indigenous populations may be punished as "wild savage beasts." Second, Europeans can take over the land they want without the consent of the people already there because anyone can appropriate uncultivated land.

---

64. Michael Hardt and Antonio Negri, *Commonwealth* (Cambridge, MA: Belknap Press of Harvard University Press, 2009). See also Tully, *Public Philosophy*, 249-67.

65. Buber, *Paths in Utopia*. For a parallel critique see Scott, *Seeing like a State*, 193-222.

66. In addition to Tully, the connections between liberalism and justifications of colonialism are also explored in Bhikhu Parekh, "Liberalism and Colonialism: A Critique of Locke and Mill," in *The Decolonization of Imagination: Culture, Knowledge, and Power*, ed. Jan Nederveen Pieterse and Bhikhu Parekh (London: Zed, 1995), 81-98, and Anthony Pagden, "Human Rights, Natural Rights, and Europe's Imperial Legacy," *Political Theory* 31, no. 2 (2003): 171-99.

67. On Locke's vested interests in such a project, see David Armitage, "John Locke, Carolina, and the 'Two Treatises of Government,'" *Political Theory* 32, no. 5 (2004): 602-27, and Barbara Arneil, *John Locke and America: The Defense of English Colonialism* (Oxford: Oxford University Press, 1996).

Underlying this argument was Locke's theory of original appropriation whereby property claims derive from mixing one's labor with what is used. Dominion fell to those able to cultivate land to its fullest capacity: an argument that, as Tully points out, specifically favors European agriculturalists over autochthonous hunter-gatherers and pastoralists.[68] Europeans were not dispossessing aboriginal peoples; they were undertaking a task that a barbarian population had failed to fulfill. Lastly, Locke justifies the nonrecognition of the title and sovereignty of aboriginal peoples on the grounds that they would be better off as a result of European settlement, as they can progress away from their state of nature and benefit from assimilation to a commercial system of agriculture and the protection of private property. Locke's view came to be enshrined in US law as exemplified in the 1823 Supreme Court ruling in the *Johnson v. M'Intosh* case.[69] More broadly, ever since Locke, economic development—and assimilation to an economic and political order seen as more advanced and rational—has been a powerful and frequent justification for the forced assimilation of colonized peoples.

Trinitarian and Augustinian Responses

Hegel's transmutation of salvation history into salvation through the processes of history provoked a theological counterreaction. The theological recovery of the finitude of time and space, the otherness of the divine, and therefore the creaturely limits of human action within history came to focus on a restatement of Trinitarian theology. In Protestant theology, the work of Karl Barth (1886-1968) is central to this restatement. In Roman Catholic theology, alongside Henri de Lubac (1896-1991) and Hans Urs von Balthasar (1905-1988), the work of Karl Rahner and Catherine LaCugna sparked renewed attention to the Trinity. The intellectual *ressourcement* of modern theology these theologians catalyzed through their engagements with Scripture, patristic thought, and the development of a constructive Trinitarian theology enabled the legacy of nominalism and voluntarism to be challenged.

With the recovery of Trinitarian theology, the exercise of a sovereign will ceases to be the basis of good order. Instead, good order is constituted

---

68. Tully, *Strange Multiplicity*, 73-74.
69. See Purdy, *The Meaning of Property*, 67-86.

through participation in right relationships as encountered and empowered through participation in the perichoretic communion of Father, Son, and Holy Spirit. In place of images of political rulers (emperors, kings, or lords), music, drama, and dance become more common analogies for the nature of God. In such accounts, God is no distant sovereign but a loving Creator who is intimately involved in creation through the ongoing work of the Son and the Spirit. In the light of this kind of God, monarchical, absolute, and indivisible claims to political sovereignty that override the freedom and dignity of the one, the few, or the many are revealed as inverted parodies of the divine nature and the true order of being, which is one of harmonious difference in relation.[70] Likewise, humans are not monadic individuals but persons in relation, with a status above and beyond any immanent social, economic, or political claims upon them.

The supposed link between monotheism and authoritarianism gave impetus to the felt need for a restatement of Trinitarian theology. For example, Moltmann sees a direct link between non-Trinitarian conceptions of God and the legitimization and sacralization of domination. For Moltmann the doctrine of the Trinity "is developed as a theological doctrine of freedom" that points toward "a community of men and women without supremacy and without subjection."[71] Key in directing attention to the Trinity as a way of countering political absolutism was Erik Peterson's response to Carl Schmitt's 1922 essay *Political Theology*. In his *Monotheism as a Political Problem* (1935), Peterson attacked the theological roots of Schmitt's theory of sovereignty, refuting the claim that sovereignty was defined—in a way that was structurally analogous to God—by the sovereign's location within and outside the law, and so, like God, the sovereign possessed the power to decide the exception to the rule of law. Following Peterson, a social model of the Trinity became a way to counter domination and violence justified on the grounds of monotheism. Some went so far as to see the Trinity as itself the basis for a social program.[72] For example, Moltmann saw a personalism grounded in the doctrine of the Trinity providing a middle way between the collectivism of communism and the individualism of liberal

---

70. As outlined in chapter 1, contemporary Trinitarian approaches pick up on and echo the passion narrative, which inverts and parodies Greco-Roman conceptions of sovereignty.

71. Jürgen Moltmann, *The Trinity and the Kingdom of God: The Doctrine of God*, trans. Margaret Kohl (London: SCM, 1981), 192.

72. Miroslav Volf, "'The Trinity Is Our Social Program': The Doctrine of the Trinity and the Shape of Social Engagement," *Modern Theology* 14, no. 3 (1998): 403-23.

capitalism.[73] However, such a sentiment can be as theologically problematic as that which it replaces, for it merely replicates the problem of presuming a mimesis between the divine nature and particular forms of social and political life, albeit more egalitarian and less oppressive ones. Here we encounter the question of whether we can ever legitimately draw direct correlations between divine and human nature.

The emphasis on the Trinity as the basis for a social program is theologically naïve. On the one hand, as Hegel's appropriation of the Trinity illustrates, the doctrine of the Trinity has been aligned with numerous forms of absolutism. On the other hand, monotheism can be used to resist political absolutism. As exemplified in the Barmen Declaration, Karl Barth's emphasis on the sovereignty of God as mediated through the lordship of Christ provided the basis for challenging the totalitarian claims of the Nazis. The lordship of Christ relativized all other claims to sovereignty. For Barth, it is the vocation of the church, as the community of faithful witness, to say yes to that which affirms, renews, and anticipates the fulfillment of the order revealed by the life, death, and resurrection of Jesus Christ. In saying yes to that, the church must say no, in both belief and practice, to those forms of rule and patterns of life that disorientate and destroy the created order as recapitulated in the Christ event. The problem is not monotheism per se, but the nature and orientation of the rule one serves. By serving themselves and not Christ, humans become subject to what Barth called the "lordless powers."[74] For Barth, the primary embodiments of the lordless powers were Leviathan (all forms of political absolutism) and Mammon (the idolatry of money, material possessions, property, and resources).[75] Against the disorder produced by the lordless powers stands the rule (*basileia*) of divine order.

The fundamental theological challenge Hegel poses, and beyond Hegel, all immanent claims to ground sovereignty, is one of time. The real challenge is the denial of an eschaton or rather the historicization of eschatology and thence the absolutization and divinization of the finite. As noted in chapter 4, if this time is all there is, then politics has no limits, as it has to bear the full weight of human meaning and possibilities. The political theorist Sheldon Wolin recognized that the great gift of Christianity to politics is time and, in particular, the relativization of historical

---

73. Moltmann, *Trinity and the Kingdom*, 199-200.
74. Barth, *The Christian Life*, 213-33.
75. Barth, *The Christian Life*, 233.

time.[76] Christians have time to hope and live in a time when change is possible and in which the communion of saints connects past and present.[77] Eschatology disqualifies any absolute claims of a political sovereign to shape human life and reasserts the need for a thicket of institutional and social forms in the wider body politic. A complex, pluralistic, cultural, and political space is theologically necessary to hold open the existence of *times* (e.g., festivals, liturgical events), *spaces* (e.g., family, church, trade unions, the commons), and *practices* (e.g., social customs such as greetings and gift exchange) that are not subject to total determination by state or market processes. On this account, part of the church's vocation as a *res publica* is to bear witness within this age to the possibilities of a common life that is in excess of and beyond this or that worldly order. Lung-like, the church breathes the works of the Spirit within any given spatiotemporal order, thereby oxygenating the work of being human.

Within the kind of Augustinian vision of politics that has become a key strand of modern Christian political thought, politics is about negotiating what is necessary for a breathable earthly peace. It is not an end in itself but serves an end—communion with God—beyond itself. Any idea that there can be a Christian society or nation needs to be treated with suspicion, as is any project of salvation or human fulfillment through politics. A confessional political theology, as distinct from a project of political theology that instrumentalizes the theological in the service of the political, must resist the temptation to render the prevailing hegemony as natural or ontologically foundational. All political formations and structures of governance are provisional and tend toward oppression, while at the same time, whether it be a democracy or a monarchy, any political formation may display just judgments and enable the limited good of a penultimate peace through the pursuit of common objects of love.

Sovereignty Distributed: A Consociational Approach

If the recovery of Trinitarian theology represents one countervoluntarist stream of theology, there is also another countermovement. This other

76. Sheldon Wolin, *Politics and Vision: Continuity and Innovation in Western Political Thought* (Princeton: Princeton University Press, 2004), 111-15.

77. Stanley Hauerwas, "Democratic Time: Lessons Learned from Yoder and Wolin," in *The State of the University: Academic Knowledges and the Knowledge of God* (Oxford: Blackwell, 2007), 147-64.

stream of Christian reflection begins not with the doctrine of God but with what it means to be a creature, and rather than reject medieval notions of sovereignty, it builds on them. This approach emerges out of reflection on the rich scriptural and theological motif of covenant and how this generates conceptions of federalism (from the Latin, *foedus*, meaning covenant or agreement). An emphasis on a plurality of covenantal associations combining together can be termed either "confederalist" or "consociationalist." I use the latter, as it brings to the fore the importance of dynamic patterns of sociality to democratic politics, whereas confederalism emphasizes process and structure. "Consociation" is a term derived from the work of Althusius and means the art of living together.[78] In contrast to Hobbes, Rousseau, and Hegel, Althusius allows for the pluralization of political order so it accommodates the diversity of associational life, whether economic, familial, or religious. In his account, to be a political animal is not to be a citizen of a unitary, hierarchically determined political society. Nor is it to participate in a polity in which all authority derives from a transcendent, monistic point of sovereignty. Rather, it is to be a participant in a plurality of interdependent, self-organized associations that together constitute a consociational or confederal polity. Echoing the work of the Spirit, in a confederal polity, commonality does not require the erasure of difference. The singularity and specificity of each are constitutive of the commonwealth of all. Such an approach entails a strong affirmation that there is a commonwealth, and it is this affirmation that sharply distinguishes it from the antipolitical visions of "minarchist" and libertarian approaches.

In a consociational commonwealth, federalism is societal and political rather than simply administrative or governmental.[79] A consociational framework differs from constitutional federalism as a way in which to limit the governmental power exercised by a sovereign authority (as exemplified in the dominant interpretations of the US Constitution). This latter approach leaves undisturbed the top-down, transcendent, and monistic

---

78. He states: "Politics is the art of associating (*consciandi*) men for the purpose of establishing, cultivating, and conserving social life among them." Johannes Althusius, *Politica*, ed. and trans. Frederick Carney (Indianapolis: Liberty Fund, 1995 [1964]), 17. It is probable that Althusius derived his use of the term from Cicero (*De re publica* 1.25-27), although in Cicero's usage its meaning is restricted to the legal bond for the organized conduct of public life. See Huegelin, *Early Modern Concepts*, 79.

79. James Skillen, "The Development of Calvinistic Political Theory in the Netherlands, with Special Reference to the Thought of Herman Dooyeweerd" (PhD diss., Duke University, 1973), 191-217.

nature of sovereignty. By contrast, consociationalism/confederalism envisages authority arising from the whole or commonweal, which itself is constituted from multiple consociations federated together for shared purposes.[80] For Althusius, sovereignty is an assemblage that emerges through and is grounded upon a process of mutual communication between covenantal associations and their reciprocal pursuit of common goods and in which unity of the whole (i.e., a common life) is sought as a noninstrumental good. Rather than being secured through either legislative procedure, the transcendent nature of sovereign authority, a centralized monopoly of governmental power, or the formation of a unitary public sphere premised on a homogeneous rational discourse, this unity is premised on the quality of cooperation and relationship building. The definitional judgment of the sovereign is not deciding the exception but the discernment and weighing up of common goods that emerge through the complex weave of social relations and customary practices that constitute the body politic and then adjudicating what to do to fulfill these goods. On a consociational account, sovereign authorities should not impose order but discover it. As laid out in the next chapter, such a process of discovery necessitates ongoing forms of deliberation and identification between those in authority and the people. In discovering a *res publica*/public thing such as a university, church, or trade union, the sovereign encounters something the state did not create but must recognize. The sovereign may well give juridical form to the public thing, but this does not create the public nature of this corporate form of life. These public things do not derive their public status from the state; rather, the state recognizes in law that here is something that has a meaning, purpose, and internal goods that contribute to the commonweal and needs coordinating with other public things, but which do not depend on the state for their existence. In encountering and recognizing these other public things, the state also realizes its limits. Claims to be the source and determine the form of all other public things are totalitarian.

The consociational approach is not as alien as it may at first appear to be. Hobbes's and Hegel's theories are one thing, historical practice is another. The medieval gothic order did not wholly disappear with the advent

---

80. As Robert Latham notes: "While commentators since the seventeenth century have read Althusius as an early formulator of ideas about popular sovereignty, they have generally overlooked how he was actually vesting sovereignty or supreme power in the webs of relations that shape the possibilities for agency across a body politic . . . rather than a collective of persons" ("Social Sovereignty," *Theory, Culture and Society* 17, no. 4 [2000]: 6).

of a "Westphalian" order of nation-states. Rather, it was displaced and redescribed so that forms of political community became relocated and renamed as "economic" or "social." For example, the joint-stock trading company—the early modern archetype of the contemporary capitalist firm—was an explicitly political community based on the concept of the *corpus politicum et corporatum* or *communitas perpetua* that went back to Roman law. The paradigmatic example of the early modern mercantile "republic" was the East India Trading Company, which, as a colonial proprietor, "did what early modern governments did: erect and administer law; collect taxes; provide protection; inflict punishment; perform stateliness; regulate economic, religious, and civic life; conduct diplomacy and wage war; make claims to jurisdiction over land and sea; and cultivate authority over and obedience from those people subject to its command."[81]

The nature of the company as a political and sovereign institution—and of all analogous company-states—is viewed as either anomalous or denied. Such entities are labeled "economic," not political. For example, the World Bank is bound by its charter to deal only with economic or technical issues, yet its work has direct political consequences and severely affects the actions of other sovereign authorities. Contrary to how it is often presented, legal and political pluralism is the norm rather than the exception in contemporary societies. Most nations are a series of overlapping political associations with varying degrees of self-government. Various local, national, regional, and international legal jurisdictions intersect them, and they deploy strategies of devolution, decentralization, federation, cross-border linkages, and other ways of recognizing "nonterritorial" collective autonomy in order to navigate "internal" plurality. Sovereignty is an assemblage that opens up different conditions and possibilities for agency, depending on where one is located. Moreover, the relationship between the governed and regimes of governance is never one of unilateral control: it is always a more open-ended negotiation involving the interplay of different stagings of the people and the procedures and institutions of governance.[82]

---

81. Philip Stern, *The Company-State: Corporate Sovereignty and the Early Modern Foundations of the British Empire in India* (Oxford: Oxford University Press, 2012), 4–6. We may speculate that firms like the East India Trading Company are the point of transition from the medieval, city-based mercantile republics such as Venice and Genoa to the modern mercantile republics that now take the form of transnational corporations such as Halliburton, Honda, or Apple.

82. Tully, *Public Philosophy*, 279.

On many fronts, a consociationalist position seems to be an increasingly prevalent, if tacit, recommendation. For example, in response to processes of globalization and the increasing cultural diversity of nation-states, some legal theorists are advocating what amounts to a more consociational approach.[83] In the realm of social policy, there is a shift toward the advocacy of the cogovernance and coproduction of services such as education and health care. With this move, there is recognition that the state and the market do not define or exhaust the parameters of provision. Noncommercial and self-governing institutions must be involved in the construction and delivery of public goods. Beyond the world of social policy and legal theory, Elinor Ostrom's work on "polycentric governance" as a form of economic and political management can also be seen as an example of the consociational approach sketched here. Her work highlights the complex interweaving of state, market, and forms of self-organized and self-governing associations in policing and managing common-pool resources such as fisheries, forests, irrigation systems, and groundwater basins.[84] The most radical and thorough, if fragile, experiment in consociational democracy is the polity established by the Kurds in northern Syria.[85] Originally established by the Kurdish leader Abdullah Öcalan (now held as a political prisoner in Turkey), its form was influenced by the work of the radical democrat and ecologist Murray Bookchin (1921–2006). The "Rojava Revolution" established a fully confederal polity. It is organized and structured from the bottom up into communes (comparable to the parish), neighborhoods of communes (similar to a diocese), and cantons or districts, constituted by

83. See Brian Z. Tamanaha, "Understanding Legal Pluralism: Past to Present, Local to Global," *Sydney Law Review* 30, no. 3 (2008): 375–411, and William Twining, *General Jurisprudence: Understanding Law from a Global Perspective* (Cambridge: Cambridge University Press, 2009). For an earlier theorization of international order as potentially "neomedieval" in form, see Hedley Bull, *The Anarchical Society* (London: Macmillan, 1977).

84. Through numerous case studies, Ostrom demonstrates that addressing the efficient management of common resources, either through their marketization via the imposing of property rights or through centralized control by the state, can have adverse consequences for resource management. This is because both marketization and centralization undermine the capacity of people to govern themselves and lead to the depletion and destruction of important forms of local wisdom and the institutions and patterns of relationship that sustain this knowledge over time. Elinor Ostrom, *Governing the Commons: The Evolution of Institutions for Collective Action* (Cambridge: Cambridge University Press, 1990).

85. As I write this, it is under military assault by the Turkish government.

a city and its surrounding area (analogous to a province), which can then be federated. This democratic confederal structure explicitly eschews any commitment to an ethnically or religiously homogenous nation-state and allows for a multiethnic, multifaith, internally differentiated polity, and it is one in which women have full equality in leadership.[86] Other civic, nonplace-based consociations such as youth organizations and women's groups also have a say in the deliberative assemblies.

In political theology, there is a set of theologically and philosophically diverse yet interlinked traditions that develop a consociational conception of sovereignty.[87] If Althusius is their progenitor, a vital mediator is the German legal historian Otto von Gierke (1841–1921).[88] Gierke directly influenced the "English Pluralists," such as the Anglican John Neville Figgis, and the subsequent development of "Guild Socialism," exemplified in the early work of Harold Laski and G. D. H. Cole, key intellectuals in the

---

86. See Michael Knapp, Anja Flach, and Ercan Ayboğa, *Revolution in Rojava: Democratic Autonomy and Women's Liberation in Syrian Kurdistan*, trans. Janet Biehl (London: Pluto, 2016), and Meredith Tax, *A Road Unforeseen: Women Fight the Islamic State* (New York: Bellevue Literary, 2016), 155–77.

87. Standard accounts of consociational democracy build on the pioneering work of the Dutch political theorist Arend Lijphart. Lijphart's initial reflections were born out of trying to understand the paradox of the Netherlands, which, on the one hand, had social and religious cleavages, yet, on the other, was a notable example of a stable democracy (*The Politics of Accommodation: Pluralism and Democracy in the Netherlands*, 2nd ed. [Berkeley: University of California Press, 1975]). However, Lijphart's conception reduces consociationalism to a form of statecraft and a technocratic means for creating a consensus between a "cartel of elites" through engineering power-sharing, voting, and constitutional arrangements. See Arend Lijphart, *Democracy in Plural Societies: A Comparative Exploration* (New Haven: Yale University Press, 1980), and Lijphart, *Thinking about Democracy: Power Sharing and Majority Rule in Theory and Practice* (London: Routledge, 2008). Lijphart's work has been much criticized, mainly for lack of conceptual clarity and theoretical depth and its empirical inaccuracies. (For a summary of these, see M. P. C. M. Van Schendelen, "Consociational Democracy: The Views of Arend Lijphart and Collected Criticisms," *Political Science Reviewer* 15, no. 1 [1985]: 143–83.) Part of the problem with Lijphart's approach is that he does not pay sufficient heed to what originally inspired it: the work of Althusius and its subsequent development in Roman Catholic and Calvinist political thought. In short, for all the richness of Lijphart's insights, he turns a diverse tradition of political thought into a technocratic set of procedures.

88. Otto von Gierke, *Community in Historical Perspective*, ed. Antony Black, trans. Mary Fischer (Cambridge: Cambridge University Press, 1990). On the reception history of Althusius and the rival interpretations of his political theory, see Stephen Grabill, *Rediscovering the Natural Law in Reformed Theological Ethics* (Grand Rapids: Eerdmans, 2006), 122–30.

development of the British Labour Party.[89] Schmitt criticized the English Pluralists and Guild Socialists, as he saw them as the alternative and threat to the position he was trying to establish. They advocated a decentralized economy based on the noncapitalistic principles of cooperation and mutuality and proposed a radical, pluralistic conception of the state. Sovereignty was not something that could be appropriated by a single agency or institution. Rather it emanated from differentiated and distributed authorities that compose the body politic. In distinction from the anarcho-syndicalists (and contemporary exponents of spontaneous order), the English Pluralists and Guild Socialists thought there was still a need for a public power, but its role was severely circumscribed. A key concern of theirs was how to maintain the freedom, specificity, and self-development of all forms of association, particularly of churches and trade unions.

The sphere sovereignty of the Dutch neo-Calvinists Abraham Kuyper and Herman Dooyeweerd represents a further strand of consociationalism.[90] For them, the sovereignty of independent spheres such as the family, schools, and workplaces is an expression of the sovereign will of God. Each sphere has a relative autonomy and specific character that need to be respected. Government has a role in ordering and protecting the general good, but it does not have the authority to interfere with or determine the character or telos of each sphere. In turn, the sovereignty of other spheres limits the sovereignty of the state. It was in the Netherlands that notions of sphere sovereignty overlapped with and found a parallel expression in the emergence of Catholic Christian Democratic thinking. Central to this current were Jacques Maritain and the development, from the papal encyclical *Rerum Novarum* (1891) onward, of Catholic social teaching. I discussed Maritain's pluralist conception of the body politic in chapter 5, but briefly

89. On the English Pluralists and Guild Socialists (read as a single movement), see Paul Hirst, ed., *The Pluralist Theory of the State: Selected Writings of G. D. H. Cole, J. N. Figgis, and H. J. Laski* (London: Routledge, 1993). There were, however, substantive differences between the frameworks developed by those associated with the English Pluralist/ Guild Socialist "school." For example, unlike Figgis, Cole and Laski had a decidedly voluntaristic anthropology. For an account of the conceptual differences among the English Pluralists (and those who subsequently developed Guild Socialism), see Cécile Laborde, *Pluralist Thought and the State in Britain and France, 1900-25* (Basingstoke, UK: Macmillan, 2000), 45-100, and Marc Stears, "Guild Socialism," in *Modern Pluralism: Anglo-American Debates Since 1880*, ed. Mark Bevir (Cambridge: Cambridge University Press, 2012), 40-59.

90. See Jonathan Chaplin, *Herman Dooyeweerd: Christian Philosopher of State and Civil Society* (Notre Dame: University of Notre Dame Press, 2011).

put, Maritain argues for a genuine plurality and a corporatist conception of civil society whereby there are multiple yet overlapping "political fraternities" that are independent of the state.[91] On this account, corporatist and personalist forms of civic association and economic organization are precisely a means of preventing the subsuming of all social relations to the demands of statecraft.[92] The kind of thinking Maritain represented was a rival to and eventually displaced the "throne and altar" authoritarianism that informed much of Schmitt's work. Animating the Christian consociationalist tradition of which the Guild Socialists, neo-Calvinists, and Catholic social teaching are a part is the sense in which we participate in a cosmic order that can disclose to us some measure of meaning and purpose.[93] That said, a consociational vision can easily become state-centric, as happened with Christian Democratic parties in Europe after World War II.[94]

On the kind of consociational account envisaged here, to arrive at wise political judgments requires practical reason, and to acquire practical reason requires training in the virtues. We are formed in the virtues through forming and sustaining schools, forms of craft production, congregations, and any form of local society that aspires, as Alasdair MacIntyre puts it, "to achieve some relatively self-sufficient and independent form of participatory practice-based community and that therefore [needs] to protect themselves from the corrosive effects of capitalism and the depredations of state power."[95] On this account, the pursuit of the virtues through forms of

91. Jacques Maritain, *Integral Humanism: Temporal and Spiritual Problems of a New Christendom*, trans. Joseph Evans (New York: Scribner's Sons, 1968), 163.

92. Given the links between Maritain and the development of Latin American liberation theology, it is interesting that Moltmann explicitly commends an Althusian-inspired framework as the necessary development within liberation theologies, warning: "Liberation theologies which do not develop into democratic federal theologies of this [consociational] kind are failing to achieve free life, and can easily become the ideology of elitist groups and their didactic dictatorships. While the Exodus is the historical foundation for liberty, the covenant is the practical form of life in freedom" (*The Spirit of Life: A Universal Affirmation*, trans. Margaret Kohl [Minneapolis: Fortress, 1992], 114).

93. It is this cosmic social imaginary that distinguishes the Christian consociationalism of Figgis, Kuyper, Maritain, et al. from their secularizing confreres, notably Émile Durkheim and the contemporary political theorist Paul Hirst. But at the same time, it connects it to Jewish confederal political thinkers who share it, for example, Martin Buber and Daniel Elazar.

94. Such tendencies have been criticized in more recent papal encyclicals. See, for example, the critical comments by John Paul II of what he calls the "social assistance state" in *Centesimus Annus*, §48.

95. Alasdair MacIntyre, "Three Perspectives on Marxism: 1953, 1968, 1995," in *Eth-*

institutionally mediated practices with substantive goods is a prerequisite for being a good citizen, that is, one who has the understanding and the ability to rule and be ruled and so can make wise political judgments. The sense of what it means to be a political animal developed here is better described as Althusian than Aristotelian.[96]

Althusius rejected Aristotle's distinction between a natural domestic rule and the political rule among free and equal citizens. For Althusius, all forms of social life, whether in the family, the guild, or the *polis*, may participate in the formation of political life. However, this does not mean that Althusius totalizes the political sphere so that it subsumes every aspect of life within it. Rather, as Thomas Hueglin clarifies: "For Althusius, each consociation or political community is determined by the same principles of communication of goods, services, and rights. The essence of politics is the organization of this process of communication. Therefore, families and professional colleges are as much political communities as cities, provinces, or realms insofar as they participate in this political process through their activities."[97] Rather than recognition and respect being given simply by dint of having a different culture or identity, they are conditional upon contributing to and participating in the shared, reciprocal work of building a common, democratic life. Failure to grant recognition renders the consociation subject to moral and political admonition. Conversely, the inherently contributory structure of consociational democracy enables making prudential judgments about how each particular consociation might contribute to sustaining the goods of communication and association that form the basis of politics.[98]

Conclusion

In political theology, sovereignty is too often overvalued, whether by those such as Schmitt, who make it the sole basis of political order, or by those

---

ics and Politics, Selected Essays, vol. 2 (Cambridge: Cambridge University Press, 2006), 155. For MacIntyre's extended account of the relationship between practical reason, economics, and politics, an account that my own account overlaps with and parallels, see Alasdair MacIntyre, *Ethics in the Conflicts of Modernity: An Essay on Desire, Practical Reasoning, and Narrative* (Cambridge: Cambridge University Press, 2016).

96. Hueglin, *Early Modern Concepts*, 56-82.

97. Hueglin, *Early Modern Concepts*, 95-96.

98. Jacob Levy develops a parallel account to mine. See Levy, *Rationalism, Pluralism, and Freedom*.

who think the only alternative to absolutist conceptions of sovereignty is to abandon any notion of sovereignty, opting instead for some kind of spontaneous order. The latter move is understandable given how transcendent, indivisible, and monist conceptions of sovereignty have justified colonial and totalitarian forms of polity. But in practice, postpolitical, utopian visions of spontaneous order—whether of the left or the right—collapse into what the feminist Jo Freeman calls the "tyranny of structurelessness."[99] The real alternative to the Hobbesian conception of sovereignty is the consociational tradition, with its distributed, bottom-up, cooperative, and pluralistic conception of sovereignty that incorporates custom and covenant alongside contract as a basis for public standing. A consociational approach offers a rich yet underexplored thickening of Trinitarian, apocalyptic, liberationist, and Augustinian responses to political and economic absolutism and tyranny. Some form of radically democratic, federal thought needs to frame contemporary theological accounts of sovereignty if they are to move beyond critique to constructive conception.

Threshold

If this chapter addressed debates about the proper form of political order, the next focuses on debates about the nature of political life. It examines what it means to be a people, how the people are the basis of a democratic conception of sovereignty, and the problems that arise within conceptions of popular sovereignty. Building on this chapter, the next chapter reflects on how a consociational conception of peoplehood reframes how to understand democratic politics.

Suggested Readings for Further Discussion

Scriptures: Deuteronomy 16:18–18:22; Judges 9:7–15; 1 Samuel 8; Psalms 8 and 9; Daniel 3–5; Matthew 22:15–21; Philippians 2:1–13; Romans 13; and Revelation 13.

Gelasius, "From *The Bond of Anathema*" and "From *Letter to Emperor Anastasius*," in *From Irenaeus to Grotius: A Sourcebook in Christian Political*

---

99. Jo Freeman, "The Tyranny of Structurelessness," Jo Freeman.com, http://www.jofreeman.com/joreen/tyranny.htm.

Thought, 100-1625, ed. Oliver O'Donovan and Joan Lockwood O'Donovan (Grand Rapids: Eerdmans, 1999), 169-79.

Thomas Hobbes, "Of the Causes, Generation and Definition of Commonwealth," in *Leviathan*. Various editions.

Johannes Althusius, "Political Sovereignty and Ecclesiastical Communication," in *Politica*, ed. and trans. Frederick Carney (Indianapolis: Liberty Fund, 1995 [1964]), 66-78.

J. N. Figgis, "The Great Leviathan," in *The Pluralist Theory of the State: Selected Writings of G. D. H. Cole, J. N. Figgis, and H. J. Laski*, ed. Paul Hirst (London: Routledge, 1993), 111-27.

Carl Schmitt, "Definition of Sovereignty" and "Political Theology," in *Political Theology: Four Chapters on the Concept of Sovereignty* (Chicago: University of Chicago Press, 2005), 5-15, 36-52.

Jürgen Moltmann, *The Trinity and the Kingdom of God: The Doctrine of God*, trans. Margaret Kohl (London: SCM, 1981), 129-32, 191-222.

Oliver O'Donovan, "The Act of Judgment," in *The Ways of Judgment* (Grand Rapids: Eerdmans, 2005), 3-12. This is a theological articulation of the nature and form of political judgment that sovereign authorities are called on to exercise. O'Donovan's account is markedly different from the kind of "decisionist theory" Schmitt puts forward.

CHAPTER 13

The People and Populism

As I outlined in the introduction, this book tries to display how talk of God and talk of politics are mutually constitutive and refract each other, and how this interrelationship shapes *both* ecclesial and political life. This is nowhere more apparent than in theological understandings of what it means to be the people of God and conceptions of what it means to be a democratic people. Central to modern conceptions of democracy and what it means to be church is the term "the people." And just as the church only exists if there is an ongoing process of forming the people of God, there is no democracy unless there are ways of forming a demos or people. The telos of the people of God and the demos may differ, but there is a direct analogy between them, and their modern conceptualization shares an intellectual and social history. Inherent in ecclesial and political uses of the term "the people" is the sense that to be a people is to be, in some way, a moral community that is an end in itself. For a people to be dominated by a foreign power (spiritual or worldly), corrupted by tyranny, or fractured through internal strife or schism is to lose a substantive good.[1] Thus, questions about how to form a people and what kind of politics is necessary to do so are not just ecclesial. The same questions lie at the heart of democracy. Churches and democratic polities also suffer the same tensions and instabilities born out of questions about the authority and legitimacy of representation intrinsic to all attempts to form a people. I contend that it is these tensions and instabilities that give rise to forms of ecclesial and political populism.

---

1. For a modern, deontological, nontheological statement of how a people is a moral good, see John Rawls, *The Law of Peoples* (Cambridge, MA: Harvard University Press, 1999), 23-30.

A central focus of this chapter is developing a political theology of what it means to be the people of God and how this connects to a democratic vision of a common life. I emphasize the political dimensions of what it means to be the people of God. A constructive vision of the relationship between politics and the formation of a people is needed to understand how to engage constructively with conflicts within churches over how to answer theological and moral questions and how best to structure the church institutionally. The former are debates about what vision of the good or flourishing life should guide the church, while the latter are disputes about what form of polity a Christian common life requires (episcopal, presbyterial, congregational, conciliar, etc.). Both are political problems requiring an ongoing dance of conflict and conciliation to generate a form of common life amid difference and disagreement between rival visions of the good and conflicting interests between friends, strangers, the friendless, and enemies. What is often forgotten or missed is that intra-ecclesial politics is indeed a form of politics, and it needs to be constructively engaged with as such rather than bemoaned as a failure or avoided because conflict per se (rather than a specific character and form of conflict) is deemed immoral or unfaithful. Alongside theological reflection, worship, and works of mercy, politics is part and parcel of forming a common life, both within and without the church. However, little attention is given to thinking about what kind of politics and polity is needed to sustain the quality and kind of relationship that can foster a Christian form of common life amidst the world. Instead, theological and moral disputes are treated as solely theoretical and hermeneutical problems, while conflicts over institutional form are increasingly dealt with in managerial terms. These ways of engaging debates about doctrine, morality, and polity put program before people and their lived reality, and suffer from the delusion that if we get the ideas, policy, or procedures right, holiness will burst forth. What is needed instead is a vision of faithful, hopeful, and loving politics.

A vision of politics is tacit within an understanding of the church as the *people* of God. The church conceptualized as the people of God involves a particular kind of politics; if this politics is not practiced, the holiness of the people is undermined. Or, to parse Stanley Hauerwas, the church does not have a political theology, it is a political theology. But contrary to Hauerwas, the political theology the church embodies—being the people of God—is not a stable category that of necessity generates separation from or distinctiveness to the world. As this chapter argues, the constitution of the people of God in this age produces its own crisis, which in turn generates forms of theological and ecclesial populism. And to be the people of God is to be formed from, by, and with the world while on pilgrimage through the world. The people of God are therefore unlike other peoples in ways that may or may not be righteous and which cannot be predetermined, but only discovered in the midst of building a common life with others. In building a common life within and without the church through politics, the way the church is like and unlike the world, for better or for worse, can be discerned.

The meaning of being a people is unstable and ambiguous. In classical usage, "the people" signifies various and sometimes contradictory things.[2] It can refer to:

- the entire people of a polity;
- the common or nonelite members of a polity;
- an assembly of the people made up of those eligible to participate in legal and political matters (historically, property-owning male citizens); and
- the source of sovereignty.

The ambiguity that arises out of these different meanings carries over into modern uses of the term in both political theory and ecclesiology. Modern conceptions of democracy, as based on the sovereignty of the people, and of the church as the people of God oscillate between two poles. On one side, there is a commitment to seeking the collective wisdom generated through an assembly's reflective deliberation (e.g., in a parliament or synod), and on the other, there is a commitment to include and consult the commoners/laity (or their representatives) in any decision affecting the entire people. A further ambiguity arises with the conflation of "people" and

2. Either *dēmos*/δῆμος or *laos*/λαός in Greek and *populus* in Latin. *Demos* carries with it a connotation of place or *terroir*, connected as it is with a *deme* or district. The demos is the assembly of the districts. *Laos* is a more generic term meaning a people in general rather than one's own people. And rather than land, *laos* is defined by a relation to a leader (e.g., a band of warriors in relation to a chief, or the group and their representative). While the use of *laos* is common in the New Testament, the use of *dēmos* is rare (e.g., Acts 12:22; 19:30-41). Given the connotation of the people being defined in relation to their leader or representative rather than in relation to their land or territory, it is not surprising that it is *laos* rather than *dēmos* that is favored to describe the people of God. On the distinction between *laos*, *dēmos*, and *ethnos*, see Émile Benveniste, *Indo-European Language and Society*, trans. Elizabeth Palmer (Coral Gables, FL: University of Miami Press, 1973), 371-76.

"nation." There is an obvious theological ambiguity deriving from the uses of these terms as synonyms in Scripture ("people of God"/"holy nation"). However, it takes on a specific valence in the modern period by eliding the people with a homogenous ethnic, racial, or cultural group.

In this chapter, I analyze how contemporary understandings of the people as a political category and the people of God as an ecclesial category share a genealogy, address a set of shared problems, and exhibit many of the same tensions and ambiguities. I do not directly address christological considerations of what it means to be the church/body of Christ or how Christ determines the nature and form of political order. These are vital considerations, and like electrons and protons, they circulate within and help constitute the matter in hand. So I touch on and reference them as needed. However, instead of beginning with an abstract account of Christology and then applying that to the church, I suggest that a *political theology* should begin with an account of politics and what it means to be a people. From this starting point, the first of the two parts into which I have divided this chapter opens by discussing scriptural and theological conceptions of the people of God, drawing out how the people is a category for understanding the social and political nature of divine-human relations. I then sketch a theologically inflected intellectual and social history of how the church as the people of God informs what it means to be a democratic people. I do this by considering the intersection between ecclesial and democratic populism from the Reformation onward, and how their interaction forms the backdrop to modern conceptions of the people as a political category. The second part of this chapter then focuses on the role of the people in understanding democracy and how the ambiguities and dynamics of rule by, with, and for the people inherently generate the conditions for the possibility of various forms of populism. Populism emerges in the space of indeterminacy about the basis of the people and who constitutes the people. This indeterminacy gives rise to crises of representation (both symbolic and institutional) that populist movements exploit. The chapter closes with a case study of the populist movement in nineteenth-century North America. The case study provides insights into the interconnection between democratic politics and populism and the ongoing relationship between ecclesial and democratic populism.

I

The People of God

The people of God are founded as a people through a civic-cultic assembly when God gives the law (Deut. 4:10; 9:10; 18:16).[3] This assembly is gathered again before entering the promised land (Deut. 31:30), and again on entering the promised land (Josh. 8:30-35). After the first assembly, all the people (including women, children, and resident aliens) were supposed to assemble every seven years (Deut. 31:10-13).[4] At crucial points in the story of Israel, it is a congregation or assembly of the people that is the basis of the reconstitution of the people of God as a holy people. For example, in Ezra 10, after a prior process of debate, the decision about how to restore the covenant is ultimately taken by an assembly of the people. And while Ezra is given delegated authority from above, he cannot act without the active consent of the people. In Nehemiah 5, an assembly of the people places limits on the power of aristocratic elites, and the completion of the city walls (depicted in chaps. 8-9) needs the approval of a civic-cultic assembly. If democracy is about more than voting, and is primarily identified with the negotiation of a common life through shared speech and action by a broad cross section of an entire polity, then all the instances cited thus far reflect how democratic assembly is a part of political and judicial arrangements in the constitution of Israel as a covenantal people. Ultimately, the fulfillment of the people of God and the fulfillment of creation are marked by an assembly of all nations before God at the eschaton (e.g., Matt. 25:31-46). In summary, a civic-cultic assembly is the means through which to constitute the people as those who stand in covenantal relation to God, each other, and the rest of creation.

The initial material basis for the constitution of the people as a people was land. To participate as a full member of the covenantal community or organized body politic originally required a landholding. Land provided the basis for the right and obligation to participate in the legal assemblies, to act in common ventures such as defense, and to be present at the fes-

---

3. קהל/*qahal* in Hebrew and ἐκκλησία/*ekklēsia* in Greek.

4. As Young-Ho Park notes: "The ἐκκλησία is the very foundation of the faith community of Israel, which is not maintained by the technical expertise of the ruling group but by all the people's continual commitment to God and his laws" (*Paul's Ekklēsia as a Civic Assembly* [Tübingen: Mohr Siebeck, 2015], 89).

tivals.[5] Possession of land was a necessary condition for participation in the assembly of tribes (the *edah*) and the sociopolitical organization of the tribe (the *shevet*), as well as the means to fulfill the obligations of the covenant with God and the duties of care owed to one's fellow Israelites.[6] For everyone apart from the Levites, to be without land meant one lacked the means to engage in relations of mutual responsibility, which therefore meant one was unable to fulfill one's covenantal obligations. This inability affected the holiness of the people, because the quality of covenantal relations broke down. Without land, *tzedakah u'mishpat* (justice and righteousness), the term for the complex of obligations and rights that forms the basis of the God-given social order, could no longer be fulfilled.[7] Thus the land in general, and familial landholdings in particular, were central to the organization and identity of ancient Israel as a body politic/people. While landholding was a vital component of who could have a say in the assembly of the people, crucially, the Levites and the temple did not own land. The political economy of Israel continues on in the formation of the church depicted in Acts, where the civic-cultic assembly of the people (an *ekklēsia*) is premised on a cooperative economy of shared property.

The primary difference between Israel as a people (*'am, laos*) and other peoples or nations (*gôy, ethnē*) is not material but formal.[8] The material life of Israel is both like and not like that of other peoples, but their end—that of covenantal relationship with God—is radically different. This formal, teleological difference is what makes it incumbent, so the theological claim goes, for all other nations to respond to Israel in appropriate ways. This end also means that the material and institutional life of the people is not static. It can be subject to radical revision in the light of what it means to fulfill the covenant. The Christian theological claim is that after Christ, the

---

5. Albino Barrera, *God and the Evil of Scarcity: Moral Foundations of Economic Agency* (Notre Dame: University of Notre Dame Press, 2005), 46, and David Novak, *Jewish Social Ethics* (Oxford: Oxford University Press, 1992), 210.

6. Daniel Elazar, *Covenant and Polity in Biblical Israel: Biblical Foundations and Jewish Expressions* (New Brunswick, NJ: Transaction, 1995), 86-91.

7. Elazar, *Covenant and Polity*, 133.

8. The primary Hebrew term translated as people is *'am*. It is sometimes contrasted with the term *gôy*, generally translated as nation. The term *gôy* is applied to a variety of entities, including the pre-Israelite Canaanite tribes (Deut. 7:1), nomadic desert tribes (Isa. 60:5ff.), and kingdoms and empires (Jer. 25:17ff.). But it can also be used for Israel. In the Septuagint (the widely read and influential Greek translation of the Hebrew Bible), the term *gôyim* is translated as *ethnē*, especially when a contrast is drawn between the chosen *laos theou* (people of God) and the gentile/non-Israelite *ethnē* (nations).

people of God includes representatives from among the nations. In effect, the eschatological vision presented in Isaiah and elsewhere is reaffirmed in the Gospels, most explicitly in Luke 13:29-30, where Jesus declares that "people will come from east and west, from north and south, and will eat in the kingdom of God. Indeed, some are last who will be first, and some are first who will be last." Jesus enacts this eschatological vision in his hospitality of sinners and gentiles and fulfills it in his hospitality to the point of death on a cross so that all who are strangers may sit and eat with God.

As a congregation, the people of God incorporate elements of an *ekklēsia* (a public assembly of the people) and a *polis* (the form and structure of a political community). As a people of God, the church does not replace Israel (this is the conclusion of Paul's wrestling in Romans 11); neither is it a new, territorially bounded polity. Rather, a distinctive pattern of relating together and to God is established, a pattern that radically reconfigures political and social distinctions between *oikos* and *polis*, gentile and Jew, native and stranger. Gentiles become grafted into Israel, yet, in other ways, they remain gentiles. Likewise, Christians are at once a distinct people yet also citizens of existing polities, strangers in their own land, yet strangers to no land (Eph. 2:19; James 1:1; 1 Pet. 1:1; 2:11).[9] Drawing on Greco-Roman usage, active and virtuous participation or communion (*koinōnia*) in the people is a marker of fulfilling what it means to be human. Noncommunion means one is subject to a realm of spiritual and moral chaos.

Before getting dewy-eyed about the scriptural precedent for a democratic politics, we must remember that a popular assembly was involved in sentencing Jesus to death. Those who gathered before Pilate were not, as is mostly assumed, a mob. Rather, they constituted an assembly of the people whose cry of acclamation carried authorizing force in both the Jewish and the Greco-Roman world. Alongside Pilate (the one), the Sanhedrin (the few)—and the forms of human authority each represents—is rule by the people (the many). Rule by the people is depicted as a key part of the proceedings by which Jesus is condemned.[10] Just as forms of rule by the one and the few are under God's judgment, so is rule by a demos/*populus*. Here the echo is with Numbers 14:1-10 when "the whole congregation" assembles and raises a loud cry, complains to Moses and Aaron, appoints captains, and

9. For early articulations of this view, see 1 Clement 1:1 and the Letter to Diognetus. For a modern articulation, see Paul VI, *Lumen Gentium*, §13.

10. This is drawn out in Jerome's use of *populus* in the Vulgate to describe those gathered before Pilate. See Jeremy D. Adams, *The* Populus *of Augustine and Jerome* (New Haven: Yale University Press, 1971), 105-8.

elects to return to Egypt. Portrayed in Numbers 14 is a process of deliberation about where the real good of the people lies and who is best fit to lead them. Things go very badly until Yahweh intervenes to prevent the stoning of Moses. But Moses is no Pilate. Rather than wash his hands of the situation, he takes up a deliberation with God on behalf of the people. Subsequently, the people repent, but their disobedience leads to military defeat.

The popular judgment against Jesus and Moses reminds us that while there is a clear preferential option for the poor and oppressed throughout Scripture, Scripture is skeptical of any beatification of the oppressed as somehow morally infallible or without sin. Rich and poor alike bear an equal dignity before God, and all need to repent, even if the heinousness of their sin varies. The common people can be stiff-necked and act in either oppressive or self-destructive ways, even as they cry out for justice. However, in stark contrast to human histories and myths, the marginal, enslaved, and colonized stand alongside God as central characters in the story of Israel. To use a term from postcolonial theory, this is a story where the subaltern speaks. Yet it turns out, the subaltern can say and do bad and evil things too. While the oppressed experience reality in a different way to the powerful and privileged, simply by dint of being oppressed they do not intrinsically or spontaneously know what is the just and loving thing to say or do. The experience and perspective of the oppressed should be given priority in any determination of the good; however, their perspective is not necessarily decisive. As Ada María Isasi-Díaz notes: "There is a triple dimension to knowing reality: becoming aware/getting to know reality, taking responsibility for reality, and transforming reality."[11] In Scripture, this process is only possible by becoming a people (to which prophecy and the cries of the oppressed contribute). Together, a people can get to know and thence make wise judgments about how to move from the world as it is to the world as it should be. Becoming a people entails a twofold, intertwined process: cycles of assembly in response to the prior work and word of God, and formation in personal and communal virtue. Through such a process, the oppressed—along with everyone else—can uphold their side of the covenant faithfully, hopefully, and lovingly, and thereby act justly with and for others and themselves. Yet the "democratic paradox" of the need to form a just and loving people out of an oppressed and idolatrous crowd is always ongoing in this age.

11. Ada María Isasi-Díaz, *La Lucha Continues: Mujerista Theology* (Maryknoll, NY: Orbis, 2004), 100.

As a people, Israel and the church are theocracies. But this should not be understood in the modern usage of the term as denoting a polity ruled by a priestly caste. The scriptural portrayal of theocracy is meant to prevent the rule by a single person or class, priestly or otherwise. Rather, the people are ruled by God, which means no human ruler or class can claim sovereignty. Theocracy in this scriptural sense means something like "no master but God"—a sensibility turned to revolutionary ends in Protestant resistance theory. God's sovereignty is distributed throughout the people rather than concentrated in a single figure or group; this dynamic is explored in the previous chapter. As Augustine notes, the divine law was given not to "a single man or even a select group of wise men," but to the people as a whole.[12] Sovereignty is thereby structurally divided. Even with the ambiguous installation of a monarchy, the legitimacy and authority of the king are institutionally negotiated and contested by prophet and priest. As distributed, God's sovereignty is not heteronomous: the people are not passive recipients of the commands of God. Rather, the fullest expression and paradigmatic form of God's rule are the assemblies where God and the people speak and hear each other, albeit often mediated by Spirit-anointed leaders such as Moses, David, Nehemiah, John the Baptist, and Peter. These public assemblies include various kinds of Spirit-anointed speech, including reasoned deliberation, prophetic indictment, legal proclamation, exhortation, cries of repentance, and shouts of acclamation, all of which help constitute the people of God.

On this account, God's command comes to the people paradigmatically through an assembly. Analogous to how preaching as a speech-act is something that takes place between the preacher and the congregation—and cannot exist without both sides of the equation—the reception of the command is an event that takes place between the people (including their anointed representatives) and God. Assembly is the fullest manifestation of God's presence. The material condition of reception is the political process of forming a people. Thus, this reception cannot happen without politics. But, conversely, a righteous politics depends on reception of God's Word. The combination of receiving God's Word and politics constitutes the faithful, hopeful, and loving mode of discovering what to do and how to do it among these people, in this place, at this time. And it makes congregating for worship/reception the paradigmatic form of encounter with God.

Pentecost represents the moment when the nature of mediation, whether of temple, priest, king, or territory, is ruptured, if not undone. The Spirit is

12. Augustine, *City of God* 10.7.

poured out on all flesh and can be manifest in any place, and among any people—Parthians, Elamites, Phrygians, etc.—without distinction, and anyone can receive the anointing needed to speak for and with God (Acts 2). The popular, the ordinary, and the vulgar can mediate God's presence, and God's presence can be articulated in one's own idiom, however uncouth. Indeed, at Pentecost, it is the marginal that speak forth God's Word, not those from the center. As Michael Welker puts it: "The Spirit gives rise to a unity in which the prophetic witness of women is no less important than that of men, that of the young is no less significant than that of the old, that of the socially disadvantaged is no less relevant than that of the privileged. The promised Spirit of God is effective in that differentiated community which is sensitive to differences, and in which the differences that stand in opposition to justice, mercy, and knowledge of God are being steadily reduced."[13]

The sociality of the people, as an assembly and *polis*, is to be characterized by relations of fellowship/*koinōnia* (analogous to the mutual sharing and solidarity of kin). A question remains, however: Should either the *ekklēsia* (and hence civic relations) or the *oikos*/household (and hence familial relations) constitute the chief paradigm for the people of God? Or is the relation between the civic and familial pattern dialectical? Different political theologies tend to prioritize one over against the other.[14] There is also the question of the most fitting way of structuring and organizing peoplehood. Is peoplehood most faithfully expressed through being a distributed, universal, nonterritorial *polis*? Or should it take on the form of a singular city-state with a diaspora or set of colonies, with Jerusalem (or later Rome) as the sovereign center to which all others must defer? An argument about how to answer this question runs through the New Testament. In the Synoptic Gospels, Jerusalem is subject to apocalyptic judgment (e.g., Mark 13).[15] And then, in Paul (e.g., Gal. 4:21-31) and in Revelation, Jerusalem as an earthly city is discursively relativized through being eschatologically relocated.[16] What eventually emerges is a distributed and catholic/universal polity that retains an association between place and civic-cultic assembly,

13. Michael Welker, *God the Spirit*, trans. John F. Hoffmeyer (Minneapolis: Fortress, 1994), 22-23.

14. On the dialectical relation between city and household in determining the sociality of the church, see Oliver O'Donovan, *The Ways of Judgment* (Grand Rapids: Eerdmans, 2005), 261-92.

15. Park, *Paul's Ekklēsia*, 148-49.

16. Richard Bauckham, *The Theology of the Book of Revelation* (Cambridge: Cambridge University Press, 1993).

and at the same time leads beyond and prevents the people of God from being overidentified with any single place, time, or people.[17]

Peoplehood and Place: Navigating the Universal and Particular Dimensions of Being Church

The institutional development of the church can be read theologically as consonant with and expanding on the scriptural framework just outlined. The formative period of the church developed a particular institutional pattern by which to answer the question of how to form a common life over time, attend to particularities of context, and pursue the good of association amid difference and disagreement. They sought a pattern of polity that attended to particular contexts but which, at the same time, connected these places into a larger, more universal set of relations. This configuration consisted of a parish/congregation, diocese, archdiocese, and province. These made up a federation of polities (Jerusalem, Alexandria, Antioch, Rome, and Constantinople) that were at once autocephalous and affiliated and which, federated together, witnessed to the geographic and synchronic catholicity of God's people.[18] This pattern of polity continued in Byzantium and its ecclesial inheritors in the Orthodox world, while in the Latin West, a single sovereign center was reasserted through claims to the supremacy of the See of Rome over all other patriarchates. Such a claim is perhaps most forcefully expressed in Pope Boniface VIII's 1302 bull, *Unam Sanctam*, which claimed ultimate authority for the papacy over both ecclesial and civil matters.[19] If the characteristic pathology of Rome is to falsely

17. This dynamic is discussed in chapter 10 on humanity. John Howard Yoder's conception of diasporic and exilic existence as the normative form of the people of God undervalues the ongoing importance of place to peoplehood even as it captures something of how, after Christ, any sense of possessing a territory or controlling history is radically relativized. See, for example, John Howard Yoder, *The Jewish-Christian Schism Revisited*, ed. Michael Cartwright and Peter Ochs (Grand Rapids: Eerdmans, 2003), 168-79.

18. "Autocephalous" denotes a distinct and sovereign episcopal jurisdiction that is at the same time constitutive of geographical and synchronic wholeness, while "affiliated" denotes a familial relation that at the same time marks the distinctness and independence of each participant in the relation. Use of the term "affiliate" can be contrasted with parallel but subtly different terms such as "affinity" or "coalition" that denote a sense of less formal, less genealogical, and more voluntaristic ties.

19. A modern restatement of the single sovereign center view is set out in *Lumen Gentium*, §8.

identify a particular place as a universal, sovereign center, that of Eastern Orthodoxy is to overidentify with the particular at the expense of any notion of catholicity. The name of this latter heresy is phyletism, defined as the move beyond ecclesial autocephaly to an identification between national and ecclesial identity. What this means in practice is that to be Greek is to be Orthodox, and, conversely, for a Greek to attend a Russian or Romanian Orthodox church is to participate in a "foreign" entity. The Synod of Constantinople in 1872 condemned phyletism. Protestant forms of phyletism are common, but today these are mostly related to a vaguer sense of being a "Christian" or "Judeo-Christian" nation rather than a "Lutheran" or "Reformed" nation. This shift represents a movement beyond phyletism, as the linkage between "the people" and Christianity no longer denotes a connection between the nation and a specific form of belief and practice. Instead, Christianity becomes a symbol untethered from doctrinal or ethical content, and so is thereby reduced to a civil religious trope deployed to buttress an exclusionary national identity.[20] Theologically, this shift represents a move from heresy to idolatry. Politically, it converts Christianity into a form of identity politics.

A Spirit-empowered, Christ-orientated form of social relations should produce a sense of place radically different from that generated by phyletism and its idolatrous offshoots. Paul's statement that the community is the "temple of the living God" points to how holiness is, in the first instance, socially rather than spatially manifested. The construction of holiness occurs through such things as ascetic practices, collective worship, patterns of gift relation and shared experience, memories, and narratives, which combine to form the constitutive elements of a "holy nation." This holy nation is, paradoxically, a people who are "resident aliens"; that is, they are unbound by commitment to territory. Such a pneumatological and eschatological sense of place provides a way in which we can steer between two problematic ways of being Christian. The first is a segregationist or sectarian Christianity, which walls off a particular form of Christianity from a common life with others. The second falsely universalizes a particular form of Christianity, equally refusing to listen to and learn from different

20. The Tea Party is a contemporary example. See Nadia Marzouki, "The Tea Party and Religion: Between Religious and Historical Fundamentalism," in *Saving the People: How Populists Hijack Religion*, ed. Nadia Marzouki, Duncan McDonnell, and Olivier Roy (Oxford: Oxford University Press, 2016), 149–66, and Ruth Braunstein and Meleana Taylor, "Is the Tea Party a 'Religious' Movement? Religiosity in the Tea Party versus the Religious Right," *Sociology of Religion* 78, no. 1 (2017): 33–59.

contexts (and what the Spirit is doing in that time and place). But instead of withdrawal, it colonizes. As noted in chapter 4, a pneumatological and eschatological sense of place is at once deeply contextual (it entails forming ways of being church among *these* people, in *this* place, at *this* time), open to a plurality of other ways of being church (it entails participating in and learning from the communion of saints in *all* times and places), and contingent (no single way of being church can claim to be definitive, as the coming kingdom of God relativizes them all).[21]

Case Study: Augustine

Augustine's reconceptualization of Cicero's definition of a people, along with his contrast between the earthly city and city of God, represents one influential attempt to crystallize how the political and theological nature of the people of God exist through time and in multiple places. Augustine divides human societies in two: there is the city of God—which combines both the true church in this age and the new Jerusalem of the age to come—and Babylon, or the earthly city.[22] Augustine characterizes the division not as a division *within* society but as a division *between* societies. Citizens of both cities seek peace; however, in the earthly city peace is achieved through the imposition of one's will by the exercise of force, and is at once costly in its creation (19.7), lacking in real justice (19.15), and unstable in its existence (19.5). For Augustine, the only true society and true peace exist in the city of God. Within Augustine's theology, the visible church participates in Babylon and thus is often directed to prideful ends. On his account, we should be suspicious of any attempt to identify one particular take on Christianity as somehow the embodiment of the new Jerusalem now. The visible church always combines the earthly city and the city of God, which are inseparable until the last judgment.

Augustine defines a people as a "multitude of rational beings joined together by common agreement on the objects of their love" (19.24; cf. 1.15; 15.18; 19.21). Thus, for Augustine, a people come to exist through the love of

21. The eschatological, relational, and temporally defined conception of place set out here contrasts with ones that emphasize a more sacramental and spatially determined theology of place. See, for example, John Inge, *A Christian Theology of Place* (Aldershot, UK: Ashgate, 2003).

22. Augustine, *City of God* 20.17. Hereafter, references from this work will be given in parentheses in the text.

goods in common. The quality and character of the people are dependent on what goods are loved and how they are loved.[23] Only the people of God assembled in the city of God are a holy people by dint of what they love, but all peoples love something, and that is the basis of their common life. With Aristotle, Augustine can thereby say that humans are naturally political animals who find fulfillment in some form of shared venture. But against Aristotle, and much other political thought, he argues that the peoples we see around us can never be the basis of fulfillment because they are fallen and orientated away from the true end of human being—communion with God—and toward their own prideful, self-destructive ends. All earthly political formations and structures of governance are provisional and tend toward oppression, while at the same time, whether it be a democracy or a monarchy, any earthly political formation may display just judgments and enable the limited good of an earthly peace through the pursuit of agreed or common objects of love. One implication of Augustine's framework is that politics is a moral realm: love and justice matter. Yet politics can never be the realm of human perfection. Any attempt for it to do so conflates the earthly city and the city of God by seeking complete fulfillment in what is created, which is inherently a form of idolatry.

Augustine's account of two peoples is an attempt to emphasize the distinctness of the people of God as the only real commonwealth and, at the same time, to recognize that this peculiar people shares mutual ground with those who do not seek God. He achieves this through contrasting two spatial realms—two cities—as commingling in a single age (*hoc saeculum*)—the time before Christ's return. The citizens of each city are inextricably interwoven in this age and cannot neatly be told apart until Christ returns.[24] Alongside their temporal coexistence, members of each city share mutual space: the earthly polities that rise and fall in this, noneschatological, age. This framework raises a profound ambiguity about the nature of the relationship between church and world that runs through the Western tradition. The visible church is a part of Babylon while also participating in the people who make up the city of God. As participants in the city of God and the earthly city, the people of God share in and are dependent on the

---

23. As Augustine puts it, "the better the objects of its loves, the better the people, and the worse the objects of its love, the worse the people" (*City of God* 19.24). Thus, while there is a difference between the Roman Empire and a band of brigands, Augustine's disquieting suggestion is that all forms of social life exist on a spectrum, which prohibits absolute, qualitative distinctions between them (4.4).

24. Augustine, *City of God* 19.17.

common objects of love of both cities and thereby share a common life with both. How to navigate the church-world distinction that Augustine is trying to articulate has divided political theologies down the centuries, with some adhering to a sharp division between church and world and others holding to a blurry line of demarcation. For Augustine, however, church and world are a field of wheat and tares that, while distinct in form and fruit, are coemergent, depend on the same soil to grow, and cannot be separated until the last judgment.

Augustine's work is also an example of a characteristic deformation of all forms of ecclesial polity, which is for them to be shot through with the patriarchal form of the classical *oikos*. One manifestation of this is the tendency to absolute claims by priests, bishops, or popes to be the *patresfamilias* of the people and thereby exercise absolute and centralized sovereignty marked by the attempt to determine the life of the polity without reference to the consent of the people/commoners/laity. However, as the ancient proverb puts it, *vox populi, vox dei*. The voice of God can be heard only where the voice of the people is heard. Listening to the whole—which includes women as well as men—is crucial to the discernment of the *sensus fidelium*—that is, coming to a judgment about what is faithful, hopeful, and loving witness.[25]

Given the primal division between Jews and Christians and subsequent disagreements that fracture the people of God, the constitution of the people is an ongoing political work that requires kaleidoscopic forms of assembly and reassembly in multiple places. As a political work, it necessarily entails forging a common life with friends, strangers, and enemies, amid radical disagreement. And so there is always an ongoing dance of conflict and conciliation. Just as with any form of political life, total unanimity is not possible. Life together in this age is ragged and fissured, with often irresolvable conflicts. Yet, even while it is fragile and very hard work, that does not make a meaningful common life impossible. But my theological claim goes beyond the practical realities of negotiating a common life amid deep disagreement and suggests that attempts at total coherence and unicity would be a theological mistake. The full realization of the whole people of God is not possible in this age. Furthermore, as outlined in chapter 4, as a Pentecostal community, the people of God should not be homogeneous. However, its symbolic and sacramental representation is possible.

25. Bradford Hinze, *Prophetic Obedience: Ecclesiology for a Dialogical Church* (Maryknoll, NY: Orbis, 2016), 95; *Lumen Gentium*, §12; *Catechism of the Catholic Church*, §§91-94.

From the perspective of Christian theology, representing the people of God raises several problems, most notably: how a sinful, stiff-necked people can represent God; how God can be represented before the people; and how a part can represent the people as a whole. I begin by focusing on the last of these issues, as it leads into the others. The people of God can never fully appear, since the communion of saints transcends time and space and the full catholicity of God's people is only fully manifested on the day of judgment. Yet the people of God do appear at a local level through characteristic gestures and performances (preaching and hearing the word of God, eucharistic assembly, singing together, acts of mercy, etc.) and in identifiable spaces (churches, chapels, festivals, pilgrimage sites, etc.). However, the nature and form of the people of God are not reducible to these gestures and spaces.

Any attempt to represent the people before God must take a symbolic and mediated form that represents the whole people by a part. And any such symbolic mode of representation can be simultaneously Spirit-inspired *and* finite and fallen. It is not a question of either/or, but of the degree of intensity a mode of representation is attuned to the work of the Spirit. Moreover, the temptation to mistake the part for the whole, and thereby subordinate the whole to the part, crouches at the threshold of all forms of representation. Clerical forms of this inversion (whereby the whole serves or is subsumed within the institutions of the church) give birth to anticlericalism and claims of direct access to God without the need for mediation. These claims take various forms, ranging from an emphasis on Scripture as the only means of encountering God, to prioritizing encounter with God through mystical or ecstatic experience (e.g., speaking in tongues), to claims about the already manifest presence of God in the work and life of ordinary people, whether of everyday life, popular culture, or popular social movements (e.g., Latin American liberation theology).[26]

The problem of representing the people of God and the question of who speaks and acts for God in relation to God's people or the people in relation to God (prophets, priests, rulers, or self-organized movements of the people) generate an inevitable instability. It is an instability that is unresolvable until the eschaton, when there will be no more temples or walls or priests or rulers or churches because God will be all in all. All forms of human representation and mediation are therefore relativized—not be-

---

26. Movements that claim to enable modes of encounter with God outside of established patterns of mediation or representation, such as Montanism, are often labeled heresies or heterodox.

cause there is no unifying truth, but because the truth is eschatological and pneumatological. Neither laity, clergy, nor political officials can ever possess or control the people who are called forth by the Spirit who blows where the Spirit wills. Echoing Hebrews 13:14, Augustine's imagery of the people of God as always on pilgrimage draws out how the people of God are ever emergent. As an eschatological and pneumatological people, whose fulfillment is at once given in Christ and yet to come, the forms of life and institutions of the people are necessarily contingent and contextually determined, and thence revisable. That said, it is important not to follow in the footsteps populist anticlericalism often treads, posing a binary between order, institution, or tradition and a spontaneous movement of the Spirit or the people. Forming the people of God involves polity *and* movement, *paradosis and* the work of the Paraclete, order *and* spontaneity, representation of *and* personal encounter with the living God.

A Christian Populism? The Turn to the Quotidian, the Popular, and the Commons

A populist impulse is a perennial feature of Christianity. It is born out of a sense that the renewal of relationship to God and the righteousness of the church come through direct, supposedly unmediated access to God. As already noted, arguments for direct access pose the reading of Scripture or the work of the Spirit in opposition to encounter with God mediated by representatives (exemplified in the administration of sacraments). This theological and ecclesial populism generates opposition to clerical and political elites, who are seen to usurp God and rule either in their own interests or in the service of idols, and thereby corrupt the people by leading them astray. It was this kind of populism that formed the backdrop to debates in the post-Reformation era, and which was central to the formation of modern conceptions of democracy. However, most accounts of the people as a political category and of populism divorce it from its theological genealogy.

With the recovery of Roman law from the twelfth century onward, there was a renewed emphasis on the role of the people as the legitimizing basis of sovereign power. With the Reformation, this Roman legal framework was combined with the hallowing of the ordinary life as a site of divine disclosure and the hallowing of popular political agency so as to generate a powerful impetus for a strong notion of popular sovereignty.[27] What emerges from the early medieval period to the Reformation era is a shift from a doctrine of royal accountability to the people, to an emphasis on direct rule by the people.[28] As noted in the previous chapter, the legal maxim of what touches all requires the consent of all (*quod omnes tangit*) was a foundation stone of this shift. Influenced by Luther and Calvin, but exemplified most clearly in such texts as Theodore of Beza's *The Right of Magistrates* (French, 1574; Latin, 1576) and the pseudonymous Stephen Junius Brutus's *A Defense of Liberty against Tyrants* (Latin, 1579; French, 1581), another building block was conceptualizing the relationship between a monarch and the people as a covenant. The failure of a ruler to keep her promises frees the people from their obligation to obey and justifies resistance to unjust rule.[29] Theories of resistance built on prior medieval accounts of legitimate resistance and were not limited to Lutherans and Calvinists. The Spanish Jesuit Juan de Mariana argued in his *De rege et regis institutione* (1598) that the people established monarchies, and under certain circumstances, monarchs could be removed or even killed by them.[30] Protestant resistance theories became radicalized during the English Civil War (1642–1651). They combined with apocalyptic thought that rejected private property, sought a restoration of Eden when the earth was a "common treasury," and sought an end to what was portrayed as "Babylonian"—that is, idolatrous and thereby illegitimate—forms of rule. An articulation of such a position is set out in Gerrard Winstanley's

27. On the hallowing of the ordinary life, see Charles Taylor, *Sources of the Self: The Making of the Modern Identity* (Cambridge: Cambridge University Press, 1992), 211-33.

28. Margaret Canovan, *The People* (Cambridge: Polity, 2005), 14-39.

29. The key distinction in play was between an illegitimate tyranny and legitimate forms of rule acting unjustly. When faced with an illegitimate ruler (whether an internal usurper or external invader), one should resist by any means necessary, including assassination. When confronted with a legitimate but unjust or wicked ruler, then individuals cannot go beyond passive disobedience. It is the role of legally constituted but lesser authorities to resist legitimate rulers acting unjustly, even to the point of armed resistance. For a review of the intellectual history of Protestant resistance theory, see Robert Kingdon, "Calvinism and Resistance Theory, 1550-1580," in *The Cambridge History of Political Thought: 1450-1700*, ed. J. H. Burns and M. Goldie (Cambridge: Cambridge University Press, 1991), 194-218. For a more schematic account of the moral and political theology of civil disobedience, see James Childress, *Civil Disobedience and Political Obligation: A Study in Christian Social Ethics* (New Haven: Yale University Press, 1971).

30. On Catholic resistance theory, see J. H. M. Salmon, "Catholic Resistance Theory, Ultramontanism, and the Royalist Response, 1580-1620," in Burns and Goldie, *The Cambridge History of Political Thought*, 219-53.

The New Law of Righteousness (1649) and manifested in the beliefs and practices of the Diggers and Levellers. Even less radical thinkers such as John Milton (1608-1674), and a host of other Protestant polemicists, came to view monarchy itself as idolatrous and thereby an illegitimate form of rule. This republican position was in turn opposed by the assertion of the divine right of kings, an early modern doctrinal innovation.[31]

The theological and political emphasis on the centrality of the people generates a reformist and a radical wing. In both, a republican form of polity is the ideal, but in the former, the people are conflated with the nation and the republic is identified with a nation-state, constituted by an indivisible sovereign, a bounded territory, one law, and a single religion.[32] Israel is still a template, but understood less as a covenantal people and more as a territorial nation. This theological debate is the backdrop to the emergence of the "Westphalian order" of liberal-democratic nation-states, which established the reformist strain of republicanism as the hegemonic one. In its radical alternative, however, the people are identified with the oppressed from any nation. Coming out of the English Civil War, this radical strand of thought circulated in the Atlantic system, encountering African religious and black Christian modes of religious/political resistance and noncompliance in such events as slave revolts and maroon spaces.[33] David Walker's *Appeal to the Colored Citizens of the World* (1829) exemplifies this process of cross-pollination. For advocates of Protestant resistance theory such as Theodore of Beza, Babylon as an idolatrous system revolved around the commodification of belief through indulgences and the anti-Christic claims of rulers to determine right belief and impose false doctrine on the people without their consent. By contrast, for the dissenting counterpublic of the "revolutionary" or "Black Atlantic," the idolatrous system of Babylon they protested was the emergent one of capitalism and colonialism and the commodification of people through slavery.

Echoing ancient and medieval conceptions of the people, the modern view of the people has a messianic quality: the people (or either a leader or vanguard acting in their name) can rise up to reinvigorate or redeem the

---

31. Eric Nelson, *The Hebrew Republic: Jewish Sources and the Transformation of European Political Thought* (Cambridge, MA: Harvard University Press, 2010), 23-56.

32. This identification is explored further in chap. 12.

33. John Donoghue, "'Out of the Land of Bondage': The English Revolution and the Atlantic Origins of Abolition," *American Historical Review* 115, no. 4 (2010): 943-74, and Peter Linebaugh and Marcus Rediker, *The Many-Headed Hydra: Sailors, Slaves, Commoners, and the Hidden History of the Revolutionary Atlantic* (Boston: Beacon, 2013).

body politic that is subject to corruption and dissolution. This redemption can be either backward- or forward-looking in its gaze. In its retrospective forms, redemption involves recovering what was lost or stolen from the people by corrupt or indifferent elites or foreign powers. The campaigns for Brexit and Trump in 2016 were successful in leveraging this retrospective vision. In the case of Brexit, it was the sovereignty stolen by the European Union. In the case of Trump, it was "greatness" lost by those portrayed as politically correct elites and racial, ethnic, and religious others.[34] In its forward-looking form, the people rise up to break with a tyrannous and dominating power and found a new polity that is to be a beacon of enlightened self-rule to all peoples. This forward-looking form was the foundation mythos of the American and French revolutions. After this founding event, populist movements retrospectively seek to recover the original moment of freedom and unity lost or stolen by present-day rulers.

A renewed emphasis on the people as the primary political subject is a turn away from a singular revolutionary consciousness housed in one set of experiences—whether of class, race, gender, or sexuality—as the primary agent of political renewal. A turn to the popular, the people, and the commons is thereby a turn away from theories of revolution that pose a subject of history (e.g., the proletariat) as the source of salvation within history. It is not just workers or the stigmatized who possess the requisite experiences to lead radical change; managers, farmers, small-business owners, indigenous peoples, etc., can contribute as part of the people. Potentially, all have gifts to bring. A contemporary example of this turn is Rev. Dr. William Barber II's invocation of "fusion politics" in the development of the Moral Mondays movement.[35] Moreover, a turn to the people is a turn away from a progressive sense that tradition, religion, and folkways are necessarily a source of oppression or, at the very least, a drag on emancipatory politics. Rather, they might be a source of it. A turn to the people can thereby be antivanguardist or anti-Caesarist: no revolutionary vanguard or single leader possesses the true gnosis by which to direct the people. The debacle of revolutionary violence culminating in dictatorial or totalitarian

---

34. Drawn on by Levellers, Chartists, and nineteenth-century radicals, there is a long-standing English tradition of "Anglo-Saxon" liberty and the ancient constitution being lost, first to the Normans and then to various Catholic or corrupt elites, and regained.

35. William J. Barber II with Jonathan Wilson-Hartgrove, *The Third Reconstruction: Moral Mondays, Fusion Politics, and the Rise of a New Justice Movement* (Boston: Beacon, 2016).

regimes, from the terror of the French Revolution, through Lenin and Stalin's gulags, Mao's Great Leap Forward, and Pol Pot's killing fields, warns against such fantasies. As the sailors, soldiers, and factory workers who joined the Kronstadt rebellion realized (before Lenin and Trotsky ordered them slaughtered in 1921 for demanding such things as free elections, free trade unions, and a free press), the people as a whole must be consulted and involved through a process of democratic politics. A contemporary focus on the people aligns with a turn to everyday life; a revolutionary event or ideology or figure will not save the day. Instead, what is needed is attention to the quotidian and recognition of the popular as bearing the seeds of change through which official and hegemonic structures can be resisted and transformed.

Contemporary political theology echoes a turn to the quotidian and the popular life of the people through an emphasis on "lived," "practical," or "ordinary" theology and a turn to a theology of the people. This turn contrasts with prior ways of understanding the people. Some Latin American liberation theology tended to draw on Marxist analysis to conceptualize the poor as the proletariat. A Marxist, class-based analysis posits an inherent conflict between the proletariat and the bourgeoisie, with no possibility of a moderately just and merciful common life existing between them. An alternative way to frame a preferential option for the poor within Latin American liberation theology, one prominent within its Argentinian strands, is to conceptualize the poor as the common people. Exemplifying this move is the influence of *teología del pueblo* on Pope Francis.[36] Francis, along with certain strands of liberation theology, is in turn highlighting a central theme in post–Vatican II ecclesiology—the emphasis on the church as the people of God.[37] In his emphasis on the priority of the people, Francis distinguishes his position from both the clerical and capitalist right and the revolutionary, Marxist left.

36. See, for example, Pope Francis's speech at the World Meeting of Popular Movements, Bolivia, July 9, 2015. On the influence of *teología del pueblo* on Pope Francis, see Austen Ivereigh, *The Great Reformer: Francis and the Making of a Radical Pope* (New York: Holt, 2014), 110-13; Juan Carlos Scannone, "Pope Francis and the Theology of the People," *Theological Studies* 77, no. 1 (2016): 118-35; and Thomas Rourke, *The Roots of Pope Francis's Social and Political Thought: From Argentina to the Vatican* (Lanham, MD: Rowman & Littlefield, 2016), 72-85. For a key official statement of this theology, see the 2007 "Aparecida document" of the Fifth General Conference of Bishops of Latin America and the Caribbean (Jorge Bergoglio served as the redactor for the final document).

37. Hinze, *Prophetic Obedience*, 1-9.

The *mujerista* theology of Ada María Isasi-Díaz develops one of the fuller and more radical expressions of such a move.[38] Isasi-Díaz's conception of the common people as *mestizaje-mulatez* attends to the mixed ethnic, racial, as well as economic histories that inform the everyday experiences of Latino/as living in the USA and elsewhere.[39] Isasi-Díaz retains liberation as a normative criterion for evaluating whether something is good or bad, but rather than focus on structural problems—as the first wave of liberation theologians did—she focuses on *lo cotidiano* or quotidian experiences, particularly of "Hispanas/Latinas."[40] She states: "*Lo cotidiano* situates us in our experiences. It has to do with the practices and beliefs that we have inherited, with our habitual judgments, including the tactics we use to deal with the everyday." But this does not make *lo cotidiano* private. As Isasi-Díaz put it: "*Lo cotidiano* is in contact on a regular basis with social systems; it impacts their structures and mechanisms. *Lo cotidiano* refers to the way we talk and to the impact of class, gender, poverty and work on our routines and expectations; it has to do with relations within families and among friends and neighbors in a community. It extends to our experience with authority and to our central religious beliefs and celebrations."[41] *Lo cotidiano* is not merely the reproduction of habit, but experiences that have been analyzed to generate "folk wisdom" about how to survive and thrive amid daily struggle.[42] And attention to *lo cotidiano* leads to questioning and even subverting established traditions and customs, especially when these reinforce structures of oppression, but these traditions and customs are still vital sources of wisdom.[43] Nor is *lo cotidiano* of Latinas unique, as Isasi-Díaz notes: "there is much we share with other communities of struggle and they with us."[44] Isasi-Díaz's *mujerista* theology represents both an extension of and a break with prior forms of liberation theology and illustrates a constructive example of the contemporary advocacy of ecclesial and democratic populism.

38. Isasi-Díaz, *La Lucha Continues*, 92–106.

39. Ada María Isasi-Díaz, *Mujerista Theology: A Theology for the Twenty-First Century* (Maryknoll, NY: Orbis, 1996), 64.

40. Isasi-Díaz, *Mujerista Theology*, 69–70.

41. Isasi-Díaz, *La Lucha Continues*, 96.

42. Isasi-Díaz, *La Lucha Continues*, 96.

43. Isasi-Díaz, *Mujerista Theology*, 72.

44. Isasi-Díaz, *La Lucha Continues*, 103.

II

In this second part I change instruments—using political theory and social history rather than political theology and church history—to play a different movement within the same composition. I review debates in democratic theory about what it means to be a people and aligned debates about the nature and form of populism. To explain the connection between parts 1 and 2, let me change from a musical to an iconographic metaphor. Like a diptych icon that has two panels connected by a hinge, parts 1 and 2 paint the same subject but from different perspectives and with different horizons in view (the first ultimate, the second penultimate). The same set of theological commitments provides the palette for each, but the distinct perspectives generate thematically and conceptually linked but different pictures. The two together are needed to see the complete work, and it is through contemplating them at the same time that the echoes and resonances between democratic and ecclesial conceptions of peoplehood become apparent. I begin this second part by considering whether the people are a political actor in any meaningful sense.

Peoplehood or Peopling?

In a democracy, the people speak and act. But how? And who is it who speaks and acts? In answering these questions, the first thing to note is that a people is always internally differentiated (not everyone is the same), under construction (who is part of the people is always changing), and only ever imagined and seen in part. The people can be staged at a rally or assembly or represented in a parliament and can appear in various physical spaces (squares, streets, courtrooms) and gestures (voting, demonstrating, occupying).[45] In contrast, the nation does not assemble. It has no need to, as it is imagined as a whole and as already existing, based on culture, blood, etc.; that is, the nation somehow already exists prior to any actual process of talking or acting together politically. It is supposedly "prepolitical." But a people must assemble to exist. And because we can never see the people in their entirety, only as a series of acts or sketches in an ongoing drama,

---

45. This builds on Jacques Rancière's theatrical framing of the concept of the people in his *Staging the People: The Proletarian and His Double*, trans. David Fernbach (London: Verso, 2011).

this means that the claim to represent the people exceeds a single space or collective gesture of appearing. Parliament cannot claim a monopoly in representing "we, the people" any more than a demonstration in Trafalgar Square, London, or the National Mall, Washington, DC, can claim definitively to represent "we, the people." However, both can make legitimate claims to contribute to the formation and determination of what the good of the people is.

Peoplehood is a form of self-articulation that is not coterminous with either the institutions of representation such as a congress or parliament or the movements and modes of contestation such as a rally or parade. Authorizing any claim to represent "the will" of the people is not at base a legal procedure. Authority for such a claim comes from the degree to which it resonates with the long, slow accretion of customary practices, bodily proprieties, symbolic gestures, and genres of speech that coalesce to form a set of normative expectations that shape the imagination of a people about what constitutes a legitimate performance and representation of peoplehood. A claim to represent the people's interests is checked at both a tacit and an explicit level against the existent social imaginary of who the people are and what it means for them to flourish. As Oliver O'Donovan notes:

> A people is a complex of social constituents: of local societies, determined by the common inhabitation of a place; of institutions, such as universities, banks, and industries; of communities of specialist function, such as laborers, artists, teachers, financiers; of families; and of communities of enthusiasm such as sports clubs and musical organisations. To have identity as a people is to be able to conceive the whole that embraces these various constituents practically, as a coordinated agency. When it is no longer possible to discern the constituent elements within the whole, each with its stock of tradition, its reserves of memory, and its communal habits of practice, then the whole dissolves before our eyes. It also dissolves when it is no longer possible to think of these elements as acting, in some sense, together and for one another.[46]

To sustain democratic legitimacy, the institutions and representatives of the people must uphold and reflect a sense of the good of the whole as perceived by those they represent. However, given the finite and fallen

---

46. O'Donovan, *Ways of Judgment*, 150.

nature of politics, there will inevitably be breaches of trust and periods of keenly felt disparity between the people and their representatives, and so crises of representation will ensue. It is into this space that populist movements move, feeding off the disconnection between rulers and ruled. The temptation is to imagine that a formal or juridical procedure can be found to fix the inherent instabilities and ambiguities of representation. This antipolitical temptation mistakenly assumes that if we can find the ideal form or procedure, then the right kind of democratic politics will ensue. By contrast, I contend that the real question is not whether it is possible to banish populism from democratic politics, but what kind of populism to foster alongside structures of representation.

The legitimacy of a claim to speak for the people is always contestable, and, contrary to a class or a nation—which tends to be monistic—the people is a pluralistic political subject. The claim to represent the interests of the people, or to embody the people, is to voice a claim that what makes for thriving among these people, in this place, at this time, needs recalibrating. Inherent in such a claim is another claim that flourishing cannot be achieved through fulfilling the needs of the one (the individual), the few (a faction or vanguard), or even the many (a class or nation). It can only be achieved through pursuing goods in common. As such, "we, the people" is a teleological, moral claim about the form of those goods that unite and serve the flourishing of the people as a whole.

A people is always appearing but never fully apprehended or assembled. It is thus always subject to expansion or dissolution. But it is not so much fugitive as fugue-like, that is, made up of a series of contrapuntal moments that continue to unfold over time. Neither are the speech-acts through which the people appear unitary. As Judith Butler puts it: "We can postulate the scene of a public assembly in which everyone speaks in one voice, but this is both abstract and somewhat frightening—invoking a kind of *Gleichschaltung* that suggests a fascist march or militaristic chant of some kind. 'We, the people' does not presuppose or make a unity but founds or institutes a set of debates about who the people are and what they want."[47]

To borrow Laura Grattan's term, it is more helpful to talk of "peopling" than peoplehood. Talk of peoplehood too easily slips into the same prob-

47. Judith Butler, "'We, the People': Thoughts on Freedom of Assembly," in *What Is a People?* ed. Alain Badiou, Pierre Bourdieu, and Judith Butler, trans. Jody Gladding (New York: Columbia University Press, 2016), 53 (49–64). On Butler's account, "we, the people" is an illocutionary speech-act that constitutes or performs that of which it speaks in the very act of it being spoken.

lem that affects talk of "the nation": it imagines an abstract, static collective subject as the expression of an organic, supposedly prepolitical spirit, essence, or identity. For Grattan, peopling names the convergence between "ongoing practices and the moments when new political actors come out of the shadows to contest the terms of the people and democracy."[48] Peopling is an ongoing, active process of becoming a people that connects horizontal experiments in everyday and radical democratic politics with vertical, hegemonic structures and discourses that order and frame the common life of a polity, thereby contesting and reconfiguring them. As will be seen, a paradigmatic example of such a process is the populist movement in North America that rose and declined between the 1870s and 1890s.[49]

The people as a political actor contrast with other ways of imagining collective political subjects, notably, class, race, gender, and sexuality. These latter forms of collective political subject focus on a part of the body politic rather than on what is common. Also, they envisage the basis of political agency as deriving from mobilizing something (class, identity, or culture) that is said to exist prior to the work of organizing and acting with others. A people or demos, by contrast, is an inherently constructed and contingent form of collective political subjectivity. It takes a political process to create it. The political process may eventuate in a sense of shared identity, and any such identity will draw on prior cultures and traditions but is itself unstable and open-ended.

The open-ended nature of a people's identity is masked by conflating it with nationality. Within the liberal international state system, a prepolitical national/ethnic moniker (e.g., the French people) is required to make legible a people's identity. Conversely, as was seen in the chapter on Black Power, the assertion of peoplehood is framed within this system as a claim to nationhood (e.g., the Palestinian people). But the people can also act to destabilize and challenge what is taken to be the identity of a nation and the hegemony and apparatus of the nation-state. For example, those gathered in Tahrir Square in 2011 asserted that they were the "Egyptian people" as a way of contesting the claims of those who managed and controlled the nation-state of Egypt to truly represent the political and economic interests of all the people living in Egypt. Likewise, those who gathered in Zuccotti

---

48. Laura Grattan, *Populism's Power: Radical Grassroots Democracy in America* (Oxford: Oxford University Press, 2016), 56.

49. Grattan, *Populism's Power*, 49-90.

Park at the outset of the Occupy movement in 2011 proclaimed they represented the 99 percent against the plutocratic 1 percent who controlled the apparatus of the American nation-state for their own selfish interests. A national moniker can also, however, be used to reassert an existing status quo or hegemony. For example, the Tea Party's claim to speak for *the* American people moves beyond a contingent political and economic claim. They do not argue for the incorporation of other interests and visions in the determination of the good of the whole. They make an identity claim that who they are fully embodies and defines what it means to be an American. Claims to represent or be a synecdoche for the people go wrong when they move beyond claims for extending or recalibrating what counts as the good of the people and instead claim to define *in toto* who is the "we" in "we, the people." This is one of the characteristic pathologies of populism.[50]

The Associational Basis of Rule by the People

If democracy at its most basic means collective self-rule by the people for the people, then we must ask what the nature and form of this self-rule should be. Many accounts of democracy conceive of self-rule as an extension of individual autonomy. A form of political order is democratic to the extent that it enables individual liberty and curtails forms of domination that limit the choices individuals may make within the context of personal and circumstantial constraints. As noted in the previous chapter, a notion of popular sovereignty derived from the sovereignty of the individual conceives of sovereignty as indivisible and singular. However, as argued in the previous chapter, an indivisible, transcendent, and monistic conception of sovereignty is not the only way to imagine and structure it: a distributed, pluralistic, and consociational vision incorporates forms of covenantal association in constituting the people.

The premise of democratic legitimacy is that each member of a polity has a say in the decisions that affect everyone. There are various ways to organize this "say," hence debates about the structuring of collective self-rule. The adjectives "representative," "deliberative," and "direct" placed before the term "democracy" denote different forms of organizing collective self-rule and constituting individuals and associations into a people. For example, deliberative democracy generates a people by generating a

50. Grattan, *Populism's Power*, 23–24, 30.

consensus through processes of rational deliberation to which all may contribute, the consensus itself being the basis of the collective self-rule. Each form of organization is given priority according to different ideological and normative accounts of what the nature and form of self-rule should be under certain conditions and within particular contexts. However, conceiving of collective self-rule—and consent—as an extension of individual autonomy hides from view the intrinsic relationship between collective self-rule and the forms of association in which the art of ruling and being ruled is learned and performed. The people as a whole is made up of associations coming into relationship with each other, and it is the negotiation of the different interests and visions of the good between associations that forms a common life—this common life being what constitutes the people qua people.

An alternative beginning point for democratic theory from individual autonomy is to start with the relationships between individuals. If democracy is the rule of the people, by the people, and for the people, then at its most basic level it demands relationships *between* those who constitute the people. Without meaningful relationships between people, there are just individuals and an atomized and disaggregated crowd. If one begins with relationships—and thence their mediation via custom, gift relations, and self-organized institutions—then one must take seriously the forms of social life through which individuals develop and sustain relationships over time. It is within these forms of life that we learn the art of making and responding appropriately to authoritative judgments about what to do and how to do it (or ruling and being ruled). This starting point for thinking about democracy is not in opposition to individual liberty; it recognizes that individual liberty depends on multiple forms of association and different kinds of relationship.[51] As Arendt notes: "A body politic which is the result of covenant and 'combination' becomes the very source of power for each individual person who outside the constituted political realm remains impotent."[52] Any account of democratic politics must take the symbiosis between individual freedom and communal formation seriously.[53]

---

51. The term "association" is used here in a generic way and encompasses both voluntary and nonvoluntary (rather than involuntary) forms of association. For a discussion of the distinction between voluntary, nonvoluntary, and involuntary, see Mark E. Warren, *Democracy and Association* (Princeton: Princeton University Press, 2001), 96–103.

52. Hannah Arendt, *On Revolution* (London: Penguin Books, 2006 [1963]), 162.

53. For accounts of the intrinsic relationship between association and democratic self-rule, see Warren, *Democracy and Association*; Paul Hirst, *Associative Democracy: New*

One of the most developed theoretical positions that begins with relationships rather than the individual is the modern restatement of civic republicanism.[54] Modern republican political theory focuses on how interdependent citizens may deliberate on and realize goods in common within a historically evolving political community. Amidst the great diversity in modern civic republican thought, there is a common emphasis on freedom, civic virtue, participation, and recognition, and how patterns of human interdependence constitute each of them.[55] But this interdependence is not based on similarity or homogeneity but on shared action and communication in a public realm. For civic republicans, rather than the upholding of individual rights, it is a commitment to and participation in a shared political project of collective self-rule and pursuit of the virtues required to sustain that project, that best guarantee and secure individual liberty. This approach is summarized in the following statement from Michael Sandel: "I am free insofar as I am a member of a political community that controls its own fate, and a participant in the decisions that govern its affairs. . . . The republican sees liberty as internally connected to self-government and the civic virtues that sustain it."[56] However, the restatement of republicanism has remained a largely theoretical enterprise. Running in parallel

---

Forms of Economic and Social Governance (Cambridge: Polity, 1994); and Joshua Cohen and Joel Rogers, *Associations and Democracy* (London: Verso, 1995).

54. Indicative of this position are the following: Hannah Arendt, *The Human Condition* (Chicago: University of Chicago Press, 1998 [1958]); Charles Taylor, *Multiculturalism and the Politics of Recognition: An Essay*, ed. Amy Gutmann (Princeton: Princeton University Press, 1992), 25-73; Taylor, *The Ethics of Authenticity* (Cambridge, MA: Harvard University Press, 1992); Michael J. Sandel, *Democracy's Discontent: America in Search of a Public Philosophy* (Cambridge, MA: Belknap Press of Harvard University Press, 1998); Ronald Beiner, *What's the Matter with Liberalism?* (Berkeley: University of California Press, 1995); Benjamin R. Barber, *Strong Democracy in Crisis: Promise or Peril?* (Lanham, MD: Lexington, 2016); Quentin Skinner, *Liberty before Liberalism* (Cambridge: Cambridge University Press, 1998); and Philip Pettit, *Republicanism: A Theory of Freedom and Government* (Oxford: Clarendon, 1997). A primary contribution of civic republicanism to modern democratic theory is to sensitize it to traditional republican themes eclipsed by late modern liberal democratic thought and practice. For Erik J. Olsen, these themes include: "the importance of cultivating habits of responsible citizenship, the public dimensions of liberty, the connection between corruption and tyranny, the patriotism of virtuous resistance to tyranny, and . . . the threat to civic virtue and public liberty that is posed by excessive acquisitiveness and commercialism" (*Civic Republicanism and the Properties of Democracy* [Lanham, MD: Lexington, 2006], 146).

55. Iseult Honohan, *Civic Republicanism* (London: Routledge, 2002), 8-11.

56. Sandel, *Democracy's Discontent*, 26.

with the theoretical rearticulation of civic republicanism as a counterpoint to political liberalism has been a growing sociological engagement with the practice and performance of citizenship in civil society and social movements.[57]

The shadow side of this way of thinking about democracy, the side that rightly worries liberals, is the way in which such a beginning point can lead to an emphasis on the collective taking precedence over and oppressing the individual. At a minimal level, the focus on relationships, and the necessary particularity of such a beginning point, is felt by some to threaten universalistic and egalitarian conceptions of citizenship.[58] There are forms of political order that inherently subordinate the individual to a collective vision of peoplehood, as is the case with nationalist, fascist, state socialist, and state communist regimes. Polities characterized by one or another of these regimes may include democratic elements, but instead of politics constituting the basis of the demos, a supposedly prepolitical species of peoplehood such as the *ethnos* or *Volk* is said to ground it. I set out a different account in chapter 3 on Black Power and black nationalism, in which I contrasted a political conception of what it means to form a people with racist and essentialist constructions of peoplehood.

I contend that beginning with "persons-in-relation" can challenge collectivist, homogenous, and racist conceptions of peoplehood and popular sovereignty. And tacit in what I have argued so far is that a focus on the relationships between people also challenges accounts of democracy built on individualistic and voluntaristic conceptions of autonomy. As exemplified in the work of John Rawls, liberalism posits a prepolitical subject: the autonomous individual self-reflexive chooser who brings to expression in politics a self-willed identity and set of interests. By contrast, a person-in-relation or covenantal approach envisages politics not as a domain of self-expression but as one arena among others in which we discover how we are always already constituted through relationship with others. At the same time, politics is a means by which to order those relationships so that all may flourish. Beginning with ongoing patterns of contingent but necessary forms of sociality that are open to change foregrounds how relationships

57. For a review of the problematic relationship between republican theory, liberalism, and the emergence of citizenship studies and sociological accounts of citizenship, see Margaret R. Somers, *Genealogies of Citizenship: Knowledge, Markets, and the Right to Have Rights* (Cambridge: Cambridge University Press, 2010), 147-70.

58. For a discussion of such concerns, see Michael Walzer, *Politics and Passion: Toward a More Egalitarian Liberalism* (New Haven: Yale University Press, 2005).

between persons take multiple forms, and the complex rather than simple nature of social and political space. Diverse centers of social formation and political power not only provide a check on totalizing forms of power but also make meaningful the ability of enmeshed persons to foster the multiple forms of association (and thence loyalties) they need to flourish.[59] In my work, I have examined how community organizing exemplifies a politics that prioritizes the relationship between distinct but reciprocally related "consociations" or covenantal associations.[60] The history of organizing and other grassroots democratic initiatives such as the labor, civil rights, and Black Power movements suggests that nonstate-centric and nonmarket-centric forms of covenantal association, and the building of relationships between them, are a vital way of generating the collective self-rule of a people/demos.

Seeking What Is Common

In a democracy, wisdom is not seen to rest with the one or the few or even with the many. It is discerned by listening to the whole, so finding it needs everyone's contribution. But how are citizens to discover that wisdom? The size and complexity of modern polities make direct input on all decisions impossible.[61] It necessitates some form of representation, which brings to the fore the communicative process through which to draw both representatives and those they represent into ongoing relationships of reciprocal and affective recognition. In a representative democracy, where an electoral procedure confers the act of legitimacy, this process is often conflated with the equally important moments of consultation and identification through which to imagine "the people" as a meaningful entity. However, if the conferral of legitimacy and processes of consultation and identification are elided, important elements are thereby eclipsed. Consultation involves listening and responding to

59. For example, Hirst uses the term "associative" to describe his conception of democracy.

60. See Luke Bretherton, *Resurrecting Democracy: Faith, Citizenship, and the Politics of a Common Life* (Cambridge: Cambridge University Press, 2015), 111–76.

61. The material conditions of a modern polity are no longer just land but also carbon, and especially oil, which generates the concentrations of energy needed to operate at the scale and complexity we see around us. See Timothy Mitchell, "Carbon Democracy," *Economy and Society* 38, no. 3 (2009): 399–432.

one's constituents. This is often achieved on an individual-by-individual basis: for example, through responding to letters and holding "surgeries" (an individual meeting with a constituent); or in an aggregative way, through elections, opinion polls, and referenda. What is missing in these modes of listening is the connection between consultation and identification of the kind that takes place in various forms of assembly, from a town hall meeting to a rally. Through forms of assembly, those gathered recognize themselves as a demos. It is thus a moment of collective self-discovery that involves an affective ritual through which "the whole" or the "people" is visualized, experienced, and represented. Alongside freedom of speech, freedom of assembly is thus a vital part of democratic politics: if the people can't assemble/congregate, there can be no people.

Ongoing forms of assembly strengthen and make more meaningful the sense of identification and communication between officeholders and the people they represent, helping ensure that representatives are responsive to a range of experiences, concerns, and proposals. Such forms of assembly guard against an elective or technocratic despotism forming wherein officeholders simply do as they see fit.[62] Populism emerges when representatives and the institutions through which a sense of a common life is mediated and communicated (e.g., schools, hospitals, political parties, banks, museums, congregations, the media, etc.) do not attend to ongoing processes of consultation and identification. They thereby grow unresponsive to the concerns and fears of those they serve and represent. These fears and concerns (whether just or not) can then be mobilized over and against established modes of representation (e.g., Fox News trades on exactly this kind of process). Crises of representation emerge serially in both churches and states, and populist movements of one kind or another are an inevitable response. Thus, the people as a political category must account for the performance of the people in various forms of populism.

---

62. On the importance of ongoing arenas of collective deliberation for sustaining political freedom and the role of self-organized associations in this, see Arendt, *On Revolution*, 223-40.

Populists and Populism

Populism is not specifically modern, neither is it solely Western.[63] It is a perennial feature of forms of rule that include democratic elements. Interpretations of populism reflect the contradictory responses to the people: the people are vicious *and* virtuous, irrational *and* bearers of a nation's true spirit, a threat to democracy *and* the holders of sovereignty. Critics of populism see it as an aberration that unless it is prevented or punctured will poison a liberal democratic body politic. Against such a view, I contend that populism is an inherent, and often benign, feature of democratic politics; yet, as with all forms of politics, it can become toxic.

Part of the difficulty in understanding populism is its protean nature. Populism is a sponge that soaks up the ideological spills and stains that surround it.[64] This feature sits alongside others, including opposing instinct and emotion against a rational legal spirit; a simplified antagonistic vision of society, in which a detached ruling class betrays the common people; and the possibility of restoring the equilibrium between the ruled majority and the ruling minority by empowering the former. But all these can serve both utopian and conservative ideological goals of either the Left or the Right.[65] For example, Hugo Chávez in Venezuela used populist discourse, but his ideology was socialism. When "people" refers to a community of blood or race or a homogenous conception of a shared culture, populism aligns itself with racist and xenophobic ideologies. Similarly, populism can incorporate religious beliefs and practices: for example, the anticommunist revolution instigated by Solidarity in Poland drew heavily on Roman Catholicism. Regarding political organization, populists can

63. See, for example, Alexander Makulilo, "Populism and Democracy in Africa," in *Contemporary Populism: A Controversial Concept and Its Diverse Forms*, ed. Sergiu Gherghina, Sergiu Mişcoiu, and Sorina Soare (Newcastle upon Tyne, UK: Cambridge Scholars, 2013), 167–202.

64. See Daniele Albertazzi and Duncan McDonnell, "Introduction: The Sceptre and the Spectre," in *Twenty-First Century Populism: The Spectre of Western European Democracy*, ed. Daniele Albertazzi and Duncan McDonnell (New York: Palgrave Macmillan, 2008), 1–11; Cas Mudde, "The Populist Zeitgeist," *Government and Opposition* 39, no. 4 (2004): 541–63; and Benjamin Moffitt, *The Global Rise of Populism: Performance, Political Style, and Representation* (Stanford, CA: Stanford University Press, 2016), 19–22.

65. A strong polarizing and dichotomizing discourse is not unique to populists: for example, socialists and Marxists denounce capitalists, while libertarians denounce socialists and bureaucrats, often in paranoid ways. In short, many ideologies deploy such a discursive framework.

build loose networks as well as formal party structures.[66] In short, populism merges with more "established" ideologies and discursive frameworks as part of a broader vision of restoring democracy and government to the people.

Part of the democratic impulse of populism is rendering politics more understandable for everyday citizens. As Benjamin Moffitt points out: "The populist embrace of the political 'low,' 'bad manners' and tendency towards simplification can provide an appealing and comprehensible contrast to the increasingly rarefied and technocratic styles of politics that characterize the contemporary political landscape."[67] Moffitt identifies two other democratic features of populism: it can include previously excluded identities within their performances of "the people," and can reveal the dysfunctions of contemporary democratic systems by pointing to corruption or elite indifference.[68] Examples include calling attention to the lack of choice provided by a two-party system in the United States (Ross Perot) and Australia (Pauline Hanson), or the democratic deficit of the European Union (UK Independence Party).

There have been various attempts to develop a comprehensive theory of populism. Much of this work takes a wholly negative view, seeing it as deviant, peripheral, and a sign of democratic decay.[69] This negative view is prevalent in Europe and North America, where journalistic and academic work on populism is focused on the emergence of right-wing, anti-immigrant parties and movements.[70] But the scope of such work is parochial and historically myopic, because it disregards the populist nature of the "third wave" of democratic revolutions that ended communism in Poland, East Germany, and Czechoslovakia, and overthrew the Marcos dictatorship in the Philippines. It also ignores phenomena such as the international peasants' movement, La Via Campesina.[71] And it overlooks the ambiguities of a figure like Pim Fortuyn, the openly gay mayor of Rotter-

---

66. An example of the former is Beppe Grillo's Five Star Movement in Italy. An example of the latter is Geert Wilder's Partij voor de Vrijheid in the Netherlands. See Moffitt, *Global Rise of Populism*, 21.

67. Moffitt, *Global Rise of Populism*, 142.

68. Moffitt, *Global Rise of Populism*, 144.

69. See, for example, Benjamin Arditi, *Politics on the Edges of Liberalism: Difference, Populism, Revolution, Agitation* (Edinburgh: Edinburgh University Press, 2007).

70. See, for example, Jan-Werner Müller, *What Is Populism?* (Philadelphia: University of Pennsylvania Press, 2016).

71. La Vie Campesina, International Peasants Movement, www.viacampesina.org.

dam, the Netherlands, a populist who adopted anti-immigrant and anti-Islamic stances in the name of defending tolerance and liberal democracy.

Within many critical readings, "populism" becomes a term of abuse whereby the common folk are labeled uneducated, vulgar, and simplistic in contrast to cultivated, educated elites—the former should not be allowed to rule, whereas the latter are the rightful rulers. The empirical basis of populist parties and movements rarely backs up such designations—elites can be populists too. But there is a latent antidemocratic suspicion among critics of populism about whether ordinary people can be allowed to govern. If they do govern, critics wonder, will they coarsen political life and generate chaotic or ruinous policies? This reflects an ancient concern that reaches back to the elites of Greece and Rome. However, there is a converse suspicion that elites are incapable of serving goods in common and instead serve only elite interests. In response, common people must give priority to and value the ordinary, the vulgar, and what is popular, as these are not merely a check on the dominance of elite interests and tastes in a democracy but are the source of a moral and political wisdom that elites ignore or disdain. The myopia of elites leads them to embark on projects of social engineering that destroy the lives of ordinary people in the name of lifting them up. They pursue policies (for example, trickle-down economics) that are proclaimed as benefiting everyone when they mostly benefit the privileged and powerful. This mutual antagonism and suspicion is an inevitable and not unjustified feature of democracies. What is popular can be idiotic and simplistic, and what is done by elites can be self-serving, corrupt, and oppressive even while it proclaims itself enlightened, progressive, and for the good of all. Democratic politics is that process through which these antagonisms are addressed peaceably rather than violently.

The ideological indeterminacy of populism makes categorizing it along a left-right spectrum a conceptual mistake.[72] Dividing populism between "democratic" and "authoritarian" forms (whether of left or right) is a more helpful way of distinguishing between different kinds of populism. But democracy itself can turn into the tyranny of the majority and, as Tocqueville observed, produce a distinctly democratic form of servility that substitutes politics for a combination of philanthropy

72. See for example, Chantal Mouffe, *For A Left Populism* (London: Verso, 2018). The logic of Mouffe's position is in keeping with a distinction between radically democratic and anti-democratic, authoritarian forms of populism.

and paternalism. Following the pioneering work of the political theorists Margaret Canovan and Ernesto Laclau, populism should not be seen as something inherently dangerous, and thus as a phenomenon to be rejected, but as playing off tensions within democracy itself.[73] For Canovan, populism is a contextual phenomenon that reacts to whatever is hegemonic.[74] And in the context of modern liberal democracies, populism is an inherent possibility born out of the oscillation between what Canovan identifies as the "redemptive" and the "pragmatic" face of democracy. When democracy, which offers government of the people, by the people, and for the people (its redemptive face), is reduced to a mechanism for negotiating and resolving conflicts of interest and distributing power (its pragmatic face), populists "move on to the vacant territory, promising in place of the dirty world of party maneuvering the shining ideal of democracy renewed."[75] Or in the words of Donald Trump, it offers to "drain the swamp."

Building on Canovan, a constructive way to distinguish between different kinds of populism is to distinguish between a "populist democratic politics" and "antipolitical" forms of populism. A *populist democratic politics* attempts to construct a common life not by denying friend-enemy distinctions but, via a heightened process of conflict and conciliation, by generating a richer sense of what is the good of the whole body politic. An *antipolitical populism* refuses the possibilities of a common life, narrowing what is considered common via exclusionary and dichotomized visions of who is and who is not part of the people. A populist democratic politics embodies a conception of politics that works to reinstate plurality and inhibit totalizing monopolies (whether of the state or market) through common action and deliberation, both of which depend on personal participation in and responsibility for tending a common life. By contrast, antipolitical populism seeks to simplify the political space rather than render it more complex. It advocates direct forms of democracy in order to circumvent the need for deliberative processes and the representation of multiple interests in the formation of political judgments. The leader rules by direct consent

73. Defining populism is a notoriously difficult conceptual task. On this see Margaret Canovan, "Two Strategies for the Study of Populism," *Political Studies* 30, no. 4 (1982): 544-52; Ernesto Laclau, *On Populist Reason* (London: Verso, 2007), 3-20; and Moffitt, *Global Rise of Populism*, 12-27.

74. Margaret Canovan, "Trust the People! Populism and the Two Faces of Democracy," *Political Studies* 47, no. 1 (1999): 4.

75. Canovan, "Trust the People!," 11.

without the hindrance of checks and balances or the representation of different interests. In antipolitical populism, throwing off established authority structures is the prelude to giving over authority to the one and giving up responsibility for the commons. The goal of antipolitical populism is personal withdrawal from public life so as to be free to pursue private self-interests rather than public mutual interests.[76] In antipolitical expressions of populism, personal responsibility is for improvement of the self, one's immediate family, institution (e.g., a congregation), or community disconnected from the interdependence of any such project with the care of the public institutions, rule of law, physical infrastructure, and natural resources that make up the commonwealth on which all depend.

Antipolitical and democratic forms of populism do, however, share the following. They both:

- emphasize the need for leadership;
- dichotomize and simplify issues;
- advocate for direct forms of rule;
- romanticize the wisdom of ordinary people;
- distrust universalist ideologies and the prioritizing of international issues;
- suspect theory, envisaging themselves as pragmatic;
- distrust party politics, elites, and bureaucracy;
- use affective rituals and symbols to generate a sense of unity; and
- mobilize dissent through the organizing theme of ordinary people/ nonelites as both the subject of grievance and the means of correction.

However, the critical differences between a populist democratic politics and antipolitical populism are fivefold. A populist democratic politics:

1. puts populist orientations and sentiments in the service of forging a shared political space—not limiting it, subverting it, or closing it down;
2. invests in long-term organization and education (e.g., the role of the "lecturer" in the Populist Movement and the "organizer" in community organizing);
3. develops a broad base of local leaders rather than relying on one charismatic leader and short-term mobilization of people who are focused not

76. Antipolitical populism is a dominant characteristic of the contemporary Tea Party movement.

on loyalty to each other and a common life but on loyalty to the single leader and the cause or issue;[77]

4. frames proposals as moral imperatives but at the same time sees compromise as "a key and beautiful word";[78] and

5. reconstitutes the sense of what it means to be a people in a way that incorporates rather than demonizes those considered other.

In short, populist democratic politics seeks to generate a common life as against a politics dominated by the interests of the one, the few, or the many. Populism corrupts the people when it claims to wholly identify the people with the interests of a part rather than the common. And as a general rule, while populist *movements* can be democratic or contain strong democratic elements, populism as a *regime of statecraft* is rarely, if ever, democratic, as it quickly degenerates into a form of authoritarianism.

Case Study: The Populist Movement

Historical examples are the best way to understand populism. Such examples enable its commitments and internal contradictions to be articulated. I will focus on the US Populist Movement. Not only is it paradigmatic for understanding modern, Western forms of populism more generally but it also represents a confluence of ecclesial and democratic populism. The Populists originated in the broad-based and fractious movement that emerged in the United States from the 1850s onward.[79] Populism reached its high point in the 1890s with the formation of the People's Party that challenged the duopoly of the Republicans and Democrats but declined rapidly as a formal movement thereafter. Yet, like an event of nuclear fission, its half-life continues to be felt long after its moment of greatest energy. The vital centers of the Populist Movement were the Midwest,

77. Harry Boyte, *Commonwealth: A Return to Citizen Politics* (New York: Free Press, 1989), 108-9.

78. Saul Alinsky, *Rules for Radicals: A Practical Primer for Realistic Radicals* (New York: Vintage Books, 1989 [1971]), 59. In the populist movement the decision to back the Democratic Party and the candidacy of William Jennings Bryan can be seen as an example of just such a compromise.

79. Use of the terms "Populist" and "Populism" as proper nouns will be reserved for reference to the Populist Movement of the nineteenth century, whereas the term "populism" will be used as a generic term.

Southwest, and Southeast, with concentrations of activity in Texas, Kansas, and Oklahoma. While primarily an agrarian phenomenon, its political impact came through forging a farmer-labor alliance. Populism is a taproot for some contemporary forms of radical democratic politics in the United States, most notably, community organizing.[80]

Like interpretations of many social movements, treatments of the Populists tend to refract the concerns and sympathies of the historian's own time.[81] The contemporary consensus among scholars of Populism seems to be that it was a broadly republican critique of the overconcentration of "money power."[82] This critique was combined with the language of evangelical Protestantism, the Methodist camp meetings, and Baptist revivals to generate a powerful rhetoric with which to challenge the status quo.[83] It thereby represents a convergence of ecclesial and democratic populism that reiterated earlier moments of similar convergences, most notably in the Second Great Awakening.[84] Populist language cut across the color line, shared as it was by black and white Populists. At the same time, however, it alienated the predominantly Catholic industrial workers in the Northeast.

80. Bretherton, *Resurrecting Democracy*, 21–36.

81. The contemporary historiographical debate begins with Richard Hofstadter's *Age of Reform: From Bryan to F.D.R.* (New York: Knopf, 1955). Writing in the 1950s in reaction against McCarthyism, Hofstadter argued that the Populists were nostalgic, backward-looking petit bourgeois businessmen who were insecure about their declining status in an industrializing America. Additionally, he claimed that they were provincial and conspiracy minded and tended to scapegoat others, a tendency that manifested itself in nativism and anti-Semitism. By contrast, Lawrence Goodwyn, writing in the wake of the 1960s, envisaged the Populists as precursors of the New Left who sought to structurally redesign American capitalism and fulfill the ideal of America's democratic promise but were thwarted by a combination of modest reformers or "trimmers" (who for Goodwyn were equivalent to contemporary "liberals") and the combined hegemonic power of media, academy, banking, party political, and industrial interests (*Democratic Promise: The Populist Moment in America* [New York: Oxford University Press, 1976]). More recently, Omar Ali casts the significant involvement of African Americans in the complex and troubled biracial dimensions of Populism as a precursor to the civil rights movement (*In the Lion's Mouth: Black Populism in the New South, 1886–1900* [Jackson: University Press of Mississippi, 2010]).

82. Goodwyn, *Democratic Promise*, xiii.

83. On the importance of theological discourse to Populist rhetoric, see Joe Creech, *Righteous Indignation: Religion and the Populist Revolution* (Urbana: University of Illinois Press, 2006).

84. See Nathan Hatch, *The Democratization of American Christianity* (New Haven: Yale University Press, 1989).

That the discursive framework of the Populists worked with the values and traditions of its participants contrasts starkly with Marxist-inspired movements, which viewed the sundering of people's traditional communal and place-based ties as the prerequisite of freedom.

The historian Michael Kazin identifies four themes that shaped Populist discourse of the 1890s and which the ongoing tradition of American populism has deployed in a multiplicity of ways. The first is "Americanism," identified as an emphasis on understanding and obeying the will of the people. Second is "producerism," which is the conviction that, in contrast to classical and aristocratic conceptions, those who toiled were morally superior to those who lived off the toil of others. Producerism maintains the belief that only those who create wealth in tangible material ways can be trusted to guard the nation's liberties. Counterpoised to producerism is a third theme: the need to oppose the dominance of privileged elites (variously identified as government bureaucrats, cosmopolitan intellectuals, high financiers, industrialists, or a combination of all four). These elites are seen to subvert the principles of self-rule and personal liberty through centralizing power and imposing abstract plans on the ways people live.[85] The final theme is the notion of a movement or crusade that is engaged in a battle to save the nation and protect the welfare of "real" America or the common people.[86]

While these themes are identifiable points of focus in the Populist movement, like all forms of populism, the movement was ideologically porous. For example, the Populists saw a need for government intervention, for to establish the conditions for fair access to public goods such as transport, credit, and a postal service, modern centralized government bureaucracies needed to exist. Elizabeth Sanders, in her history of the Populists, summarizes their approach: "Its philosophy was anticorporate, though not *anticapitalist*. It sought, as recent scholars have established, not to turn the clock back on industrial development but to harness the new technological power for social good, to use the state to check exploitative excesses, to uphold the rights and opportunities of labor (farm and factory), and to maintain a healthy and creative business competition. The program was profoundly opposed to concentrated corporate power.

85. The shadow side of the opposition to elites is the tendency of populism to adopt conspiracy theories about how "hidden" elites operate.

86. Michael Kazin, *The Populist Persuasion: An American History* (New York: Basic Books, 1995), 11–17.

Where concentration seemed inevitable, and for vital economic functions on which the well-being of the entire society depended, it was best that complete government control be established."[87] At the same time, they developed the rudiments of a "cooperative commonwealth" consisting of a huge range of autonomous institutions, educational initiatives, and mutual associations such as cooperatives in order to address their needs without being dependent on the banks or the state. However, while the Populists understood that the state must know its place, they saw the state as having an important role in securing a common life. And rather than fixate on local concerns, they sought to organize translocally and generate institutional forms at the appropriate scale in order to secure their aims.[88] Inevitably, in such a diverse movement, a wide variety of people were involved, ranging from doctrinaire socialists (of various sorts) to white nationalists.[89]

By the 1890s the Populists sought reform in three major areas: land, transportation, and money. These came to expression in what is known as the "Omaha Platform."[90] Populists called for limits to land speculation; the nationalization of railroads, telephones, and telegraphs (as these were natural monopolies and so needed operating in the interests of everyone); the formation of a central bank directly responsible to elected officials and a flexible currency created by the issuing of paper money (greenbacks) and the free coinage of silver (those who supported this were known as "silverites"). In addition, the platform endorsed the enforcement of the eight-hour working day, referendums to introduce elements of direct democracy into the system of representative democracy, and a graduated income tax. After the failure of local and regional efforts to break the crop-lien system that resulted in the debt slavery of both black and white farmers, the Populists came to endorse the "subtreasury plan," a federally backed farm commodity price support program.[91]

87. Elizabeth Sanders, *Roots of Reform: Farmers, Workers, and the American State, 1877-1917* (Chicago: University of Chicago Press, 1999), 132.

88. Theda Skocpol, Marshall Ganz, and Ziad Munson, "A Nation of Organizers: The Institutional Origins of Civic Voluntarism in the United States," *American Political Science Review* 94, no. 3 (2000): 527-46.

89. What is remarkable about Populism is that while it worked within the emerging consensus of the time in relation to gender and race, there flowered within it significant and extensive moments of biracial politics, and it actively enabled and promoted women's involvement in public life. On this see Charles Postel, *The Populist Vision* (New York: Oxford University Press, 2009), and Ali, *In the Lion's Mouth.*

90. This was adopted as the manifesto of the People's Party at its 1892 convention.

91. For an account of the devastating impact of the crop-lien and sharecropping

What these measures add up to is an attempt to reembed labor, land, and money within a social and political matrix and thereby to inhibit the destructive effects of commodification on place-based political and social relations. In terms of the Populists' own frames of reference, "money power" in the form of laissez-faire capitalism fell under a theological judgment: it was seen to be destroying the people as a moral community, and it threatened the nation with God's judgment. The government, as the embodiment of the will of the people, needed to act to make things right and thereby fulfill its covenantal role.[92] Such a view was expressed time and again in Populist speeches and pamphlets. To quote but one example, Milford Howard, writing in 1895, states: "The spirit of avarice is devouring the great heart of this nation. The greed for gain gets such possession of men's souls that they become demons. They rush into the maelstrom of money-getting, and soon lose all fear of God and love for their Fellow-men."[93] As a mode of ecclesial and democratic populism, the Populist movement was simultaneously conservative and radical. It sought to inhibit the liquefying thrust of "money power" and tried to forge a new institutional and governmental framework within the processes of modernization, one that would pluralize monopolistic forms of economic and political power.[94]

At this point I must sound a note of caution. Historical forms of populism can be democratic or authoritarian and often combine elements of both. For example, rather than being straightforwardly fascist, Peronism in Argentina and Huey Long in Louisiana are both examples of the integration of democratic and authoritarian elements. Populism (as opposed to fascism) is thus an ambiguous political phenomenon. Moreover, unlike fascists, populists insist on the values of equality (among the people) rather than hierarchy, and they prioritize the community and right relations within it, rather than the state and stable order. Kazin tells a declension

---

system on both black and white farmers, how it created a system of debt peonage, and the developments of efforts to break this system that culminated in the subtreasury plan, see Goodwyn, *Democratic Promise*, 26-33, 110-73, and Ali, *In the Lion's Mouth*, 15-77.

92. Rhys Williams and Susan Alexander, "Religious Rhetoric in American Populism: Civil Religion as Movement Ideology," *Journal for the Scientific Study of Religion* 33, no. 1 (1994): 1-15.

93. Quoted in Williams and Alexander, "Religious Rhetoric," 10.

94. Conceptualizing populism as a countermovement accords with broader accounts of the conditions for the emergence of populist movements. See Francisco Panizza, introduction to *Populism and the Mirror of Democracy*, ed. Francisco Panizza (London: Verso, 2005), 1-31.

narrative about populism in the United States wherein, from the 1940s onward, it suffers capture by the Right. By contrast, the historian Richard Hofstadter gives an ascension narrative about a move from populism to progress. The conceptualization of populism suggested here allows for a more nuanced account. Populism in the United States contains democratic and antipolitical elements, and sometimes these elements receive a greater or lesser emphasis within specific expressions of populism. The antipolitical populism of the Ku Klux Klan, Father Coughlin and the Coughlinites of the late 1930s, McCarthyism, Ross Perot, and latterly the Tea Party movement and the Trump campaigns does not exhaust nor define populism. These expressions of populism must be counterpoised with the democratic populism of broad-based community organizations such as the Industrial Areas Foundation, PICO (People Improving Communities through Organizing), the Gamaliel Foundation, and National People's Action; the development of "community unionism"; and the self-described "new populists" such as Harry Boyte, Heather Booth, and, within the Roman Catholic Church, Msgr. Geno Baroni.[95] Theological and ecclesial populism of one kind or another has contributed, for better and worse, to the discursive tropes of all of them.

Conclusion

What modern conceptions of the people and populism share with theological conceptions and ecclesial embodiments of the people of God is the indeterminacy of representation: How is the will of the people to be communicated? Can the people act directly without mediation, or can the people only ever act in part or via duly appointed representatives? If the latter, what is the best way of selecting and legitimizing representatives? And can a people be represented by a single leader, a vanguard, a class of people set apart for that task? Or is it most clearly seen in self-organized popular movements? Must a people, to be a people, be the same *kind* of people, or is a truly democratic people necessarily made up of (and therefore open to) many kinds of persons? Answers to these questions are constantly under

95. Baroni was a key figure in the development of the Community Reinvestment Act of 1977 when serving as Housing and Urban Development Assistant Secretary for Neighborhood Development, Consumer Affairs, and Regulatory Functions under President Carter.

negotiation and shape the form and character of a people, both democratic and ecclesial.

Popular democracy is no panacea, and, as already argued in previous chapters, there needs to be a tensional and mutually disciplining relationship between democracy and Christianity. Too often congregations pursue works of mercy divorced from any wider forms of political engagement. But corporeal works of mercy (burying the dead, feeding the hungry, and so on) are not just ends in themselves. They are also part of how the church constitutes itself as a body politic characterized by *koinōnia* and catholicity. And it is through the formation of healed and fruitful relations within and through congregations that the church in its catholicity contributes to the prevailing social and political order as an order not being wholly defined by an unjust status quo. However, to move beyond merely sticking Band-Aids on structural problems, churches need to be involved in wider forms of democratic politics. The church's involvement in forms of highly participatory, often agonistic forms of democratic politics is necessary because it forces local churches to recognize their need of others and to own in practice that their welfare is intricately bound up with the welfare of the demos. Conversely, the congregation, as part of a moral tradition with an eschatological vision of the good, brings a wider horizon of reference and relationship to bear upon the immediate needs and demands of the demos (whether in the form of a union, a community-organizing coalition, or a social movement). This mutual disciplining helps ensure that both congregations and democratic politics (whether place-based or work-based) remain directed toward building a common life rather than toward authoritarian and antidemocratic ends.

Threshold

Having articulated a formal framework for understanding what it means to be a people, the next chapter develops a constructive account of the kind of democratic politics through which a people is formed and sustained over time.

Suggested Readings for Further Discussion

Scriptures: Exodus 19–20; Joshua 8:30–35; Nehemiah 5:1–13; Matthew 5; 1 Corinthians 12:4–31.

Augustine, *City of God* 2.21; 14.28; 15.1; 19.21. Various editions.

Theodore of Beza, *The Rights of Magistrates over Their Subjects* (1574). Available online.

Gerrard Winstanley, *The New Law of Righteousness* (1649), chaps 6, 8, 9, and 10, and *A Declaration from the Poor Oppressed People of England* (1649). Various editions.

Paul VI, *Lumen Gentium* (1964), chaps. 2–4. Available online. A modern theological statement of the "people of God" as a central way to think about what it means to be the church, one that sits alongside the "body of Christ" as a motif shaping contemporary Roman Catholic ecclesiology.

Stanley Hauerwas, *Peaceable Kingdom: A Primer in Christian Ethics* (Notre Dame: University of Notre Dame Press, 1983), chaps. 5 and 6. Hauerwas provides a statement of the church as a distinctive people or "community of character" that embodies rather than has a social and political ethic.

Ada María Isasi-Díaz, "Lo Cotidiano: Everyday Struggles in Hispanas/Latinas' Lives," in *La Lucha Continues: Mujerista Theology* (Maryknoll, NY: Orbis, 2004), 92–106.

CHAPTER 14

Democratic Politics

This chapter picks up on the definition of politics given in the first chapter and makes explicit the vision of democratic politics tacit throughout the book. Politics as used here refers to forming, norming, and sustaining some kind of common life between friends, strangers, enemies, and the friendless amid their ongoing differences and disagreements and as they negotiate asymmetries of various kinds of power. Political agency is the ability to act with and for others in the determination of the goods, practices, institutions, and judgments that constitute a common life. Democratic politics entails the radical extension of who is considered capable and worthy of being political agents, aiming as it does to form a common life through ensuring that political agency is distributed as widely as possible. Democratic politics thereby extends politics from being the preserve of the few to something undertaken by the many for the good of the whole.[1]

Like politics as such, democratic politics should neither be collapsed into statecraft nor seen as dependent on there being a state. Democratic politics can be distinguished from democracy as a mode of statecraft (e.g., voting systems, parliamentary forms of government, etc.) even as it is a way of determining and disciplining the use of unilateral power. Democratic politics names a set of practices for generating nonviolent forms of relational power and cooperation through various kinds of shared speech and action (e.g., community organizing, unions, cooperatives, demonstrations, etc.). Democratic politics in this sense means not just participation in

---

1. The rest of the book specifies some of the ways in which democratic politics is framed within Christianity. However, I take democratic politics to be a penultimate good that can be adopted by and has analogues within a broad range of traditions of belief and practice.

decision making but also the capacity of ordinary people to act collectively to reconstitute their common life through shared speech and action. What follows in this chapter are reflections on what it means to understand democratic politics as the negotiation of a common life rather than as a way of structuring government.

A number of presuppositions guide my reflections. The first is that democratic politics involves building relationships with people you disagree with, don't like, find scandalous, or even threatening. The second follows on from the first and is that if politics is to be democratic, its most basic building block is the need to listen to others not like oneself. Listening requires certain conditions without which it cannot take place. The third is that democratic politics builds on the experience and trust that people you disagree with and don't like can show you kindness beyond what you expect or deserve; and conversely, that people who share your views can do great harm to you, themselves, and others. In short, I assume that democratic politics is premised on the recognition that love and sin are political realities.

Beginning from these three presuppositions, I explore the following as axiomatic for democratic politics:

- that it depends on forging forms of relational power and cooperation;
- that citizens are not just rights-bearing subjects but are also persons enmeshed in forms of communal and place-based relations that provide sources of meaning, purpose, and a realm of affections that must be honored if politics is to be humane and relational power is to be sustained;
- that people come before any ideological, bureaucratic, or legal program;
- that politics should be prioritized over procedure;
- that practice comes before theory;
- that institutions and forms of covenantal association, not just individuals, are a constituent element of democratic politics; and finally,
- that a precondition for a commitment to a liberal-constitutional order is not a commitment to liberalism as a political philosophy but a commitment to democratic politics, and that it is democratic politics rather than liberalism that needs prioritizing if the rule of law and a self-limiting state are to be sustained.

Before proceeding, let me make clear that when I say practice comes *before* theory, I do not mean "instead of," "as an alternative to," "as a substitute for," or "rather than." I am not establishing a dichotomy between theory and practice. It means putting first things first, giving priority to, or ordering things rightly. The same goes for other prescriptions set out here, such as people before program and politics before procedure.

Politics Needs Power

Political life always involves questions of power. So we are hopelessly naïve if we think that by getting the form, procedure, or theory right, the practice can be made good. In theological terms, the organization of power always demands attention to sin. An account of sin contends that not only is our ability to do the right thing impaired but so is our ability to think rightly about what is true, good, and beautiful. In nontheological terms, the operations of dominatory power systemically distort processes of decision making and what gets to count as common sense. Any analysis needs to face the reality of sinful power relations; that is, how are certain forms of knowledge legitimized and others marginalized, to the benefit of some and the detriment of others? But the lesson to be learned from taking sin seriously as a political reality—whether we draw on Marx, Foucault, or Augustine to develop such an account—is not that all moral claims in politics are hypocrisy. The lesson is rather that the first step to a politics that is more moral is realizing that we are not. The next step is to take responsibility for our sinfulness and establish the representation of other interests and voices in the decision-making process. We can thereby constructively address the contested nature of knowledge and judgment. But to do so involves having the humility to know that despite our expertise or experience, we do not possess a monopoly on wisdom.

Addressing the contested nature of knowledge and judgment does not of necessity warrant a species of competitive interest group politics in which politics becomes a zero-sum game. Neither does it demand a form of subcultural micropolitics that eschews all claims to power. Rather, it can undergird a common-life democratic politics where, paradoxically, contestation helps identify goods in common and the mutual interests they fulfill. This conflict involves destabilizing and disrupting the selfish or idolatrous interests of the one, the few, or the many to identify genuine goods in common. This process of contestation is as needed for the negotiation of pension remuneration rates in a company, the distribution of resources in a school, or the priorities in mission and ministry of a church as it is for tax policy in central government.

To open spaces for democratic politics and avoid abstract analysis of power, we need to focus on how people can act together to make life better. Without attention to concrete issues and the ways people act in concert and form a common life through public practices of speech and action, we have little to say other than wolves eat sheep, power corrupts, and the strong triumph over the weak. Moreover, to merely critique power in the abstract, or make critique an end in itself, results in ever-diminishing returns. Critique is no substitute for a constructive and imaginative alternative. And while oppressive uses of power are pervasive, not all power is bad.

Through acting in concert, the weak can resist the unilateral actions of money power and state power to establish goods in common on which the flourishing of everyone depends. The early labor, civil rights, women's, and environmental movements are all examples of such relational power in action. The pursuit of goods in common—better working conditions or cleaner air—is the basis of a genuinely public political life as against a practice of politics as based on the individual pursuit of private interests. As Hannah Arendt puts it: "The political realm rises directly out of acting together, the 'sharing of words and deeds.' Thus, action not only has the most intimate relationship to the public part of the world common to us all but is the one activity which constitutes it."[2] Overly deterministic accounts of unilateral power, or the domination of structural forces such as capitalism, can be antipolitical. They do not allow for the reality of the kinds of agency constituted by relational power and wily wisdom and which in turn can form the basis of a more just and compassionate common life. David (possessor of dexterity, sureness of eye, and sharp-wittedness) can beat Goliath (possessor of overwhelming force).

In democratic politics, building power takes four interrelated forms: organized knowledge, organized money, organized people, and organized action. The first generates the frameworks of analysis and understanding through which to renarrate and reimagine the world, destabilizing the dominant scripts and ideas that legitimate oppression. It entails informal, self-organized forms of "popular education" that aim to help those involved to discern and describe their political, economic, and social conditions, helping them move toward alternative ways of understanding themselves and their situation. Crucial to this process of discernment is enabling people to reflect on their conditions through broader frameworks of interpretation.

2. Hannah Arendt, *The Human Condition* (Chicago: University of Chicago Press, 1998 [1958]), 198.

Such "consciousness raising" is vital for generating an alternative community of interpretation, one with the epistemic agency to undertake the identification and analysis of an issue and thence to develop a strategy by which to articulate a position or set of demands (an "ask") and act together.

The second form, organized money, is shorthand for generating the material and economic resources and conditions to act independently from the state, one's employer, or the patronage of elites. The third—organized people—builds the relational ties, networks, trust, affective registers, and cooperation that sustain relational power over time. Such ties and networks are necessary to generate movement from the world as it is to a more just and compassionate one. One strand of such work is place-based (e.g., community organizing, community development, burial societies, neighborhood associations), and the other is work-based forms of economic democracy (e.g., cooperatives and unions). And in the contemporary context, online forms of mobilizing alongside on-the-ground forms of organizing contribute to this work.

The fourth—organized action—entails two things, either separately or combined. First, it is action that symbolically and physically contests oppressive, corrupt, or unresponsive structures, groups, and practices. This contestation aims at delegitimizing existing arrangements through various kinds of direct action: marches, demonstrations, occupations, assemblies, boycotts, and the like. Second, it is the formation of practices and institutional arrangements that prefiguratively embody and exemplify the change that is sought.

Some combination of organized knowledge, money, people, and action is the engine of democratic politics. How they are combined and performed depends in part on the context but also on how what it means to be a good democratic citizen is imagined and narrated.

Congregation and Demos

Democratic politics builds on the contention that the best way to prevent the subordination of human flourishing and mutually responsible social relationships to commodification by capitalism or instrumentalization by the state is not law or some other procedure but through power born out of associating for common action. To build and sustain relational power and forms of democratic organizing take discipline and loyalty. Loyalty or faithfulness is vital both to developing any kind of common life and to the shared action necessary for dismantling corrupt or oppressive structures. Faithfulness denotes reliability, commitment, and trustworthiness. Without it, promises are broken, relations of trust dissolve, and so the ability to deliberate and act together and the long-term reciprocal relations needed to sustain relational power evaporate.[3]

Faithfulness, by definition, is orientated to the specific. We cannot keep faith with everyone all at once in every place. We can only be faithful to these people, in this place, at this time. To modern cosmopolitan ears, faithfulness provokes a scandal of particularity: it demands boundaries and limits. However, faithfulness and the solidarity it generates are vital if democratic politics is to hold in check or change the overconcentration of either economic or political power and the monopolization of resources by a narrow range of interests.

In the American and British contexts, forms of popular, local self-organization and common action emerged within such movements as the abolitionist movement, the Chartists, the suffragists, the temperance movement, and the civil rights movement. These were aligned and had a symbiotic relationship with popular religion. A good example is the nineteenth-century Populists discussed in chapter 13, whose critique of monopolistic forms of power combined with the language of the Methodist camp meetings and Baptist revivals to generate a powerful rhetoric with which to challenge the status quo. What these movements represent, and what they offer democratic politics, is the assertion of the priority of covenantal forms of social relationships—and the loyalty and solidarity such relations generate. By prioritizing society over state or market, covenantal forms of association are vital to upholding common values and a common life over and against their instrumentalization, commodification, or destruction through state-driven and economic processes.

---

3. There is a complex interplay between faithfulness and critique in any movement for social and political change. True faith can, paradoxically, entail what appears like treachery, while what is claimed as faithful action can be hypocrisy or constitute the betrayal of the purpose and meaning of a movement. It is a theme explored in the Gospels where Jesus, who fulfills the law and the prophets, is seen by many as a traitor, while the pharisaical upholders of the law are really whitewashed sepulchers. On the centrality of this tension in feminist, queer, antiracist, and other communities of resistance, see Lisa Tessman, *Burdened Virtues: Virtue Ethics for Liberatory Struggles* (Oxford: Oxford University Press, 2005), 133-57. Echoing notions of a "loyal opposition," Tessman calls for loyal critics, contrasting such a stance over and against both a deconstructive hermeneutics of suspicion and unquestioning devotion to a cause.

As noted in the previous chapter, the congregation and the demos echo each other, and even though they serve different ends, there can be a mutually disciplining, critically constructive relationship between them. The goal of this relationship should be ensuring that when it comes to earthly politics, the proper object of democratic piety is neither the state nor some abstract notion of a nation or humanity, but the shared work of forging and sustaining a just and loving common life. To that end, the deepest gift the church offers democratic politics is that it witnesses to a horizon of reference beyond politics and economics, thereby pointing to how political economy neither exhausts nor defines human fulfillment.

Gathering for worship offers a moment of contemplation of that which lies beyond the immediate needs and demands of forming and sustaining a common life here and now. In doing so, the church insists that in the last analysis not everything is reducible to either politics or economics. Failure to abide by this truth means that a political economy ceases to serve human flourishing. Instead, it becomes an idol that humans are forced to serve. The consequence of such idolatry is that the fabric of what makes up a human life is quickly shredded and distorted. The church, by being the church, holds open times and spaces for wonder, prayer, rest, festivity, and play, all of which regenerate the human spirit and embody the reality that humans do not live by bread alone. The church also keeps open the need we have for asking questions about the meaning and purpose of life, and thence the meaning and purpose of politics and economics. That said, such contemplation cannot be the sum total and focus of life. At some level, we must engage in politics if we are to find ways of surviving and thriving by forming and sustaining a common life with and for others. The pursuit of rest, play, worship, and wonder to the exclusion of politics denies the conditions that make them possible. But politics pursued to the exclusion of rest, play, and contemplation, or the dismissal of such activities as nothing more than a reproduction of unilateral power and unjust hierarchies, makes for an intolerable and inhuman life. In the relationship between Christianity and democracy, the tension between worship and politics is an irresolvable but necessary one for the health and integrity of each. To focus on one to the exclusion of the other, or to collapse one into the other, is to lose both.

Community and Citizenship

Democratic politics requires, and is a way through which to gain, the experience to make and respond appropriately to authoritative judgments about what to do and how to do it (i.e., ruling and being ruled). As Tocqueville notes: "It is, indeed, difficult to imagine how men who have completely given up the habit of self-government could successfully choose those who should do it for them, and no one will be convinced that a liberal, energetic, and prudent government can ever emerge from the voting of a nation of servants."[4]

The ways we gain the experience of ruling and being ruled is through forms of semi-independent, self-organized practices of cooperative association like running schools or being involved in vocational, professional, and craft production; or in congregations, mutual aid societies, and the like. However, while such experience of self-rule is a necessary condition, it is not a sufficient one to make wise citizens capable of just, compassionate, and, when necessary, radical political judgments. The mere fact of associating does not determine whether a group will be civil or uncivil, democratic or antidemocratic. The crucial factor is whether an association is prepared to contribute to building a common life and communicating with others to build it. This is the key to determining whether it is democratic or not.

The experience and ability of common work *between* different associations and their particular interests and visions of the good are vital for a genuinely democratic politics. Herein lies the vocation of a political party. The point of a political party is not just to provide experience and training in ruling and being ruled, but it is also to mediate relationships between different forms of association and interests in the pursuit of goods in common. Without this kind of cross-institutional experience, institutions are vulnerable to being co-opted by the state, reconfigured within the processes of capitalism (and thereby becoming commodified), or turned against each other in competitive and intercommunal rivalry. To thrive, democratic politics requires practices that enable us to pursue a common life between multiple loyalties, while at the same time honoring our noncivic, familial, communal, and institutional loyalties as having worth and value.

4. Alexis de Tocqueville, *Democracy in America*, trans. Gerald Bevan (London: Penguin, 2003), 808 (4.6).

People before Program

If we are to attend to the lived experiences and practices through which people build power and negotiate a common life, then we must put people before program. Rather than begin with an abstract theory, ideology, or principle, democratic politics—to be democratic—contends that politics begins with what people are already doing, where they already gather to build relationship with each other, and what they hold dear. Rather than begin with a prior solution or policy (e.g., marketization, nationalization), programs should derive from listening to the people who will be most affected by a decision. Listening to people is the necessary prelude to making wise judgments about what to do now, with these people, in this place.

To truly listen necessitates taking seriously who is before us and attending to the situation. Against the ideologically driven, often paranoid politics of the extreme right and left, and their polarizing rivalries, political action born out of listening acts in trust that others not like me might have something to teach me. In short, it demands the humility to recognize that, whatever the justice of my cause or coherence of my program, I could be wrong, and I don't know all there is to know about how to live well.

A condition of truly hearing is the ability of those speaking to talk freely if they are to speak truthfully. Free speech, in the sense of the freedom to speak our mind, is therefore the complement to the need to listen. Such speech can take the form of passionate cries, stirring lament, polemic, impatient invective, and angry speeches, all of which are often vital forms of democratic communication. This is true particularly when agitating those who hold concentrated power or who are acting oppressively but who refuse to listen. Voicing and enacting (in marches, sit-ins, etc.) what we grieve for or what we are angry about is crucial for generating change. From the Hebrew prophets and Psalms onward, personal lament, anger, and grief birth public speech and action that contest an unjust status quo. However, while prophetic jeremiads can be powerful, they suffer from the law of diminishing returns, especially if they are the only form of public speech deployed. Moreover, to be sustained, both listening and free speech require anchoring in a shared commitment to the formation of a common life in which the thriving of *all* is the aim. So while there is a responsibility to listen, and thereby not merely tolerate but honor dissent as a part of democratic politics, dissent itself has responsibilities. One is to communicate in a way that can be heard. Yelling denunciations at those with whom we disagree provides invigorating compensations to the ones shouting, but screaming rarely produces understanding, let alone change. And no one is under any obligation to listen to vitriolic, ad hominem, libelous slurs, a contemporary example of which is online trolling.

If the dance of politics is a dance of both conflict *and* conciliation, there is a prudential judgment to be made as to whether free speech requires frank or fitting speech. Frank or direct speech tells it how it is without concern for others. The end in view is authenticity, candor, and sincerity of expression. The speeches of Malcolm X are a paradigm of someone who spoke truthfully in a candid and direct way. But speaking freely and truthfully also includes fitting speech, that is, conscientious and measured speech. Here the end in view is fairness and fittingness. The rhetoric of Dr. Martin Luther King Jr. is an example of this kind of free and truthful speech. The former flouts social convention, provokes, and tells it how it is regardless of how others react; the latter tends to work with the grain of social convention and seeks to be proportionate and judicious so that others may hear and respond appropriately. The call for more fitting speech is not always a curtailment of free speech. It can be what truthful speech requires at this juncture to achieve a more just and compassionate common life.

The giving and receiving of free speech, whether frank or fitting, is a vital component of what Aquinas, following Aristotle, called *euboulia*, meaning good or right counsel leading to sound judgment. Being *euboulos* involves the ability to deliberate well about what truly benefits either oneself or one's community as well the ability to recognize and receive good advice from others, even those you disagree with or who oppose you. As a virtue, *euboulia* entails being able to consider different options and viewpoints empathetically. There is a symbiotic link between democratic deliberation, giving and receiving advice, and coming to make wise judgments. A parliamentary system, which allows for fierce debate and cooperation across party lines, institutionalizes the pursuit of *euboulia*. Building on its classical usage, the deliberative process of coming to judgment, if it is to be democratic, entails a complex interplay between the need to listen equally to everyone affected by a decision, especially the poor and vulnerable (*isegoria*); the freedom to speak freely and truthfully (*parrhēsia*)—whether frankly or fittingly; and the need for coherent arguments (*logos*). Too often demands for rational, evidence-based arguments ignore the material conditions of speech and the way social hierarchies inhibit some and enable others in speaking while at the same time legitimizing certain kinds of speech over others. For those without control of state or market processes, some combination of organized knowledge, money, people, and action is the way to secure equal standing, be able to speak freely, and develop arguments for a cogent, logical, well-grounded position. Conversely, in the fierce urgency of now, the clamor for much-needed and profound change can sweep away commitments to seeking good counsel through listening to and speaking with others. But all will be ill-served—especially the most vulnerable—if, amid rallying calls to act and a desire to speak truth to power, we do not also cultivate the ability to deliberate well, especially with those we find objectionable or with whom we disagree.

Politics before Procedure

Listening is a condition of any moderately peaceable order, one derived from the pursuit of goods in common and not from the exclusion or oppression of others, particularly the friendless. Democratic government, as that which entails self-restraint and the conciliation of different interests, is not the only way to provide order. Tyranny, oligarchy, plutocracy, totalitarianism, and democratic despotism are more common ways to rule. These impose order by subverting or repressing all interests under the interest of the one, the few, or the mob. But, as should be clear, the understanding of democratic politics envisaged here is very different from that which equates democracy with legislation and bureaucratic administration (i.e., statecraft). Such state-centric and proceduralist approaches restrict democratic politics to pressure upon and action by state agencies rather than the negotiation of a common life between multiple actors of which the state is but one player. By contrast, the vision of democratic politics advocated here holds that if a group is directly contributing to the common work of defending, tending, and creating the commonweal, then they deserve recognition and respect as a vital part and colaborer within the broader body politic—whether they have formal legal status or not. Paradoxically, it is the very emphasis on participation and contribution to the building up of a common life that allows for a greater plurality and affirmation of distinct identities and traditions, as each can play a part in this common work. This common-life framework is distinct from either identity politics or multicultural approaches because recognition and respect are not given simply by dint of having a different culture or identity; recognition is conditional upon contributing to and participation in shared, reciprocal, common work. That said, the struggle is often to gain the respect and recognition for the contribution *already being made* but currently being denied, demeaned, or exploited.

If the status of the citizen is not to become absorbed into that of the producer, consumer, debtor, or volunteer, then what political philosopher Sheldon Wolin calls "politicalness" needs to be recovered. Politicalness is the "capacity for developing into beings who know and value what it means to participate in and be responsible for the care and improvement of our common and collective life."[5] In Wolin's analysis, the recovery of politicalness depends in part on local patterns of association born out of covenantal and cooperative institutions and what he calls "archaic," and in many cases very "conservative," traditions such as Christianity, Judaism, and Islam. These provide the means for the re-creation of political experience and the extension to a wider circle the benefits of social cooperation and achievements made possible by previous generations.[6]

The procedural state rarely sees and acts democratically, for to do so goes against central features of its structure. The state cannot take account of affections, meaningful relationships, or a sense of belonging. These are irrelevant to the operations of "neutral" procedures and cost-benefit calculations. Given how state actors have to proceed, moral claims are often treated as externalities to judgments about policy. They are simply not relevant to the rational administrator. Decisions about allocation of school resources and which schools to keep open are a good example. In 2013 the Chicago Public Schools closed down forty-nine schools in poor, black neighborhoods.[7] The argument was that too few children attended the

5. Sheldon Wolin, *The Presence of the Past: Essays on the State and the Constitution* (Baltimore: Johns Hopkins University Press, 1989), 139.

6. In parallel to a point made in chapter 13 in dialogue with Ada María Isasi-Díaz's emphasis on the quotidian, Craig Calhoun clarifies the sociological relationship between "archaic" traditions and the rejuvenation of a "radical" politics that challenges the status quo. Against Marx, Weber, and most other modern social theory, he contends that there is no inherent incompatibility between tradition and rationality and that political thinkers from left and right have failed to understand the "paradoxical conservatism" in revolution and the radicalism of tradition. He argues that traditional modes of association provide the social foundations and means of organization for widespread popular mobilizations and that traditional values, particularly when threatened by rapid change and modern capitalist-dominated social formations, provide the rationality for legitimating radical political action that opposes elite centers of power. Craig Calhoun, *The Roots of Radicalism: Tradition, the Public Sphere, and Early Nineteenth-Century Social Movements* (Chicago: University of Chicago Press, 2012).

7. Noreen S. Ahmed-Ullah, John Chase, and Bob Secter, "CPS Approves Largest School

schools, so it was inefficient to keep them open. Deemed irrelevant was the fact that the schools were one of the few remaining institutions in a deprived area and that they generated a range of intangible but vital civic and social goods; also deemed irrelevant was the fabric of affections and histories that circulated through these schools. The closing of the schools was primarily a bureaucratic judgment deaf to notions of loyalty, trust, reciprocity, history, and thence meaningful human relationships. These concerns fall completely outside the purview of the procedural, administrative state that makes judgments based on a utilitarian, economistic calculus that leaves little scope for discretion. The modern state manages and administers people as biology and cannot see or hear their biographies—something its social democratic and liberal advocates often fail to notice.

Listening to someone's biography rather than treating that person as merely an assemblage of biological needs enables genuine dispute and deliberation about what is the shared good in this place for these people at this time. Common goods discerned through a process of relational listening are neither the aggregation of individual self-interests nor the defense of vested interests, but goods in which the flourishing of each is dependent on the flourishing of all. The pursuit of common goods requires political judgment rather than letting a market mechanism or some technocratic, utilitarian procedure determine the good by a system of aggregation.[8] Such proceduralism constitutes a refusal to make political judgments.

While we can only discover goods in common through listening to others, listening is easily neglected or disparaged. Alongside ignoring listening by narrowing decisions to utilitarian, economistic calculations, it can be overridden by the desire to make reality fit a theory or ideology, the treatment of politics as a zero-sum game in which compromise or changing one's mind is seen as treason, or the refusal of a common world of mean-

---

Closure in Chicago's History," *Chicago Tribune*, May 23, 2013, http://articles.chicago tribune.com/2013-05-23/news/chi-chicago-school-closings-20130522_1_chicago -teachers-union-byrd-bennett-one-high-school-program. This example is discussed in Alasdair MacIntyre, *Ethics in the Conflicts of Modernity: An Essay on Desire, Practical Reasoning, and Narrative* (Cambridge: Cambridge University Press, 2016), 203-4.

8. For a pithy critique of technocratic ways of running institutions and developing policy that, at the same time, articulates a vision of democratic organizing within institutions, see Harry Boyte, *Civic Agency and the Cult of the Expert* (New York: Kettering Foundation, 2009), https://www.kettering.org/catalog/product/civic-agency-and-cult -expert.

ing and action by absolutizing friend-enemy relations. All such refusals to listen are antidemocratic.

Practice before Theory

Overly technocratic, theoretical, or ideologically driven accounts of politics fail to reckon with the nature of politics itself. As noted in chapter 1, politics is about action in time, and as such it involves questions of power (the ability to act), historicity (the time-sensitive and contingent nature of action), and wily wisdom (the local knowledge, strategic analysis, and practical skills necessary to respond appropriately to a constantly changing and ambiguous environment). The ideal ruler is not the philosopher king, but the ship's captain who can safely navigate difficult waters using craft and quick-wittedness.[9] The unpredictable and unstable nature of political life directs attention away from universal principles and general patterns toward particular contexts and historical settings.[10] There is a need to act in a way appropriate to the time/*kairos*, and hence the need for judgments about what is best for these people, in this place, at this time. As action in time, politics requires a means of judging how to put people, place, and history before any theory or program. Practical reason (*phronēsis/mētis*) is that means. I contend that in democratic politics, practical reason comes before theoretical reason.

Democratic politics sits at the intersection of our strategies for control and the recognition of our vulnerability and finitude. As a form of action in time, it involves making judgments about when, where, how, and with whom to act in a given situation, without knowing all the details or being sure of the outcomes. As Machiavelli teaches us, politics is a risk in which those acting make themselves vulnerable to fortune's wheel—that is, they act without the ability to see or control future events and outcomes.[11] To negotiate a common life between competing interests and visions of the good, with limited and imperfect knowledge, under conditions of finitude,

9. This was a frequent metaphor in classical political philosophy.

10. To recognize the unpredictable nature of political life is not to assert that it is a realm of total chaos. It is simply to recognize that political judgments address modes of action different from those of the chemist or engineer, and no amount of "evidence-based policy" can circumvent this.

11. Niccolo Machiavelli, *The Prince*, trans. Peter Constantine (New York: Modern Library, 2008), 116.

means that every action involves giving up other possible actions and outcomes. In this respect, technocratic forms of statecraft are antidemocratic: in an effort to circumvent vulnerability, loss, and contingency, they refuse to negotiate a common life by attempting to predetermine what is to be done through a program or procedure. Loss, vulnerability, and lack of control are central to the experience of acting democratically with and for others.[12] But, as should already be clear, such loss and risk demand that we view living in time and the experience of flux, change, contingency, and transition not as enemies to be defeated but as constitutive of being finite and frail creatures who need others to live. Democratic politics is a way of embracing finitude and frailty as constitutive of a just and merciful common life.

What is often missing in modern accounts of politics is an account of how, given our finitude and frailty, we may learn to make appropriate and contingent political judgments based on practical reason. Instead, politics either is concerned about the application of universally valid principles or is reduced to legal, commercial, or bureaucratic considerations. By contrast, democratic politics—if it is truly attentive to human finitude and frailty— does not work from first principles but reflects on already established practices, traditions, and customs, that is, the ways people have found for living and working together over time and through which they generate a sense of meaning and purpose. Accusations that such an approach is conservative ignore how such "conservatism" often generates radical proposals. It is worth remembering that numerous popular revolts and revolutions began among conservative, rural peasants. Against modern denunciations of tradition as inherently reactionary and the enemy of an emancipatory politics, democratic politics must take seriously the ties that bind us to our sense of place, our forebears, and the world we inherited. Rather than acts of revolutionary self-assertion (and their totalitarian debacle), it takes seriously those who appealed to and upheld common laws, common lands, and a common life as a basis for liberty and rights. Moreover, it contends that it is not a degree from Oxford or Harvard or work experience in a think tank that equips you to make prudent and, when necessary, radical political judgments. It is an apprenticeship in practices that enable you to learn the

---

12. The embrace of vulnerability and thence the contingency of political order does not necessarily imply inevitable entropy. The contrast here is with Plato, who saw all forms of political order as inevitably degenerating, so that, for example, aristocracy degenerates into timocracy.

craft of politics and thence make fitting judgments. This apprenticeship occurs in forms of self-organized institutions and mutual associations such as unions, churches, residents' associations, small businesses, and disability support groups.

Institutions and Individuals

Listening requires active involvement and commitment to a particular place, because it takes time and personal presence to build trusting and cooperative relationships. Hence, there is the vexed question of the relationship between incessant, large-scale migration and the ability to sustain the kinds of place-based, mutual, and faithful relationships on which democratic politics depends. This is a question that is both masked and exacerbated by making politics solely about individuals and their freedoms, thereby ignoring the related issue of how to sustain institutions and their practices of association. Given the disaggregating churn of economic globalization, place-based, anchor institutions (schools, universities, locally owned businesses, churches, soccer clubs, hospitals, etc.) become increasingly important. For institutions are key to generating a listening, place-based politics of a common life, rather than the individual, who is often mobile and insecure. Within anchor institutions, a mobile population congregates, however temporarily. For example, diverse kinds of students gathered in high schools can be the basis for a movement calling for gun reform. The negotiation of a common life between such *institutions*—that is, between gathered people and not just between individuals—allows for a listening, place-based politics to emerge. But institutions are fragile things that need tending in particular ways. They are not mere instruments but have internal goods that need cultivating if they are to be places of human flourishing.

Within contemporary institutions—for example, a university—what is under threat is the notion that there is a common good that requires pursuing if the institution is to flourish. Much policy and practice of universities reflect a view that the institution itself is not an arena of common life in which the individual good of each participant (whether student, faculty, or administrator) is dependent on the prior and organizing good of education. Nor is the institution viewed as having a duty of care and active interest in building up the common life of its location. Rather, universities are often subject to instrumentalizing logics of the state and education itself is seen as a commodity. The aggregation of individual interests determines what is taught (in which case there is no such thing as education as a substantive good, only individual choices and careers that make use of the university for a time); and universities are run according to the dominant interest of either managers, faculty, or students (understood as clients or customers) rather than as a negotiation of a common life between different groups that share a mutual interest in the pursuit of their good in common—education. The absence of any notion of the common good of education leaves a vacuum, rendering incoherent attempts to promote the virtues, disciplines, and standards of excellence required to fulfill this good. The result is that forms of market, legal, and bureaucratic proceduralism replace trust, loyalty, and reciprocity as ways of organizing the institution. The same process occurs in the hospitals, schools, sports clubs, libraries, and other institutions that shape and structure our common life and through which we learn the craft of politics.

Nonpecuniary institutions and forms of mutual association (i.e., those not wholly subject to logics of instrumentalization or commodification) are vital for creating spaces amid political, economic, social, and technological pressures that militate against developing such relationships. These institutions represent a legal, organizational, financial, and physical place to stand. For example, congregations can represent institutions of this kind and are places constituted by gathered and organized people who do not come together primarily for either commercial or state-directed transactions. Instead, they form institutions through which to worship God and care for each other. Without such institutions, there are few real places through which to resist the processes of commodification by the market and the processes of instrumentalization—and sometimes brutal repression—by the state. In short, if we have nowhere to sit together free from governmental or commercial imperatives, we have no shared spaces in which to take the time to listen to each other, develop mutual trust, and learn ways and means of cooperating. That said, building or strengthening such institutions, and the forms of mutual association they embody, is extremely difficult, and there is a constant need to innovate and imagine new kinds of institutional and associational life. Nevertheless, if enduring structural change is to occur, there is a need to reconfigure existing institutions or create new ones, for institutions are a means of solving shared problems, and thus pursuing, fulfilling, and ordering the goods necessary to sustain a common life across generations.

Democratic Politics Precedes a Liberal Constitutional Order

The account of democratic politics developed here is distinct from a liberal constitutional order, that is, a commitment to the rule of law and a self-limiting state. A liberal legal-constitutional order guarantees certain positive and negative liberties and equality before the law. It also sets out various procedures and institutions, such as a legal system and judiciary, for buttressing these liberties. These freedoms—which, against most current thinking, do not, of necessity, have to be conceptualized in terms of human rights—include positive freedoms such as freedom of worship, freedom of assembly, and freedom of speech, and negative freedoms, such as freedom from torture, from inhuman or degrading treatment or punishment; freedom from slavery; and freedom from arbitrary arrest and wrongful detention or exile. In short, a liberal legal-constitutional order sets a boundary *within which* democratic politics can take place. For Hannah Arendt, these rights or freedoms are not natural or self-evident. Rather, they are conventions or forms of human agreement forged through common action over time. Building on Arendt, I contend that while a liberal constitutional order seeks to guarantee a basic set of freedoms, these cannot exist without the politics to forge and actualize them. And such a politics can only occur within specific kinds of place-based and time-intensive relationships. That said, while democratic politics as defined here is not dependent on and precedes the existence of a liberal constitutional order, such an order does provide an environment which more easily sustains democratic politics over time.

There are many ways to give an account of the foundations of a liberal polity, which itself is compatible with a variety of forms of rule, including a constitutional monarchy. One justification derives from Scripture. A tenet of Scripture is the claim that human political orders should be determined not by the personal fiat of a single ruler or by an oligarchy. Rather, they should be determined in the first instance by law and "covenant" (that is to say, committed, faithful, mutually responsible social relationships orientated toward fulfilling a shared vision of the good). Justifications for a liberal constitutional order vary, but what such an order provides is the space for politics. Where a liberal understanding of the place of law and the state becomes unworkable and self-destructive is in the attempt to expand the liberal constitutional-legal order through various forms of proceduralism so that it functions as a substitute for and overrides concrete social and political relationships. In effect, instead of defining the space of politics, it seeks to become a substitute for politics.

To the extent that it is a movement beyond a commitment to a legal-constitutional space for politics and prioritizes procedure over politics, liberalism represents the attempt to eliminate frailty, historical contingency, and creatureliness from political life.[13] Thus, while democratic politics leads to and flourishes best within a liberal constitutional order, a commitment to democracy does not necessitate a commitment to liberalism as a political philosophy. Whether grounded in some account of natural rights or creation order or social contract, the freedoms that a legal-constitutional order guarantees are in practice civil and political freedoms. They have to be reappropriated and fulfilled through shared political action. But we should be in no doubt that, while they do not replace or stand in for a common life, these freedoms are precious and to be cherished more than gold. They are a hard-won inheritance that can be easily squandered or crumble through neglect. And democratic politics is the way to tend and hand them on.

Conclusion

As stipulated here, democratic politics serves three interrelated roles. First, it is *protective*, securing space for the development of different kinds of association and their respective forms of faithfulness or loyalty and the moral visions they embody. Second, it is *integrative*, enabling the forming, norming, and sustaining of a common life and the pursuit of shared goods between rival or estranged interests and conflicting visions of the good. And lastly, it is *transformative*, generating resources for the critique, accountability, and reconfiguration of an existing status quo. In keeping with this last point, democratic politics incorporates practices of dissent, protest, and lament but cannot be reduced to them. The price of meaningful protest is a creative and viable alternative. Likewise, democratic politics may begin with resistance, but it cannot be defined as resistance. It seeks not only to mourn and contest the excesses of state, market, and communal overdetermination but also to reconfigure social, political, and economic relations through generating the imagination and energy for, and movement toward, a more just and compassionate common life.

13. I am drawing here on Sheldon Wolin's argument that liberalism represents an attempt to replace politics with procedure. For Wolin, an "adequate political logic must be framed to cope with contraries and dissymmetries arising out of a mobile and conflict-laden situation" (*Politics and Vision: Continuity and Innovation in Western Political Thought* (Princeton: Princeton University Press, 2004), 60.

The account of democracy given here must be situated within the broader vision articulated throughout this book. This vision can be briefly summarized as the need for a democratized economy, in a confederal polity, with a pluralistic common life politics, undergirded by a moral commitment to generating forms of shared flourishing that are ecologically attuned. To be sustained, any attempt to ensure that market and state processes serve human and ecological flourishing requires the kind of common life, pluralistic, democratic politics outlined here. The participatory and agitational practices of democratic politics are a way to ensure that those who possess the levers of unilateral power, whether in the state or in the market, are held accountable, while at the same time ensuring that the means of accountability embody the change that is sought.

Intrinsic to democratic politics is the recognition that humans have multiple loyalties and vocations, some of which direct them to seek fulfillment beyond the limits of political and economic life. Religious commitments are but one example of such a vocation. In turn, these loyalties and vocations are vital for nourishing democratic politics. If democracy is to avoid slipping into either some form of legal, bureaucratic, or ideological proceduralism that treats humans as means to an end, or a majoritarianism that treats either minorities or the friendless as enemies, it requires people formed in a variety of virtues, with a moral vision committed to learning from and living with others not like themselves. And if the demands and exigencies of political and economic life are not to dominate everything we do and say then democracy needs people with the capacity to rest and play, as well as ponder questions about the meaning and purpose of life. In short, any kind of politics, even democratic politics, becomes pitiless if it fails to cultivate virtue, moral vision, and denies the human need for rest, play, and contemplation. Conversely, the pursuit of virtue, moral vision, and rest, play, and contemplation without any broader conception and engagement in democratic politics is pitiful, as it has no means to protect and pursue the very relationships and activities it loves and values most in the face of either their instrumentalization, commodification, or repression. Democratic politics thus conceived is a work of love. Absent love and it does not work.

Suggested Readings for Further Discussion

Jane Addams, *Democracy and Social Ethics: An Introduction* (Chicago: University of Illinois Press, 2001 [1902]). See sections headed "Charitable Effort," "Filial Relations," "Industrial Amelioration," and "Political Reform." Addams sits at the intersection of American pragmatism and the Social Gospel. In this book she develops an account of democracy as based on the sympathetic knowledge of others and the importance of reciprocity as a democratic virtue.

Reinhold Niebuhr, *The Children of Light and the Children of Darkness: A Vindication of Democracy and a Critique of Its Traditional Defenders* (London: Nisbet, 1945). This is a classic defense of democracy as the best mode of statecraft for determining the form of political order.

Martin Luther King Jr., "Letter from Birmingham Jail" (1963). A classic defense of direct action and an agitational democratic politics as a means of change.

Bayard Rustin, "From Protest to Politics," in *To Redeem a Nation: A History and Anthology of the Civil Rights Movement*, ed. Thomas R. West (New York: Brandywine, 1993), 232–35. Also available online from various sources. Rustin worked closely with King, and in this text he highlights the importance of thinking politically and how this is more than engaging in protest and direct action.

Bernard Crick, *In Defence of Politics*, 5th ed. (London: Bloomsbury, 2005), chaps. 1 and 7. Much used by community organizers, this book articulates a nonstate-centric vision of politics and why it matters. As a political theorist, Crick was involved in party politics and helped establish civic education in public education in Great Britain.

Temma Kaplan, *Democracy: A World History* (Oxford: Oxford University Press, 2015). Provides a short overview of the development of democratic movements from the ancient to the modern world.

Acknowledgments

This book draws together many different strands of my work and is the culmination of innumerable conversations over many years. Some of these conversations began many moons ago in London, others started up on my move to Durham, North Carolina. The book is also a small contribution to an ancient and ongoing conversation about the proper nature and form of politics. I cannot catalogue all those to whom I owe a debt of thanks and without whom this book would not be possible. But I can express my gratitude to those who were directly involved in its more immediate production. For funding the sabbatical year that gave me the time to complete the manuscript, I thank the Luce Foundation and the Association of Theological School for granting me a Henry Luce III Fellowship (2017–2018) and the Yale Center for Faith and Culture for their research grant. For ongoing conversation and input into and surrounding the writing of this book, I am grateful to Sarah Beckwith, Kate Bowler, Harry Boyte, Jay Kameron Carter, James Chappel, Ellen Davis, Matt Elia, Mike Gecan, Michael Gillespie, Maurice Glasman, Eric Gregory, Nicholas Hayes, Jennifer Herdt, Willie Jennings, Sean Larsen, Vincent Lloyd, Charles Mathewes, Mike Miller, Ted Smith, Gerald Taylor, Sam Wells, Brittany Wilson, and Norman Wirzba. I am particularly grateful to Stanley Hauerwas, who commented on and discussed all the chapters as I was writing them. For input on specific chapters, I am grateful to Toddie Peters for comments and feedback on chapter 2; Marvin Wickware, Bill Turner, and Joe Winters on chapter 3; Aminah Al-Attas Bradford, Mark Cartledge, Joel Haldorff, and Amos Yong on chapter 4; Nicholas Adams, Mark Chapman, Jonathan Chaplin, Gary Dorrien, Mike Higton, and Peter Sedgwick on chapter 6; Manfred Svensson on chapter 9; Eugene Rogers on chapter 10; Spencer Banzhaf, Christina McRorie, and Devin Singh on chapter 11; and Timothy Jackson on chapter 13. A special word of thanks must go to the doctoral and masters students who took part in the Political Theology Reading Group for working through drafts of each chapter and helping me clarify many of the things I was trying to say. I am particularly grateful to Matthew Elmore, Nathan Hershberger, Joseph Longarino, and Alberto La Rosa Rojas for their detailed comments. I am also especially thankful for Brandy Daniels, Nichole Flores, Paul Dayfidd Jones, Charles Mathewes, and the presenters (Lucila Crena, Creighton Coleman, and Eric Hilker) and participants in the workshop on a draft of the whole manuscript held at the University of Virginia's Center for the Study of Religion. They helped me crystallize the final shape of the book and clarify and strengthen key chapters. For his editorial input and comments, I am grateful to Matthew Jantzen. And for her invaluable editorial work and guidance, as well as ongoing conversations about genre, style, and Trollope, I thank Judith Heyhoe. Thanks must also go to James Ernest, Michael Thomson, Linda Bieze, and all those at Eerdmans involved in producing this book. Finally, my greatest thanks go to Caroline, Gabriel, and Isaac for their support. Without them I could not do this work. The book is dedicated to Michael, Caroline's brother. He was a man with an uncommon gift for nourishing faith, hope, and love in others. I miss him greatly.

Chapter 3 is a revised version of an article entitled "Exorcising Democracy: The Theopolitical Challenge of Black Power," first published in the *Journal of the Society of Christian Ethics* 38, no. 1 (2018). Reproduced with permission.

Chapter 5 is a revised version of an article entitled "Democracy, Society and Truth: An Exploration of Catholic Social Teaching," first published in the *Scottish Journal of Theology* 69, no. 3 (2016) by Cambridge University Press. Reproduced with permission.

Parts of chapter 7 are taken, with revisions, from an essay in the *Blackwells Companion to Christian Ethics*, ed. Stanley Hauerwas and Sam Wells, rev. ed. (Oxford: Wiley-Blackwell, 2011), under the title "Sharing Peace: Class, Hierarchy & Christian Social Order." Reproduced with permission.

Parts of chapter 9 draw on chapter 5 of Luke Bretherton, *Hospitality as Holiness: Christian Witness amid Moral Diversity* (Aldershot, UK: Ashgate, 2006). Reproduced with permission.

Parts of chapter 12 are taken, with revisions, from an essay that appeared in the *Oxford Handbook of Theology and Modern European Thought*, ed. Nicholas Adams, George Pattison, and Graham Ward (Oxford: Oxford

University Press, 2013), under the title "Sovereignty," by permission of Oxford University Press.

Unless otherwise indicated, the Scripture quotations contained herein are from the New Revised Standard Version Bible, copyright 1989 by the Division of Christian Education of the National Council of the Churches of Christ in the U.S.A., and are used by permission. All rights reserved.

PENTECOST 2018

Bibliography

Adams, Edward. *Constructing the World: A Study in Paul's Cosmological Language.* Edinburgh: T&T Clark, 2000.

Adams, Jeremy D. *The* Populus *of Augustine and Jerome.* New Haven: Yale University Press, 1971.

Adogame, Afe. "Reconfiguring the Global Religious Economy." In *Spirit and Power: The Growth and Global Impact of Pentecostalism,* edited by Donald Miller, Kimon Sargeant, and Richard Flory, 194-97. Oxford: Oxford University Press, 2013.

Agamben, Giorgio. *Homo Sacer: Sovereign Power and Bare Life.* Translated by Daniel Heller-Roazen. Stanford, CA: Stanford University Press, 1998.

———. *The Kingdom and the Glory: For a Theological Genealogy of Economy and Government.* Translated by Lorenzo Chiesa and Matteo Mandarini. Stanford, CA: Stanford University Press, 2011.

———. *State of Exception.* Translated by Kevin Attell. Chicago: University of Chicago Press, 2005.

Ahmed-Ullah, Noreen S., John Chase, and Bob Secter. "CPS Approves Largest School Closure in Chicago's History." *Chicago Tribune,* May 23, 2013. http://articles.chicagotribune.com/2013-05-23/news/chi-chicago-school-closings-2013 0522_1_chicago-teachers-union-byrd-bennett-one-high-school-program.

Albertazzi, Daniele, and Duncan McDonnell. "Introduction: The Sceptre and the Spectre." In *Twenty-First Century Populism: The Spectre of Western European Democracy,* edited by Daniele Albertazzi and Duncan McDonnell, 1-11. New York: Palgrave Macmillan, 2008.

Alexander, Estrelda. "Recovering Black Theological Thought in the Writings of Early African-American Holiness-Pentecostal Leaders: Liberation Motifs in Early African-American Pentecostalism." In *A Liberating Spirit: Pentecostals and Social Action in North America,* edited by Michael Wilkinson and Steven Studebaker, 23-52. Eugene, OR: Wipf & Stock, 2010.

Alexander, Jeffrey C. *The Civil Sphere.* New York: Oxford University Press, 2006.

Alexander, Michelle. *The New Jim Crow: Mass Incarceration in the Age of Colorblindness*. New York: New Press, 2010.

Alexander, Paul, ed. *Pentecostals and Nonviolence: Reclaiming a Heritage*. Eugene, OR: Wipf & Stock, 2012.

Ali, Omar. *In the Lion's Mouth: Black Populism in the New South, 1886-1900*. Jackson: University Press of Mississippi, 2010.

Alinsky, Saul. *Rules for Radicals: A Practical Primer for Realistic Radicals*. New York: Vintage Books, 1989 (1971).

Allen, Danielle. *Talking to Strangers: Anxieties of Citizenship Since Brown v. Board of Education*. Chicago: University of Chicago Press, 2004.

Allen, Theodore. *The Invention of the White Race*. New York: Verso, 1994.

Althouse, Peter. *Spirit of the Last Days: Pentecostal Eschatology in Conversation with Jürgen Moltmann*. London: T&T Clark, 2003.

Althusius, Johannes. *Politica*. Edited and translated by Frederick Carney. Indianapolis: Liberty Fund, 1995 (1964).

Anderson, Allan. *An Introduction to Pentecostalism: Global Charismatic Christianity*. 2nd ed. Cambridge: Cambridge University Press, 2014.

———. "Varieties, Taxonomies and Definitions." In *Studying Global Pentecostalism: Theories and Methods*, edited by Allan Anderson et al., 13-29. Berkeley: University of California Press, 2016.

Anderson, Benedict. *Imagined Communities: Reflections on the Origin and Spread of Nationalism*. Rev. ed. London: Verso, 2006.

Anderson, Gary. *Charity: The Place of the Poor in the Biblical Tradition*. New Haven: Yale University Press, 2013.

Anderson, Kevin. *Agitations: Ideologies and Strategies in African American Politics*. Fayetteville: University of Arkansas Press, 2010.

Ansley, Frances Lee. "Stirring the Ashes: Race, Class and the Future of Civil Rights Scholarship." *Cornell Law Review* 74, no. 6 (1989): 993-1077.

Anzaldúa, Gloria. *Borderlands: The New Mestiza = La frontera*. San Francisco: Aunt Lute Books, 1987.

"The Aparecida Document." Fifth General Conference of Bishops of Latin America and the Caribbean. Aparecida, Brazil, May 13-31, 2007.

Appiah, Kwame Anthony. *Cosmopolitanism: Ethics in a World of Strangers*. New York: Norton, 2007.

Aquinas, Thomas. *Political Writings*. Translated by R. W. Dyson. Cambridge: Cambridge University Press, 2002.

Araiza, Lauren. "'In Common Struggle against a Common Oppression': The United Farm Workers and the Black Panther Party, 1968-1973." *Journal of African American History* 94, no. 2 (2009): 200-223.

Archer, Kenneth, and Richard Waldrop. "Liberating Hermeneutics: Toward a Holistic Pentecostal Mission of Peace and Justice." *Journal of the European Pentecostal Theological Association* 31, no. 1 (2011): 65-80.

Arditi, Benjamin. *Politics on the Edges of Liberalism: Difference, Populism, Revolution, Agitation*. Edinburgh: Edinburgh University Press, 2007.

Arendt, Hannah. *The Human Condition*. Chicago: University of Chicago Press, 1998 (1958).

———. *On Revolution*. London: Penguin Books, 2006 (1963).

Aristotle. *The Politics, and The Constitution of Athens*. Edited by Stephen Everson. Cambridge: Cambridge University Press, 1996.

Armitage, David. "John Locke, Carolina, and the 'Two Treatises of Government.'" *Political Theory* 32, no. 5 (2004): 602–27.

Arneil, Barbara. *John Locke and America: The Defense of English Colonialism*. Oxford: Oxford University Press, 1996.

Asad, Talal. *Formations of the Secular: Christianity, Islam, Modernity*. Stanford, CA: Stanford University Press, 2003.

———. *Genealogies of Religion: Discipline and Reasons of Power in Christianity and Islam*. Baltimore: Johns Hopkins University Press, 1993.

Ateek, Naim Stifan. *Justice and Only Justice: A Palestinian Theology of Liberation*. Maryknoll, NY: Orbis, 1989.

Attanasi, Katherine. "Introduction: The Plurality of Prosperity Theologies and Pentecostalisms." In *Pentecostalism and Prosperity: The Socio-Economics of the Global Charismatic Movement*, edited by Katherine Attanasi and Amos Yong, 1–12. New York: Palgrave Macmillan, 2012.

Augustine. *The City of God*. Translated by William Babcock. New York: New City Press, 2012.

Augustine, Daniela. *Pentecost, Hospitality, and Transfiguration: Toward a Spirit-Inspired Vision of Social Transformation*. Cleveland, TN: CPT, 2012.

Azaransky, Sarah. *This Worldwide Struggle: Religion and the International Roots of the Civil Rights Movement*. Oxford: Oxford University Press, 2017.

Baldwin, James. *Collected Essays*. Edited by Toni Morrison. New York: Library of America, 1998.

Baldwin, James, and Audre Lorde. "Revolutionary Hope: A Conversation between James Baldwin and Audre Lorde." *Essence Magazine*, 1984. http://mocada-museum.tumblr.com/post/73421979421/revolutionary-hope-a-conversation-between-james.

Bantum, Brian. *Redeeming Mulatto: A Theology of Race and Christian Hybridity*. Waco, TX: Baylor University Press, 2010.

Banzhaf, Spencer. "Objective or Multi-objective? Two Historically Competing Visions for Benefit-Cost Analysis." *Land Economics* 85, no. 1 (2009): 3–23.

Barber, Benjamin R. *Strong Democracy in Crisis: Promise or Peril?* Lanham, MD: Lexington, 2016.

Barber, William J., II, with Jonathan Wilson-Hartgrove. *The Third Reconstruction: Moral Mondays, Fusion Politics, and the Rise of a New Justice Movement*. Boston: Beacon, 2016.

Barnett, Michael N. *Empire of Humanity: A History of Humanitarianism*. Ithaca, NY: Cornell University Press, 2011.

Barnett, Michael N., and Janice Gross Stein. *Sacred Aid: Faith and Humanitarianism*. Oxford: Oxford University Press, 2012.

Barnett, Michael, and Thomas Weiss. "Humanitarianism: A Brief History of the Present." In *Humanitarianism in Question: Politics, Power, Ethics*, edited by Michael Barnett and Thomas Weiss, 1–48. Ithaca, NY: Cornell University Press, 2008.

Barrera, Albino. *God and the Evil of Scarcity: Moral Foundations of Economic Agency*. Notre Dame: University of Notre Dame Press, 2005.

Barth, Karl. *The Christian Life. Church Dogmatics*. Vol. IV, Part 4, *Lecture Fragments*. Translated by Geoffrey Bromiley. Edinburgh: T&T Clark, 1981.

———. *Church Dogmatics*. Edinburgh: T&T Clark, 1956–1977.

———. *Community, State, and Church: Three Essays*. Eugene, OR: Wipf & Stock, 2004.

Battle, Michael. *Reconciliation: The Ubuntu Theology of Desmond Tutu*. Cleveland: Pilgrim, 1997.

Bauckham, Richard. *The Theology of the Book of Revelation*. Cambridge: Cambridge University Press, 1993.

Bear, Laura, Karen Ho, Anna Tsing, and Sylvia Yanagisako. "Gens: A Feminist Manifesto for the Study of Capitalism." *Cultural Anthropology*, March 30, 2015. https://culanth.org/fieldsights/652-gens-a-feminist-manifesto-for-the-study -of-capitalism.

Behr, John. *Asceticism and Anthropology in Irenaeus and Clement*. Oxford: Clarendon, 2000.

Beiner, Ronald. *Civil Religion: A Dialogue in the History of Political Philosophy*. Cambridge: Cambridge University Press, 2011.

———. *What's the Matter with Liberalism?* Berkeley: University of California Press, 1995.

Bejan, Teresa. "Evangelical Toleration." *Journal of Politics* 77, no. 4 (2015): 1103–14.

Bejczy, István. "Tolerantia: A Medieval Concept." *Journal of the History of Ideas* 58, no. 3 (1997): 365–84.

Bell, Daniel. *Liberation Theology after the End of History: The Refusal to Cease Suffering*. London: Routledge, 2001.

Bellah, Robert. *Religion in Human Evolution: From the Paleolithic to the Axial Age*. Cambridge, MA: Belknap Press of Harvard University Press, 2011.

Benedict XVI. *Caritas in Veritate*. 2009. http://w2.vatican.va.

———. *Deus Caritas Est*. 2005. http://w2.vatican.va.

Bentham, Jeremy. "Defence of Usury." In *Economic Writings*, vol. 1, edited by Werner Stark, 123–207. London: Allen & Unwin, 1952.

Benveniste, Émile. *Indo-European Language and Society*. Translated by Elizabeth Palmer. Coral Gables, FL: University of Miami Press, 1973.

Berman, Bruce J., Rajeev Bhargava, and André Laliberté. *Secular States and Religious Diversity*. Vancouver, BC: UBC Press, 2013.

Bernasconi, Robert. "Kant as an Unfamiliar Source of Racism." In *Philosophers on Race: Critical Essays*, edited by Julie Ward and Tommy Lott, 145-66. Oxford: Blackwell, 2002.

———. "'The Ruling Categories of the World': The Trinity in Hegel's Philosophy of History and the Rise and Fall of Peoples." In *A Companion to Hegel*, edited by Stephen Houlgate and Michael Baur, 315-31. Oxford: Wiley-Blackwell, 2016.

Berry, Wendell. *The Art of the Commonplace: The Agrarian Essays of Wendell Berry*. Edited by Norman Wirzba. Washington, DC: Counterpoint, 2003.

Bevans, Stephen B., and Roger Schroeder. *Constants in Context: A Theology of Mission for Today*. Maryknoll, NY: Orbis, 2004.

Bhargava, Rajeev. *The Promise of India's Secular Democracy*. Oxford: Oxford University Press, 2010.

Blank, Rebecca M. "Viewing the Market Economy through the Lens of Faith." In *Is the Market Moral? A Dialogue on Religion, Economics, and Justice*, edited by Rebecca M. Blank and William McGurn, 11-56. Washington, DC: Brookings Institution Press, 2004.

Bodin, Jean. *On Sovereignty: Four Chapters from "The Six Books of the Commonwealth."* Translated by Julian Franklin. Cambridge: Cambridge University Press, 1992.

Boesak, Willa. *God's Wrathful Children: Political Oppression and Christian Ethics*. Grand Rapids: Eerdmans, 1995.

Boff, Clodovis. "Epistemology and Method of the Theology of Liberation." In *Mysterium Liberationis: Fundamental Concepts of Liberation Theology*, edited by Ignacio Ellacuría and Jon Sobrino, 57-84. Maryknoll, NY: Orbis, 1993.

———. *Salvation and Liberation*. Maryknoll, NY: Orbis, 1984.

Boff, Leonardo. *Church, Charism, and Power: Liberation Theology and the Institutional Church*. Translated by John W. Diercksmeier. New York: Crossroad, 1985.

———. *Cry of the Earth, Cry of the Poor*. Maryknoll, NY: Orbis, 1997.

———. "A Theological Examination of the Terms 'People of God' and 'Popular Church.'" *Concilium* 6, no. 176 (1984): 89-97.

Boff, Leonardo, and Clodovis Boff. *Introducing Liberation Theology*. Translated by Paul Burns. Tunbridge Wells, UK: Burns & Oates, 1987.

Boggs, Grace Lee. *Living for Change: An Autobiography*. Minneapolis: University of Minnesota Press, 1998.

Boggs, James, and Grace Lee Boggs. "The City Is the Black Man's Land." *Monthly Review* 17, no. 11 (1966): 35-46.

Bonhoeffer, Dietrich. *Dietrich Bonhoeffer Works*. Vol. 6, *Ethics*. Edited by Clifford Green. Translated by Reinhard Krauss et al. Minneapolis: Fortress, 2005.

Booth, William James. "Economies of Time: On the Idea of Time in Marx's Political Economy." *Political Theory* 19, no. 1 (1991): 7-27.

Bornstein, Erica, and Peter Redfield, eds. *Forces of Compassion: Humanitarianism between Ethics and Politics*. Santa Fe, NM: School for Advanced Research Press, 2011.

Borradori, Giovanna. *Philosophy in a Time of Terror: Dialogues with Jürgen Habermas and Jacques Derrida*. Chicago: University of Chicago Press, 2003.

Bosch, David J. *Transforming Mission: Paradigm Shifts in the Theology of Mission*. Maryknoll, NY: Orbis, 2011.

Bowler, Kate. *Blessed: A History of the American Prosperity Gospel*. New York: Oxford University Press, 2013.

Bowlin, John. *Tolerance among the Virtues*. Princeton: Princeton University Press, 2016.

Boyte, Harry. *Civic Agency and the Cult of the Expert*. New York: Kettering Foundation, 2009. https://www.kettering.org/catalog/product/civic-agency-and-cult-expert.

———. *Commonwealth: A Return to Citizen Politics*. New York: Free Press, 1989.

Braunstein, Ruth, and Meleana Taylor. "Is the Tea Party a 'Religious' Movement? Religiosity in the Tea Party versus the Religious Right." *Sociology of Religion* 78, no. 1 (2017): 33–59.

Brazier, Arthur. *Black Self-Determination: The Story of the Woodlawn Organization*. Grand Rapids: Eerdmans, 1969.

Bretherton, Luke. *Christianity and Contemporary Politics: The Conditions and Possibilities of Faithful Witness*. Malden, MA: Wiley-Blackwell, 2010.

———. "Coming to Judgment: Methodological Reflections on the Relationship between Ecclesiology, Ethnography and Political Theory." *Modern Theology* 28, no. 2 (2012): 167–96.

———. *Hospitality as Holiness: Christian Witness amid Moral Diversity*. Aldershot, UK: Ashgate, 2006.

———. "Pneumatology, Healing and Political Power: Sketching a Pentecostal Political Theology." In *The Holy Spirit in the World Today*, edited by Jane Williams, 130–50. Oxford: Lion, 2011.

———. *Resurrecting Democracy: Faith, Citizenship, and the Politics of a Common Life*. Cambridge: Cambridge University Press, 2015.

Brooke, Christopher. "Rousseau's Political Philosophy: Stoic and Augustinian Origins." In *The Cambridge Companion to Rousseau*, edited by Patrick Riley, 94–123. Cambridge: Cambridge University Press, 2001.

Brown, Candy Gunther. Introduction to *Global Pentecostal and Charismatic Healing*, edited by Candy Gunther Brown, 3–21. Oxford: Oxford University Press, 2011.

Brown, Christopher Leslie. *Moral Capital: Foundations of British Abolitionism*. Chapel Hill: University of North Carolina Press, 2006.

Brown, Peter. *Through the Eye of a Needle: Wealth, the Fall of Rome, and the Making of Christianity in the West, 350–550 AD*. Princeton: Princeton University Press, 2012.

Bruni, Luigino, and Robert Sugden. "Reclaiming Virtue Ethics for Economics." *Journal of Economic Perspectives* 27, no. 4 (2013): 141-64.

Bruni, Luigino, and Stefano Zamagni. *Civil Economy: Efficiency, Equity, Public Happiness.* Bern: Lang, 2007.

Buber, Martin. *Paths in Utopia.* New York: Macmillan, 1950.

Buckley, Michael. *At the Origins of Modern Atheism.* Rev. ed. New Haven: Yale University Press, 1990.

Bull, Hedley. *The Anarchical Society.* London: Macmillan, 1977.

Burdick, John. *Legacies of Liberation: The Progressive Catholic Church in Brazil at the Start of a New Millennium.* Aldershot, UK: Ashgate, 2004.

Burgess, Richard. *Nigeria's Christian Revolution: The Civil War and Its Pentecostal Progeny (1967-2006).* Oxford: Regnum Books, 2008.

Burian, Peter. "Athenian Tragedy as Democratic Discourse." In *Why Athens? A Reappraisal of Tragic Politics,* edited by D. M. Carter, 95-117. Oxford: Oxford University Press, 2011.

Busto, Rudy. *King Tiger: The Religious Vision of Reies López Tijerina.* Albuquerque: University of New Mexico Press, 2005.

Butler, Judith. *Frames of War: When Is Life Grievable?* London: Verso, 2010.

———. "'We, the People': Thoughts on Freedom of Assembly." In *What Is a People?,* edited by Alain Badiou, Pierre Bourdieu, and Judith Butler, translated by Jody Gladding, 49-64. New York: Columbia University Press, 2016.

Calhoun, Craig. *The Roots of Radicalism: Tradition, the Public Sphere, and Early Nineteenth-Century Social Movements.* Chicago: University of Chicago Press, 2012.

Cannon, Katie. *Black Womanist Ethics.* Atlanta: Scholars Press, 1988.

Canovan, Margaret. *The People.* Cambridge: Polity, 2005.

———. "Trust the People! Populism and the Two Faces of Democracy." *Political Studies* 47, no. 1 (1999): 2-16.

———. "Two Strategies for the Study of Populism." *Political Studies* 30, no. 4 (1982): 544-52.

Carmichael, Stokely, and Charles Hamilton. *Black Power: The Politics of Liberation in America.* New York: Random House, 1967.

Cartledge, Mark. *The Mediation of the Spirit: Interventions in Practical Theology.* Grand Rapids: Eerdmans, 2015.

———. "Renewal Theology and the 'Common Good.'" *Journal of Pentecostal Studies* 25, no. 1 (2016): 90-106.

Casanova, José. "Immigration and the New Religious Pluralism: A European Union/United States Comparison." In *Democracy and the New Religious Pluralism,* edited by Thomas F. Banchoff, 59-83. Oxford: Oxford University Press, 2007.

———. "Rethinking Secularization: A Global Comparative Perspective." In *Reli-

gion, Globalization, and Culture, edited by Peter Beyer and Lori Beaman, 101-20. Leiden: Brill, 2007.

Castells, Manuel. *The Power of Identity*. Malden, MA: Blackwell, 1997.

The Catechism of the Catholic Church. http://www.vatican.va.

Cavanaugh, William. *Theopolitical Imagination: Discovering the Liturgy as a Political Act in an Age of Global Consumerism*. London: T&T Clark, 2002.

———. *Torture and Eucharist: Theology, Politics, and the Body of Christ*. Oxford: Blackwell, 1998.

César, Waldo. "From Babel to Pentecost: A Social-Historical-Theological Study of the Growth of Pentecostalism." In *Between Babel and Pentecost: Transnational Pentecostalism in Africa and Latin America*, edited by André Corten and Ruth Marshall, 22-40. Bloomington: Indiana University Press, 2001.

Chakrabarty, Dipesh. *Provincializing Europe: Postcolonial Thought and Historical Difference*. Princeton: Princeton University Press, 2000.

Chaplin, Jonathan. *Herman Dooyeweerd: Christian Philosopher of State and Civil Society*. Notre Dame: University of Notre Dame Press, 2011.

Chappel, James. *Catholic Modern: The Challenge of Totalitarianism and the Remaking of the Church*. Cambridge, MA: Harvard University Press, 2018.

———. "The Catholic Origins of Totalitarianism Theory in Interwar Europe." *Modern Intellectual History* 8, no. 3 (2011): 561-90.

Childress, James. *Civil Disobedience and Political Obligation: A Study in Christian Social Ethics*. New Haven: Yale University Press, 1971.

Chirichigno, Gregory. *Debt-Slavery in Israel and the Ancient Near East*. Sheffield: Sheffield Academic, 1993.

Chuwa, Leonard. *African Indigenous Ethics in Global Bioethics: Interpreting Ubuntu*. New York: Springer, 2014.

Clark, Christopher. "From 1848 to Christian Democracy." In *Religion and the Political Imagination*, edited by Ira Katznelson and Gareth Stedman Jones, 190-213. Cambridge: Cambridge University Press, 2007.

Clark, David J. "The Word Kosmos 'World' in John 17." *Bible Translator* 50, no. 4 (1999): 401-6.

Cleage, Albert. *Black Christian Nationalism: New Directions for the Black Church*. New York: William Morrow, 1972.

Clifton, Shane. "Pentecostal Approaches to Economics." In *The Oxford Handbook of Christianity and Economics*, edited by Paul Oslington, 263-81. Oxford: Oxford University Press, 2014.

Clough, David. *On Animals*. Vol. 1 of *Systematic Theology*. London: Bloomsbury, 2012.

Coates, Ta-Nehisi. *Between the World and Me*. New York: Spiegel and Grau, 2015.

Cohen, Joshua, and Joel Rogers. *Associations and Democracy*. London: Verso, 1995.

Cohn, Norman. *The Pursuit of the Millennium: Revolutionary Millenarians and Mystical Anarchists of the Middle Ages*. Oxford: Oxford University Press, 1970.

Coleridge, Samuel Taylor. *The Collected Works of Samuel Taylor Coleridge*. Vol. 10, *On the Constitution of the Church and the State*. Edited by John Colmer. Princeton: Princeton University Press, 1976 (1839).

Coles, Romand. *Beyond Gates Politics: Reflections for the Possibility of Democracy*. Minneapolis: University of Minnesota Press, 2005.

Colón-Emeric, Edgardo. "Human Sacrifice: Religious Act or Vicious Desire? Testing the Limits of Tolerance with Vitoria and Las Casas." *Journal of Early Modern Christianity* 4, no 2 (2017): 227-61.

Combahee River Collective. "The Combahee River Collective Statement." In *Home Girls: A Black Feminist Anthology*, edited by Barbara Smith, 264-74. New Brunswick, NJ: Rutgers University Press, 2000.

Cone, James H. *Black Theology and Black Power*. Maryknoll, NY: Orbis, 1997 (1969).

———. *For My People: Black Theology and the Black Church*. Maryknoll, NY: Orbis, 1984.

———. *God of the Oppressed*. Rev. ed. Maryknoll, NY: Orbis, 1997.

———. *Martin and Malcolm and America: A Dream or a Nightmare?* Maryknoll, NY: Orbis, 1991.

Congar, Yves. *Lay People in the Church: A Study for a Theology of Laity*. Westminster, MD: Newman, 1965.

Congregation of the Doctrine of the Faith. *Libertatis Conscientia*. 1986. http://w2.vatican.va.

———. *Libertatis Nuntius*. 1984. http://w2.vatican.va.

Copeland, Shawn M. *Enfleshing Freedom: Body, Race, and Being*. Minneapolis: Fortress, 2010.

Corney, Richard. "'Rod and Staff' (Psalm 23:4): A Double Image?" In *On the Way to Nineveh: Studies in Honor of George M. Landes*, edited by Stephen Cook and S. C. Winter, 28-41. Atlanta: Scholars Press, 1999.

Coulter, Dale. "Toward a Pentecostal Theology of Black Consciousness." *Journal of Pentecostal Theology* 25, no. 1 (2016): 74-89.

Cox, Harvey. *Fire from Heaven: The Rise of Pentecostal Spirituality and the Reshaping of Religion in the Twenty-First Century*. Reading, MA: Addison-Wesley, 1995.

Cox, Oliver C. *Caste, Class, and Race: A Study in Social Dynamics*. Garden City, NY: Doubleday, 1948.

Creative Commons. http://creativecommons.org.

Creech, Joe. *Righteous Indignation: Religion and the Populist Revolution*. Urbana: University of Illinois Press, 2006.

Creighton, Mandell. *Persecution and Tolerance*. London: Longmans, Green, 1895.

Crenshaw, Kimberle. "Mapping the Margins: Intersectionality, Identity Politics, and Violence against Women of Color." *Stanford Law Review* 43, no. 6 (1991): 1241-99.

Csordas, Thomas J. *The Sacred Self: A Cultural Phenomenology of Charismatic Healing*. Berkeley: University of California Press, 1994.

Cullen, Bernard. *Hegel's Social and Political Thought.* Dublin: Gill & MacMillan, 1979.

Curran, Charles. *The Moral Theology of Pope John Paul II.* Washington, DC: Georgetown University Press, 2005.

Curtis, Heather. "The Global Character of Nineteenth-Century Divine Healing." In *Global Pentecostal and Charismatic Healing,* edited by Candy Gunther Brown, 29-45. Oxford: Oxford University Press, 2011.

Dale, Gareth. *Karl Polanyi: The Limits of the Market.* Cambridge: Polity, 2010.

Dastur, Françoise. *How Are We to Confront Death?* Translated by Robert Vallier. New York: Fordham University Press, 2012.

Daughtry, Herbert D. *My Beloved Community: Sermons, Speeches, and Lectures of Rev. Daughtry.* Trenton, NJ: Africa World, 2001.

Davie, Grace. *Europe: The Exceptional Case; Parameters of Faith in the Modern World.* London: Darton, Longman & Todd, 2002.

Davies, J. C. "Utopianism." In *The Cambridge History of Political Thought: 1450-1700,* edited by J. H. Burns and Mark Goldie, 341-42. Cambridge: Cambridge University Press. 1991.

Davis, Angela, and Lisa Lowe. "Reflections on Race, Class and Gender in the USA." In *The Angela Y. Davis Reader,* edited by Joy James, 307-25. Malden, MA: Blackwell, 1998.

Davis, Ellen. *Scripture, Culture, and Agriculture: An Agrarian Reading of the Bible.* Cambridge: Cambridge University Press, 2009.

Dawson, Michael C. *Black Visions: The Roots of Contemporary African-American Political Ideologies.* Chicago: University of Chicago Press, 2001.

Day, Keri. *Religious Resistance to Neoliberalism: Womanist and Black Feminist Perspectives.* Basingstoke, UK: Palgrave Macmillan, 2016.

Dayton, Donald. *Theological Roots of Pentecostalism.* Grand Rapids: Francis Asbury, 1987.

Deleuze, Gilles. "Postscript on the Societies of Control." *October* 59 (1992): 3-7.

della Porta, Donatella, et al. *Globalization from Below: Transnational Activists and Protest Networks.* Minneapolis: University of Minnesota Press, 2006.

Dempster, Murray. "Christian Social Concern in Pentecostal Perspective: Reformulating Pentecostal Eschatology." *Journal of Pentecostal Theology* 2 (1993): 51-64.

De Oliveira, Pedro Ribeiro. "An Analytic Examination of the Term 'People.'" *Concilium* 6, no. 176 (1984): 81-88.

Derrida, Jacques. *Dissémination.* Translated by Barbara Johnson. London: Athlone Press, 1981.

———. *Politics of Friendship.* Translated by George Collins. London: Verso, 1997.

———. *Voyous.* Paris: Galilée, 2003.

Derrida, Jacques, and Anne Dufourmantelle. *Of Hospitality.* Translated by Rachel Bowlby. Stanford, CA: Stanford University Press, 2000.

Derrida, Jacques, and Jean-Luc Marion. "On the Gift: A Discussion between

Jacques Derrida and Jean-Luc Marion." In *God, the Gift, and Postmodernism*, edited by John D. Caputo and Michael J. Scanlon, 54-78. Bloomington: Indiana University Press, 1999.

Derrida, Jacques, and Elisabeth Roudinesco. *For What Tomorrow . . . : A Dialogue*. Translated by Jeff Fort. Stanford, CA: Stanford University Press, 2004.

Desmond, Matthew. *Evicted: Poverty and Profit in the American City*. New York: Crown, 2016.

Dixon, Thomas. "The Invention of Altruism: Auguste Comte's *Positive Polity* and Respectable Unbelief in Victorian Britain." In *Science and Beliefs: From Natural Philosophy to Natural Science, 1700-1900*, edited by David M. Knight and Matthew D. Eddy, 195-211. Aldershot, UK: Ashgate, 2005.

Donoghue, John. "'Out of the Land of Bondage': The English Revolution and the Atlantic Origins of Abolition." *American Historical Review* 115, no. 4 (2010): 943-74.

Donovan, Vincent J. *Christianity Rediscovered: An Epistle from the Masai*. London: SCM, 2001.

Dorrien, Gary J. *Imagining Democratic Socialism: Political Theology, Marxism, and Social Democracy*. New Haven: Yale University Press, 2019.

_____. *Social Ethics in the Making: Interpreting an American Tradition*. Chichester, UK: Wiley-Blackwell, 2008.

Droogers, André. "Globalisation and Pentecostal Success." In *Between Babel and Pentecost: Transnational Pentecostalism in Africa and Latin America*, edited by André Corten and Ruth Marshall-Fratani, 41-61. Bloomington: Indiana University Press, 2001.

Du Bois, W. E. B. *Black Reconstruction in America: An Essay toward a History of the Part Which Black Folk Played in the Attempt to Reconstruct Democracy in America, 1860-1880*. London: Routledge, 2017 (1935).

_____. *Darkwater: Voices from within the Veil*. New York: Harcourt, Brace & Howe, 1920.

Durkheim, Emile. *The Division of Labour in Society*. Translated by W. D. Halls. Basingstoke, UK: Palgrave, 1984.

Dussel, Enrique. *Beyond Philosophy: Ethics, History, Marxism, and Liberation Theology*. Edited by Eduardo Mendieta. New York: Rowman & Littlefield, 2003.

_____. "'Populus Dei' in Populo Pauperum: From Vatican II to Medellin and Puebla." *Concilium* 6, no. 176 (1984): 35-44.

_____. "Theology of Liberation and Marxism." In *Mysterium Liberationis: Fundamental Concepts of Liberation Theology*, edited by Ignacio Ellacuría and Jon Sobrino, 85-102. Maryknoll, NY: Orbis, 1993.

Elazar, Daniel. *Covenant and Polity in Biblical Israel: Biblical Foundations and Jewish Expressions*. New Brunswick, NJ: Transaction, 1995.

El Fadl, Khaled Abou. *The Place of Tolerance in Islam*. Boston: Beacon, 2002.

Eliot, T. S. *The Idea of a Christian Society*. London: Faber & Faber, 1939.

Elizondo, Virgil. "*Mestizaje* as a Locus of Theological Reflection." In *Mestizo Christianity: Theology from the Latino Perspective,* edited by Arturo J. Bañuelas, 7–27. Maryknoll, NY: Orbis, 1995.

Ellingworth, Paul. "Translating Kosmos 'World' in Paul." *Bible Translator* 53, no. 4 (2002): 414–21.

Ellul, Jacques. *The Meaning of the City.* Carlisle, UK: Paternoster, 1997.

Espinosa, Gastón. *Latino Pentecostals in America: Faith and Politics in Action.* Cambridge, MA: Harvard University Press, 2014.

———. *William J. Seymour and the Origins of Global Pentecostalism.* Durham, NC: Duke University Press, 2014.

Estrelda, Alexander. *Black Fire: One Hundred Years of African American Pentecostalism.* Downers Grove, IL: IVP Academic, 2011.

Eze, Michael Onyebuchi. *Intellectual History in Contemporary South Africa.* New York: Palgrave Macmillan, 2010.

Farmer, Ashley. *Remaking Black Power: How Black Women Transformed an Era.* Chapel Hill: University of North Carolina Press, 2017.

Fassin, Didier. *Humanitarian Reason: A Moral History of the Present Times.* Berkeley: University of California Press, 2012.

Felski, Rita. *The Limits of Critique.* Chicago: University of Chicago Press, 2015.

Figgis, John Neville. *Will to Freedom or the Gospel of Nietzsche and the Gospel of Christ.* New York: Scribner's Sons, 1917.

Finnis, John. *Aquinas: Moral, Political, and Legal Theory.* Oxford: Oxford University Press, 1998.

Fogarty, Michael P. *Christian Democracy in Western Europe, 1820–1953.* London: Routledge, 1957.

Follett, Mary Parker. *Creative Experience.* New York: Longmans, Green, 1930 (1924).

Forbes, James. "A Pentecostal Approach to Black Liberation." PhD diss., Colgate-Rochester, 1975.

Forst, Rainer. *Toleration in Conflict: Past and Present.* Cambridge: Cambridge University Press, 2013.

Foucault, Michel. *The History of Sexuality.* Vol. 1, *An Introduction.* Translated by Robert Hurley. New York: Random House, 1980.

———. *Security, Territory, Population: Lectures at the Collège de France, 1977–1978.* Translated by Graham Burchell. New York: Picador, 2007.

Fourcade, Marion, and Kieran Healy. "Moral Views of Market Society." *Annual Review of Sociology* 33 (2007): 285–311.

Francis. Address of the Holy Father at the World Meeting of Popular Movements. Bolivia, July 9, 2015. http://w2.vatican.va.

Franklin, Julian. "Sovereignty and the Mixed Constitution: Bodin and His Critics." In *The Cambridge History of Political Thought: 1450–1700,* edited by J. H. Burns and M. Goldie, 298–344. Cambridge: Cambridge University Press, 1991.

Freeman, Jo. "The Tyranny of Structurelessness." Jo Freeman.com. http://www
.jofreeman.com/joreen/tyranny.htm.

Funkenstein, Amos. *Theology and the Scientific Imagination: From the Middle Ages to the Seventeenth Century*. Princeton: Princeton University Press, 1986.

Gaita, Raimond. *A Common Humanity: Thinking about Love and Truth and Justice*. London: Routledge, 2000.

Gebara, Ivone. *Longing for Running Water: Ecofeminism and Liberation*. Minneapolis: Fortress Press, 1999.

Gerstle, Gary. *American Crucible: Race and Nation in the Twentieth Century*. Princeton: Princeton University Press, 2001.

Gibson-Graham, J. K. *A Postcapitalist Politics*. Minneapolis: University of Minnesota Press, 2006.

Giddens, Anthony. *The Class Structure of the Advanced Societies*. London: Hutchinson, 1973.

Gierke, Otto von. *Community in Historical Perspective*. Edited by Antony Black. Translated by Mary Fischer. Cambridge: Cambridge University Press, 1990.

Gilkes, Cheryl Townsend. "'You've Got a Right to the Tree of Life': The Biblical Foundations of an Empowered Attitude among Black Women in the Sanctified Church." In *Philip's Daughters: Women in Pentecostal-Charismatic Leadership*, edited by Estrelda Alexander and Amos Yong, 152–69. Eugene, OR: Wipf & Stock, 2009.

Gillespie, Michael. *The Theological Origins of Modernity*. Chicago: University of Chicago Press, 2008.

Gilroy, Paul. *Black Atlantic: Modernity and Double Consciousness*. Cambridge, MA: Harvard University Press, 1993.

Gitari, David. *In Season and out of Season: Sermons to a Nation*. Carlisle, UK: Regnum, 1996.

———. "'You Are in the World But Not of It.'" In *Christian Political Witness*, edited by George Kalantzis and Gregory Lee, 214–31. Downers Grove, IL: IVP Academic, 2014.

Glasman, Maurice. *Unnecessary Suffering: Managing Market Utopia*. London: Verso, 1996.

Glaude, Eddie. *In a Shade of Blue: Pragmatism and the Politics of Black America*. Chicago: University of Chicago Press, 2007.

Glissant, Édouard. *Caribbean Discourse: Selected Essays*. Translated by J. Michael Dash. Charlottesville: University Press of Virginia, 1989.

Goldstein, Alyosha. *Poverty in Common: The Politics of Community Action during the American Century*. Durham, NC: Duke University Press 2012.

Goodchild, Philip. *Theology of Money*. Durham, NC: Duke University Press, 2009.

Goodwyn, Lawrence. *Democratic Promise: The Populist Moment in America*. New York: Oxford University Press, 1976.

Gore, Charles. *Christ and Society*. London: Allen & Unwin, 1928.

Gornik, Mark R. *Word Made Global: Stories of African Christianity in New York City*. Grand Rapids: Eerdmans, 2011.

Grabill, Stephen. *Rediscovering the Natural Law in Reformed Theological Ethics*. Grand Rapids: Eerdmans, 2006.

Grattan, Laura. *Populism's Power: Radical Grassroots Democracy in America*. Oxford: Oxford University Press, 2016.

Grau, Marion. *Of Divine Economy: Refinancing Redemption*. New York: T&T Clark, 2004.

Gray, John. *Straw Dogs: Thoughts on Humans and Other Animals*. London: Granta, 2002.

Gregory, Eric, and Joseph Clair. "Augustinianisms and Thomisms." In *The Cambridge Companion to Christian Political Theology*, edited by Craig Hovey and Elizabeth Phillips, 176–96. Cambridge: Cambridge University Press, 2015.

Griffiths, Paul J. *Decreation: The Last Things of All Creatures*. Waco, TX: Baylor University Press, 2014.

Guinier, Lani, and Gerald Torres. *The Miner's Canary: Enlisting Race, Resisting Power, Transforming Democracy*. Cambridge, MA: Harvard University Press, 2002.

Gunton, Colin. *Father, Son, and Holy Spirit: Toward a Fully Trinitarian Theology*. London: T&T Clark, 2003.

Gutiérrez, Gustavo. "Option for the Poor." In *Mysterium Liberationis: Fundamental Concepts of Liberation Theology*, edited by Ignacio Ellacuría and Jon Sobrino, 235–50. Maryknoll, NY: Orbis, 1993.

———. *The Power of the Poor in History*. Maryknoll, NY: Orbis, 1983.

———. *A Theology of Liberation: History, Politics, and Salvation*. Rev. ed. Maryknoll, NY: Orbis, 1988.

———. *The Truth Shall Make You Free: Confrontations*. Translated by Matthew O'Connell. Maryknoll, NY: Orbis, 1990.

Gutmann, Amy, and Dennis F. Thompson. *Democracy and Disagreement*. Cambridge, MA: Harvard University Press, 1996.

Hahn, Steven. *A Nation under Our Feet: Black Political Struggles in the Rural South, from Slavery to the Great Migration*. Cambridge, MA: Belknap Press of Harvard University Press, 2003.

Halisi, Clyde, and James Mtume, eds. *The Quotable Karenga*. Los Angeles: US Organization, 1967.

Halldorf, Joel. "Lewi Pethrus and the Creation of a Christian Counterculture." *Pneuma* 32, no. 3 (2010): 354–68.

Harding, Vincent. *The Religion of Black Power*. Boston: Beacon, 1968.

Hardt, Michael, and Antonio Negri. *Commonwealth*. Cambridge, MA: Belknap Press of Harvard University Press, 2009.

Harris, Melanie. *Gifts of Virtue: Alice Walker and Womanist Ethics*. New York: Palgrave Macmillan, 2010.

Harrison, Robert Pogue. *The Dominion of the Dead*. Chicago: University of Chicago Press, 2003.

Hart, Keith. *The Memory Bank: Money in an Unequal World*. London: Profile Books, 1999.

Harvey, David. *Rebel Cities: From the Right to the City to the Urban Revolution*. London: Verso, 2012.

Harvey, Jennifer. *Dear White Christians: For Those Still Longing for Racial Reconciliation*. Grand Rapids: Eerdmans, 2014.

Hastings, Adrian. *The Construction of Nationhood: Ethnicity, Religion, and Nationalism*. Cambridge: Cambridge University Press, 1997.

Hatch, Nathan. *The Democratization of American Christianity*. New Haven: Yale University Press, 1989.

Hauerwas, Stanley. *The State of the University: Academic Knowledges and the Knowledge of God*. Oxford: Blackwell, 2007.

Hayek, Friedrich A. von. *Law Legislation and Liberty*. Vol. 2, *The Mirage of Social Justice*. Chicago: University of Chicago Press, 1978.

Hegel, G. W. F. *Hegel's Philosophy of Right*. Translated by T. M. Knox. Oxford: Oxford University Press, 1967.

Hehir, J. Bryan. "The Modern Catholic Church and Human Rights: The Impact of the Second Vatican Council." In *Christianity and Human Rights: An Introduction*, edited by John Witte Jr. and Franklin S. Alexander, 113–34. Cambridge: Cambridge University Press, 2010.

Held, Virginia. *The Ethics of Care: Personal, Political, and Global*. Oxford: Oxford University Press, 2006.

Hénaff, Marcel. *The Price of Truth: Gift, Money, and Philosophy*. Stanford, CA: Stanford University Press, 2010.

Hervieu-Léger, Danièle. *Religion as a Chain of Memory*. New Brunswick, NJ: Rutgers University Press, 2000.

Hesse, Barnor. "Symptomatically Black: A Creolization of the Political." In *The Creolization of Theory*, edited by Françoise Lionnet and and Shu-mei Shih, 37–61. Durham, NC: Duke University Press, 2011.

Hinze, Bradford. *Prophetic Obedience: Ecclesiology for a Dialogical Church*. Maryknoll, NY: Orbis, 2016.

Hirst, Paul. *Associative Democracy: New Forms of Economic and Social Governance*. Cambridge: Polity, 1994.

———, ed. *The Pluralist Theory of the State: Selected Writings of G. D. H. Cole, J. N. Figgis, and H. J. Laski*. London: Routledge, 1993.

Hittinger, Russell. "The Coherence of the Four Basic Principles of Catholic Social Doctrine—an Interpretation." In *Pursuing the Common Good: How Solidarity and Subsidiarity Can Work Together, Proceedings of the 14th Plenary Session, 2–6 May 2008*, edited by Margaret S. Archer and Pierpaolo Donati. Vatican City: Pontifical Academy of Sciences, 2008.

————. Introduction to *The Teachings of Modern Roman Catholicism on Law, Politics, and Human Nature*, edited by John Witte and Frank Alexander. New York: Columbia University Press, 2006.

————. "Social Roles and Ruling Virtues in Catholic Social Doctrine." *Annales Theologici* 16, no. 2 (2002): 385-408.

Hofstadter, Richard. *Age of Reform: From Bryan to F. D. R.* New York: Knopf, 1955.

Hogan, Wesley C. *Many Minds, One Heart: SNCC's Dream for a New America.* Chapel Hill: University of North Carolina Press, 2007.

Holland, Henry Scott. *Our Neighbours.* London: Mowbrays, 1911.

Hollenweger, Walter. *Pentecostalism: Origins and Developments Worldwide.* Peabody, MA: Hendrickson, 1997.

Holyoake, George Jacob. *The Origin and Nature of Secularism.* London: Watts, 1896.

Honig, Bonnie. *Antigone, Interrupted.* Cambridge: Cambridge University Press, 2013.

Honohan, Iseult. *Civic Republicanism.* London: Routledge, 2002.

Hooker, Richard. *Of the Laws of Ecclesiastical Polity.* Vol. 3. Edited by P. G. Stanwood. Cambridge, MA: Belknap Press of Harvard University Press, 1981.

hooks, bell. *Feminism Is for Everybody: Passionate Politics.* Cambridge, MA: South End, 2000.

————. *Feminist Theory: From Margin to Center.* Cambridge, MA: South End, 1984.

————. *Salvation: Black People and Love.* New York: HarperCollins, 2001.

Horsley, Richard A. *Jesus and Empire: The Kingdom of God and the New World Disorder.* Minneapolis: Fortress, 2002.

Horton, John. "Toleration." In *The Routledge Encyclopedia of Philosophy*, vol. 9, edited by Edward Craig, 429-33. London: Routledge, 1998.

Horton, John, and Susan Mendus. Introduction to *Aspects of Toleration: Philosophical Studies*, edited by John Horton and Susan Mendus, 1-15. London: Methuen, 1985.

Horwitt, Sanford D. *Let Them Call Me Rebel: Saul Alinsky, His Life and Legacy.* New York: Random House, 1989.

Hueglin, Thomas. *Early Modern Concepts for a Late Modern World: Althusius on Community and Federalism.* Waterloo, ON: Wilfrid Laurier University Press, 1999.

Huntington, Samuel P. *Who Are We? The Challenges to America's National Identity.* New York: Simon & Schuster, 2004.

Hurston, Zora Neale. *Moses, Man of the Mountain: A Novel.* New York: HarperCollins, 2009 (1939).

Ignatiev, Noel. *How the Irish Became White.* New York: Routledge, 1995.

Inge, John. *A Christian Theology of Place.* Aldershot, UK: Ashgate, 2003.

Ingham, Geoffrey. "Class Inequality and the Social Production of Money." In *Renewing Class Analysis*, edited by Rosemary Crompton, Fiona Devine, Mike Savage, and John Scott, 66-86. Oxford: Blackwell, 2000.

————. *The Nature of Money.* Cambridge: Polity, 2004.

Iremonger, F. A. *William Temple, Archbishop of Canterbury: His Life and Letters*. New York: Oxford University Press, 1948.

Isasi-Díaz, Ada María. *La Lucha Continues: Mujerista Theology*. Maryknoll, NY: Orbis, 2004.

——. *Mujerista Theology: A Theology for the Twenty-First Century*. Maryknoll, NY: Orbis, 1996.

——. "Strangers No Longer." In *Hispanic/Latino Theology: Challenge and Promise*, edited by Ada María Isasi-Díaz and Fernando F. Segovia, 367–74. Minneapolis: Fortress, 1996.

Ivereigh, Austen. *Faithful Citizens: A Practical Guide to Catholic Social Teaching and Community Organising*. London: Darton, Longman & Todd, 2010.

——. *The Great Reformer: Francis and the Making of a Radical Pope*. New York: Holt, 2014.

Jantzen, Matthew. "Hermeneutics of Providence: Theology, Race, and Divine Action in History." ThD diss., Duke University, 2017.

Jeffries, Judson. *Huey P. Newton: The Radical Theorist*. Jackson: University Press of Mississippi, 2002.

Jennings, Willie James. *The Christian Imagination: Theology and the Origins of Race*. New Haven: Yale University Press, 2010.

Joas, Hans. *Faith as an Option: Possible Futures for Christianity*. Translated by Alex Skinner. Stanford, CA: Stanford University Press, 2014.

John XXIII. *Pacem in terris*. 1963. http://w2.vatican.va.

John Paul II. *Centesimus Annus*. 1991. http://w2.vatican.va.

——. *Christifidelis Laici*. 1988. http://w2.vatican.va.

——. *Dives in Misericordia*. 1980. http://w2.vatican.va.

——. *Evangelium Vitae*. 1995. http://w2.vatican.va.

——. *Laborem Exercens*. 1981. http://w2.vatican.va.

——. *Redemptor Hominis*.1979. http://w2.vatican.va.

——. *Veritatis Splendor*. 1993. http://w2.vatican.va.

Jordan, Wilbur. *The Development of Religious Toleration in England*. 4 vols. Cambridge: Cambridge University Press, 1932–1940.

Joseph, Peniel E. "The Black Power Movement: A State of the Field." *Journal of American History* 96, no. 3 (2009): 751–76.

——, ed. *Neighborhood Rebels: Black Power at the Local Level*. New York: Palgrave Macmillan, 2010.

——. *Stokely: A Life*. New York: Basic Civitas Books, 2014.

——. *Waiting 'Til the Midnight Hour: A Narrative History of Black Power in America*. New York: Holt, 2006.

Kaiser, Wolfram. *Christian Democracy and the Origins of the European Union*. Cambridge: Cambridge University Press, 2007.

Kalu, Ogbu. *African Pentecostalism: An Introduction*. Oxford: Oxford University Press, 2008.

Kalyvas, Stathis. *The Rise of Christian Democracy in Europe*. Ithaca, NY: Cornell University Press, 1996.

Kant, Immanuel. *Kant: Political Writings*. Edited by Hans Reiss. Cambridge: Cambridge University Press, 1991.

———. *The Metaphysics of Morals*. Translated by Mary Gregor. Cambridge: Cambridge University Press, 1996.

Kantorowicz, Ernst. *The King's Two Bodies: A Study in Mediaeval Political Theology*. Princeton: Princeton University Press, 1957.

Kapoor, Ilan. *The Postcolonial Politics of Development*. London: Routledge, 2008.

Kärkkäinen, Veli-Matti. "Are Pentecostals Oblivious to Social Justice? Theological and Ecumenical Perspectives." *Missiology: An International Review* 29, no. 4 (2001): 417-31.

———. *Creation and Humanity*. Grand Rapids: Eerdmans, 2015.

Katznelson, Ira. *When Affirmative Action Was White: An Untold History of Racial Inequality in Twentieth-Century America*. New York: Norton, 2005.

Kauffman, L. A. *Direct Action: Protest and the Reinvention of American Radicalism*. London: Verso, 2017.

Kazin, Michael. *The Populist Persuasion: An American History*. New York: Basic Books, 1995.

Keel, Othmar, and Christoph Uehlinger. *Gods, Goddesses, and Images of God in Ancient Israel*. Translated by Thomas Trapp. Minneapolis: Fortress, 1998.

Kerridge, Eric. *Usury, Interest, and the Reformation*. Aldershot, UK: Ashgate, 2002.

Kim, Kirsteen. *The Holy Spirit in the World: A Global Conversation*. Maryknoll, NY: Orbis, 2007.

———. *Joining In with the Spirit: Connecting World Church and Local Mission*. London: SCM, 2012.

Kingdon, Robert. "Calvinism and Resistance Theory, 1550-1580." In *The Cambridge History of Political Thought: 1450-1700*, edited by J. H. Burns and M. Goldie, 194-218. Cambridge: Cambridge University Press, 1991.

Kirk-Duggan, Cheryl. *Exorcizing Evil: A Womanist Perspective on the Spirituals*. Maryknoll, NY: Orbis, 1997.

Knapp, Michael, Anja Flach, and Ercan Ayboğa. *Revolution in Rojava: Democratic Autonomy and Women's Liberation in Syrian Kurdistan*. Translated by Janet Biehl. London: Pluto, 2016.

Koslofsky, Craig. "The Kiss of Peace in the German Reformation." In *The Kiss in History*, edited by Karen Harvey, 18-35. Manchester: Manchester University Press, 2005.

Kothari, Uma. "Power, Knowledge and Social Control in Participatory Development." In *Participation: The New Tyranny?*, edited by Bill Cooke and Uma Kothari, 139-52. London: Zed, 2004.

Kselman, Thomas A., and Joseph A. Buttigieg. *European Christian Democracy: His-*

torical Legacies and Comparative Perspectives. Notre Dame: University of Notre Dame Press, 2003.

Kymlicka, Will. "Two Models of Pluralism and Tolerance." In *Toleration: An Elusive Virtue*, edited by David Heyd, 81-105. Princeton: Princeton University Press, 1996.

Laborde, Cécile. *Pluralist Thought and the State in Britain and France, 1900-25*. Basingstoke, UK: Macmillan, 2000.

Laclau, Ernesto. *On Populist Reason*. London: Verso, 2007.

Laderchi, Caterina Ruggeri, Ruhi Saith, and Frances Stewart. "Does It Matter That We Do Not Agree on the Definition of Poverty? A Comparison of Four Approaches." *Oxford Development Studies* 31, no. 3 (2003): 243-74.

Lakeland, Paul. *The Politics of Salvation: The Hegelian Idea of the State*. Albany: State University of New York Press, 1984.

Lancaster, Carol. *Foreign Aid: Diplomacy, Development, Domestic Politics*. Chicago: University of Chicago Press, 2007.

Land, Steven. *Pentecostal Spirituality: A Passion for the Kingdom*. Sheffield: Sheffield Academic, 1993.

Langholm, Odd. *Legacy of Scholasticism in Economic Thought: Antecedents of Choice and Power*. Cambridge: Cambridge University Press, 1998.

Latham, Robert. "Social Sovereignty." *Theory, Culture and Society* 17, no. 4 (2000): 1-18.

"The Lausanne Covenant." Lausanne Movement. August 1, 1974. https://www .lausanne.org/content/covenant/lausanne-covenant.

La Via Campesina/International Peasants Movement. www.viacampesina.org.

Le Goff, Jacques. *Your Money or Your Life: Economy and Religion in the Middle Ages*. Translated by Patricia Ranum. New York: Zone Books, 1990.

Leo XIII. *Rerum Novarum*. 1891. http://w2.vatican.va.

Leshem, Dotan. "Oikonomia Redefined." *Journal of the History of Economic Thought* 35, no. 1 (2013): 43-61.

Levy, Jacob. *Rationalism, Pluralism, and Freedom*. Oxford: Oxford University Press, 2015.

Lewis, C. S. *Mere Christianity*. New York: HarperOne, 2001 (1952).

Lijphart, Arend. *Democracy in Plural Societies: A Comparative Exploration*. New Haven: Yale University Press, 1980.

———. *The Politics of Accommodation: Pluralism and Democracy in the Netherlands*. 2nd ed. Berkeley: University of California Press, 1975.

———. *Thinking about Democracy: Power Sharing and Majority Rule in Theory and Practice*. London: Routledge, 2008.

Linebaugh, Peter, and Marcus Rediker. *The Many-Headed Hydra: Sailors, Slaves, Commoners, and the Hidden History of the Revolutionary Atlantic*. Boston: Beacon, 2013.

Lipsitz, George. *The Possessive Investment in Whiteness: How White People Profit from Identity Politics*. Philadelphia: Temple University Press, 2009.

Lloyd, Howell. "Constitutionalism." In *The Cambridge History of Medieval Political Thought, c. 350–c. 1450*, edited by J. H. Burns, 267–68. Cambridge: Cambridge University Press, 1988.

Lloyd, Vincent. *Black Natural Law*. Oxford: Oxford University Press, 2016.

———. *Religion of the Field Negro: On Black Secularism and Black Theology*. New York: Fordham University Press, 2018.

Locke, John. *Locke: Political Essays*. Edited by Mark Goldie. Cambridge: Cambridge University Press, 1997.

Longenecker, Bruce. *Remember the Poor: Paul, Poverty, and the Greco-Roman World*. Grand Rapids: Eerdmans, 2010.

Loomer, Bernard. "Two Conceptions of Power." *Process Studies* 6, no. 1 (1976): 5–32.

Lorde, Audre. *Sister/Outsider: Essays and Speeches*. Trumansburg, NY: Crossing, 1984.

Lovett, Leonard. "Black Holiness-Pentecostalism: Implication for Ethical and Social Transformation." PhD diss., Emory University, 1979.

———. "Liberation: A Dual-Edged Sword." *Pneuma: The Journal of the Society for Pentecostal Studies* 9, no. 2 (1987): 155–77.

Loy, David. "Religion of the Market." *Journal of the American Academy of Religion* 65, no. 2 (1997): 275–90.

Machiavelli, Niccolo. *The Prince*. Translated by Peter Constantine. New York: Modern Library, 2008.

MacIntyre, Alasdair. *Dependent Rational Animals: Why Human Beings Need the Virtues*. London: Duckworth, 1999.

———. *Ethics and Politics, Selected Essays*. Vol. 2. Cambridge: Cambridge University Press, 2006.

———. *Ethics in the Conflicts of Modernity: An Essay on Desire, Practical Reasoning, and Narrative*. Cambridge: Cambridge University Press, 2016.

———. "Incommensurability, Truth and the Conversation between Confucians and Aristotelians about the Virtues." In *Culture and Modernity: East-West Philosophic Perspectives*, edited by Eliot Deutsch, 104–22. Honolulu: University of Hawaii Press, 1991.

———. "Moral Relativism, Truth and Justification." In *The MacIntyre Reader*, edited by Kelvin Knight, 202–20. London: Polity, 1998.

———. "Toleration and the Goods of Conflict." In *The Politics of Toleration: Tolerance and Intolerance in Modern Life*, edited by Susan Mendus, 133–56. Edinburgh: Edinburgh University Press, 1999.

MacKinnon, Donald M. *Explorations in Theology 5*. London: SCM, 1979.

Macpherson, C. B. *The Political Theory of Possessive Individualism: Hobbes to Locke*. Oxford: Clarendon, 1962.

Maddox, Randy L. "'Visit the Poor': John Wesley, the Poor, and the Sanctification of Believers." In *The Poor and the People Called Methodists, 1729-1999*, edited by Richard P. Heitzenrater, 59-81. Nashville: Kingswood, 2002.

Mahmood, Saba. *Religious Difference in a Secular Age: A Minority Report*. Princeton: Princeton University Press, 2016.

———. "Secularism, Hermeneutics, and Empire: The Politics of Islamic Reformation." *Public Culture* 18, no. 2 (2006): 323-47.

Makulilo, Alexander. "Populism and Democracy in Africa." In *Contemporary Populism: A Controversial Concept and Its Diverse Forms*, edited by Sergiu Gherghina, Sergiu Mişcoiu, and Sorina Soare, 167-202. Newcastle upon Tyne, UK: Cambridge Scholars, 2013.

Maritain, Jacques. "The Concept of Sovereignty." *American Political Science Review* 44, no. 2 (1950): 343-57.

———. *Integral Humanism: Temporal and Spiritual Problems of a New Christendom*. Translated by Joseph Evans. New York: Scribner's Sons, 1968.

———. *Man and the State*. Washington, DC: Catholic University of America Press, 1998 (1951).

Marks, Jonathan. *What It Means to Be 98% Chimpanzee: Apes, People, and Their Genes*. Berkeley: University of California Press, 2002.

Markus, Robert A. *Christianity and the Secular*. Notre Dame: University of Notre Dame Press, 2006.

Marrow, Stanley. "κοσμος in John." *Catholic Biblical Quarterly* 64 (2002): 90-102.

Marshall, Katherine, and Marisa Van Saanen. *Development and Faith: Where Mind, Heart, and Soul Work Together*. Washington, DC: World Bank, 2007.

Marshall, Ruth. *Political Spiritualities: The Pentecostal Revolution in Nigeria*. Chicago: University of Chicago Press, 2009.

Martin, David. *Pentecostalism: The World Their Parish*. Oxford: Blackwell, 2002.

———. *Tongues of Fire: The Explosion of Protestantism in Latin America*. Oxford: Blackwell, 1990.

Marty, Martin E., and R. Scott Appleby, eds. *Fundamentalisms Observed*. Chicago: University of Chicago Press, 1991.

Marx, Karl. "Comments on James Mill, *Éléments D'Économie Politique*." 1844. Marxists Internet Archive. https://www.marxists.org/archive/marx/works/1844/james-mill/.

Marx, Karl, and Friedrich Engels. *The Communist Manifesto*. Translated by Samuel Moore. London: Penguin Books, 1967.

Marzouki, Nadia. "The Tea Party and Religion: Between Religious and Historical Fundamentalism." In *Saving the People: How Populists Hijack Religion*, edited by Nadia Marzouki, Duncan McDonnell, and Olivier Roy, 149-66. Oxford: Oxford University Press, 2016.

Mathewes, Charles. *A Theology of Public Life*. Cambridge: Cambridge University Press, 2007.

Mauss, Marcel. *The Gift: Forms and Functions of Exchange in Archaic Societies*. New York: Norton, 1967.

McCartney, John T. *Black Power Ideologies: An Essay in African-American Political Thought*. Philadelphia: Temple University Press, 1992.

McGinn, Bernard. *The Calabrian Abbot: Joachim of Fiore in the History of Western Thought*. London: Macmillan, 1985.

McRoberts, Omar M. *Streets of Glory: Church and Community in a Black Urban Neighborhood*. Chicago: University of Chicago Press, 2003.

McRorie, Christina. "The Emptiness of Modern Economics: Why the Dismal Science Needs a Richer Moral Anthropology." *Hedgehog Review* 16, no. 3 (2014): 120-29.

Medina, Lara. "Nepantla." In *Hispanic American Religious Cultures*, edited by Miguel de la Torre, 403-8. Santa Barbara, CA: ABC-CLIO, 2009.

Medina, Néstor. *Mestizaje: (Re)Mapping Race, Culture, and Faith in Latino/a Catholicism*. Maryknoll, NY: Orbis, 2009.

Meeks, M. Douglas. *God the Economist: The Doctrine of God and Political Economy*. Minneapolis: Fortress, 1989.

Mehta, Uday. *Liberalism and Empire: A Study in Nineteenth-Century British Liberal Thought*. Chicago: University of Chicago Press, 1999.

Meikle, Scott. "Aristotle on Money." *Phronesis* 39, no. 1 (1994): 26-44.

Mell, Julie L. "Cultural Meanings of Money in Medieval Ashkenaz: On Gift, Profit, and Value in Medieval Judaism and Christianity." *Jewish History* 28, no. 2 (2014): 125-58.

Mendelsohn, Isaac. *Slavery in the Ancient Near East: A Comparative Study of Slavery in Babylonia, Assyria, Syria, and Palestine from the Middle of the Third Millennium to the End of the First Millennium*. New York: Oxford University Press, 1949.

Mendus, Susan. *Toleration and the Limits of Liberalism*. London: Macmillan, 1989.

Metz, Johannes Baptist. *Poverty of Spirit*. Translated by John Drury. Glen Rock, NJ: Newman, 1968.

Midgley, Mary. *Evolution as a Religion: Strange Hopes and Stranger Fears*. London: Routledge, 2002.

Mikkelsen, Jon. "Translator's Introduction." In *Kant and the Concept of Race: Late Eighteenth-Century Writings*, edited and translated by Jon M. Mikkelsen, 1-40. New York: State University of New York Press, 2013.

Milbank, John. *Being Reconciled: Ontology and Pardon*. London: Routledge, 2003.

———. *Theology and Social Theory: Beyond Secular Reason*. Oxford: Blackwell, 1990.

———. *The Word Made Strange: Theology, Language, Culture*. Oxford: Blackwell, 1997.

Miller, Donald E., and Tetsunao Yamamori. *Global Pentecostalism: The New Face of Christian Social Engagement*. Berkeley: University of California Press, 2007.

Miller, Mike. "The Student Movement and Saul Alinsky: An Alliance That Never

Happened." In *Too Many Martyrs: Student Massacres at Orangeburg, Kent, and Jackson State during the Vietnam War Era*, edited by Susie Erenrich. Forthcoming.

Miller, Vincent J. *Consuming Religion: Christian Faith and Practice in a Consumer Culture*. London: Continuum, 2004.

Mills, Charles W. *Blackness Visible: Essays on Philosophy and Race*. Ithaca, NY: Cornell University Press, 1998.

Mills, C. Wright. *The Sociological Imagination*. Oxford: Oxford University Press, 1959.

Mitchell, Timothy. "Carbon Democracy." *Economy and Society* 38, no. 3 (2009): 399–432.

Mitchem, Stephanie. "Healing Hearts and Broken Bodies: An African American Women's Spirituality of Healing." In *Faith, Health, and Healing in African American Life*, edited by Stephanie Mitchem and Emilie M. Townes, 181–91. Westport, CT: Praeger, 2008.

Modood, Tariq. "Establishment, Multiculturalism, and British Citizenship." *Political Quarterly* 65, no. 1 (1994): 53–73.

Moessner, David. *Lord of the Banquet: The Literary and Theological Significance of the Lukan Travel Narrative*. Minneapolis: Fortress, 1989.

Moffitt, Benjamin. *The Global Rise of Populism: Performance, Political Style, and Representation*. Stanford, CA: Stanford University Press, 2016.

Moltmann, Jürgen. *The Coming of God: Christian Eschatology*. Translated by Margaret Kohl. Minneapolis: Fortress, 2004 (1996).

———. *The Spirit of Life: A Universal Affirmation*. Translated by Margaret Kohl. Minneapolis: Fortress, 1992.

———. *The Trinity and the Kingdom of God: The Doctrine of God*. Translated by Margaret Kohl. London: SCM, 1981.

Monahan, Arthur. *Consent, Coercion, and Limit: The Medieval Origins of Parliamentary Democracy*. Montreal: McGill-Queen's University Press, 1987.

Moore, Leonard. *Carl B. Stokes and the Rise of Black Political Power*. Urbana: University of Illinois Press, 2003.

Morefield, Jeanne. *Covenants without Swords: Idealist Liberalism and the Spirit of Empire*. Princeton: Princeton University Press, 2005.

Morris, Aldon D. *The Origins of the Civil Rights Movement: Black Communities Organizing for Change*. New York: Free Press, 1984.

Morris, Jeremy. "Secularization and Religious Experience: Arguments in the Historiography of Modern British Religion." *Historical Journal* 15, no. 1 (2012): 195–219.

Mouffe, Chantal. *The Democratic Paradox*. London: Verso, 2000.

———. *For a Left Populism*. London: Verso, 2018.

———. "Religion, Liberal Democracy, and Citizenship." In *Political Theologies: Public Religions in a Post-secular World*, edited by Hent de Vries and Lawrence E. Sullivan, 318–26. New York: Fordham University Press, 2006.

Mudde, Cas. "The Populist Zeitgeist." *Government and Opposition* 39, no. 4 (2004): 541–63.

Muhammad, Khalil Gibran. *The Condemnation of Blackness: Race, Crime, and the Making of Modern Urban America*. Cambridge, MA: Harvard University Press, 2011.

Müller, Jan-Werner. *What Is Populism?* Philadelphia: University of Pennsylvania Press, 2016.

Muñoz, José Esteban. *Disidentifications: Queers of Color and the Performance of Politics*. Minneapolis: University of Minnesota Press, 1999.

Murray, John Courtney. *The Problem of Religious Freedom*. London: Geoffrey Chapman, 1965.

Myers, Ched. *Binding the Strong Man: A Political Reading of Mark's Story of Jesus*. Maryknoll, NY: Orbis, 1988.

Nagel, Thomas. *Equality and Partiality*. Oxford: Oxford University Press, 1991.

Nandy, Ashis. *Time Warps: The Insistent Politics of Silent and Evasive Pasts*, 61–88. Delhi: Permanent Black, 2001.

Nederman, Cary. "Sovereignty, War and the Corporation: Hegel on the Medieval Foundations of the Modern State." *Journal of Politics* 49, no. 2 (1987): 500–520.

———. *Worlds of Difference: European Discourses of Toleration, c. 1100–c. 1550*. University Park: Pennsylvania State University Press, 2000.

Nederman, Cary, and John Laursen, eds. *Difference and Dissent: Theories of Toleration in Medieval and Early Modern Europe*. London: Rowman & Littlefield, 1996.

Nelson, Eric. *The Hebrew Republic: Jewish Sources and the Transformation of European Political Thought*. Cambridge, MA: Harvard University Press, 2010.

Nelson, Julie. *Economics for Humans*. Chicago: University of Chicago Press, 2006.

Nelson, Robert. *Economics as Religion: From Samuelson to Chicago and Beyond*. University Park: Pennsylvania State University Press, 2002.

Nembhard, Jessica Gordon. *Collective Courage: A History of African American Cooperative Economic Thought and Practice*. University Park: Pennsylvania State University Press, 2014.

Neusner, Jacob, and Bruce Chilton, eds. *Religious Tolerance in World Religions*. West Conshohocken, PA: Templeton Foundation, 2008.

Newman, Jay. *Foundations of Religious Tolerance*. Toronto: University of Toronto Press, 1982.

Nicholls, David. *Deity and Domination: Images of God and the State in the Nineteenth and Twentieth Centuries*. London: Routledge, 1994.

Niebuhr, Reinhold. *The Children of Light and the Children of Darkness*. London: Nisbet, 1945.

———. "The Test of Tolerance." In *Religious Pluralism in the West*, edited by David Mullan, 281–96. Malden, MA: Blackwell, 1998.

Nixon, Rob. *Slow Violence and the Environmentalism of the Poor*. Cambridge, MA: Harvard University Press, 2011.

Noel, James A. *Black Religion and the Imagination of Matter in the Atlantic World*. New York: Palgrave Macmillan, 2009.

Nongbri, Brent. *Before Religion: A History of a Modern Concept*. New Haven: Yale University Press, 2013.

Noonan, John T. *The Scholastic Analysis of Usury*. Cambridge, MA: Harvard University Press, 1957.

Novak, David. *Jewish Social Ethics*. Oxford: Oxford University Press, 1992.

———. *Natural Law in Judaism*. Cambridge: Cambridge University Press, 1998.

Novak, Michael. *The Spirit of Democratic Capitalism*. New York: Simon & Schuster, 1982.

Oakeshott, Michael. *Rationalism in Politics and Other Essays*. New York: Basic Books, 1962.

O'Donovan, Joan Lockwood. "The Theological Economics of Medieval Usury." *Studies in Christian Ethics* 14, no. 1 (2001): 48–64.

O'Donovan, Oliver. *The Desire of the Nations: Rediscovering the Roots of Political Theology*. Cambridge: Cambridge University Press, 1996.

———. *On the 39 Articles: A Conversation with Tudor Christianity*. Carlisle, UK: Paternoster, 1986.

———. *Resurrection and Moral Order: An Outline for Evangelical Ethics*. Grand Rapids: Eerdmans, 1986.

———. *Self, World, and Time*. Grand Rapids: Eerdmans, 2013.

———. *The Ways of Judgment*. Grand Rapids: Eerdmans, 2005.

O'Donovan, Oliver, and Joan Lockwood O'Donovan, eds. *From Irenaeus to Grotius: A Sourcebook in Christian Political Thought, 100-1625*. Grand Rapids: Eerdmans, 1999.

Olsen, Erik J. *Civic Republicanism and the Properties of Democracy*. Lanham, MD: Lexington, 2006.

Olson, Joel. *The Abolition of White Democracy*. Minneapolis: University of Minnesota Press, 2004.

O'Neill, Kevin. *City of God: Christian Citizenship in Postwar Guatemala*. Berkeley: University of California Press, 2009.

Ostrom, Elinor. *Governing the Commons: The Evolution of Institutions for Collective Action*. Cambridge: Cambridge University Press, 1990.

Padilla, Elaine, and Dale Irvin. "Where Are the Pentecostals in an Age of Empire?" In *Evangelicals and Empire: Christian Alternatives to the Political Status Quo*, edited by Bruce Ellis Benson and Peter Goodwin Heltzel, 169-84. Grand Rapids: Brazos, 2008.

Pagden, Anthony. "Human Rights, Natural Rights, and Europe's Imperial Legacy." *Political Theory* 31, no. 2 (2003): 171-99.

Pandey, Gyanendra. *A History of Prejudice: Race, Caste, and Difference in India and the United States*. Cambridge: Cambridge University Press, 2013.

Panizza, Francisco. Introduction to *Populism and the Mirror of Democracy*, edited by Francisco Panizza, 1-31. London: Verso, 2005.

Parekh, Bhikhu. "Liberalism and Colonialism: A Critique of Locke and Mill." In *The Decolonization of Imagination: Culture, Knowledge, and Power*, edited by Jan Nederveen Pieterse and Bhikhu Parekh, 81-98. London: Zed, 1995.

Park, Young-Ho. *Paul's Ekklēsia as a Civic Assembly*. Tübingen: Mohr Siebeck, 2015.

Parry, Jonathan. "The Gift, the Indian Gift and the 'Indian Gift.'" *Man* 21, no. 3 (1986): 453-73.

Patterson, Orlando. *Slavery and Social Death: A Comparative Study*. Cambridge, MA: Harvard University Press, 1982.

Paul VI. *Apostolicam Actuositatem*. 1965. http://w2.vatican.va.

————. *Lumen Gentium*. 1964. http://w2.vatican.va.

Payne, Charles. *I've Got the Light of Freedom: The Organizing Tradition and the Mississippi Freedom Struggle*. Berkeley: University of California Press, 1995.

Pearce, Fred. *The Land Grabbers: The New Fight over Who Owns the Earth*. Boston: Beacon, 2012.

Perkinson, James. *White Theology: Outing Supremacy in Modernity*. New York: Palgrave Macmillan, 2004.

Perreau-Saussine, Emile. *Catholicism and Democracy: An Essay in the History of Political Thought*. Translated by Richard Rex. Princeton: Princeton University Press, 2012.

Peterson, Erik. *Theological Tractates*. Translated by Michael J. Hollerich. Stanford, CA: Stanford University Press, 2011.

Pettit, Philip. *Republicanism: A Theory of Freedom and Government*. Oxford: Clarendon, 1997.

Pew Forum of Religion and Public Life. *Global Christianity: A Report on the Size and Distribution of the World's Christian Population*. Washington, DC: Pew Research Center, 2011.

Pfau, Thomas. *Minding the Modern: Human Agency, Intellectual Traditions, and Responsible Knowledge*. Notre Dame: University of Notre Dame Press, 2013.

Phillips, Anne. *The Politics of the Human*. Cambridge: Cambridge University Press, 2015.

Pimblott, Kerry. *Faith in Black Power: Religion, Race, and Resistance in Cairo, Illinois*. Lexington: University Press of Kentucky, 2017.

Pitts, F. H., and A. C. Dinerstein. "Corbynism's Conveyor Belt of Ideas: Postcapitalism and the Politics of Social Reproduction." *Capital and Class* 41, no. 3 (2017): 423-34.

Pitts, Jennifer. "Empire and Legal Universalisms in the Eighteenth Century." *American Historical Review* 117, no. 1 (2012): 92-121.

————. *A Turn to Empire: The Rise of Imperial Liberalism in Britain and France.* Princeton: Princeton University Press, 2005.

Pius XI. *Divini redemptoris.* 1937. http://w2.vatican.va.

————. *Quadragesimo Anno.* 1931. http://w2.vatican.va.

Pius XII. *Christmas Address.* 1942. http://w2.vatican.va.

Pleij, Herman. *Dreaming of Cockaigne: Medieval Fantasies of the Perfect Life.* Translated by Diane Webb. New York: Columbia University Press, 2001.

Pleyers, Geoffrey. *Alter-Globalization: Becoming Actors in a Global Age.* Cambridge: Polity, 2010.

Pocock, J. G. A. *Virtue, Commerce, and History: Essays on Political Thought and History, Chiefly in the Eighteenth Century.* Cambridge: Cambridge University Press, 1985.

Polanyi, Karl. *The Great Transformation: The Political and Economic Origins of Our Time.* 2nd ed. Boston: Beacon, 2001.

————. *Primitive, Archaic, and Modern Economies: Essays of Karl Polanyi.* Edited by George Dalton. Garden City, NY: Doubleday, 1968.

Post, Gaines. "A Roman Legal Theory of Consent, *Quod Omnes Tangit,* in Medieval Representation." *Wisconsin Law Review* 1 (1950): 66–78.

Postel, Charles. *The Populist Vision.* New York: Oxford University Press, 2009.

Purdy, Jedediah. *The Meaning of Property: Freedom, Community, and the Legal Imagination.* New Haven: Yale University Press, 2011.

Quayesi-Amakye, Joseph. *Christology and Evil in Ghana: Towards a Pentecostal Public Theology.* Amsterdam: Rodopi, 2013.

Ragir, Sonia. "Diet and Food Preparation: Rethinking Early Hominid Behavior." *Evolutionary Anthropology* 8 (2000): 153–55.

Rancière, Jacques. *Staging the People: The Proletarian and His Double.* Translated by David Fernbach. London: Verso, 2011.

Rasmussen, Larry L. *Earth Community, Earth Ethics.* Maryknoll, NY: Orbis, 1997.

Rawls, John. *The Law of Peoples.* Cambridge, MA: Harvard University Press, 1999.

————. *Political Liberalism.* New York: Columbia University Press, 1993.

————. *A Theory of Justice.* Rev. ed. Oxford: Oxford University Press, 1999.

Reagon, Bernice Johnson. "Coalition Politics: Turning the Century." In *Home Girls: A Black Feminist Anthology,* edited by Barbara Smith, 343–55. New Brunswick, NJ: Rutgers University Press, 2000.

Reeves, Marjorie. *Joachim of Fiore and the Prophetic Future.* London: SPCK, 1976.

Reid, Marcella Althaus. *Indecent Theology.* London: Routledge, 2000.

Rhonheimer, Martin. *The Common Good of Constitutional Democracy.* Washington, DC: Catholic University of America Press, 2013.

Riggs, Marcia Y. *Awake, Arise and Act: A Womanist Call for Black Liberation.* Cleveland: Pilgrim, 1994.

Riley, Patrick. *The General Will before Rousseau: The Transformation of the Divine into the Civic*. Princeton: Princeton University Press, 1986.

Rist, Gilbert. *The History of Development: From Western Origins to Global Faith*. New ed. London: Zed, 2002.

Robbins, Joel. "The Globalization of Pentecostal and Charismatic Christianity." *Annual Review of Anthropology* 33, no. 1 (2004): 117-43.

———. "Pentecostal Networks and the Spirit of Globalization: On the Social Productivity of Ritual Forms." *Social Analysis* 53, no. 1 (2009): 55-66.

Roberts, Neil. *Freedom as Marronage*. Chicago: University of Chicago Press, 2015.

Robertson, Roland. *Globalization: Social Theory and Global Culture*. London: Sage, 1992.

———. "Global Millennialism: A Postmortem on Secularization." In *Religion, Globalization, and Culture*, edited by Peter Beyer and Lori Beaman, 9-34. Leiden: Brill, 2007.

Robinson, Cedric. *Black Marxism: The Making of the Black Radical Tradition*. London: Zed, 1983.

Rodgers, Darrin, and Nicole Sparks. "Pentecostal Pioneer of Earth Day: John McConnell, Jr." In *Blood Cries Out: Pentecostals, Ecology, and the Groans of Creation*, edited by A. J. Swoboda, 3-21. Eugene, OR: Pickwick, 2014.

Roediger, David R. *The Wages of Whiteness: Race and the Making of the American Working Class*. Rev. ed. New York: Verso, 1999.

———. *Working toward Whiteness: How America's Immigrants Became White*. New York: Basic Books, 2005.

Rogers, Eugene. *After the Spirit: A Constructive Pneumatology from Resources outside the Modern West*. Grand Rapids: Eerdmans, 2005.

Rogers, Mary Beth. *Cold Anger: A Story of Faith and Power Politics*. Denton, TX: University of North Texas Press, 1990.

Rosario-Rodriguez, Ruben. *Racism and God-Talk: A Latino/a Perspective*. New York: New York University Press, 2008.

Rose, Nikolas. *Governing the Soul: The Shaping of the Private Self*. 2nd ed. London: Free Association Books, 1999.

Rourke, Thomas. *The Roots of Pope Francis's Social and Political Thought: From Argentina to the Vatican*. Lanham, MD: Rowman & Littlefield, 2016.

Rousseau, Jean-Jacques. "A Discourse on the Origin of Inequality." In *The Social Contract and Discourses*. London: Everyman, 1993.

———. *The Social Contract and Other Later Political Writings*. Edited by Victor Gourevitch. Cambridge: Cambridge University Press, 1997.

Rubenstein, Jennifer. *Between Samaritans and States: The Political Ethics of Humanitarian INGOs*. Oxford: Oxford University Press, 2015.

Rufinus of Sorrento. *De Bono Pacis*. Hannover, Germany: Hahn, 1997.

Russell, Letty. *Just Hospitality: God's Welcome in a World of Difference*. Louisville: Westminster John Knox, 2009.

Rutenberg, Jim. "A Dream Undone: Disenfranchised." *New York Times*, July 29, 2015.

Ryan, John. *Distributive Justice*. New York: Arno, 1978 (1916).

Sacks, Jonathan. *The Home We Build Together: Recreating Society*. London: Continuum, 2007.

Said, Edward. *Orientalism*. New York: Vintage Books, 1979.

Salmon, J. H. M. "Catholic Resistance Theory, Ultramontanism, and the Royalist Response, 1580-1620." In *The Cambridge History of Political Thought: 1450-1700*, edited by J. H. Burns and Mark Goldie, 219-53. Cambridge: Cambridge University Press. 1991.

Salvatore, Armando. *The Public Sphere: Liberal Modernity, Catholicism, Islam*. New York: Palgrave Macmillan, 2007.

Sandel, Michael J. *Democracy's Discontent: America in Search of a Public Philosophy*. Cambridge, MA: Belknap Press of Harvard University Press, 1998.

Sanders, Cheryl. *Empowerment Ethics for a Liberated People: A Path to African American Social Transformation*. Minneapolis: Fortress, 1995.

————. *Saints in Exile: The Holiness-Pentecostal Experience in African American Religion and Culture*. Oxford: Oxford University Press, 1996.

Sanders, Elizabeth. *Roots of Reform: Farmers, Workers, and the American State, 1877-1917*. Chicago: University of Chicago Press, 1999.

Sanneh, Lamin. *Translating the Message: The Missionary Impact on Culture*. Maryknoll, NY: Orbis, 1989.

Sartre, Jean-Paul. *Anti-Semite and Jew: An Exploration of the Etiology of Hate*. Translated by George Becker. New York: Schocken Books, 1948.

Scannone, Juan Carlos. "Pope Francis and the Theology of the People." *Theological Studies* 77, no. 1 (2016): 118-35.

Schillebeeckx, Edward. *Jesus: An Experiment in Christology*. Translated by Hubert Hoskins. New York: Seabury, 1979.

Schmitt, Carl. *The Concept of the Political*. Translated by George Schwab. Chicago: University of Chicago Press, 2007.

————. *The Leviathan in the State Theory of Thomas Hobbes: Meaning and Failure of a Political Symbol*. Translated by George Schwab and Erna Hilfstein. Westport, CT: Greenwood, 1996.

Schooyans, Michael. "Democracy in the Teachings of the Popes." *Proceedings of the Workshop on Democracy*, December 12-13, 1996. Pontificiae Academiae Scientiarum Socialum.

Schwöbel, Christoph. "Recovering Human Dignity." In *God and Human Dignity*, edited by R. Kendall Soulen and Linda Woodhead, 44-58. Grand Rapids: Eerdmans, 2006.

Scott, James C. *Seeing like a State: How Certain Schemes to Improve the Human Condition Have Failed*. New Haven: Yale University Press, 1998.

Scudder, Vida. *Socialism and Character*. Boston: Houghton Mifflin, 1912.

————. *Socialism and Spiritual Progress: A Speculation*. Boston: Church Social Union, 1896.

Sheehan, Johnathan, and Dror Wahrman. *Invisible Hands: Self-Organization and the Eighteenth Century*. Chicago: University of Chicago Press, 2015.

Shelby, Tommie. *We Who Are Dark: The Philosophical Foundations of Black Solidarity*. Cambridge, MA: Belknap Press of Harvard University Press, 2005.

Sigmund, Paul E. "Catholicism and Liberal Democracy." In *Catholicism and Liberalism: Contributions to American Public Philosophy*, edited by R. Bruce Douglass and David Hollenbach, 217-41. New York: Cambridge University Press, 1994.

Simmel, Georg. *The Sociology of Georg Simmel*. Translated by Kurt H. Wolff. New York: Free Press, 1950.

Singer, Peter. *The Life You Can Save: How to Do Your Part to End World Poverty*. New York: Random House, 2010.

Skillen, James. "The Development of Calvinistic Political Theory in the Netherlands, with Special Reference to the Thought of Herman Dooyeweerd." PhD diss., Duke University, 1973.

Skinner, Quentin. *Liberty before Liberalism*. Cambridge: Cambridge University Press, 1998.

Skocpol, Theda, Marshall Ganz, and Ziad Munson. "A Nation of Organizers: The Institutional Origins of Civic Voluntarism in the United States." *American Political Science Review* 94, no. 3 (2000): 527-46.

Somers, Margaret R. *Genealogies of Citizenship: Knowledge, Markets, and the Right to Have Rights*. Cambridge: Cambridge University Press, 2010.

Sontag, Susan. *Regarding the Pain of Others*. New York: Farrar, Straus & Giroux, 2003.

Stamatov, Peter. "Activist Religion, Empire, and the Emergence of Modern Long-Distance Advocacy Networks." *American Sociological Review* 75, no. 4 (2010): 607-28.

————. *The Origins of Global Humanitarianism: Religion, Empires, and Advocacy*. Cambridge: Cambridge University Press, 2013.

Stears, Marc. "Guild Socialism." In *Modern Pluralism: Anglo-American Debates Since 1880*, edited by Mark Bevir, 40-59. Cambridge: Cambridge University Press, 2012.

Stein, P. G. "Roman Law." In *The Cambridge History of Medieval Political Thought, c. 350-c. 1450*, edited by J. H. Burns, 37-47. Cambridge: Cambridge University Press, 1988.

Stern, Philip. *The Company-State: Corporate Sovereignty and the Early Modern Foundations of the British Empire in India*. Oxford: Oxford University Press, 2012.

Stout, Jeffrey. *Blessed Are the Organized: Grassroots Democracy in America*. Princeton: Princeton University Press, 2010.

Studebaker, Steven. *A Pentecostal Political Theology for American Renewal: Spirit of the Kingdoms, Citizens of the Cities*. New York: Palgrave Macmillan, 2016.

Stuurman, Siep. "Common Humanity and Cultural Difference on the Sedentary-Nomadic Frontier: Herodotus, Sima Qian, and Ibn Khaldun." In *Global Intellectual History*, edited by Samuel Moyn and Andrew Sartori, 33–58. New York: Columbia University Press, 2013.

———. "Herodotus and Sima Qian: History and the Anthropological Turn in Ancient Greece and Han China." *Journal of World History* 19, no. 1 (2008): 1–40.

Swanson, Judith Ann. *The Public and the Private in Aristotle's Political Philosophy.* Ithaca, NY: Cornell University Press, 1992.

Sykes, Stephen. *Power and Christian Theology.* London: Continuum, 2006.

Tamanaha, Brian Z. "Understanding Legal Pluralism: Past to Present, Local to Global." *Sydney Law Review* 30, no. 3 (2008): 375–411.

Tanner, Kathryn. *Christ the Key.* Cambridge: Cambridge University Press, 2010.

———. *Economy of Grace.* Minneapolis: Fortress, 2005.

Tax, Meredith. *A Road Unforeseen: Women Fight the Islamic State.* New York: Bellevue Literary, 2016.

Taylor, Charles. "Can Secularism Travel?" In *Beyond the Secular West*, edited by Akeel Bilgrami, 1–27. New York: Columbia University Press, 2016.

———. *The Ethics of Authenticity.* Cambridge, MA: Harvard University Press, 1992.

———. *Modern Social Imaginaries.* Durham, NC: Duke University Press, 2004.

———. *Multiculturalism and the Politics of Recognition: An Essay.* Edited by Amy Gutmann. Princeton: Princeton University Press, 1992.

———. "The Polysemy of the Secular." *Social Research* 76, no. 4 (2009): 1143–66.

———. *A Secular Age.* Cambridge, MA: Harvard University Press, 2007.

———. *Sources of the Self: The Making of the Modern Identity.* Cambridge: Cambridge University Press, 1992.

Temple, William. *Christianity and Social Order.* New York: Penguin Books, 1942.

———. "Christianity and the Empire." *Pilgrim* 6 (1926): 447–57.

———. *Personal Religion and the Life of Fellowship.* London: Longmans, Green, 1926.

Tessman, Lisa. *Burdened Virtues: Virtue Ethics for Liberatory Struggles.* Oxford: Oxford University Press, 2005.

Thompson, E. P. "Time, Work-Discipline, and Industrial Capitalism." *Past and Present* 38 (1967): 56–97.

Tocqueville, Alexis de. *Democracy in America.* Translated by Gerald Bevan. London: Penguin, 2003.

Townes, Emilie M. *Breaking the Fine Rain of Death: African American Health Issues and a Womanist Ethic of Care.* New York: Continuum, 2001.

———. "Living in the New Jerusalem: The Rhetoric and Movement of Liberation in the House of Evil." In *A Troubling in My Soul: Womanist Perspectives on Evil and Suffering*, edited by Emilie M. Townes, 78–91. Maryknoll, NY: Orbis, 1993.

———. *Womanist Ethics and the Cultural Production of Evil.* New York: Palgrave Macmillan, 2006.

Tronto, Joan. *Caring Democracy: Markets, Equality, and Justice*. New York: New York University Press, 2013.

Tully, James. *Public Philosophy in a New Key*. Vol. 2, *Imperialism and Civic Freedom*. Cambridge: Cambridge University Press, 2008.

———. *Strange Multiplicity: Constitutionalism in an Age of Diversity*. Cambridge: Cambridge University Press, 1995.

Turner, William C. "Pneumatology: Contributions from African American Christian Thought to the Pentecostal Theological Task." In *Afro-Pentecostalism: Black Pentecostal and Charismatic Christianity in History and Culture*, edited by Amos Yong and Estrelda Alexander, 169–89. New York: NYU Press, 2011.

Tutu, Desmond. *Hope and Suffering: Sermons and Speeches*. Grand Rapids: Eerdmans, 1984.

Twining, William. *General Jurisprudence: Understanding Law from a Global Perspective*. Cambridge: Cambridge University Press, 2009.

Valentín, Benjamín. "Mestizaje." In *Hispanic American Religious Cultures*, edited by Miguel de la Torre, 351–56. Santa Barbara, CA: ABC-CLIO, 2009.

Vallely, Paul. *Pope Francis: Untying the Knots*. London: Bloomsbury, 2013.

Van Deburg, William L. *New Day in Babylon: The Black Power Movement and American Culture, 1965-1975*. Chicago: University of Chicago Press, 1992.

Van Schendelen, M. P. C. M. "Consociational Democracy: The Views of Arend Lijphart and Collected Criticisms." *Political Science Reviewer* 15, no. 1 (1985): 143–83.

Vásquez, Miguel. *More Than Belief: A Materialist Theory of Religion*. Oxford: Oxford University Press, 2011.

Veer, Peter van der. *Imperial Encounters: Religion and Modernity in India and Britain*. Princeton: Princeton University Press, 2001.

Visser 't Hooft, Willem Adolph, and Joseph Houldsworth Oldham. *The Church and Its Function in Society*. London: Allen & Unwin, 1937.

Voegelin, Eric. *The New Science of Politics: An Introduction*. Chicago: University of Chicago Press, 1952.

Volf, Miroslav. "Materiality of Salvation: An Investigation in the Soteriologies of Liberation and Pentecostal Theologies." *Journal of Ecumenical Studies* 26, no. 3 (1989): 447–67.

———. "'The Trinity Is Our Social Program': The Doctrine of the Trinity and the Shape of Social Engagement." *Modern Theology* 14, no. 3 (1998): 403–23.

Vondey, Wolfgang. *Pentecostal Theology: Living the Full Gospel*. London: Bloomsbury, 2017.

Wacker, Grant. *Heaven Below: Early Pentecostals and American Culture*. Cambridge, MA: Harvard University Press, 2001.

Wacquant, Loïc. *Deadly Symbiosis: Race and the Rise of Neoliberal Penalty*. London: Polity, 2009.

———. *Punishing the Poor: The Neoliberal Government of Social Insecurity*. Durham, NC: Duke University Press, 2009.

Walker, Alice. *In Search of Our Mothers' Gardens: Womanist Prose.* San Diego: Harcourt Brace Jovanovich, 1983.

Walker, Cardinal Aswad. "Princes Shall Come out of Egypt: A Theological Comparison of Marcus Garvey and Reverend Albert B. Cleage Jr." *Journal of Black Studies* 39, no. 2 (2008): 194–251.

Walls, Andrew F. *The Missionary Movement in Christian History: Studies in the Transmission of Faith.* Edinburgh: T&T Clark, 1996.

Walzer, Michael. *On Toleration.* New Haven: Yale University Press, 1997.

———. *Politics and Passion: Toward a More Egalitarian Liberalism.* New Haven: Yale University Press, 2005.

Ward, Graham. *Cultural Transformation and Religious Practice.* Cambridge: Cambridge University Press, 2005.

Ware, Frederick. "On the Compatibility/Incompatibility of Pentecostal Premillennialism with Black Liberation Theology." In *Afro-Pentecostalism: Black Pentecostal and Charismatic Christianity in History and Culture*, edited by Amos Yong and Estrelda Alexander, 191–208. New York: New York University Press, 2011.

Wariboko, Nimi. *The Charismatic City and the Resurgence of Religion: A Pentecostal Social Ethics of Cosmopolitan Urban Life.* New York: Palgrave Macmillan, 2014.

———. *Nigerian Pentecostalism.* Rochester, NY: University of Rochester Press, 2014.

Warren, Mark E. *Democracy and Association.* Princeton: Princeton University Press, 2001.

Warren, Mark R. *Fire in the Heart: How White Activists Embrace Racial Justice.* Oxford: Oxford University Press, 2010.

Waterman, A. M. C. *Political Economy and Christian Theology Since the Enlightenment: Essays in Intellectual History.* New York: Palgrave Macmillan, 2004.

Weber, Max. *From Max Weber: Essays in Sociology.* London: Routledge & Kegan Paul, 1948.

———. *The Protestant Ethic and the Spirit of Capitalism.* Translated by Stephen Kalberg. Oxford: Oxford University Press, 2010 (1904).

Welker, Michael. *God the Spirit.* Translated by John F. Hoffmeyer. Minneapolis: Fortress, 1994.

Wellman, Christopher H. "Liberalism, Samaritanism, and Political Legitimacy." *Philosophy and Public Affairs* 25, no. 3 (1996): 211–37.

West, Cornel. "The Paradox of the African American Rebellion." In *Is It Nation Time? Contemporary Essays on Black Power and Black Nationalism*, edited by Eddie S. Glaude Jr., 22–38. Chicago: University of Chicago Press, 2002.

Williams, Bernard. "Tolerating the Intolerable." In *The Politics of Toleration: Tolerance and Intolerance in Modern Life*, edited by Susan Mendus, 65–75. Edinburgh: Edinburgh University Press, 1999.

———. "Toleration: An Impossible Virtue." In *Toleration: An Elusive Virtue*, edited by David Heyd, 18–27. Princeton: Princeton University Press, 1996.

Williams, Delores. "Sin, Nature, and Black Women's Bodies." In *Ecofeminism and the Sacred*, edited by Carol J. Adams, 24-29. New York: Continuum, 1993.

———. *Sisters in the Wilderness: The Challenge of Womanist God-Talk*. Maryknoll, NY: Orbis, 1993.

Williams, Peter, Jr. "An Oration on the Abolition of the Slave Trade; Delivered in the African Church in the City of New York, January 1, 1808." University of Nebraska-Lincoln, https://digitalcommons.unl.edu/etas/16/.

Williams, Raymond. "Class." In *Keywords: A Vocabulary of Culture and Society*. Oxford: Oxford University Press, 1976.

Williams, Reggie. *Bonhoeffer's Black Jesus: Harlem Renaissance Theology and an Ethic of Resistance*. Waco, TX: Baylor University Press, 2014.

Williams, Rhonda. *Concrete Demands: The Search for Black Power in the 20th Century*. London: Routledge, 2015.

Williams, Rhys, and Susan Alexander. "Religious Rhetoric in American Populism: Civil Religion as Movement Ideology." *Journal for the Scientific Study of Religion* 33, no. 1 (1994): 1-15.

Williams, Rowan. *Anglican Identities*. Cambridge, MA: Cowley, 2003.

———. "Hegel and the Gods of Postmodernity." In *Wrestling with Angels: Conversations in Modern Theology*, edited by Mike Higton, 25-34. Grand Rapids: Eerdmans, 2007.

Wilmore, Gayraud. *Black Religion and Black Radicalism: An Interpretation of the Religious History of African Americans*. Maryknoll, NY: Orbis, 1998.

Wilson, Bryan. *Religion in Sociological Perspective*. Oxford: Oxford University Press, 1982.

Wolin, Sheldon. *Politics and Vision: Continuity and Innovation in Western Political Thought*. Princeton: Princeton University Press, 2004.

———. *The Presence of the Past: Essays on the State and the Constitution*. Baltimore: Johns Hopkins University Press, 1989.

Wood, Diane. *Medieval Economic Thought*. Cambridge: Cambridge University Press, 2002.

Wood, Richard, and Brad Fulton. *A Shared Future: Faith-Based Organizing for Racial Equity and Ethical Democracy*. Chicago: University of Chicago Press, 2015.

Woodberry, Robert. "Pentecostalism and Democracy: Is There a Relationship?" In *Spirit and Power: The Growth and Global Impact of Pentecostalism*, edited by Donald Miller, Kimon Sargeant, and Richard Flory, 119-37. Oxford: Oxford University Press, 2013.

Wright, N. T. *Jesus and the Victory of God*. London: SPCK, 1996.

Wyschogrod, Michael. *The Body of Faith: God in the People of Israel*. San Francisco: Harper & Row, 1983.

Yancy, George. *Christology and Whiteness: What Would Jesus Do?* London: Routledge, 2012.

Yoder, John Howard. *The Jewish-Christian Schism Revisited*. Edited by Michael Cartwright and Peter Ochs. Grand Rapids: Eerdmans, 2003.

Yong, Amos. *Discerning the Spirit(s): A Pentecostal-Charismatic Contribution to Christian Theology of Religions*. Sheffield: Sheffield Academic, 2000.

———. *Hospitality and the Other: Pentecost, Christian Practices, and the Neighbor*. Maryknoll, NY: Orbis, 2008.

———. *In the Days of Caesar: Pentecostalism and Political Theology*. Grand Rapids: Eerdmans, 2010.

———. *The Spirit Poured Out on All Flesh: Pentecostalism and the Possibility of Global Theology*. Grand Rapids: Baker Academic, 2005.

———. "A Typology of Prosperity Theology: A Religious Economy of Global Renewal or a Renewal Economics?" In *Pentecostalism and Prosperity: The Socio-Economics of the Global Charismatic Movement*, edited by Katherine Attanasi and Amos Yong, 15-32. New York: Palgrave Macmillan, 2012.

Young, Philip. *Mestizaje and Globalization: Transformations of Identity and Power*. Tucson: University of Arizona Press, 2014.

Zizioulas, John. *Being as Communion: Studies in Personhood and the Church*. New York: St. Vladimir's Seminary Press, 1985.

Index of Names

Index of Subjects